AFRICA
SOUTH OF THE
SAHARA

AFRICA
SOUTH OF THE
SAHARA

BY

A. T. GROVE

LECTURER IN GEOGRAPHY
AND FELLOW OF DOWNING COLLEGE
UNIVERSITY OF CAMBRIDGE

SECOND EDITION

OXFORD UNIVERSITY PRESS

1970

Oxford University Press, Ely House, London W. 1

GLASGOW NEW YORK TORONTO MELBOURNE WELLINGTON
CAPE TOWN SALISBURY IBADAN NAIROBI DAR ES SALAAM LUSAKA ADDIS ABABA
BOMBAY CALCUTTA MADRAS KARACHI LAHORE DACCA
KUALA LUMPUR SINGAPORE HONG KONG TOKYO

FIRST EDITION 1967
SECOND EDITION 1970

PRINTED IN GREAT BRITAIN
AT THE UNIVERSITY PRESS, OXFORD
BY VIVIAN RIDLER
PRINTER TO THE UNIVERSITY

Preface

To write the regional geography of a continent undergoing a revolution is a hazardous undertaking. The old order in Africa collapsed around 1960 and one cannot forecast which of the new political structures will survive and what forms they will take. Much that seems important fades into obscurity after a few months; federations break up, unions dissolve, and economies fluctuate with the rise and fall of governments and of world commodity prices.

Away from the capital cities and development projects people continue to live as they have for so long, planting and harvesting and herding their cattle. It is tempting to concentrate attention on the traditional societies, living in conformity with tribal custom and the physical environment. But, it may be argued, these are the people of the past, not the future, and in a few decades they will be as unrepresentative as the crofter is of Scotland or the milkmaid of Holland. It is far from certain that this will be so. The various stages from the technically backward to the technically advanced, from the tribal to the emancipated, can be seen in the space of an hour's walk at the edge of almost any large town, and Africa is likely to retain this museum-like quality for a long time to come, with 'primitive' societies and economies embedded in remote areas and surviving, possibly in a scarcely modified form, quite close to modern towns. An attempt has been made here to find a balance, and to write within a limited space a geography of modern Africa which takes into account the traditional and historical background while dealing mainly with present conditions and trends.

The scope of the book is limited to the continent south of the Sahara for three reasons: firstly, because it is hoped that another book in this series may deal with the Mediterranean region of which the Maghreb and Egypt form an integral part, physically and culturally; secondly, the Sahara remains a barrier, easy to cross by air, but still costly; thirdly, because Africa south of the Sahara is the land of the negro. There may be a few million white men in the south and several hundred thousand Asiatics along the east coast; Hamitic and Semitic peoples inhabit the Sudan zone and the countries bordering the Red Sea, but the sub-continental area south of the Tropic of Cancer is predominantly the land of the negroes. This gives it a character of its own, for these are the people who have not shared until recent centuries in the literary civilizations, these are the people who have been hewers of wood and drawers of water, in the Middle East, in the Maghreb, in the Americas. They have been the world's second-class citizens and it colours their attitude to the rest of the world. They have their own traditions of art and social organization and now they feel their own worth and distinctiveness and are anxious to catch up with the rest of the world economically.

The national state is used as the basic regional unit. If the Addis Ababa Conference of 1963 had ended as President Nkrumah had hoped, with the various states coming together in some form of political union, abandoning at least some of their sovereignty, it might have been necessary to write this book differently. But the states of Africa, curiously shaped in the chaos of eighty years ago, show every sign of retaining their individuality.

Economic and social conditions are becoming, by degrees, integrated within national boundaries, and statistics and plans for development are prepared on a national basis.

Though these are sound reasons for choosing the national states as the primary units for description, there is no denying that they provide an unsatisfactory framework from many points of view. There are over fifty of them, they vary enormously in size, and their arrangement is disorderly. Chapters 1, 2, and 3 are intended to give a set of physical and human patterns to form a background against which they can be set. Chapter 4 gives examples of traditional economies that overlap national frontiers. Chapter 5 traces the more important historical stages in the evolution of the continent as a whole and the present political units.

In the regional studies the individual countries have been grouped together into a number of blocks about which generalizations of a higher order can be made. The composition of such blocks has not been easy to decide. Should Rwanda and Burundi be attached to the Congo, for all of them were administered by the Belgians for forty years, or should they be lumped with east Africa to which many of the people migrate? The decision is an arbitrary one and the blocks I have chosen are not entirely satisfactory, but none would be; they simply seem to be the most convenient for my purpose.

Within each state, even the smallest ones no larger than an English county, there is considerable diversity. An attempt is made to indicate this but there is no room to deal with more than a few elements of the micro-structure. Here particular attention is paid to the characteristic features of each country, not merely its peculiarities, but to special aspects of the social organization and economy that give a flavour to the country as a whole, or a certain large part of it, for instance, the cattle contract in Rwanda and Burundi, population pressure in Mauritius, and irrigation in the northern Sudan. For more detailed treatment it is necessary to turn to country and local studies, many of which are mentioned in the bibliography.

Sources of information for a study of Africa's geography are very scattered. The bibliography at the end of the book lists several books and articles relating to each chapter. The names of a number of journals regularly containing useful articles are also given and a list of bibliographies that enable one to keep up to date with the literature. Primary sources of information which are not listed include government departmental and special reports, and statistical data on the population censuses, censuses of production, crop-yield estimates, mining returns, tax returns, government accounts, imports and exports, and employment.

The list of African Studies centres has been compiled by Miss Julia Allen, Secretary of the Cambridge Centre, who was also good enough to read the typescript. Mrs. M. J. Clegg read the early chapters and I am grateful for her helpful criticism. The maps have been drawn by Miss G. Seymour. For the coloured maps at the end of the volume I am indebted to the Clarendon Press and especially to Miss W. Knight of the Cartographic Department who helped to select them.

A. T. G.

October 1965

Contents

PREFACE   v

LIST OF FIGURES AND TABLES   ix

LIST OF ILLUSTRATIONS   xi

1. THE PHYSICAL ENVIRONMENT   1

RELIEF AND ROCKS, evolution of the structure and relief, the coastline, the effects of climatic change, rock weathering, residual crusts, and stripped landscapes   1

CLIMATE, wind systems and the pattern of precipitation, rainfall reliability, tropical cyclones, temperature, humidity, evaporation, man's response to the climate   12

RIVERS AND LAKES   16

2. VEGETATION, SOILS, FAUNA, PESTS, AND DISEASES   23

VEGETATION, tropical forest, tropical savanna, steppe and desert, high montane vegetation   23

SOILS   26

FAUNA, mammals   30

PESTS AND DISEASES, locusts, termites, the mosquito and malaria, the tsetse-fly and trypanosomiasis, parasitic worms, rinderpest   33

3. THE PEOPLE   40

RACE, racial tension   40

CULTURE, language, society, religion   43

POPULATION DISTRIBUTION, numbers of people, towns   45

MIGRATIONS, migrant labour, the pilgrimage to Mecca   49

4. TRADITIONAL HERDING, FARMING, AND FISHING   52

PASTORALISM, the Tibu, the Turkana and Jie, the Nuer, the Baggara, the Fulani, the future of pastoralism   52

AGRICULTURE, forest cultivators, savanna cultivators, dry-land cultivators   57

FISHING   62

5. AFRICAN PREHISTORY AND HISTORY   64

PREHISTORY   64

EARLY HISTORY, the western Sudan in medieval times, Portuguese exploration, the slave trade, the settlement of South Africa, nineteenth-century exploration   65

THE COLONIAL ERA, the division of Africa, the beginning of the colonial era, railway construction, the First World War, the inter-war years   75

INDEPENDENCE, the Second World War and its sequel   81

6. SUDAN REPUBLIC   83

The Three Towns, the Gezira, pump irrigation from the Nile, rainlands west of the White Nile, clay plains east of the White Nile, the South, development trends

7. THE SOUTHERN SAHARA AND ITS BORDERLANDS   92

THE SOUTHERN SAHARA   92

CHAD REPUBLIC   95

NIGER REPUBLIC   97

MALI   98

MAURITANIA   101

SENEGAL   102

GAMBIA   105

8. WEST AFRICA   106

THE WESTERN TRIANGLE   106

SIERRA LEONE   108

GUINEA   110

PORTUGUESE GUINEA   111

LIBERIA   112

THE MIDDLE OF WEST AFRICA   113

GHANA, early development, cocoa, the forest landscape, timber, minerals, industry and the Volta dam, agricultural development, fisheries, the coastal lagoons and Volta delta, the Volta basin, Kumasi, northern Ghana   115

IVORY COAST   122

UPPER VOLTA   124

TOGO AND DAHOMEY   125

NIGERIA 126
    Physical diversity 127
THE TWELVE STATES, Western, Lagos, Mid-
western, Rivers, South-Eastern, East-Central,
Kano, North-Central, North-Western, North-
Eastern, Kwara, Benue-Plateau 132
    Prospects 148

9. THE CONGO BASIN AND
    CAMEROON 149
CONGO KINSHASA, transport, agriculture,
mining, economic and political developments 149
GABON 156
CENTRAL AFRICAN REPUBLIC 158
CONGO BRAZZAVILLE 159
CAMEROON 161
EQUATORIAL GUINEA AND THE
    PORTUGUESE ISLANDS 165

10. ETHIOPIA AND SOMALIA 166
ETHIOPIA, the central highlands, the other
parts of the Empire, political and economic
development 166
SOMALIA, economic and political development 173

11. EAST AFRICA 175
TANZANIA, Zanzibar and Pemba, mainland
Tanzania, Dar-es-Salaam, Tanga and its
hinterland, less successful ports and railways,
Sukumaland, Bukoba, the western and southern
highlands, possibilities for economic develop-
ment 176
KENYA, the coast, the drylands, the highlands,
west to the lakeshore 182
LAKE VICTORIA 191
UGANDA, Buganda, other heavily settled areas,
northern and western Uganda 193
RWANDA AND BURUNDI 200

12. SOUTH CENTRAL AFRICA 204
ANGOLA 204
RHODESIA, European settlement, the Central
African Federation, agriculture, mining, in-
dustry 207
ZAMBIA, mining, African agriculture, Euro-
pean farming, fishing, future prospects 217
MALAWI 220
MOZAMBIQUE 224

13. INDIAN OCEAN ISLANDS 228
MADAGASCAR 228
MAURITIUS 232
RÉUNION 234
COMORO ISLANDS 235
SEYCHELLES 235

14. SOUTH AFRICA 237
The physical environment, the Orange river
scheme, the pattern of economic activity, racial
patterns and problems
SOUTHERN TRANSVAAL AND
    NORTHERN ORANGE FREE STATE 240
SOUTH-WEST CAPE 246
DURBAN AND THE EASTERN PLATEAU
    SLOPES 250
BANTU HOMELANDS 252
SOUTH-WEST AFRICA 253
SWAZILAND 254
LESOTHO 255
BOTSWANA 257

15. A SUMMING UP 259

GUIDE TO FURTHER READING 262

INDEX 269

COLOURED MAPS AND
    STATISTICAL TABLE at end

List of Figures and Tables

1. Physical features of the continent	1
2. Africa as part of Gondwanaland	4
3. The high plains of Africa	5
4. Longshore drift near Lagos	6
5. Shifting lakeshores and desert limits in west central Africa	7
6. Cross-section of the Chad basin	7
7. The past and present extent of blown sand	7
8. The glaciers of Kilimanjaro	9
9. Elephants in the Sahara	9
10. The development of a landscape by weathering and stripping	11
11. Air masses and precipitation in January and July	12
12. Diurnal and seasonal variation in relative humidity	15
13. Longitudinal sections of the Nile, Niger, and Congo	17
14. The discharge of the Niger and Benue	19
15. The seasonal and annual discharge of the Nile	21
16. The catenal arrangement of soils in a part of Ghana	30
17. Areas frequently infested by desert locusts	34
18. The main races in Africa	41
19. Widely spoken languages	43
20. The main migratory movements	50
21. Subsistence economies	52
22. Distribution of some important crops	58
23. The village of Oko in eastern Nigeria	59
24. African empires and trade routes	66
25. *a*. Africa after the Berlin Conference	77
b. Africa at the outbreak of the First World War	
26. *a*. Africa at the outbreak of the Second World War	80
b. Africa in 1969	
27. Khartoum, Omdurman, and Khartoum North	83
28. The Gezira irrigation scheme and the Managil extension	85
29. Irrigation schemes in the Sudan	86
30. The southern limits of the Sahara	92
31. Irrigation from the Niger in Mali	99
32. Mauritania and Nouadhibou	101
33. Senegal and Gambia	103
34. The site of Dakar	103
35. The western triangle of west Africa	107
36. The middle of west Africa	114
37. Southern Ghana	115
38. Field systems in southern Ghana	116
39. Nigeria	128
40. The twelve states	133
41. Eastern Nigeria	137
42. North-east Nigeria	144
43. Congo Kinshasa	150
44. The lands around the lower Congo	157
45. The Cameroon Republic and Central African Republic	162
46. Ethiopia and Somalia	167
47. Zanzibar and Pemba	177
48. Tanzania	179
49. A Kenya transect	183
50. Kenya	189
51. Lake Victoria, north shore	191
52. Uganda	194
53. Rwanda and Burundi	201
54. Angola	205
55. The port of Lobito and the Benguela railway	206
56. Rhodesia, Zambia, and Malawi	209

57. Irrigation on the Rhodesian lowveld   213

58. The Zambian Copperbelt   219

59. The levels of the Great Lakes and the discharge of the Zambezi   223

60. Mozambique   224

61. The western Indian Ocean   229

62. Madagascar   230

63. A schematic section across Madagascar   231

64. Mauritius   232

65. Seychelles   235

66. Land use and minerals in South Africa   237

67. Facilities for development and native reserves in South Africa   240

68. Location map of South Africa   241

69. Bushveld basin, Bankenveld, and Vaal river   241

70. The south-west Cape   249

71. South-West Africa   253

72. Swaziland   254

73. Botswana   257

Geological Table   3

Table of Statistics   at end

Table of Maps (at end)

1. Africa—physical

2. Geology

3. Mean Annual Rainfall

4. Moisture Regions

5. Climatic Diagrams

6. Mean Annual Accumulated Temperature

7. Vegetation

8. Soils

9. Tsetse and Trypanosomiasis

10. Tribes and Languages

11. Population 1—Rural

12. Population 2—Urban

13. Population 3—Urban

14. Railways

15. Accessibility to Main Roads

16. Electrical Power

List of Illustrations

The summit of Mount Kenya. (Kenya Information Services)   5

Mount Kenya from the air. (R.A.F., 13A/20. 5132–3)   8

Saharan engraving of an elephant   9

Half-dome inselberg   10

Castle koppie   11

Flooding resulting from heavy rains in Zambia. (Federal Information Office)   13

Murchison Falls, Uganda   18

Gully erosion, eastern Nigeria   22

Creek near Lagos. (Hunting Technical Services Ltd.)   24

Coffee under forest remnant. (Hunting Technical Services Ltd.)   24

Derived savanna   25

Vegetation arcs. (USAAF, 379/RI/49 and Blackwell Scientific Publications Limited)   26

Ruwenzori high-level vegetation. (J. Harrop)   27

Soil erosion on the Chad–Niger watershed in Nigeria. (R.A.F., 82E/242/5258–9)   28

Elephant trap   31

Game reserve in Uganda. (East African Railways and Harbours)   32

Band of Desert locust hoppers. (FAO and Anti-Locust Research Centre)   33

Desert locust invasion. (FAO and Anti-Locust Research Centre)   34

Aircraft spraying a locust swarm. (Desert Locust Control Organization for Eastern Africa and Anti-Locust Research Centre)   34

Termite heap patterns in Kenya. (R.A.F., CPE/KEN/125/5514–5)   35

Tsetse country   37

Rock painting from South Africa. (South Africa House, London)   40

Trader travelling a country district in central Nigeria   45

King Mtesa's palace in Buganda   47

Parliament buildings in Kampala. (E. S. Adams)   48

A Ugandan lad moves into town. (W. B. Craik)   49

Rock engraving of a humpless cow   52

Sheep and goats   53

Pastoralists on the move in northern Kenya. (Kenya Information Services)   54

Baggara pastoralists' huts under trees. (Hunting Technical Services Ltd.)   55

Fulani camp on agricultural land   61

Fishing boat leaving the harbour at Walvis Bay. (South Africa House, London)   63

Terracing in Kigezi. (Uganda Information Dept.)   65

Zimbabwe ruins. (S. T. Darke, by courtesy of Federal Information Office)   65

The city of Timbuktu   67

Fort Jesus, Mombasa. (Kenya Information Services)   68

Dutch farmers returning from a day's sport. (South Africa House, London)   70

A Boer's wife taking her coffee   71

'Skirmish with the natives'   72

Speke and Grant at King Mtesa's levee   74

A sectional steamer being hauled from the Lower to the Upper Congo   76

Léopoldville about 1884   78

A pump scheme on the Blue Nile. (Hunting Technical Services Ltd.)   87

The Jebel Marra massif. (Hunting Technical Services Ltd.)   88

A modern waterhole in the Sudan. (Hunting Technical Services Ltd.)   88

The crater of Jebel Marra. (Hunting Technical Services Ltd.)   89

Haraz trees in cropland. (Hunting Technical Services Ltd.)   89

Desert mountain scenery in Tibesti, southern Sahara   93

Reed boats on the shore of Lake Chad   97

A camel caravan on the route from Maradi to Kano   98

Sailing boat off Freetown   108

Pepel iron-ore loading pier, Sierra Leone. (Taylor Woodrow)   109

Guma dam, Sierra Leone. (Taylor Woodrow)   110

Takoradi Harbour, Ghana. (Taylor Woodrow)   117

The Achiasi–Kotoku railway, Ghana. (Taylor Woodrow)   117

Ambassador Hotel, Accra, Ghana. (Taylor Woodrow)   119

Farmland of the Tiv people in central Nigeria   129

Mumuye people of the Nigerian Middle Belt   129

Waterfall on the Jos plateau, northern Nigeria   129

Cactus-hedged village on the Jos plateau   129

Ancient dunes, now cultivated, in north-east Nigeria. (R.A.F., 82E/201/5388-9)   131

The Chalawa river near Kano in northern Nigeria   132

Truck assembly plant at Apapa, near Lagos. (Jack Barker, by courtesy of United Africa Company Ltd.)   135

Log raft at Sapele ready for loading on to steamer. (Jack Barker, by courtesy of United Africa Company Ltd.)   135

Brewery at Aba, eastern Nigeria. (Jack Barker, by courtesy of United Africa Company Ltd.)   139

Oil being pressed out of palm fruit   140

Docks at Port Harcourt, eastern Nigeria. (Taylor Woodrow)   140

Raft for transporting palm-oil on the Niger. (Jack Barker, by courtesy of United Africa Company Ltd.)   141

Barges being pushed up the Niger. (Jack Barker, by courtesy of United Africa Company Ltd.)   142

Hausa weaver at work   142

Hamdala Hotel, Kaduna. (Taylor Woodrow)   143

The Yobe river in Bornu   146

Cattle being watered from artesian bore-holes in Bornu   147

The banks of the Upper Congo   152

Harvesting latex on a Congo plantation. (United Africa Company Ltd.)   153

A cocoa plantation in the Congo. (United Africa Company Ltd.) 154

Harvesting bananas on a West Cameroon plantation. (Elders and Fyffes Ltd.) 163

Flood plain in West Cameroon 164

The stelae at Aksum, Ethiopia 168

A Coptic church under construction in Eritrea 168

A farm near Addis Ababa, Ethiopia 169

Roadside settlement alongside the Massawa–Addis Ababa highway, Ethiopia 169

Africa House, Addis Ababa 171

Masai women. (Kenya Information Services) 184

Floating dredger on Lake Magadi. (Kenya Information Services) 185

Market scene in Meru District, Kenya. (Kenya Information Services) 186

Cattle on a European farm in the highlands of Kenya. (Kenya Information Services) 187

A new village in Kenya 188

Nairobi 190

Steamer on Lake Victoria. (East African Railways and Harbours) 192

Kiganda market. (Uganda Department of Information) 195

Sugar cane in Uganda. (Uganda Department of Information) 196

Kigezi, Uganda. (B. B. Whittaker) 198

Picking cotton in West Nile, Uganda. (East African Railways and Harbours) 199

Ankole cattle. (R. N. Sanders) 199

Virunga volcanoes. (Uganda Information Department) 200

Port of Lobito in Angola. (Portuguese State Office, London) 205

Rhodes. (Federal Information Office) 208

The Victoria Falls. (Federal Information Office) 210

Kariba. (Federal Information Office) 212

Rhodesian tobacco field near Umtali. (Federal Information Office) 213

The Shabani asbestos mine, Rhodesia. (Federal Information Office) 214

Aerial view of Salisbury, capital of Rhodesia. (Federal Information Office) 215

Wankie colliery, Rhodesia. (Federal Information Office) 215

Rhodesian Iron and Steel Company's plant at Redcliff, Que Que. (Federal Information Office) 216

The Barotse plains of western Zambia. (Federal Information Office) 217

The Kuomboka; the migration of the people across the flooded Barotse plains. (Federal Information Office) 218

Roan Antelope copper mine, Luanshya, Zambia. (Federal Information Office) 218

Plucking tea on one of the estates in the Cholo area of Malawi. (Federal Information Office) 222

Chapel and walls of S. Sebastião fortress, Island of Mozambique. (Portuguese State Office, London) 227

Johannesburg. A view over the city showing the mining dumps. (South Africa House, London) 243

A factory at Germiston on the eastern Rand. (South Africa House, London) 244

xiii

Natives ploughing on the contour. (South Africa House, London)   245

Citrus farms in the Rustenburg area, Transvaal. (South Africa House, London)   246

Cape Town in the early eighteenth century   247

Cape Town from the air. (South Africa House, London)   247

Municipal flats in the Malay quarter of Cape Town. (South Africa House, London)   248

Cultivation patterns in Lesotho. (R.A.F., 82/E489/5107-8)   256

The pairs of air photographs on pages 8, 28, 35, 131, and 256 are intended to be viewed through a pocket stereoscope. With practice, one can obtain a three-dimensional impression without the aid of such an instrument.

1

The Physical Environment

RELIEF AND ROCKS

A LINE drawn across the map from northern Angola to western Ethiopia divides the continent into Low Africa and High Africa (Fig. 1 and Map 1). Low Africa, in the north-west, is largely made up of upland plains and sedimentary basins, 500 to 2,000 feet above sea-level, comprising the Sahara, and the catchments of the Congo, Nile, Lake Chad, Niger, and Senegal. Land rising above 3,000 feet is mainly confined to the Saharan massifs, Ahaggar and Tibesti, Jebel Marra in the Sudan Republic and

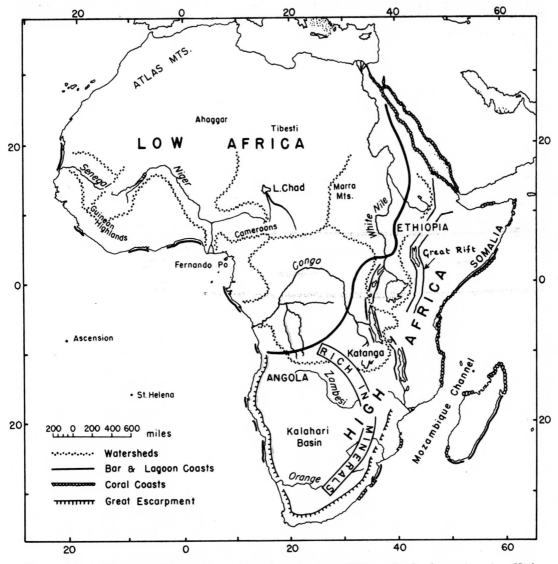

FIG. 1. *Physical features of the continent. A line from Angola to Ethiopia divides the continent into High Africa, mainly above 3,000 feet, and Low Africa, mainly below that level.*

the highlands of the Cameroon Republic and in the headwaters of the Niger. Nearly all of High Africa, to the south and east, rises above 3,000 feet, with the exceptions of Somalia, broad lowlands on either side of the Mozambique Channel, and relatively narrow coastal plains and valley strips elsewhere. Even the Kalahari basin is 3,000 feet or more above the sea, except in the vicinity of the Zambezi, Limpopo, and Orange rivers, and in east Africa the surface of Lake Victoria stands more than 3,700 feet above sea-level.

Evolution of the structure and relief

The mining areas in the south have been carefully studied, and geological surveys of a reconnaissance type have been made over most of the continent. In 1952 a geological map of the whole of Africa was prepared on a scale of 1:5 million. This has subsequently been modified to provide the basis for UNESCO's Geological Map of Africa, 1963, and for Map 2 in this book. More detailed surveys are slowly being extended to other parts of the continent where oil and other minerals are likely to occur. Air photographs, geophysical and geochemical methods of surveying and prospecting are being employed. Teams of Soviet and American geologists are working in certain territories, but even including these, geologists in Africa number less than a tenth of those in the U.S.S.R.

Ore bodies are often quite small at the surface; a heavily mineralized zone at Tsumeb in south-west Africa, for instance, is only 400 feet by 50 feet, so there must be many others of similar size lying undiscovered under the forests and deep soil layers in many parts of the continent. Exploration must be done with great care if potential supplies are not to be missed. However, the future seems to lie mainly with vast deposits of ore, deposits that can yield, either directly or after concentration, high-content ores able to be evacuated by heavy-load transports. Between 1960 and 1966 African production of bauxite and manganese-ore tripled and of iron-ore quadrupled.

Although it had long been suspected that oil was to be found in the Sahara and southern Nigeria, it was not until the late fifties that the size of the oil and natural gas reserves began to be appreciated. No doubt other mineral discoveries will yet be made and improvements in techniques of enriching and transport will allow ores to be worked that have long been known but are at present uneconomic.

The geological structure of the continent is much more complicated than the usual general statement that 'Africa is a rigid and ancient Pre-Cambrian

shield' might lead one to suppose, and it will be many years before the evolution of the structure and relief is known at all well. The account that follows is merely a brief introduction to a long and complicated history of earth movements, erosion by wind and running water, and the accumulation of a great variety of volcanic and sedimentary rocks.

Ancient crystalline rocks of Pre-Cambrian age underlie the whole area and outcrop at the surface very widely in High Africa. They form the highlands flanking the inland Niger basin, giving the rugged massifs of Aïr and Ahaggar as well as the dissected plateaux of the Guinean highlands, and Northern Nigeria. They build the Cameroon highlands and all the western rim of the continent from the Crystal Mountains on either side of the lower Congo to the Orange River in the south. Granites, gneisses, and schists, exposed in hill ranges or masked by the products of long-continued weathering, form the low watersheds between the Nile, Congo, and Chad basins. In east Africa they appear more extensively than anywhere else, building the plateau country between the Transvaal in the south and the Red Sea hills in the north.

The oldest of the crystalline rocks are intensely folded schists and banded gneisses, resistant to erosion, but generally less resistant than granites and quartzites intruded into them. Over wide areas, these old rocks are characterized by extensive, gently sloping surfaces, the solid rock being concealed beneath a deep weathered layer or by comparatively youthful transported material. The granites and some of the gneisses form rugged hill masses or dome-shaped inselbergs, rising sharply from the surrounding plains, and quartz dykes stand up as long, narrow ridges.

Rocks in the vicinity of igneous intrusions of Pre-Cambrian and later age have commonly been mineralized. In certain very restricted areas the ores of gold and other metals are present in sufficient quantities and concentrations, either in the crystallines or in alluvium derived from them by erosion, for large-scale mining to be worth while.

The latest of the Pre-Cambrian rocks have not been strongly folded in most areas. They include extensive sheets of volcanic lavas in South Africa and the very important gold-bearing quartzites of the Rand. Of considerable scientific interest are Pre-Cambrian tillites, found in both the Transvaal and Congo; they are boulder clays, now very much hardened or lithified and believed to have been laid down by ice-caps that seemed to have covered much of Africa south of the equator at one stage or more in Pre-Cambrian times.

GEOLOGICAL TABLE

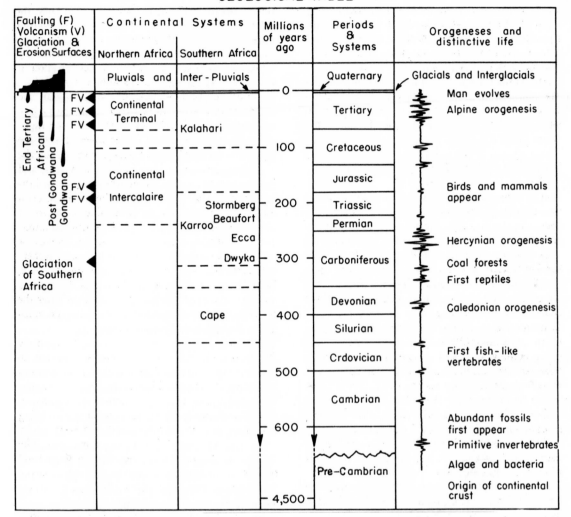

The old rocks were lifted above sea-level and strongly eroded before the Cambrian period began, and on this ancient land surface various continental sediments and lavas accumulated. Then in the Cambrian period much of the continent was covered by a sea in which sandstones and limestones were laid down, sedimentation in some areas continuing into the Carboniferous period. The Lower Palaeozoic rocks hardened into quartzites, crystalline limestones, and slates, some of them very resistant to erosion and standing up as steep-sided ridges and escarpments. Good examples are the tough sandstones of the Cape Series building Table Mountain behind Cape Town, Silurian sandstones rising from the desert plains in Tibesti and the Tassili des Ajjers, and the scarps at the margins of the Voltaian sandstones in Ghana.

The Lower Palaeozoic rocks were tilted and fractured by earth-movements about the time of the Caledonian orogeny, but folding in Africa was less intense than in Europe and North America. Later, while the coal measures of north-west Europe were accumulating, the continental areas of the southern hemisphere, including southern Africa, lay under an enormous ice-cap that probably covered as large an area as the European and North American ice-sheets of Pleistocene times and may well have lasted much longer. In parts of South Africa the lithified boulder clays are several hundreds of feet thick and, where glacial sediments have been removed by natural erosion or stripped off in quarries, scratched rocks and roches moutonnées can still be distinguished. This glaciation took place at such a remote time, 250 million years ago, that glaciated landscapes comparable to those of high latitudes have not survived. The effects of ice sculpture in Africa are confined to mountains like Ruwenzori and the Atlas ranges, high enough to harbour glaciers during the cooler periods of the last few hundred thousand years.

While the Carboniferous ice-caps still persisted, the southern tip of the continent was convulsed by violent earth movements comparable in age to the Hercynian in Europe (see Geological Table). The rocks of the Cape were strongly folded, and subsequent erosion of the strata has given the ranges of hills running parallel to the coast south of the Great Karroo.

The folded structures of certain old mountain blocks on the eastern side of South America resemble those of southern Africa in about the same latitude. These and other similarities in the geology of the two continents, and indeed of all the southern continents, have been taken as evidence that they were all united at this time to form a super-continent called Gondwanaland (Fig. 2). It may or may not have existed, there is no general agreement on the subject, but the resemblances in the build of Brazil, Africa, peninsula India, and Australia are so striking as to make the idea attractive to many earth scientists.

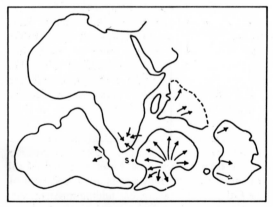

FIG. 2. *Africa as part of Gondwanaland. The Southern Continents may have been grouped together 250 million years ago, possibly in this kind of arrangement near the South Pole* (S). *The arrows show the directions of ice movement at the time of the Permo-Carboniferous Ice Age.*

The Karroo is the name applied to a system of rocks laid down over much of south and central Africa in those ages known in Europe as the Upper Carboniferous, Permian, Triassic, and Lower Jurassic. (The region in South Africa from which the name is taken is commonly spelled Karoo nowadays. We have retained the old form for the

sake of consistency.) The system includes the glacial tillites already mentioned, debris eroded from the Hercynian fold mountains, sandstones that accumulated in lakes and deltas, some deep-water clays, thick beds of coal and enormous sheets of volcanic lavas. In Lesotho the lavas are over 6,000 feet thick. In north Africa the *Continental Intercalaire*, a system of rocks varying to a similar degree, but much thinner than the Karroo, accumulated at a somewhat later stage. These rocks include some of the water-bearing beds, aquifers, under the Sahara that are now being tapped by deep boreholes.

The hypothetical super-continent of the southern hemisphere is supposed to have broken up in early Mesozoic times, the African continent acquiring roughly its present outline as the fragments drifted apart. Great fractures appeared in the east about this time, letting down blocks of Karroo sediments, which subsequently guided the evolution of the relief and drainage. In the west, the Newer Granites of northern Nigeria were introduced in the Jurassic period, and other granites in the highlands around the Chad basin are probably of comparable age. From about this time onwards the geological history of the south-eastern part of the continent is quite different from that of the north-west. The former was left high and upstanding with only its margins covered with marine sediments; the latter was flooded by seas advancing south from Tethys, the Alpine geosyncline of which the Mediterranean is a surviving fragment, as well as north from the Gulf of Guinea.

In late Mesozoic and Tertiary times, stresses within the crust resulted in the folding of the sediments accumulated in the Tethys geosyncline. From these structures the Atlas Mountains have been derived by long-continued erosion and intermittent uplift. The southern boundary is clear-cut, a series of faults separating the folded rocks from the rigid Saharan block. South of the Atlas, rocks and strata were not strongly folded by the late Mesozoic and Tertiary earth movements, except in the Benue trough where Cretaceous sandstones and clays were folded and have since been dissected to give scarpland topography. Elsewhere the stresses in the crust caused large-scale faulting and accentuated the basin form of certain depressions, but there is nothing in tropical Africa to compare with the great fold ranges of the Western Cordillera of North America, the Andes, Alps, and Himalayas.

The relatively undisturbed nature of the old massive shelves and huge sedimentary basins is of some economic significance in that it has been favourable to the deep development of altered and impregnated mineral deposits for which demand is increasing.

Throughout most of the continent evidence is to be found of successive uplifts during late Mesozoic and Tertiary times. Each uplift was followed by the cutting of an erosion surface graded to a lower base-level than the one preceding it and many geomorphologists look upon the continent's relief as consisting essentially of broad erosion levels and intervening erosional escarpments. The most spectacular erosional escarpment of all is the Drakensberg in the Republic of South Africa, with its extensions north into Angola and Rhodesia.

Dating of the erosion surfaces and the stages in the evolution of the relief is difficult, and the way in which the surfaces have been cut is still a matter for discussion and further research. F. Dixey has been inclined to distinguish a large number of stages and has supposed that the surfaces were probably formed in the manner described by W. M. Davis in his 'normal cycle of erosion'. L. C. King groups the surfaces together into a few major 'cycles' (Fig. 3) and attributes them to pediplanation involving scarp retreat over long distances. King has attempted to show that the earliest group of surfaces was formed before the break-up of Gondwanaland, and that the same cycles can be traced not only throughout Africa, but also in the other continents. The problem is a very difficult one because so many pages in the geological history of the continent are missing. Datable material is restricted to the products of erosion—mainly sands and clays, which were either carried down to the oceans or deposited in interior depressions and now underlie the great sandy plains of the Niger, Chad, and Kalahari basins and the swamps of the White Nile and Congo. As more deep bores are put down into these coastal and basin deposits in the search for oil and water, so will knowledge of the erosional history of the continent be deepened. But fossils are not common in the continental formations, so they are difficult to date, and there is much uncertainty in linking up coastal sedimentary formations with the erosion surfaces from which they were derived.

The most striking physical feature of the continent, at least as it appears on a structural map, is

The summit of Mount Kenya. Standing on the Equator, the mountain rises to 17,058 feet. This photograph, taken from the Upper part of the Lewis Glacier, looks south towards Top Hut, which appears at g on page 8.

the rift-valley system which stretches one-seventh of the way round the world, from the valley of the Jordan to the mouth of the Zambezi. In east Africa two fault systems can be distinguished. The eastern rift cuts across the Kenya highlands to Lake Rudolf, then turns north-east, splitting the Ethiopian plateaux and diverging into the much wider trenches of the Red Sea and Gulf of Aden. The western rift can be traced from the upper Nile and Lake Edward, through Lakes Tanganyika and Malawi, to the coast near Beira with a branch along the Luangwa valley.

The general pattern of the rift valleys seems to correspond with the lines of ancient structures in the crystalline floor. In the southern part of the system, some of the troughs such as the Luangwa valley appear to have been excavated out of relatively weak sediments that had been let down between parallel faults at the end of Karroo times. They are essentially erosional features. In others, like Malawi and Tanganyika, the form of the valleys

FIG. 3. *The high plains of Africa. Some writers describe the relief of the continent in terms of erosion surfaces. The cyclic landscapes shown here in diagrammatic profile are the groups of erosion surfaces distinguished by L. C. King (Morphology of the Earth, p. 226).*

has been sharpened in late Tertiary or Quaternary times by dislocations along earlier fault-planes, sometimes involving vertical movements of thousands of feet. Locally, at least, faulting has continued into the Recent period. Movements intense enough to produce very strong earthquakes still take place not only along the rift fractures but also in coastal areas, such as Ghana, where the continental mass is bounded by faults. Geophysical investigations indicate the likelihood of some connexion between the east African rift system and the mid-ocean ridges of the Atlantic and Indian Oceans.

Attention has been drawn by R. Furon and others to evidence for the existence of major fault systems in the west, notably a great rift running north-east from St. Helena, through Fernando Po and western Cameroon, beneath the Chad basin sediments to Tibesti. Other faults running north-east to south-west and north-west to south-east are seen as controlling the rectilinear courses of the middle Niger and the Nile in the northern Sudan.

Many of the Indian Ocean and Atlantic islands are the fragments of old volcanoes. The islands stretching south-west from Mount Cameroon mark the line of weakness associated with the hypothetical fault system just mentioned; others rise from the ocean floor or stand on mid-ocean ridges, like Mauritius. A volcano on Réunion is still active and so are Mount Cameroon and a number of the volcanoes in the vicinity of the Rift Valley, notably the Virungas near Lake Kivu.

The coastline

The coastline, like that of Gondwanaland generally, is remarkably free from indentations. This is probably to be explained by its faulted character, by the lack of folding in late geological times, by continental uplift being dominant, and by the deposition of river-borne sediments along the coast as sandbars and deltas. In consequence, natural harbours are few and far between. The tropical coasts of the Indian Ocean and Red Sea are fringed with coral reefs that can tear the bottom off a boat driven inshore by the easterly winds. Heavy swell generated by steady onshore winds, with a long fetch over thousands of miles of open ocean, gives heavy breakers along all the exposed coasts. In the days of sail African coasts were rightly considered dangerous for shipping. Ships still have to anchor well offshore at some 'surf ports', where both cargo and passengers must be carried to and from the shore by small boats specially designed to cope with the difficult conditions, but in the last few decades, artificial harbours have been constructed in several

territories and absence of ports no longer hampers development seriously.

Alongshore drift of beach material is very strong in many areas where the prevailing winds and waves approach the coast at an angle to the perpendicular and harbour works built to keep shipping channels clear have been difficult to construct and expensive to maintain because at the same time they have to prevent excessive coast erosion on the downdrift side. Lagos in particular has suffered in this way; a million tons of sand are pumped annually on to Victoria beach to try to stop erosion east of the harbour (Fig. 4).

The low alluvial shores have been shaped by the powerful waves. Barrier beaches sprinkled with coconut palms stretch for hundreds of miles along the Gulf of Guinea and the east coasts of Madagascar and Mozambique, and very long sandspits directed towards the equator are characteristic of Senegal and Angola. Such bars and spits seal off the rivers and prevent easy access from the sea. But the lagoons behind provide useful waterways for small boats and are often very well stocked with fish.

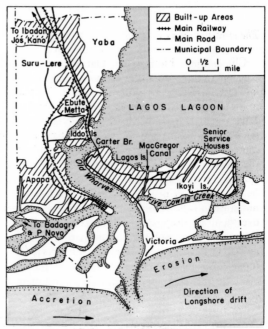

FIG. 4. *Longshore drift near Lagos. In the Bight of Benin, the waves approaching the soft, sandy coast from directions west of south cause beach material to be carried rapidly from west to east and if at any point the drift is interrupted by artificial structures, such as the harbour entrance works at Lagos, accretion takes place on the west and erosion on the east side.*

6

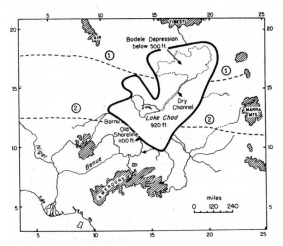

FIG. 5. *Shifting lakeshores and desert limits in west central Africa. The importance of Quaternary climatic fluctuations in Africa is indicated by the landforms of the Chad basin. The southern limit of vegetated dunes (2) lies far to the south of the southern limit of moving dunes of the present day (1). Old strandlines at 1,100 feet indicate an old lake, much larger than the present one, which overflowed into the Benue.*

The effects of climatic changes

Climatic conditions all over Africa have varied considerably during the Quaternary period of the last million years. The changes can be deciphered in the soils and drainage systems of the present day. Lake Chad, for example, which is less than 25 feet deep for the most part, and was reduced to little more than a swamp early in this century, was about the size of the Caspian Sea, possibly as late as 5,000 or 10,000 years ago. The old shoreline can be traced across Bornu in Nigeria and far to the north-east (Figs. 5 and 6). The lake must have been over 500 feet deep, its waters overflowed into the Benue valley to reach the Atlantic, and there can be no doubt that the Sudan zone at that time was much more humid then than it is now.

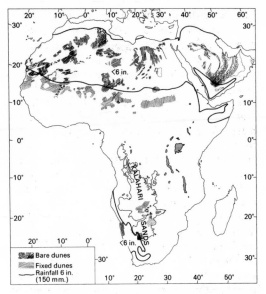

FIG. 7. *The past and present extent of blown sand. Moving sand is confined mainly to the very gentle slopes of basin-shaped areas with mean annual rainfall totals of less than 6 inches—about 150 mm. Old dunes extend into more humid areas and indicate that the deserts have at times been more extensive. The Kalahari Sands are shaped into dunes in the south, and include wind-blown sands further north. Note that the directions of the dune lines correspond broadly with those of the prevailing winds of the present day.*

Conditions drier than those of the present day are indicated by deep soils derived from blown sands that cover tens of thousands of square miles far beyond the present limits of the Sahara and Kalahari deserts, and ancient dune fields can be easily detected from the air in country that has been well watered and under cultivation for several centuries (Fig. 7). The deserts have evidently expanded and contracted from time to time as the climate fluctuated.

The climates of the more humid zones nearer the equator also varied in the course of the Quaternary

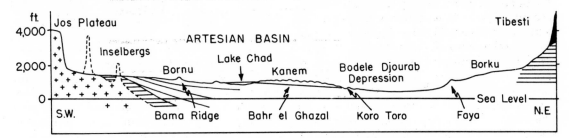

FIG. 6. *Cross-section of the Chad basin.*

7

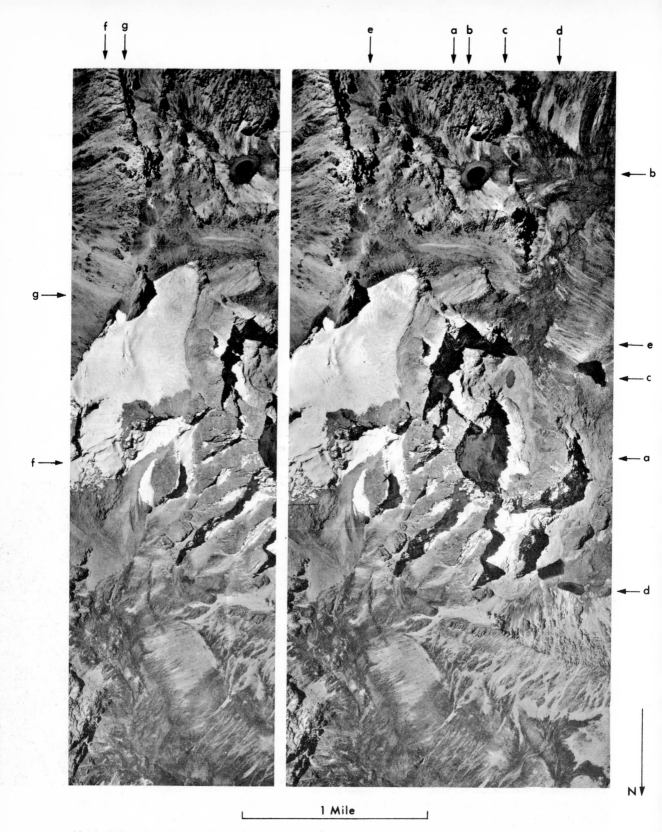

Mount Kenya from the air. This pair of air photographs, when viewed stereoscopically, gives a three-dimensional impression of Mount Kenya's summit. a—Batian the highest peak; b, c, and d—the Teleki, Tyndall, and Hausburg Tarns; e and f—the Lewis and Gregory glaciers; g—Top Hut. The glaciated valleys and moraines, formed when the ice was more extensive, can easily be distinguished.

1 Mile

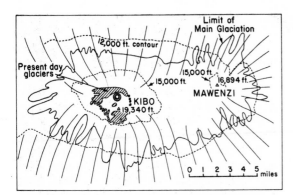

FIG. 8. *The glaciers of Kilimanjaro. At present confined to levels above 15,000 feet, moraines show they descended below 12,000 feet in the past, and, as now, came lower on the south side than on the north. Adapted from C. Downie,* Geol. Soc. America Bull., *1964, 1-16.*

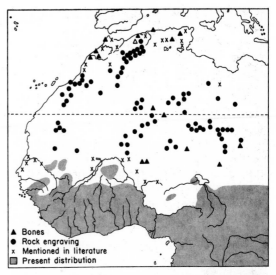

▲ Bones
● Rock engraving
x Mentioned in literature
▢ Present distribution

FIG. 9. *Elephants in the Sahara. The distribution of elephants in the Sahara at present and earlier times is shown in this map by R. Mauny ('Repartition de la grande "faune éthiopienne" du Nord-Ouest africain du Paléolithique et à nos jours', Proc. 3rd Pan-Afr. Cong. Prehist.,* Livingstone 1955, 102-5). *Increasing aridity in the last ten thousand years plus hunting are the main reasons for the reduction in the area where they are found.*

period. On the slopes of Ruwenzori and the high volcanic mountains in east Africa, old glacial moraines now overgrown with high forest indicate that glaciers must have descended several thousands of feet lower than now, implying lower temperatures and greater precipitation in the form of snow (Fig. 8). Lower temperatures would have reduced evaporation losses from drainage basins and lakes, and may help to explain the greater size of lakes at certain stages.

A great deal remains to be learned about these intertropical climatic fluctuations. It is commonly assumed that rainfall totals on the borders of the African deserts were greater during glacial advances and smaller during interglacial periods than they are now. This was probably the case, but it has not been conclusively proved. Indeed, some evidence has been found that pluvial or humid periods of low latitudes are to be correlated with the interglacial periods of high latitudes, and that the deserts shifted bodily towards the equator in the glacial periods. Yet again, certain meteorologists envisage the climatic zonation as being intensified in glacial periods and subdued in interglacial times. This complicated question is gradually being elucidated by the analysis of sediments containing sub-fossil pollen grains which indicate the vegetation in the past, and by using radioactive (C-14) methods of dating deposits. Recent work indicates that the southern margins of the Sahara abounded in lakes as late as 9,000 years ago, and many of the numerous paintings and engravings found in the middle of the desert, showing elephant, giraffe, and other savanna animals, probably date from this period, or an even later humid phase (Fig. 9). However, the climate has

Saharan engraving of an elephant on volcanic rock in the wadi Ganoa in western Tibesti. The climate there now is far too dry for elephant and other savanna animals.

probably changed very little over the last 4,000 years.

The results of research into climatic history are of interest to both naturalists and technicians. The present distribution of animals and plant associations in Africa must be explained largely in terms of the fluctuations of climate that modified their habitat; at the same time studies of distributions by botanists and zoologists can help to throw light on these fluctuations. The movements of early peoples no doubt responded in some degree to the climatic shifts, and the distribution of artifacts can be useful in helping to date recent geological deposits. Excavations and borings made by engineers reveal layers of sediments that provide information about the past climates, and engineers are anxious, on occasion, to learn more about the climates in order to gain a greater understanding of the nature and reliability of certain underground sources of water. Such studies involve the co-operation of scientists and technicians engaged in several different fields, and the findings are of practical importance as well as being of great interest in themselves.

Rock weathering, residual crusts, and stripped landscapes

Most of the earth's surface is mantled by a layer of weathered debris; solid rock comes to the surface only where the products of breakdown have been removed suddenly or as quickly as they formed, for example on steep slopes. The debris and drift mantle, sometimes called the regolith, is the parent material from which soils are derived and so an understanding of its nature is of some importance

Half-dome inselberg. This hill, near Zaria in northern Nigeria, shows curved joint plains in the rock mass and residual joint-bounded blocks near the summit.

in attempting to appreciate the interaction of the elements of the environment.

In Africa chemical weathering is more active than in higher latitudes because the high temperatures cause rock minerals to decay rapidly. Furthermore, weathering has not been interrupted by glaciation and so crystalline rocks, particularly in humid areas of moderate relief are decomposed to depths of 50 feet or much more. In some places sources of fresh rock and gravel for road-metal, harbour works and general constructional purposes are quite rare, and rocky inselbergs are then valuable economic assets as well as scenic attractions. In the wetter regions the thick regolith and soil are protected from erosion under natural conditions by an absorbent surface layer of decaying vegetable matter. When forests are cleared, more water runs over the ground and within a few decades hill-sides may be gashed by gullies and landslips, and streams clogged with the debris. In the drier parts of the continent, where the rainfall is too low to give much percolating water, chemical weathering is inhibited and solid rock is generally near the surface, except in structural basins filled with great thicknesses of youthful sediments, or where the products of weathering from a past humid period persist.

In many regions soil-forming and weathering processes that were at work thousands or may be millions of years ago have resulted in the accumulation of certain distinctive layers in the regolith. When these layers are exposed by erosion of the overlying soil horizons, they emerge as thick, hard surface crusts, sometimes called duricrusts. Three main kinds can be distinguished called ferricrete, calcrete, and silcrete.

Ferricrete is rich in iron or alumina, so rich that some types have been used as iron-ore by African iron-smelters. It covers quite extensive areas in the savanna lands and is typical of old upland plains, over many kinds of rocks. The original enrichment of the soil layer with oxides of iron and alumina was probably the result of long-continued leaching away of the more soluble products of weathering in areas of low relief where erosion by running water had practically ceased. The hardening of the iron-rich layer may have taken place either as a result of the soil being dried out following uplift and rejuvenation of the streams, or in consequence of the climate getting drier. Some ferricrete has formed in other ways, and many problems regarding its origin remain to be solved. How is it that some beds of residual ironstone tens of feet thick are found in areas where the rocks have such a low iron content that hundreds of feet of rock would have to be

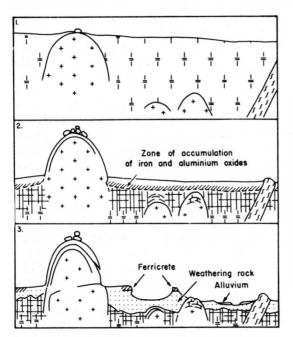

Castle koppie. It stands near the left bank of the Niger a little way down-stream of the Benue confluence.

FIG. 10. *The development of a landscape by weathering and stripping. The three diagrams show how inselberg landscapes of the savanna lands may have developed. 1. Crystalline rocks are planed off and deeply weathered. 2. Stripping of the weathered layer reveals resistant masses of rock; renewed weathering on the plains leads to the formation of lateritic soils. 3. Renewed downcutting leads to the formation of duricrusts, new valleys, and the exposure of slightly weathered rock. The inselberg residual is split along joint planes parallel to the surface but remains resistant to further erosion.*

weathered and selectively removed to give the iron-rich surface layer? Presumably some of the iron has in fact been carried into the area in suspension or solution and is not truly residual.

When streams cut down into a ferricrete layer, steep valley-side slopes retreat while fragments of ferricrete remain to a late stage capping mesas and smaller flat-topped hills, known as buttes. The debris from the edges of the ferricrete cappings moves gradually downslope to the new erosion surface and is incorporated in the soils developing there to form what is sometimes called secondary laterite. The sequence of iron enrichment, induration and dissection may be repeated, and flat residual surfaces with their ferricrete caps of different kinds provide some kind of record of the physical evolution of the landscape.

Silcrete, or surface quartzite, with a very high content of silica underlies wide tracts of country in Botswana and in the Cape Province of South Africa. Calcrete, or surface limestone, is very widespread in the northern Sahara, especially in areas underlain by lime-rich rocks and it also occurs very extensively in the Kalahari.

Wherever duricrusts are the parent materials, soils are shallow and usually of little value for agriculture because the lower layers of the profile are too dense to allow satisfactory root development and nutrients are inadequate to support crops or pasture. But they are sometimes useful materials for building roads and for other constructural purposes.

Many geomorphologists are inclined to visualize the development of the relief in many parts of Africa as being essentially discontinuous. Instead of assuming that weathering and erosion take place simultaneously, they believe that the present landforms are to be explained most satisfactorily in terms of long-continued weathering being followed at a later stage by rapid erosion of the regolith—perhaps as the result of uplift or a change in climate. Inselbergs and koppies are then seen not as monadnocks or the final remnants of a rock mass reduced by the parallel retreat of steep slope units, but as the rock cores resistant to weathering, revealed when the regolith has been stripped away (Fig. 10). This approach to the study of African landforms, which was outlined by Falconer early in the century, found favour with Bayley Willis, Wayland, and

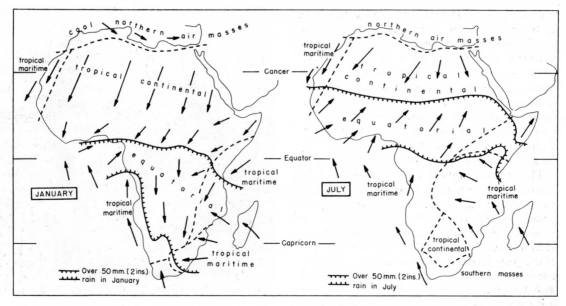

FIG. 11. *Air masses and precipitation in January and July. The arrows indicate the directions of the prevailing winds at low altitudes.*

later workers in east Africa and appears to have much to recommend it.

CLIMATE

Almost the whole of Africa lies within 35° of the equator; it is the most tropical of all the continents. Regional differences in river régimes, vegetation, and land-use can be explained primarily in terms of the variation from place to place in the amounts and seasonal distribution of the rainfall. This variation depends on the atmospheric circulation about which much remains to be learned and the description that follows is much simplified.

Wind systems and the pattern of precipitation

The basic pattern of air movement over much of the continent is towards the equator, from the northeast in the northern hemisphere and from the southeast in the southern hemisphere. These two floods of air are derived from sub-tropical cells of high pressure where air is descending and is consequently warm and dry near the surface. The descending air in each hemisphere diverges to flow towards the equator and towards the pole, and because of the rotation of the earth is diverted to the right in the northern hemisphere and to the left in the southern hemisphere.

Until quite recently the explanation usually given for the seasonal occurrence of the rains and hence the arrangement of the climatic regions of tropical

Africa was in terms of an inter-tropical front formed by airstreams moving to lower latitudes from northeast and south-east and coming together (the south-easterlies swinging round to become south-westerlies on crossing the equator, and the north-easterlies likewise becoming north-westerlies). The front was said to lie across the continent in July from Senegal to Eritrea and to shift south as the sun moved towards the Tropic of Capricorn until in January it ran near the Guinea coast and, swinging far to the south, stretched across southern Africa in about latitude 18° south. Rain was described as occurring in association with the front and in the humid air on the side nearer the equator.

According to B. W. Thompson (1965), however, the inter-tropical front is recognizable only to the west of the Kenya–Ethiopian plateau and its movements appear to be confined to the zone between the Tropic of Cancer and latitude 5° north. Furthermore the rainfall belt on the equatorial side begins 200 miles from the front's surface position.

For rain to fall, moist air is needed. In general, the easterlies over Africa, the trade winds, are dry except for the lower layers which have collected moisture on the ocean passage, whereas the westerlies have moisture distributed in depth throughout the current. What is more, the westerlies have a greater tendency to rise, and moist air must rise and cool if condensation is to take place. Upward motion occurs mainly, however, in meteorological situations in which the lower layers of the atmosphere, up to about 5,000 to 10,000 feet, converge horizontally, giving linear areas of low pressure called equatorial troughs; uplift due to relief and convection are of secondary importance. Such horizontal convergence commonly takes place south of the inter-tropical front. It can also result from the funnelling of air flowing between two anticyclonic systems, and in the case of winds blowing onshore it can be a consequence of deceleration caused by the greater frictional drag over the land.

The extreme south-west and north-west of the continent receive rain in the winter months from eastward moving, mid-latitude, cyclonic depressions. The Sahara, and to a lesser degree the Kalahari, are occupied by subsiding, diverging air, at least above the surface layers, throughout most of the year. In the inter-tropical part of the continent a broad rainfall belt moves north and south with the sun, as shown in Fig. 11, rainstorms being mainly associated with the convergence of westerly airstreams in equatorial troughs. In consequence, two rainfall peaks per year are experienced at most equatorial stations and single summer rainfall peaks nearer the Tropics.

The pattern of the rainfall distribution is complicated by the relief, with the mountains and escarpments particularly of High Africa receiving more rain than the sheltered valleys to leeward. Certain low coastal belts are remarkably dry and their aridity is usually explained in terms of cold water offshore brought by currents or welling up from great depths. The extreme aridity of the Namib desert and the extension north of coastal desert almost to the mouth of the Congo is attributed to the Benguela current. Similarly the Canaries current is seen as intensifying the aridity of the northwest fringe of the Sahara, and cool upwelling water off the Horn of Africa as chilling and stabilizing the lower layers of moist air approaching Somalia and Kenya from the east. The anomalous dry zone in south-east Ghana also has relatively cool water lying offshore. Thompson, however, is more inclined to explain such coastal aridity in terms of locally high atmospheric pressure and associated subsidence.

Rainfall reliability

Climatic fluctuations are on various time scales. Shorter period fluctuations of a few centuries are superimposed on the longer period oscillations of the Quaternary period mentioned earlier. Such fluctuations giving, say, more frequent droughts, were probably severe enough within the last few

Flooding resulting from heavy rains in Zambia. In early 1962 these floods cut off Luapula Province from the rest of the country.

thousands of years to affect the history of communities in sensitive areas such as the desert borderlands but the evidence is too scanty to be conclusive.

Of greater moment are variations in rainfall from one year to another, and sporadic floods and droughts such as those that caused much damage in east Africa in 1961. As Map 3 indicates, the chance of the rainfall total in any one year being within 10 per cent. of the mean is less than 40 per cent. over most parts of the continent and, in general, the reliability expressed in these terms varies with the mean annual rainfall. There are, however, some notable exceptions to this general rule; for example, Beira and Durban on the east coast have quite high annual rainfall means but low orders of reliability.

Poor rainy seasons can affect very wide areas; 1913, for instance, seems to have been a dry year throughout the Sudan zone. There is also a tendency for rainy or dry years to occur in bunches. The 1940's were dry in the western Sudan; the early 1960's were rather wet in east Africa, rather dry in south-central Africa.

In time meteorologists may be able to predict the precipitation for a coming rainy season, but as yet this cannot be done. Many have attempted to find cyclic variations in the rainfall which might be extrapolated into the future. At one time it appeared that such fluctuations, recorded in the varying levels of east African lakes, were related to the eleven-year sunspot cycle, but recent records do not give much support to such speculations.

Most of the rain in tropical Africa is the outcome of convergence and uplift in equatorial troughs and convectional activity within humid, unstable air masses, giving strong vertical development of clouds. Thunder-storms are common, and are especially violent in the first weeks of the rainy season as the warm, wet air advances. Strong gusty winds accompanying them are responsible for most of the wind erosion in semi-arid lands, and much of the accelerated water erosion also happens at the opening of the rainy season, when the vegetation forms a less effective cover than later in the year and the first heavy storms of rain falling on bare soil cause severe erosion.

Studies made in east Africa indicate that a high proportion of the rain in any year is concentrated in a few spells each lasting about a week. The sky is rarely overcast for very long periods except in such very wet areas as western Cameroon and Gabon, and at the height of the rainy season elsewhere. Normally the sun shines for several hours on most days of the year, and an African living in England can miss it sadly (see Map 6).

It is commonly supposed that rain falls most frequently in the late afternoon and early evening, and it is usually assumed to be the result of convectional activity increasing through the day as surface heating generates increasingly strong upward currents of air. Statistical studies do not give much support to these ideas and they may apply only locally.

The prediction of rain is no easy matter in tropical Africa even a few hours ahead, for convectional storms are local, usually only a few miles in diameter, and while one place may receive an inch of rain in half an hour, another only a mile or two away from the track of the storm-centre may record no rain whatsoever.

Tropical cyclones

Between November and April, violent revolving storms are generated from time to time in the southern Indian Ocean, and move in a westerly direction towards east Africa. Small cyclones very occasionally cross Zanzibar and the extreme southern coast of mainland Tanzania, causing severe damage over small areas and Mozambique is also liable to be affected. But the risks of damage are greatest on the islands of Madagascar, Mauritius, and Réunion, the storms usually curving away to the south and south-east before reaching the continent itself. Damage is inflicted not only by the very high winds, which may exceed 100 m.p.h. but also by big waves and a temporary rise in sea-level. Torrential rain, several inches falling in a few hours, may add to the destruction.

Temperature (see Map 6)

The south-eastern part of the continent is considerably cooler than the north-west because of its greater altitude, stations on the high plateau experiencing many days in the year with mean temperatures well below 15° C. (59° F.). The highest mean annual temperatures are recorded in the interior of Somalia. In all the countries bordering the southern Sahara mean daily temperatures exceed 25° C. (77° F.) for a substantial part of the year and they must be rated as amongst the hottest parts of the world (see Map 5, climatic diagrams for Sokoto and Gao). At most stations the mean daily range of temperature exceeds the difference between the mean temperatures of the warmest and coolest month. Both daily and monthly temperature ranges increase towards the continental interior.

Between the tropics, the highest temperatures are recorded just before the onset of the main rainy season; it is cooler after the first rains and then as the rainy season closes temperatures rise again but not so high as before. Daily ranges of temperature are at a maximum during the dry season when clear skies allow surface cooling by radiation at night and strong surface heating in the daytime. The figures quoted in climatic statistics are, of course, those recorded in meteorological screens under standardized conditions; temperatures on the bare ground have a much greater range and under a dense forest cover a smaller one than these figures indicate.

The importance of the high temperatures is very great. They result in high rates of evaporation from the soil and from water surfaces, annual rates about four times those normal in the British Isles being recorded. The effects of the heat on people's behaviour and efficiency are difficult to assess. Africans as well as Europeans find it unpleasant to work hard, manually or mentally, when shade temperatures exceed 30° C. (86° F.), especially if at the same time the humidity is high. Both appreciate air conditioning and this is being introduced to hotels, offices, and some homes. But the equipment is expensive and electricity is needed, so its use is mainly confined to highly paid staff in the largest towns.

Humidity

The dampness of the air, as indicated by figures for relative humidity, fluctuates through a wide

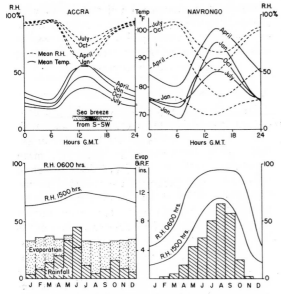

FIG. 12. *Diurnal and seasonal variation in relative humidity. At Accra on the coast of Ghana and at Navrongo in the north of the country the relative humidity reaches a maximum at dawn and a minimum in the early afternoon. The seasonal variation in relative humidity is much greater in the interior than on the coast. Navrongo's climate is typical of the Sudan zone. Accra's climate has rather a special character. The sea-breeze that sets in towards midday and reaches its maximum strength a few hours later helps to keep the temperature down in the mid-afternoon. In contrast to many parts of west Africa with two rainfall peaks, the second peak at Accra is very subdued. Except in June the mean monthly values for evaporation from a free-water surface exceed the mean rainfall and as the climate diagrams show on the maps, the water balance is small.*

daily range, reaching a maximum at dawn and a minimum in the early afternoon, so care must be taken in comparing the humidity at different places to see that the figures apply to the same times of day. Variations in the mean relative humidity from season to season correspond fairly closely with the distribution of rain through the year, figures rising when humid air masses cover the country and falling when dry air from the sub-tropics replaces it.

In the dry season of the Sudan zone, wood warps and splits and visibility is reduced for days or weeks at a time by dust, consisting in large part of diatoms from ancient lake beds, carried seawards from the Sahara; this is combined in many areas with smoke particles from bush fires. On the coastlands of

Guinea and in the northern parts of the Congo basin the air is humid throughout the year. In such damp climates fungi thrive, many materials deteriorate rapidly and human energy is not displayed to advantage. These are all 'costs of the environment' not easily quantified; heavy, but possibly no heavier than those that have to be borne in lands of severe ice and snow.

Evaporation

Losses of water from the surfaces of African lakes and rivers, and transpiration from the leaves of growing plants are greater than in higher latitudes, particularly where high temperatures are combined with low relative humidity. The depth of water lost from lakes and reservoirs by evaporation varies from 750 mm. (about 30 inches) per annum in the more humid and cooler regions to over 2,000 mm. (80 inches) in the Sahara. The actual amount lost from bare ground surfaces is smaller because moisture losses are greatly reduced when the soil surface dries out. Over most of the continent the drying capacity of the air, the water need, or more precisely the potential evapotranspiration, is in excess of the rainfall in a majority of months in the year. This helps to account for the numerous basins of inland drainage; they occupy the areas shown with a negative moisture index in Map 4.

Rain water is protected from direct evaporation once it has percolated into the ground to a depth of a few feet, and from transpiration when it sinks down below the level of roots. If geological conditions are favourable and the regolith and rocks are pervious, percolating water feeds ground-water held in the pore spaces. It slowly moves laterally through the ground in the direction of the slope of the water-table and eventually emerges in springs, river-beds, or swamps fed by seepage. So although the beds of many rivers are dry during much of the year, water can still be obtained from most of them by digging pits a few feet deep into the sand. Away from rivers, deeper wells and bore-holes allow people to obtain water from greater depths where geological structures are favourable. In the last half century exploitation of underground water has opened up many thousands of square miles for herding and cultivation.

Water within the root zone is liable to be brought back to the surface and transpired from the leaves of grasses and trees. Consequently, if the trees are cleared by cultivators, losses of water may be reduced and more of it sinks down to feed the ground-water at depth. Deforestation may explain why water-tables in many sandy parts of northern Nigeria have been rising in recent years. In other areas, where soils and rocks are less pervious, clearing the woodland has increased runoff and reduced percolation to such an extent that water-tables have fallen.

In Africa the evaporation from the ground is so strong and the demands of plants for water so great that land receiving 20 inches of rain annually or even more may be of very little use for cultivation unless it is irrigated. An inch or two of rain falling in a month is not enough for growing crops. At the height of the rainy season on the other hand, when over 15 inches may fall in a month, water losses by evaporation may be reduced by high humidity and cloudy skies to a small percentage of the rainfall and a big surplus is available not only to supply plants abundantly, but also to fill the river channels and feed water-bearing strata underground (see Map 5, climatic diagram for Freetown). Evaporation thus tends to emphasize the effects of the uneven seasonal distribution of the rainfall and to sharpen the distinction between years or places with adequate and inadequate rainfall totals. This is illustrated in the diagrams (Map 5) showing graphs of precipitation and potential evapotranspiration superimposed.

At the beginning of the growing season, soil moisture conditions in intertropical Africa are quite the opposite to those in Britain or the Mediterranean lands. The soil profile is dried out, and so if there are gaps of a few days between storms at the time of sowing there is no supply of moisture stored in the soil that the young plants can fall back on. They quickly wilt and die. In the drier areas the crop season may continue as a running fight between evaporation and transpiration, in which evaporation gains the upper hand as the rains decline. Agriculture in Africa is consequently more precarious, at least in this respect, than in higher latitudes.

Man's response to the climate

The lives of the people are adapted to the vagaries of the climate and above all to the seasonality and uncertainty of the rainfall. Townsmen are less affected than the more numerous country people, for life in modern African cities, as in cities elsewhere, has a stronger daily than seasonal routine. But the cultivator's life is geared to the seasons. He works hard on his land during the rains, planting, weeding, and keeping off pests, and then after the harvest he attends to his house, visits his friends, or he may leave his home to seek work in the mines or plantations. Economists are fond of pointing to the possibilities of raising incomes by extending the period when work could be done by growing a wider range of crops and irrigating them in the dry season. Dry-season cultivation is becoming more popular,

wherever rural populations are densely settled and especially in the vicinity of large towns.

The annual cycle of activity on the land varies from one climatic belt to another, and from one year to another, according to the rain. Pastoralists move their herds from well-drained ranges occupied in the rainy season to riverine and marshy regions in the dry season. Their customs and social relations are governed by their movements and by the alternating dispersal and concentration of family groups they involve. Here again, the traditional rhythm appears to be rather inefficient to western eyes; a less mobile existence would allow the herds to produce more milk and meat, and attempts are being made to settle the pastoralists by improving both grazing and dry-season water supplies so that there will be less need for them to move.

Fluctuations in crop yields depending on the rains also provide economic problems. Most African territories are very dependent on exports of a few crops and the uncertainty of the returns from these, because of the climate amongst other factors, makes it very difficult to prepare long-term investment programmes and development schemes. The economic uncertainty cannot be entirely blamed on the African climates for other climates are just as variable, but African peoples and economies are more sensitive to climatic vicissitudes than many others because they depend on nature so directly. More advanced industrialized countries with their better transport systems and integrated economies are less dependent on locally produced primary products and agriculture, and so can meet local shortages more easily by importing goods from a distance.

RIVERS AND LAKES

Most African rivers are dry for half the year and in flood during the rains. Variations in precipitation from season to season dominate river régimes, whereas in higher latitudes seasonal variations in evaporation are commonly more effective. Except for a few streams rising in Lesotho and some high mountain torrents in east Africa, melting ice and snow are of no importance as sources of supply, and do nothing to even out discharges through the year.

The levels of most of the big rivers, including the lower Niger, rise and fall through 20 feet or more, greatly reducing their value for many purposes. Bridges are very expensive to construct when they must include long approaches across marshy tracts liable to be flooded for several weeks at a time. Navigation is impeded in the dry season by sandbanks and rocks, and during the rains strong currents impede boats moving upstream.

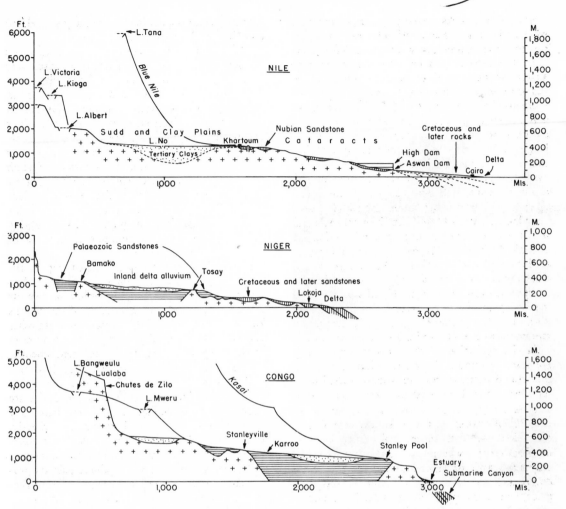

FIG. 13. *Longitudinal sections of the Nile, Niger, and Congo. The profiles of the big African rivers are very irregular, with rapids stretching up-stream and down-stream of long reaches between 1,000 and 1,500 feet above sea-level. The steep course of the Congo below Stanley Pool is particularly noteworthy.*

Rapids and waterfalls which interrupt the courses of nearly every river on the continent are additional obstacles to river traffic. The Congo is a prime example; between Stanley Pool and the head of the estuary at Matadi the river falls nearly 900 feet in 150 miles by a series of great cataracts (Fig. 13). These and other falls are the outcome of intermittent uplift in Tertiary and later times. In the past such falls have been regarded as troublesome hindrances to navigation, which they undoubtedly are, but now they are seen more often as potential sources of energy on an enormous scale. On the rivers of the west coast between Guinea and Angola there are numerous sites suitable for power-stations, on falls within a few tens of miles of the coast, just where river discharges are at a maxi-

mum. The Congo is in a class by itself; it has been calculated that the falls on the lower river are capable of providing as much electricity each year as the whole of western Europe consumed in 1960.

Several spectacular projects for generating electricity have been completed and others are under construction (see Map 16). Construction costs are high because large dams are needed to even out the seasonal fluctuations in discharge and assure a steady flow through the turbines. Though primarily constructed for power production, the dams bring other benefits; for example, by regulating discharge they improve navigation and can provide water for irrigating flood plains downstream.

The rivers with the steadiest discharges are in the equatorial zone. The Congo's vast basin lies across

The Murchison Falls, Uganda. A short distance before it reaches Lake Albert, the Victoria Nile falls about 120 feet to the level of the lake. From S. W. Baker, Albert N'yanza, Great Basin of the Nile, vol. ii, London, 1866.

the equator, so the lower river is supplied one-half of the year mainly from the northern hemisphere and in the other half from the southern. As a result, the mean ratio between its mean maximum discharge of $2\frac{1}{2}$ million cubic feet per second and mean minimum flow of 0·8 million is remarkably low for any African river. The White Nile too has a very steady flow, not only because its waters are derived from an extensive equatorial region with two rainy seasons, but also because the great lakes, Victoria and Albert, have a regulating effect on its behaviour appropriate to bodies of water bearing such august names.

Both the Congo and the White Nile provide useful waterways in country which is still difficult to traverse overland. The river steamers operating on

them are not unlike those on the Mississippi and Rhine. Most of them are no longer stern-wheelers but diesel-engined, propellor-driven boats, pulling, or in the more modern style, pushing trains of barges between forest-covered banks and through reedy swamps.

Traffic in the Nile Sudd and on Lake Mweru in the Congo system has always been impeded by blockages caused by papyrus and floating water weeds. A new enemy has appeared since the mid-1950's in the form of *Eichornia crassipes*, the floating water hyacinth, which has immigrated from America and colonized many of the navigable reaches of both rivers. It has been proving very difficult to eradicate. It chokes the water intakes of cooling systems on boats and if it spreads much further down the Nile could foul the pumps used for irrigation in the central Sudan and, further downstream, block irrigation canals.

Artificial lakes created by new dams on the Zambezi and Volta have disadvantages as well as bringing benefits. The crests of the dams themselves can be used as highways, and boats can link together lakeshore settlements. Freshwater fisheries may be developed. However, drowned forest trees poking through the surface are serious obstacles to shipping and fishing, and the seasonal rise and fall of the water-level presents real difficulties. Some of the ecological consequences of creating these big lakes are impossible to predict. Soon after the completion of Kariba, a water-weed called *Salvinia auriculata* began to spread over the lake; fortunately the prevailing winds drift it westwards away from the turbine intakes, but it may obstruct navigation for some years. It remains to be seen how the Volta lake will behave. With a bigger area than any other man-made lake, it has necessitated a rearrangement of the trunk-road system linking north-east Ghana to the coast. On the other hand, it may allow certain iron-ore deposits to be exploited, which would otherwise have remained untouched, and may well prove to be an attraction to tourists who wish to cruise into the interior.

Rivers in general flow from wet to drier areas, mountains at the source usually attracting more rain than plains near the mouth. In Africa, where drainage basins commonly stretch across climatic belts from very wet to extremely dry country, the consequences are more pronounced than elsewhere, many rivers dwindling downstream with interesting physiographic effects. The waters of the Logone and Shari, for instance, which are supplied by tributaries rising in a wide arc from Cameroon to Jebel Marra, flow across the gently sloping plains

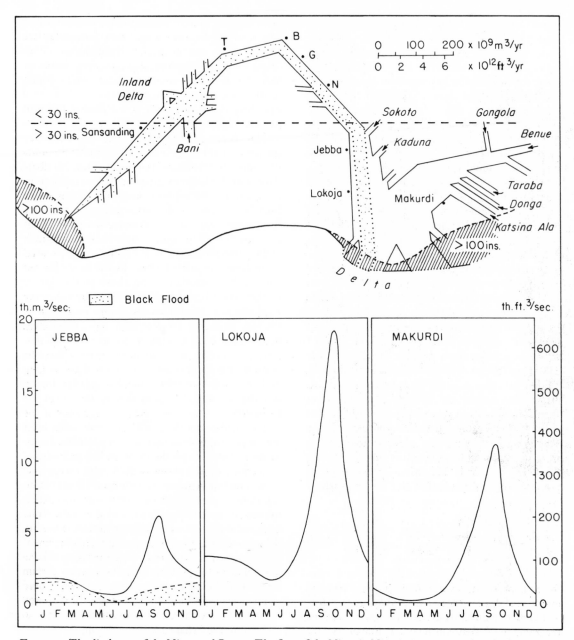

FIG. 14. *The discharge of the Niger and Benue. The flow of the Niger in Nigeria is maintained in the first quarter of the year by the Black Flood, water which fell as rain on the highlands of Guinea several months earlier and has made its way slowly through the 'Inland Delta'. Little water is added to the river where annual rainfall totals are less than 30 inches. The width of the diagrammatic river is a measure of the discharge according to the scale in the top right-hand corner. T.—Tombouctou, Timbuktu; B.—Bourem; G.—Gao; N.—Niamey.*

of north-central Africa for several hundreds of miles and eventually spread out to form Lake Chad. The water at the southern edge of the lake is quite fresh, but salinity gradually increases towards the north as the high evaporation takes effect, and along the sandy northern shores salts crystallize out, notably sodium carbonate. The complicated shape of the north-east side of the lake and numerous elongated low islands within it are believed to be the remains of ancient sand dunes, formed in a drier period several thousands of years ago and now flooded by the southern rivers. From the south-east corner of the lake, a broad shallow channel known as the Bahr-el-Ghazal can be traced north-east for about 200 miles to the lowest part of the basin, the Bodelé depression at about 500 feet above sea-level. Chad itself is quite close to the western rim of the basin at a level of about 920 feet and no doubt its waters have at times spilled north-east, along the Bahr-el-Ghazal as well as westwards into the Benue in still more humid periods (Fig. 5).

In south-eastern Angola a similar hydrographic situation exists (Fig. 73). The Cubango and Cuando diminish in volume as they approach the Kalahari desert, and eventually break up into distributaries which form a swampy delta in the Okavango basin of northern Botswana, comparable in size to the delta of the Nile. Water escaping from the upper end of the swamps occasionally reaches the Zambezi via the Linyanti channel and the lower end of the delta overflows annually to feed Lake Ngami and to run down the Botletle channel into the Makarikari depression. Both of these hollows show signs of having held much more water at times in the last century and the more distant past than they do now.

Some other large rivers enter extensive saucer-shaped depressions and manage to escape from them. The Chambezi, one of the main headstreams of the Congo, enters the marshes bordering Lake Bangweulu in Zambia, and splits up into several branches some of which feed the lake. From the south-west corner of the marshy tract a reconstituted river emerges, called the Luapula, which eventually reaches the main Congo by way of the Luvera and Lualaba.

The Niger is a better-known example. During a dry period of the Quaternary it formed a big inland delta south-west of Tombouctou (Timbuktu). At a later humid stage a lake filled the basin and overflowed the eastern rim at Bourem to join a river, of which the Tilemsi depression or *dallol*, now usually dry, formed the headwaters. When drier conditions returned, the Niger continued to follow its new course to the sea, and the sets of rapids between Gao and Niamey, and further down between Bussa and Jebba, point to its recent emergence as one of the world's great rivers.

The complicated forms of the great river basins, with their swamps and lakes, plus the varied climatic zones they traverse, produce complex river régimes. At Jebba on the Niger, water-levels rise owing to local rains from July to early October when the peak level is reached. The river then falls until December when the fall is balanced by a second flood, derived from the July to October rains in the hills of Guinea and retarded by the swamp area formed by the ancient delta south-west of Tombouctou. This 'black flood', so called because its waters are clearer than those of the silt-laden local 'white flood', results in a period of sustained water-levels until March or April, when there is a further fall continuing to June (Fig. 14).

The régime of the Nile was once dominated by the floodwaters brought down in summer from the Ethiopian highlands by the Sobat, Blue Nile, and Atbara, and in Upper Egypt the flow was maintained in winter by the constant discharge of the White Nile. Now the river's discharge in Egypt is regulated by storage reservoirs upstream. The Jebel Aulia dam south of Khartoum ponds back the summer and autumn flow of the White Nile. The floodwaters of the Blue Nile are conserved in part by the Sennar and Er Roseires dams, and those of the Atbara by the dam at Khashm el Girba (see Fig. 15). Since 1968 the new High Dam at Aswan takes care of the rest. Standing 250 feet high and 3 miles long, it can hold back enough water to even out seasonal discharges and conserve water from wet years for use in dry ones. At a cost of about £400 million, it will increase Egypt's acreage of cultivable land by 30 per cent. and double the output of electricity.

The Vaal in South Africa is the only other river where control is so complete. The southern Transvaal's industry depends on its waters and so they are conserved and allocated with great care.

Seasonal shortages of water remain a great handicap in most parts of the continent and other possibilities for conserving water and diverting rivers have naturally attracted much attention. Many of the schemes proposed are quite impracticable. Some of the most spectacular involve creating great lakes to ameliorate the climates of lands now dry. A dam across the Congo above Stanley Pool, it has been claimed, would produce a lake in the Congo basin overflowing into the Chad basin and flooding much of the southern Sahara. Or again, the upper Zambezi should be diverted to supplement the rivers entering the Okavango basin and create a lake in the northern Kalahari. But the Zambezi is needed to generate power at Kariba. In any event, even if the topography and evaporation losses would allow such vast lakes to be formed, their benefits are unlikely to repay initial costs. The air over the Sahara and Kalahari already contains huge masses of water. The cause of drought is the lack of dynamic processes capable of producing ascending currents that cause adiabatic cooling and hence cloud formation

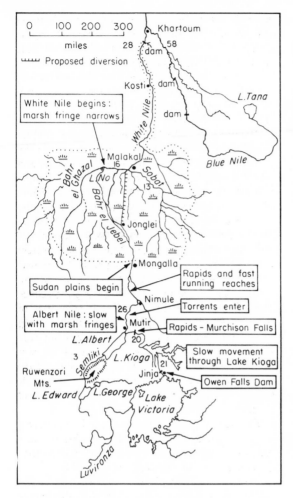

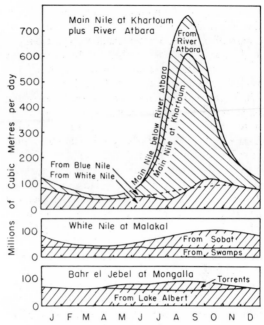

FIG. 15. *The seasonal and annual discharge of the Nile. The numbers alongside the rivers give the approximate mean annual discharges in units of cubic kilometres or milliards. They show that about half the Nile water entering the swamps of the Sudan plains is lost by evaporation between Mongalla and Malakal. A study has been made of a scheme to divert and canalize the river north of Jonglei in order to reduce these losses. Adapted from* H. E. Hurst, The Nile, *1957, and* P. P. Howell, Geog. Journal, *1952, 33-48.*

—the indispensable first stages of getting any of the water down to the earth's surface. Only the broad oceans can provide the raw material for the bulk of continental precipitation. The Red Sea is an extensive source of water vapour, well over a hundred miles wide, but its low coasts are amongst the driest lands in the world. Whatever is done by man, the Sahara and Kalahari, except for spots here and there, will remain dry for a very long time. The best results are likely to be obtained by conserving existing rainfall and reducing to a minimum wasteful evaporation losses.

It has been realized for several decades that the total discharge of the Nile could be increased and the Great Lakes used to even out the discharge of the lower river by canalizing the White Nile's course through the Sudd. In the early fifties a survey was made to determine the best line for the diversion canal and the extent to which altering the régime of the river would affect the people who live nearby

and at present take advantage of its natural fluctuations. It appears that with careful planning a canal cutting across from Jonglei to Malakal, a distance of 150 miles, would allow thousands of acres more land to be irrigated further downstream and could also open up new possibilities for economic and social development of the local clay plains. The scheme has been shelved for the present because all attention is being directed towards the High Dam which it would supplement. This is the kind of scheme that could be employed in the Okavango basin to make productive use of the waters that at present run to waste there.

The only very large irrigated area in Africa south of the Sahara is the Gezira and its extensions watered from the Sennar dam on the Blue Nile. One of the most successful planned agricultural enterprises in the world, its success is the outcome of favourable natural conditions, a good labour supply and careful preparatory work over a number

Gully erosion, eastern Nigeria. Tertiary rocks in the Awka area, formerly covered with high forest, have been deeply dissected by systems of gullies hundreds of feet deep.

of years followed by close supervision of the farming operations. An almost equally ambitious French scheme on the inland delta of the Niger has been far less rewarding because of poorer soils, higher costs, and an inadequate labour supply. Other projects are being developed on the Kafue flats of Zambia, in the Sabi valley in Rhodesia and near the Rufiji river of Tanzania.

It becomes increasingly difficult to make proper use of rivers because clearing of woodland and cultivation have altered the hydrological characteristics of drainage basins. Rates of runoff have increased and drainage systems are responding to the new conditions in various ways. Gullies cut into the hill slopes thereby increasing the length of watercourses in each square mile, that is increasing the drainage densities of catchments. Downstream, sand accumulates in river beds, river channels shift sideways cutting away alluvial plains, floods are higher and more frequent than in former times. If the water resources of the continent are to be used to the best advantage great efforts will have to be made to conserve the soil and water on the uplands and to control the rivers throughout their courses.

2

Vegetation, Soils, Fauna, Pests, and Diseases

VEGETATION

IN most parts of Africa the character of the landscape depends on the quality of the vegetation, the spacing of the trees and their size, the height of the grasses and the resulting textural patterns in green and brown. While the general aspect of the vegetation is primarily controlled by the climate, its floristic composition varies with distance from the Euro-Asian landmass. Broadly speaking the plants of north-west Africa are comparable with those of the Mediterranean area as a whole; those of the Sudan zone and the Sahara resemble plants from similar climatic regions in south-west Asia, while the species characteristic of southern Africa, and particularly those of the macchia in the south-western Cape, have evolved in greater isolation. The flora of Madagascar, separated from the rest of Africa since mid-Tertiary times, has its own peculiar features and some affinities with the flora of south-east Asia.

Few extensive tracts of country remain where the plant cover has not been modified by man: cultivators have cleared the forest for agriculture, hunters have burned savanna grasslands to drive out game, pastoralists have grazed their herds over all the drier lands. Remnants of the primeval plant cover allow some impression to be gained of the pattern of the vegetation as it would have been without human interference, and so maps of what is called the natural vegetation can be prepared. The distribution pattern of this somewhat hypothetical natural vegetation, as might be expected, corresponds fairly well with the climatic zonation, but is modified over considerable areas by local soil and drainage conditions (see Map 7).

Tropical forest

Tropical moist forest, or rain forest, is the most imposing structure in the plant world. It still covers large parts of west and central Africa, but has been treated so wantonly as to be sadly in need of care and protection if it is to impress posterity. The forest is made up of a large number of species of trees of different heights and ages, related only distantly to species in the forests of India and Malaya. In virgin forest, or a near approach to that rare state, the forest floor is fairly open with a shallow layer of decomposing leaves and rotting branches covering the mineral soil. Wherever a large tree has fallen, lianas, vines, and young trees crowd together in dense tangles. Elsewhere, leaves and branches form canopies or layers at two levels, one at a height of 40 or 50 feet above the ground, and another at about 100 feet; the tallest trees, called emergents, push through the top canopy to heights of 150 feet or more.

Rain forest is confined to lowland areas where the precipitation is well distributed through the year and annual rainfall totals exceed 1,500 mm. (about 60 inches). In such humid areas temperatures fluctuate between about 21° and 32° C. (70° and 90° F.). Towards the drier margins, the number of species of evergreen trees diminishes, the proportion of deciduous trees increases, and soil differences have a greater effect on the floral composition.

The composition of the forest also varies with altitude, forests above about 3,000 feet including only one-tenth of the species normally found in the lowland rain forest. Such montane forests are scattered all across Africa, from Cameroon mountain to the highlands bordering the rift valley and beyond to the slopes of the east African volcanoes; yet the assemblages of species found in each of them show striking similarities. To explain this situation it has been suggested that at times during the Quaternary period when the climate was cooler than now, forest of the montane type may have reached down much further to occupy a continuous belt across the upland country of central Africa of which the present patches are merely remnants.

On low-lying, swampy areas near the Niger delta and on the floor of the Congo basin where rivers flood wide areas for months at a time, the forest trees are adapted to life in fresh-water swamps and stand high on stilt roots. Near the coasts of east and west Africa, but especially in the Niger delta, where alluvium is inundated for much of the time with fresh or brackish water, the mangroves *Rizophera* and *Avicennia* have colonized the muds and overhang winding creeks and pools.

The rain forest is being depleted rapidly, for the tall trees and enriched soils can be very profitably exploited. Montane forests have suffered from cultivators clearing the hill-sides and transforming

Creek near Lagos, Nigeria

them into open woodland or coffee plantations. The soils of the deciduous forests have been particularly attractive to west African cultivators, who have cleared very wide areas. Everywhere the rate of encroachment on high forests has accelerated in the last few decades to such an extent that little will remain by the end of this century unless they are deliberately preserved.

Man's activities have not been entirely destructive. Trees producing fruit or valuable for their timber have been preserved and continue to regenerate when the rest have gone. Forest transformed by this artificial selection has an enhanced value and has been the main source of palm-oil and kola nuts. But the costs of harvesting wild forest produce are high and plantations are being established ever more widely.

Of the high forest remaining, large blocks are now conserved in forest reserves where indiscriminate clearing is prohibited and lumbering is organized in such a way that natural regrowth can keep pace with felling. Much depends in the future on the ability of central governments to resist pressure from both local communities and foreign businessmen wishing to make use of the trees and land, with an eye to short-term profit rather than long-term gains. Once forest has been cleared it is both costly and technically difficult to re-establish it by planting; for the rain forest is a very complex association of plants, appearing at the climax of a long sequence of developments in the formation of the soil and the establishment of larger and more specialized plants, a natural resource to be used with care and deliberation.

The protection of forests on the main watersheds of the continent is essential to prevent erosion, and the preservation of at least some large representative blocks is also important to scientists. As Richards has written in *The Tropical Rain Forest*: 'The rain forest flora with its immense wealth of species belonging to thousands of genera and scores of families has acted in the past as a reservoir of genetic diversity and potential variability. During at least the more recent epochs in the earth's history it has been a centre of evolutionary activity from which the rest of the world's flora has been recruited.'

Tropical savanna

The term savanna is used to denote the sub-humid tropical woodland or grassland that occupies the plateau country of south-central and east Africa, and extends westward along the northern margins

Coffee under forest remnant, West Cameroon.

of the Congo basin to the Atlantic coast south of the Gambia river. Many of the species in the north are closely related to those of India; others are more typical of south-central Africa. The savanna flora south of the equator is very rich and a remarkable number of the plants there are able to resist fire and drought. *Brachystegia*, which are amongst the most typical trees of south and east Africa, are absent from the west.

Some of the tall woodlands, such as the *chipya* and *Marquesia* woodland of Zambia, are not clearly distinguishable from rain forest. The savannas of the more humid areas of west Africa include many high-forest species and are sometimes called derived savanna because they are believed to have replaced rain forest as a result of human interference. There are other formations, dominated by evergreen trees which lack the physiognomic characteristics of rain forest and so are generally regarded as savanna.

Quite commonly the boundary between savanna and high forest is distinct, being sharpened every year by grass fires which are held up by islands and peninsulas of forest and sweep through dry grasses between gnarled, fire-resistant trees typical of savanna woodland. Patches of high forest sheltering villages or following the winding courses of rivers extend far outside the main rain-forest belts. Elsewhere the pattern is inverted, and savanna advances well into humid country, possibly because the soils happen to be dense and clayey, with sub-surface water hardly available to trees during the dry season but supporting a dense growth of tall inflammable grasses.

There is a good deal of disagreement about the relative importance of the different factors involved in the distribution of savanna and its variation in character from place to place. The overriding importance of climate is indisputable, the rain forests giving way to savanna where the winter dry period becomes marked. Burning has certainly been important more than locally. But there is a growing realization that vegetation patterns are to be explained in large part by soil and drainage conditions related to the geomorphology. As M. Cole writes on Zambia: 'undulating areas fashioned by current dissection are generally well drained and have mature soils able to support forests, whereas level areas subject to deposition or planed by erosion generally have impeded drainage and soils subject to alternating waterlogging and moisture deficiency which support only grassland' (*Geog. Journal*, 1963, p. 291).

Though savanna plants supply few commodities in demand for export to industrial countries, with

Derived savanna. Tall grass savanna with woodland that includes forest trees on the Benue plains of Shendam, south of the Jos Plateau in Nigeria.

the exceptions of shea-butter and gum arabic, they play an important part in the economy of the local people, providing all manner of wild fruits, medicaments, dyes, timber, and firewood. The leaves of certain trees are useful in soups; wildfowl and other game are abundant in remote areas, and honey can be won from the nests of wild bees. Domestic animals graze and browse at large. The climate allows both grain and root crops to be grown and crops such as cotton and groundnuts for local use and export are raised locally. But sleeping-sickness, river blindness, poor soils, or a combination of these and other factors has restricted settlement and population growth in most savanna areas.

Steppe and desert

Towards the margins of the deserts, as the mean annual rainfall diminishes to less than 20 inches, the proportion of thorny species in the woodland increases, grasses are shorter than in the more humid savanna, and plants are more specialized in their adaptation to drought conditions. As the rainfall diminishes still further, the gaps between plants increase and eventually vegetation is confined mainly to the margins of storm-water channels and the borders of temporary lakes where trees such as date-palms, tamarisk, and certain acacias can obtain water from soil at depth.

In southern Africa the savanna merges southwards into wooded steppe, and thorn scrub in the

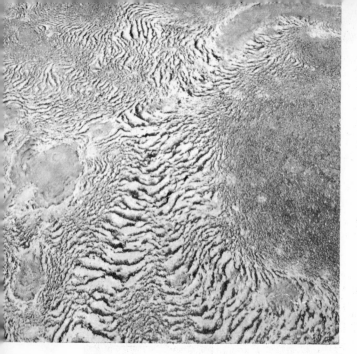

Vegetation arcs in Somalia. (From S. B. Boaler and C. A. H. Hodge, 'Observations on vegetation arcs in the northern region, Somali Republic', pp. 511–44, Journal of Ecology, 1964.)

Karroo and finally into the sclerophylous bush of the Cape of Good Hope, which is largely made up of evergreen shrubs with some low trees and bulbous plants. Various exotic grasses have been introduced from other continents, and trees able to survive the harsh conditions, like poplar and Australian wattle, have transformed the scene.

Air photographs have revealed that the sparse 'steppe' vegetation of parts of semi-arid west Africa, the central Sudan, and Somalia is commonly arranged in linear patterns. Strips of bush or grass are seen to run along the contour with wider bare strips separating them. In general such patterns are best developed on gently sloping clayey plains over which water moves as a sheet after heavy storms, carrying along silt and organic matter in suspension. Some of the material may be deposited when flow ceases, giving a long low mound, possibly slightly convex upslope which, it has been suggested, might be colonized by grass and bushes and collect more debris. Recent studies envisage vegetation patterns like those shown in the air photograph above as developing in a formerly continuous plant cover, the linear spaces forming, in the first place, as a result of climatic deterioration or heavy grazing. French writers have called such striped vegetation in the western Sudan *brousse tigré*.

High montane vegetation

Vegetation persists to very high altitudes on mountains near the equator and zones of vegetation can be distinguished which correspond to some slight degree with those found at progressively higher latitudes. Above the savanna woodland of the plateaux are forests of great white-trunked trees and bamboo thickets. Giant groundsel, lobelia, and other strange plants make their appearance at about 10,000 feet and higher still these give way to grasses, herbs, sedges, and bracken of moorland country. The flora becomes more specialized towards the snowline and is comparable to that found at high altitudes in the Alps.

The montane climates at the equator are peculiar in that seasonal fluctuations are far less marked than in extra-tropical areas with comparable mean annual temperatures. At the top of Mount Kilimanjaro, for example, the mean annual temperature of every month is comparable with that of the cooler parts of the British Isles in January, but the sun is much higher in the sky and the hours of sunshine are much greater, so the conditions for plant growth are rather peculiar.

SOILS

African soils are very variable and it is difficult to summarize their characteristics. Broadly speaking they are similar to soils developed in Brazil, peninsula India, and Australia. There are no wide tracts of highly productive soil like the chernozems of the wheatlands of Ukraine and North America, nor are there such extensive irrigable lowlands as the Indo-Gangetic plain of northern India. Nevertheless, irrigated soils in the Nile valley are highly productive and no doubt parts of the Niger and Chad basins and some of the flat-floored valleys of Zambia and Tanzania hold possibilities for the future. In the humid regions, the illusion of fertility given to early travellers by the luxuriance of the forests has long since been dispelled and the fragility of the soils is recognized. Once the natural vegetation has been cleared, the organic matter in the soil is rapidly burned up by the high temperatures and not replenished, crop yields diminish, the structure of the soil deteriorates and erosion accelerates. The soil is washed away. This sequence has been followed in many areas and is not easy to halt.

The full potentialities of the land have still to be realized. Yields in Europe were low in medieval times and soils tended to deteriorate rather than improve under cultivation. As agricultural techniques

Ruwenzori high-level vegetation. Giant lobelia and groundsel at about 12,000 feet.

improved cultivation began to increase soil fertility and now production from well-farmed land is greater than from virgin soil. In most parts of Africa, farming methods giving big returns and appropriate to the several geographical environments are still being worked out. Substantial increases of yields can be obtained by controlling disease, planting high-yielding material, and using fertilizers. In Ghana it has been shown that improved methods can give yields of up to 3,000 lb. per acre of dry cocoa compared with the farmer's average of 240 lb. In Liberia, the Firestone Rubber Company has obtained yields of more than 1,000 lb. per acre compared with the small growers' 200 lb. per acre in Nigeria and Ivory Coast. It would seem that improved methods could multiply yields from African soils between three and six times, but such methods are costly to employ.

In each and every climatic region of the continent there are both productive soils and poor soils, their quality depending on the parent material from which they are derived and the history of the use made of the land. The pattern of the soils is a very complicated one, being compounded of the climatic, geological, and relief patterns superimposed on one another.

An attempt has been made by the Belgian pedologist d'Hoore to compile a soil map of the entire continent. He has assembled information from the individual countries in which soil surveys have been made and has extrapolated from these data into the unmapped regions. Map 8 is based on that of d'Hoore and we may attempt to consider some aspects of the pattern it presents.

The desert soils are shallow, have poorly developed profiles and lack organic matter. Desert plains are commonly underlain by calcrete or silcrete; bare sand and pebbly reg are characteristic of the driest areas; upland soils are usually thin and stony. In depressions, water seeping through the regolith evaporates and leaves behind salty or calcareous deposits either in the soil profile or forming a surface crust. A good deal of publicity has been given to the discovery of fossil soil profiles in the Sahara, formed in a more humid period of the past, and it has been suggested that they would be very

27

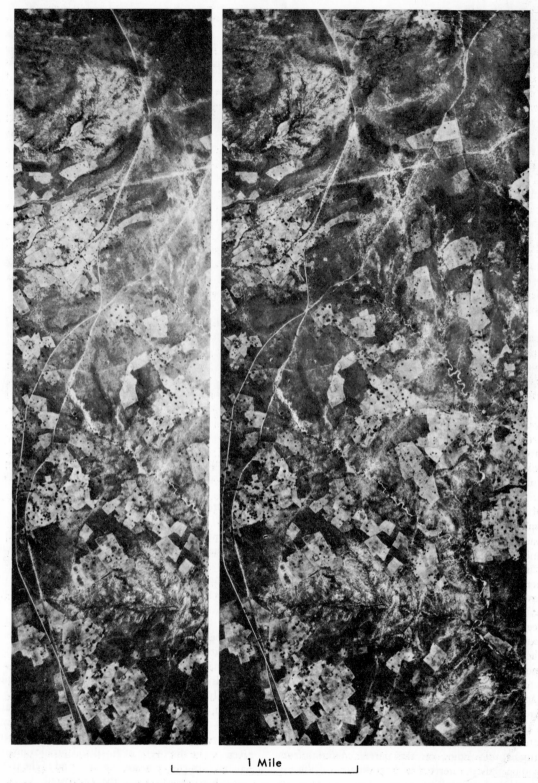

1 Mile

Soil erosion on the Chad–Niger watershed in Nigeria. Water running off an old trackway and overgrazed streambanks has caused soil wash and gully erosion. The black dots are trees, mainly locust bean trees, on the cultivated land. Compounds are scattered through the farmland. The grey area is rough grazing land.

fertile if they were to be irrigated. Their potentialities are probably very limited.

In semi-arid lands with 10-25 inches of rain annually the brown soils and ferruginous tropical soils are occasionally alkaline, but heavy rains concentrated in periods of a few weeks each year generally wash the bases away and as a result of this leaching the soils are commonly found to be slightly acid. Duricrusts, mainly ferricrete, outcropping widely on low watersheds are of little value for agriculture. Much more useful are the brown sands, such as those of the Sudan zone derived from ancient dune formations, which are particularly suitable for groundnuts. Superphosphate fertilizers give good responses on these soils. They are susceptible to wind erosion if overcropped or overgrazed. Low-lying areas in the semi-arid parts of the continent, flooded by local rains or by large rivers rising at a distance, are floored by dark-brown or black, deeply cracking non-kaolinitic clays. They are sometimes called Black Cotton Soils, though cotton is rarely grown on them, or margalitic from the Latin *marga* meaning marl, because they are heavy and calcareous, or simply Tropical Black Earths. Such soils occupy wide areas in the White Nile basin of the Sudan Republic and also in the south-eastern quarter of the Chad basin.

In the sub-humid savanna lands, with rainfall totals of 30 to 50 inches annually, the upland soils are usually red and ferruginous with lateritic ironstones developed locally. An association of gently rolling plain with inselbergs rising sharply from it, and savanna woodland covering a more or less dissected lateritic ironstone crust, is very characteristic of west Africa north of the high forest zone and the central African plateaux at the margins of the Congo basin.

Soils of the humid regions are deeper than elsewhere on account of the intense weathering, the great activity of biological and chemical processes involved in soil formation at temperatures around 27° C. (80° F.), and because high forest protects the regolith from erosion. Red or yellow coloration extends several tens of feet below the surface, yet the top horizon, rich in organic matter, is seldom more than a few inches thick, for leaves, branches, and even tree-trunks break down with great rapidity under the attack of termites and bacteria and other large and small organisms. These acid soils are commonly called latosols from the word laterite, commonly applied to thoroughly leached tropical soils. In recent years the term ferralitic has also been used, referring to the presence of alumina as well as iron oxides.

Amongst the best soils are those which are still youthful and retain quantities of soluble minerals useful to plants. The deep loamy clays formed under high forest, chocolate brown in colour at high altitudes, red at lower levels, derived from basalts and other volcanic rocks of Pliocene and later age, are richer than most other soils in Africa. The red, gritty earth at the base of rocky outcrops is also well liked by cultivators; it remains moist long into the dry season on account of seepage from the hills behind, is well drained and easy to till, but liable to be eroded by gullies cutting back towards the hill masses. Such fertile areas are too small to appear on a map with a scale of 1:25 million. There are other good soils, but wide tracts of the continent, above all on the upland plains where weathering has continued for millions of years, have soils that are thin, lack plant nutrients or essential minerals, or for some other reason are at present of little value for agriculture.

The vegetation is often a useful guide to soil potential. Shifting cultivators judge when the land is fit for cropping by the nature and the density of the plant cover, and soil surveyors are always on the look-out for plant indicators. Over much of west Africa borassus palms are found to be growing on moist alluvial land. The borassus is a curious tree with a bulge or two near the top of its slender trunk, and producing yellow nuts the size of tennis balls which are relished by goats and used by humans in time of famine; the timber is stringy but useful because of its resistance to attack from termites. Small thorny trees with grey-green trunks, *Acacia seyal* often characterize heavy black earths derived from basic lavas or clayey limestones in the savanna zone. Coconut palms thrive on freely drained sandy soils at the coast; oil-palms flourish on well-drained red loams, ferrallitic soils derived from sedimentary rocks; cocoa grows most satisfactorily on deep clayey soils underlain by crystalline rocks, rich in bases, from which high forest has lately been cleared.

Although the soil and vegetation map is occasionally so complicated as to have very little discernible pattern or order, the arrangement of the soil and vegetation in many parts of the continent conforms to some degree with the relief and drainage, and a certain sequence of soil types and related vegetation associations is found to be repeated time and time again across country. Such a sequence is called a soil-vegetation catena, the sequence of soils across a section of a river valley being likened to the links of a suspended chain (Fig. 16). From the soils on the crests of upland facets material is constantly

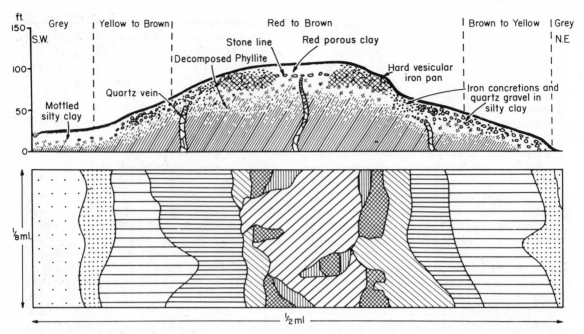

ft.
150
Grey | Yellow to Brown | Red to Brown | Brown to Yellow | Grey
S.W. | | | | N.E
| | Stone line | Red porous clay | |
| | Decomposed Phyllite | | Hard vesicular |
100 | | | | iron pan |
| Quartz vein | | | Iron concretions and
| | | | quartz gravel in
50 | | | | silty clay
Mottled | | | |
silty clay | | | |
0

⅛ml.

½ ml

½ ml

FIG. 16. *The catenal arrangement of soils in a part of Ghana. In many parts of the tropics soil catenas are developed between upland erosion surfaces and alluviated valley floors. This cross-section shows the distribution of soils overlying phyllites in the rain forest region of southern Ghana. Red clay soils on the erosion surface remnant are underlain by a stone line. Such lines, which commonly appear in soil sections in tropical Africa, are the outcrops of layers of stones more or less parallel to the surface and several feet below it. Some represent old land surfaces, others probably mark the depth to which termite activity penetrates. Ironstone outcrops at the breaks of slope bounding the erosion surface remnant; fragments of quartz and concretionary debris appear in the slope soils. Alluvial terraces on valley slopes and bottoms, probably associated with Pleistocene climatic changes, introduce complexities to the lower part of the catenas. From H. Brammer (1962) 'Soils', in J. B. Wills (ed.)* Agriculture and Land Use in Ghana, *London, OUP.*

being removed by eluviation, by washing out of soluble constituents through the soil profile and washing away of particulate material in water flowing over the surface. On the hill slopes, colluvial soils consist in part of material derived from upslope and in the process of moving, by degrees, to the slope foot. At the border of the valley floor, slope material accumulates giving deep soil profiles sometimes with impeded drainage; towards the stream successively younger soils are encountered, derived from alluvial deposits of various ages. In many cases the vegetation distribution shows some relationship to the soil sequence and occasionally farmers are found to have adopted their cropping pattern and even the shapes of their holdings to this topographical arrangement of the soils.

The soil map presented here (Map 8), in spite of its apparent complexity, conceals a multitude of important soil differences within small areas. Its practical usefulness is limited, but it is at least an attempt to find some order in a mass of scattered

surveys and field observations by pedologists and soil scientists with different backgrounds and using different terminologies.

FAUNA

Mammals

Africa's mammalian fauna is remarkably rich, consisting of thirty-eight families (excluding bats). Fossil remains indicate that many of the animals now confined mainly to the centre and east were much more widely distributed thousands of years ago, roaming the foothills of the Atlas mountains and the basin of the Vaal river (see Fig. 9). Ancient rock engravings and paintings of hippopotamus, giraffe, and other large beasts have been found in remote desert regions from which they have long since disappeared. The periods of great aridity during the Pleistocene probably drove many species out of north Africa, and in more recent times the demands of the Roman amphitheatres disposed of

Elephant trap. 'In what manner the Hottentots catch the Elephants.' From P. Kolben, The Present State of the Cape of Good Hope, *vol. i, London, 1731.*

most of the lion, elephant, and other large animals that had managed to survive. In west Africa, with its high population densities, larger mammals have been all but eliminated by native hunters armed with bows or muzzle loaders, and by cultivators steadily encroaching on grazing lands, so that game is now restricted to a few remote swampy or mountainous regions. Within living memory elephant have vanished from parts of northern Nigeria and ostrich from the Algerian Sahara. In east and south Africa great numbers of antelope and other animals have been slaughtered for sport and also in attempts to eliminate game held to be carriers of diseases harmful to cattle. Most Africans who travel abroad or live in towns have their first sight of lions, rhinoceroses, and such creatures on television or in the cages of zoos.

The fauna that remains is of very great value because it provides scientists with the opportunity to study the complex interactions of a rich fauna of vertebrates such as must have once existed more widely. Such a resource should not be allowed to disappear. National parks have been demarcated where hunting is forbidden, and nearly everywhere licences are required to kill the larger animals. But regulations alone cannot prevent poachers killing rhinoceroses when the horn can be sold for large sums because of its reputed medicinal value. Crocodiles and snakes are real dangers to people living in the bush. Baboons, monkeys, and elephants damage farmers' crops, and to a person living on a 1,500-calorie carbohydrate diet an antelope, no matter how graceful, is going to mean only one thing—meat. Parks and reserves have to be guarded and controlled, and this is costly. Furthermore, the governments of some territories are not easily persuaded that they can afford the land needed to ensure the preservation of wild life.

Game reserve in Uganda. Elephant coming down to drink near the Murchison Falls.

The situation will probably get worse before it improves, but there are some grounds for optimism. Large tracts of sparsely settled country persist in all the larger territories and surveys are being made to distinguish those parts which are unsuitable for human settlement and might well be set aside as game reserves. It has even been claimed that game preservation can give a return in cash as well as in pure enjoyment. In several reserves the animals already have to be 'cropped' in order to prevent overstocking. In Kenya, for instance, elephant in the Gulara River Reserve became so numerous that they devastated the vegetation, flattening nearly every tree including the portly baobab, until Waluangula tribesmen, who were formerly hunters and the most troublesome of Kenya's poachers, were employed to help in the control work; they were glad to kill the surplus beasts and dispose of the carcasses. Moreover, it has been argued that on marginal and poor land the potential meat production of indigenous fauna is higher than that of domestic animals. The reasons for this have been given by E. B. Worthington (1961). 'The wild flora', he writes, 'usually comprises herb layer, shrub layer and trees, and in the wild state this is utilised by a dozen or more species of animals from the pig tribe rooting underground to giraffes feeding on the tree tops, with a range of grazers and browsers in between. Also the animals are immune to trypanosomiasis and several other indigenous diseases which are dreaded by cattlemen. In order to eliminate tsetse and to tame such land for the purpose of cows and sheep, it is necessary to eliminate or depress the upper storeys of vegetation and concentrate upon the pasture, inevitably introducing at the same time the dangers of accelerated soil erosion.'

One may hope that 'game-cropping' will be shown to be economic and practicable, but it would be a little surprising if careful hunting turned out to be more productive than careful herding. The strongest argument for wild-life conservation in practice is the foreign currency obtainable from tourists armed with cameras. The countries of east and southern Africa are paying a great deal of attention to their game reserves now and tourism is a major industry.

PESTS AND DISEASES

No one seems to be very concerned about preserving the smaller creatures; few of them are in danger of extinction, though much of the scientific interest they attract seems to be directed towards their destruction. *Quelea* birds, which consume enormous quantities of grain annually, are one of the main targets. Some of the small creatures are obviously beneficial, bees for instance; wild honey is an excellent dish. But many are harmful to man, damaging crops and carrying diseases. Some are a greater menace between the tropics than in higher latitudes because climatic conditions allow them to live and breed easily. Others present problems because standards of hygiene, water supply, and sanitation are lower in Africa than in countries with higher standards of living. From all these creatures and organisms a few have been selected for more detailed discussion here because they are particularly interesting ecologically and play an important part in the human geography of the continent.

Locusts

Locusts are amongst the traditional plagues of Africa. They are large grasshoppers and normally live in small groups or singly in a solitary state, but occasionally they congregate into large swarms, probably, in the first place, as a result of their food supplies being restricted to a small area. A grown locust needs to eat its own weight of food every day, and a swarm will eat up the green leaves and crops over several square miles.

In the 1930's locust damage in Africa alone was estimated at £15 million annually. To prevent food shortages, an International Locust Organization was set up for the Red Sea area during the Second World War and has continued in existence since then. As a result of its activities a certain degree of control has been obtained. The work is difficult, for swarms normally originate at the desert margins and rapidly move out to the Mediterranean and savanna lands of Africa and south-west Asia. Experts fly out from the organization's headquarters

Band of Desert locust hoppers. Somalia.

in London as soon as an outbreak is reported and teams of local people are organized to deal with it before damage has become severe.

The three main kinds of locust south of the Sahara, the Red locust, the African Migratory locust, and the Desert locust, all need two kinds of habitat: bare ground for egg-laying and vegetated country for feeding. They are found living permanently mainly in areas of vegetation transition at the desert margins or near the limit of woodland and grassland.

The Red locust has at different times afflicted the whole of south-central Africa, notably in 1847-54, 1892-1910, and 1930-44. It has two outbreak areas, one in the grassy plains around Lake Rukwa in south-west Tanzania, the other in the marshes between Lakes Mweru and Tanganyika (see Fig. 48). Experts keep the locusts under observation from a research centre at Abercorn, and immediately it is noticed that the locusts are increasing, and laying eggs in larger numbers than usual, poisoned bran or poisoned dust is spread in the area to kill the young locusts, the hoppers, before they get their wings. If outbreaks had not been treated in good time, many swarms would probably have emerged from the Rukwa valley in 1954.

Desert locust invasion. Locusts squashed by cars are immediately preyed upon by the survivors.

Aircraft spraying a locust swarm. A de Havilland Beaver aircraft of Desert Locust Survey spraying a desert locust swarm at Borama in Somalia.

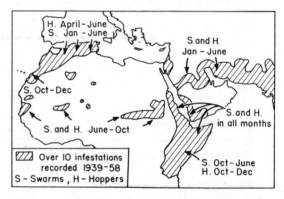

FIG. 17. *Areas frequently infested by desert locusts. Locusts multiply when the soils at the desert margins are moist after rain. Hoppers, the young locusts keeping to the ground, eat out the local vegetation and having exhausted the food supply come together in swarms that take to the wing and move with the wind. The Red Sea coast of Ethiopia and the Horn of Africa seem to breed more swarms than any other part of the continent.*

The African Migratory locust emerges from swampy country a little to the north of the Niger bend between Macina and Tombouctou. The last invasion during the decade 1928–37 spread to the whole of west Africa, Kenya, the Sudan, Tanganyika, and south-west Africa, affecting many areas for two consecutive years. Although this species now seems to be under control continued vigilance is essential to deal with any future outbreak in the early stages.

The Desert locust has proved a more difficult problem than the others because its breeding places are much more variable, being scattered over a wide belt stretching from Morocco to Pakistan (Fig. 17). Outbreaks of this species at intervals of about ten years have affected individual areas for two or three years at a time. The most recent outbreak began in 1947 and subsided in 1960. The locusts were tackled in their breeding grounds with poisoned bran and spraying from the air. One swarm destroyed by aircraft in northern Somalia in 1960 was estimated to weigh 30,000 tons.

Research into the movements of locusts has shown that swarms move down wind. Consequently they are impelled towards the intertropical convergence where storms of rain occur, producing conditions suitable for breeding. Locusts hatching out from eggs laid after winter and spring rains in the northern Sahara often move south under the influence of the Etesian winds. They roost by night and fly by day. They breed again at the southern fringe of the desert and at the end of the short summer rainy season, when the food supply diminishes, swarms may move south again to be carried by the winds in the wake of the intertropical convergence, arriving in east Africa about October. Movements of swarms can thus be forecast from the wind systems and this is a considerable help to those attempting to control an outbreak. In 1965 it appeared that the Desert locust was no longer a serious threat. Three years later there were signs of new outbreaks developing; a quarter of a million acres of the Sudan were reported to be infested, threatening the cotton crop.

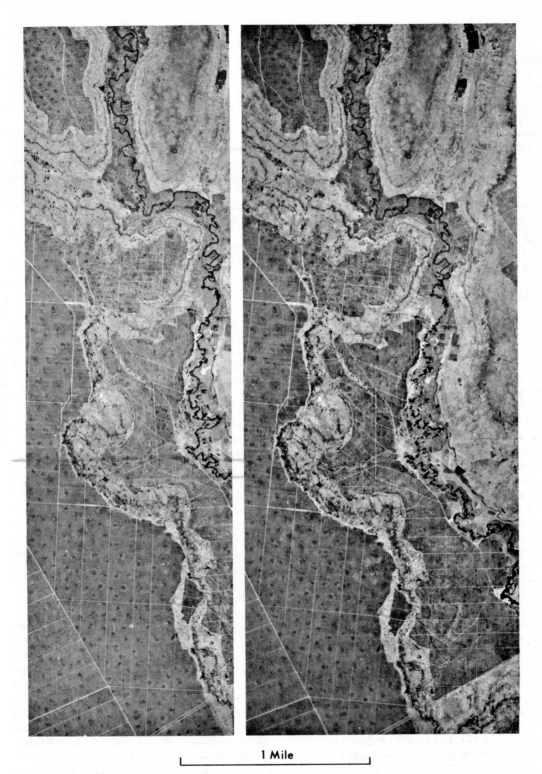

1 Mile

Termite heap patterns in Kenya. The remains of the heaps appear as dark dots spaced about 100 to 200 yards apart in the big fields on the left side of the photographs. Notice the very small field plots on an alluvial terrace near the meandering stream. The steeper slopes, cut into beds of volcanic lavas, remain uncultivated.

Termites

Often miscalled white ants, termites are a primitive type of creature related to cockroaches. In fact they are neither white, nor ants. Like wasps, bees, and ants, termites invariably live social lives; they cannot exist in the solitary state as locusts can, but only in the group. Nearly 400 species are known in Africa south of the Sahara, some living entirely underground, some in wood, others in mounds protruding above the ground. They are probably the most numerous macroscopic creatures in Africa.

Termites play an important part in the ecosystems of both forest and savanna. Forest species commonly build their nests in trees, while termites in open woodland are more commonly subterranean or dwell in mounds. Several species, some living in damp forests, others in humid savanna with tough ironstone soils, build mushroom-shaped dwellings. Deep red earths are often characterized by skyscrapers 20 or more feet high. Flat cones like miniature volcanoes are distributed over wide stretches of semi-arid country; each mound being surrounded by a bare patch and the whole area showing up on an air photograph as a dense rash of white dots. In swampy or clayey areas largely grass-covered, trees are found to be confined to termitaria and their ruins which rise a foot or two above the general level of the ground and provide relatively well-drained sites; such is the case on the south-east coast of Ghana, in Uganda west of Lake Victoria, and in parts of Barotseland in Zambia.

Termites consume dead plant and animal remains and perform functions comparable with those of the earthworm in high latitudes. Leaves and stems and roots of plants are not allowed to decompose gradually; they are comminuted by termites to a state in which further more complete decomposition is rapid. This helps to explain the small amount of raw humus in tropical African soils and the rapid turnover in plant remains. Dinka in the Sudan, and some other tribes, make use of termites to rejuvenate sheet-eroded land. They chop branches off trees, with the leaves adhering, and cover the ground with them to a depth of up to two feet. By the time termites have rendered the branches into dust, the land is once more fit for cultivation. Some termites seem to concentrate fertility in their mounds by feeding on the dead or dying plants of the surrounding area, and analyses of earth from the termitaria show the earth to be less acid and to contain more soluble bases than elsewhere. Other mounds are built of sub-soil and are less fertile. Some soil scientists have suspected that termite activity might explain the vesicular or sponge-like structure (though not consistency) of certain tropical soils and ferricretes, but the weight of evidence is now against this idea. They probably are responsible for the stone line, a layer of stones at a depth of several feet which is a characteristic feature of the soils in many parts of Africa; it is widely held to mark the lower limit of termite activity.

To the householder, termites are a menace threatening to eat up any paper, wood, or cloth; to the historian they are the destroyers of buildings and documents that might have thrown light on the past; to the modern farmer they are pests whose termitaria can impede cultivation and form dangerous traps for mechanical equipment.

The mosquito and malaria

It is sometimes suggested that memorials should be raised in the capitals of the newly independent states of west Africa to commemorate the mosquito, because this creature, by spreading malaria and yellow fever, was mainly responsible for discouraging European settlement and thereby prevented the introduction to the west coast of those plaguey inter-racial problems that appear to be so intractable in the southern end of the continent. There may be a grain of sense in this idea, but the disease and misery the mosquito has brought to Africans and continues to bring them would be held by most people far to outweigh its benefactions.

Infant mortality caused by malaria is enormous. Amongst adult Africans the disease is rarely fatal because they have acquired a measure of resistance. Furthermore, the common form of malaria in Africa is *Plasmodium falciparum* which is less lethal to those people who possess in their blood the abnormal haemoglobin S and sickle-cell haemoglobin. On the principal of the survival of the fittest for local conditions, this abnormality has increased in malarious parts of Africa, in some of which it reaches a frequency of 30 or 40 per cent. Nevertheless, attacks of fever reduce physical energy and the general state of health, and farmers are liable to be affected at the beginning of the rainy season, at the very time when they need all their strength for preparing the land and planting crops. Some forms of malaria can be fatal to expatriate Europeans, but they are usually able to protect themselves by proofing their houses against mosquitoes and by regularly taking protective drugs of one kind or another in the form of small pills; few Africans can afford, or indeed would feel it necessary, to do this.

Of the several species of mosquito capable of transmitting malarial parasites of one kind or another, some are more attracted to human blood

36

than others. The most prevalent in Africa is *Anopheles gambiae*, and malaria eradication on the continent is made unusually difficult because this mosquito feeds on animals as well, so that they can survive even if they are temporarily prevented from feeding on man. As mosquitoes usually breed in standing water and are most numerous near swamps and rivers, risks of infection are greatest in riverside towns and during the rainy season.

Malaria can be controlled in several ways. The larvae can be killed by draining swamps and spraying pools; insecticides can be painted on the walls of dwellings; drugs can be used to suppress the activity of malarial parasites in the blood. On islands such as Mauritius the disease has been eliminated, and schemes on the Copperbelt of Zambia show that malaria can be almost completely dislodged from towns. But it is now realized that control must be really effective or anti-malarial projects could conceivably do more harm than good. If the people in a treated area lose their resistance to the disease and then mosquitoes infest the area once more, infection may be fatal instead of merely producing a mild fever. Or Africans who lose their resistance in one country may go to find work in another where malaria remains endemic; if they become infected they may die, and if they live they carry the disease back to their homes.

Mosquitoes can also transmit a virus disease called yellow fever. Essentially this is a disease of monkeys but it can be transmitted from them to man by several species of forest mosquitoes. Once it becomes established in an urban centre, *Aedes aegypti* acts as a very efficient carrier from one man to another. The disease is commonly fatal, but a vaccine has been known for several decades and migrants to and from African territories are always inoculated against the fever. Millions of Africans have also received prophylactic treatment.

Finally it should be noted that small parasitic worms called *filariae* are also transmitted by mosquitoes and can cause great distress to persons infected by them. There is now an efficient treatment for this disease.

The tsetse-fly and trypanosomiasis *of Problem*

The tsetse is a large, bustling brown fly, like a horse-fly, with greyish stripes or spots on the thorax, and wings that overlap when it is at rest. It is the main but not the only vector of trypanosomiasis. If a tsetse bites a man or animal suffering from the disease, it swallows blood containing parasites called trypanosomes. These develop and multiply within the fly, and if the tsetse should subsequently

bite another animal or man, they are injected into the blood and the disease has been transmitted. The victim usually falls ill within a few days, but in the case of man several days or even months may elapse before death occurs. There are drugs for treating the disease in man, where it is usually known as sleeping sickness, and preventative inoculation is now partly effective in man and animals.

Most of Africa within 14° of the equator is infested with tsetse-flies of various species, except for grassy highlands rising to levels above 4,000 feet which are too cold, and open country where the dry season is too hot and desiccating for the fly to breed successfully. Such open country is broadly of two kinds; firstly, semi-arid country such as occurs in the Horn of Africa with less than 20 inches of rain annually, and secondly, heavily settled regions in the savanna zone, near Kano in Nigeria for instance, where population densities exceed 200 to the square mile and game animals on which the fly normally depend for their food supplies have been wiped out. Typical tsetse-ridden country can be characterized as sparsely settled savanna woodland, with 30 to 60 inches of rain and poor soils (see Map 9).

Amongst man the disease is now under control, but its past ravages have probably influenced the geographical distribution of the continent's population quite strongly. It has denied vast areas of Africa to cattle and horses and indeed to most other domestic animals except poultry, and this helps to

Tsetse country. Fire resistant trees and tall grasses in a sparsely settled part of the Benue valley in the Nigerian Middle Belt.

37

explain why cultivation nearly everywhere is by the hoe and not by draught plough. Surveys are now carried out regularly to discover victims of the disease so they can be treated in the early stages and before infection can be transmitted to others living nearby. Villages have been shifted to new sites free of tsetse-fly, and woodland where tsetse might breed near villages has been cleared. Attention is now directed mainly towards preventing trypanosomiasis amongst cattle. Many pastoralist groups long ago devised systems of transhumance by which they pasture their cattle on highlands or dry lands free from tsetse-fly during the rains, and move down to the lowland savannas only during the dry season when the fly usually keeps to cool moist woodland bordering streams and pools.

More positive measures have been taken in recent years, by dealing with the hosts of the trypanosomes or the food supply and breeding-places of the tsetse-fly. In parts of Uganda and Rhodesia game animals, especially antelope, have been killed off in large numbers because they carry the disease and are always a source of infection to cattle. In some parts of Nigeria, wide areas of grassland have been made safe for cattle by clearing clumps of infested woodland. Since the introduction of new drugs such as dimidium bromide and antrycide, cattle can be inoculated and so survive for several months together in areas from which they were formerly barred; then they have to be inoculated again. Various poisonous sprays and smokes have been developed, but they are not very discriminating, and have to be used carefully for fear of killing useful insects and upsetting the natural balance entirely; they are also expensive.

The actual methods or combinations of methods used against trypanosomiasis vary from one area to another according to the local vegetation and the species of tsetse and trypanosomes involved. Each species has its own habits of breeding and feeding. In Uganda, it was found that *Glossina palpalis*, the waterside tsetse, could be eradicated by spraying 6·2 per cent. dieldrin on to the water-edge vegetation, and when an epidemic of Gambian sleeping sickness broke out in northern Lengo in 1957 the new technique was applied very successfully. While the Medical Department carried out mass surveys and treatment of all cases found, the Department of Tsetse Control sprayed the banks along 75 miles of the Moroto river and 230 miles of its tributaries and almost immediately this treatment resulted in the elimination of *Glossina palpalis* throughout the 500 square mile outbreak area. Within two years human infection had dropped to a very low level.

The eradication of *Glossina morsitans*, the most widespread savanna tsetse and the most important vector of the animal disease, requires quite different methods. In Ankole, Uganda, an effective technique has been worked out which consists of applying a single coating of 3·1 per cent. dieldrin to the most favoured daytime resting sites of the fly, which have been found to be the undersides of horizontal branches and the boles of the larger *acacia* and *euphorbia* trees.

Studies of the food preferences of tsetse have allowed greater discrimination to be used in dealing with game; it has been found that hartebeest, water buck and oribi, impala, zebra, klipspringer, and leopard can be spared because tsetse rarely feed on them, and attention is now concentrated on killing off the buffalo, bushbuck, reedbuck, duiker, warthog, and bushpig. Such methods have resulted in 7,000 square miles of Uganda being reclaimed from savanna tsetses, and their occupation by many thousands of cattle.

Parasitic worms

Many Africans are infected with worms, some of them living in the blood and tissues, others in the intestines. Amongst the latter, the most common is the hookworm which feeds on the blood of its host producing symptoms similar to those of malnutrition. The affliction can be treated fairly easily, but unless local sanitary arrangements are improved or the patient takes to wearing shoes he is likely to be reinfected from the microscopic eggs of the worm in excreta. Infection by guinea-worm, which is very common in parts of west Africa and causes ulceration of the legs incapacitating people for weeks at a time, can be avoided if surface water is boiled or filtered before drinking, or if reliance is placed on clear water from wells. In both cases the keys to better health are education in hygiene and sanitation together with quite small improvements in household equipment.

The borders of streams and lakes are commonly unhealthy because such places are attractive to the carriers or vectors of diseases. Mosquitoes and tsetse-flies have already been mentioned in this connexion, and certain parasitic worms that cause blindness are other hazards. River blindness, *onchocersiasis*, is one of the worst diseases in Africa, afflicting millions of people. It is caused by a tiny worm that is transmitted by a small black fly called *Simulium damnosum*. The larvae of the fly usually live in the vicinity of falling water, and in certain areas it is particularly dangerous to bathe near waterfalls for this reason.

Bilharzia, another worm afflicting millions of

Africans, seems to be more prevalent than a few decades ago. It lives in the bladder or intestine of man and lays eggs that may be passed out into fresh water. If snails of a suitable species are present, embryos of a different character are liberated from the snails into the water and may penetrate the skin or mucous membranes of persons who drink or bathe in it. Again, treatment is effective, but it may not be of much value because the cause of infection remains and is rather difficult to eliminate. All workers in irrigated areas are liable to be infected and some schemes have been held up because of the risk of bilharzia. Much research is being carried on to find a solution to the problem.

Rinderpest

This is the old cattle plague, a virus disease, that afflicted Europe at intervals until the middle of the nineteenth century when it was virtually eliminated by concerted action to ensure the effectiveness of quarantine regulations and the slaughter of infected beasts. The disease seems to have been introduced from eastern countries; it was highly contagious and caused heavy mortality amongst cattle. In south Africa rinderpest does not seem to have been known before 1896 and in central Africa it may not have occurred until about that time. It seems to have arrived on the continent in 1889 when Italian armies invaded Ethiopia from Somaliland. It reached Masailand and Uganda in the same year and, according to local accounts, cattle had never been known to die in such numbers. In 1892 it entered the country north of Lake Nyasa and early in 1896 was reported on both sides of the Zambezi, and shortly afterwards in the Transvaal, Orange Free State, and Angola. A barbed-wire fence a thousand miles long, erected to prevent the southward movement of cattle into Cape Province, checked the disease only briefly. It got through in 1897 and spread right to the southern tip of Africa. West Africa did not escape; thousands of pastoralists lost their entire herds and were forced to take up sedentary agriculture for at least a few years. Eventually the epidemic subsided, in the way of an influenza epidemic, but its indirect effects persisted.

Some of the consequences were less evidently harmful than others. When rinderpest wiped out the antelope in the Rhodesias the tsetse-fly were deprived of their chief source of food and they disappeared from wide areas. As a result, stock-rearing was for a time possible in areas that had previously been closed to cattle. This was the first indication to the early white settlers that eliminating the game deliberately might be a practicable method of controlling trypanosomiasis.

Since the end of the last century rinderpest has broken out in different parts of the continent and has been one of the main preoccupations of veterinary departments. Inoculation is very effective and is being organized with increasing efficiency. The disease is now of little importance south of the equator and an intensive campaign to eradicate it from Nigeria, Cameroon, Chad, and Niger began in 1962 under an American aid programme.

In controlling this disease and many others in Africa, much depends on international co-operation. In the colonial era it was necessary for only a few metropolitan governments to work together, but now a large number of independent states must co-operate. Various organizations mostly under the auspices of the United Nations were set up for the purpose, but the membership of Portugal and the Republic of South Africa was disliked by many of the other countries and so they have not functioned very efficiently at times. Here, as in every sphere of activity in Africa, the part played by politics cannot be ignored. Recently the Organization of African Unity has shown increasing interest in the organization of research and technical services for the continent as a whole. The main problem now is shortage of staff at the professional level.

3

The People

WITHIN its boundaries, Africa has more peoples, tribes, and cultures than any other continent. Map 10 indicates the complexity. Here we can attempt to distinguish the larger groupings, starting with race.

RACE

Any set of physical characteristics that may be chosen to distinguish a particular race is somewhat arbitrary and unsatisfactory; individual racial groups have recognizable characteristics and can be typified but, like geographical regions, they are very difficult if not impossible to delimit precisely. Terms such as Nilotic, though in general use, are difficult to define. In many cases terms used to denote racial groups are in fact the names of languages, and names such as Hausa, Bantu, and Hamitic have acquired a racial connotation for which no sound basis exists. Racial and linguistic boundaries where they can be defined seldom correspond exactly, and a different nomenclature should ideally be used for each.

The largest racial group is formed by negroes, typically dark brown or black people, with crinkly hair, wide noses, and thick lips. They occupy most of the continent south of the Sahara, and a few thousand years ago were probably the dominant race in Ethiopia, the northern Sudan zone and Sahara, regions which have since been invaded by paler-skinned people from the north and east. Bushmen and negrilloes or pygmies probably preceded the negroes and are often regarded as the aboriginal inhabitants. The negroes have interbred with them, with pale-skinned Caucasoid and Armenoid peoples moving down from the north, and with people of Indonesian origin who came across the Indian Ocean to Madagascar (Fig. 18).

Bushmen have yellow-brown skins and are not really negroid in appearance; they have thin lips and hair so tightly spiralled as to form tufts; peppercorn hair it is called. Their language, Khoisan, is characterized by a large number of clicking noises. Early ancestors of the bushmen may have been the skilful artists responsible for rock paintings widely distributed over the central and southern parts of the continent. Now bushmen are confined to the Kalahari and its borders where they probably took refuge from invading negroes and Europeans. Only a few thousand remain untouched by newcomers; they live in small bands, hunting all manner of animals and collecting food from wild plants. Some interbred with cattle-owning people from the north, the Hottentots, who roamed south-west Africa south of the Cunene river. Most of the Hottentots were eventually absorbed into people of mixed origin, the Cape Coloureds of Cape Province.

Pygmies, the other aboriginal group, are mainly confined to the equatorial forests of the Congo. Hunters, trappers, and collectors, they are dark-skinned, shy people with an average height of only 4 ft. 8 in. They seem to live on good terms with their

Rock painting from South Africa. Such paintings are found mostly in the west of the Orange Free State and in the Drakensberg of Natal, under rock shelters and in caves. Similar paintings are found much further north in the Windhoek area, Rhodesia, and east Africa. They are believed to be the work of Bushmen and vary in age a good deal. Notice that the painting of the eland partly obliterates a Bushman with a bow and arrow and is clearly a later addition.

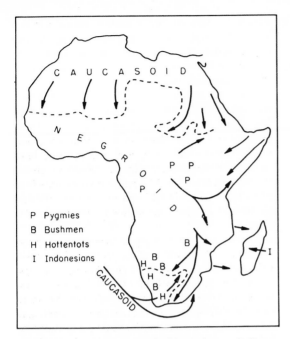

P Pygmies
B Bushmen
H Hottentots
I Indonesians

FIG. 18. *The main races in Africa. Arrows indicate, in a very generalized way, their movements over the centuries.*

negro lords, receiving grain and bananas from them in exchange for meat; in recent years they have been attracted to the roads and now many pygmies rely on tourists who give them tobacco and money when they agree to pose for photographs.

Negroes can be roughly divided into two great groups of approximately equal size, a north-western group speaking languages which have been variously classed as Nigritic, Sudanic, and (as in Map 10) West African, and a south-eastern group mainly speaking Bantu languages. In addition, a smaller number, notably in Chad, speak certain central African languages. The negroes of the west and the Congo basin are primarily agriculturalists. Some keep goats and cattle which are not usually milked. Specialists engage in fishing and various handicrafts. The other negroes in the east and south are more typically cattle keepers. This difference may be associated with a greater degree of inter-mingling of negro and Caucasoid peoples on the east side of the continent than on the west, many of the Caucasoids having been immigrant pastoralists who found conditions more favourable to stock on the eastern plateaux than in the western river basins.

Caucasoid or Amenoid people usually have pale skins and features more 'European' than negroid. The terms Hamitic and Semitic are often applied to them, words derived from the biblical names of the sons of Noah, but these should be reserved for the languages most of them speak. The Caucasoid people include Arabs who have infiltrated into the eastern Sudan and east Africa seaboard over the last thousand years. Originally traders or nomadic pastoralists, many of them have settled down to become sedentary cultivators; they continue to speak Arabic, a Semitic language, and are mainly Muslims. The Hamitic-speaking peoples in all probability also originated in Asia, though they seem to have been in Africa for several thousands of years. Typically, the Hamitic-speaking peoples are yellowish or coppery in colour.

As a result of miscegenation all gradations can be found, from typical negro to typical Caucasoid. Many with mixed physical characteristics have acquired the language and culture of later Arab invaders. In the areas lying north-east of Lake Victoria, where the intermixture of negro and Caucasoid has been complex, groups of people called Nilotes, Half-Hamites, and Nilo-Hamites have been distinguished; they are typically tall, dark-skinned pastoralists. But the pattern of peoples and cultures in east Africa is very complicated and no analysis of their movements, mixtures, and origins can be more than partial.

Europeans south of the Sahara number only about 4 millions, about 2 per cent. of the total population, but their importance politically and economically is out of all proportion to their num-bers. The majority live in the Republic of South Africa where more than half are descended from Dutch and German settlers of the seventeenth and eighteenth centuries, and the remainder mainly from Britons arriving within the last 150 years. The next largest European groups are made up of about 300,000 whites in Rhodesia, mainly of British origin, and a similar number of Portuguese in Angola and Mozambique. About 70,000 Euro-peans, mainly British, live in Zambia, mostly in the Copperbelt towns, and in Kenya there are about 50,000, the majority in Nairobi. The Belgian population of Congo Kinshasa has declined since independence when it stood at about 50,000. Euro-pean settlement has evidently concentrated in the relatively cool south and on high plateaux near the equator. Elsewhere in the continent smaller groups, not permanently settled, are employed by govern-ments, commercial and engineering firms, and international agencies. Finally, there are the mis-sionaries from Europe and America, diminishing in number now, as they train Africans to take their places in churches, schools, and hospitals.

Asiatics live mainly along the east coast. They

arrived in large numbers in the latter half of the nineteenth century to provide labour for railway construction and to work on plantations. Kenya, Uganda, and Tanzania have about 350,000, and the Province of Natal a similar number. Most of them are Indians and Pakistanis but the diversity is considerable. Some are Hindu, some Muslim, and within both groups there are differences of belief and allegiance to religious authority. They do not form a homogeneous bloc.

The Europeans and Asiatics are divided amongst themselves and separated from the Africans by language and culture as well as by colour. In the towns where most of the newcomers are concentrated, Europeans, Asians, and Africans have until recently lived in separate quarters, each group retaining its peculiar ways of life and scarcely ever intermarrying. Naturally, there are exceptions. In Angola and Mozambique, Portuguese and Africans have intermarried and interbred for centuries, and in the Republic of South Africa about a million Cape Coloureds, living mainly in and near Cape Town, are the outcome of white, negro, Hottentot, and Indonesian miscegenation over the last three centuries. In the past the interbreeding of black and white usually involved European men and African women; now the reverse is perhaps more often the case. While the Republic of South Africa has laws against miscegenation, African professional men from the newly independent states, who have spent long years studying in Europe, quite often return to their homes with white wives.

Perhaps as many as three-quarters of the Asians and Europeans, who have been described here as newcomers, were born in Africa and quite naturally regard it as their home. Some families have been living, sometimes on the same land, for several generations; their roots are in the continent and they are not easily to be dislodged as unwanted intruders who must return to their proper countries. One might as well suggest the expulsion of all Chinese from Malaya or for that matter, Greater Russians from central Asia. Even if all the Asians and Europeans were to leave Africa, differences in language, colour, and religion would remain amongst the 'native' peoples to cause dissension of the kind with which we are familiar in Nigeria, the Congo, and Sudan, where no serious problems have been caused by European and Asiatic settlers.

Racial tension

Racial tension arises where one section of a community assumes that it is superior to the others and seeks privileges not accorded to the rest. As Philip Mason has written (in his *Essay in Racial Tension*, 1954): 'When the sections involved correspond with racial groups, then the tension is displayed to the world and becomes intensified in the minds of the contestants with racial differences.'

There are no sound scientific grounds for believing that differences between races allow them to be placed in an order of precedence, some being superior and others inferior. Clearly there are physical differences and tests could perhaps be devised to discover the relative physical efficiency of different racial groups so long as the confusing influence of variations in diet and care of children could be eliminated. But to compare the mental capacities of racial groups is a much more difficult task, for tests are likely to indicate a person's cultural environment rather than his inherent intelligence, whatever may be implied by this term. That the bushman and pygmy are incapable of reaching as high a level of performance as other African peoples would be extremely difficult to prove or disprove for, although their ability in most intellectual spheres would appear limited to the outsider, their attainments in certain specialized fields are undoubted. Again, there is no conclusive evidence as to the relative ability of brown, black, and white people. Coloured people can certainly compete very successfully with the best of white peoples in sport, sculpture, music, and scholarship. Average ability is more difficult to assess; but the fact that black Africans are in general less advanced technically and economically than Europeans does not imply that they are incapable of reaching the same level. They have had a different history, they have their own cultures and traditions, and they are making their own contributions to the sum total of human knowledge and awareness; therefore, it can be argued, different criteria should be used for assessing their performance.

Racial tension appears to be the expression of antagonism based not so much on the inherent aversions of one race for another, but on the fear of one group for another stimulated by economic or other differences. In Africa the early white settlers were separated from the black Africans by a wide cultural gulf, which can largely be attributed to the fact that until the sixteenth century Africa had been isolated from the rest of the world. It had not shared in the accumulation of knowledge and wealth that began in the riverine areas of Egypt, Iraq, and India and which, from a European viewpoint, culminated in the spread of Roman civilization from the Mediterranean basin to north-west Europe. The art of writing and all that it involves in historical continuity was largely unknown. Africa south of the

Sahara escaped the culturally unifying influences of medieval Islam and Christendom. There could be no African Renaissance. To the seventeenth-century European the African was a savage; the white man was master, the black man, slave. It is not very surprising that difference in race should have been automatically associated with difference in status, and since social stratification in Europe was at that time associated with all manner of economic and political privileges and restrictions, class reinforced colour in the differentiation of native and European. This class/colour stratification has persisted anachronistically into the second half of the twentieth century and continues to influence human affairs in many parts of the continent.

CULTURE

Language

It has been estimated that there are more than 800 African languages, some spoken by millions of people and some by only a few hundreds. Attempts have been made to trace their genealogy but without very much success so far. The Bantu languages which are spoken by most of the peoples of the east and south appear to be derived from one ancestral language; from linguistic data it would seem possible that the progenitors of the Bantu-speaking peoples of today lived at one time on the southern edge of the equatorial forest roughly midway between the Atlantic and Indian Oceans.

In a country like Nigeria where about thirty languages are in common use, the multiplicity of tongues causes difficulties in education and commerce and hinders the spread of ideas. It is also a great obstacle in the way of creating a national feeling amongst all the peoples of this large and very varied country. In many countries, like Ghana, no one African language is dominant and so the language of the former imperial power has been adopted to transact official business. In such countries English or French is now being spoken at home, especially in families where mother and father are educated and come from different tribes.

In the Sudan Republic, Arabic has been adopted as the official language, in the face of southern opposition. Hausa is widely used in Northern Nigeria and further afield in west Africa and the Sudan. In the Belgian Congo both French and Flemish were official languages, as they are in Belgium. Both French and English are official languages in the Cameroon Republic. A student in Ethiopia who has spoken, say, the Cushitic language Galla at home must learn Amharic at school, and

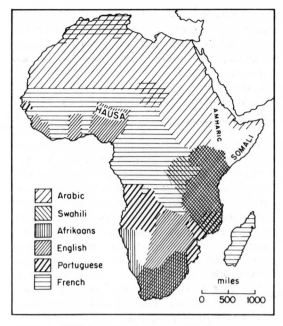

FIG. 19. *Widely spoken languages. The language map is extremely complicated but some languages are now spoken over wide areas, at least by educated Africans, as shown here.*

English at the university. The time and costs involved in learning and translating are very great, and unless African nationalism objects too strongly, English and French are likely to emerge as the main common languages (see Fig. 19). In time to come many African languages will be spoken only in remote rural districts, as Gaelic is in Scotland.

Society

African society is based on kinship, the network of relationships woven by descent and marriage. Descent is reckoned in various ways, patrilineally, that is from father to son over most parts of the continent, matrilineally amongst the southern Bantu living in the zone between Angola and Mozambique. The patrilineal system might have been brought from the north by Caucasoid peoples speaking Hamitic languages, but the fact that most of the negro peoples of west Africa seem to be also patrilineal does not lend support to this hypothesis.

The unit of the social organization is the family, not just a man, his wife, and children, but the extended family embracing three or four generations and including cousins. The lineage, the group tracing its descent back through three or four more generations, retains its cohesion, and people belonging to the same clan with a common ancestor say

43

ten generations back recognize certain ties and in some circumstances may act in concert. The membership of these clans and lineages is thought of as including the dead as well as the living.

In most African societies, lineages and clans are exogamous. Sexual relations between members of the same lineage are regarded as incestuous and marriages take place only with people outside that lineage. This leads to the development in time of a web of interconnecting strands between individuals in villages through a wide area.

The transference of bridewealth from the husband's family to that of the bride signals the completion of a marriage. This is not simply a payment for property; amongst other advantages it has the effect of helping to stabilize marriage. Polygamy, according to which a man may have more than one wife at a time, is traditional in most African societies. This does not mean that there are more women than men. The women marry early and often marry again later; the men marry late and may then have more than one wife at a time.

Cutting horizontally across the lineages and clan structures are age-grade organizations, craft guilds, and other associations. Several hamlets and villages or lineages and clans may recognize certain individuals as having particular religious status or function, perhaps as oracles or rain-makers. The people interlinked in these ways with similar traditions, sharing a common ancestry, speaking the same language, and perhaps occupying a particular tract of country constitute a tribe. The word 'tribe' like the word 'native' is not popular in some quarters these days, but it seems a better word than 'nation' which has been suggested as an alternative. A tribe might not occupy and claim as its own a well-defined piece of country. It might grade almost imperceptibly into a neighbouring tribe, or it might have been scattered by war or divided by a nine-teenth-century frontier. Some tribes have chiefs and a paramount chief, others have no important rulers. Perhaps language is the best guide to tribal identity, but languages have dialects and some peoples speak more than one language fluently.

In spite of the difficulty of defining a tribe, there is no doubt that tribalism is still important in present-day Africa. Membership of the tribe, and tribal education, impose upon boys and girls standards of behaviour which are to be expected from them in adult life. The kinship structure within the tribal context provides links between rich and poor, and between town and country dwellers. Associated restraints and responsibilities continue to be felt even in countries where a majority of the children attend school and a large proportion of the population is now urban. This kinship system is the aspect of African society that seems to distinguish it most clearly from Western society, in which kinship ties rarely stretch far outside the small family unit.

Religion

Details of religious observance vary from one tribe to another. In most of them some form of ancestor worship is practised and the existence of a supreme being is recognized together with a number of other spirits believed to have some control over natural phenomena. Various practitioners act as intermediaries between the spirits and the individual or group, and in some cases these priests are regarded as chiefs or kings. Religion forms an integral, everyday part of the life of the individual person and the community, but is particular to the clan or larger social group.

Islam and Christianity brought into Africa ideas about God that were in some ways new. (To write about this from the outside is difficult; the meaning of a religion is only fully apparent when you are a part of it.) These new religions, claiming to be universal, made little impression on Africa south of the Sahara before the colonial period. Christian missionaries until that time were confined to certain coastal stations. Muslim missionaries and traders had made a greater impact and had been at least partly responsible for the emergence of large political states, which evolved in the Sudan zone from medieval times onwards, and embraced several tribes. But until the end of the last century the impress of Islam had been restricted mainly to the big towns at the southern end of the trade routes across the desert; the mass of the people, country-dwellers, remained pagan.

The improvement of communications about the turn of the century was the most important factor promoting the dissemination of the new religions, Islam as well as Christianity; ideas as well as people and goods were able to travel quickly and easily. Tribes and tribalism were never static, but the rate of change has greatly accelerated in the last few decades. People have been moving from the country into the towns; traders have been travelling the country districts, and under the new stresses of a money economy the old cults are breaking down. The individual person is no longer confined to his tight tribal home. He goes to school, he reads newspapers and listens to the radio, works in the mines and in offices and shops, and soon realizes his place in a wider world. Some old beliefs and ceremonies may be retained, but in the new settings of time and

space, Islam and Christianity have provided super-
natural ideas that have been widely accepted.

Now a large proportion of the people north of
latitude 10° N. are Muslims and increasing numbers
of Muslim converts are being made towards the
Guinea coast particularly in western Nigeria, and
also down the east coast into Tanzania and Mozambique. It is not easy to indicate the numbers
or proportions of the people who now belong to
either Islam or Christianity because there are many
intermediate stages between being a pagan and
being a monotheist. In time, both the new religions
are likely to be influenced by Africa as much as they
have influenced Africans.

POPULATION DISTRIBUTION

Numbers of people

The population of Africa south of the Sahara,
standing at over 220 millions in 1968, is slightly
greater than that of the United States of America
and somewhat less than that of the Soviet Union.
The figure is approximate, for reliable counts have
yet to be made in most territories. A full census is
costly and succeeds only if sufficient trained enu-
merators can be obtained and if the people being
counted are sufficiently willing and able to give the
information required. Numbers in the Republic of
South Africa are known with a fair degree of
accuracy and in most other territories the estimates
given, for instance, in the United Nations Demographic Yearbook are probably within about 15 per
cent. of the truth. Uncertainty about the population
of Ethiopia is unusually great and the population
there may differ by several millions from the figure
given in the statistical table at the end of the book.
In Nigeria the situation has been confused because
the seats in the Federal House of Assembly, and the
Federal revenue, were distributed between the regions on a basis of their population, and censuses
made in 1962 and 1963 are suspected to have been
highly inaccurate as a result of each region attempting to push up its own numbers to get 'a bigger slice
of the cake'. In general, however, governments everywhere are coming to realize that census data are
essential for sound economic planning and development of all kinds, and so population statistics are
gradually becoming more detailed and reliable.

Rates of population increase, which are probably
the most important figures needed by planners, are
seldom available. In most countries the first counts
of any reliability were made after 1948 and later
figures to compare with them are only now beginning to appear. An alternative means of assessing

Trader travelling a country district in central Nigeria.

rates of change, by comparing birth- and death-
rates, can seldom be used because records, if they
are kept, are incomplete. However, information of
one kind or another is beginning to accumulate;
taxation figures are useful, sample surveys can be
revealing, and it is usually agreed that African
populations are increasing at rates of between $1\frac{1}{2}$
and 3 per cent. annually. If these rates are maintained, numbers will have doubled by the end of
the century, and it is very likely that they will be
exceeded.

The present trend is for rates of growth to increase
as health improves and death rates decline, so the
population of Africa south of the Sahara may rise
to more than 500 millions by the year A.D. 2000.
Numbers in Central and South America are growing even faster. In Europe, on the other hand, with
its higher standards of living, and much lower
mortality amongst children, rates of increase are
relatively low because parents usually limit deliberately the number of children in the family. But
most Africans are still anxious to rear as many
children, certainly boys, as they can, and it is impossible to foresee if and when they will adopt the
restrictive attitude of Europeans. Greater numbers
provide additional supplies of labour and a growing market and both these are prerequisites of
economic growth. But unless the labour can be
employed productively, rapid population growth
merely aggravates problems of housing, food
supply, and land shortage.

Extensive areas remain sparsely settled, with

fewer than ten persons to the square mile (see Map 11). They include the deserts of the north and south-west, swampy plains in south-east Angola, Zambia, and the central Congo, and the tsetse-ridden plains of the Congo watershed. In such country people live either in small groups exploiting the natural resources of the wide tracts extensively, or in larger groups spread at wide intervals, farming intensively. Belonging to the first group are the pygmies in the eastern Congo, and the Kalahari bushmen, both of whom are collectors and hunters. In the second group are the oasis dwellers of the Sahara. In such difficult environments the people are usually not entirely dependent on their own surroundings, but their ways of life are so finely adjusted to their habitats that they find it extremely difficult to change; so unless they abandon their homelands for more favoured areas they have little opportunity of sharing in any overall improvement in national standards of living. They continue to retain their old customs and occupations; they are anachronisms, interesting specimens for the anthropologist, traveller, and tourist, but a source of some embarrassment to their progressive compatriates in the towns.

Most sparsely settled regions, if they lack mineral deposits, are likely to remain poor and empty. Agricultural development is difficult when labour is short for clearing bush, building roads, and digging for water. High costs of developing such land deter large-scale investment. So the empty lands of Africa are liabilities rather than assets to the countries possessing them, increasing the costs of transport between more productive regions and oftentimes absorbing capital that could more profitably be invested elsewhere.

The heavily settled regions have an economic importance out of all proportion to their extent. With the exceptions of the Johannesburg–Durban industrial and mining regions and the Copperbelt of Katanga and Zambia, they are essentially agricultural regions with population densities generally between 100 and 500 to the square mile, rising locally to over 1,000. Although greater congestion is known in western Europe and other highly industrialized parts of the world, these densities are as high as those in most rural areas, with the exception of the irrigated rice-growing regions of the world.

Of the largest densely settled regions, two are in west Africa and one is in the east. They differ from one another both physically and economically; if they have anything in common, it is possibly the relative youth of their soils.

The largest populous region borders the Gulf of Guinea, including the southern parts of Nigeria,

Dahomey, Togo, and Ghana. Lying mainly in the high forest belt, it receives for the most part over 50 inches of rain annually. Some 35 million people there depend on root crops and plantains (large bananas) for food; their external trade is based on exports of tree crops, notably cocoa, palm produce, and kola nuts.

Hausaland in northern Nigeria is very different. The rainfall of 20–45 inches comes in only five months of the year, and the majority of the people are mainly engaged in growing sorghum and millet for themselves, and groundnuts and cotton for export.

About 20 million people live on either side of the equator within about 200 miles of Lake Victoria, in country with 40 to 60 inches of rain falling in two seasons and producing all manner of tropical tree, root, and grain crops. Southern Uganda, on the north side of the lake, includes some of the most prosperous African farmers; the highlands of Rwanda and Burundi to the south-west help to supply labour for the cotton- and coffee-growers; Sukumaland and Nyanza on the south and north-east sides of the lake are populous lowlands with numerous livestock; and the highlands on either side of the eastern rift, between Nairobi and Kitale, though less evenly settled, have a high population density overall.

Other closely settled areas of lesser extent are distributed along the east coast between East London and Durban, and at intervals further north. The hinterlands of Freetown and Dakar on the west coast and the borders of the rift valleys in Ethiopia and Malawi are all populous areas in each of which a few million people live on 10,000 or 20,000 square miles. In all, about 25 per cent. of the population lives in a few regions constituting little more than 2 per cent. of the whole area.

Nearly all the heavily settled lands are important producers of crops for export. Of all the cocoa grown in Africa, 90 per cent. comes from the populous belt near the Guinea coast. About 50 per cent. of the palm produce entering world trade is from the same region; Hausaland exports between half and one million tons of groundnuts annually besides a considerable amount of cotton, hides, and skins. Cotton, coffee, and tobacco are valuable exports from the country bordering Lake Victoria. These sales of cash crops give the peoples of the heavily settled lands higher material standards of living than those of the sparsely settled lands. The explanation is to be found, it would seem, in the greater fertility of their land, but still more in the greater opportunities for specialization of production in the heavily populated areas where local markets are

King Mtesa's palace in Buganda. '. . . a magnificent sight. A whole hill was covered with gigantic huts, such as I had never seen in Africa before.' This is one of the hills on which the capital of Uganda, Kampala, now stands. From J. H. Speke, Journal of the Discovery of the Source of the Nile, *London, 1863.*

numerous and where road and rail services and marketing organizations allow quick and cheap movement of produce.

Towns

Africa is the least urban of the continents; only a tenth of the people live in towns with more than 5,000 inhabitants. Until the end of the last century nearly all Africans were subsistence cultivators, herdsmen, and fisherfolk, living in small settlements, groups of huts clustered on hill-tops scattered through the forest or savanna, or strung along the coast and river banks.

A number of towns, some of them hundreds of years old, stood at the termini of trans-Saharan caravan routes, and essentially Arab ports were dotted along the east coast. In the interior, Kampala, Addis Ababa, and Kumasi were the capitals of martial states, and attracted large numbers of chiefs and their retainers and slaves. These were exceptional. In the Congo basin and the lands to the south

there seem to have been no towns of any size except those established by European traders and settlers. Only in Yorubaland in south-west Nigeria was any large proportion of the population not rural. Ibadan, Oyo, Abeokuta, and a number of other Yoruba towns had populations running into tens of thousands, but they were 'agrotowns'—not typically urban, for most of their inhabitants were still directly dependent on agriculture in the surrounding country.

In the colonial period, many of the towns already in existence were adopted as administrative and commercial centres and were linked together by railways and roads. Old towns, by-passed by the new means of communication, declined. The fastest-growing towns were those chosen to be the ports, coastal or riverine, at the termini of the railways. They were the obvious centres for trade and commerce and in many cases they were chosen to be colonial capitals.

Some large towns seem to have started by chance;

the site of Nairobi was first selected as a suitable site for railway workshops on the new railway being built from Mombasa to Lake Victoria at the very end of the last century. Other towns are mining towns which have become communications centres and have subsequently developed in other directions. Johannesburg, springing up on the spot where gold was discovered on the Rand, is now a great commercial and industrial city. On a much smaller scale, Enugu, established in connexion with the newly discovered coal seams in the Udi escarpment, and linked by rail about 1917 to the new creek port of Port Harcourt became the capital of Eastern Nigeria.

New towns are likely to develop in the future near new mineral discoveries or as a result of government planning. The Copperbelt towns in Zambia are only a few tens of years old. Tema in Ghana was a little fishing village until the 1950's when a great artificial harbour was constructed there to serve the Volta dam and Accra the country's capital. However, it would seem likely that future urban growth will take place mainly in cities that are already important. Minor ports are declining as the harbour installations and overland links of major ports improve. Government spending on public works and the employment

offered in government offices attracts ever more people to the main administrative centres, above all to the national capitals. The big towns, with their good water supplies, schools, hospitals, shops, cinemas, and bright lights attract swelling numbers of young and old, rich and poor, and the rate of increase of population within the cities is high, higher than in the country. The big cities are getting bigger, doubling in size every ten years; it is a world-wide phenomenon, and the problems it presents are immense (see Maps 12 and 13).

Most African cities differ from European ones in their spatial arrangement. In Europe we are accustomed to large towns in which the central areas are the main shopping and business districts. Further from the centre is often a ring of decaying residential property possibly being taken over for offices and rebuilt. Then come the sprawling residential areas of this century and new factories. This ring-structure is less apparent in Africa; there the towns are mainly remarkable for distinct quarters or sectors. In southern Africa and at least until recently in east Africa, Europeans, Asians, and Africans lived in separate parts of the town, either because of legal restraints on mixing or because

Parliament buildings in Kampala.

48

only Europeans and a few others could afford the high-class houses, and the Africans had to be satisfied with the third-class residential areas. In west Africa the government offices and the houses for the European civil servants were commonly built a mile or two away from the 'native' townships for reasons of health and security; the commercial area lay near the docks or railway station, and one or more stranger settlements sprang up, each dominated by a particular ethnic group. The old government areas retain their character, with roads laid out often in a rectangular grid and shaded by avenues of flowering trees. In the business districts rising land values are causing multi-story buildings to be erected. The African townships, many of them sordid slums built of mud and beaten-out petrol drums, are slowly being cleared and replaced by concrete and aluminium boxes.

In the Republic of South Africa about one-third of the people are urbanized and in Rhodesia and Zambia the proportion is one-fifth. In the Congo, where the urban population multiplied five times in the fifteen years after the war, the proportion in towns is well above the average for Africa as a whole, but in several countries of the east and west only one person in twenty is a town-dweller. Even in these last the importance of the towns is very great. Their inhabitants have a higher income than the country people, they are more conscious politically and set the fashions in thought and behaviour for the youth of the country. They provide a market for agricultural produce and everywhere provide the nuclei for development. At the same time they present immense problems. In most towns the influx of people combined with the natural increase exceeds the opportunities for employment, jobless youths turn to crime in the absence of other means of getting a living, and the kinship system of social security functions less effectively than in the villages, leading to destitution and neglect of children.

MIGRATIONS

Migrant labour

The history of an African tribe, when it can be traced over a few hundred years, is usually found to have involved movements over tens or hundreds of miles, with groups splitting or combining with neighbouring peoples perhaps several times. Under present conditions, with recognized territorial boundaries and central governments capable of extinguishing local conflicts, wholesale tribal migrations are rare. Tribal lands were crystallized with the coming of European law and order, and

A Ugandan lad moves into town.

the earlier processes of growth and movement were checked. In Kenya a section of the Masai were induced to leave the highlands early in this century for the semi-arid steppes further south, and in recent years mass movements of tribes have been caused by river-development projects, such as those on the Zambezi, Nile, and Volta rivers. But such events are exceptional and to some degree planned.

The ending of tribal migration has been accompanied by the development of labour migration, perhaps the most characteristic feature of the human geography of Africa today. Men, usually unaccompanied by their women-folk and children, move long distances to work for a few months or a few years in factories, in mines, and on farms, and then return home. In South Africa alone there are some 2 million such workers. The movements are largely from rural areas with subsistence economies into wage-labour in a money economy. In west Africa the migrants, coming mainly from heavily settled areas such as Mossi country in the Volta Republic, are attracted to the mining areas of Ghana and the Jos plateau, the cocoa farms of southern Ghana and western Nigeria, and to the main cities.

E

49

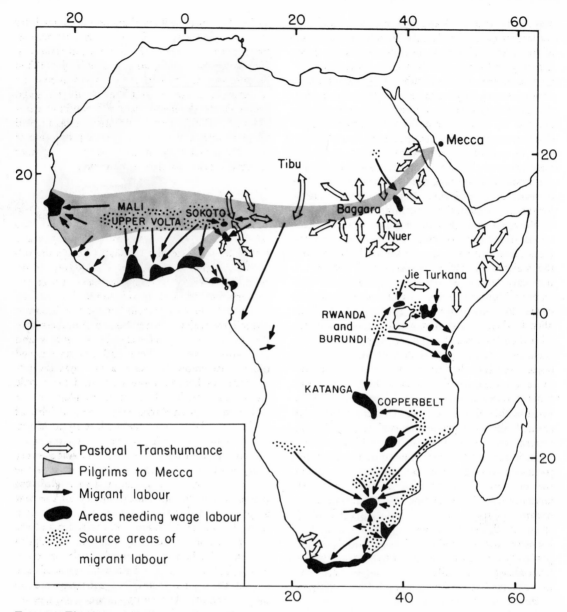

FIG. 20. *The main migratory movements. They are of three kinds; pastoralists shifting their grazing grounds seasonally, Muslim pilgrims going to and from Mecca, and labourers moving to the mining areas and export crop regions and back to their homes.*

From some districts, such as Sokoto in north-western Nigeria, the proportion of people moving out is very large, but since the majority are away for only a few months during the dry season, when farm work ceases, the effects are less drastic than in other parts of the continent. In south and east Africa, problems arising from migrant labour are on a larger scale. Take Malawi, for instance: of the total number of able-bodied adult males,

one-third at any one time are working abroad as wage-earners, mainly in Rhodesia and the Republic of South Africa (Fig. 20).

The basic reason why Africans have moved from their tribal areas into employment as wage labourers is the growth of mining, industrial, and agricultural enterprises in places remote from the centres of African population, particularly in that area rich in minerals stretching from Katanga through Zambia and Rhodesia to the Rand, where white capital and settlement have stimulated economic development of all kinds. This has engendered a very great demand for labour. To meet it, the Africans have been lured from their old subsistence economies in various ways; they have learned to value money and the things it can purchase; governments have assisted by exacting forced labour and by imposing many taxes which could be paid only if people went away to work for wages; transport, even by air, has been provided by recruiting agencies. Underlying the whole situation has been the poverty and lack of opportunity, and sometimes the shortage of land for the migrants in their own homes.

Whereas in Europe, and indeed in most countries, people have been moving into the towns from rural areas for a century and have settled in the towns, the majority of African workers have not settled but have continued moving periodically to and from their villages. In part this has been their own desire, for the environment of the town has been alien to them and they have wished to retain ties with their homes and to return to them as soon as they have earned sufficient cash to achieve the objects for which they originally emigrated. Furthermore, the colonial governments of Nyasaland and other territories encouraged labourers to return because they formed the man-power on which, it seemed, the food production and family life and general well-being of these countries depended. Most important has been the attitude of the companies employing labour, and the governments of the territories receiving migrants. Both have been anxious to avoid responsibility for establishing communities of immigrants, and the expense of housing them. In the past a labourer was provided with bachelor quarters only, and there was little opportunity for him to lead a normal family life. He looked back to his village as his real home, where his relatives lived, where he had his land or rights to land, and where he was secure.

In spite of the difficulties, many Africans have been able to settle in the towns and raise families, with the result that a new generation of Africans has grown up, with slackened tribal ties and having the town as their natural environment. Industrial development has required the services of Africans in semi-skilled occupations. Such workers are unobtainable amongst the migrants. Settled, experienced labour is needed, and so employers have been forced to adopt a new attitude. Governments have come to regard migrant labour with disfavour because it prevents rural areas adopting more advanced agricultural practices and weakens rural society by depriving it over long periods of the fitter and more progressive elements in the male population; it is also very wasteful in time and resources. Temporary labour migration cannot be prohibited because so many people in rural areas depend on remittances sent or brought home by migrants and economic development could not continue without them. But increasing attention is being paid to the problems of settling a greater proportion of the wage labour force and everywhere the number of African town-dwellers is increasing.

The pilgrimage to Mecca

A quite different migratory pattern is traced across north Africa, where the Sudan merges into the Sahara, by Muslim pilgrims travelling to and from Mecca. According to Islamic beliefs the pilgrimage should be made by every Muslim, and for centuries groups of believers have set out from the western Sudan to walk or ride to the shores of the Red Sea. Some have travelled across the Sahara to Tripoli, the majority east to Suakin. Numbers have fluctuated according to the state of the country, and the disturbances of the nineteenth century reduced them considerably, but since about 1920 the pilgrimage has become more popular. Poor people still walk for much of the way; others ride on lorries and trains through Kano, Fort Lamy, Abéché, El Fasher, and Khartoum; the wealthy fly to Mecca and back in three weeks, at a cost of about £100.

Ten thousand travel over the land routes every year, many of them taking several years over the journey, stopping for a year or two at different places *en route* to earn enough money for the next stage. Cotton picking south of Khartoum is a favourite source of income and the success of the Gezira scheme can be partly attributed to pilgrim labour at the harvest season. Many thousands of Hausa, Fulani, Kanuri, and other 'Westerners' have settled there permanently, though they are no longer permitted to take up tenancies. Others are concentrated in railway towns such as El Obeid, where Hausas work as porters and follow various trades and crafts. Most of the rest live in 'Westerner' villages, mainly in southern Kassala where the riverain conditions are similar to those of their homes in the western Sudan and the rainfall régime approximates to that of northern Nigeria. It has been estimated that the total number of Westerners who have settled in the Sudan Republic since 1900 exceeds a quarter of a million. Many of them retain their own customs and languages and their assimilation presents a political problem of considerable magnitude.

51

4

Traditional Herding, Farming, and Fishing

MOST Africans depend for a livelihood on the produce of their own farms and herds. Traditional economies persist alongside modern methods of production and exchange, and vary from place to place according to local physical conditions, especially climate, and also according to tribal custom. Methods of holding land, which are closely bound up with the social organization of the tribe and its rules of inheritance, have an important bearing on agriculture. Thus the traditional economies are fittingly seen against a physical and ethnic background, whereas the modern economies, which owe much to former colonial policies and current development plans, can best be considered later in this book, within the framework of national boundaries.

PASTORALISM *find largest group*

Pastoralists are mainly confined to the drier parts of the continent with mean annual rainfall totals of less than 35 inches and to highland areas in more humid regions (Fig. 21). Although they are often described as nomadic, the vast majority do not move

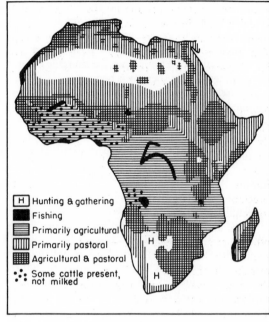

H Hunting & gathering
⬛ Fishing
≡ Primarily agricultural
▥ Primarily pastoral
▦ Agricultural & pastoral
•:• Some cattle present, not milked

FIG. 21. *Subsistence economies.* (*After Murdock.*)

Rock engraving of a humpless cow. Inscribed in volcanic lava rock in the Ganoa area of western Tibesti, where the mean annual rainfall today is about 2 inches, too dry for cattle; this engraving dates back to a more humid period a few thousand years ago.

at random but with a seasonal regularity. Many of the cattle, possibly most of them, are now owned by sedentary cultivators. Livestock are not entirely absent from the humid forest regions, infested though they may be with trypanosomiasis and other diseases, for there are certain breeds of dwarf cattle, goats, and sheep that are unusually resistant to disease and the forest people value them not so much for their milk or meat but for ceremonial and investment purposes. The table of statistics at the end of the book probably underestimates numbers very seriously because the figures available are normally based on taxation returns which are not comprehensive.

Cattle in African ownership are humped animals for the most part, descended from *Bos indicus*, the Zebu first domesticated in the steppe country of central Asia and introduced to Africa several centuries ago, possibly about the time of the first Muslim invasions. They have mixed with earlier Dwarf Shorthorns, of uncertain origin, and with

Hamitic Longhorns like those depicted on ancient Egyptian monuments and on rock carvings in various parts of the continent. The variety of breeds is now very great, many different strains having emerged, suited to local environments and able to survive conditions much more rigorous than they would be exposed to in north-west Europe or North America.

Pure-bred cattle introduced from Europe are acclimatized in the south and are proving successful in dairy herds in east Africa. They do not thrive unless they are carefully protected from disease; also they need supplementary feeding. Crossing European cattle with native breeds has been found to increase meat and milk production, provided that nutrition is also improved and the South African Zebu, for example, a cross between European cattle and the hump-backed Zebu kept by the Hottentots, weighs 1,100-1,500 lb. as compared with the 600-900 lb. of east and west African Zebus. However, the opportunities for livestock improvement appear to lie mainly in selection and breeding from native stocks which has been shown to treble milk yields and double meat production.

Goats and sheep are more numerous than any other domestic animals and are found very widely, wandering with herds of camels at the desert margins, in the company of cattle and donkeys in the Sudan zone, scampering through oil-palm gardens and native townships in the forest zone. They are able to browse off shrubs and trees, can tolerate being without water for several days, and have some resistance to trypanosomiasis. Goats provide many of the essentials of life for the villager, but European farmers usually regard them as unprofitable and so careful breeding has received little attention. With goats as with cattle the African pastoralists' main object has been numbers rather than quality. An exception to the rule is the Red Sokoto and certain other goats in west Africa which have been selected and improved for the sake of their appearance and the quality of their skins. Native African breeds of sheep bear quite a strong resemblance to goats, having hairy coats and, in the dry lands, a lank appearance, with long legs and ears. Both Merino and mutton-sheep have been introduced to south Africa and the tropical highlands and have done well; the majority being owned by European farmers.

Throughout the continent the seasonal distribution of rainfall and long periods of drought cause fluctuations in the quality and quantity of grazing and water. Each pastoral group has its own methods of overcoming the difficulties and making the best use of the resources available. In the desert regions,

Sheep and goats. The scene is a Hausa market in the Katsina area of northern Nigeria.

nomads move to and fro over hundreds of miles, crossing international frontiers and creating political disturbances. Their families are commonly split into two sections, one wide-ranging and the other more restricted in its movements or even settled in a farming area. The farms of cultivators are obstacles to the free movement of herds and the enmity of pastoralist and sedentary is a recurring theme in the human geography of the steppe and dry savanna.

The Tibu

The Tibu of the south-central Sahara, like many other desert pastoralists, were once notorious as professional brigands, depending for their livelihood and recreation on raiding camel caravans as well as engaging in trans-Saharan trade themselves. Most of them have homes in the wadis of the Tibesti mountains, but some groups are settled as far afield as Kufra and the southern Fezzan, on the shores of Chad and in Darfur. Members of a family set out from Tibesti in winter to wander with their camels and goats far south across Borku. If the grazing is good and political conditions are favourable, they may remain in the Chad basin for several years, a constant coming and going being kept up between the part of the family left behind in the Tibesti oases and the herdsmen out on the plains. If the rains fail or political conditions deteriorate, the nomads return to their homes in the mountain massif to recuperate. Always there is expansion and pastoralism in good times, the return to the mountains when times are difficult. Such advances and

Pastoralists on the move in northern Kenya. This particular group of tribesmen use donkeys to transport their huts and belongings. The basket-work forms the framework of their huts.

retreats may be repeated on several occasions in the life of the individual Tibu. They are adaptable people; they have to be, to persist in such a harsh environment.

The Turkana and Jie

The Turkana, living west of Lake Rudolf in northern Kenya, number about 80,000 and roam an area half the size of England and Wales. They own a quarter of a million animals; cattle, camels, donkeys, sheep, and goats. The annual rainfall varies from 2 inches on the plains to 20 inches on the massive granite hills rising 4,000 feet above the general level. Since the cattle need grass and must be watered at least every day or two, they spend most of the year near water-courses, and in the driest season retire to the hills where there is always some grazing. Only occasionally are they driven quickly over the plains to take advantage of new grass springing up after local storms. The camels, on the other hand, need to browse and, for much of the year they wander over the plains in charge of herdsmen who also look after most of the sheep and goats. Only during the driest season is their range limited to the water-courses and hill foot zones. Consequently individual families split up for at least a part of the year to cater for the differing needs of their livestock. They are in part

nomadic, in part transhumant. Members of different families who may meet each other briefly on the plains during the rains are separated by hundreds of miles the following dry season when all retire to the widely scattered hill masses.

The Jie who live in north-east Uganda where the rainfall is heavier, 15 to 35 inches annually, are believed to stem from the same tribe as the Turkana. The two tribes having separated only about two centuries ago continue to have much in common. Both depend on their cattle for food, clothing, and utensils; cattle enter into their ritual and, as bride-wealth, pass from one family to another. In both tribes, rights to property involve not land and water as such, but wells.

Now that the Jie and Turkana live in different environments they are evolving in different directions. The herds of the Jie, numbering more than 100,000 head of stock, depend for their dry-season water on eight main water-holes near the centre of their grazing grounds. For about ten months of the year the women and children live in homesteads near the water-holes, growing sorghum and other crops, while the men of the tribe are on the move, scattered with their herds, living near the cattle in temporary camps, and seeing little of each other. They travel west to catch the early rains, then move across to the drier east for the peak of the rains in

54

July and August and back to the west for the last rains and early dry season. In this way they make the best use of the grazing. Towards the end of November, however, they all settle down to spend a month or two near the wells and water-holes and for a while at least the tribe is reunited. This probably explains why the Jie have come to live a much more social life than the Turkana who are split up into tiny groups throughout the year and lack any large-scale political cohesion.

The Nuer

The Nuer are a pastoralist tribe in the southern Sudan whose seasonal movements are controlled by the flood levels of the Nile and its tributaries. From May to November when they are confined to land rising only a few feet above the flooded clay plains, they grow millet and a little maize and tobacco near their compounds and pasture their cattle on dry land nearby. As the floods recede they lead their cattle on to wide grassy plains uncovered by the falling waters, and while the women and children stay behind to gather the harvest, the men live in temporary cattle camps scattered over a very wide area. By February, grazing on the higher flooded land has deteriorated and families reassemble to move down to the *toich* or river-side grazing. At this season the men spend as much time spearing and catching fish as in herding their cattle. Eventually, the rising waters necessitate a return to higher ground.

Some Nuer families move long distances, 80 miles or more across country every year. Others are far less mobile because there happens to be an adequate variety of land within a few miles of their rainy season encampments. All of them are primarily pastoralists and they are not anxious to give up their nomadic way of life. To depend on cultivation in such an environment with a variable rainfall and poor drainage is rather precarious. Also tilling the heavy clay soils is very hard work.

The Baggara

The Baggara Arabs live north of the Nuer in a belt of country stretching from the White Nile through the central and southern parts of Kordofan and Darfur and as far west as Lake Chad. They are descended from camel-owning Muslim pastoralists who moved south from Egypt several centuries ago, interbred with the local negroid peoples and took to herding cattle, which are better suited than camels to this wetter region with heavier soils. In Kosti District, the pastoralist families grow some crops in the wetter areas. The cattle cannot stay near the cropland during the rains, mainly because

Baggara pastoralists' huts under trees. This wooded country lies west of the Nile on the Qoz, the fixed dunes of Kordofan.

of biting flies that abound at this season, and the herdsmen drive their flocks and herds to the well-drained sands of the Qoz where the rainfall is lighter and there is less surface water. At the end of the rains they return to help with the harvest, bringing their cattle to feed on the crop residues. Then local pools of water dry up and the cattle are taken down to the river front for the end of the dry season to feed on the marshy grasslands until the first rains, when all return to the farmlands of the hinterland.

The Fulani

The Fulani or Peuhls have been established in the Sudan zone of west Africa for five or six centuries and in the last 200 years have pushed south on to the highlands of the Fouta Djallon and northern Cameroon. After the pacification of Pagan tribes by the British at the beginning of this century, Fulani also moved on to the Jos plateau in Nigeria and the Bamenda highlands of west Cameroon. In the north their movements are comparable to those of the Baggara, being from well-drained upland sites in the rains to river-side pastures in the dry season. Further south their seasonal movements are mainly a response to disease risks. In the rains, herds in Nigeria concentrate on plateaux above 4,000 feet because tsetse-fly, at that season, are widespread over the plains of the Niger and Benue valleys. The density of stocking on the highlands in the rains exceeds a hundred to the square mile. With the arrival of the dry season, about November, the cattle are driven to lower levels, and later to pastures alongside the Benue and its tributaries, care being taken to avoid patches of woodland where tsetse seek refuge from the dry heat of the open plains.

Most Fulani families depend to some degree on corn bought in the local market with cash derived from sales of surplus milk and butter. Many grow millet and beans near their wet-season encampments, some of which are inhabited through the year by at least a few family members. There are several tens of thousands of people in Nigeria who call themselves Fulani but who are now settled in villages and are hardly distinguishable from neighbouring negroid cultivators with whom they have intermarried, though they usually retain strong interest in cattle and own more stock than the others. Many of these settled Fulani are descended from groups that revolted against their Hausa rulers in the early nineteenth century and now form a ruling class and also a proportion of the peasantry in northern Nigeria. Some of them lost their cattle in the rinderpest epidemics at the end of the last century; others were forced to depend on agriculture after their cattle died in the widespread droughts about 1913. Stenning (1959) mentions certain Fulani chiefs in the vicinity of Potiskum who were persuaded by British administrators to establish permanent settlements in the 1920's to ease the problem of collecting cattle tax. Usually, however, the pastoralist is averse to giving up his mobile way of life and only does so when compelled by natural disaster or political constraints.

The future of pastoralism

Although the pastoralist commonly makes use of land that is unattractive to the agriculturalist because of its aridity or remoteness, local or central administrations tax his cattle quite heavily; at a rate of several shillings per beast annually. He usually avoids paying in full but still the amount extracted from him makes a large contribution to the costs of government and helps to provide social services, such as schools, which benefit mainly the sedentary inhabitants. Until veterinary services expanded the pastoralist did not receive much in return, but he was content so long as he was left to arrange his own affairs with the minimum of state interference. The new African governments, even more anxious to control and count and educate their peoples than were the old colonial administrations, are also more concerned than the old régimes that the pastoralist should contribute more effectively to the national economy, and are making efforts to persuade him to settle down. On a European farm, beef cattle are slaughtered at the age of 18 months to 3 years, giving a rapid turnover and good returns on capital

whereas amongst some pastoralist tribes cattle are sold only when cash is urgently required for some specific purpose and slaughter is delayed until the death of a beast appears imminent. The difference can be attributed in part to the fact that on a ranch run commercially livestock are raised primarily as a means of making money for purchasing other goods, whereas amongst many pastoralists, owning animals is an end in itself as much as a means to an end. Like the ownership of a car by a town-dweller, it promotes a feeling of pride and a status that could not easily be acquired otherwise.

The family herds have often been compared to a bank balance that can be drawn upon when unusual demands are made on the family finances. Such demands are greatest when marriage by one of the male members is in view and the young men who perform the hard and tedious work of tending the animals are anxious to see their flocks and herds grow in size, so that they may have wives themselves and rear children who will enable them, as soon as possible, to lead the more leisured existence of their fathers. Furthermore, people like the Fulani depend on milk for their food, and since lactation depends on calves, the main interest of the herd owner is in a steady yearly increase in his herds. In the past when losses by disease were greater and political conditions less favourable, numbers in herds probably fluctuated violently. In recent years numbers of cattle have generally been increasing and many rangelands show signs of being overgrazed, with deteriorating pastures and eroding soils.

Governments are anxious to prevent overstocking and at the same time to increase the meat protein in diets. If herd owners could be persuaded to dispose of a greater proportion of their stock each year, both problems would be solved. Improved transport facilities have increased the demand for young animals which might not have had the stamina to walk the long distances to markets. Auctions have proved quite popular in east Africa. Slaughterhouses and canning factories built in the stock-rearing areas are increasing local demand, and stock prices are rising with the increasing number and prosperity of city-dwellers. Some years will elapse before pastoralists generally look upon their herds as sources of wealth rather than wealth itself, but a younger generation with new values is growing up, and there is a possibility that some will decide that the traditional life, in a harsh environment, is not sufficiently rewarding. In various ways, then, the pastoralists are being drawn into the economic life of the states they roam, and increasing numbers are settling down to a more sedentary existence.

Little is known about the origins of agriculture south of the Sahara. North African winter rainfall crops were not very suitable for the tropical summer rainfall habitat and it is possible that cultural evolution south of the desert was held up until rice, millets, and sorghum were domesticated from local plants. It is also possible that agriculture began quite independently of the Nile valley and Asia, perhaps, as Schnell has argued, in the rice-growing area of west Africa. There is as yet too little evidence to come to any firm conclusions. The plough appeared south of the Sahara at a very late stage and cultivation for subsistence over most of the continent is still with the hoe. Yams, cocoyams, and bananas appear to have been introduced from south-east Asia over a thousand years ago; maize, cassava, sweet potatoes, and a number of other very important crops were brought over from America by the Portuguese.

Many, possibly most, cultivators these days grow something for sale, but primarily their crops are for the consumption of the grower and his family. Agriculture is as much a way of life as an economic activity.

Some staples such as sorghum, cassava, and maize are grown very widely, from the rain forest to the desert margins; others are much less tolerant and more restricted in their distribution. Three main crop regions might be distinguished. In the first, with rainfall totals exceeding 50 inches, roots, oil-palms, bananas, and plantains are important, with rice the staple in certain areas. In the sub-humid to semi-arid savanna lands, various cereals and legumes are dominant. Where mean annual rainfall totals fall below 10 inches, cultivation is mainly confined to irrigated garden crops, bulrush millet and date palms (Fig. 22).

In any particular climatic zone, the assemblage of crops grown, the implements used, and the customs of holding land vary from tribe to tribe.

Within a single tribal area, the intensity of farming varies with the pressure on the land, and in detail on soil conditions and the distance of a farm plot from the farmer's dwelling-place. Plots cropped annually, their fertility maintained by manuring, may lie within a few hundred yards of land that is cleared, cultivated for a year or two and then allowed to revert to bush for a decade or more. The same family commonly employs intensive methods in one area and extensive methods in another, varying them according to local drainage and soil conditions. The pattern of cultivation is sometimes simple but rarely uniform.

Forest cultivators

Relatively few African farmers have the opportunity to clear high forest for cultivation, for much of the remaining high forest is included in reserves or persists only in very sparsely settled country.

Some of the Mayumbe, who live in small villages on forested hills north of the Congo, are among this minority. Their houses are surrounded by vegetable gardens and plantains which are manured with domestic refuse and night-soil. Groves of oil-palms, coconut-palms, and fruit-trees encircle the villages, and paths radiate through them to cultivated patches scattered through the forest. Clearing of the forest trees by the men takes place in the dry season when the smaller trees are lopped off 3 feet from the ground and a ring of bark is stripped from the larger ones. Oil-palms and other useful trees are left unharmed, and as the years go by they become dominant. The debris is burned shortly before the rains, the charred trunks of the larger trees are felled and the ground is then ready for the women to plant their crops before wild plants spring up again. Seeds of maize, cuttings of cassava, seedyams, and banana clones are planted here and there, bananas in well-manured patches, cocoyams in moist depressions. Three or four months later the maize is harvested and a second crop may be procured before the root crops are ready for lifting at the end of the rains. A new plot is cleared the following year, though the women return to collect bananas and cassava roots from the abandoned plots for the next two or three years as the forest reclaims them.

Methods of cultivation like this can support only a sparse population because so much land is required if there is to be time for forest to grow up and restore fertility. Livestock play a negligible role. Only a small area can be manured and cropped annually, and a family can manage to clean, weed, and cultivate only about 2 or 3 acres at most each year. Diets consist largely of starchy foods and there is little surplus available for sale.

With a heavier population when the period of resting diminishes to ten or fifteen years, the forest is unable to recover after cultivation, and the system can then be described as rotational bush-fallow farming. This stage has been reached on the rainy uplands of Sierra Leone, for instance, where the Mende plant upland rice and a very wide range of other crops.

The Ibos of south-east Nigeria are very thick on the ground and in an area where the mean annual rainfall is between 60 and 70 inches, the resting period has been reduced to a stage at which grasses

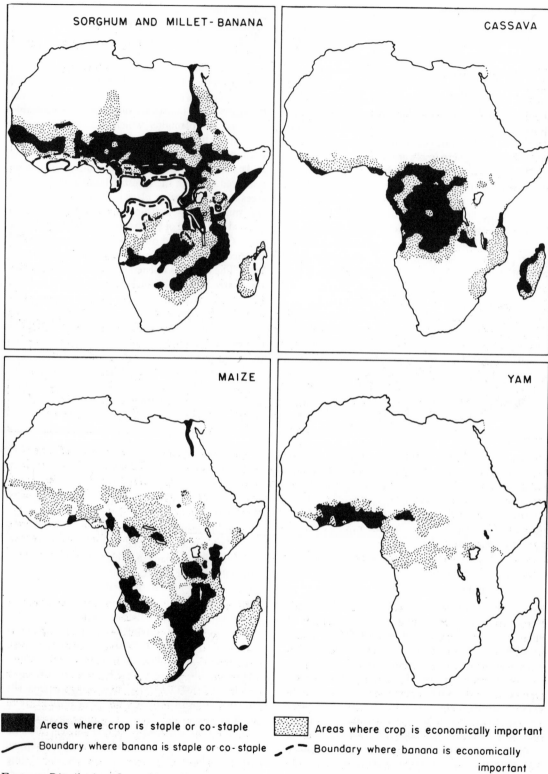

SORGHUM AND MILLET-BANANA

CASSAVA

MAIZE

YAM

■ Areas where crop is staple or co-staple

⬚ Areas where crop is economically important

— Boundary where banana is staple or co-staple

‒‒ Boundary where banana is economically important

FIG. 22. *Distribution of some important crops.*

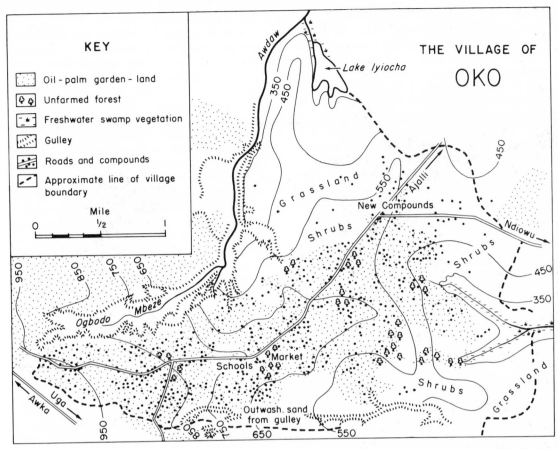

FIG. 23. *The village of Oko in eastern Nigeria lies on the east-facing escarpment a few miles south of Awka (see Fig. 41) in the headwaters of the Mamu river. The Awdaw, a tributary of the Mamu, rises in a very large and deep ravine which is probably the result of headward recession of a spring issuing from the Tertiary sandstones and erosion accelerated by clearing of the forest and an increased run-off. The people, Ibos, live in large compounds scattered through oil-palm gardenland that merges with similar wooded land in adjacent villages along the Uga-Awka road. The eastern outskirts of the village consist of poor grassland which is slowly being planted with shrubs and trees as the population increases. Lake Iyiocha in the north appears to have been formed as the result of sediment from the big gully Ogbodo Mbeze accumulating on the valley floor and blocking a small tributary of the Awdaw.*

have replaced trees over wide areas of upland. Forest trees are now confined to the vicinity of villages, where they have been either deliberately preserved or planted through extensive garden plots near the houses. Undisturbed high forest persists only around spring-heads and pagan shrines. Open grassland stretches between the villages, providing only thatching grass and rough grazing for a few dwarf cattle; it is almost useless for cultivation. Shrubs like *Acioa barteri* have been planted at the edge of the woodland to restore fertility to the exhausted soils (Fig. 23). Food crops are mainly grown under the village trees on land benefiting from leaf-fall, dung from goats and sheep kept in the compounds, and household refuse.

From such heavily settled areas, young people emigrate to find work in the growing towns or to seek farmland in less populous country west of the Niger. Those who remain rely heavily on local trading or remittances from migrants; they buy much of their food from markets to which yams, cassava, and maize are imported by lorry from less congested districts.

In these examples, the settlements of the cultivators remain fixed, even though different plots may be farmed each year. Cultivators who shift their dwellings from time to time are less numerous.

Amongst them are some of the Zande who live on the borders of the rain forest where the Sudan Republic adjoins the Congo and Central African Republic. They are made up of some fifty small tribes assimilated by a conquering group nearly 200 years ago and now speaking, in the main, a single language. Explorers who visited the region a century ago described the Zande as primarily hunters and collectors. Now they cultivate a very wide range of crops, and individual groups have evidently been borrowing new crops from their neighbours.

The Zande, or at least one section of them, have been described by de Schlippe in *Shifting agriculture in Africa* (1956). He emphasizes that an orderly arrangement can be detected in what appears at first sight to be a chaotic distribution of farm plots and bush around the settlements. Homesteads are usually built on the valley slopes, particularly on the fertile soils at the edge of gallery forest, that is, forest bordering streams, while the upland plains, underlain by ironstone at a shallow depth and where the grass is burned every year, are mainly left unused except for hunting. Crops are planted here and there around the living huts; tobacco in the shade of the eaves, bananas on old refuse heaps, pumpkins and sweet potatoes on rich soil swept from the courtyard and receiving ashes and other household waste. The main farms are established in forest clearings where eleusine millet and groundnuts are planted in the first year, followed by maize and gourds in the second, with cassava interplanted for harvesting in the third year when the plot is reverting to woodland. The gardenland near the houses is planted up with oil-palms, mangoes, and bananas, and as the years go by they cover an increasing area, expanding down the slope, eventually as far as plots of dry-season maize near the stream bed. But every year the main food farms have to be established further away from the homesteads on the upland, and after a decade or two the distance to them is so great that the decision is made to move home to another site. Usually there are other reasons for moving; poor harvests, misfortunes of one kind or another may have as much influence on the decision as the effects of local soil exhaustion. So a man may move several times in the course of his life, but as each shift is likely to be in response to some particular event the removals are not looked upon as being in any way regular. The farming activities of the Zande, like those of many subsistence cultivators, are a succession of improvisations involving adjustments not only to soil conditions and the weather but also to any number of other circumstances out of the individual's control.

Savanna cultivators

The studies made by Trapnell and Clothier in north-western Zambia show how cultivation methods vary with the type of country and with tribal agricultural tradition. On the northern plateau, cultivation of the *citemene* (ash-planting) type is practised. It involves felling trees over a much larger area than the one to be planted, lopping off the branches, taking care to preserve the leaves, and laying them in stacks or flattened piles for burning. The thick patches of ash are then cultivated. On the northern Kalahari soils, the woodland is thicker and the system is a little different; the entire cleared area being covered indiscriminately with lopped branches and the trunks of smaller trees, the larger trunks left standing, and nearly all the clearing cultivated. Such methods allow sorghum, millet, maize, cassava, and numerous lesser crops to be grown for a year or two before soil exhaustion and weeds force the cultivators to move on.

Shifting cultivation of this kind can support a population of up to fifteen persons to the square mile. With greater densities, the equilibrium is liable to be upset for the fallow period has to be reduced, fertility declines, larger areas have to be cultivated each year and so the resting period is still more abbreviated.

In some of the savanna lands, increased pressure on the land appears to have led to the adoption of more conservative and advanced systems of agriculture. These are possible where soils are inherently good and animals can be introduced into the farming system. Such is the case in the Sudan zone of west Africa where a large proportion of the well-settled country is cropped every year.

The Hausas of northern Nigeria maintain fertility by applying animal manure to their fields. Because of the high population densities, commonly exceeding 200 persons to the square mile, wild game has almost been eliminated and woodland where tsetse can breed is very limited, so trypanosomiasis is not a serious menace. Goats, sheep, and cattle that go out daily to graze on the uncultivated land at the village outskirts and on patches of poor land nearer the centre are kraaled at night near the houses or within compounds and their dung, together with other waste from the houses (usually not including night soil), is carried out to the fields by donkeys. The plant nutrients from a large area of the village left uncultivated are thereby concentrated on the cultivated fields. After the grain harvest, herds of cattle belonging to nomadic pastoralists pass through the heavily settled agricultural districts, on the way from wet season grazing lands to riverside pastures. The cultivators welcome them and may be ready to build huts, dig wells, or pay a considerable sum of money just to persuade them to spend a few days or weeks in the neighbourhood, the stock feeding on crop residues and in recompense leaving dung, enriching the fields.

Farmers living near the larger towns rely to some degree on the waste products of the towns to enrich their fields. Slaughter-houses, pit latrines, and other sources of waste in big towns like Kano enable the small fields of the surrounding country to remain under cultivation year after year, the manure being carried away by donkeys. Most of the people are no longer subsistence cultivators in such heavily settled areas. Benefiting from being within easy reach of markets and transport systems, they sell a proportion of their crops for processing in the towns or for export abroad and with the cash buy foodstuffs, cloth, and other goods. Many of them are artisans or craftsmen as well as being farmers; some are weavers, others are mat-makers, petty-traders, leather-workers, butchers, and so on.

Dry-land cultivators

Crops in areas with mean annual rainfall totals of less than about 10 inches are largely dependent on flooding or artificial watering and so cultivation in the semi-arid lands and deserts is confined to relatively small areas with favourable soils and water supplies.

The volumes of water required for irrigation are very large when compared with these needed by stock or human beings; while a cow or a man can manage with about 4 gallons of water per day, an acre of millet demands about 200 gallons of water every hour of the day. Such large volumes of water, free from salts, can only be obtained cheaply in restricted areas. Deep holes tapping underground water are expensive to drill, costing over £1 per foot for bores with a diameter of only 2 inches. Then, unless the water is under pressure, there is the expense of pumping it to the surface and distributing it.

Soils in the dry lands are commonly derived from dune sands which allow the irrigation water to disappear rapidly by percolation; others are derived from alluvial clays in which salts concentrate rapidly in the surface layers. Ideal soil conditions are rare and so settlement sites have generally been restricted to quite small areas with a fortunate combination of physical conditions, notably on the banks of the Nile and in a number of widely scattered depressions in the Sahara.

In Saharan oases life has always been based on the

Fulani camp on agricultural land. These cornstalk shelters were being used in the late dry season near Zaria in northern Nigeria.

date-palm, a tree which can withstand great heat, high rates of evaporation, and soil-water containing a moderately high content of common salt in solution. The fruit is hard and floury, very different from the fruity dates imported into Europe. As an acre of date-palms, say fifty trees, requires about a million gallons of water annually, they cannot rely entirely on water hauled from wells but their roots must be able to draw on sub-surface water at a shallow depth. Estimates have been made of $2\frac{1}{2}$ million date-palms growing in the Sahara south of the Tropic of Cancer. Only about one-third of these bear dates, for summer rains towards the south prevent proper maturing of the fruit. Some are wild and are visited every year by nomadic groups only for the harvest season, about August. But the most productive palmeries have been carefully established from root suckers, selected to give a distribution of one male palm to every fifty females, the trees that bear the fruit. Natural pollination is not very effective and unless a good deal of labour is expended in the spring months pollinating the females with the efflorescence from a male tree, much of the fruit is uneatable. One man can deal with only forty trees in a day and this one factor effectively limits the number of productive trees.

Various crops are grown beneath the date-palms; wheat and barley as winter crops are most important in Algeria, Libya, and Egypt, but in the southern Sahara the main cereals are millets, sown in August and September after the date-harvest and harvested three or four months later. Tobacco and onions are grown in nearly every oasis, together with small tomatoes for drying and use in soups, and henna, valued by the women as a cosmetic, for staining teeth. Peas, beans, and melons are locally important; occasionally figs and vines manage to survive in the shade of the palms.

While the date-palms rely chiefly on sub-surface water, the annual crops have to be irrigated. A single well, say 12 feet deep, might water a tenth of an acre, and all through the day the squeaking of the balancing arms of the *shadufs* sounds through the oasis. If a donkey or camel is used to haul the rope over a pulley, lifting a large leathern bucket, the well may irrigate an acre or more, but additional manual labour is then required to handle the beast and lead off the water. Although less arduous methods can be used when running water is available, labour is still required to maintain such works as *foggaras*, the conduits gathering water from a water-bearing layer of rock and leading it by tunnel to the oasis. Spring water is rarely available and when it is, a reservoir is needed to store the water overnight; the flow must be directed from one farm-plot to another, and on each plot every square yard must receive its due. So oasis cultivators must remain at their work all the year round to produce their meagre harvests. They use various manures to increase yields; sheep and goat, even bat, dung are used, but yields are not remarkably high and there may be little more than 200 lb. of corn per head for a year. These people are living quite close to starvation level.

Many of the cultivators are slaves settled in the oasis by Arab, Tibu, Touareg, or other master peoples who depend largely on livestock but found it useful to have slaves working gardens for them. Now the slaves have become croppers or tenants, but are little better off than they were before. Many of them are moving off to more favoured lands and the pastoralists must reluctantly assist with the cultivation. In the northern Sahara, new oil-wells have brought improved artesian water supplies, cheap fuel, and employment to many oasis dwellers, but in the south there are no oil-wells yet, and the oases are dying settlements.

FISHING

Although fish constitutes only a minor part of the diet of most Africans, it is an important part not only because it supplies much of the protein people living in forested areas badly need but also because dried fish is a powerful condiment much relished where food largely consists of starchy porridges. The fisherfolk consume large quantities of fish themselves and the surplus is preserved, often by the women, who dry, smoke, or salt it. Fresh fish

will keep long enough to be sold little more than half a dozen miles from where it has been caught; preserved fish is traded over distances of hundreds of miles and may finally be sold for several shillings per pound.

African sea fisheries have not been fully exploited by traditional methods, partly because the most productive grounds lie off sparsely settled desert coasts. Cool upwelling waters, partly responsible for the aridity inland, are rich in nutritive salts and the plankton they support provide the food supply of great quantities of sardine, pilchard, tuna, hake, and a variety of other fish. The cool seas off the coasts of south-west Africa and Angola and between Morocco and Senegal have attracted much attention from commercial companies in recent years, and motorized fishing-boats now land large catches at ports equipped with refrigerating and processing plants. Some of the fish is sold to the interior, but most of it is exported to countries outside Africa in the form of oil and fish-meal.

The fisheries of the Guinea coast, less productive than those in the Benguela and Canaries currents, are of considerable local importance. The Ewes are amongst a number of coastal people who put out to sea in dugout canoes and employ long seine nets hauled in from the shore. The nets are costly and a good deal of financial enterprise and organization are required to operate the large companies involved. New techniques and equipment are adopted as they are found to be economical; nylon nets and outboard engines fitted to the traditional canoes being amongst the most important recent developments. Distribution of the fresh fish has been a weakness and fish from Europe both dried and frozen can still undercut local produce in the large towns. African governments are introducing larger fishing vessels and centralized marketing and refrigeration in attempts to increase efficiency.

Inland fisheries are very varied in character. On some lakes modern, heavily capitalized methods can be employed successfully. Fish from Lake George and Lake Mweru have been frozen for export by road and even by air to mining towns which provide a ready market. Shallow lakes like Naivasha and Lake George may yield 50 tons of fish annually per square mile of surface area. The waters of deeper lakes are not so rich; below a certain depth the water is cool and stagnant and incapable of supporting many fish. Lake Kivu is particularly noteworthy in this respect. As a result of its violent history in recent geological times it contains few species of fish, and the water a few hundred feet below the surface is so saturated with

sulphuretted hydrogen and methane as to make fish
life at depth impossible. Recent attempts to utilize
the methane as a source of fuel were accompanied
by attempts to improve the fisheries. The water
brought to the top for the extraction of the methane
contains much carbon dioxide and nutrient salts in
solution, photosynthesis is stimulated by its release
into the surface waters, and species of fish have been
introduced from Lake Tanganyika to feed on the
new supplies of plankton made available. The
Belgians have estimated that such methods would
allow fish production from Lake Kivu to be raised
from the present 800 to about 35,000 tons annually.

Amongst the most productive inland fisheries are
the great swamps, not those that are stagnant, for
the decaying vegetation reduces the oxygen content
of their waters, but those with a through flow, like
Bangweulu, the Malagarasi swamps of Tanzania,
Lake Rukwa and Lake Chad. They yield millions
of fish annually, chiefly *tilapia*. Livingstone, who
died near Bangweulu after struggling through the
swamps for days on end, described the fishing
industry in his journal. 'The great numbers of fish
caught by these weirs, baskets and nets now, as the
water declines, is prodigious. The fish feel their
element becoming insufficient for comfort and
return from one *bouga* [pool] to another towards the
lake; the narrower parts are duly prepared by weirs
to take advantage of their necessities; the sun's heat
seems to oppress them and forces them to flee.' The
same fishing methods are in use today as a century
ago, but now there is a flourishing bicycle and lorry
traffic in dried fish to the Copperbelt towns.

The Malagarasi swamps were rather neglected
until 1946 on account of the sparse population and
the lack of easily accessible markets. Since then the
fisheries have expanded. Great numbers of fish can
be caught there, in spite of the fact that the waters
of the swamps are remarkably clear and have a sparse
plankton population. According to Hickling, the
abundance of fish life is due to the presence of two
species of small fish which are able to feed on the
water lily and its seeds and on other plant material.
They pass out a partially digested mass which forms
the main food of other species of fish, especially
tilapia.

Fishing methods in creeks and river deltas are
comparable to those in lakes and swamps. Some
tribes are more skilful and employ a greater variety
of methods than others. Upstream two kinds of
fisheries can be distinguished, those dependent on
the flood and those on the low-water stages. African
rivers in flood spread over the valley floors forming
vast lakes, lagoons, and marshes. The people with

*Fishing boat leaving the harbour at Walvis Bay. The
waters off the south-west African coast are very rich in
fish and about half a million tons are landed annually,
one-fifth of the total African catch. The Walvis Bay
area, a 434-square-mile enclave, though administered
as a part of south-west Africa is actually a part of
Cape Province.*

their homes on the natural levees, which rise above
the level of all but the highest floods, catch the
migrating fish by constructing barriers of reed
fences supported by wooden poles that guide the
fish into basketwork traps. Such fences show up
clearly on air photographs, enmeshing tens of
square miles of flooded plains and lagoons.

On the upper Nile in the southern Sudan, Arab
fishermen from the north set up temporary encampments and catch the fish in the main stream in seine
nets and gill nets for sale salted and dried to the
Congo. The Nilotic peoples such as the Nuer,
primarily herdsmen, are active fishermen too. In
November and December they construct dams to
trap fish attempting to move back from the river-
side swamps into the falling waters of the mainstream and use their spears to good effect. Later in
the dry season, when grain and milk are scarce, fish
become the mainstay, being speared and caught by
hand in great quantities as pools dry up.

Fish farms have been established in several
African countries since 1946, especially in the
Congo. *Tilapia* are normally reared and if the pools
are carefully tended good crops of fish can be
obtained year after year.

5

African Prehistory and History

INTEREST in African history has been greatly stimulated by the upsurge of nationalism and the emergence of dozens of self-governing African states. New institutes and university centres are sponsoring research into the subject, not only in the advanced countries, but also in the new states themselves. African leaders anxious to establish links with the pre-colonial period give their support. They feel that many assumptions commonly made about African beliefs and cultures are based on racial prejudice, and educated Africans generally are irritated by European writers who have attributed so many cultural achievements to outside Egyptian, Arabic, or Portuguese influences without appearing to recognize the possibility of any essentially African contribution having been made. Now that African scholars are beginning to study their own traditions and histories, the pendulum shows signs of swinging towards the other extreme.

Most of Africa, it must be admitted, has no written history before the sixteenth century; writing was introduced with Islam and Christianity. Before the coming of these universal religions, written contracts and codes of law were unknown amongst the negro peoples. Tribal histories have been preserved in folk-lore, but events have been so symbolized and distorted in transmission by word of mouth that fact and fiction are difficult to disentangle and much reliance must be placed on artifacts—tools, pottery, buildings—evidence of great value, but incapable of telling a very full story of the past, except in the minds of fanciful writers.

PREHISTORY

The very early pre-historic record is more complete (or less incomplete) than anywhere else in the world. Fossil remains of anthropoids, from apes of Miocene times to *Homo sapiens*, form a more continuous sequence in the east and south than in any other continent, and have caused some authorities to claim that man originated in Africa. The most outstanding discoveries of early man and his tools have been made by Dr. L. S. B. Leakey and his wife in the course of their excavations in the region lying east of Lake Victoria, above all at Olduvai gorge in northern Tanzania. A great thickness of alluvium

that accumulated through the Quaternary period west of the Ngorongoro crater has yielded to the Leakeys huge quantities of animal remains and implements which allow a remarkably long story of faunistic and cultural changes to be traced.

The most ancient human implements found in Africa and elsewhere are of crude workmanship and are similar to those found all over the world. Later tools vary from one region to another; African specimens are as specialized as those of about the same age found elsewhere. Although stone and bone implements were still in general use when the Portuguese first arrived, objects of gold, copper, and iron had been known throughout the continent for hundreds of years. Recent excavations in Nigeria, for instance, have revealed iron tools at about the same level as charcoal dated by radioactive methods as being more than 2,000 years old. This and other evidence suggests that in some parts, at least, the Iron Age in tropical Africa began as early as in north-west Europe. Slag-heaps associated with old iron-workings are widely distributed. Those of Meröe on the Nile, a hundred miles down the river from Khartoum, are more than 2,000 years old and so enormous that Sayce, an archaeologist, writing fifty years ago, was tempted to call Meröe the Birmingham of ancient Africa.

The Sahara and the empty forest lands separating tribe from tribe restricted the spread of ideas. Although the Egyptians were in quite close contact with the Nubians in the north of the present Sudan Republic, and the Greeks and Romans penetrated south to the Sudd, the Nile valley did not provide an easy route into the continental interior. Further west, rock paintings of chariots in the southern Sahara seem to indicate that some Romans were able to cross the desert, but it was not until the second century A.D. that camels were widely used in the region and there is little information in classical writings about intertropical Africa.

The first close contacts of Africa south of the Sahara with the civilizations of the Mediterranean basin and Mesopotamia were made by sea. Greeks and Arabs sailed down the Red Sea to African ports quite regularly and a pilot book of about A.D. 120, the *Periplus of the Erythraean Sea*, written in

Alexandria, gives some details of the coast as far south as the Mozambique channel, and indicates that ships from India occasionally visited the western shores of the Indian Ocean. Recent discoveries of Chinese porcelain of the twelfth century at various points along the coast and on the offshore islands of Tanzania show that trade with the Orient was on a considerable scale for several centuries before the arrival of the Portuguese.

Very little is known of the early history of south and east Africa behind the coast. Well-built systems of terraces in the north of Cameroon, the Jebel Marra, and in several areas between Ethiopia and Mozambique suggest that fairly advanced agricultural communities lived there centuries ago. Old irrigation channels in the Nandi country of Kenya, ancient wells, and other structures point in the same direction. It has been suggested that the people who constructed them were dispersed by immigrant pastoralists, but there are no written records or other information at present to make this more than a guess. More is known about the stone structures of Rhodesia because their rare workmanship has attracted the attention of several archaeologists. The buildings at Zimbabwe, towers, gateways, and walls 30 feet high, are believed to have been constructed by Africans between A.D. 1000 and 1400. The work is African, but the stimulus for the construction and the cultural development associated with it may well have been oriental trade, for Chinese porcelain, beads from India, and other foreign goods have been discovered there, almost certainly imported through the ancient port of Sofala, 250 miles away to the east.

EARLY HISTORY

The western Sudan in medieval times

The early history of the western Sudan is relatively well known because camel caravans linked the region to the Mediterranean, and accounts of the states on the southern margins of the desert were brought back to Europe by Arab travellers. The medieval states depended on their control of north–south trade; gold and slaves from the forests, salt from the Sahara, and European goods from the Mediterranean (Fig. 24). The earliest was Ghana, the name adopted by Gold Coast in 1957 on gaining independence from Britain. Old Ghana, with its capital probably at Kumbi Saleh about 200 miles north of Bamako near the Senegal–Niger divide, controlled the trans-Saharan trade in Guinea gold. The negroes gave their gold in exchange for salt excavated from ancient lake-beds in the Sahara,

Terracing in Kigezi, Uganda.

Zimbabwe ruins. The most spectacular ruins in southern Africa. They stand in broken country in south-east Rhodesia. The walls, skilfully built of roughly dressed local granite, probably formed a chief's palace and may have been erected in the fourteenth century. Excavations have shown that Zimbabwe was an important centre of trade about that time. Gold and other objects were looted from the ruins at the end of the nineteenth century.

F

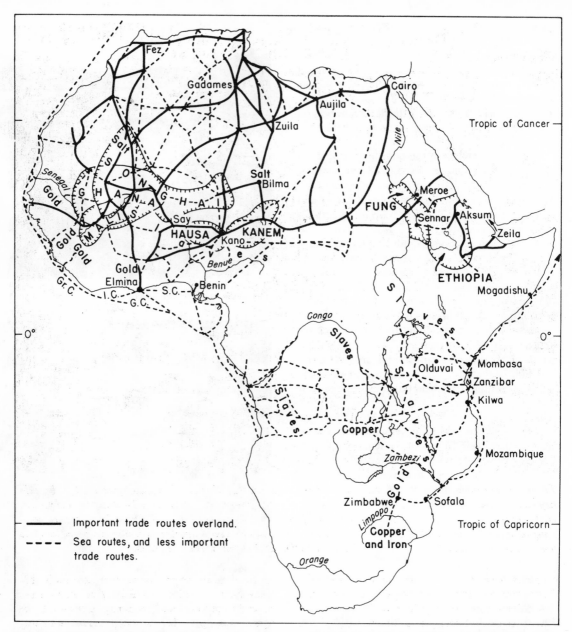

FIG. 24. *African empires and trade routes. The trade routes of northern Africa are better known than those else-where. Their importance varied from time to time, as did the extent of the empires. Ghana flourished in the ninth to eleventh centuries, Mali in the thirteenth to fifteenth centuries. Songhai reached its peak about 1520. Gr.C.—Grain Coast, I.C.—Ivory Coast, G.C.—Gold Coast, S.C.—Slave Coast.*

and the gold paid for European goods brought south by desert Arabs and Berbers from Morocco. Many of the northern traders who came to settle in the town were Muslims. They attracted many converts to their religion amongst the leading members of the community, and their influence increased.

About A.D. 1040, a warlike Muslim sect, the Almoravids, gained many adherents among the nomadic peoples of the region. One group moved north and quite rapidly conquered Morocco and Spain; the remainder took control of Ghana. According to legend the people who fled south and east from the

The city of Timbuktu. From Réné Caillié, Travels through Central Africa to Timbuctoo, *vol. i, 1830. Travelling inland from Senegal, Caillié was the first European traveller to reach Timbuktu (or Tombouctou) and return. He found the city 'at first view, nothing but a mass of ill-looking houses built of earth'. 'Still . . . there was something imposing in the aspect of a great city, raised in the midst of sands, and the difficulties surmounted by its founders cannot fail to excite admiration.' Its population at that time was about 10,000.*

original Ghana at this time were the ancestors of the Akan peoples of the modern state of Ghana.

A federal union formed in 1960 by the former French colonies, Senegal and Sudan, adopted the name Mali which had belonged to a Mandingo kingdom, a successor to ancient Ghana. Flourishing in the thirteenth century, its capital lay on the upper Niger far to the south-west of Kumbi, but like its predecessors it traded in Saharan salt and Wangara gold. Mali's ruler, Mansa Musa, made a pilgrimage to Mecca in the early fourteenth century and displayed so much wealth at Cairo and elsewhere *en route* that his fame spread to Europe and he is to be seen depicted on several maps of the period. At his death the Mali Empire extended across the southern Sahara and western Sudan from the Atlantic coast

to Aïr. Like all the great states that have evolved in this region it was a loose confederation, consisting of several large towns and tribes paying tribute to the paramount chief when he was powerful and going their own ways in time of stress. After Musa's death, the Songhai people of Gao in the east broke away from the empire and troubled times followed, though Ibn Battuta, travelling there in the 1350's, found it still possible to move about freely and his reports indicate that commerce remained active.

In the fifteenth century the Songhai people extended their influence towards the west, and under Mohammed Askia their empire became the most powerful state in the western Sudan. Later it came to include the Hausa states on the Niger-Chad watershed, which had been established in the

Fort Jesus, Mombasa. An old Portuguese fort in east Africa.

eleventh century, possibly by Berber immigrants from the north. In 1586 Songhai was attacked by an army from Morocco whose rulers wished to gain control of trans-Saharan trade and the gold-producing lands of the south. The Moorish army, having suffered heavy losses in the desert crossing, managed to defeat the negroes but its efforts brought no benefit to Morocco. The Moors were unable to gain control of the gold-mines or the elusive people who worked them; trade declined in the turmoil following the invasion, intertribal conflict spread, and Touareg raiders from the desert, always ready to exploit any weakness of their more sedentary neighbours, added to the confusion. The surviving Moors established their capital at Timbuktu and in time became independent of the Shereef of Morocco; to this day Moorish influence is discernible in the pottery, dress, and diet of the people of the middle Niger.

The modern states of the western Sudan are far from being directly derived from their medieval predecessors, but they all have a great deal in common as a result of their former commercial and political connexions. Islam has inspired a certain

cultural uniformity in the zone; the languages of the old imperial peoples are spoken more widely than most African tongues, and tribalism is less divisive than in other parts of the continent.

Portuguese exploration

The Portuguese were as anxious as the Moroccans to reach the source of Guinea gold and, in the fifteenth century, they systematically explored the west coast. About 1470 they at last discovered a land where gold was mined and built the castle of Saõ Jorge da Mina (now Elmina in Ghana) to be the headquarters of a royal governor and to try to ensure that none but Portuguese merchants should trade in the area. Their captains continued to explore further south but after the rounding of the Cape of Good Hope in 1498 their attention was directed mainly towards the Indian Ocean and we hear little from them about the forestlands of west Africa at this time.

The voyage of Vasco da Gama, round the Cape and across the Indian Ocean to Calicut, began a new era in the history of Africa. Within ten years the Portuguese had conquered the Arabs in the east coast ports and they continued to dominate the trade of the Arabian Sea until the end of the sixteenth century. Settlements were established along the east and west coasts of Africa in connexion with the trade. Numbers were few and the mortality was high, the settlements were little more than stopping-places on the way to the Indies for watering and repairs, yet several notable journeys into the interior were made by the Portuguese and in most cases their routes were not to be followed again until the great exploring days of the mid-nineteenth century. In the west, an official Portuguese embassy penetrated to Mali in 1534. Edward Lopez travelled in the Kingdom of the Congo, south of the lower course of the river, for four years in complete security. Pires was well received by the Oba of Benin; da Silveira reached the court of Monomotapa more than 200 miles up the Zambezi. Conditions in Africa at this time it seems are not to be compared too unfavourably with those in contemporary Europe.

One of the early motives of the Portuguese in exploring the African coast was to find the legendary kingdom of Prester John, to obtain its ruler's assistance in fighting the Moors. The kingdom they sought seems to have been Coptic Abyssinia. In the sixteenth century the Abyssinians were themselves more hard pressed than the Portuguese, and in 1541 they asked the Portuguese king for military aid against Mohammedan invaders from the north-east. They were supplied with 400 musketeers who fought valiantly in many battles, the last of them near Lake Tana, and saved the kingdom for Christianity. The remnants of the Portuguese army stayed in the country and their number was augmented from time to time by missionaries and artisans, but in 1633, after Jesuit priests had succeeded in converting the Emperor to Roman Catholicism and were striving to convert his subjects, there was a popular uprising and all the Portuguese were expelled from Ethiopia. Further south the Portuguese were involved in intermittent fighting with the Arabs and various Bantu tribes, which at this time were moving south. By 1740 they had been expelled from much of east Africa.

In west Africa, where they were mainly confined to coastal settlements, Portuguese influence seems to have been comparable with that of the earlier Arab traders on the east coast. New towns sprang up around their trading posts, peopled by members of several different tribes of the surrounding region and acknowledging the jurisdiction of no traditional African chief. Portuguese in the local garrisons chose wives from the local women, and in course of time communities developed that seem to have been as much European and Christian as they were African and pagan. On the east coast there was little expansion inland from the old Arab ports. No permanent settlement was made at the Cape and it was left to the Dutch, the successors of the Portuguese as the chief maritime power, to plant the first colony there in the future stronghold of white supremacy.

The Portuguese effort was spectacular, but it was the incidental features of their activity, above all the introduction of new food crops from the New World, that had the most far-reaching consequences. Bananas and yams had been brought in from Asia in earlier times and were already growing in the extreme west of Africa long before Columbus discovered America. Sorghum, bulrush millets, species of rice, pulses, oil-palms, and yams were native to the continent. But the arrival within a few years at the beginning of the sixteenth century of maize, groundnuts, cassava, and sweet potatoes from the newly discovered Americas must have altered economic and social life at least as much as the potato did in Europe. Maize is now the chief food crop in large parts of south and east Africa as cassava is in the west. The greater diversity of cropping allowed by the new plants must have eased the food situation and improved nutrition and may well have caused numbers to increase, first in the coastlands to which the new crops were initially introduced, and then further inland.

The slave trade

In 1530 the first slaves for sale in America were carried across the Atlantic to work in the mines and plantations of the Spanish West Indies, the first, it has been estimated, of some 15 millions. In the sixteenth century, when the trade was almost entirely in Portuguese hands, less than a million were exported. The demand then spread to Brazil and North America. All the European maritime countries competed for the profits and the numbers mounted each year until in the eighteenth century about 100,000 were being shipped annually. At that time Britain was the principal maritime power, and half the slaves were carried in British ships, bringing great profits to the merchants and stimulus to the British economy.

The slaves were procured from the hinterland by African traders who were careful to prevent the Europeans from travelling far inland. The Europeans stayed on the coast, living in forts built along the rocky shores of the Gold Coast, for example, or in hulks tied up in the creeks of the Niger delta. The great numbers of men, women, and children exported at this time must have been a considerable drain on the tribes living within, say, 150 miles of the coast. Their populations are, of course, quite unknown; one might make a guess of 20 million between Senegal and Angola and, since the natural rate of increase was probably less than that of the present day, some areas may well have been depopulated.

Nearly everywhere, it seems, social life was disrupted by the trade. The coastal peoples, armed with European firearms, raided for slaves far into the interior. States like Dahomey and Ashanti grew strong and wealthy, but for most of the west-coast people the years between 1550 and 1850 must have been years of turmoil, with armed bands and mercenary troops a constant threat to settled life. African works of art discovered in recent decades, mostly undated but clearly of some antiquity, such as the Ife bronzes and the brass figurines from Igbo in Nigeria, point to earlier streams of cultural development that seem to have been dammed back at this period. Some would regard it as a dark age, reaching its nadir a century ago. Now, the new countries of Africa may be able to look back to the more distant past, and see the present time of economic and political development as being not merely an offshoot of 'westernism' but as a resurgence of their own streams of development after the years of confinement and dissipation.

Slavery was accepted in most countries of northwest Europe and America. To merchants and plantation owners it was an economic necessity; if it were to be abolished, they would be ruined. If one country were to prohibit the trade, other countries persisting in it would profit at the expense of the first. Nevertheless, slavery in England was recognized as being illegal in 1772 and about 15,000 slaves there were set free as a result. Some of them, with 1,200 negroes from Nova Scotia who had fought on the British side in the American War of Independence, were shipped to Freetown. They settled to a European way of life under the influence of Christian missionaries and formed the nucleus of the British colony of Sierra Leone. In 1820 free negroes from the U.S.A. were settled by the American Colonization Society at Monrovia, later to become the capital of Liberia. The black colonists belonged to tribes from other parts of Africa or to no tribe at all; they were as much American as African. Nearly all of them stayed at the coast and to this day the inhabitants of Freetown and Monrovia form groups quite separate from the indigenous peoples inland.

The settlement of South Africa

By the beginning of the nineteenth century a distinct nation had emerged in south Africa from the descendants of Dutch and German Protestants and French Huguenots, all of whom had arrived in the latter half of the seventeenth century. The original Dutch supply station, founded at the Cape in 1652 to provide corn and cattle for ships *en route* to the Indies, had formed a civilized compact community.

Dutch farmers returning from a day's sport. This aquatint by Samuel Daniell gives an excellent idea of the mode of life of the men about 1800.

On farms within 50 miles of Cape Town wheat and vines were grown, with Malay, west African, and local slave labour. As the settlers increased in number and spread north-east into drier country more remote from Cape Town, they took to rearing cattle and sheep because the climate was more favourable to pastoral than arable farming and it was easier to walk the animals to Cape Town than to carry corn over miles of difficult country. Farms were large, often covering several square miles, and as they were inherited according to Roman–Dutch law by the eldest son, younger sons constantly pushed north and later east, cutting out new holdings for themselves from country which appears to have been scarcely inhabited. The birth-rate was high and the frontier of settlement advanced rapidly into the interior.

On their great lonely farms, isolated by distance and steep mountain ranges from the civilized life of Cape Town, a new people emerged in the eighteenth century. Their language, Afrikaans, had a simpler pronunciation and grammar than the Dutch from which it was derived and included in its vocabulary many African and eastern words. They were Calvinists clinging to the harsh orthodoxy of the seventeenth century and finding in the Old Testament justification for the master and slave relationship between themselves and their Hottentot servants. These rough country farmers formed the nucleus of the new nation, the Afrikaner or Boer (farmer) element in the Union and Republic of South Africa, a country with a strong colour consciousness, with the white man master of the black.

The main conflicts now apparent in South African society began to develop early in the nineteenth century. While the Dutch settlers advanced steadily inland and then east along the valleys and plains south of the Nieuwveld Range, Bantu tribes were continuing to move down the east side of the continent as they seem to have done for at least several decades. Both were immigrants to a land which appears to have been only sparsely settled by nomadic Hottentots and Bushmen. Boer and Bantu met in the vicinity of the Great Fish River, which reaches the sea between Port Elizabeth and East London, and there were several clashes between them even before 1800 (Fig. 67).

During the Napoleonic Wars the Cape came under the control of the British government. About 1820 several hundreds of British immigrants arrived and many of them were settled in the eastern districts to populate the frontier area against the Bantu. Each colonist was allocated 100 acres of land to encourage him to farm intensively. Before long most of them had sold their farms, which they found

A Boer's wife taking her coffee. 'The women of the African peasantry lead a life of the most listless activity.'
'Most of them, in the distant districts, can neither read nor write, so that they have no mental resources what-
soever.' John Barrow, Travels into the interior of Southern Africa, *London, 1806.*

too small to be very rewarding, or had rented them to Bantu tenants and moved to the towns. A large Bantu population built up east of the river where today a high proportion of the country in eastern Cape Province is included in native reserves. The British have continued to be predominantly town-dwellers and in the rural areas are far exceeded by Boers.

Friction arose between the Boers and British in the Cape. The colonial authorities attempted to enforce laws that were foreign to the Dutch settlers, refused to annex African territory to satisfy the farmers' demand for more land, and in 1834 forbade the Boers to keep slaves. Boer farmers began to trek to the west of the Bantu territories across the Orange river to escape British interference and found good pasture land on the high veld. Taking their possessions on ox-wagons they occupied the plateau by degrees as far north as the Limpopo and set up their own Republics of the Orange Free State and Transvaal. Others moved east through

the passes in the Drakensberg and coming down towards the wetter lands of Natal encountered the Zulu and came into conflict first with them and then with the British settlers already established in the Durban area. The British government intervened in 1843 to establish the colony of Natal which has remained to this day the most British part of the country. Bantu tribes that had been suffering under Zulu rule swarmed into Natal from the north and, lacking chiefs or tribal organization, were settled like refugees in locations, later to become native reserves.

The Trekkers who occupied the high plains numbered only about 10,000 and they took what land they wanted. The Africans in the area at the time were few in number because throughout the eighteenth century and until the arrival of the Trekkers they seem to have been involved in inter-tribal warfare that depopulated wide areas. In any case, they were primarily pastoral people with tribal areas large enough to allow a considerable degree of nomadism. After the Trek, the land most suitable for farming and grazing was quickly taken up by the white settlers and only a relatively small area was set aside for the Bantu.

Along the coast of Natal a number of sugar plantations were established before 1850. They needed a big supply of labour. There were many natives in the reserves nearby, but they had no desire to work for the white man and so the planters were allowed to import labour from India. Of the several thousands of Indians shipped across, some returned home at the end of their contracts, but most of them elected to settle in the country and sent home for their families. Indians continued to arrive until 1913, when further immigration of Asiatics was stopped by law. Since then they have increased faster than the other racial groups in the country.

Nineteenth-century exploration

At the beginning of the century, little was known in Europe about the African interior, far less than about South America. Much of the map remained a blank. The rivers, which had so far been rather unhelpful in giving access to the interior, provided the pretext for several of the most important exploratory journeys. Tracing their courses seems to have

'Skirmish with the natives.' From S. W. Baker, Albert N'yanza, Great Basin of the Nile, vol. i, London, 1866. Turco-Egyptian troops firing on tribesmen in the southern Sudan.

been particularly attractive, for some unknown reason, to Scotsmen.

Amongst the earliest scientific explorers was James Bruce, a Scottish laird who travelled through Ethiopia and the Sudan about 1770 with the source of the Blue Nile as his main objective. He found the Abyssinian highlands divided between a number of independent feudal lords warring amongst themselves. In spite of the fact that Semitic immigrants from the Yemen had brought the art of writing to northern Ethiopia hundreds of years before the time of Christ, and the kings of Axum (or Aksum) had been converted to Christianity by Byzantine priests as early as A.D. 300, the country was little more advanced than the rest of Africa. For nearly a thousand years Ethiopia had been isolated from the world, not only by its formidable mountain rim and desert borders, but also by the hostility of Muslims and pagans surrounding it on all sides. Wars against Somalis and Arabs attacking with Turkish support in the sixteenth century had been successfully concluded, after much destruction, with the help of the Portuguese. Then came invasions of Galla nomads from the south-east, and Ethiopia fell into the depressed state in which Bruce found it; backward, disunited, and with rulers whose cruelty was extraordinarily revolting. The utter disregard for life and the sadistic caprices of chiefs are amongst the features of African life at the time that strike the reader of explorers' journals most forcibly, and this is particularly true of the accounts of Christian Abyssinia.

Ethiopia remained in a fragmented state until the middle of the nineteenth century when the regional chiefs were conquered in turn by the Emperor Theodore. He died in 1868 after failing to repel a British expeditionary force led by Napier, but his new empire recovered from the attack in time, to defeat the armies of Egypt pushing south from the Sudan. Later, by destroying an Italian army at Adowa, the Abyssinians preserved their independence for another forty years.

The Egyptian advance up the Nile had begun in the 1820's, when Mohammed Ali conquered the northern Sudan, hoping to find gold and other precious minerals. There was little gold to be had, but the Egyptians remained in the country and for several decades it suffered under a savage administration that imposed extortionate taxes and openly traded in slaves. Several Europeans were engaged as governors about 1863; conditions improved somewhat and the area under Egyptian rule was extended from the predominantly Muslim north towards the Congo watershed and Red Sea and south into pagan country near Lake Albert.

By the 1880's Egypt was in a state of collapse and bankruptcy and the Sultanate in Constantinople, on whom the British had depended for exerting influence throughout the Middle East, was in a similar state. The golden age of Islamic insolvency it has been called. Britain, partly because of the need to safeguard the Suez canal, intervened and took control of the Egyptian government thereby, it has been suggested, setting off the international rivalry that led to the partition of Africa (Robinson, Gallagher, and Denny, 1961). At almost the same time a militant Islamic revolt swept away the Egyptian administration in the Sudan and the entire country, after the death of the Mahdi, the religious leader of the revolt, relapsed into anarchy. Order was not restored until an Anglo-Egyptian force under Kitchener defeated the Mahdist army at Omdurman in 1898. Then, for half a century, the Sudan was in effect ruled by Britain.

In 1822 the Sultan of Muscat, on the Persian Gulf, whose ancestors had driven the Portuguese out of the east African ports, was recognized by Britain as overlord of the east African coastlands. He had captured Mombasa and transferred his capital from Arabia to the island of Zanzibar. Twenty miles from the continental shore and with a good harbour, it was in an excellent position for trading along the coast. Cloves were introduced from the East Indies and soon became an important export, but for long their value was exceeded by that of slaves and ivory from the mainland.

The Arabs, unlike the Europeans on the west coast, did not depend on African middlemen for their supplies of slaves but sent caravans far inland, and by the middle of the century had established small settlements at several places like Tabora in the centre of the Tanganyika plateau and Ujiji on the east side of Lake Tanganyika. The slaves brought to the coast were sold in the market at Zanzibar and exported to Turkey, Arabia, Persia, and India. The treaty of 1822, recognizing the Sultan, had been aimed at limiting the trade, particularly with India, and British naval patrols attempted to stop the traffic. Yet, in the middle of the century, about 15,000 slaves were still passing through the Zanzibar market every year, and as many were perishing on the way to the coast. Explorers like Speke and Livingstone, who followed the slavers' routes on their journeys to the interior, brought back to Europe horrifying accounts of the suffering and destruction they encountered and suggested that the raiding and enslaving went far to explain the emptiness of the lands they traversed. Public opinion in Britain was aroused, and by 1873 naval and diplomatic pressure had eliminated the slave trade along the coast, though in the interior it was rooted out only at the end of the century when European administration was properly established.

The early missionaries in east and central Africa entered the country as explorers. Rebmann discovered the snow-capped mountain Kilimanjaro, and Krapf first saw Mount Kenya. But Livingstone's travels in southern Africa were unrivalled; they were so extensive and revealing that he must be regarded as the greatest of all African explorers. By the last quarter of the century, missionary influence was being felt in many parts of east Africa. At Zanzibar, the cathedral church was built on the site of the slave market; French Catholic and English Protestant missionaries were received at the court of the Kabaka of Buganda, and attempts were made to undertake work in the neighbourhood of Lake Tanganyika. Besides making converts and providing information about the interior, the Christian missions compiled dictionaries of the native languages, introduced all manner of trade goods and, above all, brought new ideas, schools, and a freedom from old fears. Little though they may have wished it, their activity necessarily had political implications, and in many cases the flag of his country followed the missionary inland.

While the course of the Nile was attracting the attention of explorers in east Africa, the Niger was the initial stimulus to much activity in the west. Mungo Park, travelling there under the auspices of the African Association, which had been founded in 1788 to promote the discovery of the interior parts of Africa, was able to show that Leo Africanus had been wrong in describing a great river at Timbuktu as flowing west. The Niger flowed to the east. But at the beginning of the nineteenth century it was still not realized that the Oil Rivers, where Europeans had been trading for centuries, were in fact a network of creeks forming the delta. Park was drowned in the great river far above the delta at the Bussa rapids, and when Oudney, Denham, and Clapperton were sent to the western Sudan by the British government in 1823, tracing the course of the Niger was still a pretext for their journey, though there was a greater anxiety in some quarters to secure treaties with the rulers of the interior both to put a stop to the slave trade and stimulate legitimate commerce.

Clapperton's party followed an old caravan route across the Sahara from Tripoli to Bornu on the west side of Chad and then while Denham explored the country round the lake, Clapperton travelled west to Sokoto. At this time the Shehu of Bornu, whose

Speke and Grant at King Mtesa's levee. From J. H. Speke, Journal of the Discovery of the Source of the Nile, *London, 1863.*

influence extended through all the Chad territories and north to the Fezzan, was at war with the Fulani of Sokoto. Nomadic Fulani pastoralists had been infiltrating into the northern parts of Nigeria for several centuries and settling near the towns. They revolted against the rulers of the Hausa states in 1804 under the pretext of reviving the Islamic faith, succeeded in taking over the reins of government, and then pressed south and east and continued to threaten Bornu for several decades. The country between the two empires and on their southern borders was devastated by fighting and slave-raiding but the explorers brought back to Europe a vivid picture of active commercial life still managing to persist in the western Sudan. 'Kano', Clapperton wrote, 'may contain some 30,000 to 40,000 resident inhabitants of which more than one half are slaves. This number is exclusive of strangers who come here in crowds during the dry months from all parts

of Africa, from the Mediterranean and the Mountains of the Moon, and from Sennar and Ashanti.' The market was well regulated, with fair prices, and produce from the local country and afar displayed for sale. One large section was for slaves; 'slavery is here so common', writes Clapperton inconsequentially, 'that they always appear much happier than their masters'. The explorers were unable to secure the Sultan of Sokoto's signature to a treaty ending the trade and it continued until the end of the century.

The very detailed descriptions of the country between the Niger bend and Lake Chad in Barth's journals of his travels in the 1850's would seem to show that the heavily settled rural areas of a century ago differed little in appearance from the present day, but the more remote pagan areas at that time were always liable to be devastated by warring bands and the villagers driven off into slavery.

Between Hausaland and the Atlantic coast the Fulani ruled over several states in the early nineteenth century of which the most important were on the highlands of Fouta Djallon and centred on Massina. Towards the end of the century, three of the states were united under a warlike leader El Hadj Omar. When he died his successor was unable to resist growing French pressure from the west. The French rapidly advanced east from their old-established bases in Senegal, continued to Chad, and eventually reached the banks of the Nile at Fashoda.

On the west coast, in the 1830's and 1840's, the slave trade was still vigorously alive and the number of slaves carried overseas was increasing rather than diminishing even though the trade had been made illegal for most north-west European nationals for many years. A British naval patrol based on Freetown operated in west African waters specifically for the purpose of searching ships for slaves. More than 130,000 were found and released between 1825 and 1865, many in Freetown, but nearly 2 millions are believed to have been exported in the same period. It was clear that more positive measures were required.

In the 1830's, after the Lander brothers had shown that the Niger reached the sea via the Oil Rivers, two expeditions were sent up the Niger to trade, establish mission stations, and to plant a model farm at Lokoja. The paddle-steamers used were more manœuvrable than sailing vessels, but the enterprises failed, mainly because of the many deaths from malaria. Some years later, however, in 1852, when news arrived that Barth had reached the upper Benue, an expedition under Baikie sailed far up the river to try to meet him, quinine was used and no one died. From that time forward the Niger could be used as a route to the interior; safe, except for the hostility of local people anxious to prevent trade in the hinterland falling to the Europeans.

Legitimate trade along the west coast steadily expanded and by 1840 the palm-oil trade alone was worth a million pounds a year to British merchants. The French at that time were mainly interested in the Senegal area and as late as 1870 would have been willing to exchange French rights on the seaboard from Ivory Coast to the Cameroons for the Gambia. While other countries lost interest in west Africa, Britain's influence grew. British missionaries were active in Freetown, on the Gold Coast, and in Yorubaland and their schools were largely responsible for spreading European ways of thought and political aspirations. On the Gold Coast, agreements made with chiefs of the coastal states led to

intermittent conflict with the Ashanti further inland. Lagos was annexed in 1861 to stop slave trading there. By 1870 Britain was too deeply involved in west African affairs to relinquish her interests, but she failed to take the opportunity to secure a monopoly along the coast, a momentous failure or restraint which has resulted in the present political and economic fragmentation.

By 1870 the Great Lakes of east Africa had been discovered, the White Nile was known to emerge from Lake Victoria, and Livingstone had traced the course of the Zambezi and explored the southern headwaters of the Congo. The falls on the lower Congo still prevented any expedition penetrating up the river, and all the centre of the basin remained unknown to European geographers until Stanley reached the Lualaba from the east coast and in 1877 sailed down the Congo to Stanleypool and reached the mouth of the river. The accounts he brought back were of especial interest to Leopold II, King of the Belgians, who was already organizing expeditions to explore central Africa from a base at Zanzibar. Stanley met him and agreed to lead an expedition to build a road from Stanley Pool to the sea and open up the Congo basin. Within five years, treaties had been made with hundreds of native chiefs, five steamers were sailing on the river above the falls, and the Congo Free State had begun to take shape.

THE COLONIAL ERA

The division of Africa

Most African states first took shape at the end of the nineteenth century when the continent was carved up by European powers and shared between them. Why this imperialist scramble took place is not clear; it was looked upon as rather absurd by many of the statesmen involved. A good deal seems to stem from the British interference in Egypt which marked the end of a period of Anglo-French collaboration in overseas affairs; after 1882 the French were looking for places to put pressure on Britain. The carve-up does not seem to have been a calculated attempt to acquire exploitable territory. In fact, British governments, much occupied by events elsewhere, in India, Canada, and Australia, where British investments were very much greater and prospects for the future far more attractive, would have preferred to remain unencumbered with the costs and responsibilities of administering such pestilential and unproductive territories. However, increasing trade or missionary activity resulted in consular and military interference in native affairs

A sectional steamer being hauled from the Lower to the Upper Congo. From H. M. Stanley, The Congo, *vol. ii, London, 1885.*

and although at first there was no intention of procuring territory, British influence in the critical coastal areas grew stronger. In the early 1880's French and German activity in these areas caused some friction and when Leopold's ambitions in the Congo conflicted with those of Britain and Portugal, a pretext was provided for calling a conference of the powers involved. At the Berlin Conference (1884) it was agreed that new annexations on the African coast were not to be recognized as valid unless they were accompanied by effective occupation. Activity on the continent was intensified; this was the beginning of the colonial period that lasted until 1960 (Fig. 25a).

In west Africa the French advanced rapidly east from Senegal, engulfing the remains of El Hadj Omar's empire and a Mandingo empire further south, and sweeping on to Lake Chad. Their advance barred the way to British expansion into the interior and prepared the foundations for modern Muslim states such as the new Mali. Behind the Guinea coast Britain had already gained the most productive chunks, the French merely prevented them from spreading laterally by pushing into the interior from their coastal bases at Conakry, Abidjan, and Porto Nuovo. Upstream of Bathurst, which had long been in British hands, the Gambia was confined to a narrow strip on either side of the river which was consequently no longer able to serve its natural hinterland. Sierra Leone blocked direct access to the sea from the interior of French Guinea. The British penetrating inland from Accra and the Germans from Lomé agreed on a frontier between Gold Coast and Togoland that split both the Ewe and Dagomba peoples. British trading companies on the lower Niger and Benue united to resist competition from other countries and managed to secure sole trading rights in the region from the Emir of Sokoto. The British government, mainly to prevent the French taking over the lower Niger and raising a tariff barrier, declared a Protectorate over that region and handed it over to be ruled by the Royal Niger Company.

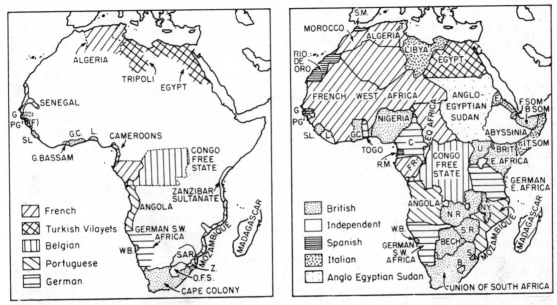

FIG. 25 a. *Africa after the Berlin Conference.*   b. *Africa at the outbreak of the First World War.*

In west-central Africa, Britain, Germany, and France sought access to Lake Chad, which was one of the few definite features appearing on maps of the interior and was thought to have greater potentialities than in fact it possessed. From a short coastal strip in the Cameroons, where Britain had long been influential, Germany rapidly acquired a large triangle stretching inland to the lake, and French expeditions pushing north from the forests of the Congo at Brazzaville linked up with their compatriots advancing across the desert from Senegal and Algeria. In the Congo Free State, exploration and occupation went on simultaneously, with the Belgians keeping Mahdists from the Sudan out of the Uele basin in the north-east and forestalling the British in Katanga.

South Africa shared in the revolution. Diamonds were found near Hopetown, south of Kimberley, in 1867. Prices of agricultural produce in the neighbourhood soared as Africans came out of their reserves to earn money in the mines. Exports trebled in value, capital was attracted from abroad, and a railway was soon built from Cape Town to Kimberley. Rhodes, Beit, and Barnato gained control of the mines by buying out small operators, and when gold was discovered in the Transvaal in 1886 the financiers of Kimberley were able to supply or attract the capital required for its exploitation. Gold-seekers from Britain flocking into the Boer Republics soon outnumbered the early settlers and the tension between the two peoples which

eventually led to the Anglo-Boer War gradually increased. By the end of the century the Rand was producing a quarter of the world's gold supply and the Boers and British were at war.

The Germans established themselves in south-west Africa. In 1886, before they could link up with the Boers in the Transvaal, Rhodes, who was then the Prime Minister of Cape Colony, succeeded in annexing Bechuanaland. He thereby succeeded in securing a British routeway to the north along the tracks followed a few decades earlier by the missionaries Moffat and Livingstone. The chief of the Matabele was persuaded to grant mining concessions to Rhodes, and by 1890, when the British South African Company assumed responsibility for administering the lands north of the Limpopo, British influence extended north to the headwaters of the Congo and the far northern end of Lake Nyasa.

The French gained an early foothold in Madagascar and subsequently occupied the whole of that great island, but their activities on the mainland of east Africa were limited to Djibouti in Somaliland. Britain and Germany, both operating from Zanzibar, were the main competitors, and in contrast to the situation in west Africa, government interest was greater than that of the merchants. German claims to the land south of Lake Victoria were recognized by Britain in 1886 partly to gain support over Egypt, and a few years later the Imperial British East Africa Company took over the administration of the territory stretching from the lake north and east to the indeterminate borders of Sudan and Ethiopia.

The Italians arrived late on the scene. Britain and Germany warned them off the Sultan of Zanzibar's southern possessions and they proceeded to occupy the desert coasts of Eritrea and Somaliland. A resounding defeat at Adowa in 1896 halted their advance on to the Abyssinian highlands, and this was not resumed until 1935, when Ethiopia, though a member of the League of Nations, was conquered by Fascist Italy.

The beginning of the colonial era

By 1900 the colonial governments of the European powers were busy delimiting frontiers, assessing the economic resources of their new possessions, and organizing the administration of the African peoples they had come to rule. They stamped out the slave trade and after some initial disputes brought peace to a continent that was sorely in need of a period of tranquillity. The nineteenth century had been a time of wars and uncertainty. Many pastoral peoples had lately suffered from rinderpest, and black military states had terrorized their neighbours. Rebellions in German East Africa were crushed with marked severity, and Leopold's administration in the Congo gained notoriety for

Léopoldville about 1884. The new town, named after Léopold II, King of the Belgians, is in the foreground, the native village Kintamo, behind. Taken from H. M. Stanley, The Congo, vol. i, London, 1885.

its harsh treatment of native labour. But for most Africans, it would seem, conditions probably improved under the new order; fear abated and individuals moved more freely about the countryside.

There was little thought at this time of systematic economic development of the new colonies. Governments had far less control over world capital resources than they have today, and the bankers and financiers were unwilling to invest in countries that seemed to be so poor and unprofitable. Local colonial governments were short of cash and relied on territorial incomes derived from import duties and head taxes. On the west coast, where people had long traded with Europe, exports of groundnuts from Senegal and palm-oil from the Guinea coast steadily increased. Cocoa was introduced from Fernando Po to the Gold Coast in 1879 and in a few decades exports of cocoa exceeded gold in value. But the continental interior remained scarcely touched until communications improved, allowing bulky produce to be exported economically.

Railway construction (see Map 14)

The railway routes of today are the outcome of various economic and political motives and rivalries. Many of the first railways in Africa were built from coastal ports to new mining centres inland, notably in south Africa. Here, as elsewhere, economic interests did not always coincide with political ones. The Transvaal government, afraid of having to rely on the lines first constructed to the Rand from the British ports, Port Elizabeth and Durban, gave financial backing to a line reaching the sea at Lourenço Marques in Portuguese East Africa and refused to allow the line from Cape Town to Kimberley to be extended north through Transvaal to Rhodesia. Eventually the railway to Rhodesia was laid across the fringe of Bechuanaland, reaching Bulawayo in 1902 and over the next few years it was extended to Wankie with the prospect of traffic from the coalfields, to Broken Hill where lead and zinc had been discovered, and finally to the enormously rich deposits of copper extending from Northern Rhodesia across the frontier into Katanga. There is still no direct rail link between the Transvaal and Rhodesia.

The Congo railways were designed originally to supplement the navigable reaches of the river and its main tributaries. First the essential link was constructed from the seaport of Matadi to Léopoldville above the falls, a difficult task for which forced labour was employed. Since then the railway has gradually been extended so as to involve fewer switches from rail to river and back to rail, especially between Katanga and Léopoldville.

In Nigeria, reliance on the river diminished at an earlier stage. Although Baro on the Niger was first visualized as the main outlet for the north, Kano was soon connected by rail right through to the coast at Lagos by a line crossing the Niger at Jebba and joining the Kano–Baro line at Minna. Traffic on the Niger and Benue remained moderately heavy, but most of the groundnuts of the north and the tin from the Jos Plateau took the direct rail route to Lagos. In the Gold Coast, the railway built primarily to serve the goldfields at Tarkwa was extended to Kumasi and provided carriage to the coast for Ashanti cocoa.

Many of the railways that were built primarily for military or political reasons have never been very profitable and continue to carry far less traffic than they could manage. The early railway from St. Louis to Dakar greatly stimulated groundnut production in Senegal and was a profitable enterprise, but other French lines directed from ports on the Guinea coast towards the inland Niger basin were designed in the first place for rather vague strategic purposes and have always lost money.

In east Africa, Germany and Britain were anxious to establish rail links between the coast and Lake Victoria. The British line from Mombasa to Kisumu was rapidly completed at a cost of £5 million and got there first. Much of its total length of 884 miles lay across unproductive country, there appeared to be little prospect of it ever paying its way, and it was partly to alleviate the financial burden of the railway that white settlement on the highlands was encouraged a few years later. Meanwhile the German line west from Tanga towards Victoria was left uncompleted to serve the fertile highlands of Meru and Kilimanjaro while efforts were concentrated on a line further south from Dar-es-Salaam following the old slave route to Tabora and on to Kigoma on Lake Tanganyika.

The new railways and the steamers on the main lakes and rivers reduced the costs of transport in the interior to a small fraction of those for head-loading or rolling barrels, which in many cases were the only alternatives. Long-distance trading in bulky goods became profitable, and agricultural production for export in the interior was greatly stimulated. Furthermore, telegraph lines alongside the railways allowed administrative instructions and business orders to be transmitted rapidly from the coast instead of being carried by runners. The ports served by the railways had to be extended to cope with the new bulky traffic generated, while others with restricted hinterlands stagnated and fell into disuse. Large numbers of Africans who had never before worked for wages were employed by railway contractors as labourers and learned to use and need cloth, matches, and metal goods. In some areas where local supplies of labour were inadequate, foreigners were brought in. Punjabis were shipped over to east Africa from India and many remained after the completion of the railway. They were amongst the forerunners of the 365,000 Asiatics now living in Kenya, Uganda, and Tanzania (1962).

The First World War

By 1914 most of the colonies had been pacified and organized into new administrative units sometimes, but not always, conforming with tribal and other traditional areas (Fig. 25b). Tribes and villages found their boundaries had suddenly become more rigid than hitherto. The position that happened to have been reached when the Europeans arrived was crystallized. The rule of law was at times confusing but it brought obvious benefits; people descended from the hills where they had taken refuge in the troubled times and taxation gradually became effective. Roads were built to link the main settlements to the railways and navigable rivers. Traditional markets that happened to be well placed grew in importance and quite new market towns developed. Then for six years during and after the First World War progress was limited. The German territories in the west were occupied after relatively little fighting, but the campaign in east Africa dragged on for years, involving only small forces, but causing much general destruction and heavy loss of life, particularly amongst native porters, in country which had still to recover from earlier upheavals. Veterinary work was neglected and once again rinderpest spread through much of east Africa.

After the war the German colonies were administered by individual allied powers, at first as League of Nations Mandates and after the Second World War as United Nations Trust Territories. Their future was always uncertain and by discouraging investors this hindered their economic development. Eventually in the 1950's South-West Africa was absorbed into the Union of South Africa, in fact if not in law; western Togoland joined Ghana, and while the southern part of the British Cameroons attached itself to the new Republic to the east, the north joined the Federation of Nigeria. The French sectors of Togoland and Cameroons were larger and had been administered as separate colonies; they acquired independent status. Ruanda–Urundi, the heavily settled, mountainous part of German

79

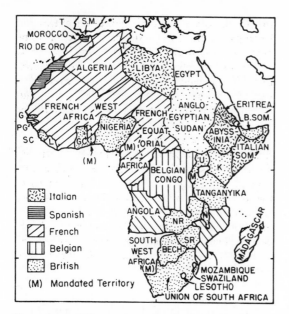

FIG. 26 a. *Africa at the outbreak of the Second World War. b. Africa in 1969.*

East Africa, administered by Belgium, split into two independent states, Rwanda and Burundi (Fig. 26b).

The inter-war years

Prices for agricultural products were high for a time in the early 1920's and some territories such as the Gold Coast embarked on ambitious development projects. Soon produce prices slumped with the general contraction of world trade between 1930 and 1936, government revenue shrank and, since a large proportion of it was required to maintain administration and pay the interest on loans for railway construction, programmes for expansion were curtailed. Roads, water supplies, and schools were sorely needed everywhere, the industrial countries of Europe needed the work, but development practically ceased. In some fields, steady, unspectacular progress continued. District officers touring their areas on horseback and in boats gradually introduced new ideas to rural areas; they supervised native courts and treasuries, made maps and built bridges. Technical officers, pitifully few as they were, began to make an impression on agricultural methods and to control diseases amongst humans and livestock. Missionaries built churches and helped to collect support for them by building schools too, for which the demand in some areas was rapidly growing. Educated Africans in small numbers were reaching universities and joining the professions, and as the possibility of acquiring wealth and power equal to that of the Europeans became more apparent, so did the fermentation begin which was to culminate in the post-war struggles for independence.

The nature of the changes in the interwar years varied from one territory to another according to the size of the white settler element and the policy of the administering power.

In the Union of South Africa nearly everything achieved in agriculture, mining, transport, and industry was the result of European skill, capital, and organization combined with non-European labour. Africans were prohibited from owning land except in the reserves which formed only 13 per cent. of the country. Laws restricted their movements and prevented them from performing a large number of skilled jobs, and while class distinction throughout the world was weakening, South African life became increasingly based on colour distinction. Nevertheless, the whites could claim that standards of living amongst Bantu in the Union were higher than anywhere else in Africa and could point to immigration from surrounding countries as an indicator of worse living conditions outside its frontiers.

In Southern Rhodesia the trend of events was similar, after it became a self-governing colony in 1923. Separate European and native areas were delimited, the former close to the railway and on the best land with reliable rainfall. Africans in towns were required to carry passes and were discriminated against in industry, but policies were generally more liberal than in the Transvaal.

Nearly 17,000 square miles of good land in the Kenya highlands were reserved for European ownership, yet there was this difference; whereas in Southern Rhodesia there could be no question but that the whites intended to remain in control, Kenya was recognized by British governments as being primarily African territory, where the interests of the African must be paramount.

British policy in Africa was not based on any general theory of colonialism and the pattern of government varied widely from one colony to another according to local circumstances. In the territories with few white settlers, much reliance was placed on traditional native rulers in both the administration of justice and local government affairs. The same was true to a lesser degree in other territories, because it was the only practical way in which small numbers of Europeans could rule large numbers of Africans cheaply. Whereas the French swept away the higher traditional offices and operated through small chiefs, the British often retained the full traditional administrative hierarchy and confirmed the native rulers in their powers. On the other hand, the British have been criticized for being less willing than other Europeans to accept educated Africans on an equal footing socially.

While the government of each British territory had a good deal of responsibility for the policies adopted, the French colonial administration was much more centralized in Paris. Each French colony was represented in both houses of the French parliament by elected delegates and was regarded as an integral part of the French Union. Within each colony, government was highly centralized and authoritarian. More attention was paid to the towns by French administrators than to rural areas; the reverse seems to have been the case in British territories. The underlying French philosophy was to regard the colony as actually or potentially a part of the motherland; the African was to be turned into a black Frenchman. The results are apparent in the political scene of the present day.

The Belgians were able to concentrate on governing their one great colony, a hundred times the size of the mother-country, and they ruled it in a businesslike way, in effect from Brussels. Educated Africans were given special privileges but there were few of them because very little attempt was made to develop higher education. The emphasis was placed on technical training. Native institutions were carefully studied and, where possible, supported. Little attempt was made to educate the people politically; such luxuries could come later when the economic basis had been prepared and the people were ready for it. Standards of living in Katanga and the large towns elsewhere came to be higher than in most other parts of tropical Africa, thanks to the copper, gold, and diamond mines. But African leaders remained inexperienced, they were known only to their own tribal groups and lacked national support when the time came for independence to be granted.

Portuguese policy was and still is somewhat akin to that once followed by France, but more extreme. There is the same desire to produce a native *élite*, which it is hoped will owe allegiance to Portugal as the source of civilization. Mozambique and Angola are looked upon as provinces of Portugal, permanently linked to the mother-country, and any growth of national feeling is purposefully prevented by allowing political rights and privileges to neither Portuguese nor Africans.

INDEPENDENCE

The Second World War and its sequel

Colonial rule seemed well established throughout Africa in 1939. Only the Union in the south was an independent state and Southern Rhodesia had dominion status. Liberia, though politically independent, relied heavily on the great rubber plantations of the Firestone Rubber Company and its voice was unheard in international affairs. The Ethiopian Empire was being modernized by its Italian conquerors. In many of the tropical dependencies a few Africans were gaining experience in legislative assemblies, but as these were dominated by European officials and had little real authority, the African members were often looked upon by their compatriots as tools of the white man.

As the European nations rearmed, prices of tropical produce rose uncertainly, but before new development projects could gain momentum, the war supervened. France and Belgium were occupied by Germany and in consequence their possessions in Africa enjoyed somewhat greater responsibility for their own affairs than hitherto. While shortage of shipping space and the blockade of continental Europe reduced the demand for agricultural produce, tin, copper, and other mines yielding metals vital in wartime rapidly increased production. Manufacturing in the Union of South Africa expanded enormously and the value of Southern Rhodesian manufactures multiplied five times in the 1940's. Many airfields were built to serve supply routes to the Middle East from across the South Atlantic. In general, however, economies stagnated for lack of skilled technicians and equipment, and

G

progress remained slow for several years after the end of the war for the same reasons.

Political development during and after the war, accelerated. Africans who joined the allied forces were promised better conditions after the war. They fought in Ethiopia against the Italians and defeated them, and they saw service in India where the movement towards independence was far advanced. They mixed with European soldiers in Africa and overseas and greater familiarity with the whites revealed their frailty as never before and provoked envy of their wealth. In west Africa, the circulation of nationalist newspapers increased and demands for independence swelled in volume. To most Europeans it still seemed that several decades of economic and political growth lay ahead before Africans would be in a position to govern their own countries, and many of the African intelligensia seem to have thought likewise.

In 1948 riots in the Gold Coast instigated by ex-servicemen and the nationalist party received much popular support. They were followed by a commission of inquiry that recommended far-reaching constitutional changes giving much greater responsibilities to the Africans. In Nigeria the same year saw a new constitution come under heavy fire because it offered too little power to the Nigerians. At the same time African affairs began to attract attention in the United Nations Assembly where a number of Asian states which had recently thrown off European rule were itching to fight imperialism wherever it persisted. The colonial powers were suffering repeated rebuffs at the hands of the Chinese in Indo-China and in Korea, the Persians over the oilfields, and in Egypt. The Mau-Mau rebellion in Kenya seems to have been an unusual expression of anti-white emotion that existed in many parts of the continent.

British and French governments were by this time aware that no profit or prestige was to be gained from resisting nationalist movements once they had gained momentum with popular backing. On the contrary, events in India showed it would be advantageous to Europeans and Africans to settle their differences by the granting of self-government in the shortest possible time. Sudan, Tunisia, and Morocco became independent, the Gold Coast and Nigeria saw the road to freedom stretching broadly ahead, and Tanganyika moved gently forward. In France a change in the régime in 1958, chiefly dictated by the long-drawn-out struggle for Algeria, resulted in her African colonies being given the opportunity to decide their future relations with the mother-country. Guinea chose full independence. The other territories, including those held in trust for the United Nations, decided to remain at least temporarily within the French Union, mainly in the expectation of receiving badly needed economic assistance.

The Congo demanded independence and all unprepared was granted it by Belgium with a delay of only a few weeks, to fall into a state of anarchy from which it took years to emerge. The Federation of the Rhodesias and Nyasaland fell to pieces when Nyasaland and Northern Rhodesia asserted their independence of white domination. Uganda and Kenya patched up their internal divisions and followed Tanganyika to independence, and by the end of 1963 the only African countries of any size remaining under European rule were those bordering South Africa, now a Republic outside the Commonwealth. The Portuguese territories which for long had appeared to lie aside from the mainstream of nationalism felt the cold touch of the floodwater but still resisted the pressure from within and outside.

Until the last war the colonial powers had been satisfied to keep the peace, and leave the economic development of their territories to private enterprise. They had little thought of developing the colonies as independent economic units. After the war a new approach manifested itself; the idea of a planned expansion of the tropical African countries. The United Kingdom made funds available for colonial development; Belgium initiated a ten-year plan for the Congo, and France invested very large sums in her overseas territories. Several international organizations were instituted under the aegis of the United Nations to provide financial and technical assistance to the under-developed territories, notably the International Bank for Reconstruction and Development (World Bank), the Economic Commission for Africa (E.C.A.), and the Commission for Technical Co-operation in Africa (C.C.T.A.). Since about 1957, aid from the U.S.A., U.S.S.R., and China has reached big dimensions and has more than counterbalanced the withdrawal of capital by private investors.

Several Pan-African organizations have been established, notably the Organization of African Unity (O.A.U.) set up by thirty-one African nations in 1963. This Organization took over responsibility for C.C.T.A. in 1964. The structure of the O.A.U. was greatly weakened in 1964–5 by differences of attitude towards the Congo situation amongst the member states and since then it has failed to find a solution to the problem of Biafra.

6

Sudan Republic

THE Sudan Republic with a population of 14 million and an area of almost a million square miles is the largest state in Africa. It is a flat country, stretching from the Red Sea and the Abyssinian highlands in the east across the middle of the Nile valley to the Chad basin in the west. In spite of the low relief, the contrasts within the country are very striking. The north is desert with its Nubian and Arab population mainly confined to the banks of the Nile. The extreme south, within 5° of the equator, is forested country with negroid peoples. The Sudan is part Muslim, part animist and Christian; at the same time African and Middle Eastern.

The Arabs came down from the north and east as pastoralists and by the fourteenth century they had forced the negroid peoples living west of the Nile to retire to the Nuba mountains and Jebel Marra. East of the Nile, where the Arabs were less strong, the pagan sultanate of Fung emerged in the sixteenth century and managed to persist for about 300 years. Its capital, Sennar, which had a population reckoned to be over a quarter of a million in 1700, traded with Abyssinia, the Red Sea ports, and with the state of Darfur which arose later in the far west.

Fung, Darfur, and other sultanates of less importance fell apart when Turco-Egyptian armies advanced up the Nile early in the nineteenth century. Under Egyptian rule the diverse lands now making up the Republic of the Sudan were brought together in one state ruled from a capital deliberately chosen to be at the confluence of the Blue and White Niles. The old dynasties were swept away and successors of the ancient states have since played little part in the political life of the country. In the disturbed conditions of the rest of the century there was much movement and inter-mixing of the peoples living north of the clay plains of the White Nile. Thousands were drafted away from Kordofan, then the richest province, to fight the battles of the Khalifa, while the fertile Gezira, the neck of land between the two Niles, was left almost deserted. The south, though raided for slaves, remained relatively isolated from these events and retained its ancient tribal structure. With the defeat of the Mahdists, the Sudan

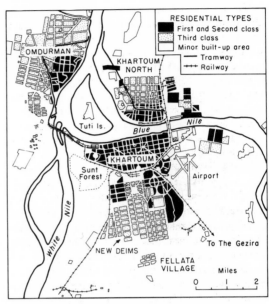

FIG. 27. *Khartoum, Omdurman, and Khartoum North. The three towns at the confluence of the Blue and White Niles. (After Hamdan, 1960.)*

became nominally a joint Egyptian and British Protectorate. In fact it was ruled by a British governor and his administrative staff very much as if it had been a colony. Their main aim for many years was to repair the damage of the preceding decades and build up the economy. Efforts were made in the 1930's to give greater responsibility to native rulers but by that time it was too late, for traditions of regional autonomy had all but disappeared. Since independence in 1956 authority has been concentrated more than ever in Khartoum, and the government has been in the hands of the Muslim Arabs of the capital.

The Three Towns

The confluence of the two Niles is the focus of the Sudan's political, intellectual, and economic life. Khartoum between the two Niles is the seat of government (Fig. 27). Alongside the ministries lining the left bank of the Blue Nile stand the Gothic brick buildings that once housed the Gordon

Memorial College and are now a part of the much larger university which has sprung from it. Behind lies the shopping and commercial centre and the older high-class residential areas where Italians, Greeks, and Levantines live in separate ethnic islands. A newer residential area has sprung up south of the railway tracks, running from expensive villas housing the diplomatic corps, to the New Deims, a huge 'grid-iron' colony of one-storied mud hovels and more than 50,000 inhabitants. South again, a shanty town separate from the main city houses 15,000 immigrants from west Africa.

Omdurman, the Mahdi's capital on the other side of the White Nile, is a low mud-built town of 200,000 people, larger than Khartoum itself. The native market, or Suq, is one of the biggest in Africa, with all manner of local produce for sale, and hundreds of artisans and craftsmen making and selling their wares.

Khartoum North in the third angle of the confluence is a growing industrial town, with textile, footware, and other factories.

These three towns together hold over 50 per cent. of the urban population of the Sudan. The people and the economic activity are concentrated here because Khartoum was chosen to be capital, and the Three Towns stand at a nodal point in the sparse communications system of the country, centrally placed in relation to the main areas of commercial agriculture.

The Nile was for long the most important routeway in this part of Africa. Stern-wheelers plied up the White Nile in the days of Turco-Egyptian rule and, after channels had been cleared through the Sudd, took traders and administrators to the south where overland routes were, and often still are impassable in the rains. The Blue Nile was never very convenient because of sandbanks in the dry season and currents in flood; north of Khartoum the cataracts prevent large boats going far downstream. River steamers, which still carry some 2 million tons of cargo annually are meeting strong competition from road and rail. Passengers go by air; from Kosti to Juba is only three hours by plane, but six days by steamer. Some of the older boats, no longer required as carriers, have been tied up alongside Khartoum's waterfront and for some years took the overflow of guests from the Grand Hotel.

A railway was constructed south from Wadi Haifa to bring up supplies for Kitchener's troops when they advanced south to reoccupy the Sudan, and after the defeat of the Mahdi at Omdurman it was continued to Khartoum on a somewhat different alignment. The capital was soon afterwards linked to the coast at Suakin and Port Sudan by a line joining the north-south one at Atbara. The old Red Sea port of Suakin with its small and inconvenient harbour has declined while Port Sudan, capable of taking ocean-going ships, has steadily grown in importance and now handles about 1·5 million tons annually.

At the beginning of the century the Sudan had little to sell to the rest of the world. Lebanese, Greek, and Italian merchants who had been established in Khartoum and some outlying towns for many years exported little else but ivory and gum arabic, a resin derived from certain species of acacia, notably *Acacia senegalensis*. The most productive parts of the country at that time were the narrow terraces of the Nile downstream of Khartoum, where crops were grown on lands flooded seasonally by the river or watered from it by *shadufs* and ox-powered lifting devices called *saquiya*. A good deal of corn was also grown on the clayey soils of the Gezira, where the rainfall was considerably greater than that of Khartoum (about 6 inches) but very unreliable.

The Gezira

Soon after the British occupation of the Sudan, Sir William Garstin proposed that the Gezira should be irrigated, either by converting Lake Tana into a reservoir or by building a barrage across the Blue Nile in the Sudan. The second alternative having been adopted, surveyors began work almost immediately and produced a closely contoured map of the area between the two Niles to provide the basis for planning a canal system. Experimental plots showed that long-staple cotton would grow well, and by 1913 an experimental pump scheme at Tayiba near Wad Medani had proved the suitability of the central Gezira for this crop.

The Nile flood in 1913 happened to be the lowest on record for nearly 200 years; only two floods were known to have been lower for a thousand years. The next year the flood was not much higher and it was evident that Egypt, at this time under British tutelage, required in such years all the dry season flow of the Nile after the middle of January. So it was decided that the dam to be built would have to do two things, firstly raise the waters of the Blue Nile to a level at which they would flow through canals to irrigate the Gezira, and secondly store a part of the summer flood for use in the Sudan in the latter part of the dry season when Egypt required all the natural flow. The dam was built at Sennar between 1919 and 1925. It was two miles long and provided water for over 300,000 acres of the Gezira. The main canal runs along a slight eminence a few miles west of the Blue Nile, with branch canals running off at right angles to feed major distributary channels through which the water flows day and night during the winter growing season (Fig. 28).

At the beginning of the rains, in July, the reservoir is practically empty and the river flows freely down into Egypt. The Gezira tenants plant a little millet at this time. From mid-July the sluice gates are partly closed to raise the level of the river and at the end of the month, when water begins to flow along the main canal, the cotton is planted. Most of the silt-laden water of the flood continues north until the end of October when the flood peak has passed; then the sluices are closed and the water level rises behind the dam to provide maximum storage by early December. This level is maintained until early February and is then gradually reduced, the natural discharge of the Blue Nile being allowed to pass down to Egypt, the stored waters going into the Gezira canals and on to the cotton fields.

The agricultural operations on the Gezira are carefully controlled by a central organization under the direction of a Sudan government board. (Until 1950 the managers of the scheme were the agents of a commercial firm, the Sudan Plantations Syndicate.) The farmers are tenant cultivators, holding their land from the government which in turn rents it from the original owners. The land is cultivated in blocks, each block being sown with a single crop in order to facilitate crop treatments and watering. Each tenant has several plots in different blocks. He may have 5 acres under cotton, 7 under corn and legumes, and 6 resting. The food and fodder crops are kept by the tenant for his own use; the cotton crop is handed over to the management for sale, and the tenant receives a share of the profits proportional to the weight of cotton he has delivered.

The importance of the Gezira to the economy of the Sudan can hardly be exaggerated. In most years it provides nearly one-half of the country's total exports by value and a fifth of the government's revenue. The income is fairly widely distributed. There are no rich Gezira landowners living in Khartoum on the profits of the cotton fields. The chief beneficiaries are the 30,000 tenants and their families. In addition, some 150,000 or more labourers find seasonal employment in the Gezira and some 2,000 people are permanently employed in supervising the scheme. The commercial centre for the Gezira is Wad Medani, linked by rail to Khartoum, Sennar, and Port Sudan. The capital benefits from the purchasing power of the large community to the south and from the taxes it pays directly and indirectly to the central government.

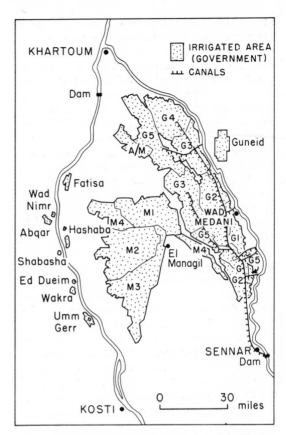

Fig. 28. *The Gezira irrigation scheme and the Managil extension. (After Barbour, 1961.)*

The profitability of the Gezira naturally stimulated interest in the possibility of extending the present scheme and creating new ones. The high prices paid for cotton on the world market in the early and mid-fifties and the greater availability of capital for development projects were further encouragements. An important obstacle to the greater use of Nile water was the agreement with Egypt that had been made by Britain for the Sudan, in 1929, which restricted Sudanese consumption to 4 million cubic metres of water annually. A new agreement was drawn up in 1959 giving the Sudan the right to 17 million cubic metres and the irrigated area was extended west over the Managil plain towards the White Nile. The cultivable area is now about 2 million acres, about a quarter under cotton. Another dam has been built at Roseires further up the Blue Nile to irrigate a million acres in the tribal area of the Kenana Arabs, provide water to new extensions of the Gezira scheme, and generate electricity.

There is no doubt that the huge area of irrigated

land south of Khartoum will continue to be the economic power-house of the Sudan for many years to come. The future of the country depends very heavily on the maintenance of high levels of production there and the possibility of selling its chief product, long-staple cotton, at a good price on the world market.

Pump irrigation from the Nile

Below Khartoum the Nile flows across clayey plains, hot and dusty in the dry season with vegetation confined to the river banks. It heads for a great mass of ancient volcanic rocks about 30 miles north of the city and cuts across them in a deep gorge. This is the Sabaloka gorge, the site of the sixth and highest cataract. Below Sabaloka crystalline rocks form the plains on the east side of the river and are overlain by Nubian sandstones on the west side. (The river was probably superimposed from a continuous Nubian sandstone cover to give the gorge.) The Nile itself is confined to a narrow valley trenched into these rocks, with alluvial terraces entirely lacking where the river cuts across the crystallines and rarely more than a mile wide where it has transgressed on to the sandstones (see Fig. 13).

Cultivation north of Khartoum is confined to these long narrow alluvial strips alongside the river. In the past they were irrigated by floodwaters of the Nile soaking the ground enough to give a single crop, or by *shadufs* and *saquiya* allowing two or even three crops to be taken. *Saquiya* are water-wheels powered by bulls; each wheel can lift enough water to irrigate 5 acres when the river level is high, or about 2 acres at low water. But there is very little grazing to be had away from the river in the northern areas and so the bulls eat up a good proportion of the corn and fodder crops grown by their own efforts. Both the Arabs in the south and the Nubians further north are very poor, land is scarce and costly, and many of the men go far afield in search of work, most of them to Khartoum.

Pumps powered by diesel engines introduced in recent decades allow the basins that once depended on the annual flood of the Nile to be irrigated throughout the year and new areas that were difficult to water at all by traditional methods have been brought under cultivation. Unhappily standards of living for the local people have not been much improved by this innovation because the pumps belong to wealthy Sudanese in Khartoum. *Saquiya* are still common because many holdings are so small that protracted negotiations would be necessary to bring enough together to make a pump scheme worth while.

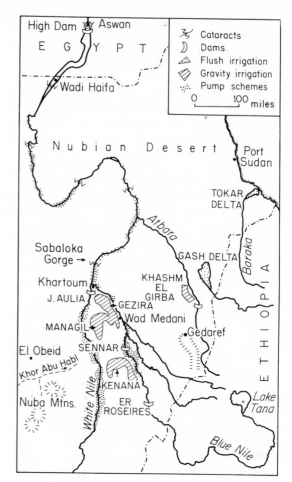

FIG. 29. *Irrigation schemes in the Sudan. The period since 1925, when the Sennar Dam was completed, has shown a great increase in the irrigated area of the Sudan, especially in the area south of Khartoum.*

The water behind the new High Dam at Aswan flooding Wadi Haifa near the frontier and stretching 70 miles south into the Sudan, has forced some 50,000 Nubians living on the banks of the Nile to leave their homes. In compensation the Egyptian government paid the Sudan £15 million towards the costs of resettling the displaced people on a new irrigation scheme at Khashm el Girba, 220 miles east of Khartoum, where the Atbara river has been dammed to provide water (Fig. 29).

South of Khartoum the opportunities for large pump schemes are much greater than to the north because so much of the dry plain is flat, soil covered, and suitable for irrigation. The land alongside the Blue Nile could not be irrigated in the past because the river is deeply incised and the lift is too great

86

for animal power. Diesel pumps are quite capable of doing the job and in many places it has been made easier for them by dams raising the water-level far upstream. The effect of the Sennar dam is felt for 50 miles upstream throughout most of the cotton-growing season. The Jebel Aulia dam on the White Nile, which was intended mainly for storing water for use in Egypt, assists pumping schemes as far up the river as Kosti, and the water can usually be relied upon to stay high enough for the pumps to use it until February. For all these reasons the number of large pump schemes above Khartoum is increasing faster than downstream, nearly all of them financed by private investors.

Rainlands west of the White Nile

Towards the south, where the rainfall increases to more than about 15 inches, settlement and cultivation away from the river is possible. A fairly productive and populous region stretches west of the Nile across the undulating, lightly wooded plains of Kordofan. This is the Qoz, an area of wind-blown sands which accumulated in drier periods of the Pleistocene era. They stretch from near the Nile westwards to the flanks of the Jebel Marra massif and southwards to the southern clay plains. Mostly they are formed into gently undulating reddish dunes, sometimes 100 feet high, and there is little or no sign of surface drainage except for a few large wadis. They are covered by scrub woodland becoming dense in the south. Huge areas in the west are almost deserted and only visited by summer graziers, but the east is a populous and fairly prosperous region.

Nomadic camel Arabs in the north range far towards the desert during the rains and return to the wells and pastures of the northern Qoz for the dry season. Nomadic cattle Baggara in the south graze their herds on the Bahr-el-Ghazal in the winter dry season, coming north to the Qoz in the rains (see p. 55).

The central Qoz is settled by tribal people. They are mostly concentrated to the east of El Obeid, where numerous wells yield abundant water, and along the railway line. The people are mixed: Nubians, Arabs, and others are concentrated in small villages clustering round small wells or ponds. When they dry out the people either move *en masse* to deep boreholes, drilled by the government near large towns such as El Obeid and En Nahud, or send out camel expeditions to carry water back—often a journey of several days. Trucks carry large drums of water to outlying villages and the government is now drilling a great number of bore-holes

A pump scheme on the Blue Nile. Pumping station and settlement near the river, irrigated land in the background, at Guneid near the Gezira.

to tap supplies very deep underground. The railway was extended west to Nyala in 1960, new bore-holes have been put down, and these improvements are expected to attract more settlers to the southern Qoz where the higher rainfall is more favourable for agriculture. The current main farming areas, in the north, suffer from drought and only in occasional years is there a surplus of corn for sale outside the region. The main crops here are maize and 'simsim', an oil-seed. Oil-seeds and groundnuts are the main exports and many farmers supplement their incomes by collecting gum in the winter months, but they remain poor and the area seems to be less prosperous than, for instance, the comparable region of Hausaland in northern Nigeria.

Irrigation in the Qoz is on a very limited scale. After 1945 the flood waters of the Khor Abu Habl coming from the Nuba hills in the south were used to grow some 5,000 acres of cotton. This fairly isolated tract produced seed from strains developed at government research stations for distribution over a wide area of the Rainlands. A second area with irrigation is in the neighbourhood of the Jebel Marra in the west, where a number of small schemes are operated. Near Suni, for example, perennial springs are used to irrigate citrus orchards in carefully tended smallholdings, and near most of the larger settlements fruit and vegetable gardens are watered with *shadufs*. Tiny clay flats between lines of low dunes in the north of the Qoz are irrigated in the same way, but their importance is very slight.

The Nuba mountains lying south-east of the Qoz are mainly populated by pagan negroes,

The Jebel Marra massif seen from the east, from the perennial stream just below Suni village.

A modern waterhole in the Sudan. Many pits of this kind have been excavated by machinery in recent years to store water for the dry season.

numbering about three-quarters of a million. They moved down from the hills on to the plains early in the century and took to growing short-staple cotton on a considerable scale in the twenties. Between 100,000 and 200,000 acres are now devoted to this crop, the seed coming in part from the

multiplication centre on the Khor Abu Habl. Cotton cultivation is to be greatly extended in the future. The rest of the population, about a quarter of a million, are Arabs. Some are traders in the towns. Others came into the mountains as pastoralists, staying only for the dry season and moving out to the Qoz during the rains. Many of them began to settle down to farming and they were ready to take up cotton-growing before the Nuba pagans. In the last twenty years a great many reservoirs have been excavated in the clayey plains between the granite mountains to store water into the dry season and open up wider areas for cultivation. The Arabs have settled near them, but the Nuba prefer to remain at the foot of the hills, where the soils are lighter and better drained and where they are nearer to the homes of their ancestors.

One of the most beautiful parts of a country which, admittedly, is not famed for its scenic attractions, is Jebel Marra, a highland region of volcanic hills with a giant crater forming the culminating feature, its rim rising to 10,000 feet. A striking feature of the region is the artificial terracing of the lava slopes, rising to within a thousand feet of the summit. Some terraces are still used, being manured by cattle kraaled there in the dry season and producing crops of millet. Most have been abandoned now that settlement on the plains is possible and many of the Fur have moved down to compact villages on the wadi floors at the outskirts of the highlands. There they are in close contact with Arab tribes and produce crops for export via the railway at Nyala.

A good deal of the country stretching west of the Jebel towards the Chad frontier has been observed from the air to be terraced in a rudimentary fashion, and the population may once have been much greater. Cultivation at present is mainly confined to the alluvial terraces of wadis running towards Chad. Sorghum, millet, and other crops are grown beneath *haraz* trees (*Acacia albida*), which are peculiar in that they shed their leaves at the end of the dry season and are in new leaf in October, just before harvesting begins. After immigrant and local cattle have grazed on the crop residues, the 'bean' pods falling off the *haraz* trees provide additional feed. This useful tree is widely distributed through the Sudan zone and fits very well into traditional farming systems.

Clay plains east of the White Nile

The plains lying north-west of the Abyssinian highlands are very different from the Qoz. The rainfall is comparable but the soils are heavy clays for

The crater of Jebel Marra. It is rather more than 3 miles in diameter and rises to a height of about 10,000 feet.

the most part, derived from ancient alluvium near the major rivers, and weathered from crystalline rocks in the south and east. Trees growing on these impermeable soils have great difficulty in obtaining moisture in the dry season, and the vegetation of the clay plains is comparable in density and species to that of areas on the sandy Qoz receiving much less rain.

The plains north-west of the 15-inch isohyet are bare or only sparsely clad in acacia scrub or grasses. When seen from the air their monotony is relieved by the appearance of two kinds of pattern. One of these is natural and is caused by the grasses and trees being concentrated in narrow parallel arcs and stripes covering very wide areas. This arrangement is not noticeable on the ground and was first seen from the air and on air photographs; it has still to be explained satisfactorily. The other type of pattern is rectilinear and clearly man-made. The lines are low earth banks a foot or two high, built to trap the summer rains running down the gentle slopes so that the water will soak into the ground and allow a crop of quick-maturing millet called *feterita* to be grown. It takes only eighty days to mature after the seed has germinated. A comparable technique is employed on the claylands west of Lake Chad in Nigeria.

The plains people are now concentrated mainly on the Gezira and the other irrigated areas (see Fig. 29). Another productive area lies near Gedaref where the railway crosses a tongue of basalt projecting to the north-west, and a combination of good rainfall, about 24 to 30 inches annually, and fertile soils derived from the volcanic rocks allows over a million acres to be cultivated without irrigation. Grain and cotton are collected by lorries and taken

Haraz trees in cropland. The trees form a closed cover on the lower terraces alongside the watercourses on the floors of the main wadis.

to market at Gedaref. The government sponsored mechanized agricultural schemes in the neighbourhood from 1944 until 1954 when private companies took over. Several local farmers have tractors and employ local labour, but most of the land is in the hands of entrepreneurs from outside the area. In 1968 it was believed that 750,000 acres were being cropped, sorghum being grown year after year. Conflict has developed between pastoralists, local cultivators, and new tractor farmers; erosion and decline of fertility are both severe problems.

Gedaref is far from typical of the clay plains. They are generally much drier and, away from the main rivers and the canal to the Gezira, such people as there are live in small nucleated settlements for mutual protection against the nomads who still roam the plains. There are few wells in this area of impermeable soils and rock, and a good deal of reliance is placed on *hafirs*, pit reservoirs excavated in the last twenty years by machinery. No doubt many of the local Fung and Arabs, and the stranger settlers from west Africa, will be attracted to the new irrigation scheme on the Atbara, for although about two-thirds of the land to be irrigated by the Khashm el Girba dam will be reserved for the Nubians displaced by the High Dam, several tens of thousands of acres will be available for the locals.

In the dry north-east the main agricultural areas depend on two torrents from the Ethiopian hills. The Baraka and the Gash have carried down heavy loads of sediment to form extensive alluvial cones, usually referred to as deltas, where the water soaks away. The Gash delta, on the east side of the railway from Kassala to Port Sudan, and which is flooded to a varying extent each year, was regularly used by Beja pastoralists as a dependable dry-season grazing area. Since 1929 six canals have been dug to lead the floodwater on to fields where cotton is sown after the soil has been soaked for several days. The cultivators are Hadendowa, belonging to the pastoralist Beja tribe. Very wisely they continue to depend mainly on their animals, for the flood varies in size each year and the cultivated acreage varies accordingly. The Baraka watering the Tokar delta of the Red Sea hills is even more unreliable and uncontrolled. From one year to another the total area cultivated in the two deltas varies between 50,000 and 200,000 acres.

The South

The areas bordering the Nile and the Nyala-Port Sudan railway are the populous and productive parts of the country, containing over half the people in a tenth of the total area. The other nine-tenths of the Sudan are remote, sparsely settled, and contribute little to the national economy.

The Nilotic peoples living on the clay plains flooded annually by the White Nile and its tributaries are primarily stock-rearers (see p. 55). They depend for their food on grain as much as animal products but their life is orientated mainly towards the well-being of their herds. There is little to make them change their outlook on life at present. Transport is difficult, education makes slow progress where people are so mobile, and the pastoralists are so little acquainted with towns that they are not greatly disposed to want goods their own economies cannot provide.

The scheme to canalize the White Nile from Jonglei to Malakal, in order to reduce evaporation losses from the floods and increase the total discharge of the river, would have involved a transformation in the environment of the Nilotics. The floods that now provide dry-season grazing for the herds of the Dinka, Nuer, and Shilluk would have been greatly reduced in effectiveness and the people would have been forced to change their ways. They might have become cultivators, growing sugar-cane, rice, and other crops by irrigation. The decision to build the High Dam has reduced the need for the scheme and it has been shelved for the present. But if population pressure in the Sudan begins to be felt seriously, and the demand for water in Egypt continues to grow, the Jonglei scheme may be taken out of its pigeon-hole and engineers begin to dyke and drain the southern clay plains and turn the Nilotics into good productive citizens.

In the south-western corner of the country an attempt was made amongst the Zande after the last war to raise the level of economic activity. This is one of the most remote parts of Africa (see p. 60). Transport costs to the outside world were so high that it was difficult for the producer to get a reasonable return for exporting his crops and so it was decided to use local resources in small local industries, manufacturing goods with a higher value per unit weight than the bulky raw materials and exporting the finished products. The British government put about £1 million into the scheme, mainly for machinery to produce cotton goods and soap. To provide the raw materials the Zande were resettled on regular-shaped plots running back from paths and roads in a way resembling the strip-fields that have evolved elsewhere in Africa. They were supplied with high-yielding oil-palms and other crops and got away to a good start. High prices were being offered for cotton grown there in the early 1950's and incomes increased. Later on the sugar and soap factories were closed down, and although it has been claimed that many of the original aims were achieved, the scheme does not seem to have formed a secure basis for economic growth in the area as a whole, and little has been heard of it recently. Tobacco is being widely grown in the south to supply the cigarette factories of Wad Medani and Khartoum, and other crops such as rice are being developed. In 1962 a railway extension to the south from Babanusa reached Wau, and in time it may be carried down to Juba. Perhaps this link to the outside world will give a new stimulus to development in Zande country.

As it stands, the southern half of the Sudan, the

part south of Malakal, contributes very little to Sudanese exports or northern markets. It remains racially and culturally as well as economically a land apart, in every way more akin to Uganda and the Congo than to the Muslim north. Until the 1950's the southerners were educated in Christian mission schools. Most, if not all, of these have been closed. The new generation is being led into Islamic society. Arabic is taught in the schools now, not English, and it is intended that the young people shall learn to conform with the Sudanese way of life as it is lived in the Arab north.

Development trends

The economy of the Sudan is founded on Khartoum and the lands irrigated from the Blue Nile. Outside this well-populated core, distances between towns are great, roads are very bad, productivity is low. The very size of the country is a great handicap to development. In education, for example, secondary schools outside the Three Towns must cater for students coming from a very wide area and so they must be boarding schools. The expense of education is therefore high and a school's influence is scarcely felt in the places from which the students come. They are taken away from their home environment, have difficulty in adapting themselves again on leaving school, and so gravitate towards the capital. This is but one factor tending to accentuate the predominance of the capital in the life of the country, a trend, it must be added which is not confined to the Sudan.

The economy depends on the sale of cotton to pay for imported goods of all kinds, and to provide government revenue. In 1964 cotton and cottonseed products made up two-thirds of the country's exports by value and the proportion is unlikely to decrease. Long-staple cotton is usually able to command a good price in world markets; nevertheless, with individual investors putting their money into pump schemes and the government building new dams, all with the object of producing more cotton, the reliance on a single crop would seem to be excessive. Up to a few years ago gum arabic, in which the Sudan has a virtual monopoly, was the second export by value. Now it has been displaced by groundnuts. The two together are worth about £13 million compared with the £35 to £45 million received from sales of cotton and cottonseed.

Industry is just beginning: until 1955 no factories employed more than fifty people, but now local raw materials are being used for making cotton cloth, footwear, and paper. Cigarette factories and flour mills that started by using imported materials are turning over to Sudanese crops. The usual assortment of breweries and cement works is to be found, mainly in the Three Towns, with some plants in Wad Medani and Port Sudan. But most of the people remain poor farmers and pastoralists, living far from Khartoum and little affected by economic development there.

7

The Southern Sahara and its Borderlands

THE SOUTHERN SAHARA

THE Sahara stretches 3,000 miles across the widest part of Africa from the Nile to the Atlantic, a nearly empty land between the Sudan zone on the south, and the Mediterranean and the Atlas mountains on the north. It is the largest desert in the world, bigger than the United States of America—with the population of a single large city. Effectually it makes west Africa a peninsula of the main mass of the continent to the east, in something the same way that western Europe is a peninsula of the Euro-Asian landmass. The trans-Saharan trade-routes are more difficult, less-used equivalents of the ocean shipping lanes, and the desert oases are islands as rarely visited as the Azores or Ascencion.

In spite of the distances separating them, the lands around the desert have much in common. They all suffer from seasonal or perennial shortage of water that forces livestock herders to be nomadic and cultivators to irrigate their crops. Arab pastoralists and traders have carried their language far into the tropics, Islamic culture has spread into the wooded steppe zone south of the desert, and negro blood has been introduced to the lands bordering the Mediterranean. Much in the same way that one can speak of a North Sea culture or of the western Mediterranean as a cultural region, so can one detect a likeness, based on their heritage from the past, amongst all the Saharan borderlands.

In the course of the nineteenth century almost the whole of the western Sahara came under French

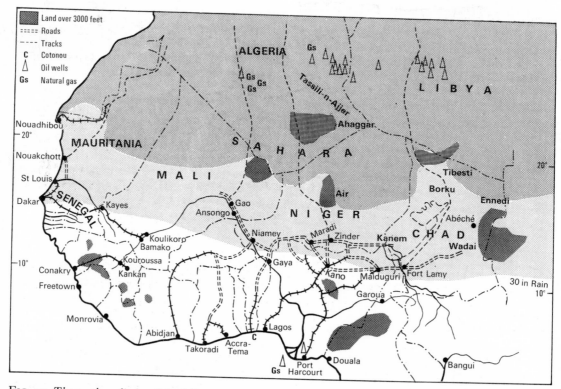

FIG. 30. *The southern limits of the Sahara. The shaded area represents desert vegetation as indicated by Capot-Rey on Map 1 of his book* Le Sahara français. *It will be seen that the boundary shown on the vegetation map at the end of this volume is slightly different.*

a. An ancient volcano, Ehi Mousgou.

b. Trou au Natron, a giant caldera, 5 miles in dia-meter and about 2,000 feet deep.

c. Old schists and phyllites, closely dissected in the background and with a layer of coarse sediments a few feet thick covering a rock pediment in the foreground.

d. Isolated sandstone hill, capped with volcanic lavas, rising sharply from sandstone plains near Bardai.

control and the area has thereby retained some cohesion. Lord Salisbury's attitude to French Saharan ambitions, 'Let the Gallic cock sharpen his spurs on the desert sands!', seemed to be appropriate until the 1950's when the empty tracts of bare rock and sand acquired a new value as the result of oil and natural gas being discovered there in very large quantities. Most of the important finds of minerals lay in the north, in Algeria and Libya; in the southern Sahara, within the boundaries of the old colonial federations of French West and Equatorial Africa, large deposits of iron ore are the only

minerals so far being exploited on any scale. France attempted to maintain her influence in the area by instituting an Organization of the Sahara Regions (O.C.R.S.) which was to co-ordinate and finance the development of Saharan resources, but this Organization was swept aside with Algerian independence. Now the new states of the Saharan borderland regard each other with considerable suspicion.

The southern Sahara, with which we are mainly concerned here, consists largely of rocky and sandy plains broken by low escarpments (Fig. 30). The Ahaggar and its southern projections, Aïr and the

Adrar of the Iforas, are upwarped masses of crystalline rocks, with volcanic peaks rising from them to high altitudes. In Tibesti, the mountain massif is largely built of Palaeozoic sandstones resting on a crystalline floor, and with a much more extensive cover of volcanic rocks than in the Ahaggar region. In both these highland areas the relief bears a very close relationship to the kind of rock outcropping, and in both areas there is clear evidence in the form of potholes and alluvial gravels of the important part played by running water in shaping the landscape.

The deep, steep-sided wadis of the massifs merge into wide shallow wadis in the open desert which run for hundreds of miles towards the centres of shallow depressions mainly in about latitude 17° N. On the gentle slopes of the depressions lie extensive tracts of sand, called *ergs*, composed of material deposited by streams in the past and derived from the weathering of crystalline and, above all, sandstone rocks. The sand has been sorted and transported by the wind, and shaped into dunes of various kinds, the forms of which are difficult to distinguish from the ground but show up clearly on air photographs. Most imposing are the great whaleback dunes, about a mile wide, tens or hundreds of feet high, running almost straight across country for tens or hundreds of miles, in the direction of the prevailing winds. Other lines of dunes lie at right angles to the wind. Vast areas simply consist of gentle sandy undulations, a few feet high and spaced 500 feet apart, called *méréyé* after a region in the south-west Sahara from which they have been described. Outside the main sand seas stretches the pebbly *reg* or *serir*, the pebbles having been waterborne in the past or weathered out of underlying pebbly sandstones. Near the Atlantic coast and in Borku, north of Lake Chad, fields of crescentic dunes called *barchans* move between south-west and west at rates of several tens of yards every year under the influence of unusually strong winds from a single direction. Slight depressions are marked by muddy sediments, by deposits of salt, or a light dusty rock called diatomite, made up of the siliceous skeletons of microscopic organisms that lived in the lakes of a more humid period that seems to have lasted until less than 10,000 years ago.

Vegetation is scarce or absent, but the traveller who has crossed a barren waste may be surprised if he returns a few weeks later to find that a storm of rain has produced a carpet of fine grasses and flowering plants. Nomads with their flocks take advantage of the fresh growth where they can; although their camels may be able to survive without water for several days on end, their sheep and goats need watering every day or two, and where there are no wells the grass seeds and dies unused.

Most of the desert people live in oases, in the shade of the date-palm, watering their crops from wells and springs and wringing a bare living from the soil. The date-palm makes life bearable. Its fruit is a basic food for both the nomad and the sedentary cultivator. The fermented sap provides a refreshing drink in places where the water is often salty and unpalatable. Its wood and fibre are used for building and making ropes, and even the date-stones are pounded into a flour and used to feed animals. From afar, the silhouette of the date-palm indicates the presence of man in the desert, and to the scorched traveller the prospect of water and shade. As the rainfall increases towards the south, the date-palm is still to be seen, even at Kayes on the Senegal and Bamba on the Niger. It mingles with baobab-trees near the northern frontiers of Nigeria, and with forked doum-palms in the valleys of Borku. But in these low latitudes its fruit is of little value and the people import dried dates from the north.

The more humid lands where the rainfall exceeds about 5 or 6 inches are called the *Sahel* from the name of the region between the Senegal and upper Niger, about 15° N. Here the dunes are fixed and grey, only locally golden and active. Not only is the vegetation more varied and continuous than in true desert, with acacia and tall grasses of various kinds often arranged in arcs and stripes as in the Sudan, but animal life is much more prolific. The wells are thronged with hundreds of animals being watered, and besides the desert sounds of camels burbling, and the bleating of sheep and goats, you can hear the lowing of cows and braying donkeys. From the air, the wells appear as white spots with paths radiating in all directions from the bare ground surrounding them. Nights are no longer still and empty, but disturbed by the buzzing of mosquitoes. You sleep on a bed for fear of snakes and scorpions, no longer on the ground with only a blanket. Game is abundant with large numbers of gazelle, and in places, elephant and giraffe. Termite nests appear and are sometimes so numerous that the pale-coloured circles of bare ground form a dense pattern on air photographs. Clearest indicator of all that the desert has been left behind is the ubiquitous presence of *cram-cram*, a grass with very prickly seeds, which Capot-Rey, the author of *Le Sahara Français*, chooses to mark the limit of the Sahara.

Plant life in the Sahelian zone has a precarious hold on the soil. If the grasses are too heavily grazed, the soils trodden by too many hoofs and the bush cleared, wind erosion begins and plants have difficulty in recolonizing the raw sand exposed. This has happened over wide areas and some observers have reported that the Sahara is advancing. But a clear distinction should be made between this man-made desert and the natural one. There is little possibility of improving the plant cover of the Sahara; but if an area in the Sahel remains protected and undisturbed for about twenty years a remarkable improvement can take place. There is hope for the desert margins, though so far, conservation measures have not been very effective because the inhabitants object so strongly to restrictions on their movements and on the size of their herds.

CHAD REPUBLIC

Chad was once the northernmost territory in French Equatorial Africa, an enormous colonial federation which had its capital at Brazzaville on the Congo and its northern extremity in the central Sahara. The independent Republic retains political and economic links with Cameroon and the Central African Republic. It also continues to rely on French technical, economic, and military assistance, for, like the other states further west with their front doors opening on to verdant gardens bordering great rivers and their backyards desert, Chad is a remote and poor country.

The north receives a mean annual rainfall of less than 10 inches. Infrequent storms in the Tibesti and the sandstone plateaux of Erdi and Ennedi produce short-lived floods that die out in sandstone canyons before reaching the plains. These ephemeral streams bring no water to Lake Chad, but they do contribute to the sub-surface movement of water in the sandy beds of wadis and thereby to the water supplies of flocks and herds. Unless valuable minerals are found there (and geological surveys do indicate possibilities of oil), the north of the country will remain an economic backwater, attracting explorers in search of fantastic scenery, adventure, and discomfort, but repelling investors.

The Tibu who predominate in the north are a tough, wiry people, some resembling Arabs, the majority of them more negroid in appearance (see p. 53). Several thousands are concentrated in the Enneri Bardagué of northern Tibesti, where water, seeping down the sandy floors of wadis draining high volcanic mountains to the south, emerges in springs at a constriction in the Enneri and is used to irrigate date-palms and gardens. Some of the Tibu spend all their lives in the mountain oases, living in small villages, where the houses are perched on terraces

above the wadi floors, out of reach of the occasional floods. Others move long distances away from the mountains to seek grazing for their animals, sometimes performing extraordinary feats of endurance. Quite commonly, they will take camels and goats across hundreds of miles of desert country to Kufra or Gatroun in Libya where small colonies of their countrymen live, and return to Tibesti with loads of dates, matches, perfumes, and other goods. Such trading is less profitable than formerly, because, at least in the winter season, a lorry convoy runs at monthly intervals from Tunis to Fort Lamy bringing to Zouar and Faya supplies for the military detachments and for the Tripolitanian merchants who have settled amongst the Tibu.

While the Tibesti mountains afford some of the most spectacular natural scenery in the world, the desert plains to the south are amongst the most desolate and monotonous anywhere. They once formed the bed of a greater Lake Chad; now there are only shallow wadis, salt flats, dunes, and a few small lakes, of which those at Ounianga are perennial and contain crocodiles descended from ancestors that lived there in a wetter period. Near the present Lake Chad, the ground is littered in some places with fish bones. The north-easterly winds, funnelled between the high ground of Tibesti and Ennedi, drive the loose sand before them, abrading the old lake sediments and carrying the dust far away to the south-west where in the winter months it obscures the skies of northern Nigeria.

Between the Bodélé depression and Lake Chad sand ridges, running NNW. to SSE., are grown over with grasses and trees. This is Kanem, a country that formed the centre of an empire several centuries ago, encompassing at its maximum extent Hausaland, the Fezzan, and Darfur. The pastoral inhabitants are mixed, some Tibu and Fulani, the majority Arabs who have migrated into the area from the east and north. They are all divided into a number of different, mutually suspicious tribes, amongst whom the Shuwa Arabs are the most numerous.

The undulating country of Wadai, rising gently towards Darfur in the Sudan Republic, is more heavily settled. This is a problem area, where half a million impoverished people are short of water, without schools and lack any opportunity for development. Wadai lies hundreds of miles from a railway; whereas in Senegal a ton of groundnuts will buy 3 tons of cement, in Wadai it will buy only a quarter of a ton. The people cannot produce much for export under these conditions except cattle. To get cash they emigrate to the Sudan to pick cotton and gather gum, following the pilgrim route from Abéché to El Fasher (Fig. 20).

Towards Lake Chad the density of the human and cattle population increases and people are engaged in farming as well as herding. Large numbers of animals are exported to Nigeria and the Central African Republic. The Kanembu people of this area are descended in large part from groups who came south from Tibesti several centuries ago. Their tongue evolved into the Kanouri language which was disseminated through the Kanem Empire and became a lingua franca of the central Sudan, spoken by peoples of diverse tribal origins. Kanouri continues to be a unifying force, the language being adopted by many of the Arab immigrants to the region.

The lakeshore and the numerous dune islands in the lake are occupied in part by the Buduma. They tend their cattle and engage in various other pursuits. Wheat is cultivated on polders along the eastern shore by farmers whose main farms are on the higher sandy soils. Yields are variable because of imperfect control of the water. Blocks of natron (sodium carbonate), used as a cattlelick and condiment, are dug from the hollows near the northeastern lake shore where salty water evaporates, some 5,000 tons being won annually. Thousands of tons of fish are caught each year, mainly in nets. They are dried and, with blocks of natron, carried on reed boats by the Buduma to Fort Lamy and certain villages on the Nigerian side of the lake. From the villages, they go by camel and lorry to Maiduguri in Bornu for distribution further afield.

In the past the people of the southern lakeshore used to suffer a great deal from slave-raiding by Muslim northerners. They managed to retain their freedom and culture, and today the tables are turned and they form the *élite* in the towns of southern Chad. Though they are divided into many tribes, the French language helps to unify them. In the country, they live in beehive-shaped houses, grouped closely together into compact villages where pigs and small hardy cattle are to be seen.

The flat plains south of the lake are frequently flooded by the Logone and Shari rivers overflowing their banks. Most of the country is covered in sedges and grasses, and trees are confined to termite heaps rising above the general level of the waters. In such alluvial areas where a few feet make all the difference between a well-drained site and a bog, the sandy banks of the rivers are the most attractive settlement sites. Fort Lamy, the capital of Chad, stands on the right bank of the Shari about 50 miles south of the Lake and roads running along the banks of

the main rivers connect it to Bongor and Fort Archambault. Another road runs west across the northern tip of the Cameroon Republic to the nearest railhead at Maiduguri (Fig. 45). There are no railways in Chad itself, and in the rains most of the roads are unusable, though some of the main rivers are navigable at this season.

Since the last war, the French have taken much interest in the possibilities for irrigating the deltas of the Logone and Shari, and further upstream, near Bongor, a large area has been reclaimed for cultivation by constructing embankments to control flooding. Rice is being cultivated and is replacing sorghum as the staple crop in many places. But costs are high, the embanking has reduced the area of dry-season feed available to cattle and, in the absence of better equipment, the people are unable to cultivate more land than they have already.

Cotton which provides about 80 per cent of the country's exports was forcibly introduced by the French in 1929. Now it occupies some half million acres, mainly in the extreme south of the country. A little is irrigated, but most of it depends on the rains and is grown by peasants on land newly cleared of bush and burned over. The seed is sown in July, when the farmers have got their grain crops well established, and is harvested in the dry season. State-controlled factories gin the crop; some of the seed is reserved for planting and the lint is compressed into bales for export. Exports vary from 20,000 to 100,000 tons. Some goes by road to the Nigerian railhead and Port Harcourt; some via Garoua and down the Benue to Burutu in the Niger delta; most of the rest goes via Bangui to Brazzaville and Pointe Noire. A little has been known to go to Douala by air.

The long journey to the coast is costly and consequently when world prices are low the price received by the producer is very low indeed. A farmer working the land with his family can deal with only an acre or two of cotton, so his cash income in a year may be only £5 or £10. When he has paid his taxes and goes to a store with what is left he may decide to buy cloth which could conceivably have been made from his own cotton, which has travelled all the way to northern France and back. Naturally, the price of imported goods is high and so the returns for his work in the fields are trifling. Some of the tribes, like the Massa, prefer to invest their money in cattle; with eight or ten of them a new wife can be won. Sara living further south are in the tsetse-belt and the young men are said to be more inclined to buy clothes and bicycles.

Reed boats on the shore of Lake Chad. They are used for transporting fish, salt, and passengers.

NIGER REPUBLIC

In the Niger Republic, 3 million people live in an area of half a million square miles. Most of the population is concentrated along the southern frontier and near the Niger river; the rest of the country is virtually uninhabited. Its communications with the coast are little better than those of Chad. Although Niamey, the capital, stands on the left bank of the Niger, rapids at Ansongo prevent boats moving upstream into Mali, and navigation downstream to the Niger delta, via the Kainji lake, has yet to be developed. The main links with the outside world are south through Nigeria, and south-west via the bridge across the Niger at Gaya to the coast at Cotonou in Dahomey (Fig. 30).

Niamey is a thriving town of some 30,000 people, with a large international airport and handsome public buildings and shops. A fairly good road runs south-east to Dosso; there, a right-hand fork runs down to the Niger bridge at Gaya, the road to the left keeps within about 50 miles of the Nigerian frontier, passing through Maradi and Zinder to N'Guigmi at the north-west corner of Lake Chad. Though the going is difficult for long stretches because of soft

sand, it is motorable for most of the year, and a regular weekly bus service traverses the whole route.

Travelling along this road to the east from Niamey, one sees a good deal of the economically productive part of the country. As far as Zinder, most of the people are Hausa and Fulani farmers growing millet and groundnuts in the sandy soils and keeping a few animals. Groundnuts form the country's main exports; large numbers of cattle and goats are trekked across the frontier for sale in Kano and the other northern towns.

Maradi stands on the banks of a seasonal stream that rises in Nigeria and eventually drains via the Rima into the Niger. The stream channel silted up, probably as a result of accelerated erosion following the clearing of woodland in the vicinity of the headwaters, and the old site of Maradi was threatened by floods. A new town has been built on a bluff overlooking the site of the old one on the floodplain. A good road runs 160 miles south-east to Kano, and Maradi is the market and distribution centre for much of the country.

The military post of Zinder, which was capital of the territory until 1926, stands amongst rocky

97

hills on the watershed between seasonal streams draining west to the Niger and east to the Chad basin. A motorable track runs north to Agadès, the chief settlement in Aïr, and continues north across the desert to Tamanrasset and Algiers. It follows an old caravan route, and for a time was used by a bus service between Kano and Algiers. This has been discontinued because of the competition from air lines, but trans-Saharan car travellers still make use of the track which provides some of the finest mountain scenery in Africa. Rainfall totals in Aïr are higher than in Tibesti, with frequent thunder-showers between June and September, and the Touareg inhabitants, though primarily pastoralists, manage to raise some meagre crops on the wadi terraces.

Zinder, with a mean annual rainfall of about 20 inches, is the centre of a countryside producing groundnuts and millet. It has an oil-mill; crafts-men are engaged in leatherwork and weaving, and there is a considerable trade with Kano, which is the commercial centre for much of the Niger Republic as well as for northern Nigeria. Although lorries are now the main carriers, long camel cara-vans in the charge of veiled Touaregs are still to be seen in the winter months, following the old hedged ways to the south, and avoiding the modern tarmac roads.

Towards the east, the rainfall and productivity of the soils diminish. The Manga and other peoples cultivate flat-floored depressions within the main mass of fixed dunes stretching to the northern edge of Lake Chad. Gum collected from the acacias is carried down to Geidam and Nguru in Nigeria for export by rail. Nomadic herdsmen graze their animals on the rolling sandhills and move freely across the frontier, from dry-season grazing grounds in north-east Nigeria to wet season pastures along-side the great wadis traversing the sandy plains east and west of Aïr.

Water is scarce nearly everywhere, except in the south-west where the lands bordering the Niger are well favoured because the river is at its highest in the dry season and can be used to irrigate riverside farms. Artesian water is being developed in the Tahoua area and north-west of Lake Chad. Gener-ally men and animals depend on wells for over half the year, crops are liable to suffer from drought, people are poor, and it is difficult to see how their lot can be improved. With the exception of uranium recently found in the north and a little tin-ore in Aïr, minerals worth exploiting have yet to be discovered and the country's economy is very insecurely based.

A camel caravan on the route from Maradi to Kano.

MALI

A greater proportion of Mali lies outside the Sahara, and although it is about the same size as Niger, its population at 4 million is considerably greater. The majority of the people live in the river-side lands and further south.

Bamako, the capital, resembles Niamey in being situated at the south-west extremity of the country, on the Niger river, and about 500 miles from the sea. Though it lies in the heartland of the old empires of Ghana and Mali, where routes following the Senegal river inland from the coast approach nearest to the Niger, there was no more than a village on the site of Bamako in 1883 when the French arrived and built a military post. A railway reached the town in 1904, linking it to Kayes on the navi-gable waters of the Senegal river, and twenty years later this line was extended to Dakar. Upstream of Bamako the Niger is navigable for 200 miles to Kouroussa and is used for the carriage of provisions to the gold-mines of Siguiri in Guinea and for local canoe traffic. Downstream, for 30 miles, the river is broken by rapids and the Dakar railway has been extended to Koulikoro, below which the river is navigable for 875 miles to Ansongo. Thus Bamako is an important route centre.

For a few months after the French West African territories gained their independence, Mali was united with Senegal in a federation which appeared to be a logical consequence of their economic inter-dependence. Most of Mali's external trade, notably its exports of groundnuts and rice, were directed westwards along the railway to Dakar, a fine port, closer to western Europe than any alternatives in west Africa. Senegal depended on this traffic for operating its railways and ports economically, and also relied on Mali migrant labour. But political dissension soon arose between the leading politicians in the two countries, and while feeling still ran strong, they separated. Senegal cut Mali's rail communications with Dakar, and Mali decided to develop other means of access to the outside world, so that in future it should not be at the mercy of Senegal and the strong French community in Dakar. For a time much of its trade was directed south-west using lorries to the railhead at Kankan in Guinea. There was talk of building a railway to give a through line from Bamako to Conakry and an old project to extend the Abidjan line to the Niger was revived. But in 1963 relations between Mali and Senegal were re-established and it is unlikely that either line will ever be built.

Mali faces that awkward problem common to all the under-developed countries; it lacks capital. At present it depends heavily on French and other foreign aid, and the past record of investment in the country is not one that is attractive to potential investors.

In the interwar years the French attempted to irrigate the country lying north of the Niger a little way downstream of Ségou, where a deltaic fan of Pleistocene sediments provides some 5,000 square miles of gently sloping land. A barrage at Sansanding was completed in 1946 to raise the level of the Niger and divert the water along the Sahel and Macina channels, occupying the sites of old river distributaries that ceased to function long ago (Fig. 31). Villages and roads were built and Africans given plots of land, with the aim of growing cotton to supply the French textile industry as the Gezira supplied Lancashire. It was hoped to put 2 or 3 million acres under cultivation. Over £30 million have been spent on the scheme, but by the early sixties only about 100,000 acres were being cropped successfully. The soils are not as fertile as those of the Nile valley, nor are climatic conditions so favourable for cotton. The colonists who number about 30,000 are growing mainly rice for local consumption. The scheme relies on subsidies—and the cash might well be invested more profitably elsewhere in the country.

Less ambitious schemes designed to improve irrigation near the mainstream have been more successful and far less costly. The possibilities for such schemes in the future are very great. Downstream of the ancient delta the Niger flows across the gently sloping bed of a Pleistocene lake and splits up into several channels bordered by natural levees. When the river overflows its banks the water flows into the neighbouring depressions to form semi-permanent lakes alongside which crops of rice and grain are grown as the water recedes. Control works would allow much greater areas to be brought under cultivation.

There are some objections to such developments. The floodplains are very important dry-season grazing areas, and if the extension of arable land were to restrict the areas available to cattle at that time of year and block traditional routeways, the livestock economy of the areas would suffer severely. Another danger seemed to lie in the fact that the soils derived from dune sands near the lake margins might be eroded by the wind if the level of the water was to be lowered. This possibility has been investigated by Tricart whose geomorphological study has shown that the risks are negligible. Erosion is caused mainly by stock trampling down the vegetation, and as their numbers are likely to be reduced as the cropland expands, the danger of wind erosion should diminish. Furthermore, the

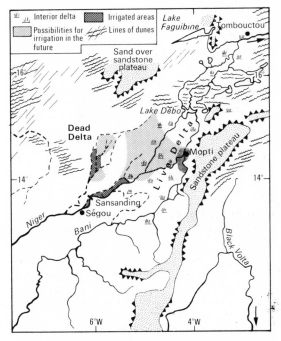

FIG. 31. *Irrigation from the Niger in Mali. The barrage raises the river water to a level at which it can flow along canals following old courses of the river running north towards the desert. Down-stream lies the seasonally flooded distributary system of the present day. Notice the lakes on the western side of the hills in the north-east, lying in hollows formed by the wind on the lee side of the hills when the climate was drier than now.*

lake-shores, which suffer most from trampling and erosion, are on the less erodible silts and, in any case, the new gardens would be protected from animals by fences which would serve to reduce the strength of the wind nearby and so prevent soil drifting.

The Niger is confined to a single channel to the east of Lake Faguibine and the old town of Tombouctou lies on the north side of the river, about 5 miles from its banks where the crossing is easier than in the swampy reaches further upstream. The town was once an important trading centre, where the nomads of the Sahara met the cultivators of the Sudan. It was also the goal of caravans bringing great blocks of salt 400 miles across the desert from Terhazza and Taoudenni, old lake beds in the northernmost corner of Mali, where the climate is so dry that the houses were built of salt. The mines were a source of wealth to the medieval empires of the Mandingoes and Songhai, and for a time the Songhai emperor lived at Tombouctou. Merchants from Cairo and Fez visited the town, and in 1513 Leo Africanus brought back glowing accounts of it to Europe. Its prosperity declined after its capture by the army of the Sultan of Morocco, and every European traveller who has gone there since Réné Caillié in 1828 has expressed his disappointment. Now a town of some 10,000 people, its importance is entirely local, a provincial headquarters and nothing more—save to the romantic (see p. 67).

For 250 miles east of Tombouctou the Niger flows across semi-desert country, a broad stream flashing back the sun and with a colourful fringe of green reeds and bare red dunes. The river level is highest in the early dry season and so the riverside land is readily irrigated for growing rice and cotton. Gao, one of the few old cities of the western Sudan that has retained some importance, is sited pleasantly on a curve of the river where trees overhang a waterside crowded with travellers and traders. Big dugout canoes are poled slowly upstream, and out in the middle of the river boys can be seen casting their nets from small dug-out canoes. Behind stand the brown, squarish mud houses of the town, the camel market, a comfortable hotel or two, and a mud pyramid marking the tomb of one of the last and greatest rulers of the Songhai empire.

Motor tracks by the river run south to Niamey and north to Bourem. The latter forks left to Tombouctou, right along the bed of the great wadi Tilemsi to the rugged hills of the Adrar of the Iforas and on across the empty stretches of the Tanezrouft to the wadi Saoura and Bechar on the far side of the Sahara. At least until the Algerian troubles, a fortnightly bus service operated in the winter between

Gao and Colomb Béchar, taking four or five days over the journey. Most travellers would prefer to travel by air, but the road crossing is a rewarding if strenuous experience. If current proposals to improve the road with outside assistance are put into effect, the overland journey may be shortened considerably. Tourists would certainly use the road and there might be some growth in the traffic of livestock, millet, dates, and petroleum.

Since most of Mali is free of tsetse-fly, livestock abound and large numbers of animals are exported to the Ivory Coast, Ghana, and Nigeria. In the riverine areas most of the stock is in the charge of Fulani, whose herds include cattle, sheep, and goats belonging to cultivators who have invested in this kind of stock—the Fulani acting as bankers. Camels and goats and cattle further north are mainly owned by Touareg. In recent years the Mali government has tripled the cattle tax to 8s. 6d. per head and has attempted to collect the full amount. The Touareg have responded by smuggling their cattle into Niger or Upper Volta to avoid the tax collectors and there have been uprisings amongst nomads in the Iforas hills.

Vast tracts in the north are uninhabited because of the shortage of water or fodder or both. The dune-covered area of the Majâbat al-Koubrâ which lies astride the frontier with Mauritania is the subject of a fine study by Th. Monod; its sub-title is *The Empty Quarter of the Sahara*.

The finest scenery in the country is probably given by the Palaeozoic sandstones that build the Hombori plateau and the Bandiagara escarpment within the loop of the Niger. The jointed rocks have been scoured by north-easterly winds in past dry periods, pagan villages huddle against the steep margins, and on the nearby plains, long parallel dunes, now fixed by vegetation, swing away from their usual NE.–SW. alignment to run parallel with an escarpment that deflected the dry winds of the desert past.

The wealth of the country appears to lie mainly in its livestock and the opportunities for developing irrigation. With the exception of rather unpromising deposits of gold in the south-west of the country, and some bauxite, its minerals are of little value. The male population has long been attracted by the better opportunities for wage labour in Senegal, the Ivory Coast, Ghana, and France, and in view of the limited prospects in Mali, this flow is likely to continue.

Politically the government aligned itself for a while with Ghana and Guinea and attempted to adopt socialistic methods of distribution and production. These were not very effective and in 1968 there was a *coup d'état* which has resulted in less government control of the economy.

MAURITANIA

Mauritania is almost entirely desert, and though comparable in area with Niger and Mali, its population is only half a million. Most of the people live in the extreme south near the Senegal river, where the rainfall is more than 10 inches and cultivation without irrigation is possible but precarious. The majority of the people are negro cultivators. Further north are the Moors—Arabs and Berbers who have interbred with negroes formerly their slaves. They vary in colour from fair to dark but usually refer to themselves as whites. They are pastoralists: cattle-owners in the south, camel-herders in the north. The people with any schooling number only a few thousand, but Mauritania is now an independent state, at least nominally, and is represented in the United Nations.

French influence in state affairs remains strong, for France has a very big financial stake in the country, its largest in Africa. Several tens of millions of pounds have been invested in the development of a very rich body of iron-ore in the hill ranges of Kedia d'Idjil near the south-east corner of the Spanish Sahara, believed to contain some 200 million tons of ore, almost pure haematite with an iron content of 63 per cent. Its exploitation has involved the construction of a mining town to house about 7,000 people at Fort Gouraud, which is supplied with water pumped from a depth of 130 feet. The ore is carried to the coast by diesel-electric trains on a specially constructed railway, built at very great expense. Because Spain was unwilling to co-operate, the line could not take the shortest route inland from Nouadhibou, but had to skirt the frontier and pass through a mile-long tunnel. It also traverses two belts of stabilized dunes and other stretches of active dunes (Fig. 32).

Mauritania benefits from the duty paid on the

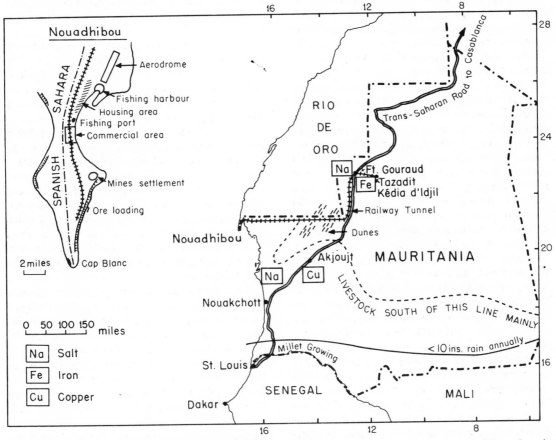

FIG. 32. *Mauritania and Nouadhibou (formerly Port Etienne). Mauritania's iron-ore is carried by rail to the coast for export from Nouadhibou. The capital is Nouakchott.*

101

goods imported in connexion with the mines, and its government's revenue mainly consists of a share in the profits from the project. Other indirect benefits include the construction of a new capital. Until 1957 the administration was based at St. Louis in Senegal. A new site for the capital of independent Mauritania was then chosen on the coast about 150 miles north of the Senegal river, at Nouakchott. This lies between the predominantly negro south and the more numerous Moorish population of the north and it is hoped that this choice for a site will help to prevent the country being divided between the two chief ethnic groups. In addition Nouakchott has the advantage of a climate less hot than most of the country, with cool northerly winds for much of the year.

The liveliest town in the country is Nouadhibou, a fishing port on the inner side of the peninsula of Cape Blanc, hard against Spanish Sahara. The frontier runs down the middle of the peninsula. Formerly, as Port Étienne, it had little contact with the rest of the country. Now it forms the ocean terminus of the iron-ore railway, where 7 million tons of ore are automatically loaded every year into ships supplying the hungry furnaces of western Europe and North America. The fishing fleet has benefited from greatly improved facilities. Formerly the fish were dried in the sun for export, and the whole town was pervaded with the smell; now there are plans to build refrigerators and canning factories. For fresh water the town used to depend on tankers and, later, on two plants distilling sea water; soon a piped supply will be provided, and there will be electricity too.

With these resources Mauritania will be in a healthier economic position than some of its neighbours to the east. Other resources are to be developed. The main trans-Saharan track from Dakar to Casablanca passes quite close to an important deposit of copper at Akjoujt. Although the deposits are on a much smaller scale than those in Katanga, the U.S.A., or Chile, about half a million tons of the metal are estimated to be available. In addition, the coast is part of a great sedimentary basin where the discovery of petroleum would not be very surprising.

How the people of the territory will react to becoming an economic appendage of industrial Europe remains to be seen. It will not be easy to prevent the pastoralists of the interior flocking into the towns if they so desire. A number of irrigation projects are planned for the southern districts, but development of the northern deserts presents a more difficult problem.

SENEGAL

Senegal is smaller, less arid, and somewhat less sparsely settled than the other countries of the Saharan borderland. The mean annual rainfall exceeds 10 inches over the whole country and reaches as many as 50 inches in the Casamance area south of Gambia.

The production of groundnuts, about three-quarters of a million tons annually, is greater than that of any other country in west Africa, with the exception in some years of Nigeria. Dakar is one of the greatest cities in intertropical Africa. In fact, groundnuts and Dakar dominate the economy of the country. While it was capital of the whole of French West Africa, Dakar's great size was reasonable, but since the individual territories became independent, and the Mali Federation broke up, the city tends to upset the balance of a small country which has a total population of less than 4 million. The near-exclusive reliance on groundnuts is also a more serious matter now that Senegal is no longer part of a larger and more varied economic unit.

This part of west Africa has been in close contact with France and other European countries for more than 250 years, trading with them in hides, ivory, gum, and wax, whereas the interior lands were not directly in touch with Europe until after 1890. Groundnuts were first introduced as a commercial crop about 1840. At that time, the French headquarters on the west coast were at St. Louis, on an island at the mouth of the Senegal river (Fig. 33). Shifting sandbanks hindered navigation, and in 1854 the greater possibilities of Dakar were recognized. Jetties were built there and in 1885 a railway was completed between the two towns. Almost immediately villages and towns sprang up along the line and the land nearby was planted with groundnuts. The French made Dakar a naval base and improved the port facilities, so that boats on the South African and South American runs made it a regular port of call; in 1924 the railway to Bamako was completed and Dakar became the outlet for the French Sudan as well as for Senegal. Extraction of oil from groundnuts increased, especially during the last war. As the nearest point in Africa to South America, Dakar's strategic importance in the war was considerable, and a large military aerodrome, for use by planes crossing the Atlantic, was constructed near the city. This later became an international airport. In addition, Dakar was the capital of all French West Africa. With these developments its population increased rapidly, from a few thousands at the beginning of the century to half a million in 1968.

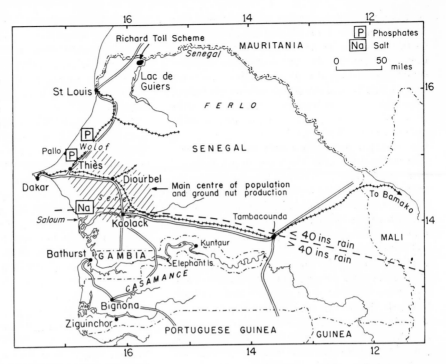

FIG. 33. *Senegal and Gambia. The most productive area in Senegal lies within a hundred miles of Dakar.*

Dakar has a larger European population, 38,000 in 1960, than any other city in west Africa; Frenchmen have been attracted by the opportunities for employment that existed in trade, constructional work and, under the colonial administration, in government service. It is quite close to France, and the climate, tempered by cool breezes from the Canaries current, is more pleasant than either the interior with its high temperatures and violent seasonal contrasts, or the west coast nearer the equator with its high humidity. Many of the Europeans live in the expensive residential area of Fann, overlooking a bay on the west side of Cape Verde peninsula; the port and industrial areas lie 2 or 3 miles away on the east, and between is the African sector of the city, gravely overcrowded with immigrants from the countryside (Fig. 34).

The capital of Senegal remained at St. Louis until the formation of the Mali Federation, by which time its population had grown to 60,000 and the town had spread from the island in the river over to the sandspit on the seaward side. As a port, St. Louis is now of little consequence, mainly because of the rapid extension southwards of the sandspit Langue de Barbarie at the mouth of the Senegal river. But the new town on the spit has become one of the largest fishing centres in west Africa. The coast north to Nouadhibou is one of the richest fishing grounds around Africa, with different kinds

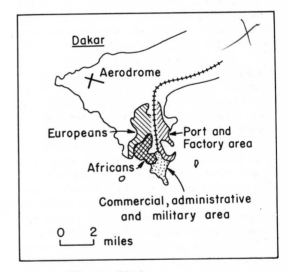

FIG. 34. *The site of Dakar.*

of fish appearing there in large quantities according to the season. The total catch exceeded 80,000 tons in 1963. Much is dried and exported to other parts of Africa; some fish are salted, the salt being obtained from saline swamps fringing the estuary of the Senegal river. With the construction of new refrigeration plants at St. Louis and Dakar, the outlook for the industry is bright.

The alluvial deposits and fixed dunes near the mouth of the Senegal river provide a record of the fluctuations of climate and of sea-level in this part of west Africa during the Pleistocene period; morphological maps of the region have been prepared to assist in planning agricultural development, for there is a very close relationship between the nature of the soils and the landforms in such areas of recent sedimentation.

One of the most important projects to be carried out in Senegal has been the Richard Toll scheme which has involved controlling the movement of water in a distributary of the Senegal river about 70 miles upstream of St. Louis. Floodwaters from the main stream flow along this distributary in September to fill the Lac de Guiers. A barrage was completed in 1948 which retains in the lake fresh water when the level of the Senegal river falls and prevents salt water entering in the dry season. This has allowed about 20 square miles of land north of the lake to be irrigated and produce about a ton of rice to the acre. As with many large irrigation schemes in west Africa the high costs of development, about £6 million up to 1962, have not been entirely justified and several smaller schemes in nearby areas which together yield a larger quantity of rice have been much less expensive. However Senegal's need for rice, which at present necessitates an annual import of 150,000 tons, is likely to lead to further expansion of the Richard Toll scheme.

South of the river, youthful dunes lie behind the smooth coast of Cayor, between St. Louis and Cape Verde. Behind these again are older dunes, running NE.-SW., formed in a past arid period. The wind-blown deposits obscure horizontally bedded Cretaceous and Tertiary marine sedimentary rocks, and few points rise more than 200 feet above sea-level. The sandy soils have been cleared of woodland and are now much impoverished, with overgrazing by Fulani herds and overfarming by Wolof groundnut cultivators. Much of the land that was brought under cultivation in the early days of the railway has been exhausted of its fertility and left abandoned. The Serer people living near the coast further south, in more humid country with somewhat heavier soils, are better farmers, applying animal manure to the land and preserving useful trees. Their careful methods were perhaps applied because they have long been short of land and so have been accustomed to treating the soil carefully.

The Saloum river appears to mark the southern limit of the old dune soils which are so well suited to groundnuts. The district around Kaolack, with a mean annual rainfall of 40 inches, accounts for about half Senegal's production. A large part of the crop is evacuated down the Saloum river, despite the fact that a bar at the river mouth limits navigation to ships drawing less than 11 feet of water, and despite the existence of a rail link to Dakar.

At the present time the country's economy depends very heavily on its enormous exports of groundnut oil. Improved varieties and the use of more fertilizers have been responsible for an increase in commercial production of groundnuts, but output varies according to the rains from 0·6 to 0·9 million tons (in shell). Other crops, such as millet, rice, beans, and market-garden produce have shown little progress, but it is hoped that improved tools and the adoption of fertilizers will soon begin to show results. At present the country is far from self-sufficient in food; in fact more foodstuffs are imported per head of population than almost anywhere else in Africa, largely to feed Dakar.

Mineral production is at present confined mainly to phosphates and common salt. Various phosphate deposits have been discovered in the last half century, but none of them appeared to be economically workable until those at Taiba were investigated in the 1950's. They lie about 70 miles north-east of Dakar, between the St. Louis-Dakar railway and the sea, and consist of a bed of phosphate about 20 feet thick, covered by an average thickness of about 60 feet of aeolian sands. The water-table lies only 30 or 40 feet below the surface and so floating bucket dredges are used to excavate the phosphate after the sterile sands have been stripped off by a giant dragline. The phosphate, mixed with water, is then piped to a factory where it is treated and enriched for export from Dakar. Other phosphate deposits are also being worked at Pallo nearer Thiès. Phosphate production in 1966, about a million tons, represented only 2 per cent. of world consumption, and was worth less than a tenth of Senegal's groundnuts. Salt comes from the saline flats in the estuary of the Saloum, about 50,000 tons being produced annually, for use locally and for export to other parts of west Africa.

Industrial development has mainly involved the crushing of groundnuts, almost the entire crop being treated before export. Processing developed in Senegal much more quickly than in Gambia and Nigeria, mainly because of private French investment in plant and the protected market available in north Africa. Cement and cotton factories are in production and it is expected that a large oil refinery and a fertilizer industry, based on local raw materials, will soon be operating. There are plans to take industries to other centres outside the Dakar region and to make the Bignona–Ziguinchor area south of Gambia a centre for textiles and fruit and vegetable canning.

The economy of Senegal has been harmed by the break-up of French West Africa and the Mali Federation but less seriously than might have been expected, and the country appears to be developing more rapidly than the bigger countries to the east. It has the advantages of a coastal position, a good system of communications, and perhaps most important, a large number of economically active people, with capital, living in Dakar.

GAMBIA

The indented outline of the coast stretching south-east of Cape Verde to Sierra Leone very strongly suggests that the land has sunk relative to the sea and that old river valleys have been drowned. This may help to explain the great depth of the Gambia river in comparison with the Senegal. It is certainly a much better waterway, and even in the dry season is tidal and navigable for 300 miles. Kuntaur can always be reached by ships drawing 17 feet of water, and if Gambia were to become a part of Senegal the river would no doubt be used much more than at present.

This natural and economic routeway was lost to Senegal, at least temporarily, by some agreement made a century or two ago, according to which the land stretching either side of the river was claimed by Britain. It is true that British merchants have been trading there for 300 years, but until the last decade or two of the nineteenth century, few people in Britain would have been troubled by its loss. Once the French had occupied the hinterland, however, the Gambia river became a potential bargaining counter in Britain's hands—though as it happened a counter that was never employed. In time the boundaries of the long riverside colony became important features of the environment, not merely customs barriers, but frontiers between the British and French ways of doing things. When the other west African territories gained their independence about 1960, Gambia remained a colonial problem-child, unwanted and expensive to support, but too small, it seemed, to be capable of looking after itself. The country has practically no valuable mineral resources, and although the possibility of oil being found cannot be ruled out, its future is likely to depend on agriculture. Its economy relies on groundnuts even more than that of Senegal. About 60,000 tons are exported annually; practically none are milled locally.

A fine set of maps of Gambia has been produced by the Directorate of Overseas Surveys in England from air photographs which give a good picture of the way in which the land is used. The majority of the people live in nucleated villages and hamlets situated on sandy plains that rise from alluvial flats bordering the river. Groundnuts, together with millet and sorghum, are grown mainly within a mile or two of the village centres, and for another mile or two around the villages savanna woodland has been cleared for fuel supplies and intermittent cultivation. Large areas are under rice, nearly all of it being grown in grass marshes near the Gambia river. Above Kuntaur, where the river is about a quarter of a mile wide, the grass swamps and rice fields stretch for about 2 miles on either side of the river. Further downstream, where salt water penetrates in the dry season, reed swamps lie close to the river and grass swamps near the bounding bluffs. From Elephant Island to the mouth for 93 miles, the river is flanked by mangrove swamps with grass marshes and paddy fields behind.

Rice is now the country's basic food, more important than millet, but there is still a shortage each year in the upper-river districts and inferior foreign rice has to be imported. Production could, no doubt, be increased, but the funds are lacking for equipment, and such funds as exist are needed for many other things. Roads are bad, ferries inefficient, and there is only a weekly freight and passenger service along the river. This whole country of 300,000 people was until recently served by only two doctors and two secondary schools. A third of the annual budget was expended on expatriate staff living mainly in the capital.

Bathurst, the capital, handles about 100,000 tons of cargo annually. Its harbour can accommodate ships of 20,000 tons and the water at the wharf is over 30 feet deep. It could take over the functions of Kaolack and Ziguinchor in Senegal and compete with Dakar for Mali's trade, but its hinterland is limited at present to the 4,000 square miles alongside the river and it remains a pleasant small town with a population of about 24,000.

Union with Senegal, which might appear to be inevitable, does not appeal to all the people and politicians of Gambia for they would find themselves a partly anglicized minority in a country that maintains closer ties with France than any other in tropical Africa. They would also cease to profit from smuggling goods into Senegal. Nor does Senegal appear to be anxious to absorb a neighbour which is not self-supporting and would not help at all to diversify its own economy.

8

West Africa

THE country lying between the Gulf of Guinea and the semi-arid lands bordering the Sahara is more heavily settled and more productive agriculturally than any other part of tropical Africa of similar size. It is relatively well watered, with moderate relief and a varied landscape. The dry interior is grain and cattle country; forestlands within 150 miles of the coast produce a variety of roots, tree crops, maize, and rice, and between these two zones lies a sparsely settled belt of savanna woodland, often referred to as the Middle Belt.

Political frontiers and lines of communication run inland from the coast, cutting across the latitudinal zones of climate, vegetation, and cropping. Consequently many of the countries within the region vary considerably from one end to the other and the railways and roads, originally built to develop overseas trade, link complementary areas and serve internal trade within each separate territory. Only Upper Volta is entirely cut off from the coast and depends on communications through neighbouring territories. In general, the individual countries are independent of their neighbours economically and their products compete on world markets. The value of Nigeria's trade with Ghana amounts to only about £1½ million annually, compared with £150 million with Britain; and Ghana's trade with Upper Volta, Togoland, and Ivory Coast adds up to only £8 million out of a total of £260 million. East-west movements of goods are not very important, but could develop in the future if communications improve. It is too late to develop a rail network and hopes are pinned on an international highway system for which plans were prepared in 1961. If it is to be put to full use, various restrictions at present in force for political reasons on the movement of people and commodities between the different countries will have to be relaxed.

All the countries are politically independent with the exception of Portuguese Guinea. They are divided by language and politics. The French-speaking territories form a single block, with Nigeria, Ghana, Liberia, and Sierra Leone forming English-speaking enclaves. To some degree political alignments have cut across the language divides; Ghana contrived to establish closer links with Mali and Guinea about 1959 within the framework of what was known as the Casablanca group of African states, which also included Morocco and Egypt. Nigeria, Liberia, and the Ivory Coast were the leaders of a less radical, loose organization of African states known as the Monrovia Group. These groups were disbanded in 1963 with the formation of the Organization of African Unity. Since then, proposals have been put forward for a free-trade area between Liberia, Guinea, Sierra Leone, and the Ivory Coast, and agreement was reached at a meeting in Dakar in 1967 on the aim of a west African common market. Niger, Nigeria, Chad, and Cameroon have set up the Chad Basin Commission to develop the lake and the surrounding lands, and representatives of Guinea, Mali, Mauritania, and Senegal have established an interstate committee to develop the Senegal river.

Hitherto political and economic groupings have proved to be ephemeral and their future is uncertain so they have not been used here as a basis for subdividing the region. Instead the long strip of west Africa is treated in three convenient chunks, consisting of the Federation of Nigeria in the east, the four countries looking to the south-west windward-coast, and the five countries between.

The Western Triangle

The coast of Liberia, Sierra Leone, Guinea, and Portuguese Guinea runs athwart the south-western, rain-bearing winds. Rainfall totals over the coastal plains reach 100 inches annually, and still more at Freetown and to the south-east. Most of the rain comes between May and October; early in the year, crops like cocoa and coffee can suffer from drought. South into Liberia the rains are spread over a longer period of the year, with a pause in late July or early August. To the north and in the lee of the Guinea highlands the rainfall is lower and confined to a shorter period of the year.

The cliffed coast of Liberia is prolonged by sandy barrier islands running north-west to Sherbro island; further north, wide creeks and low shores are bordered by mangrove swamps, or locally by fields of rice where the mangroves have been

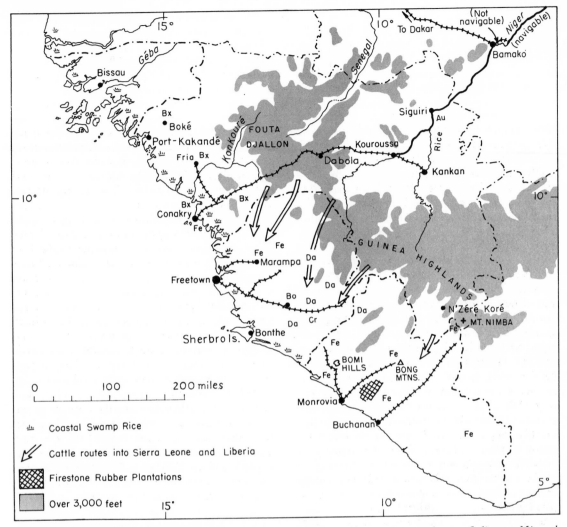

FIG. 35. *The western triangle of west Africa. The windward coast has a monsoonal type of climate. Minerals constitute the most valuable exports. Fe—iron, Bx—bauxite, Da—alluvial diamonds, Cr—chromite, Au—gold.*

cleared. Low coastal plains rising to about 200 feet are backed 50 miles inland by crystalline hills and plateaux. Further inland still, on the watershed between the coastal rivers and the Niger, ancient sandstones several hundreds of feet thick build the Fouta Djallon and dip gently west to the Atlantic coast. The steep margins of the Fouta Djallon are deeply dissected and difficult to traverse, but on the crests of the ranges great stretches of open grassy plains have attracted large numbers of Fulani well south of their usual ranges. Many of them, though still herding cattle, have settled down to cultivation. Their lands are not highly productive, for the soils of the high plateaux are poor with wide outcrops of lateritic ironstone. To the south-east, where the sandstone is lacking, steep-sided crystalline hills rise to more than 6,000 feet in the Nimba and Loma mountains. This entire highland zone is a considerable obstacle to communications between the coastlands and the interior of Guinea, a natural obstacle which the frontiers with Sierra Leone and Liberia accentuate (Fig. 35).

These countries, all rather small and poor, have benefited in recent years from the exploitation of their mineral resources, notably iron-ore. Government revenues have thereby been increased, and new railways built to export the ore have opened up the interior of Liberia and to a lesser degree Sierra Leone and Guinea. Agricultural production has made slow progress, industry is still negligible.

The peaks behind Freetown, where the thunder rumbles like a roaring lion, have given their name to the whole country though the hilly peninsula is very different from the mainland behind. Decaying villages with names like Leicester and Regent straggle along the forested slopes, and the surf breaks on shell sand beaches, where the sea is a clear pale green. For long the ocean-going vessels riding at anchor in the immense harbour formed by the estuary of the Sierra Leone river linked Freetown to the outside world more closely than the difficult trails across the neck of the peninsula tied it to the interior. The Creoles of Freetown had their own language; they were Christians descended from Africans of diverse origin, returned from the Americas or released from slave-boats. They had little in common with the Mende and Temne and the dozen other smaller tribes on the mainland. Houses in Freetown were built of brick, many of them with slate roofs. Fourah Bay College had been founded as early as 1827. The people of the Protectorate on the other hand were tribal, shifting cultivators, growing rice on the hills and clearing the forest by degrees until hardly any remains.

Trade until the end of the nineteenth century was mainly coastwise and along the lower courses of the rivers. Large boats with lateen sails, manned by Bulom sailors who had learned how to make the sails from the Portuguese, plied between the little coastal settlements. Bonthé on Sherbro Island was one of the largest towns a century ago, shipping to Britain rubber and fresh coconuts and piassava, the long stiff bristles from the raffia palm used for making brooms.

Sailing boat off Freetown.

The completion of the railway to Bo in 1889 brought Freetown's isolation to an end. Palm-oil and palm kernels collected from trees growing wild in the south-east of the country were railed to the coast for export, and later on cocoa and coffee also. For long, the ships taking them to England had to anchor offshore but recently Freetown harbour has been improved and even the bigger ships can now moor alongside the quay. But the character of the town has changed more radically, for so many immigrants have come in from the Protectorate, especially during and since the last war, that the Creoles now find themselves in a minority in the capital.

Agricultural production has failed to increase very rapidly and the railways, though only narrow-gauge lines, have never been supplied with enough traffic to make them pay. In recent years exports of palm-oil have ceased entirely, and in place of a rice surplus the country has been importing a million pounds worth or more each year from abroad. The remnants of high forest in the east and south-east have been constituted reserves and provide a steady supply of timber, but this is hardly enough to supply home requirements, and the small plantations are only beginning to yield additional small quantities. The majority of people in the interior are agriculturalists, still at the subsistence stage, growing rice and cassava in the south, and millet in the north. Yields are low, for the soils on the more heavily settled lowlands are derived from sandy schists and thoroughly leached by the intense rains, and the upland soils are not much better.

Goats, sheep, and poultry are quite numerous. Pigs are restricted to those parts of the country without a Muslim population. Tsetse-flies and lack of grazing restrict the number of cattle, and many of the chief tribes keeping them seldom slaughter beasts but use them as currency. Ndama cattle in the northern part of the country, which may number as many as 200,000 and have some resistance to trypanosomiasis, have suffered heavy losses from rinderpest.

The coastal peoples rely mainly on fish for supplies of protein. Nets and lines are used from dug-out canoes and the shore to catch bongo and other fish in the shallow coastal waters, and several privately owned trawlers supplement supplies from time to time. The fishing industry is largely in the hands of women traders who provide the capital required for nets and other equipment and arrange the drying, smoking, and sale of the fish. Dried bongo are traded up-country and there is a return trade in rice and tomatoes.

Pepel iron-ore loading pier, Sierra Leone. It runs out to sea for about half a mile and allows ships of up to 30,000 tons to be loaded at the rate of 2,000 tons per hour.

The best opportunities for agricultural development would appear to lie in the mangrove and grass swamps along the coast and the smaller areas of swamp land, called *boli*, on the valley floors of the interior. In the Scarcies estuary in the north, much of the mangrove swamp has been cleared for paddy and attempts have been made to introduce mechanized methods of cultivation. These have been only moderately successful, for labour supplies dropped off in the early 1950's when people were lured away to the diamond fields of the east, where anyone might have the luck to make a fortune in a few weeks. Now that the diamond diggings are less remunerative, the diggers—unwilling to go back to farming—are moving into Freetown.

The economy of Sierra Leone has come to depend increasingly on its mineral resources, above all iron-ore and diamonds. The iron-ore of the Marampa chieftancy situated on the crests of inselbergs rising from the coastal plains was mined as early as the 1930's, being carried down to the coast at Pepel on a railway built by the mining company. The higher-grade haematite is now worked out and most of the ore exported is powder ore from the underlying schists. Production has been running at about $1\frac{1}{2}$ to 2 million tons for several years. Other larger deposits are known to occur, of which the ore body forming the crest of Simbili mountain in Tonkolili district is the most important. Its exploitation would involve extending the Marampa line 100 miles further inland. Although the ore has an iron content of 56 per cent. it may be several years before

this deposit is worked, because other ore bodies elsewhere in west Africa are even richer.

Diamonds were first discovered in eastern Sierra Leone in 1930. They occur in layers of alluvial gravel a few feet thick underlying swamps and forming river terraces. The concession to work them was obtained by the Sierra Leone Selection Trust which paid an annual rent of £7,000 and a quarter of net profits to the government. Production was running at about half a million carats annually when, in the 1950's, native diggers found they could win diamonds too. To avoid taxes they smuggled their diamonds out of the country. Government revenue benefited indirectly from the increased sales of beer, tobacco, and motor cars, but the situation could not be allowed to continue. Eventually it was agreed that the Trust should relinquish its exclusive prospecting and mining rights, except for an area of 450 square miles where it had already proved or developed the ore reserves, while African miners were enabled to obtain leases to mine in certain areas totalling 9,500 square miles.

The Trust is intensifying production and has commenced deep mining operations at Yengema, working towards the kimberlite forming the main pipe from which the diamonds are believed to originate. The methods of the African miners are wasteful, a third to a half of the diamonds not being recovered. Total production, about $1\frac{1}{2}$ million carats worth over £20 million annually, of which the Trust is responsible for nearly a half, represents two-thirds of the country's exports. Since 1964

Guma dam, Sierra Leone. It holds four and a half million gallons to augment the water supply of Freetown and supply a 2·5 MW hydro-electric plant.

an increasing proportion of the diamonds mined by Africans has been smuggled out of the country instead of being sold through the government purchasing office, seriously undermining the economy.

A small diamond-polishing factory was established in 1966. It employs about 60 Sierra Leone workers and in 1967 processed about 20,000 carats of rough diamonds.

Chromite was mined in the 1950's about 180 miles up the railway line from Freetown. Production declined on account of falling world prices and ceased in 1963. Alluvial gold deposits are widespread in the eastern highlands, but the richer surface deposits are worked out and deeper ones have yet to be opened up. Bauxite has been found in the Mokanji hills and elsewhere in the central parts of the country and is being worked by a Swiss firm. The ore is hauled by road for 21 miles to Nitti Island and loaded into lighters which convey it several miles downstream to sea-going ore carriers in the Sherbro river. Mining of rutile, required in the manufacture of paint, glass, and light metals, has started in the Mogbwemo area of the south-east. Production is expected to reach 100,000 tons

annually in the late sixties and shipment will also be from Nitti Island.

Development plans look forward to improvements in communications and power supplies which may allow more use to be made of mineral resources such as the bauxite. Efforts are also being made to encourage tourism. A good deal is to be spent on education; at present only about half the students at Fourah Bay College are Sierra Leoneans, the local secondary schools being unable to supply enough students reaching the necessary standard for entry. In agriculture, reliance is being placed on the further development of swamp rice cultivation, and on oil palm and other plantations employing a large labour force and relatively little capital.

GUINEA

The Republic of Guinea, which occupies about half the western triangle, is much bigger and more varied than Sierra Leone, but its population is scarcely larger. Its resources include important ore bodies, conveniently near the coast, and abundant water power.

The country is divided into three parts, the highlands of Fouta Djallon separating savanna plains in upper Guinea from coastal lowlands. The highlands are the home of Ndama cattle, a breed resistant to trypanosomiasis. The valleys of the south-western slopes are well settled, with many orange, coffee, and pineapple plantations on the hill-slopes, and irrigated bananas in the valley bottoms. Many of the plantations were established by Europeans. Productive forest country on the north side of the highlands extends far to the east. In recent years the construction of a road from N'Zérékoré in Upper Guinea to Monrovia has resulted in big increases in the export of palm kernels and coffee from that area, and an agreement made with the iron-ore mining company, Lamco, provides for the carriage of produce along the new railway to Buchanan.

While the highlands are inhabited by Peuls, the name given to Fulani and people with whom they have intermarried, the interior plains in the head-waters of the Niger are occupied by Malinke. The majority of both these Sudan zone peoples are Muslims, though Islam has been diluted a good deal by its transmission through the Berbers with their saint cults, and on account of the persistence of fetish beliefs and practices.

The opportunities for agricultural expansion in the interior would seem to be very considerable, for the climate is suitable for rice growing, and flood control works would allow vast areas bordering the

Niger and its tributaries to be irrigated for rice. But the people are not enthusiastic farmers. In the early days of the French occupation many of the Malinke were attracted by the chances of getting rich quickly by collecting rubber, hunting elephant, and digging for gold. The rubber and ivory were soon exhausted and the ancient gold-mines that supplied the trans-Saharan trade are not very rewarding these days. Many people lost the desire to work in the fields and now emigrate for long or short periods, to find work in Senegal, Sierra Leone, or Conakry with the result that the Guinean interior remains under-developed.

Conakry and the adjoining area is the most productive part of the country. The capital and chief port, it resembles Freetown in standing on the end of a rocky peninsula with quite deep water close to the shore. The dunite rocks of the Kaloum peninsula have weathered in such a way as to concentrate the iron content of the original rock into a residual deposit containing more than 50 per cent. iron, a hard surface layer 10 to 20 feet thick overlying softer ore. The workable deposits can be quarried over an area of several square miles, all within a few miles of the port. Production is highly mechanized, with equipment enabling a ship to be loaded with 10,000 tons of ore in 10 hours. Less than a thousand Europeans and Africans are employed on the workings. Production, little more than half a million tons in 1966, could easily be multiplied several times within a few years. Other richer deposits of ore occurring in the Nimba and Simandou mountains near the frontier with Liberia will probably be exploited by means of the railway being constructed to evacuate the ore on the Liberian side of the mountains to the coast at Lower-Buchanan.

Bauxite formations very favourably situated for export are at present Guinea's most valuable resource. Shipments from the Los Islands began in 1952. A large deposit about 80 miles north of Conakry is being worked by an international consortium, FRIA, which includes U.S., French, British, and Swiss interests. Local water power is used for converting the ore to alumina, half a million tons of which is exported annually to Europe, North America, and Douala in the Cameroon Republic (p. 163). The biggest deposits, amongst the richest in the world, are near Boké, 120 miles north of Conakry. An American firm has obtained the concession which provides for an eventual export of 3 million tons of bauxite and 200,000 tons of alumina. The bauxite will be carried by rail to Port-Kakandé on the coast.

A French plan to develop electricity from the Konkouré river in eastern Guinea may be carried out by the Russians. Two dams would provide for a generating capacity of 1,720 MW, enough to manufacture 150,000 tons of aluminium metal each year, plus chemicals.

The ultimate value to Guinea of its mineral resources depends largely on the nature of the agreements made with the foreign concessionaires and on the way in which the government invests the proceeds. The mines and plants are so highly mechanized that the number of jobs open to local people is small. The construction of hydroelectric plants such as that planned for the Konkouré river should provide some basis for industrial growth in the Conakry area, but how long it will be before such developments take place depends on a number of imponderables. Several other sites for power-stations and aluminium smelters occur along the west African coast and for several years after independence investors were put off by political uncertainties in Guinea. Industrial growth is hampered, as in Sierra Leone, by the poverty and small size of the local market. Factories making furniture, cement and shoes, canning fish and pineapples, and milling rice contribute a small amount to the Guinean economy, and in 1965 a large textile factory, which at first will use American raw cotton, was completed near Conakry. In the future Conakry could become the industrial centre for this part of west Africa, but much depends on trade barriers between Guinea and its neighbours being reduced, and on the efficiency of its nationalized concerns.

PORTUGUESE GUINEA

Lying between Senegal and Guinea, Portuguese Guinea is a small country about half the size of Sierra Leone or one-third that of Portugal. On the low, laterite-covered plateaux of the interior, Mandingo and Fulani people herd cattle and grow millet and groundnuts. The coastlands are more humid and varied in character. The inhabitants are animists and Christians, not Muslims, belonging to a number of tribes of which the Balante are the most important. They are a hard-working people who have cleared great stretches of mangroves around the highly indented coastland and up the lower courses of the Géba and Cacheu rivers. From the air the seaward parts of the country present a multi-coloured picture, with wide, dull-green rivers meandering down to an island-studded ocean, the shores of the coastal creeks bordered with networks of bright-green paddy fields, and red-brown soils on the higher ground sparsely wooded with coconut, oil-palm, and savanna trees. It is a country of hamlets and villages. Bissau, the capital, is the only town of any size; most of the older Portuguese settlements are decaying. There is no railway and few good roads, and transport is mainly by means of the numerous watercourses.

LIBERIA

Liberia, about one-third larger than Sierra Leone, has a smaller population, only about $1\frac{1}{2}$ to 2 million spread over 43,000 square miles. The people of the capital, Monrovia, are like those of Freetown, the descendants of negro slaves who had lived for some time in America and were returned to Africa in the first half of the nineteenth century. Until about 1920 they had very little contact with the tribal interior. Then a colonial system of administration was introduced on the British pattern, with elected native chiefs answerable to provincial and district commissioners appointed by the central government in Monrovia. It was not a very efficient system and quite wide areas remained unadministered and unfriendly to the government until the 1940's. Road construction in later years improved access to the interior; but many tribes still remain little affected by the new administrative centres. The native people continue to refer to the Liberians of Monrovia as Americans, while many of the Monrovians regard themselves as quite distinct from the natives. They form a black-settler minority dominating the country, about 2,000 American Liberian families controlling the Liberian government and economy.

Monrovia, thanks to American activity during and after the war, has a deep-water harbour and modern docks, a fine airfield, and large public buildings. At present it is the only free port on the west African coast; merchandise can be unloaded and stored there for re-export without duty being paid and it is steadily growing in importance as a distribution centre for west Africa as a whole.

Broad, well-surfaced highways have been pushed into the interior, capable of carrying far more traffic than will be available for many years. The country inland is more hilly than near the coast, and from the air is seen to form a patchwork of high forest and clearings. Most of the people are still subsistence cultivators, growing hill rice on fields they crop for a few years, and then moving on. The villages are small, usually consisting of some 30 to 100 circular huts grouped round an open space. Few feeder roads have been built and where villages have been linked to Monrovia, the result in many cases has been to reduce rather than increase production of crops for

sale; the best land along the new highways being bought up by Monrovians. As for the villagers, many have been put to work on the new plantations and few have gained much from the change.

The money economy of the country depends mainly on foreign enterprise in two fields, iron-ore and rubber. The rubber plantations were started by the American Firestone Company in the 1930's, and until 1950 rubber constituted about 90 per cent. of the country's exports. Most of it comes from Harbel about 50 miles inland from Monrovia where some 12 million trees are planted over about 100,000 acres—the biggest rubber plantation in the world. Yields are good, as much as 1,400 lb. of dry rubber per acre, and fertility is being maintained. Although wages are not high, the standards of living for the workers on the foreign plantations are much better than those of the ordinary population, with hospitals and schools available to them. Rubber is also produced on smaller plantations owned by Liberians. This is processed and exported by the Firestone organization.

The exploitation of Liberia's iron-ore is a much more recent development, for the first shipments of ore did not take place until 1951. The early workings were in the sparsely settled Bomi Hills about 45 miles north of Monrovia where a main band of high-grade magnetite (68 per cent. iron) is surrounded by 200 million tons of lower grade ore. The railway built from Monrovia to the Bomi Hills by the American company mining the ore has been extended 50 miles to the Mano river where other deposits have been mined since 1961. Another new railway has been constructed from Monrovia to the Bong Hills. Here the ore is treated before export to convert it into a pellet form ready for immediate use in the blast furnaces of the United States and Europe. By far the largest iron-ore project in Africa is the Mount Nimba mine at an altitude of about 4,000 feet near the Guinean border. The ore is carried down the hill-side on a conveyor belt 2 miles long and is then railed 170 miles to the coast at Lower-Buchanan. The iron content of the ore is 60 to 70 per cent. and it is estimated that after 1968 about 10 million tons will be produced annually. The project, which involved the investment of £100 million, includes a harbour at Lower-Buchanan accommodating 45,000 ton ore-carriers. Eventually this port may be the site of a steelworks supplying the west African region.

Although the economy of Liberia is growing very quickly, in the sense that the value of goods produced is increasing at a rate of 15 per cent. annually, nearly all this is in the form of iron-ore, exported to

Europe and North America. Exports reached the huge total of 20 million tons in 1967. Up to 50 per cent. of the profits are paid to the Liberian government, and the opportunities for investment in capital equipment of various kinds would appear to be good. At present, however, it appears that government funds are not being applied in a manner that will increase the productivity of the country as a whole, mainly because the black settler families in Monrovia remain in charge of the government of the country and operate it for their own benefit instead of for the good of the whole of Liberia. In thirty or forty years time the iron-ore will have been worked out, the rubber plantations may no longer be able to meet the competition from synthetic material, and the country may have little to show for the loss of its mineral wealth.

The Middle of West Africa

Ghana and the territories grouped round it form a much larger block than the western triangle. With the exception of the Nimba mountains in the extreme west and isolated hills in the Togo ranges, the entire area lies below 2,000 feet. Rainfall totals exceed 100 inches in the south-west of Ghana and the south-west of the Ivory Coast, and drop below 30 inches in Upper Volta and near the Volta delta.

The dry zone along the coast between Takoradi and Cotonou, with mean annual rainfall totals on the Accra plains dropping locally to about 20 inches, is the most striking feature of the climatic pattern. In this coastal strip, low woodland and open grassland lie between the sea and the rain and deciduous forests on the dissected uplands further inland. Air photographs show woody thickets aligned in patches and strips running SSW. to NNE. in many flat areas, and it seems likely that this pattern is the result of grass fires being driven in a NNE. direction by the sea breezes of the dry season.

Although the natural vegetation was originally denser than we see it now, accounts of eighteenth-century travellers indicate that the dry-zone country even at that time was already rather open. The fact that European traders found conditions more congenial than along the coasts further east and west may help to explain the large number of forts constructed there by Portuguese, Dutch, British, and Danish companies. Most of them persist to this day, and are well cared for by the Ghana government.

An entirely satisfactory explanation for the low rainfall along the coastal strip has yet to be produced. It is noteworthy that the rainy season develops normally until June, by which time the intertropical convergence has moved well to the north and the winds get round to the WSW., blowing parallel to this part of the coast. Under these conditions surface water might be drifted offshore, allowing cool water to well up from some depth quite near in, thereby preventing the development of instability and of a second rainfall peak such as the Guinea coast to the east and west normally experiences.

The continental shelf all along the Ivory and Gold coasts is very narrow, the sea-bed plunging down 12,000 feet and more within 50 miles of the shore. Palaeozoic and later sedimentary rocks in the coastal zone are faulted and dip seawards, and quite severe earthquake shocks occur from time to time. These phenomena point to crustal instability which is possibly associated with downwarping of the coast towards the ocean deeps. Volcanism is absent, except for the possibility that Lake Bosumtwi in southern Ghana may lie in a caldera of some kind. Its origin is uncertain and a meteor impact has been given as an alternative explanation.

The coast of the Gulf of Guinea hereabouts is arranged in two shallow arcs symmetrically disposed about Cape Three Points in western Ghana. Along the western sectors of both arcs, ancient folded rocks run SSW. to meet the coast almost at right angles, giving low cliffs and headlands. Beach material moves generally towards the east. This movement may be related to the Guinea current which flows eastward with a speed of about one knot for most of the year and with twice that speed between May and July. But the transport of sand, which is mainly involved, is more probably caused by waves approaching the coast from slightly west of south causing longshore drift. East of Fresco and again east of the Volta delta, Mesozoic and Tertiary rocks fringe the coast. Sandy barrier beaches, which accumulated along these stretches at different times in the latter part of the Quaternary period, separate long and, locally, quite deep lagoons from the sea.

Along these shores, both cliffed and sandy, there are no deep, natural harbours. Until artificial harbours were constructed in the last forty years ships of any size were forced to anchor some distance offshore for loading and unloading, surf boats carrying the cargo between ship and shore. The names of the early commodities are preserved in the names given to the coast from west to east; the Ivory, Gold, and Slave coasts. With the need to build up stocks over a considerable period, forts and warehouses were built and people along this

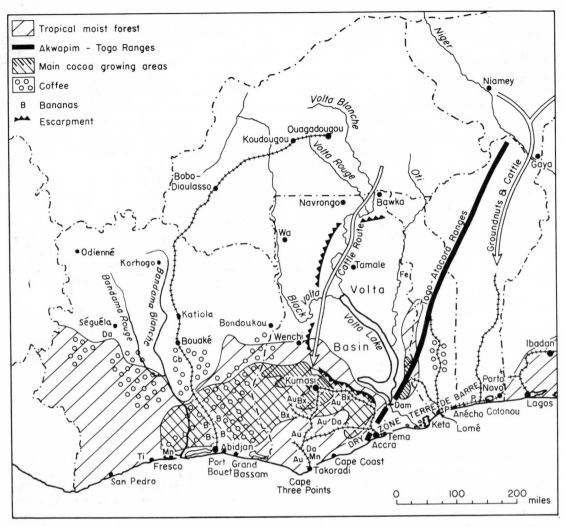

FIG. 36. *The middle of west Africa. The most productive areas lie within a radius of 250 miles of Cape Three Points.* Au—gold, Da—alluvial diamonds, Mn—manganese, Bx—bauxite, Fe—iron, P—phosphates, Cb—columbite, Ti—titanium.

coast have been in quite close touch with Europeans for three centuries and more.

Penetration inland was limited by the lack of navigable rivers; rapids on the Volta prevented even the small ships that could cross the bar at the mouth from sailing more than about 50 miles upstream. Now conditions have been transformed by the artificial harbours constructed first at Takoradi then at Abidjan, where a canal was dug across the barrier beach sand bar, and lately at Tema, 20 miles east of Accra. Lomé, Cotonou, and some other ports continue to trade on a considerable scale, but most of the old ones have reverted to fishing villages (Fig. 36).

As in the western triangle, where similar crystalline rocks occur, gold and diamonds are present, particularly in Ghana. Iron-ore plays a much less important part in the economy, and bauxite is being exploited on only a modest scale. The money economy of the Ivory Coast and Ghana is underpinned by coffee and cocoa, the value of which in the area as a whole far exceeds that of all other exports put together. World prices fluctuate violently, but these crops provide a sounder basis for development than iron-ore, because the proceeds remain in the producer countries. The Ivory Coast and Ghana are two of the most prosperous countries in the tropical world.

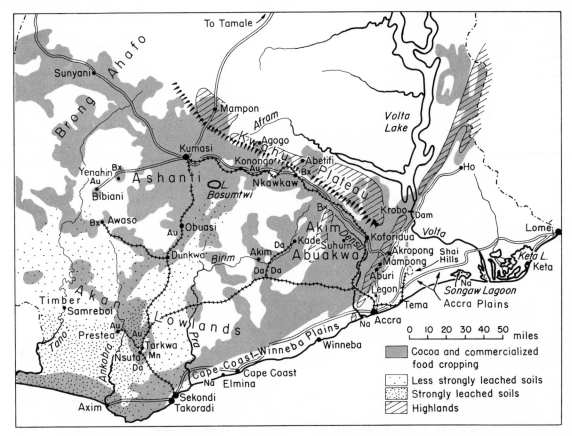

FIG. 37. *Southern Ghana. Au—gold, Da—alluvial diamonds, Bx—bauxite, Na—salt (from sea water).*

GHANA

Ghana can be divided into two contrasting areas by drawing lines across the map NW. and NNE. from the Volta dam. These lines correspond very roughly with both the southern margin of Palaeozoic rocks underlying the Volta basin and the northern limit of high forest. The south-western part of the country and the sliver of territory running north from the Volta delta, on the east are on the whole much more productive than the remainder, and they are likely to remain so. The south produces the cocoa on which the national economy depends, and also most of the timber, minerals, and manufactured goods (Fig. 37).

Early development

The first railway was built inland from Sekondi to serve the gold-mines at Tarkwa. Until its completion in 1901 cargo was taken up the winding Ankobra river (Ankobra means serpent) by surf boats from Axim and then headloaded 20 miles to the mines. The western line was soon extended to new gold-mines at Obuasi and in 1903 reached

Kumasi. By this time the first cocoa plantations were being established inland of Accra by the Akwapim people, at first on their own hill-sides and later in the sparsely settled forests west of the Densu river in Akim Abuakwa. The construction of another railway line in the east, from Accra towards Kumasi, allowed the crop to be evacuated easily to Accra for export. Thus the foundations of the country's economy and relative prosperity were laid in the decades on either side of 1900 when the railways to Kumasi were completed, the gold-mines were opened up and most important, tens of millions of cocoa-trees were planted every year.

The expansion of the land under cocoa in the Akim Abuakwa area has only been described at all fully in quite recent years, Hill and others having traced the process from maps prepared by the Gold Coast Department of Agriculture which show the ownership of cocoa farms in areas devastated by swollen-shoot disease. The pioneer farmers involved were the villagers of Akwapim and their neighbours from the Accra plains, the Shai and Krobo who used

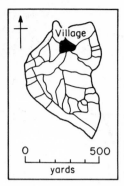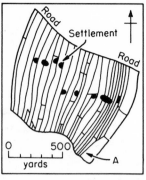

FIG. 38. *Field systems in southern Ghana.* a. *A nucleated settlement surrounded by a patchwork pattern of smallholdings making up a matrilineal family land of about 54 acres.* b. *A typical* huza *settlement pattern covering nearly 200 acres. Company land belonging to the patrilineal Shai has been divided into strips and each farmer has a house on his strip.* (*Taken from J. M. Hunter, 'Cocoa migration and patterns of land ownership in the Densu valley, near Suhum, Ghana',* Trans. Inst. British Geographers, *No. 33, 1963, pp. 74 and 80.*)

to dwell on hills not far from the site of the Volta dam, and the Ga and Adangbe whose homeland is near the coast. These stranger-farmers, as members of syndicates or family groups, bought land in the uninhabited forest west of the Akwapim hills and divided up the plots they purchased into strips varying in width according to the contribution of each individual member. Each farmer planted cocoa in his strip, doing the work himself or hiring labourers. These ribbon plots still persist (Fig. 38).

By 1911 exports of cocoa had risen to 40,000 tons annually, most of it coming from the country within a radius of 50 miles to the north-west of Accra. Since that time Ghana has remained the world's largest cocoa producer. Many of the migrant farmers grew rich; they invested their money in new farms ever further to the north-west, built large houses in their hometowns on and near the Akwapims, and paid for the education of their children. Cocoa-trees were planted at that time in all the forest land of southern Ghana; but in areas too dry, too infertile, or badly drained the crop failed, and gradually the main producing areas became established and recognized.

The period following the First World War was one of unprecedented prosperity in the country. Hundreds of miles of roads were built. People moved away from their houses in search of tillable land. Lorries carried cocoa down to the coast, not only from the old farms in the south-east but also from new ones established by immigrant and local farmers in Ashanti. From the railway joining Sekondi and Kumasi a branch line was constructed eastwards to Kade. A new harbour was opened in 1928 at Takoradi, a little to the west of Sekondi, and it immediately became the chief port. Equally important, Achimota College was instituted near Accra, and from this sprang the University of Ghana, which now occupies a fine hill site at Legon a little to the east of Achimota.

Cocoa

In the slump of the thirties, cocoa prices fell sharply and production declined. The decline was partly the result of lower prices but various diseases were also beginning to take effect. Swollen shoot was one of them. It was not until the forties that its seriousness was recognized and by that time a very large part of the oldest cocoa-growing area around Koforidua was infected with the disease, a virus transmitted by a mealie bug. Attempts were made to control swollen shoot by cutting out infected trees and, in spite of a good deal of opposition to the programme in the late forties, 100 million trees had been cut out by 1961. Cutting out still appears to be the most effective way of dealing with the disease. In the newer cocoa areas of Ashanti, infected trees were cut out in good time, and swollen shoot has not yet gained a firm grip. Since 1942 the region within 25 miles of Kumasi has been the main source of cocoa, but the danger of swollen shoot spreading there cannot be disregarded.

When prices of cocoa rose to very high levels in the early fifties, at times exceeding £500 per ton, cocoa production did not respond. There were too many old trees; planting had dropped off because of the low prices in the thirties and forties and other diseases besides swollen shoot, such as capsid bug and black pod, affected yields very seriously. Nevertheless, the economy of the Gold Coast was greatly strengthened by the rise in the income from cocoa and the Marketing Board, established during the war with the aim of stabilizing prices for the producer, accumulated very large surpluses. It has been complained since then that these funds were invested in London when the value of sterling was declining so that the Gold Coast did not obtain full benefit from them. The fact remains that these big sterling balances, under the control of the local government, were of considerable importance in allowing the country to feel it could be independent of Britain economically as well as politically.

Ghana's development plans envisaged cocoa production rising to 450,000 tons by 1970. In 1960–1

Takoradi Harbour, Ghana. Extensions to the wharf in recent years have allowed the volume of export and import cargoes handled to increase from one to three million tons.

exports were about 423,000 tons, about twice the early post-war figures, and the 1964–5 crop reached 600,000 tons. This rapid increase seems to have been due to new plantations coming into bearing and, above all, to the success of spraying against capsid and other diseases. However, it may not be easy to maintain this level of production, for yields decline after trees reach the age of 25 or 30 and quite a high proportion of the suitable land is already planted. Over half the production now comes from Ashanti and Brong-Ahafo. The area under cocoa has been spreading into the western forests, but the coastal sectors where much of the free land remains have a very high rainfall, especially in the months of May and June, and the soils seem to be too thoroughly leached of plant nutrients to be suitable for the crop. A good deal depends on experiments with new strains and fertilizer treatments at the Cocoa Research Station, Tafo. Attempts are also being made to re-establish strains resistant to swollen shoot in the devastated areas of the east, but it is not certain that cocoa can be established successfully on land that has already supported one crop. Meanwhile, the price of cocoa on world markets in 1965 fell disastrously to little more than its 1945 price, £100 per ton, and Ghana's income from the crop, in spite of a doubling of production, was no more than in the early fifties. Since then prices have risen again. In 1964 and 1968 the cocoa harvest was spoiled locally and transport to the coast interrupted as a result of unusually heavy rains in the producing areas. Supplies to the world market fell below demand and prices climbed sharply.

The Achiasi-Kotoku railway, Ghana. This line, 51 miles long, was driven through dense forest, bush, and swamp in 1954–6 and halves the rail journey between Accra and Takoradi. Notice the deeply weathered layer exposed in the cutting.

The forest landscape

Most of the forest region of Ghana behind the strip of coastal savanna consists of a mosaic of cocoa plantations, food farms, and secondary regrowth. The cocoa-trees are not planted in orderly rows but in scattered patches of a few acres, under the shade of large forest trees, with crops like yams, plantains, and peppers growing alongside and dense tangles of young trees and creepers engulfing recently farmed plots. The tarmac road from Accra to Kumasi, running parallel to the sandstone Voltaian escarpment, switchbacks up and down ridges and valleys developed on the crystalline schists and granites. The bush on either side appears to be sparsely populated—superficially quite untamed and it is not unusual to find a diversion where a giant tree, uprooted in a storm, has fallen across the road. The villages are nearly all tucked away in the forest and are approached by paths and tracks leading off the main roads.

Timber

The main source of timber is in the west, not in the rain forest near the coast where the majority of the trees on the leached soils are too spindly for timber, but further inland where the rainfall is not excessive in any part of the year and the number of massive timber trees is much greater. Production increased rapidly after the last war but levelled off in the sixties at 30 million cu. ft. Nearly 90 per cent. is exported, mostly from Takoradi. At one time only mahoganies were in demand but now many trees formerly of little value find a ready market. A soft white wood called *obeche*, or *wawa* in Ghana, coming from the rather abundant *Triplochiton scleroxylon* comprises two-thirds of the logs exported. About a half of the timber by value is still exported in the form of great cylindrical logs, but sawmills and plywood factories have been established by British and American firms, the biggest being at Samreboi. Ghanaian craftsmen and small factories are producing handsome furniture to traditional and modern patterns and the woodwork in the University of Ghana at Legon beautifully exhibits the value of local timber.

Of the 15,000 square miles of high forest that remain, about one-third is in forest reserves. These should continue to yield a steady supply of timber in the future, but it is unlikely that the present high rates of production of mahogany and certain other trees can be maintained indefinitely. As the timber contractors drive their roads into the unreserved forests and fell the big trees, they are followed, or too often preceded, by farmers planting food crops and cocoa. The forest is disappearing.

Minerals

Economic minerals occur mainly in the forest zone, in Birrimian rocks outcropping south-west of the Voltaian sediments. Gold, long won by primitive methods from alluvial deposits, is mined underground and Ghana is about sixth in order of gold-producing countries. The future profitability of the industry depends mainly on financial conditions, the world price for gold, the relative value of Ghanaian currency, taxation, and labour costs.

From the top of one of the steep hills overlooking the railway near Tarkwa one looks down on the pit-head gear of gold-mines to the north and west. Nearby are neat villages for the workers and pleasant bungalows for the senior staff. A few miles to the south appear the raw, red, benched hill-sides where manganese is quarried at Nsuta. The ore is rich, with a 50 per cent. metal content, and the output in 1965 was worth nearly £4·7 million, about half that of gold. The manganese ore is railed to Takoradi and loaded into the ships by a special conveyor.

From the road leading south to Takoradi, African diamond diggers can be seen at work on the floor of the Bonsa valley, sinking shallow pits through the fine alluvium to diamond-bearing gravels underneath. Several hundred labourers are employed there. The main diamond fields lie to the north-east in the Birim valley where European companies work more extensive alluvial formations systematically, using machinery and a smaller labour force. All Ghanaian diamonds are, unfortunately, of the small kind used for industrial purposes. Exports in 1965 were worth £6·8 million.

Bauxite is mined near Awaso, to which a branch line was constructed from Dunkwa in the last war, and 336,000 tons were exported in 1966. The bauxite occurs on the flat top of a hill, probably the remnant of an ancient planation surface. Other bauxite formations are known in comparable positions at Yenahin, Ejuanema, and Alewa.

Industry and the Volta dam

Industrial growth in Ghana is beginning to make an impression. Several factories processing or semi-processing local primary products such as timber and cocoa have been in existence for some years. Fruit juices are made for local consumption. Beer, tobacco, matches, and the usual assemblage of miscellaneous consumer goods such as plastics and textiles are manufactured or finished using local and imported materials. Bread and other foodstuffs are prepared, both in large-scale plants and by individual women. Cloths are woven in traditional patterns, notably the brilliantly coloured and rather expensive Kente cloth.

Most of the industrial activity is concentrated in the Accra area which provides the largest single market in the country and which, since the com-

Ambassador Hotel, Accra, Ghana. West Africa's first luxury hotel.

pletion of Tema harbour about 1960, is in a good position for importing and exporting raw materials and manufactures. Accra and Tema are being planned as a single city, with Accra retaining its administrative, commercial, and educational importance while Tema becomes the chief port and industrial centre. Factories producing margarine, plastics, aluminium, household ware, and a number of other goods have been built as well as an oil refinery capable of handling a million tons of petroleum annually and a small steel plant that depends on local supplies of scrap.

Abundant cheap power is available from the Akosombo dam about 50 miles north of Tema. About a third of the electricity produced is consumed in an aluminium smelter which has been constructed by a consortium of aluminium companies under the name VALCO. Alumina is imported from America and after processing at Tema the aluminium ingots are exported to America and West Germany; production is running at about 100,000 tons annually. The company pays the Ghana government £2½ million each year for electricity, enough to cover the interest payments on the loans for Akosombo dam. At a later stage Ghanaian bauxite may be used, but this would involve the building of another expensive plant.

It is planned to export electricity from Akosombo to Ghana's neighbours to the east, Togo and Dahomey. When the Ghanaian economy gains strength once more no doubt there will be further industrial expansion in the Accra–Tema area and elsewhere in the country, making use of the power from the Volta.

On the plains between the Volta delta and the Akwapim ranges there is no lack of room for more people. In fact the landscape is much more typical of the Sahelian zone in the neighbourhood of Lake Chad than of an equatorial coast, with big herds of cattle, many of them in the charge of Fulani herdsmen wandering over open grassy plains. Great stretches of deeply cracking black clays derived from the old basic gneisses are scarcely cultivated at all. Rising from the plains are massive inselbergs, the Shai and Krobo hills, which have long been deserted by the tribes whose names they bear. They have moved north-west into the more fertile rain forest lands.

Agricultural development

Accra and the other large towns in Ghana depend for their food supplies mainly on lorries bringing regular supplies of yams, cassava, and fruit from the high-forest region and the savanna lands lying within a hundred miles of the forest limits. Dried fish are carried down to Kumasi from the Niger bend. Cattle trek down to Accra from Nigeria through Togo, and about 200,000 cattle plus sheep and goats that cross the northern frontier annually from Upper Volta and Mali are brought down to Kumasi by lorry. Flour, fish, meat, and various frozen and tinned foodstuffs are imported from overseas.

In order to conserve foreign exchange, reduce the price of food for the growing urban population, and absorb the unemployed, the Nkrumah administration set up State Farms. Large tracts of forest and savanna were cleared, using machinery from Russia and a number of other countries. These enterprises lost money and produced very little food and many of them have been abandoned.

Proposals have been made in recent years that parts of the Accra plains should be irrigated from the Volta lake. American consultants to the Ghana government consider that 440,000 acres are suitable for such development and have proposed large-scale mechanized schemes for producing sugar, vegetables, fruit, and rice. Irrigating a rolling erosional plain is more difficult than dealing with an alluvial plain, and the risks are likely to be considerable because of the problems presented by the relief and soils. Whatever the outcome, the bulk of agricultural production in Ghana will remain in the hands of African capitalist smallholders for many years to come.

Fisheries

Fishing in the sea and lagoons is traditionally the main source of income for certain coastal peoples, notably the Ewe who have migrated west from their home-towns on the sandbar at the seaward margin of the Volta delta and are now to be found all along the coast as far west as Abidjan. They use dug-out canoes purchased from forest people living 50 miles or more inland. Nylon nets have come into general use, the smaller ones made in Ghana, the larger ones imported, and many of the dug-outs are now fitted with outboard motors, greatly increasing their radius of action. Special harbour facilities are being provided for the boats at a number of ports.

Marketing of fish is being modernized. A government Corporation was set up in 1961 which was intended to organize the distribution of fish throughout the country from cold stores situated at strategic centres. Privately owned concerns and individual traders continue to handle a large proportion of the catch which is bought from the fishermen by local women, often the fishermen's wives, who smoke it in simple wood-fired ovens or salt it.

The Fishing Corporation had five vessels in 1964 which caught about 7,000 tons of fish annually. It is intended to expand the size of the fishing fleet and also to increase the efficiency of the traditional craft. In 1965 motorized fishing vessels numbered 355 of which 182 had an over-all length below 32 feet. They were operating from natural havens at Ada, Apam, and Axim, and from artificial harbours at Tema, Elmina, and Takoradi. The continental shelf is narrow and there are some signs that catches by the traditional canoes could be reduced by the larger craft coming into use. However, the opportunities for the expansion of deep-sea fishing are still considerable.

The coastal lagoons and Volta delta

The coastal lagoons are the outcome of the submergence and drowning of small river valleys followed by the accumulation of barrier beaches across their mouths which are liable to be broken through by the river floods during the rains. Some of them provide fish, others salt. The main source of salt used to be Keta lagoon in the Volta delta, but in recent years the water in the lagoon has been much deeper because of higher rainfall totals in its catchment, and the salt has not crystallized out. The unfortunate town of Keta has suffered trebly; there has been no salt, the town has been flooded by the lagoon and on the seaward side the waves have swept away schools, a hospital, and houses. Many of the people are moving south to a broader part of the sandbar nearer Cape St. Paul. But there is one compensation for them; the lagoon fishing has prospered.

One of the most striking features of this densely settled Ewe area, between Keta and Anloga, is the intensive production of shallots, maize, and other vegetables grown in irrigated plots carefully sited at the edge of the Keta lagoon, and in long narrow hollows between low ridges building the sandy foreland of Cape St. Paul. Watered from shallow wells, manured with crop residues, fish manure, and bat dung, and producing as many as three crops a year, this land must be more productive than almost any in Africa. Much of the produce is taken to Accra for sale, the lorries travelling 130 miles along tarmac roads and crossing the Volta at the head of the delta by a modern ferry, soon to be replaced by a bridge.

A little to the west of Accra, the Densu river has almost filled the lagoon at its mouth with silt forming a wide, flat evaporating basin. A salt works has been established by a Lebanese firm, salt water being pumped over the sandbar from the sea and into a series of basins where its salinity progressively increases. About 20,000 tons of salt are produced here annually and this, together with a smaller quantity obtained at Elmina in a similar fashion, goes far towards making the country self-sufficient in this commodity. Salt could probably be got from other lagoons and an export trade developed.

The expanding city of Accra has encircled the Korli lagoon alongside which the early settlement grew up. The lagoon, which takes much of the waste from the town and frequently flooded the lower parts, has been deepened and given a new outfall to the sea, and land reclaimed from the lagoon is being used for factory buildings. Future expansion of the city is planned to be eastwards towards Tema.

The Volta basin

Tall deciduous forest climbing the scarp of the Voltaian sandstones between Koforidua and Wenchi advances 10 to 30 miles north-east across the watershed formed by the Kwahu plateau. Many of the early mission stations were established on the plateau because of the pleasant scenery and relatively cool climate, and the schools of Abetifi, Agogo, and Mampon continue to have a considerable reputation.

In the extreme south of the plateau, the Krobo employ a method of acquiring land called the *huza* system, which seems to have been a precursor of the arrangement by which land was purchased by groups planting cocoa. The *huza* or tract of land bought by a company is divided into strips running away from a footpath along one side of the purchase; settlement is dispersed, houses associated with each strip being strung along the footpath or a stream frontage (see Fig. 38*b* for a similar type of Shai pattern). The Krobos have the reputation of being the best farmers in Ghana. Certainly they produce great quantities of yams and palm-oil for sale in Accra and other centres. Their main market is Asesewa from which numerous lorries carry away the local produce to Koforidua and Accra every Monday and Friday.

Within the arms of the V formed by the Kwahu plateau and the Togo ranges lie plains and low plateaux, mainly at 300 to 500 feet, excavated in the gentle structural basin of Voltaian sandstones and shales. The basin is shaped like a leaf, with the tributaries of the Volta forming the smaller veins and the man-made lake an asymmetrically placed main vein. Most of the country is sparsely settled savanna woodland. Only 70,000 people were displaced by the lake, an average of about twenty to the square mile and most of them lived in the south by the Afram and Pawmpawm rivers. The thin soils are underlain by sandstone or lateritic ironstone, tsetse-fly abound, river blindness affects a great many people, and communications are poor.

It will be interesting to see how far the lake will change conditions. At first it will disrupt communications, but new roads avoiding it are to be constructed from Accra to Tamale and it is hoped that eventually the lake will provide a useful waterway, by which cattle can be carried to the south, tourists to the north. It might produce more than 10,000 tons of fish annually, but tall trees, some projecting above the surface, are likely to hinder fishing and navigation for many years. The seasonal rise and fall of the lake will also create difficulties. On the other hand, the fluctuations of level may allow several thousands of acres along the shores to be irrigated for rice-growing. Apart from the Volta lake, the region has other possibilities, ranching for example. But the difficulties of the environment are considerable, as they are throughout the middle belt of west Africa to which the basin belongs.

Kumasi

Kumasi, founded in the decades around 1700, was the capital of the Ashanti confederacy and the seat of its ruler, the Asantehene. It lay on one of the subsidiary routes of trans-Saharan traders and in 1820 was estimated to have a population of 15,000 to 20,000. Since the completion of the railway to Sekondi it has grown steadily and is now second only to Accra, a vigorous commercial city of some 250,000 people serving the chief cocoa-producing areas of the country in Brong Ahafo and Ashanti, and as a distribution centre for the whole of northern Ghana. Industries connected with timber are well established, and new industries such as the manufacture of beer, soft drinks, and jute bags are springing up. About half the people are Christian and about one-quarter Muslim; half are Ashanti, the other half belong to tribes from other parts of Ghana and other parts of west Africa. The University on the outskirts of the town concentrates on scientific and technical studies.

Northern Ghana

The general level of the crystalline rocks west of the Voltaian sandstones rises from about 200 feet near the coast to about 800 feet at Kumasi and remains within a couple of hundred feet of that altitude right up to the far north of Ghana and into Upper Volta.

North of Wenchi, where the scarp face of the Voltaian sandstones fades out, population densities on the crystallines are no greater than in the Volta basin to the east. North of latitude 10° N., however, settlement quite suddenly becomes much denser, particularly in the Kusasi and Frafra country overlooked by the Gambaga escarpment in the northeast and also around Lawra in the north-west. Numbers exceed 100 to the square mile and locally, near Bolgatanga, 200 to the square mile.

The pattern of settlement is characteristically dispersed. The people live in large compounds, each consisting of several neatly constructed round mud houses, arranged in a circle and linked by walls to give one or more central courtyards. Such a compound, holding about a dozen people, is set in the middle of the family holding, and is separated from its nearest neighbour by a distance of about 100 yards—a bowshot distance, it is said.

The main crops are guineacorn and millet. Yields are rather low, for though the land is cropped every year, farmyard manure and household wastes are applied only to about one acre in ten. Nearly every year many people in the area are short of food from March to June, and although maize and yams are imported from the south, many are unable to afford to buy them and have to make do with beans from the dawdawa and shea trees and other wild produce. Groundnuts and poultry are exported by lorry to Kumasi and, from the north-west, large numbers of cattle are sold to the south. Most of the stock are exported during the early rains when fewer animals are entering Ghana from Mali and Upper Volta and local stock-owners want money to buy food and seed.

While the population contrives to increase, the area under cultivation appears to be shrinking as people retire from the wooded river margins where river blindness has incapacitated large numbers. It is not surprising that immigration to the south is growing.

The country around Navrongo, Bolgatanga, and Bawku has been constituted a Land Planning Area in an attempt to improve rural conditions. Contour bunds have been laid out to reduce erosion and earth dams constructed to irrigate vegetables and rice, and provide water for domestic use and stock. Tomatoes are being grown on the irrigated plots and canned at Bolgatanga. A factory nearby produces corned beef and frozen meat for carriage south

in refrigerated vans. It depends on imported cattle. Opportunities for increasing output from this heavily settled and rather isolated region are limited; many of the young people who will have to move out are unwilling to farm and so it is particularly important that they should be trained to read and write. At present most of the school buildings in the north are quite inadequate and considerable difficulty is being experienced in persuading teachers from the south to teach in the north, living there amongst a strange people with whom they have very little in common.

The Akan, Ewe, Ga, and other peoples of southern Ghana differ from each other in language, customs, and political sympathies and differ much more from the Dagomba, Frafra, and other northern tribes. Under the old colonial régime each group was able to exercise a degree of autonomy, but under the strongly centralized administration of President Nkrumah, an attempt was made to obliterate tribal differences in order to build a new nation in Ghana owing allegiance to the Ghanaian state not to the tribe and traditional ruler. A break was made with the past, and the attention of the people was directed towards a future modern, industrialized Ghana. In 1966 the President was ousted and it remains to be seen how far tribalism has been rejected.

IVORY COAST

The Ivory Coast resembles Ghana in many ways, having the same latitudinal extent, but it has a larger area and smaller population. The coasts of the two countries are morphologically similar, but Ivory Coast is much wetter and rain forest there comes right down to the sea. This difference helps to explain why contact with Europe was delayed until the late nineteenth century, by which time Gold Coast's castles were already old. Amongst the most advanced, populous, and productive parts of the country are the eastern deciduous high-forest lands which came under Ashanti influence in the eighteenth and nineteenth centuries. West of the Bandama river, there are no signs of the former existence of any organized state, in fact the people of the sparsely settled south-west were notorious as cannibals.

The main coastal towns are situated on lagoons and sandbars in the east. Port Bouet, for example, which was the ocean terminus of the railway for many years, stands on a sandbar, and Abidjan, the capital, is on the landward side of a lagoon. Since the end of the last war, the Vridi canal has been cut through the sandbar separating Abidjan's lagoon from the sea, and ships drawing 30 feet of water can now tie up alongside. Port Bouet and Grand Bassam, a former capital, have been unable to compete with Abidjan and have fallen into deep decay. Now unrivalled, Abidjan is a thriving city. Its population rose from 46,000 in 1946 to 400,000 in 1968. Some 20,000 of the inhabitants are from France.

Exports from Abidjan give a good impression of the main features of the Ivory Coast's money economy. About one-half by volume consists of timber, mostly in the form of logs, though the proportion of sawn timber increases as bigger mills are constructed. Logs from the great forests near the coast are floated down the lower courses of the rivers to the three lagoons, Grand-Lahan, Ebrie, and Aby, which have been dredged to provide a protected waterway running a hundred miles either side of the port. The forest area exceeds that of Ghana and the timber industry has grown at a phenomenal pace in recent years. In 1965 over 100 million cu. ft. were produced, most of which was exported to Common Market countries, notably the German Federal Republic. There is an urgent need for forest conservation.

The most valuable export from the Ivory Coast is coffee, most of which is grown by African small-holders. The quality is high, but it seems unlikely that the quantity produced by the Ivory Coast can continue to increase. By 1966 exports had reached about 180,000 tons, but the total output was 268,000 tons, and in spite of the Ivory Coast's special relationship with the Common Market, difficulty was experienced in disposing of stocks. In 1968 several thousands of tons of surplus coffee were burned. Prospects for cocoa are a little better. The crop, which is mainly grown by local farmers, though there are several European estates, was not grown on a large scale until the 1920's. Production having been static for many years, as in Ghana, has risen rapidly in the sixties and cocoa could replace coffee as the main cash crop. Exports fell from a record 102,700 tons in 1962–3 to 88,000 tons in 1963–4.

The two other main export crops are bananas and kola. The bananas are grown mainly within a hundred miles of Abidjan to ensure rapid shipment to Europe. French plantations are numerous and an increasing number of Africans have been growing bananas for sale. Production was stimulated in the late fifties when France bought fewer bananas from independent Guinea, and the Common Market relationship gave Ivory Coast an advantage over most alternative suppliers. Figures for the kola trade are uncertain, but it appears that some 20,000 tons are exported annually to Mali, Upper Volta, and Senegal; in 1960 they were worth about £3 million, the same as banana exports. Large areas are being planted with oil palms with the intention of increasing oil production to 135,000 tons by 1975.

Although mineralized Birrimian rocks outcrop widely, mining is much less important than in Ghana. Gold output is negligible. Diamonds are mined near Katiola and Séguéla, with thousands of native diggers attracted to the diamond fields as in Sierra Leone. According to official statistics, diamond production increased from 7,000 carats in 1948 to 184,000 carats in 1966, but these figures are not reliable because of the concealment of diamonds mined locally and smuggling of stones from Guinea and Liberia. The biggest mining concern in the country, which started operations in 1960, is exploiting very large manganese deposits a few miles inland of Grand-Lahou. The ore is carried by road to the creek port and then by large barges along the lagoon to Vridi. Exports, expected to level out at about 100,000 tons annually, reached 245,000 tons in 1966.

The industrial sector of the economy is growing rapidly under the impetus of foreign private investment; the value of industrial production was £34 million in 1964 and the annual growth rate exceeds 25 per cent. The textile industry is the largest in operation. This is centred at Abidjan and most of the factories producing paint, pesticides, veneers and plywood, and assembling cars, radios, and bicycles are also in the capital. Power is provided by generating stations on the Bia river which supply almost 90 per cent. of the country's present consumption of electricity. Bouaké, the second largest town in Ivory Coast with a population of 150,000, and the only other industrial centre, has a textile mill, sisal, and tobacco factories.

Most of the people of Ivory Coast live in the east of the high-forest zone. Like other people in the same zone they rely for food on yams, plantains, maize, and rice. Production of cassava seems to be increasing and cocoyams decreasing, trends which are typical of the zone and probably responses to the growing urban population with a consequent emphasis on crops which are easily preserved. The main source of protein is fish. About 45,000 tons are caught annually, probably more than in Ghana. The completion of the Vridi Canal allowed a modern fishing harbour to be constructed at Abidjan, and by 1961 a fleet of fifty motor vessels was based there supplying three tuna fish canneries. Cattle are brought down from the north; in part they come from the Korhogo and Odienné areas of north-west Ivory Coast where about a quarter of a million cattle, many of them of the Ndama breed, are kept by Malinke people. The majority of the 80,000 head of cattle and 150,000 goats and sheep imported annually come from Mali and Upper Volta.

The Ivory Coast is one of the most prosperous of the former French territories. Under the colonial régime the country formed a part of the federation of French West African states and had to contribute towards the support of weaker brethren. It has continued to subsidize Upper Volta, Niger, and Dahomey to some extent, but more of the territorial revenue can now be invested internally. The Ivory Coast government has received financial assistance in various forms from France with which close ties have been maintained. Private enterprise, mainly French, is strong. Relations with Ghana, pursuing a more independent political line have been strained. The situation has not been eased by the fact that cocoa from Ghana finds its way across the frontier in considerable quantities when producer prices are higher in Ivory Coast. Road communications between the two countries are not good, being confined to a highway from Kumasi to Bondoukou, but they may improve with better relations following the departure of Nkrumah from Ghana.

In 1965 an agreement was announced with the United Nations Special Fund for economic and social development in the far west of the Ivory Coast where it is planned to build a deep-water port at San Pedro, 60 miles from the Liberian frontier, and to construct a road–rail network. Diversification of export crops is also being attempted and efforts are to be made to develop the relatively poor north by expansion of rice and cotton production.

UPPER VOLTA

Upper Volta is entirely landlocked, for the headwaters of the Volta are no use for navigation, and the nearby reaches of the Niger are equally valueless for exporting produce. Ghana lies on the direct route to the coast, and more than half Upper Volta's external trade is with that country. Most of the rest is with the Ivory Coast, Ouagadougou the capital of Upper Volta being linked by rail to Abidjan.

Upper Volta belongs to the Sudan zone, and like other parts of that zone to the east and west it is rather heavily settled, with population densities exceeding 100 to the square mile locally, a high figure in view of the fact that the rainfall is only 20–45 inches annually and the soils are not very fertile. Ghana, though smaller, has twice as many people as Upper Volta and far greater agricultural and mineral resources.

It has long been evident that Upper Volta could not be self-supporting economically and, for this reason the greater part of the colony was attached by the French to the Ivory Coast in 1932, the rest being divided between the French Sudan and Niger Territory. But the Mossi people of Upper Volta form a well-organized, cohesive tribal group, and after the last war they prevailed upon the French to reconstitute the colony. It has since become a precariously independent state.

Half the total population of 3 million belong to the Mossi nation, which seems to have sprung from a number of different tribes that were united about the eleventh century under a conquering aristocracy. They remained animists and withstood the pressure from the Islamic Mandingo and Songhai empires of the fifteenth and sixteenth centuries. Probably at this time, they congregated for defence in the vicinity of Koudougou and Ouagadougou, and this would help to explain the dense population round these towns at the present day. Both Muslim and Roman Catholic missionaries are now gaining many converts amongst the Mossi, especially in the main towns, and the cohesion of the nation is being undermined by the large-scale emigration of its menfolk to the more prosperous countries on the Guinea coast.

With the exception of Bobo-Dioulasso, which was for long the terminus of the railway, and Ouagadougou the capital, there are few towns of any size. Most of the people live in villages, spaced at intervals of 10 miles or more, or alternatively in large compounds scattered through the countryside. Baobab and shea-butter trees, both of which yield useful fruits and nuts, are scattered through fields of millet and sorghum, and between the villages herds of cattle wander through acacia woodland. Groundnuts are cultivated in the south-west, the most productive part of the country, and some 10,000 to 20,000 tons are exported annually through Abidjan. Fulani herdsmen graze their cattle mainly on the tsetse-free pastures of the drier north, and there is a considerable export of livestock to Ghana and the Ivory Coast. The cattle are driven to check points on the frontier for inspection and if necessary quarantine and inoculation, before being allowed to proceed to the south. Traders from Upper Volta seem to retain the organization of the lorry transport to Kumasi and other southern towns in their own hands.

Upper Volta exports labourers as well as livestock to the cocoa farmers of the forestlands. Tens of thousands, possibly as many as a quarter of a million, leave the heavily settled districts every year, some on foot, some by lorry. After months or in some cases years they return home with new clothes, or it may be a bicycle or sewing-machine. About half a million are believed to be living more or less permanently in Ghana and a lesser number in the Ivory Coast. The migration has given rise to a new type of commercial activity along the routes followed; the preparation and sale by women of rice, millet balls, and food cakes. As the economy of the Guinea coastlands gains momentum and the interior stagnates, more and more northerners are attracted south.

Upper Volta would probably benefit from closer association with one or other of its more prosperous neighbours. Ghana would probably be most satisfactory commercially, but an attempt to create a customs union between the two ran into difficulties. Historically, Upper Volta's links are closer with the rest of French-speaking Africa. Furthermore, the railway to the coast runs through Ivory Coast, and although Ghana once had plans to build a railway with Russian assistance from Kumasi to Ouagadougou, it will be some years at least before these come to fruition.

TOGO AND DAHOMEY

These two countries stretching inland for 300 or 400 miles from narrow frontages on the lagoon and sandbar coast of the Gulf of Guinea are two of the most striking examples of the irrationality of African state formation. Togo is the remnant of a German colony; Dahomey was a French one. They lie side by side, squeezed between much bigger and more prosperous neighbours, with the Ewe in southern Togo cut off from their brothers in Ghana to the west and Yoruba in Dahomey separated from their kin in Nigeria to the east. Neither country is big enough to be economically self-supporting and both have relied on grants from France.

The climate and vegetation are less varied than the considerable latitudinal extent would lead one to expect, for the southern parts lie within the coastal dry zone and the rainfall inland is scarcely great enough to support high forest except on the Togo ranges where annual totals locally exceed 50 inches.

The hill ranges extending NNE. from the trans-Volta region of Ghana, reach their maximum width and altitude in western Togo, and continue into northern Dahomey. Though deeply dissected they are fairly well settled and well wooded. The greater part of both countries consists of planed-off crystalline rocks covered by savanna woodland with some forested residual hills rising above the general level. Near the coast, Tertiary sandstones and clays give rise to upland country reaching about 300 feet above the sea. This is called *La Terre de Barre*, the word *barre* being derived from the Portuguese word *barro* meaning clay (Fig. 36). The red loamy soils are similar to the Benin Sands of southern Nigeria, and are likewise covered by oil-palm woodland and farms growing maize, cassava, sweet potatoes, and beans.

Rivers cutting across the *terre de barre* flow into lagoons which are linked to the sea through only two gaps, one to the east of Grand Popo and the other at Cotonou. There are no good natural harbours, and but for the political frontier, southern Dahomey would fall within the hinterland of Lagos and Apapa. But Dahomey must have its own port to handle traffic from the Niger Republic as well as its own meagre trade, and so the new harbour of Benin has been constructed near Cotonou, where the railway from Pobé and the main line from the north reach the sea. The capital is Porto Novo founded by the Portuguese in the seventeenth century, and linked by the Ouémé lagoon to Lagos (Fig. 4).

The coast of Togo is very short, for the Dahomey frontier swings about 12 miles west from Grand Popo, so that Anecho, the site of an early European trading settlement, is only 2 miles from the frontier. On the other side Lomé, the capital, is only 2 miles from Ghana (Fig. 36).

The people of the main coastal towns include the descendants of slaves returned from Brazil, and as a result, some of the larger buildings are in the Portuguese style. In Togo, some of the old people can still speak German and some of the early German churches and other buildings still survive. Outside the towns the people depend mainly on fishing and gardening. Because of the lack of big trees inland, the fishing boats have to be imported from Ghana and Nigeria, to which many of the fishermen are accustomed to migrate seasonally unless prevented by political conditions. The fishing villages are in the shade of coconut plantations, most of which were established early in this century with German encouragement. Near Anecho, where population densities locally reach 400 to the square mile, gardens similar to those near Keta in Ghana are cultivated in the same intensive fashion; the farmers specializing in raising maize and vegetables for sale.

The most important commercial development in recent years has been the exploitation of the phosphate deposits at Akoumapé in Togo, only a dozen miles from the sea. Some 100 million tons of 80 per cent. ore are believed to be available, occurring in late Tertiary sediments as a layer 10 to 20 feet thick. Exports began in 1961. The ore is concentrated at Kpémé and then taken to the ships by conveyor belt along a new pier, nearly a mile long, going out beyond the breakers. Production is expected to reach about 1 million tons annually, and the value of the phosphates will be about equal that of all other Togo exports put together. But, of course, the investment comes mainly from outside the country; the Togo government owns only 20 per cent. of the capital and only about 500 Togolese are employed, so the country does not greatly profit from the mines.

Apart from the phosphates, the main source of income for both countries lies in their oil-palms. Plantations in Dahomey were originally established by the kings of Dahomey and Porto Novo who happened to have large numbers of slaves on their hands when the slave trade was interrupted in the mid-nineteenth century and put them to work planting trees. The plantations are well laid out, mainly on the *terre de barre* but also further north, and are highly productive.

The central areas are poor and, for the most part, sparsely settled compared with the south. However, a number of villages at the foot of the Togo ranges are surrounded by cocoa and coffee plantations in valleys running up into the hills. In the Lama–Kara area, where the Kabré people took refuge from invading Gurma, population densities reach 600 to the square mile locally. The basic rocks give better soils than those round about, and the Kabré farm them very carefully. Stone banks prevent erosion, animals are stall-fed, and the tiny fields are manured. The land has acquired a cash value and is rented and sold. The extreme north-west of Togo is, like the adjacent parts of Ghana, another well-settled area, with population densities of more than 100 to the square mile. Here again the explanation appears to lie in tribal history, for the Moba, once a powerful people, were forced to concentrate in a smaller area than they formerly occupied as a result of pressure from neighbouring tribes.

Nigeria

Nigeria is easily the biggest country on the coast of Upper Guinea, and its population of some 55.6 million, according to an untrustworthy 1963 census, is greater than that of all the other west African territories put together. The Northern Region alone, as it was then, with nearly 30 million, had more people than any other African state, and both the East 12.4 million and West 10.3 million were more populous than, for example, Ghana.

Regionalization was introduced after the Second World War in recognition of the fact that the majority of the people belong to one or other of three main tribal groups, Hausa in the north, Ibo in the south-east, and Yoruba in the south-west. The Northern Region corresponded with the Protectorate of Northern Nigeria which had been governed as a territory separate from the rest of the country until the First World War. What had been the Protectorate of Southern Nigeria was divided along the Niger into East and West. The federal government in Lagos was responsible for foreign affairs, customs, defence, control of the banking system, railways, and trunk roads; it shared control of agriculture and police with regional governments; other matters such as local government and schools were in the hands of the regions.

None of the regions formed a homogeneous ethnic unit. Within all three there was considerable diversity of language and religion. The most striking internal division was between the Muslim and non-Muslim peoples of the North. The Muslims in the North are mainly Hausa, Fulani, and Kanuri of the older Emirates in the Sudan zone; the non-Muslims belong to smaller tribal groups in the Middle Belt, many of which have been ruled for several decades by Muslim chiefs. From time to time movements had gathered strength in support of a separate Middle Belt Region, but such a region would have been so diverse and feeble in comparison with the others as to be in constant danger of fission and its economic foundations would have been weak. In the south-west of the Middle Belt most of the people near Ilorin are Muslim Yorubas, having strong links with their kin further south, while the Tiv in the south-east have resented interference from the northerners and have always been anxious to manage their own affairs.

The East was comparatively well knit with Ibos forming about 75 per cent. of the population, Ibibio, 11 per cent. almost entirely confined to the Ikot Ekpene-Calabar area in the south-east corner, and most of the rest Ijaw and Idoma. A relatively dense network of roads, a widespread enthusiasm for education, and rapidly growing towns all tended to promote greater uniformity throughout the region.

The Western Region was the richest part of Nigeria. The Yoruba in the west grow cocoa and have a standard of living similar to that of southern Ghana. The Edo and Ibo people further east were and still are more dependent on palm produce, rubber, and timber.

In 1958 the British Government appointed the Willink Commission to examine the wishes of the tribal groups forming important minorities within all three regions and at the end of the Inquiry advised that independence for Nigeria would be delayed if the aspirations of all the minorities were to be ascertained to determine whether new regions should be created. Nigerian nationalists were in a hurry, and when independence came in 1960 Nigeria still consisted of Northern, Eastern, and Western Regions, within each of which government was in the hands of a political party based on the dominant tribe of the core area.

Social and economic development in independent Nigeria was uneven, the central areas of the regions tending to be favoured and receiving more investment funds than peripheral areas. The minority leaders were dissatisfied and felt insecure. During a constitutional crisis in the Western Region the Edo, Itsekiri, Urhobo, and Ibo peoples of the Old Benin Empire broke away, following a referendum, to form the Midwest Region. Rivalry and tension continued between the 'Big North' and the much smaller, but richer southern regions. The regions came to operate more and more as independent states leading to much duplication in economic development and competition rather than interdependence in all fields. Census counts in 1962 and 1963 were generally believed to have been wildly inaccurate, with each region exaggerating its own numbers to get more representatives in the federal parliament and a greater share of the national budget. Public dissatisfaction with the politicians reached a peak when an election in the Western Region was blatantly rigged and eventually, early in 1966, the army forcibly removed regional and federal governments.

The Ministers and army officers killed in the coup were mostly Yoruba, Hausa, and Fulani. The head of the new military government, Ironsi, was an Ibo and so were most of his advisers. The suspicions and fears of the non-Ibos were aroused when it was said that appointments and promotions in the Civil Service would be based on merit and, soon after he announced that Nigeria was to be a unitary state, Ironsi was killed and replaced by a non-Muslim northerner, Gowon, as the result of another military coup. Subsequently, hundreds of Ibos living in several towns of northern Nigeria were attacked and killed by northern soldiers and civilians. The survivors fled back to the East and Ibos living in other parts of Nigeria also returned to their homeland. The Eastern Region government proceeded to dissociate itself for most purposes from the rest of the Federation.

In mid-1967, the federal government proposed to divide Nigeria into twelve states. Iboland was to become the East Central State, deprived of the oil-rich coastlands and Port Harcourt by the new Rivers State, populated mainly by Ijaw. The Eastern Region government under Ojukwu responded by declaring its independence as the Republic of Biafra. Efforts made by the federal military government in Lagos to prevent the secession of the East led to civil war which continued into 1970. As federal troops slowly advanced, the Ibos retired into the very densely settled Ibo heartland around Orlu and there was much loss of life mainly as a result of the disruption of trade and the shortage of food in the south-east of the country.

Physical diversity

Nigeria is on the whole less than 3,000 feet above sea-level, higher ground being mainly confined to the Jos plateau in the centre, and highlands along the frontier with Cameroon. As a result of the low relief, the zoning of the climate, vegetation, and crops from south to north is remarkably regular.

From the creeks and mangrove swamps of the delta and lagoon coast, with rainfall totals of about 100 inches, the level rises gradually inland and Tertiary and Cretaceous sedimentary rocks give rise to yellow and red sandy soils. The rock strata dipping towards the coast thicken to reach depths of as much as 7 or 8 miles offshore. Under the delta they are faulted and folded as a result of gravitational sliding towards the ocean during deposition and have entrapped great reservoirs of oil and gas. Drilling is taking place in several areas and many wells have been brought into production. By mid-1966, oil had been reached by 136 of the 261 exploratory wells drilled, a remarkably high success ratio, and production exceeded half a million barrels per day. About 60 per cent. of the oil was produced in what is now the Rivers State.

Much of the rain forest of the humid south has been replaced within the last century by cocoa, oil-palms, kola, rubber, and other useful trees (Fig. 39). West of the lower Niger, crystalline rocks outcrop widely and the altitude rises to over a thousand feet on dissected upland plains surmounted by inselbergs. Forested and with cocoa in

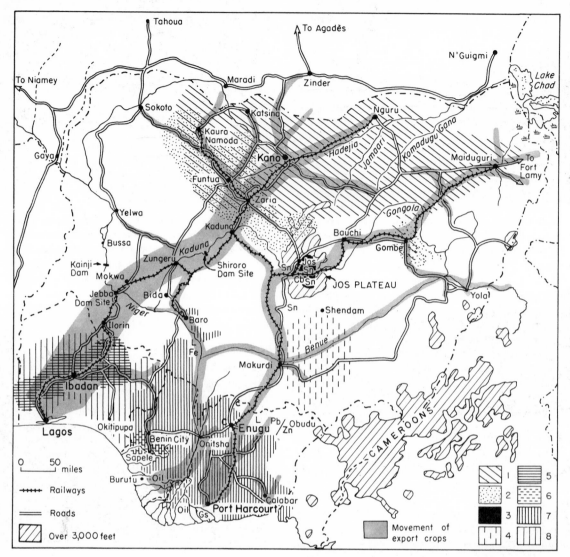

FIG. 39. *Nigeria. This shows the areas from which the main crops and minerals for export are derived. 1—ground-nuts, 2—cotton, 3—tin, 4—benniseed, 5—cocoa, 6—rubber, 7—palm-oil, 8—palm kernels, Sn—tin-ore, Cb—columbite. Other minerals indicated are Gs—natural gas, Pb/Zu—lead-zinc, L—limestone, C—coal, Fe—iron.*

the south, savanna-covered further north, this part of Nigeria is comparable with much of Ghana and the Ivory Coast in the same latitude. East of the Niger the sedimentary rocks stretching almost to the foothills of the Cameroon highlands and Jos plateau have been gently folded along NE.-SW. axes and then dissected. Two main upland areas are bounded by east-facing scarps, the heavily settled and well-wooded Awka-Orlu uplands nearer the Niger, and the higher and more open Udi plateau to the east (Fig. 41). Important coal-bearing beds outcrop in

the escarpment of the Udi plateau overlooking Enugu and also further north in Benue-Plateau State. At the foot of the scarp, limestones inter-bedded with shales and mudstones underlie the Cross river plains and the left-bank tributaries of the Benue. East of the Cross river, big rocky spurs and outlying hills of the Cameroon highlands rise sharply from the plains. They provide tsetse-free grasslands above 3,500 feet, near Obudu in South-Eastern State for instance, but are a considerable barrier to east-west communications.

Farmland of the Tiv people in central Nigeria. As their numbers increase, the Tiv are clearing the woodland further afield. In the background are the foothills of the Cameroon highlands.

Mumuye people of the Nigerian Middle Belt. These are amongst the most backward people in Nigeria. Many of them came down from the hills to work on the new road constructed across their lands in the 1950's and now live down on the plains.

Waterfall on the Jos plateau. The stream, a headwater of the Gongola river, plunges over a granite dyke near the eastern margin of the plateau.

Cactus-hedged village on the Jos plateau. The hedges may have been planted originally for protection against mounted raiding parties. Beyond the village, granite hills in the distance and open farmland.

On either side of the Niger and Benue rivers, where the land lies below 1,000 feet, low-level erosion surfaces cut across the Cretaceous sandstones and shales, and extend on to crystalline rocks outcropping at the margins of the valleys. About the confluence of the Gongola and Benue, where the Cretaceous strata are thick and have been folded along ENE.–WSW. axes, the drainage systems seem to have been superimposed from a cover of younger rocks, for the rivers cut through steep sandstone ridges forming the limbs of eroded anticlines and in general are unconformable with the structure of the country (Fig. 42). This steep cuesta landscape provides some of the finest scenery in West Africa.

The Niger and Benue valleys form part of the Middle Belt of Nigeria. This region has been defined in various ways, none of them altogether satisfactory, for the idea of the Middle Belt is rather vague and seems to mean different things to different people. In general it consists of the country between the predominantly Muslim areas of north

Nigeria and the southern boundary of what was called until 1966 the Northern Region. Quite extensive areas of savanna woodland, infested with tsetse and other pests, are practically uninhabited, but the Tiv, Nupe, and Yoruba areas are well populated and several small tribes, each numbering several tens of thousands, are clustered on rocky hills and escarpments especially on the northern side of the Benue valley. They are believed to have taken refuge there a century or two ago from marauding Juken and Fulani horsemen. The lack of settlement over wide areas and the poverty of the Middle Belt —it exports only small quantities of crops—have been attributed at various times to the rainfall being suitable for neither tree crops nor grain, the infertility of the soils, sleeping-sickness, and slave-trading. Any or all of these may have been effective, but there is no doubt that the settled area is expanding as the Tiv and Mumuye, for instance, farm over wider areas. As they clear the woodland where tsetse-fly breed, and as they kill off the game that forms a reservoir for the trypanosomes, Fulani are willing to keep their cattle through the year where once they hesitated to stay just for the dry season. A big scheme for growing groundnuts near the railway north of the Niger at Mokwa failed dismally in the early fifties, but human factors were more to blame for this than the Middle Belt environment. Now rice and tobacco are being grown more widely and the hydro-electricity scheme for the Niger at Kainji which also provides for the irrigation of the flood plain down-stream of Jebba, may perhaps attract settlers.

The granite bastions of the Jos plateau rise suddenly 3,000 feet from the floor of the Benue valley. The surface of the plateau, declining gently northwards, forms the hydrographic centre of northern Nigeria, with rivers rising in marshy hollows draining to the Niger, the Benue, and Lake Chad. It is pleasant, open, grassy country with cactus-hedged villages huddled at the foot of granite koppies and inselbergs and bare ironstone-capped mesas and buttes, the remnants of ancient lava flows rising a hundred feet or more above the general level. Youthful volcanic cones, some quite recently active, are surrounded by red and chocolate-coloured clayey soils, terraced and yielding quite good crops of millet and of a small grain called *acha*. But the most striking features of the Jos plateau are the pits and spoil heaps, the dams and sediment-choked streams resulting from alluvial tin-mining. Tin-ore (cassiterite) plus columbite, from which the metal niobium is obtained, are both present in the Younger Granites emplaced in Jurassic times.

Mine-workings are located in the alluvial formations of old river systems in which tin-ore, derived from long-continued weathering of the Younger Granites, has been concentrated by the sorting action of running water. To this mining industry the plateau owes its good road network and its power supplies, the electricity being generated on streams toppling over the steep south-western and western escarpments.

The watershed between the Chad and Niger drainage systems runs through the centre of the tin-mining area from Barakin Ladi to Bukuru and Jos and then curves round towards Funtua. It was approximately followed by the old narrow-gauge railway from Jos to Zaria, the 'Bauchi Light' which was dismantled about 1957. The Hadejia, Jamaari, and other rivers rising on the plateau and north of it flow north-east in rocky courses until they arrive on the sandy plains of the Chad basin where they lose most of their water by infiltration and by evaporation from swamps. The Gongola begins to flow in the same north-east direction but swings round to the south and cuts across the folded Cretaceous rocks to reach the Benue. On the west side of the plateau, the Kaduna river bends round in a similar fashion and flows through the Shiroro gorge to enter the Niger not far from Bida. A dam on the Kaduna at Shiroro will form the third stage of the Niger dams project, providing power supplies during the early rains while the flood-waters of the Niger have yet to raise levels behind the Kainji and Jebba dams. The flashy rivers of the north-west, running in broad shallow valleys, are collected by the Sokoto river and led into the Niger.

All the plains north of the Jos plateau bear traces of Pleistocene climatic changes. Some 12,000 square miles of Kano and North-Eastern State are covered with long, low mounds of sand running from ENE.-WSW., the remains of an ancient erg formed when the Sahara extended some hundreds of miles further south. Now they are covered with open savanna woodland and fields of millet and groundnuts. The mean annual rainfall exceeds 30 inches and there is plenty of water to be obtained from wells in the underlying sedimentary rocks, though often it lies at a considerable depth. Near the main watershed north of Kano, desert sands blown west by the dry winds of Pleistocene times have been diverted either side of abrupt quartz ridges near Kazaure in such a way that the sand streamed between the ridges and accumulated in strips stretching some 50 miles downwind of the gaps. Now we find the sandy soils are almost entirely under cultivation while the intervening strips of old

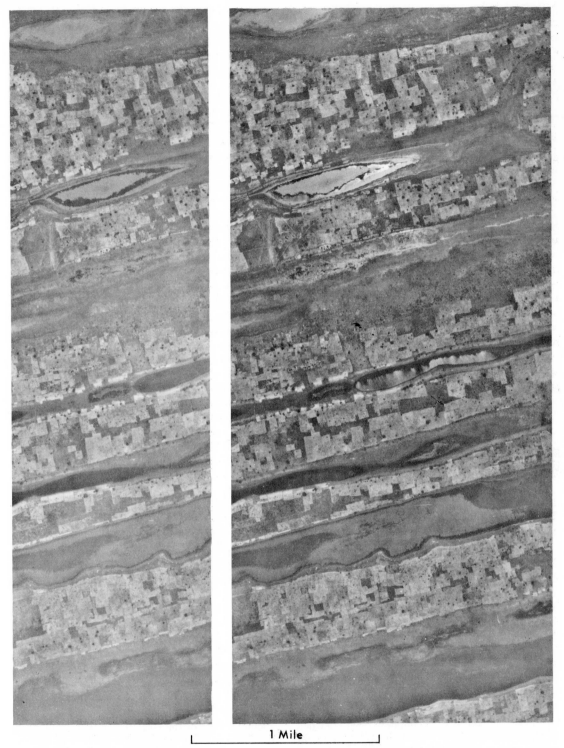

1 Mile

Ancient dunes, now cultivated, in north-east Nigeria. The small squares are cultivated fields, each an acre or two in size, on the dune crests. The intervening hollows still hold water from the preceding rainy season which ended about two months before the photographs were taken.

The Chalawa river near Kano in northern Nigeria. The building on the left is a pumping station supplying Kano with water from the river. Gullies are stripping sandy drift from the slopes in the foreground.

ironstone soils which were not covered with sand are left uncultivated and used for rough grazing (Fig. 42). Near Kano itself, weathered rocks and laterite are covered with several feet of 'drift', much of which appears to consist of wind-blown sand, rather finer and more productive than the sands of the ancient sand-sea lying further east. Fine sandy soils of this kind in the area north of Zaria are very compact and the heavy rains of July and August running rapidly off the surface have cut many deep gullies through the sands into the weathered rock beneath (see page 28).

Indications that the climate at other times in the Pleistocene was much more humid than now are to be seen in the neighbourhood of Lake Chad. A ridge running south-east through Maiduguri and Bama, nearly 100 miles from the lake, is believed to be a barrier beach formed near the margin of Chad when its waters stood 180 feet above their present level. This immense lake overflowed to the Benue via a low area near Bongor on the Logone river which has often been referred to as a zone of capture, for the flood-waters of the Logone occasionally overflow into the Maio Kebbi, a tributary of the Benue, and it has commonly been regarded as an instance where river capture is imminent (Figs. 5 and 6). A permanent diversion of the Logone into the Benue would reduce the level of Lake Chad, which would not be agreeable to the

fishermen living on its shores, but risks of this happening do not seem to be very great. At present the waters of the lake are not used to any great extent for irrigation and the region is rather sparsely settled. But there are fertile soils there, notably deep blackish clayey soils called *firki* which lie between the old high strandline and the present lake and which are derived from fine sediments that accumulated, possibly not very many centuries ago, when the lake stood 20 feet or more higher than now.

In the lands stretching from the dry north of Nigeria up to the Sahara the vegetation cover has deteriorated as a result of clearing for farming and grazing by cattle, sheep, and goats. In some places, even in Nigeria, soils deprived of their plant protection from the wind have begun to blow. Some people visiting this part of the western Sudan have concluded that the Sahara is advancing and, at the beginning of the century, when Lake Chad happened to shrink to an unusual extent, it seemed possible that the climate was steadily getting drier. However, the lake began to rise again in the 1950's and has since reached higher levels than ever before in this century. In general, desiccation causes less concern than it did a few decades ago, nevertheless, extensive soil and water conservation measures are planned for the basin of the Sokoto river where the accumulation of sand in widening river beds and erratic floods are creating difficulties for farmers cropping the flood plains.

The Twelve States

By 1968 some progress had been made towards the division of the four regions into twelve States. Western State with a population of 9·5 million, reduced a little in size with the enlarging of Lagos, is still more populous than any country in West Africa. North-Eastern with slightly fewer people than Western is comparable in size and population with Ghana. It is interesting that the state boundary lines, as they stand at present, follow portions of the old provincial boundaries of the colonial period.

Western State

The most populous and productive area in the West is the strip of country centred on Ibadan and stretching north-east from Lagos to Ilorin on either side of the main railway and roads to the north; it includes most of the large towns that characterize Yorubaland, and most of the cocoa and kola on which the economy of the region depends is produced in this area, as well as great quantities of palm produce and other food crops (Fig. 40).

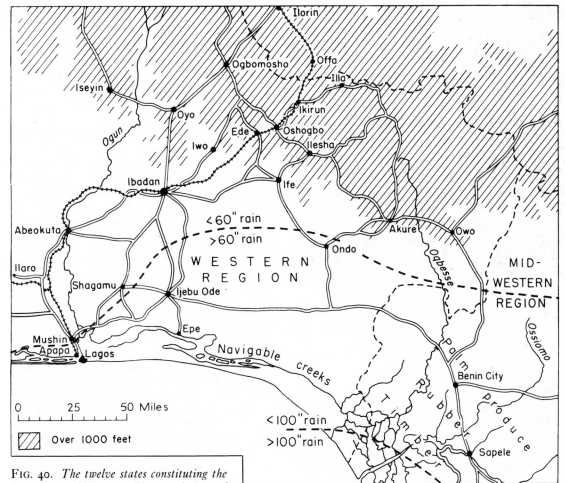

FIG. 40. *The twelve states constituting the
Federation of Nigeria. The population of
North-Central is about 4·1mn., of Rivers 1·5mn., and of East-Central 7·2mn.*

Of the 132 urban centres in Nigeria, according to the 1952 census, that is towns with more than 5,000 people, as many as 120 are in the Yoruba West. Most of them go back to the nineteenth century and many can trace their origin further back to Ile-Ife, which was probably established about a thousand years ago when Yoruba first immigrated into this part of Africa. Daughter settlements laid out on the same plan as Ile-Ife reproduced its social and political institutions. The walled palace of the Oba priest-king stood in the centre with the market alongside; wide roads radiated out to neighbouring towns. The traditional unit of settlement was the compound which consisted of a number of rooms grouped round a central square courtyard, the whole compound covering half an acre or more. Such compounds lined rectangular networks of streets between the main roads, and the whole town was surrounded by a wall and ditch.

Early in the nineteenth century the Yoruba towns were being attacked from the north by the Fulani and were fighting heartily amongst themselves. Refugees from defeated towns fled to those that remained, swelling their populations. Owu was destroyed in 1824 and the Egba towns allied to it were overcome in turn. Abeokuta was founded in 1830 by a large body of Egba refugees and other new towns were established well south into the forest zone. These new settlements were amongst the first to come into contact with European missionaries as they made their way inland from the coast. Ibadan, which escaped destruction in these wars, became a big centre for military operations, and has since succeeded in retaining its dominant position, both politically and economically in the region. The military authorities became more important than the civil arm as a result of the fighting; sanitation was neglected and this has been given as an explanation for the dirty and squalid appearance of the towns at the time, qualities they have still not entirely lost.

After the British arrived in Yorubaland, several of the bigger towns continued to grow faster than the rest. The railway, starting from Iddo island, linked Lagos to Abeokuta, Ibadan, Oshogbo, and Ilorin, and all of them flourished. Under indirect rule, much power was left in the hands of the Obas, and administrative headquarters were set up at the outskirts of the main towns where the traditional rulers lived. The growing class of educated Nigerians was attracted from the crowded old settlements to the new quarters with their stores and offices and new-style single-family houses. Consequently, many of the large towns now have two distinct parts; an older one, rather broken-down and congested, with the big compounds split up into a large number of separate parts, and a newer quarter with modern buildings, good water supplies, and a car-owning population. Ibadan now has more than half a million people and is reputed to be the largest native African city south of the Sahara; Lagos in 1967 exceeded 600,000, and the populations of Ogbomosho, Ile-Ife, Iwo, and Abeokuta are all about 100,000 or more.

In some ways, these Yoruba towns resemble medieval European cities or city states. Although the biggest towns have some industry, and Lagos above all is dependent on large-scale commercial activity, in many of the other towns a high proportion of the people continue to depend on food grown within a few miles of the town. Womenfolk are engaged in farming though trading is their main preoccupation. Specialization of labour has not been carried very far; only a small number of people work in factories, though great numbers are involved in crafts such as weaving, dyeing, and leatherwork. One reason why people have not moved out of the towns is that the crop on which many of them depend for a livelihood, namely cocoa, does not require a great deal of attention once it has been established. But lineage ties within the towns are probably the main centripetal influence. Many of the people who do live in the surrounding country are strangers from the north, hired as labourers by town-dwelling Yoruba owning the land to tend the cocoa and grow food crops. The towns still retain much of their ancient character, with social ties still depending on family inter-relationships. But as slums are cleared and people are moved to single-family dwellings on new housing estates at the outskirts of the towns, the old bonds slacken.

The economy of the south-west of Nigeria remains based on agriculture, cocoa being the main source of wealth. The region produces as much as Brazil, thus placing Nigeria second in the list of world producers. The earliest plantings near the coast, on soils derived from sedimentary rocks, were less successful than those further inland on the crystallines. Of the million acres now under cocoa, most lie in the belt curving eastwards from the railway near Ibadan into Ondo where the area under the crop is still expanding.

Swollen shoot has affected a few hundred square miles in the middle of the belt but has never been as destructive as in Ghana. Capsid and black pod diseases which have been more serious are being brought under control by spraying, and this, together with increased planting, is expected to bring production up to 200,000 tons by 1973. The rainfall is less than in the main cocoa belt of Ghana, about 45–55 inches, and the dryness may help to explain why the cocoa is more restricted by soil conditions; it grows best on the clays and clay loams of ridge tops and the upper slopes of the hills. On the sandy soils of the south, kola nuts are now more important than cocoa, and large quantities are exported to the north from Abeokuta and Agege. Cocoa has raised standards of living in the west higher than those elsewhere in Nigeria. The area is quite well supplied with foodstuffs; kola nuts are exported to the north, palm kernels to the United Kingdom. Roads are quite good and nearly all school-age children attend primary school. But the state lacks valuable minerals and industrial development is very limited. One gets the impression that there are too many big towns, too great a dependence on a single crop, and too many unemployed school-leavers.

Lagos

In 1877 John Whitford wrote in his book on *Trading life in western and central Africa* that 'Lagos undoubtedly rejoices in the best situation for trade in the Bight of Benin, and the merchants are alive to its importance; for notwithstanding the natural difficulties caused by winds, tides, the rainy season, the rough bar and the ocean steamers being obliged to anchor for safety far out to sea, they have organized efficient cargo-cutters sent out on the decks of steamers from England for the purpose, and also small steamers to work the traffic'. Since then, the harbour has been improved by the construction of a mole on the west side of the entrance to the lagoon, and vessels drawing 27 feet of water can tie up alongside the quays at Apapa (Fig. 4).

Lagos was founded on the slave trade, for it was ideally located for handling the human exports made available by the wars in Yorubaland. After its occupation by the British in 1861, people from the interior flocked to it as an island of security. Freed slaves from Freetown and Brazil also arrived and the town owes much of its character to them. Freetown Protestants formed a nucleus of intellectual and literary life in the town. The Catholic Brazilians had been trained as carpenters, cabinet-makers, tailors, and painters. Brazilian masons brought a strong Portuguese influence into the architecture of Lagos, as they did to certain other towns on the Guinea coast. A British residential area developed on Lagos island, on the east side, away from the crowded, unhealthy city to the west. Now, as the slums behind the handsome water-front, the Marina, are being cleared and the inhabitants removed to the mainland, various new social problems are arising, with sections of families finding themselves hours away from their relatives, and craftsmen miles from their customers.

Lagos is easily the biggest port in the country handling 3 million tons of cargo annually, and serving much of northern Nigeria and the countries beyond as well as the west. Numerous factories are in production or under construction on the mainland north of Apapa; cement, textiles, margarine, flour, soap, and as usual beer, are all produced here, and the range of articles is constantly increasing. Land for industry has become so scarce and costly that hundreds of acres of swampland are being reclaimed for industrial development, and many factories are being built north of the city at Mushin, Oshodi, and most particularly Ikeja.

Midwestern State

The low-lying country between the main cocoa belt and the Niger is inhabited by the Bini (Edo) of Benin and Ibos, many of whom have crossed over from the heavily settled country east of the river. This is relatively sparsely settled country with less than 200 people to the square mile.

Rubber and timber are the main products of Benin and the country stretching west. Some of the earlier rubber plantations were established in the vicinity of Sapele early in the century and a number of plantations in the area are owned by Africans. Now 90 per cent. of Nigeria's rubber exports, worth more than £10 million annually, come from the mid-west. Only about a tenth of the rubber comes from plantations, the rest from small growers whose trees receive little attention and are in many cases over 30 years old. Much more land could be planted

Truck assembly plant at Apapa. Cab being mounted on chassis at one of the many new factories in the Lagos area.

Log raft at Sapele ready for loading on to steamer.

up with rubber and with proper care and good stock yields of more than 1,000 lb. to the acre could be obtained as compared with 200 from small farms. But the rubber market is very erratic, Malayan production is increasing rapidly, and so the return from investments is uncertain.

Nigerian timber production is concentrated in the area south of Benin where the largest remnants of high forest in the country are reserved for timber exploitation. The tropical timbers of the kinds found here are well suited to new techniques of veneering and bonding. Exports, which rose by 50 per cent. between 1955 and 1960, are now increasing slowly. Prices have fluctuated, but the growing demands of the home market should help to give the industry greater stability in the future.

The plywood factory at Sapele, operated by the United Africa Company, is one of the biggest factories of its kind in the world and the largest single industrial plant in Nigeria. Logs from the forests inland are floated down to Sapele or towed down river in rafts of up to 300 logs. The best logs are exported as cylinders or squared-off, the rest, with more waste, are converted into plywood. Sawdust and chippings go to the furnaces to provide power for the plant.

Oil was discovered near Burutu in 1964, when a 'wildcat' well situated in 30 feet of water, about 7 miles offshore in the western delta, was successfully tested with a production rate of 2,000 barrels per day. Many other wells have since come into production both in the Ughelli area east of Warri and offshore. Exports from the area continued to increase during the Civil War and the Midwest now has all the opportunities and the problems of an oil-rich state.

Rivers State

The small Rivers State consists of the south-eastern part of the Niger delta. Its people are mainly Itsekiri and Ijaw living in fishing villages scattered here and there along the creeks, but the dominating feature of the economy is oil and natural gas. The name Oil Rivers earned in the old palm-oil trading days has a new connotation. In 1966 about two-thirds of Nigerian oil production came from oilfields distributed all round the perimeter of the new state.

The capital of Rivers State is Port Harcourt which, until the civil war, was the collecting centre to which oil flowed on its way by pipeline to the Bonny terminal. Near Port Harcourt, too, is the oil refinery completed at a cost of £10 million and capable of supplying all Nigeria's petrol and kerosene requirements and a little for export. Port Harcourt was, and no doubt again will be, second only to Lagos as a port and an industrial centre. Factories making rubber tyres, rolling aluminium,

milling flour, and producing glass-ware were under construction or in operation. An industrial estate was being supplied with 5 million cubic feet of gas daily and an electric generating plant at Afam was powered from the same source. All these were damaged in the early stages of hostilities.

The factories can be repaired but the big question that arises is that of Port Harcourt's future population. Before the war it was largely Ibo. Will they be allowed to return and, if so, what part will they be allowed to play in the economic and political life of the new state? Another question concerns the uncertainty of the disposal of oil revenues. Will Rivers State have at its disposal large sums of money for investment, and, if so, will this be devoted to agriculture, for example, rice-growing in the Delta, or to further industrialization around Port Harcourt?

South-Eastern

The densely settled, low-lying parts of South-Eastern State lying west of the Cross river estuary around Uyo and Ikot-Ekpene are within the main oil-palm belt and compare with the heavily settled areas of Iboland to the north-west. They contrast strongly with the sparsely peopled and remote hill country of the interior which has been looked upon as providing potential settlement areas for the congested country to the west. Communications were improved in the fifties but a settler scheme in the virgin forest country north of Calabar was a failure. Further inland, cocoa-growing has prospered in the Ikom area and rice-growing is important in the north between Ogoja and Abakaliki. Expansion of the rice-growing took place about 1950 with the introduction of small but efficient machines for milling and cleaning rice. The growers were mostly young Ibo immigrants, not entirely welcome to the local people, but with lots of energy. They lifted production to 80,000 tons annually of which a quarter was exported to Lagos. There are opportunities for rice-growing elsewhere on the alluvial plains of the Cross river. But the greatest opportunities in the state are likely to be those arising from the discovery of oil in 1968 within the boundaries of the South-East. Without this source of income its economic viability would seem to be rather precarious.

East-Central

This is Iboland, an area which had a population of 7 million before the civil war and a mean population density in excess of 500 persons to the square mile, with well over 1,000 in considerable

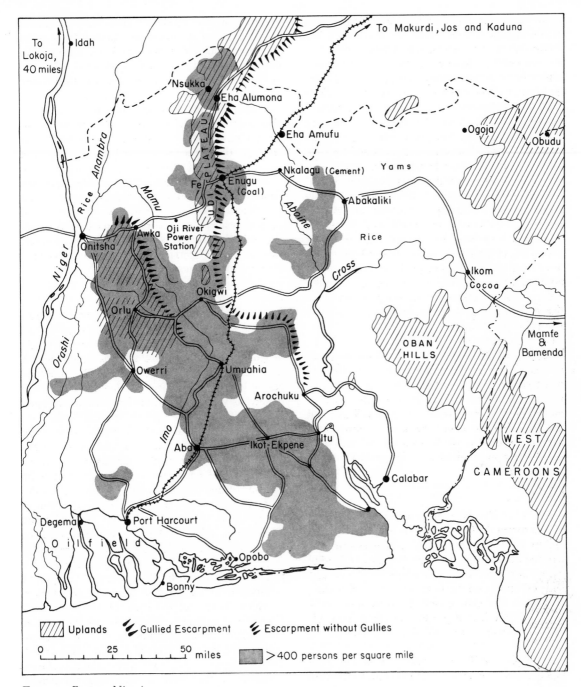

FIG. 41. *Eastern Nigeria.*

areas around Orlu and Okigwi. Figures like these are comparable to those for irrigated ricelands in south-east Asia, yet the agricultural resources of this country are far from outstanding. The sandy soils derived from the sedimentary rocks are well suited to oil-palms and, when carefully farmed, produce good crops of yams, maize, and vegetables. But they are unsuitable for cocoa and are liable to deteriorate rapidly unless well manured.

Traditionally the people are village-dwellers, living in rectangular huts thatched with straw or palm-fronds and surrounded by fences or mud walls. In general compounds are spaced some tens of yards apart, surrounded by gardens where root crops and vegetables grow in the shade of oil-palms and other useful trees. In the old days these wooded villages were commonly surrounded by an earthen wall and a belt of forest. All the people in a village or a village group traced their descent from a single ancestor, and the villages formed self-sufficient units, both socially and economically. Several of them have populations of 10,000 or more, but they are still villages, not towns. Those on the Udi Plateau form quite large islands of trees in a sea of open grassland. In Awka, Orlu, and Okigwi the wooded compound land stretches almost uninterrupted from one village to the next, with little woodland or open country between. In less-congested districts, belts of uninhabited palm groves remain between the villages; there are big patches of scrubby woodland cleared for farming every few years; raffia palms crowd the stream banks and occasional patches of high forest—Juju bush or forest reserve—preserve the deep shade of the past.

Some of the most heavily settled areas have suffered from soil erosion. The escarpment on the east side of the Udi plateau is deeply scored by systems of gullies cut a hundred feet or more into soft red earths and white sandstones forming the crest of the scarp, and the eastern margins of the uplands south of Awka are dissected by sprawling ravines that have penetrated Tertiary sandstones to expose weak clays beneath. Coarse sediments, eroded out of the raw gashes in the hill-sides, have accumulated on the floors of nearby valleys, causing flooding and in places blocking tributary streams to form small lakes (Fig. 23). Hundreds of acres have been ruined for agriculture. The cause of the erosion appears to be rainwater running off roofs, market-places, and impoverished open farmland, rushing down footpaths leading to the scarpfoot springs. The springheads were probably cut deeply into the hill-sides quite naturally, but were once protected by forest growing on the slopes. When the trees were cleared, the falling water cut back the springheads very quickly, starting the large-scale gullying that now attracts attention from nearly all foreign visitors to the area.

The gullies are a nuisance, it is true, interrupting communications as well as despoiling farmland. Less spectacular but more important has been the impoverishment of the soil over far wider areas resulting from the clearance of forest and its replacement by open tussocky grassland. Much of it is hardly capable of producing any crop at all, except thatching

grass, and so the villagers must rely very largely on the produce of the gardens round their houses. As the population grows, and the canopy of oil-palms and other trees thickens, more and more land at the outskirts of the wooded villages is planted up with oil-palms and enclosed for growing vegetables. Most of this expansion takes place alongside the roads, and the ribbon development gives one an impression, when driving through this country, that it is better wooded than is in fact the case.

The income of the villagers is small, and there has been a great deal of emigration from the heavily settled areas which, as a result, normally have a disproportionate number of women and elderly people. Many of the emigrants moved away to the towns elsewhere in Nigeria, Port Harcourt which was chosen to be the terminus of the railway inland to the Enugu coal-mines attracted many because of the constructional work in connexion with the nearby oilfield. Some went to Aba and Umuahia, both important market centres on the railway, to Enugu the administrative capital of the east, to Onitsha or much further afield to Lagos and the north where every town had its Ibo quarter thronged with mechanics, traders, and clerks. Other migrants found spare land to cultivate, it may be only a few miles from their homes or much further afield on the west side of the lower Niger or between Abakaliki and Ogoja to the north-east.

The opportunities for employment were increasing, but not fast enough to absorb all the school-leavers. The people in the heavily settled east have long been keen on education. Large numbers of primary and other schools were built under the guidance of Christian missions in the first half of the century and, of recent years, the government of eastern Nigeria was spending 40 per cent. of its revenue on education. As a result large numbers of students were being produced, nearly all of them determined not to go back to the land. The government saw the answer to this problem of under-employment as lying in two directions; labour-intensive agricultural schemes and industrialization.

Exports of oil-palm produce which usually brought into south-east Nigeria about £15 million annually, were the main source of wealth until mineral oil production began. The volume of palm-oil exported had remained stationary for many years and efforts were being made to increase it. In 1960, 97 per cent. of the oil came from semi-wild trees and only 3 per cent. from plantations. Production from the semi-wild palms is very inefficient; they vary in numbers from 10 to 100 to the acre; they grow 60 feet high and yield poorly. The only flesh of the fruit is thin, the useless shells of the kernels are thick, and it has been shown that an acre of planted palms, reared from good seedlings, properly spaced and carefully tended, will give six times the oil, three times the kernels, and five times the cash income of an acre of semi-wild palms.

Evidently plantations could greatly increase the productivity of the region, and both small plantations run by communities and larger ones operated by state organizations have been established. These larger blocks of trees have the additional advantage that they allow more efficient presses to be introduced, capable of dealing with a larger volume of fruit and extracting 90 per cent. of the oil instead of the 60 per cent. extracted by the hand presses.

Rice-growing has expanded near the confluence of the Niger and Anambra rivers upstream of Onitsha and further extension of the area under this crop is possible in the future.

Before the civil war about £5 million worth of dried fish was imported annually from Norway and most of it was traded north into Iboland. Live cattle were driven down from the north, from Niger and Chad to the market at Umuahia. Yams were brought in by lorry from Ogoja. No doubt trade in these commodities will recommence when peace returns, but there will be a greater deficit of foodstuffs than before the war (unless the death toll is even greater than has been feared) and the question will arise as to where the Ibos are to earn money to buy the food.

Until the fifties, industry in eastern Nigeria was very limited in scope. There was a soap factory at Aba and *gari* was produced there (*gari* is fried cassava flour—a useful food on which town-dwellers and travellers depend). Hand-presses for extracting palm-oil were widely distributed through the palm-oil belt and some larger mills had been established for pressing the fruit and cracking the nuts to extract the oil-rich kernels. The biggest single employer of labour was the coal-mining industry at Enugu.

In the fifties a power-station was constructed on the Oji river, Enugu coal being carried across the hills to it on overhead wires. The cement works at Nkalagu were opened, based on local limestone formations and also using coal from the mines nearby. But coal production declined because Nigerian

Brewery at Aba. Aba is well placed as a collecting and distributing centre for the densely settled parts of the region.

Oil being pressed out of palm fruit. This is the old-fashioned way of doing the job and it can be seen in use today only in the most remote parts of the country.

railways changed to diesel locomotives and coal could not compete with natural gas and oil from the Port Harcourt area.

For a time it seemed that Enugu might be chosen as the site of a large steel mill. Nigerian iron and steel consumption exceeds 150,000 tons annually

and there are plans to produce this quantity using either the oolitic ores from the flat tops of hills west of Lokoja, which have an iron content of 50 per cent., or lateritic ores with a 30–32 per cent. iron content on the crest of the Udi plateau. A steel plant located at Enugu would have been conveniently placed on the railway, near limestone, and the Udi supplies of ore. However, the local coal is unsuitable for coking by the usual methods and local supplies of water are limited. Other sites considered were near Onitsha, Lokoja, and Idah. A final decision will probably depend a good deal on the political situation as it develops after the war.

At the time of writing Biafra persists, but it is assumed that East-Central State will eventually be established as one of the twelve States making up Nigeria. It is possible that it will receive economic assistance from outside sources to repair the war damage. Much of this can soon be made good. The long-term problem remains of providing opportunities for productive employment to the massed population. In 1966 tens of thousands of Ibos, no one knows exactly how many, returned to their homeland from the north and west of Nigeria. As the federal armies moved in from north and south, so the townspeople retired to their home villages in the already congested central districts of Iboland. There is no work for them there. It would seem to be essential for their welfare, and eventually for

Docks at Port Harcourt. Extensions completed in 1960 doubled the port's capacity.

that of Nigeria as a whole, that they should be allowed and encouraged to move back to the towns, especially Port Harcourt, where they can live full and useful lives. To restrict them to their homeland would only cause more distress and store up more trouble for the future.

Kano State

The largest populous region in northern Nigeria is centred on Kano city and extends westwards into North-Central state. Numbers around Kano city exceed 500 to the square mile, some 2 million people living within 30 miles of the city. The mean population density for the state as a whole approaches 400, though pressure on the land is less in the riverine swamps of Hadejia and the hilly savanna country in the south.

The vast majority of the people in the state are Hausa-speaking Muslims, most of them sedentary cultivators growing sorghum, millet and beans to feed themselves; cotton and groundnuts for sale. They live in towns and villages and in dispersed compounds scattered through the fields. Most farmers cultivate 5 to 10 acres and own some sheep and goats and possibly a cow or two or a donkey. Some have much larger acreages and own several cattle. These may be handed over to the care of a village herdsman or an arrangement may be made with a Fulani stock-owner for him to look after the cattle, keeping the milk for himself and possibly a proportion of the progeny. Most of the smaller farmers are craftsmen as well, making leather articles, weaving, dyeing, making mats from the leaves of the young doum-palm. There are traders, Koran-teachers, butchers, and local government employees in the villages. Here we are reminded of medieval village life.

The countryside in the most closely settled areas has a well-kempt appearance, with plots of land demarcated by grass strips, cactus, or other hedges. Useful trees provide shade, corn-stalks are neatly stacked. The stock graze on crop residues, donkeys carry manure from kraals and compounds to the fields; Fulani may be invited to stay with their herds on the cropland for a few days as they move towards the south after the harvest. Thus enriched, a large proportion of the state's farmland is kept under cultivation year after year, about a quarter of it under groundnuts.

Near the big towns, especially around Kano itself, farmers supplement their incomes by carrying wood for sale as fuel or using their donkeys for local transport.

A large proportion of the three-quarters of a

Raft for transporting palm-oil on the Niger, near Oguta at the apex of the Niger delta.

million tons of groundnuts annually exported from the north are brought into Kano, and for several months after the harvest great green pyramids of sacks covered with tarpaulins look down on the station surroundings. Increasing quantities of nuts are being processed in Kano and the oil railed south in tankers. Most of the groundnut cake is also exported, as in the case of cottonseed because local demand is lacking. One of the most surprising features in this Muslim area is the existence on the outskirts of the city of one of the biggest piggeries in the world, utilizing groundnut meal for feed. The pigs are railed to Lagos for conversion into bacon and ham, and the Kano piggery plus another near Minna supply most of Nigeria's commercial pig-meat requirements.

Kano city is the greatest commercial centre of the western Sudan. Its population increased slowly from about 35,000 in the middle of the nineteenth century to about 50,000 in 1921, and has grown much faster in recent decades, reaching 130,000 in 1952 and over 300,000 in 1968. The old cubical mud buildings remain within the crumbling red-brown

Barges being pushed up the Niger, near Onitsha, by the diesel-engined Trenchard.

Hausa weaver at work. He makes a very long, narrow strip of cloth, using his hands and feet.

mud walls of the old city. A new commercial and residential area has arisen outside them in the neighbourhood of the railway station, and as in the case of every large northern town, a sprawling Sabon Gari accommodates the southerners and other strangers.

The range of industries steadily grows; beer, cigarettes, soft drinks and perfumes, soap and shoes, meat-canning and tanning are amongst the most important. They benefit from low labour costs, local raw materials, a large market near at hand, and the protection afforded by the long haul from the coast. In the future, the rate of expansion is likely to increase because Kano is the most prosperous state in the north and the area may no longer have to contribute as much as it has in the past to the support of its poorer neighbours.

North-Central State

Consisting of the former Provinces of Katsina and Zaria, North-Central is a much more varied state than Kano. The south is poorer than the north, with soils derived from lateritized crystalline rocks, and quite wide areas of dense woodland infested with tsetse-fly. From Zaria northwards conditions resemble those in Kano State, though the population is not quite so dense and the west, against the border with Sokoto, is sparsely settled. It was depopulated by a Fulani ruler of Katsina in the middle of the last century in the course of his conflict with Gobir. In recent decades it has been the goal of immigrants from further east and recently the woodland has been opened for grazing.

In the region of Katsina city and in Daura Emirate in the north-east of the state, the mean annual rainfall is only about 20 to 30 inches. In nearly every year there is a period of a few months at the end of the dry season when grain is scarce and the people depend at least in part on corn brought in by lorry, it may be from as far away as the Middle Belt. When harvests are poor in successive years many people, particularly the very old and very young, are liable to suffer severely. Livestock have to be sold off to buy food and seed, many people make their way to the towns, and young men go off to find work in the cocoa-growing areas. Katsina city has no rail connexion with the south and has ceased to grow. Its prospects would improve if trading relations between Nigeria and the Niger Republic became closer.

The country around Funtua and Zaria is the main cotton-growing region of Nigeria. Yields are low at present but methods of cultivation have been worked out by the Samaru agricultural research

Hamdala Hotel, Kaduna. The central tower block contains 78 air-conditioned bedrooms all with private bathrooms. An open-air swimming pool is close by in the hotel grounds.

station that could increase them many times. The difficulty lies in discovering why the local farmers are so slow to adopt the new methods. Near most of the large towns in the north, especially near Zaria, increasing numbers of farmers are employing irrigation. They use *shadufs* to lift water from shallow wells sunk in the terraces or scooped from the sandy floors of dry water-courses, and grow sugar-cane, tobacco, and various vegetables.

Zaria town at the junction of the railway lines to Nguru and Gusau is in a more favourable situation than Katsina. The University for the north lies a few miles from the city together with the Samaru research station. A number of small industries have been established in the area.

Kaduna, unlike Zaria, has no long history. It was merely a railway camp at the bridge over the Kaduna river until Lugard chose it to be the capital of the north, its site being more convenient than that of Zungeru, the capital from 1902 to 1917. It was within reach of Zaria and Kano and yet outside the immediate sphere of influence of the Emirs.

Later it was chosen to be the junction for the railway lines from Port Harcourt and Lagos which were for many years the main transport links to the south for passengers as well as commodities. Like every other administrative centre in Africa, Kaduna grew rapidly in the decades after the Second World War as government took on more and more responsibilities. An important industrial area developed near the railway junction on the south side of the river, the largest plant, a textile mill established in 1956, producing some 40 million yards of cotton cloth and employing over 3,000 people in 1965. Other textile mills have since been opened and consume a large proportion of the total Nigerian cotton crop. Public buildings, tree-lined streets, and suburban sprawl cover several square miles, but uninhabited savanna woodland comes to within a few miles of the city, and women of the Gwari tribe can still be seen trudging through the streets, stooping under great baskets of firewood on their hunched shoulders. What will happen to Kaduna now that it is merely a state capital and no longer

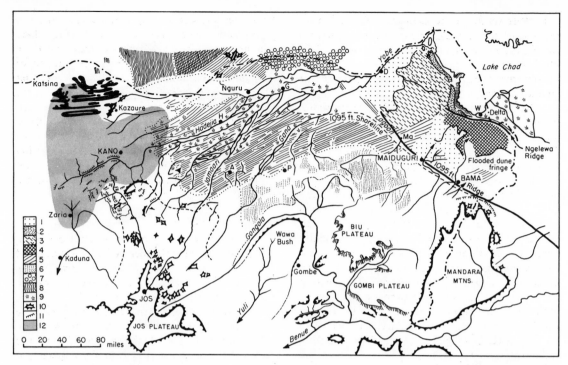

FIG. 42. *North-east Nigeria is made up of the Chad basin, floored with Pleistocene sediments, and dissected plateau country drained by the Benue river. The populous region around Kano lies on the Chad-Niger water parting. 1—old deltas formed in a larger Lake Chad, 2—sandhills bordering the present lake, 3—NW./SE. sand ridges, with lake sediments between the ridges nearer Chad, 4—black lagoonal cracking clays, 5—longitudinal dunes, covered in vegetation and running ENE./WSW., 6—open woodland showing a N./S. banded pattern, 7—sandy plain with closed depressions, some of which contain lakelets, 8—N./S. dune patterns, 9—seasonal swampland, 10—rocky hills, 11—gullied banks of watercourses, 12—heavily settled country with well over 200 people to the square mile. H—Hadeija, G—Geidam, D—Damasak, Ma—Magumeri, P—Potiskum, A—Azare, W—Wulgo.*

capital of the great Northern Region? Its offices may perhaps continue to house organizations co-ordinating certain activities of at least some of the northern states, but it is likely to become predominantly an industrial town relying on the momentum it has gained, its public utilities, its central position, abundant water in the Kaduna river, and power from Kainji and, eventually, the Shiroro gorge.

The southern districts of North-Central State are sparsely settled by small tribal groups which until recently have not been Islamized. This was an area that suffered from slave-raiding in earlier centuries. Although much progress has been made in recent years, and a large proportion of the children attend school, much of it is still remote hill country, poorly served by roads.

North-Western State

Whereas most parts of North-Central State can be reached from Zaria in three or four hours by road, North-Western is a sprawling state, with the capital Sokoto, near the northern extremity, 400 miles from the Nupe areas of the south-east, around Bida. Since the leader of the Fulani, Shehu Usman dan Fodio, took over control of the Hausa states early in the nineteenth century, Sokoto has been the political and religious focus of the Muslim north. Slaves were sent as tribute from the other rulers, trade flourished, and the country bordering the valleys of the Sokoto and Rima rivers became well settled. Early in this century many Hausas crossed into Sokoto from French territory, to escape military service or attracted by the numerous wells sunk by the Nigerian government. Woodland was cleared as the farmed areas expanded and poor sandy soils were eroded and locally abandoned. This may help to explain the great numbers of people who emigrate seasonally from the Sokoto region; some of the northern districts lose half their menfolk in the dry season to the cocoa-growing areas of Ashanti and Western State.

Further south, in the Zamfara valley, opportunities exist for cotton-growing and irrigation but the numbers attracted from the over-populated far north have not been very great and attention is mainly directed at present towards improving conditions in the northern river valleys. Detailed contour maps have been prepared from air photographs to assist in soil and water-conservation measures, and attempts to control flood levels in the rivers. Fears have been expressed that the Sokoto and Rima may become 'dead rivers' like the dallols of Niger Republic further north. They are not likely to deteriorate to that extent, for mean annual rainfall totals exceed 20 inches, but there is no doubt that sand accumulating in the river beds, severe bank erosion, and increasingly destructive floods are all hindering agricultural development of the flood plains. Artesian water has recently been discovered in parts of Sokoto at relatively shallow depth. Its exploitation will probably be delayed until experience in Bornu has indicated the ways in which it can be used for the long-term benefit of the area. A cement factory has been built at Sokoto and a textile mill at Gusau.

South of the Zamfara valley in the old Niger Province population densities are less than 50 persons to the square mile with wide areas uninhabited south of Kontagora. The Kainji dam lies in this empty country where the river is confined by hills on either side. Here a concrete dam has been built, 200 feet high and 14,000 feet long, to provide the storage and head of water for twelve electricity generating units each with a capacity of 80 MW, capable of meeting Nigeria's electricity requirements for some years to come. Below the dam is a bridge across the Niger. Until it was constructed the bridge at Jebba, used by the trains and road traffic, was the sole link between Lagos and the north.

The Niger dams project is the chief single development project, not only in the Middle Belt but in Nigeria as a whole. Additional dams at Jebba and Shiroro, constituting the second and third stages of the scheme and expected to be built in the eighties, will raise the total power output to over 1,700 MW. These dams too will be in North-Western State but the consumers of the power will be mainly in the Kaduna–Kano area to the northeast and Ibadan–Lagos to the south. No doubt south-east Nigeria will depend on thermal plants using natural gas from the delta region.

There appear to be reasonable opportunities for growing sugar-cane, rice, and other crops on the floodplain of the Niger downstream of Kainji. The dam has reduced the difference between high- and low-water levels on the Niger from 20 feet to about 5 feet and a large part of the floodplain, which will no longer be inundated naturally, could be irrigated by pumps. River traffic on the Niger should benefit from the dam, locks allowing barges to travel upstream to Yelwa throughout the year and to Niamey in the Niger Republic except for part of the dry season. This may perhaps stimulate agricultural developments in the western areas of the new state by allowing cheap evacuation of produce. River fisheries are already important in the area and these will be supplemented by the new lake above Kainji.

North-Eastern State

Comprising the old provinces of Bauchi, Bornu, and Adamawa, plus the former Trust Territory of Sardauna, North-Eastern State is extremely large and varied. It was at first stated that the capital would be the Hausa-Fulani town of Bauchi in the west. Now it has been settled that Maiduguri in the far north-east is to be the seat of the administration.

Maiduguri is the chief town in Bornu, the country lying south-west of Lake Chad where the majority of the people are Kanuri. There are about 2 million people in Bornu, mostly farmers settled in villages and hamlets, growing sorghum, millet, and groundnuts and keeping cattle. Shuwa Arabs and certain Kanuri-speaking groups who have immigrated from east of the lake over the last century or two are much more interested in cattle than farming and many of them continue to lead a nomadic life, shifting with their herds from well-drained sandy country in the centre of Bornu, where they spend the rains, to the neighbourhood of Lake Chad and the swampy valleys of the rivers draining to it for the dry season. Fulani, who are most numerous in the western parts of the state, have penetrated to the vicinity of the lake along the Yobe river in the north. They and the Shuwa look after cattle belonging to Kanuri farmers, keeping them with their own herds for the sake of the milk they give. Cattle numbers seem to be increasing rapidly, possibly doubling between 1950 and 1963, and the over-all density of stocking is now about fifty to the square mile, a high figure in view of the poor nature of the grazing. Over a half of these cattle are believed to be settled, not nomadic, and the proportion of village cattle is increasing, probably because farmers are making more money than in the past. Elsewhere in northern Nigeria, where pressure on the land is higher, the proportion of nomadic cattle is lower still and livestock numbers have ceased to increase. In Bornu there is still room

L

The Yobe river in Bornu. It is April, near the end of the dry season, and flow has ceased. The high bank on the right is probably not far from the margin of the ancient Lake Chad.

for shifting cultivation in some of the more remote areas, but this will probably soon come to an end as the remaining woodland is cleared and as the people begin to concentrate more in towns and villages along the new roads.

Costs of transport to and from Bornu have decreased with improvements in the roads to Jos and Kano. Production of groundnuts has become much more worth while than before in the area that was not served by the railway to Nguru. The new Bukuru-Maiduguri line, running south of the main roads, should further improve the position. Stock-owners should get better returns from their cattle, sheep, and goats when normal trade links with the south-east are re-established. Feeder roads are being constructed to extend the influence of the railway further afield. One of the longest of these, and one of the most expensive to build because of the lack of good constructional materials in the area, is the road from Maiduguri to Abadan, near the lakeshore and on the frontier with Niger. This will greatly improve the accessibility of the towns on the lakeshore dealing in fish. Several thousands of tons are already being caught annually and dried for export by lorry to the south. The deplorable state of the roads until recently has kept costs at a high level, both for the carriage of the fish and return loads. The potentialities of the Chad fisheries are being investigated and appear to be considerable, so Bornu's position as the chief supplier of protein to the rest of Nigeria is likely to be enhanced.

Since 1959 the people living within 80 miles of Lake Chad have benefited from a drilling programme which has provided them with good supplies of water from some 200 bore-holes which tap an artesian aquifer about 1,000 feet below the surface and far below the level of the lake and unconnected with it. The bore-holes have caused stock-herders to keep more cattle in the rainy season grazing areas right through the year, and the grazing is suffering as a result. Some form of organization appears to be needed to ensure that best use is made of the new water supplies.

One of the most striking features of the region is the great area under sorghum, growing green and tall at the height of the dry season. This *masakwa* is restricted to the *firki* soils of eastern Bornu, where the moisture accumulating in the black clays during the rains is sufficient to grow a crop, planted in September, to be harvested in February. The farmers live in villages situated on old sand dunes that protrude through the clays and are surrounded by watery mud during the rains. Flocks of *Quelea*, enormous numbers of these little birds, steal a good deal of the grain and attempts have been made to eliminate them by exploding dumps of petrol placed in the thicket patches where they roost—without much success so far.

The presence of abundant fresh water in the lake and seasonal supplies in its tributary the Yobe, quite close to great stretches of gently sloping ground, has naturally suggested the possibility of large-scale irrigation. Onions and other crops watered by *shadufs* are grown already at various places along the Yobe and its tributaries. In the early fifties, a pilot project to grow rice near Chad was flooded out by the progressive rise of the lake level in recent years. Other schemes have since been started with the aim of growing rice and wheat. But costs are high and risks of salt accumulation in the surface layers of the soil may prevent these schemes becoming of great importance. Proposals have been made for irrigating very large areas, following Israeli examples, by pumping large volumes of water from the lake and distributing it over the plains by pipe-lines. But such schemes involve agreement with the other lacustrine states, Chad, Cameroon and Niger, as to the allocation of the lake waters.

Maiduguri is the commercial centre of Bornu, at the junction of roads from Abadan, Fort Lamy, and Bama and is now the railhead for the region. It has a new meat-packing plant and factories have been built for crushing groundnuts and making cattle cake.

The southern half of the state, in contrast to the north, is hilly and locally mountainous, with many rivers draining to the Benue. It is populated by a myriad of pagan tribes amongst whom Fulani have infiltrated over the last two centuries. Most of the country, when the British arrived, was subject to the Fulani rulers of Bauchi, Gombe, and Adamawa. The last of these takes its name from Adamu, Lord of the South, who was commissioned by Usuman dan Fodio to propagate Islam from the Nile to the Bight of Biafra. In the first half of the nineteenth century he assembled by war and diplomacy an empire, founded on the ruins of several smaller pagan kingdoms, that stretched over the whole of the upper Benue valley east of the Shebshi mountains, including a large part of what is now the northern part of the Cameroon Republic. In Adamawa, Gombe, and Muri, in contrast to Kano and the country to the west, the Fulani retain their ethnic distinctiveness and the Fulfulde language continues to be used in everyday life.

The lower Gongola is a well-settled and productive region where cotton production expanded rapidly in the fifties. Here and further north around Azare the people are mainly Fulani cultivators and stock-raisers living interspersed with pagan villagers. Other well-settled areas in the state include a number of small tribal areas around the south-western, southern, and south-eastern fringes, from the margins of the Jos Plateau and along the frontier

with Cameroon, to the Mandaras south of Lake Chad. This is very varied country where the people are commonly little touched by modern ways of life. By degrees many of them are adopting the Muslim faith and many of the social attitudes and ways of life that go with it.

Kwara

Four hundred miles long and with an average width of little more than 60 miles, Kwara is one of the most awkwardly shaped of the new states. It runs along the south side of the Niger from the remotenesses of Borgu, through well-settled Yoruba areas around Ilorin, the capital, and extends east into Igala country south-east of the Niger-Benue confluence. The most prosperous part of this Middle Belt state is the well-populated section in the middle along the main roads and railway running through Offa and Ilorin to the Niger crossing at Jebba. The outlying parts of the state have poor communications with the centre and considerable difficulties can be foreseen in its administration.

It is one of the poorest of the new states. Developments associated with the Niger Dams Project may assist the economy. At Bacita, 10 miles downstream of Jebba, a sugar plantation has been established on the flood plain of the river and a refinery with a capacity of 35,000 tons is expected to supply a large part of Nigeria's requirements. Harvesting of the cane provides seasonal labour for migrants from

Cattle being watered from artesian bore-holes in Bornu. Sheep can be seen in the background. The largest tree, a gawo, Acacia albida, is in leaf. This is the dry season, and the other trees are leafless.

Sokoto, local labour being neither mobile nor plentiful. Lokoja at the Niger-Benue confluence has been mentioned as a possible site for a steel mill. Its poor communications with the populous parts of the country do not recommend it, but access by river to the oilfields of the south might prove to be an advantage; crystalline limestones are near at hand as well as the oolitic iron-ores behind the town, coal and oil could be brought upstream on barges, electricity is available from Kainji, and natural gas might be piped from the delta.

Benue-Plateau

Benue-Plateau occupies a central position in Nigeria in the sense that it adjoins six other states as well as Cameroon. The Benue river divides it into two parts of similar size. The Tiv, a vigorous people numbering over a million, occupying much of the area south of the river and have been colonizing the plains to the north for several decades. The Idoma, a less virile group, are established on both sides of the Benue further downstream. The remnants of the Jukun live in the sparsely settled country upstream. Elsewhere in the state, especially on and around the Jos Plateau, a large number of tribal groups, varying in number up to about 100,000, occupy small areas often centred on rocky defensible sites. Many of the people have been converted to Christianity and quite a high proportion are well educated. Many of them are playing an important part in the current political developments in Nigeria. But in the remote parts of the state are some of the most colourful and interesting survivals of ancient communities, preserving their own languages, shrines, and dances and a fascinating variety of houses, implements, ritual equipment, and decorative clothing.

The capital of the state, Jos, in the extreme north, is the commercial centre of the tin-mining industry and standing at an altitude of 4,000 feet it is also an attractive Hill Station with comfortable hotels and a very fine museum. The state should have no difficulty in attracting personnel from Europe and America. Besides its scenic and climatic attractions, Jos is well served by transport links with the rest of Nigeria. The railway to Kafanchan gives access to Port Harcourt and through Kaduna to Lagos. From Kuru, a few miles south of the town, the new line runs north-east to Gombe and Maiduguri.

Fairly good roads run south to the river crossing at Mukurdi, south-east to Pankshin and the Shendam area south of the Plateau, and east to Bauchi and North-East State.

The tin-mining industry, which is centred on the high rocky plains stretching 30 miles south of Jos, has suffered a temporary setback as a result of the Ibo clerks and mechanics being driven out. The future of the industry is uncertain but it seems likely that production will continue at present rates, with production approaching, 10,000 tons of cassiterite annually for some time to come. Some industrial development may take place in Jos and Bukuru, benefiting from their central position, the availability of water and electricity, and a labour force accustomed to operating machinery. There are opportunities for the extension of the areas under rice, tobacco and other crops on the flood plains of the Benue and its tributaries. Stock-raising will no doubt increase in importance as control is gained over the tsetse-fly on the plains south of the Plateau. But for the next few years at least the state is likely to be short of funds unless it receives a subsidy from the central government.

Prospects

The creation of the twelve states has not by any means solved Nigeria's political problems. Nearly all the states have important minority groups and the problem of the collection and division of the federal revenue remains. Now there are twelve state governments making decisions instead of four regional governments and the variation in size and wealth of the constituent parts is almost as great as ever it was. The north it is true has been broken and ceases to loom over the rest of the country. Perhaps the central government at Lagos, eccentrically placed though it is, will more easily dominate the states than it did the regions. The balance between state and federal powers is of very great importance for the future development of Nigeria. This will determine the way in which funds are distributed and the detailed pattern of industrial growth. Nevertheless, the concentrations of population and resources in a few areas of limited size, between Enugu and Port Harcourt, Ilorin and Lagos, Kano and Kaduna, plus the oil resources of the Delta are likely to dominate the future development of the country as they have in the recent past.

9

The Congo Basin and Cameroon

THE greater part of the Congo basin falls within the territory formerly known as the Belgian Congo and now called Congo Kinshasa to distinguish it from the former French colony on the north side of the river, Congo Brazzaville. Kinshasa and Brazzaville, the capitals of the two states, face each other across the waters of Stanley Pool. Here the Congo widens to about 13 miles before plunging over the first cataracts of the Livingstone falls on the steep descent to Maradi, which lies 200 miles away at the head of the estuary, nearly a thousand feet lower than Stanley Pool. The Central African Republic to the north stretches from the Congo basin across a low watershed into the Chad basin. Of the Cameroon Republic only the south-east corner is drained to the great equatorial river. Gabon, though completely outside the Congo basin, is included here because it forms a portion of the main block of west central Africa and was a part of French Equatorial Africa. Equatorial Guinea, formerly Spanish Guinea, made up of Rio Muni and the island of Fernando Po, comes in the same general area.

Although these territories taken together approach the size of Europe, their total populations scarcely exceed 25 million. In all of them most of the people speak Bantu languages, and except in the former Spanish territories government business is conducted mainly in French. Well over half the people are agriculturalists. The rainfall throughout almost the entire region is high, exceeding 50 inches annually, and except on the periphery the main food crops grown are roots and plantains.

The coastal peoples have long been in touch with Europe. The Bakongo, for example, numbering about 3 million today, who live on either side of the river below Stanley Pool and are split up between Angola and the two Congos, were once united in a kingdom that was well known to the early Portuguese and persisted for some 200 years after their arrival. Further inland, the Baluba of eastern Kasai and northern Katanga, and the Balunda of southern Katanga, are both large tribal groups with memories of times a few centuries ago when they lorded over neighbouring peoples. With Europe they had very few contacts until the end of the last

century. On the east side of the basin, Arabs arrived before Europeans, and the Baluba, amongst other tribes there, suffered much in the nineteenth century from Arab slave-raiding. A lasting consequence of Arab penetration of the country bordering the western rift valley, is the use of Swahili as a lingua franca in parts of the eastern Congo.

The main centres of population are at the fringes of the region, notably on the volcanic highlands bordering the rift valley, on the Cameroon highlands, and near the mouth of the Congo. Very wide areas in the centre of the basin are sparsely settled, for the forest, which in west Africa is a populous and productive zone, remains untamed and uninhabited here. The flat country near lakes Tumba and Leopold II is flooded for much of the year, and higher country to the east has infertile soils derived from sandstones of the Karroo system.

CONGO KINSHASA

This great country, second in Africa south of the Sahara in extent and fourth in population, may well have greater natural resources than any other in Africa. Its mineral resources are enormous and already support, in Katanga, the largest economic complex between the Sahara and the Republic of South Africa. About a half the total area is cultivable, though only a very small fraction is under crops at any one time. The Congo's system of navigable waterways is unrivalled in all the continent (Fig. 43).

Until the 1880's the falls at the head of the estuary prevented traders and explorers reaching the interior from the west and the basin remained unknown to the outside world. The completion of the railway from Matadi to Stanley Pool in 1898 quite transformed the situation and Leopold II tried to make up for lost time. His administration aimed to make the Congo a paying concern and to achieve this end were ready to make use of forced labour. For several years the Congolese people were subject to all manner of brutalities, until Morel and Roger Casement drew the attention of the civilized world to their abuses. The Belgian government took over responsibility for the Congo from the King and from being a personal estate it became a more normal type of colony.

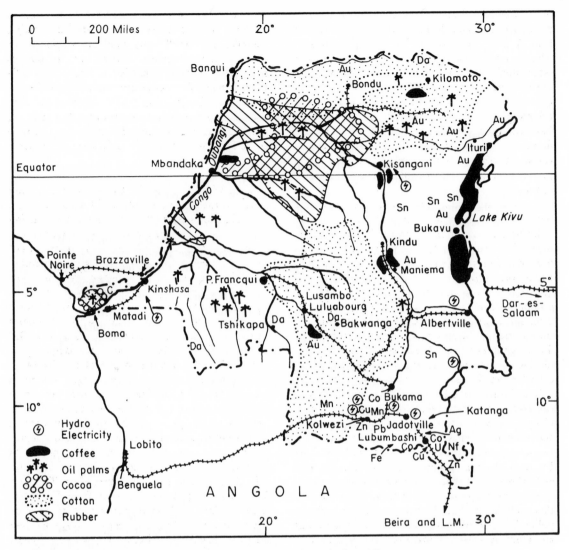

FIG. 43. *Congo Kinshasa. The navigable rivers are shown by a thickened line.*

It was soon realized by the Belgians that economic minerals were particularly abundant in the Katanga Province, far away in the south of the country. Development of these resources evidently required large-scale investment in transport and all manner of equipment. The Belgian government encouraged large monopoly companies to provide the capital and take responsibility for developing the country's resources. Shares in these companies were held by Belgian, American, and British banks and by the Belgian government. In addition, private concessionaires were given the opportunity to buy monopoly rights to the collection of rubber, ivory, palm produce, and timber over great tracts of land. Many plantations were established, and the scale of

European agricultural enterprise has no parallel elsewhere in western Africa, except in Liberia. Between 1887 and 1953, £5,700 million, it has been estimated, flowed into the country for investment. It went mainly into communications, plantations, and mining and the economic progress that resulted was extremely impressive.

The Belgians divided the country into six provinces for administrative purposes, each of them larger than most African countries. The capital, which was first established at Boma, a port on the estuary, was transferred to Léopoldville in 1929 and has remained there since then. The country round about the new capital was sparsely populated, and the Bakongo people of the region were hostile to the Belgians. Labour was attracted to the new capital from all over the rest of the Congo, and even from Angola. The Bangala from the upper Congo, who were very ready to adopt western ways, soon established themselves in a dominating position in the city, and when eventually the resentment of the Bakongo had worn off and they began to move into Léopoldville in larger numbers, they found the Bangala already established as an *élite*. The Bakongo founded the Abako party in 1950 to enable them to reassert their influence; it was the leader of this party, Kasavubu, who became the first President of the Republic.

The provincial administrations under the colonial régime were responsible to the governor at Léopoldville; he took his orders from the Belgian government in Brussels. No democratically elected parliament existed, and neither White nor Black had a vote until 1957 when a limited form of self-government was introduced. The Belgians put economic development in the forefront. Unless the economic foundations of the country were sound, so they argued, political development meant nothing. They were not concerned with those 'abstract idealogies' that were causing so much disturbance elsewhere in the continent in post-war years.

The Church stood alongside the companies and the State as the third pillar supporting the colonial Congo. Roman Catholic and other missions were active nearly everywhere, not only spreading the Gospel, but also providing schools and hospitals. By 1960 some 4 million natives were recognized as Catholics and about 1 million as Protestants.

To many people in Europe and America it seemed that the Belgians had the key to successful colonial policy. The administration was remarkably thorough and efficient, the economy was thriving, standards of living were higher than those amongst any other native peoples in intertropical Africa outside Ghana. About 1 million people were in paid employment at the time of independence, some 36 per cent. of the adult male population. Production of minerals between 1952 and 1959 increased by 30 per cent. Sisal, cotton, and palm-oil production were increasing. The population, so far as the age-structure could show, was about to increase rapidly. Léopoldville had expanded from 47,000 in 1940 to over 360,000 in 1960. The Congo appeared to be the most stable and secure state in mid-twentieth-century Africa.

Education had not been neglected. At the time of independence about half the Congolese children were receiving primary education. About 500 Africans had been trained for the priesthood and ordained. But there were places for only 10,000 students in secondary and vocational training schools, and hardly any graduate engineers or doctors, and not many lawyers. Lack of politics meant that no national parties evolved and no politicians were able to establish country-wide followings. So the Congo, in spite of its apparent stability, was ill-prepared for self-government; but after all, the Belgians had not intended self-government to come for several years, probably several decades.

Transport

The Belgians made the Congo river the main artery in the transport system of the country, for, natural difficulties and the high costs of construction ruled out roads and railways for most of the country, particularly the sparsely settled, swampy regions of the central basin. The water routes were operated by OTRACO, a Belgian company which has now become the property of the Congo government. The river fleet, which had a total displacement of more than a million tons, made use of 8,750 miles of rivers and another 810 miles of lake routes. Old stern-wheelers have largely been replaced by modern diesel-engined boats, mainly propeller-driven tugs that push along trains of several barges. The main waterways had lighted buoys, and boats were fitted with radar and searchlights so they could move by night as well as by day. Much of this equipment was destroyed in the troubled years after independence.

The great advantage of river transport is its cheapness; rates are about one-third of those by rail. On the other hand, it is very slow. To reach Mbandaka, 437 miles upstream from Kinshasa, takes 3½ days, and Kisangani is another week or more upstream. The boats creep slowly up the river much as they did half a century ago when Conrad described them in *The heart of darkness*: 'Trees, trees, millions of trees, massive immense, running up high, and at their foot, hugging the bank against the stream, crept the little begrimed steamboat, like a sluggish beetle crawling on the floor of a mighty portico.'

The railways supplement the river system, by-passing reaches obstructed by rapids, and linking the river to areas lacking navigable waterways. From time to time the track has been extended to reduce the amount of loading and unloading that leads to loss, damage, and theft, adds to the costs, and increases the time for the journey. In Katanga the railways have been electrified; elsewhere diesel engines are in use.

The Katanga system links up with the lines to Lobito and Beira which, in the early sixties,

The banks of the Upper Congo. 'We were in a channel two hundred yards wide, walled in by a bank of vegetation that rose 150 feet high. Two lofty fortress walls could not have been more inhospitable to us.' From H. M. Stanley, The Congo, *vol. ii, London, 1885.*

carried a high proportion of the Congo's mineral exports. Matadi's total exports, which largely consist of agricultural produce, were about three-quarters of a million tons annually, and Boma's less than 150,000 tons, mostly timber.

The road network is one of the best in Africa and though the rains render long stretches unusable for days at a time, road transport has been competing very effectively with the railways. Between Bukavu and Uvira a modern paved highway has entirely replaced the old railway, and near the coast the traffic of the Mayumbe line has been absorbed by the Boma-Tshela highway.

For Africa the transport system was a good one. As in most other territories it was designed mainly to expedite the movement of goods in and out of the country and, in spite of the disturbances in the early sixties, it has continued to do this effectively.

As the economy begins to grow again, more consideration is being given to interregional communications and less to movement of materials from the periphery to Kinshasa.

Agriculture

Most Congolese are still cultivators, growing cassava in every region, plantains and root crops in the wetter areas, guineacorn, beans, and groundnuts in the drier ones, mainly for their own consumption. Many of them are shifting cultivators, more are bush-fallow farmers. About one in ten of them was involved in peasant farming schemes initiated by the Belgian administration in the 1930's in an effort to organize shifting cultivation. Under these schemes, village lands were divided into parallel, rectangular strips, and each farmer, at least in theory, advanced down his strip each year by the same distance as his neighbour, so that all should plant the same crops side by side and then leave the land to recover during a twenty-year fallow period. This arrangement, combined with other improved farming practices allowed machinery to be used in preparing the land for planting and sowing and also in harvesting. Advice was given by INEAC, an agricultural research institute which gained international recognition. Its principal research station was at Yangambi near Kisangani, where, at one time, 400 European scientists were employed. One of its main jobs was to distribute very large quantities of improved seeds and plants. Farmers in the peasant farming schemes are said to have doubled and trebled their incomes by growing cotton and rice for sale within these organizations. At the same time, with the more intensive farming and greater concentration of the population, schools and dispensaries could be provided and co-operative marketing organized. Interregional trade in food-crops was developing at the time of independence, with Kasai farmers living near the railway, growing foodcrops for sale in the mining towns of Katanga.

About two-thirds of the export crops were and probably still are produced on plantations and farms managed by Europeans and providing employment for a quarter of a million Congolese. Large companies, like Unilever, had been granted concessions at an early stage that gave them the right to the wild produce over wide areas of country. Even in the 1950's about half the country's oil-palm produce came from wild palms. Now it is being found, as in Nigeria, that plantations are more profitable, the planted palms giving a higher yield of better-quality fruit, a more regular supply, and easier harvesting because the planted trees are much shorter than the wild ones—an important consideration now that cutters are scarce. The large companies operate their own mills for extracting the oil from the fruit and also for crushing the kernels. The oil is carried by rail and tank barges to bulk storage tanks at Mosango, Mbandaka, Kinshasa, and Boma to await export. The kernels are exported uncrushed. Largely as a result of the development of the plantations, which cover more than 80,000 acres, exports of palm-oil from the Congo increased from 70,000 tons before the last war to 170,000 tons in 1964, whereas exports from Nigeria over the same period remained static at about 170,000 tons annually.

The other main plantation crops, rubber and cocoa, are grown in various parts of the central basin on about 30,000 acres of land. The output of rubber

Harvesting latex on a Congo plantation.

is expanding rapidly; over half the young trees are owned by Africans. Cocoa is mostly on European plantations below 2,000 feet. Very large areas have a suitable climate for the crop; the deep friable clay soils it needs are less widely distributed, but prospects for expansion appear to be good. A few sugar-cane plantations are in production and have sugar mills attached. Pyrethrum and cinchona are speciality crops in the Kivu area.

Stock-raising is not very important because the climate, pastures, and disease are all against it. There are hardly more than a million head of cattle in the entire country, and perhaps two or three times that number of sheep and goats. A large proportion of the cattle are, or were, owned by Europeans living near Kinshasa and the high country of Kivu, Katanga, and Ituri. But it must be noted that there were never more than about 1,500 European farmers, and they were settled in groups so as to avoid coming into conflict with Africans over land rights.

In general, animal protein is deficient in diets, and fish is generally more important than meat. In recent years some hundreds of fish ponds have been created, fertilized with waste material and yielding good crops of *Tilapia*.

A cocoa plantation in the Congo.

Mining

Minerals form a very large proportion of the Congo's exports; most of them come from Katanga, where the production of copper alone reached nearly 300,000 tons annually in the period 1959–68. This represents about 8 per cent. of world production of this metal. The ores, which are extremely rich, richer than those of Chile and the United States, are won from an ore-body some 200 miles long and about 30 miles wide on the Zambian frontier.

There are three principal copper-mining areas. In the south, the copper-zinc sulphide ores are mined underground at Kipushi, where there is also a plant for concentrating the ore. The concentrates are railed about 15 miles east to Lubumbashi for smelting and conversion to blister copper. In the central area, copper and cobalt oxides are quarried from open pits and the concentrates are refined at Jadotville where there are also foundries, metal-working and electrical plants. The most important mining area is in the west where Kolwezi is the focus for processing the ores.

The enriching of the ores, carried out to reduce their bulk before the long journey to the coast, involves the most advanced methods available and the consumption of large amounts of electric power. This is mainly supplied by four hydro-electric stations on the falls of the Lufira and Lubilash rivers with a combined capacity of 500 MW.

As well as copper, Katanga supplies between half and two-thirds of the world's cobalt, a metal widely used in steel alloys, most of it coming from the Kolwezi area. Other mines produce between 100,000 and 200,000 tons of zinc concentrates annually, plus cadmium, silver, and germanium sulphide ores, and practically all the world's supplies of radium. Treatment of the sulphide ores at Jadot-ville and elsewhere yields sulphuric acid as a by-product and this is used for treating the copper ores and for many other industrial purposes. Manganese ores are quarried near the Angolan border, quite close to the railway to Lobito.

Before the Congo's independence, the mining companies were induced to export a large part of their output from Katanga via Port Francqui and Kinshasa in order to make better economic use of the internal water and rail transport systems. The alternative route through Angola to Lobito is shorter, and when Katanga cut itself off from the rest of the country after independence, minerals were taken out by this route and by the other line to Beira on the east coast.

Outside Katanga, the chief mining areas are in southern Kasai where Tshikapa is the centre of a diamond-mining area producing gem-stones. Industrial diamonds, which form the bulk of the Congo's production, come from Bakwanga. Katanga produces half the tin, the remainder comes from the Kivu–Maniema area in the east. Gold is less important than it used to be, because the world price has not risen as much as for other metals and so many of the less-efficient mines have been abandoned. The chief centre now is at Kilo–Moto where a few big companies operate highly mechanized mines and employ a much smaller labour force than before the last war.

Economic and political developments

The Congo was unprepared for independence either politically or economically. The initial breakdown of the administration came in July 1960, a few days after independence, as a consequence of the revolt of the army against their European officers. Then came the breakaway of Katanga, which for a time ran its own affairs under a government headed by Tshombe backed by European industrial and mining companies and was only forced back into the Congo by United Nations forces. Since then the central government has divided the old Katanga Province into three parts, the North, East, and Lualaba on the west, presumably with the intention of reducing the overwhelming economic importance of Katanga as a whole. The period during which it asserted its independence was long enough for it to become apparent that Katanga was capable of forming a viable state, so long as it could maintain its trading links with the outside world via the Lobito railway. Under the Belgian régime, it contributed about 50 per cent. of the Congo's public finances, and without it the Léopoldville government could not have balanced its budget. On the river and rail systems, freight from Katanga constituted much of the traffic and prevented the systems being run at a loss. It accounted for 37 per cent. of the Congo's industrial output and 80 per cent. of the country's electrical generating capacity. Clearly its wealth is of critical importance for the economy of the Congo as a whole.

Fortunately for the future of the Congo there was and is little basis for the development of Katangan nationalism. The people are very mixed. The Balunda, who are strong in the south-west, the new Lualaba province, are far from being homogenous. The northerners are mainly Baluba. The townspeople are largely immigrants, drawn from all over the Congo and neighbouring territories by the chance of wage employment; one-third of the total Katangan population is from other provinces or countries. Outside the towns the population is sparse, less than ten to the square mile, less in fact, than in any other province; the size of France, Katanga contained only 2 million people. Now the secessionist spirit seems to be dead, and the mining companies ask only to be allowed to carry on producing copper and other minerals with the minimum of disturbance. In the early sixties they were remarkably successful, for mineral production in Katanga was scarcely interrupted.

With eighty major tribes spread over an area the size of western Europe, a weak central government, and foreign interference from several directions,

it is not surprising that the country is continuing to suffer from revolts and disturbances. The Baluba people have probably suffered more from the disorders than any other tribal group. They are an energetic, intelligent people who were ready to work as labourers, building railways and working in the mines, in the early years of the Belgian régime. Later they took up trading, lorry-driving, and growing cash crops. As a result they are now widely distributed through the Congo and, as in the case of the Ibos in Nigeria, their success has earned them the dislike of their neighbours. After independence, while the Bakongo were able to take over the administration of the lower Congo, Kinshasa, and eventually the whole country, the Baluba were scattered and badly placed to seize power. Their homeland was divided between northern Katanga and southern Kasai. In both they attempted to form their own governments, but in both they were minorities, and while the Baluba in Katanga suffered at the hands of the secessionist state's army, those in Kasai came under the pressure of Kinshasa forces.

By 1964 the European population in the Congo had dropped to about 50,000; of these, Belgians numbered about 25,000, compared with 113,000 in 1958. Now in 1968 there are not enough Congolese capable of replacing Europeans in the higher posts of the commercial and industrial concerns and both efficiency and production have declined. The mines continue to produce, the plantations to yield, and many of the services, such as the river steamers, continue to function. During the fighting and confusion people flocked into the towns and villages from the rural areas for greater security, foodstuff production declined and half the urban population was unemployed. The Congo franc was reduced to only a fraction of its official value and early in 1964 devaluation took place. When United Nations forces left, civil war broke out again and for a time the central administration was in danger of a complete breakdown. Now there are some signs that stability is returning.

Over the years 1910 to 1960 the Congo made faster and steadier progress than any country in Africa, perhaps in the world. The total output of goods and services increased at an average rate of over 4 per cent. annually. This was possible because of the abundant natural resources, above all minerals, and because of the colonial-type economy. Only the big companies in the Congo were in a position to obtain capital from Europe. They maintained wages at a fairly low level and this enabled them to invest large sums every year in new

155

machines and equipment of every kind. The smaller companies were short of capital but managed to continue operations, again because of low wages. With independence this situation is changing. Wage rates are increasing while efficiency declines. As a result, many of the smaller firms have gone out of business. Others have closed down with the departure of their Belgian owners and managers. So unemployment is increasing and it seems that eventually the rate of investment will decline and the economy may cease to expand.

For the future, much depends on the speed at which a new form of economic organization develops from the old colonial system, and the stability or otherwise of the administration. The basic resources of the Congo are immense. Many of the people have received a primary education and are accustomed to wage labour. The population at least until recently has been growing rapidly. But the problems of adjustment to the new conditions are enormous.

GABON

Gabon is a small country lying astride the equator between Congo Brazzaville and the Atlantic. In shape it compares with Sierra Leone, having a lagoon coast in the south, and creeks, estuaries, and deltas further north. Like Senegal, it has old ties with France. The citizens of Libreville, the capital, were French subjects as early as 1839; as a result many of the people speak French and mulattoes make up 10-15 per cent. of the town's population.

For many years Gabon formed a part of French Equatorial Africa. Having greater resources than its neighbours, it was required to help pay for their development, notably for the new towns and communications in Congo. After independence Gabon, though ready to strengthen its ties with France, was anxious to slacken those with its neighbours, so as to ensure that the profits from its own exports should be invested locally rather than for the benefit of others. The parallel with Katanga in relation to the Belgian Congo is obvious.

The relative wealth of Gabon is based on the exploitation of its extensive rain forests and rich ore deposits. Over a third of the export revenue is brought in by lumber and wood products. The most valuable timber is okoumé, a soft-wood that grows in extensive pure stands on abandoned bush-fallow land, i.e. as 'secondary regrowth'. It is in great demand for making veneer and plywood. The wood is light enough to float as soon as the trees are cut down, and great rafts of okoumé are floated down the Ogowé river to the coast (Fig. 44).

Before the Second World War a large labour force of some 20,000 was employed in forestry, many of the labourers having been forced to take up the work. After the war, forced labour ceased, wages rose, and so the timber companies found it paid to mechanize. Until this time a number of small African firms had been involved in the trade, but only the large companies could afford the tractors and motorized lumber barges that now came into use. Furthermore, the cost of permits for cutting was constantly being increased, with the result that most of the African timber contractors were forced out of the trade. Only about 12,000 wage-earners, about a quarter of the entire labour force in the country, are now employed in the wood industry, and many of them are immigrants from Nigeria, Togo, and Dahomey. Of the 0.8 million tons of timber produced in 1966, a large part was processed in the big plywood factory at Port Gentil at the mouth of the Ogowé river. One of the largest of its kind in the world, it failed to operate at full capacity for some time because French home-based manufacturers were afraid of the competition and successfully opposed the Gabon exporters.

Internal transport is very difficult indeed. Until 1960 there were no railways in the country and in spite of some efforts to build roads, the mileage is still low partly because of the natural obstacles to construction. The rainfall exceeds 160 inches locally and the coastal lowlands are interrupted by lagoons and creeks lined with reeds and mangrove swamps. The Crystal mountains and southernmost parts of the country are very rugged. Until recently the hinterland of Libreville, in the estuary of the Gabon, has been very restricted by lack of roads and railways. Its exports have been almost entirely timber. New roads are being built and work began in 1968 on a new port, Owendo, 10 miles outside Libreville.

Port Gentil at the mouth of a navigable river, the Ogowé (or Ogooué), has developed considerably in recent years. It handles over 1½ million tons annually, though vessels still have to anchor offshore and load and unload by lighter. It has benefited from the search for oil in the coastal area. The first wells came into production in 1957 and about 1·5 million tons of oil were exported in 1966. A refinery was completed in 1968 with a capacity of 630,000 tons to process oil from Congo Brazzaville as well as from Gabon. The search continues in the hope that heavy oil will be found to complement the Saharan light petroleum.

The country is rich in other mineral resources and their exploitation is leading to a great improvement in the transport system, since the largest ore

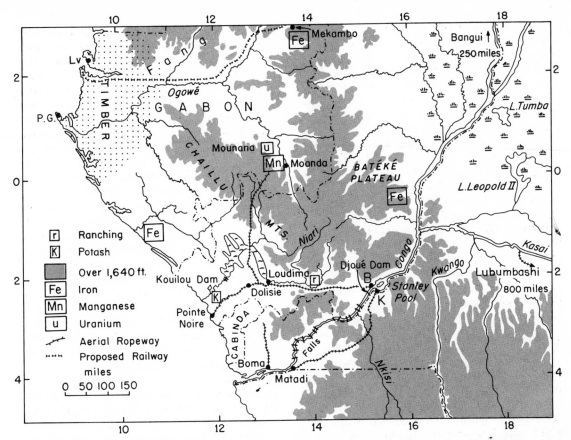

FIG. 44. *The lands around the lower Congo. Kinshasa (K) and Brazzaville (B) on either side of Stanley Pool are the capitals of the two Congo states. Cabinda is Portuguese, a part of Angola. The main ports of Gabon, Libreville (Lv), and Port Gentil (P.G.), have poor communications with the interior. The commercial crop production area in the Niari valley lies east of Loudima.*

bodies occur in the interior. Gold and diamonds are now far less important to the economy than manganese, uranium, and iron. One of the most important sources of manganese in the world lies in the southeast, at Moanda on the west side of the Ogowé river. The ores have a 50 per cent. manganese content and form a surface crust about 40 feet thick, with known reserves of 200 million tons. To exploit them, an aerial ropeway was completed across the Chaillu mountains in 1962, to link up with a railway running south to the Ocean railway at Dolisie in Congo Brazzaville. The manganese ore is treated at Moanda to remove fine material and increase the metal content. About 1·3 million tons of enriched ore was produced in 1966 making this mine the greatest manganese producer in the free world. The project provides direct employment to only 3,000 Gabonese but there are indirect benefits to the country's economy.

A few miles to the north of Moanda's manganese deposits, mining of uranium began at Mounana in 1961. World prices for uranium have been quite low but are rising, and the Mounana mines provide a source of supply which France can hope to control for her own purposes.

Two big deposits of iron-ore have been investigated, and at the time of writing a decision has still to be reached on which is to be worked first. The more accessible one lies within 25 miles of the coast at Milingué, but with an iron content of only 43 per cent. it would have to be enriched for export. The other lies in the extreme north-east of the country at Mekambo, and extraction would involve building a railway line 435 miles long across difficult country to the Gabon estuary. The cost would be heavy, but the ore is high grade, about 60 per cent. iron, and the reserves have been put at 700 million tons as compared with the 80 million at Milingué.

157

In both cases, the distance to consumers in the U.S.A. and north-west Europe is considerably greater than from Nouadhibou, and if the ore is to compete with Mauritanian ore it may be worth smelting it locally, using hydro-electric power, and exporting the cast-iron.

Agricultural development in the interior has been slow. The rural population is very sparse indeed; transport is poor and expensive so prices for the producer are low, and in any case, the people are not very keen on farming. About a quarter of the Gabonese population belong to the Fang nation which numbers altogether about half a million. Many of the Fang used to live in the northern Cameroons, but they were driven out by the Fulani about 200 years ago and many of them shifted south from the savanna into the forest lands near the Ogowé river, conquering the small forest tribes. By the end of the last century many of them were settled in villages sited on trade routes and were profiting from the export of rubber and ivory to the coast and by distributing salt and other goods through the interior. More recently, many of the young men have been either attracted to the timber industry or forced into it, staying away from their homes for months or years at a time. Three-quarters of the unmarried workers, it has been reckoned, never return to their own villages and wander aimlessly from one forest camp to another. The social cohesion of the Fang has broken down as a result, particularly near the southern limits of their distribution where they are intermingled with other peoples, and their numbers have diminished. Further north, however, many have settled down as peasant farmers, and some have become quite enthusiastic cocoa-growers.

Cocoa is now the country's third export by value, but the amount is small as compared with the figures for west African output; a mere 3,000 tons annually. Much of it finds its way to the coast at Douala, in Cameroon, which is more accessible to the producing areas than Port Gentil (Fig. 45). Some goes abroad clandestinely by way of Equatorial Guinea where prices are sometimes higher. Rice production near Tchibanga in the south has been increasing, but in 1959 was little more than a thousand tons. Some of it was flown to market in Port Gentil where it was found to be more expensive and poorer in quality than rice imported from Madagascar and elsewhere.

Meat production is negligible, and in the past supplies have been flown in from Cameroon and Chad. Fish are a more important item in the diet; the rivers yield some 10,000 tons annually. From time to time whales have been caught off the coast and the meat sold locally. In general food in the towns is scarce and expensive, and is likely to remain in short supply until communications improve.

The prospects for Gabon are relatively bright because of the income it is likely to obtain from the development of its mineral resources. Port Gentil and its immediate neighbourhood are likely to form the focus of industrial development in the immediate future. Later on, if the railway to Mekambo is constructed, its ocean terminus on the peninsula opposite Libreville might form another centre of industrial activity. But the population of the country is too sparse at present to be able to make full use of the resources to hand. In west Africa, such a situation would be transformed by large-scale migration from the interior; here the interior is just as sparsely settled as the coast.

CENTRAL AFRICAN REPUBLIC

Formerly known as Ubangi-Shari, the Republic stretches north from the humid equatorial forests bordering the Congo's main right-bank tributary to the dry plains of the Chad basin. It owes its name to M. Boganda, an unfrocked priest who was the leading politician in the territory from 1952 until his death in an air crash in 1959. He had hoped that the countries of French Equatorial Africa would form a central African state with its capital at Brazzaville. But this the other states were unwilling to do, and only the name of the proposed union now survives as that of one of the smallest of the new African states.

The Republic is indeed central African. Its main commercial link with the outside world is Bangui, the capital, on the Oubangui or Ubangi river, at the head of navigation from Brazzaville. Thirty miles of rapids prevent boats from continuing further upstream, though above the rapids, boats of up to 100 tons can use the river from mid-June to November. There are no railways in the country. A line from Bangui to Chad has long been under consideration, but is unlikely to be constructed. The projected lines to Mekambo in Gabon and in Cameroon from Yaoundé to the north would provide useful outlets to the more productive western part of the country. The road system, largely owing to the efforts of a single colonial governor, is one of the best in tropical Africa (Fig. 45).

The people belong to several different tribes, none of them large. At the beginning of the century settlements were dispersed, and there was not a single town with a population of more than 2,000.

Since the last war the settlement pattern has been transformed by the movement of most of the people into village clusters round the main administrative centres. In these new villages the houses are lined up along the roads, with no regard to family relationships which used to determine the old house pattern. At the beginning of the rains, people leave the urban clusters to go farming on land at a distance, and stay away through the growing season. Then they return with the harvest and sell their surpluses in the towns. As a result of the movement to the towns, many areas are more sparsely settled than ever they were, and much of the region is completely empty for much of the year.

This attraction of the towns is known throughout Africa, and indeed the rest of the world, but in the Central African Republic it seems to be peculiarly well marked. The explanation is uncertain. The French administrative centres were established on trade routes where rubber and ivory were collected together for export. Some people were attracted to them by the opportunities for paid employment; others came originally to visit the dispensaries or were sent to school in the towns and decided that they liked the freer social life. The French accelerated the process by forcing farmers to grow cotton, an unpopular crop, and many moved into the town to escape the coercion. In the bush, the old small social groups began to disintegrate and the remaining people left.

Greater contact with civilization has not led to much agricultural improvement; shifting cultivation is still the norm. Cotton, the main commercial crop, remains rather unpopular and the acreage has declined in recent years. Improved strains have maintained production at about 40,000 tons, representing about 40 per cent. of the country's exports, but this level of production had already been reached by 1941. Returns to the cultivators are small because the costs of transport to Europe are so high; and this applies to every crop. Coffee-growing was encouraged after rubber production declined in the 1920's, European plantations were established, and now coffee exports stand at about 10,000 tons annually. Natural conditions are favourable for sisal and the acreage increased in the early fifties when prices were high; but with lower prices the Republic's crop cannot compete with sisal grown nearer the coast in east Africa.

As in the Zande country of south-west Sudan some attempt has been made to process crops to supply the local market, small as it is. A power-station on the Bouali falls completed in 1955 supplies power for a textile mill using local cotton;

palm-oil from the southern tip of the country is used for making soap; Bangui has a few small tanneries and sawmills. In recent years, alluvial diamonds have accounted for about half the total export receipts and Africans are being trained in diamond cutting. But the economic outlook of the country is not bright. Perhaps it would benefit from inter-regional trade with Chad if a railway were ever to be built from Fort Lamy to Bangui—but construction costs would be high. In any case a line from Douala to N'Gaoundéré is under construction and there have been discussions about a project to build a branch line to Bangui. At present the Central African Republic is one of Africa's pauper states, relying heavily on subsidies from France and support from neighbouring states.

CONGO BRAZZAVILLE

Moyen Congo was the poorest of all the poor countries of French Equatorial Africa, lacking both natural resources and people. In 1961 its population was estimated to be about 850,000 giving an overall density of seven persons to the square mile. The soils are mainly sandy and leached and give poor returns. The northern part of the country, drained by the Congo, stagnates under equatorial forest; the Atlantic coast is marshy and backed by infertile plains and rugged mountains. In spite of this unpromising background, the territory benefited more from capital investment under the French than any other part of the Federation.

The reason for the high rate of investment is to be found in the position of the country, between the coast and the navigable Congo. Most of the money went into transport—above all into the construction of the Ocean railway and the port of Pointe Noire. Until 1925 there were no roads. Supplies for half the Federation were carried to Brazzaville by the railway on the Belgian side of the river. So in 1921 the line was started from Pointe Noire across the Mayumbe mountains. It took thirteen years to complete and only came into full operation in 1946 when the port of Pointe Noire was properly equipped. In the north of the country, transport is still almost entirely by river (Fig. 45).

Brazzaville, at the terminus of the Ocean railway, grew into a thriving city after 1945. Its hinterland could not compare with that of Léopoldville, but it was the capital of the Federation and much money was spent on developing it accordingly. People were attracted to the new towns. Into Brazzaville came the young men of the Mboshi, who live in the northern forests to settle in the native township, Poto-Poto. The Vili tribe living near the coast gravitated towards Pointe Noire. Between the two towns lived the Balati and various branches of the Bakongo nation, the most evolved and enterprising people in western equatorial Africa who form nearly a half of the total population of the country. At first hostile to the French administration they adapted themselves to the colonial conditions quite successfully and came to dominate the new state. They retain a strong feeling of solidarity with the Bakongo across the frontiers of Angola and Congo Kinshasa and this is likely to have a persistent influence on political developments in the region.

Political parties in Congo Brazzaville, as in the neighbouring state to the south, have a tribal basis. Friction between the tribes and parties has led to bloodshed on more than one occasion, especially in the capital where different tribes live side by side and the situation is aggravated by the large number of young men who have come in from the bush to seek work and have been unsuccessful. Brazzaville's population had grown to 145,000 by 1958; since then it has ceased to be federal capital, industrial development is slow, and the demand for labour has diminished.

Pointe Noire appears to be more favourably placed for future development in spite of the fact that the seat of government for the country has been shifted to Brazzaville. Its population has increased rapidly and traffic through the port, mainly on account of shipments of manganese ore from Moanda in Gabon, rose from 300,000 tons in 1953 to 2·2 million tons in 1965. Several important projects recently set in motion depend on Pointe Noire for imports and exports. The town takes its name from black seepages of bitumen at the base of cliffs nearby and a small oilfield associated with the bitumen produces about 60,000 tons of petroleum annually. More important are potash deposits about 25 miles north-east of the town, at a depth of 1,000 to 2,000 feet, which are believed to be amongst the world's largest. Mining, which is expected to begin in 1969, may be at a rate of half a million tons annually, representing about 4 per cent. of world consumption. Hopes for the future are based on the Kouilou hydro-electric project which it was hoped to complete in the sixties.

At present the economy of the country depends heavily on exports of timber, especially the tree called *limba* which grows most extensively in the valley of the Sangha river. Some is used locally in Brazzaville and Kinshasa, but most of it is exported to West Germany. The resources are large and an effort is being made to conserve them by replanting. In the Mayumbe hills an example set by the Belgians is being followed; entrepreneurs are allowed to clear forest if they agree to plant banana-trees afterwards and care for *limba* trees planted amongst the bananas by the Forestry Service. The contractors benefit from the sale of the timber and bananas, and it is hoped that at the end of the contract the government will be able to take back established plantations of *limba*.

Cassava is the staple food everywhere except on the north-western plateaux. Production of export crops has not made much progress. A post-war scheme for growing groundnuts on the Batéké plateau failed sadly on account of droughts and poor soils. Cocoa has been introduced to the Souanké area near the Cameroon frontier and the area under this crop is now expanding slowly east towards the Sangha river. Extraction of the crop is difficult. Large oil-palm plantations have been established near the Congo river in the vicinity of Ouesso, and African farmers have begun to grow Virginia tobacco in various places both for export to France and for use in locally produced cigarettes.

Livestock rearing has never been important and the large towns have been supplied in the past with frozen meat flown in from Chad. In the future there seems to be a chance that meat will be produced locally, for a large herd of some 10,000 Ndama cattle is thriving on well-watered pastures in the Niari valley near the railway line and no more than 80 miles west of Brazzaville. Country folk rely mainly on fish caught in the local rivers for their animal protein. In the last few years Africans on the coast have been instructed in modern methods of sea fishing, and some 3,000 tons of tuna and sardine are being landed annually at Pointe Noire.

The most important agricultural developments in the country have taken place in the Niari valley, which is followed by the Ocean railway for 60 miles. About 1,000 square miles of fertile soils were found to occur there in a sparsely settled stretch of country and European settlers were attracted by the possibilities. Amongst them were former members of the French wartime resistance movement, maquisards from Aubeville, who emigrated to the Niari valley in 1946 and have since worked hard together under their wartime leader. In the first five years they suffered badly from pests, diseases, and hail but managed to build houses for themselves and to raise groundnuts, tobacco, and rice, plus a variety of market-garden crops to supply a growing market in Brazzaville. They were assisted by the agricultural advisory services who turned the valley into a kind of field laboratory where new crops and methods of cultivation could be tested. African farmers were encouraged by their example to try new methods; land was ploughed for them, and it is said that their income has increased fivefold. In addition, cane plantations and a refinery in the valley supply most of the sugar requirements of the country, and several thousand tons of rice are grown for sale in the towns. Kayes-Jacob which did not exist until 1955 had grown to 12,500 in 1961.

These developments in the Niari valley give some basis for hoping that with improvements in communications agricultural production will increase. But much depends on the attitude of the local people; at present it seems that the young men would prefer to live on the edge of starvation in the towns rather than live frugally in the bush.

CAMEROON

The Cameroon Federation is made up of two former Trust Territories; the eastern one, a large triangular country with a population of about 3 million, was administered by France; Western Cameroon, very much smaller but with a population approaching one million, was administered by Britain as a part of Eastern Nigeria. Together, they formed before the First World War, the greater part of the German colony of Kamerun, which was conquered by the French and British and divided between them. The British part consisted of two narrow strips on either side of the Benue river, both of which have now been incorporated in northern Nigeria, and a broader area including the Bamenda highlands and Cameroon mountain which formed the Southern Cameroons. The people of the latter area are ethnically closer to their eastern neighbours than to Nigeria and in 1961 they voted to join the Cameroon Republic. The two territories thus reunited are experiencing some difficulties arising from having been administered separately under two different colonial systems for over forty years, and acquiring in the process different languages, and legal and monetary systems. In 1965 a customs frontier still separated them.

Although the steep western escarpments of the Bamenda highlands and Mandara mountains form a distinct physical barrier between Cameroon and Africa to the west, there are many resemblances between the new federation and the countries of west Africa. Like Nigeria, Cameroon combines a Muslim-dominated northland of savanna and steppe, and southern forestlands with mission-educated negroes. Of the northerners, three-quarters of a million are pagans belonging to many different tribes who found refuge in the Mandara mountains from raiding parties of horsemen, coming

down from Kanem and Bornu. Another half million people, mainly Muslims, live on the Sahelian plains stretching north-east of the mountains towards the Logone river and Chad. The majority of the southerners are concentrated on volcanic highlands in the west, and on the lower plateau near Yaoundé. Between the well-settled lands in the north and south lie 300 miles of sparsely settled country including the Adamawa plateau and savanna plains north of the upper Sanaga river.

Although a main road runs north from Douala through well-settled country to Foumban and on via N'Gaoundéré to Garoua, Maroua, and Fort Lamy, most of the northern produce is still exported by the Benue river. River steamers, pushing trains of barges laden with petroleum and cement, begin to reach the port of Garoua in late July, and then return 1,200 miles to the Niger delta, carrying hides, skins, groundnuts, and cotton. The last of the boats must be clear of Garoua within six weeks of the opening of the shipping season, for the level of the river can fall rapidly, stranding tardy boats until the following rainy season. The main harvests come later on, so crops must be stored for six months or more before they can be shipped, thereby increasing costs of storage and transport. The season of navigation could be lengthened by constructing a dam above Garoua, to store some of the floodwater and release it by degrees in September and October. A less expensive way to improve navigation would be dredging further downstream, especially below the confluence of the Benue and the sediment-laden Faro river.

The nearest railway to the producing areas of the north is the Maiduguri extension of the Nigerian railway system. This could easily be extended a little further to serve the north of Cameroon, but for political reasons, the Cameroon government is more inclined to favour the construction of a line from Yaoundé north to Fort Archambault in Chad Territory (Fig. 45). Such a line would be expensive to construct and is unlikely to pay because of the long stretches of empty country providing no traffic, and because road transport would be a strong competitor. The first stage is to be an extension of the Yaoundé line up the Sanaga valley to N'Gaoundéré which will allow the exploitation of very large bauxite deposits, estimated to exceed a thousand million tons, near Mantap a little to the south of N'Gaoundéré. This line will also provide access to parts of the Central African Republic, offering a more direct route to the sea than the alternative one by river steamer to Brazzaville, and the Ocean railway to Pointe Noire. But the traffic available is

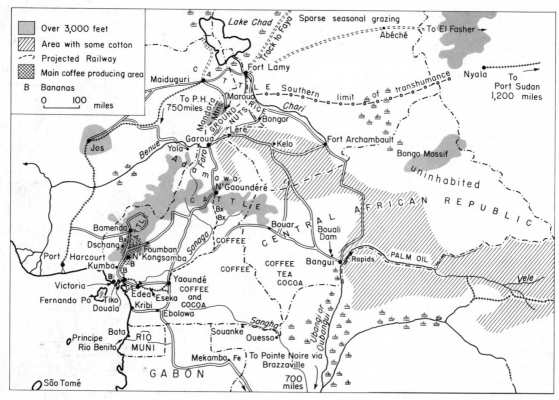

Over 3,000 feet
Area with some cotton
Projected Railway
Main coffee producing area
B Bananas
0   100 miles

Lake Chad Sparse seasonal grazing
To El Fasher
Abéché
Track to Faya
Fort Lamy
Maiduguri
CATTLE
Southern   limit   of   transhumance
Nyala
To Port Sudan 1,200 miles
To P.H. 750 miles
Maroua
RICE
Chari
GROUNDNUTS
Bongor
Léré
Kelo
Fort Archambault
Mandara Mts.
Garoua
Yola
Benue
Jos
Faro
Adamawa
N'Gaoundéré
CATTLE
Bx
Bx
Bongo Massif
uninhabited
CENTRAL   AFRICAN   REPUBLIC
Bamenda
Dschang
Bx
Foumban
N'Kongsamba
Sanaga
COFFEE
Bouar
Bouali Dam
Port Harcourt
Kumba
B
B
COFFEE
COFFEE
COFFEE TEA COCOA
Bangui
Rapids
PALM OIL
Vele
Victoria
GS
Yaoundé
COFFEE and COCOA
Fernando Po
Tiko
Edea
Eseka
Kribi
Ebolowa
Douala
Sangha
Ubangi or Oubangui
Principe
Rio Benito
Bata
RIO MUNI
Souanke
Ouesso
São Tomé
Mekambo Fe
To Pointe Noire via Brazzaville
GABON
700 miles

FIG. 45. *The Cameroon Republic and Central African Republic. The area between Lake Chad and the upper Oubangi is over 700 miles from the sea and will probably be very slow to develop economically. The most productive area lies within a hundred miles of Douala and is quite close to Port Harcourt and the populous region of south-east Nigeria.*

not very great, and is unlikely to be enough to make both rail and river routes pay.

The main feature of north–south trade is the movement of cattle from the northern plains and the Adamawa plateau, where Fulani herdsmen graze about a million head of cattle. Hundreds of wells have been provided for them by the central government in recent years and a stock improvement centre has been established in Adamawa. In order to avoid deaths from disease and loss of weight amongst cattle on the long trek to the coast through country infested with tsetse-fly, refrigerated stores have been built at Maroua and N'Gaoundéré so that meat from cattle slaughtered locally can be frozen for export by air to Douala and Yaoundé and even as far afield as Gabon and Brazzaville.

Lines of communications in southern Cameroon radiate from the embayment overlooked by Cameroon mountain. Douala, situated 15 miles from the sea on the left bank of the Wuri river, is by far the largest port, with a mile of quays and handling a million tons annually. A long bridge curving

for nearly a mile across the Wuri river links it to the country on the west side of the estuary and carries the railway to N'Kongsamba, a town 3,000 feet up in the heavily settled highlands. The country immediately around Douala is forested, sparsely settled, and not very productive. Foodstuffs are brought 30 miles down the river by canoe from Yabassi and others from Mungo west of the estuary. Plenty of fish are caught locally, and cattle for meat are driven down from the Bamiliké plateau. But as in most African towns, the local population is coming to rely more and more on imported rice and wheat flour. Of the population of Douala, some 200,000 in all, the majority are immigrants from the heavily settled Bamiliké plateau. About a quarter of them have no regular employment and the suburb of New Bell (named after a local chief) presents all the usual problems of growing African towns—crime, prostitution, and political unrest.

A dam across the Sanaga river at Edea, about 40 miles from the river mouth and 30 miles south-east of Douala, harnesses the energy of falls 60 feet high

162

to generate electricity on a large scale. The capacity of the plant in 1963 was 160 MW. Most of the energy is absorbed by an aluminium plant alongside the dam which produces 46,000 tons of metal yearly. The Edea scheme accounts for a large part of the big French investment in Cameroon, but its effects on the country as a whole are limited. Only about 2,500 people are employed on the power plant and factory together; the alumina is imported from Guinea, and the ingots are shipped to north-west Europe for further processing. Nevertheless, a number of Africans are gaining experience in modern industry and engineering; in time, the reserves of bauxite in Adamawa may be exploited, and quite soon, aluminium utensils will probably be made locally for African markets. Power from the scheme is also employed in a rubber factory at Edea, and by sawmills and various small factories in Douala producing soap and cloth.

The nearby ports of Victoria-Bota and Tiko with populations of about 20,000 are far less important and may suffer from the competition of Douala as the latter extends its hinterland north to Kumba and along the road to Mamfe. Both small ports depend heavily on the produce of the plantations between Cameroon mountain and the boundary with East Cameroon. Most of these plantations were started by the Germans and confiscated from them after the First World War, but by the outbreak of the Second World War some quarter of a million acres were again in German hands. After the war they were leased to the Cameroons Development Corporation which further extended the area under bananas, rubber, oil-palms, and cocoa. Other plantations are in the hands of commercial companies and three large timber firms operate in the area. The labour force for these concerns, totalling about 25,000, is mainly made up of migrants from the north, who leave their homes about April and return about Christmas time. Before the separation of the two countries many of the immigrant labourers came from Nigeria.

The people living behind Victoria and Tiko have themselves begun to grow crops for export. Land available for cultivation has become scarcer and, as a result, customary methods of tenure are being ignored and land is being bought and sold. Cocoa and coffee are planted on land that has already been cropped for some years with food crops such as cocoyams, cassava, and maize, until yields have begun to diminish, and the young trees are left to grow up amongst oil-palms that survived the initial clearing. A co-operative movement which started with government stimulus in 1952 has flourished;

Harvesting bananas on a West Cameroon plantation. The fully developed bunch, now ready for harvesting, is being severed from the plant by a worker with a machete.

it sold nearly 1½ million stems of bananas in 1958. Since then the banana crop has suffered from low prices, disease and tornadoes, and oil-palms have become the most profitable crop.

Tree crops are also produced on a large scale

163

Flood plain in West Cameroon. Rising on the hills in the background, a headwater of the Katsina Ala meanders over a broad swampy plain formed by a lava flow which has partly filled a pre-existing valley. A little way downstream the river plunges over a waterfall cut in the lavas.

north of Douala, where the low coastal plain underlain by sedimentary rocks is widely covered with wild oil-palms which are not fully exploited because of labour shortage. Banana plantations have been established near the railway ensuring rapid movement to the port, and in spite of the same difficulties as those experienced in the west, production has increased rapidly. Cocoa, coffee, and timber are other products of this area, mainly in the hands of companies directed by Europeans, but with growing African participation.

Inland, the grassy highlands of Bamenda stretch eastward into Bamiliké and Bamoum. This is beautiful open country on volcanic hills rising to 6,000 feet and more, with bamboo forests on the higher peaks, fine waterfalls, and neatly built villages sheltering alongside forest remnants in the valley heads. The cool freshness of the atmosphere is a great attraction to Europeans tired of the heavy humidity of the coast and many of them come to stay at Bamenda and Dschang. Because of the high rainfall and strong relief, communications are difficult; only one all-season road links Bamenda and Nigeria, and access is easier from the east.

A succession of invaders has entered the highlands from the north; the Tikar were driven south by the Chamba, and the Chamba in turn by the Fulani. These people with well-developed chief-

taincy systems are now settled on the highlands, while descendants of the earlier inhabitants are scattered about in numerous small groups through the forested areas at lower levels. The Fulani have continued to arrive on the grasslands, and their herds have greatly increased in numbers over the last half century, much to the displeasure of settled agriculturalists who already have insufficient land. Attempts have been made to check the movement of more cattle into the area from the north in the interests of controlling rinderpest, but it is difficult to stop them coming because herds are always moving from place to place, from wet-season high-level pastures to dry-season grazings at lower levels. The agriculturalists are keeping more animals too; some are left in the hands of Fulani herdsmen, others are being incorporated into the local farming system, to provide manure for the coffee and other crops.

Fertile soils derived from recent volcanic ash in the higher areas of the west are the main sources of coffee and tea. Red soils derived from older lavas are less productive, but are carefully terraced in the heavily settled areas and support a wide variety of crops. Laterite soils at lower levels are more sparsely settled but are not attractive to the people of the congested villages. They prefer to migrate to the coast.

The capital of the federation, Yaoundé, with a population of 100,000, lies 150 miles north-east of Douala, on a rolling plateau with a pleasant climate, just north of the equatorial forest zone. As the centre of one of the richest agricultural areas in the country producing coffee, cocoa, and palm-oil, and linked by rail to the coast, and by road to Bangui and Brazzaville, it has considerable commercial importance.

Outside these well-settled areas of the south, economic activity is very limited. European companies exploit the timber of the forests south-east of Douala, where the sawmill at Eseka is one of the best equipped in the world, and have established some rubber, cocoa, and oil-palm plantations. The small port of Kribi ships cocoa from the Ebelowa area about 100 miles inland. Nearby iron-ore deposits may be worked in the future, and power developed from the falls on the Lobé river. In general, soils are poor, the population sparse, and hunting and shifting cultivation persist.

The economy of the Cameroon federation has benefited from heavy investment in the post-war years and is in a healthier state than that of many African countries. But its resources are limited; the chief minerals, bauxite and iron, are unlikely to be worked for many years, and much will depend in the future on relations with western Europe.

Politically the country seems to have settled down well after a turbulent period, about 1960, when the heavily settled Bamiliké area suffered from terrorists opposed to the government. The main centre of political unrest in the future is likely to be Douala with its jobless immigrants.

EQUATORIAL GUINEA AND THE PORTUGUESE ISLANDS

Equatorial Guinea consists of Rio Muni, between Cameroon and Gabon, with an area of about 10,000 square miles, Fernando Po, about one-tenth that size, plus Annobon, $6\frac{1}{2}$ square miles, and several other even smaller islands. They became independent of Spain towards the end of 1968.

Rio Muni was very much neglected until after 1945, because Fernando Po was so much more attractive to European investors and settlers, but in recent years European concessionaires using Nigerian labourers have been busy extracting mahogany and okoumé from the great forests of the coastal plans, and floating the logs down the Benito and Muni rivers to the sea. Local Africans grow coffee on the central uplands east of Bata, the capital, and the Fang who live in the east, cut off from their countrymen in Cameroon and Gabon, grow a certain amount of cocoa.

Fernando Po, like the other smaller islands to the south-west, is of volcanic origin; the harbour of St. Isabel the capital is a crater breached by the sea. From a narrow coastal plain occupied by large European cocoa and coffee plantations and small African farms, the ground rises quite steeply to a height of nearly 9,500 feet in the Pico de Santa Isabel. The southernmost part of the island is so steep and entrenched by streams fed by the heavy rains, some 400 inches annually, that it is almost impenetrable and is scarcely inhabited. The middle levels between 3,500 and 5,500 feet have been cleared of forest and are used as pasture for cattle; as a result the island is self-sufficient in dairy products. In the sixteenth century, slaves were brought to the island from Gabon and Angola to work on sugar plantations, and later when the Royal Navy leased Santa Isabel as a base against the slave trade, freed slaves were landed here and settlers came from Sierra Leone. Still the labour supply is inadequate; the total population is only about 70,000, of whom 6,000 are Europeans, and the plantations rely on Ibo labourers from eastern Nigeria numbering about 20,000.

At one time all the islands were Portuguese possessions but Fernando Po and Annobon were ceded to Spain in 1778 in return for Spain's recognition of Portuguese rights in Brazil, and now Portugal is left with Príncipe and São Tomé, 42 and 330 square miles respectively. They are smaller editions of Fernando Po. Cocoa is the main crop, in fact the two islands were the world's main cocoa producers for the first few years of this century, until complaints of slave labour scared away British chocolate manufacturers. Cocoa still accounts for three-quarters of the exports but oil-palm products and copra are also of some importance. Both islands are heavily settled, but they are so fertile and intensively cultivated that additional labour is required and contract labourers are brought mainly from Mozambique to work on the plantations.

All the islands are closely tied economically either to Spain or Portugal and trade is mainly with these countries. The plantations are owned by Europeans and worked largely by immigrant labour. Nevertheless, standards of living are not low by African standards. Perhaps in time to come the islands will attract tourists of the tougher kind, ready to put up with equatorial rains and a humidity that would deter the crowds ready to flock to the Canaries.

10

Ethiopia and Somalia

RUGGED escarpments overlooking the Sudan, and desert plains in north-east Kenya, separate the highlands of Ethiopia and the Horn of Africa from the rest of the continent. The highlands, shaped in plan like the outspread wings of a butterfly, are well watered with 80 inches of rain falling annually in the south-west, between 15 and 25 inches in the north-east. They are built of volcanic lavas overlying Mesozoic sandstones and limestones. From Lake Rudolf a rift valley runs north-east across the highlands. Several lakes, some fresh and others brackish are strung along the south-west end of the trough, which is about 30 miles wide and overlooked by scarps some 3,000 feet high. The trough floor rises to about 6,000 feet near Addis Ababa. The Awash river enters from the west and flows north along the trough, eventually petering out on a marshy plain, where the rift broadens into the dry Danakil depression. This triangular desert depression, which locally descends 400 feet below sea-level, corresponds in shape with the south-west corner of Arabia, strongly suggesting that the two land masses on either side of the Red Sea and Gulf of Aden have been roughly torn apart. In fact, Ethiopia and Somalia have much in common, both physically and culturally, with Yemen and Arabia across the straits of Bab-el-Mandeb.

Most of the high country lies within Ethiopia, the Empire created by Menelik during the last decades of the nineteenth century in the face of Turco-Egyptian and European imperialism. Eritrea in the north, which takes its name from Mare Erythraeum, as the Romans called the Red Sea, was federated to Ethiopia in 1952; Somalia came into existence in 1960 on the fusion of British Somaliland with the Italian Trust Territory to the south-east. French Somaliland (now Afar and Issa) is no more than a small enclave, owing its importance to the port of Djibouti which is the terminus of the only railway to the central highlands (Fig. 46).

ETHIOPIA

The central highlands

The core of Ethiopia is the mountainous region, which may properly be called Abyssinia, stretching from the borders of Eritrea to the headwaters of the Awash river, where the majority of the people are Amharic-speaking Christians. 'The Amhara', in the words of R. E. Cheesman, 'is a Semitic immigrant to Abyssinia and is believed to have come from the Yemen. Hamitic peoples from Asia came over first and had already colonised the Abyssinian plateau and had driven the aborigines, possibly negroes, down to the lower levels. When the Amhara, a virile and warlike race arrived, the Hamitic occupants were pushed down the slope in their turn, and the Amhara, who are now the ruling class occupied the best lands. So the state of affairs today might be briefly explained by saying that on top of the plateau are the Amhara tribe, lower down on the escarpment are found the Hamitic peoples, and at the bottom in the hot lowland are the negroid tribes.' This over-simplifies a very complicated ethnic pattern and neglects the Galla, a light-skinned people who occupied much of the central highlands about three or four centuries ago and form about one-third of the total population of Ethiopia, about the same proportion as the Amharas.

A Semitic civilization brought from the Yemen over 2,000 years ago first struck roots in Tigrai near the borders of Eritrea, a sparsely populated plateau now strewn with the ruins of ancient cities; Aksum (or Axum), was the largest. Today it is no more than a village where small boys search the fields after heavy rainstorms and come upon corroded coins, 1,500 years old. Near the cathedral where the emperors are crowned, a few stone stelae, huge granite monoliths, still stand; the largest have fallen and the village goats play about the pieces. The people of Aksum were converted to Christianity about the fourth century and Gez, the language they spoke at the time, which is related to the dialects of south-west Arabia, is still used by the Ethiopian Coptic Church. The head of the Church, incidentally, was always an Egyptian appointed by the patriarch of Alexandria, but that link with the past has recently been severed, and the present *Abuna* is an Ethiopian appointed by the Emperor.

Muslim occupation of the coastlands in the ninth century cut Abyssinia off from the outside

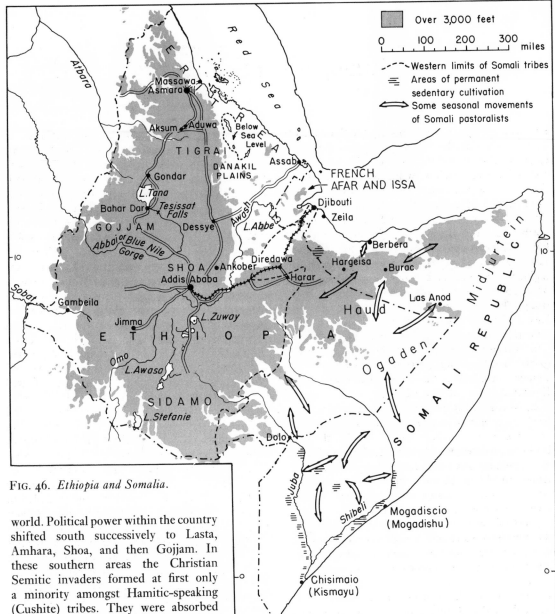

FIG. 46. *Ethiopia and Somalia.*

world. Political power within the country shifted south successively to Lasta, Amhara, Shoa, and then Gojjam. In these southern areas the Christian Semitic invaders formed at first only a minority amongst Hamitic-speaking (Cushite) tribes. They were absorbed racially, but still managed to retain their ancient cultural heritage. The Amhara language which evolved in the south is more akin to Cushite, while Tigrai and Tigrinya in the north are still basically Semitic.

The Agaw-speaking people who live north of Lake Tana may represent the old Cushitic or Hamitic sub-stratum in the population. A group of Agaw called the Falasha still practise a peculiar form of Jewry which was probably transplanted from southern Arabia some 2,000 years ago. Their adherence to Hebraic beliefs and customs is analogous to the persistence of monophysite Christianity amongst the Amharas. Survivals of this kind in Ethiopia, the preservation more or less intact of the languages, religions, and customs of a variety of peoples, give the country a museum-like quality. Ethiopia is an African microcosm.

The great variety of climates and the physical fragmentation afford a variety of niches for different biological and cultural groups. The Central Highlands, reaching a general level of 7,500 feet, are

The stelae at Aksum, Ethiopia. The tallest monolithic tower, grey granite and 70 feet high, is carved to represent a building of nine stories. One can pick out the door, windows, and also the rounded ends of logs supporting the imaginary stories. Sacrificial altars associated with the stelae indicate their pre-Christian age, and it follows that they must have been erected before A.D. 327 when Christianity was permanently established as the state religion.

crossed by high volcanic ranges of which the mountains of Semien north of Lake Tana exceed 14,000 feet above sea-level. Flat-topped hills with precipitous slopes, called *ambas*, rise above rich grassy plains studded here and there with volcanic cones and craters. Gorges, cutting through the volcanic rocks into sandstones and crystallines underlying them, divide the highlands into a number of separate blocks. Gojjam, for instance, is almost isolated by the circuitous course of the Blue Nile or Abbai river. Routeways cling to the watersheds and avoid the deep wooded valleys.

A Coptic church under construction in Eritrea. Its ancient faith and the Amharic language form the basis of Ethiopian nationalism.

The Abyssinians are very well aware of the affect of altitude and aspect on living conditions and distinguish between a number of altitudinal zones. The high plains above 8,000 feet, rich in springs, often cool and windy, are known as *dega*. The valleys and hot plains sunk far below the plateau, malarious and so far as possible avoided by the highlanders, are called *kwolla*. Between the two lies the *woyna dega*, literally the vine country, well-settled rolling country, dotted with villages and reminiscent of parts of upland central Europe.

Little is known about the soils, but they are derived from volcanic rocks and give the impression of being considerably more fertile than soils in most parts of Africa.

Woodland has been cleared from the *dega* and *woyna dega* and is now mainly confined to the major valleys; degraded savanna covers the steep slopes and tall forest trees are mainly confined to the wet, western scarps and the wide valley floors. The flat areas on the plateau are bare and cultivated. Excellent systems of terracing permit cultivation of steeply sloping hill-sides and locally permit irrigation. Churches and villages, often perched on hilltops, are surrounded by native trees, and plantations of eucalyptus provide firewood and building poles. Eucalyptus were first introduced by a French forester in 1895. Their extraordinary rapid growth attracted the Emperor's attention, he encouraged their distribution, and now they are characteristic of the highland landscape. Addis Ababa itself appears from a distance as a city of shining corrugated-iron roofs sprinkled through a forest of eucalyptus trees.

The number of plants indigenous to Abyssinia is not large, but a striking feature of the flora is the amazing diversity of the varieties of field crops, notably wheat and barley. The Russian plant breeder and geneticist, N. I. Vavilov, was led by the diversity to regard the Central Highlands as one of the eight independent centres of origin of the world's most important cultivated plants. It is interesting that the diversity existed here, whereas wheat and barley seem to have been unknown further south in High Africa until they were introduced by Europeans within the last few centuries.

The highlanders depend chiefly on *teff* (*Eragrostis abyssinica*), a small grain which they grow intensively at middle and high altitudes. They make it into a flat porous bread, called *enjera*, which is eaten with *wot*, a hot peppery sauce. Oats, barley, and wheat are also grown in the *dega* zone; oats for human consumption, not for animals, barley for brewing as well as making bread. Maize, introduced by the Portuguese, is best suited to the humid southwest. Chillie peppers are used to flavour most dishes, and *kat*, a mild intoxicant, is chewed or made into a stimulating drink.

Agricultural techniques are more advanced than in most parts of Africa not settled by Europeans, but still compare in many respects with those of medieval Europe. Ox-ploughs are normally used to prepare the ground for planting and most farmers keep a number of cattle to breed replacements for their plough teams. Beef is only eaten on special occasions, often uncooked. Many farmers will buy or rent a piece of land in the valley so that livestock can descend in the rainy season to warmer conditions while pastures on the high-level land are rested. The ploughs, which are lightly built of wood with a steel point, do not turn the soil but break it into chunks and ploughing may have to be repeated three or four times before an adequate seed-bed is prepared. F.A.O. experts have tried to persuade the farmers to try light, mouldboard ploughs but without much success so far. Seed is sown broadcast, sickles are used to harvest the corn, oxen trample the outspread sheaves to thresh the grain which is then tossed in the air for the chaff to be blown away by the wind.

Much could be done to increase the low yields and give the farmer a larger cash income. At present he sells only 10 to 20 per cent. of his produce and so his material standards of living are low. But most of the people are well fed; the land is not overcrowded, and there is no certainty that new ways

A farm near Addis Ababa, Ethiopia. Oxen trample the outspread sheaves to thrash out the grain, a few miles from the capital.

Roadside settlement alongside the Massawa–Addis Ababa highway, Ethiopia. The mud houses are roofed with corrugated iron. Trees in the background are eucalyptus.

would bring them greater contentment. Most European residents in Abyssinia are torn between the urge to modernize and a desire to preserve so much that is peculiarly charming; the Abyssinians in their own fashion and their own time contrive to do both.

Most of the people live in thatched mud-walled houses, usually circular and grouped together in farmsteads which stand isolated or in clusters around a church. Small towns which have grown up here and there are used as market centres rather than for habitation and every second house seems to be an inn. Of the big towns, Addis Ababa, with a population in 1968 of 500,000, is easily the largest and is attracting most of the modern industrial development. Dessye, at the crest of an escarpment where it is frequently cold and misty, is a big commercial centre at the junction of roads to Addis, Asmara, and Assab. Gondar, with its ruined palaces, its school of religious learning and sacred music is the regional centre of the country north of Lake Tana. Bahar Dar, on the south shore of the lake, is to be a new planned town, where factories are to be built making use of electricity generated by a new plant about 30 miles away at the Tesissat Falls on the Blue Nile. Very different are towns marking the caravan routes of old; ancient capitals such as Debra-Behran, still the centre for various local fairs, and Ankober, almost forgotten now, far away from the main roads on the eastern side of Shoa.

The other parts of the Empire

The Central Highlands formed the nucleus of the Empire. From his own chiefdom of Shoa, Menelik conquered the rich regions to the south, inhabited by Galla-speaking Muslims and by the Guraje who hold a wide range of religious beliefs. In 1889, when the Emperor John was killed fighting Mahdist invaders from the Sudan, Menelik became Emperor. He proceeded to establish his capital at Addis Ababa and then turned his attention to the highlands east of the rift, using the old Muslim city of Harar as a base to subdue the Galla-speaking peoples of the surrounding region. In later years he extended the circumference of the Empire in all directions to take in the Somali of Ogaden on the semi-arid eastern plains, the Afar or Dankali bordering French Somaliland and the negroid and Nilotic peoples on the escarpments and piedmont plains of the west and south.

The south-west highlands are the wettest part of Ethiopia with most rain between June and September and quite large amounts falling every month. In addition to the usual grain farming, many communities depend very largely on the cultivation of a species of plantain, *Ensete edule*. This plant, which looks like a banana plant growing 10 to 25 feet high, is usually planted around the houses on plots well manured with dung and ashes. The pseudostem formed by the sheaths of the leaves is the edible part, yielding a starch of high nutritional value, which can be used for making bread or a kind of porridge. Population and cattle densities in the *ensete*-growing areas are both high.

Communications in the south-west are being improved with new roads linking the outlying districts to Jimma and Addis Ababa, and it should prove to be one of the most productive parts of the country yielding timber, oilseeds, grain, cotton, coffee, and livestock.

The eastern plateaux and plains are much drier, the rains mainly being confined to April–May and October–November, and the country is mainly covered with acacia scrub and low grass except on the more humid heights bordering the rift. The Gallas who came into the area as nomadic pastoralists about the sixteenth century are now settled herders of cattle and agriculturalists. A few have adopted the plough, but the implements of most are very primitive, their hoes often consisting simply of poles with nails fixed in the heads. Towards the eastern plains where the rainfall diminishes to less than 15 inches, Galla and Somali pastoralists intermingle. In winter they congregate near water-holes or move up into the hills; in summer the light rains allow the flocks and herds to spread out over the plains where the Ethiopian government's control is uncertain. They are a tough people amongst whom a man was not considered to have proved himself until he had killed another.

The Danakil or Dankali depression is a dry, desolate area, one of the last parts of the world to be explored. Its nomad tribes earned such a reputation for savagery that the people of the highlands avoided the escarpments bordering the desert to be out of reach of their raids. The Galla took advantage of the vacuum when they invaded Ethiopia, colonizing the western escarpment as far north as Tigrai and forming a buffer between the highland and lowland peoples. To meet the Dankali on equal terms they had to remain warlike and until a few years ago remained as savage as their neighbours on the plains.

Now the desert can be crossed in a few hours by a new road linking the port of Assab to the main Massawa–Addis Ababa road at Dessye. The journey is still not without risk, for the country is extremely inhospitable with barren black lava flows, hot dusty salt-flats, and temperatures in July and August commonly reaching 120° F.

Eritrea, the newest addition to the Empire, provides Ethiopia with a coastline. About one-eighth the size of Ethiopia, and with a population of about 3 million, it is extremely heterogeneous, including almost the full range of physical conditions represented in the rest of the Empire and a great variety of ethnic groups. The highlands of Tigrai, which extend to the shores of the Red Sea and receive about 15–25 inches of rain and upwards of 40 inches locally, north of Asmara, support about half the population, principally Tigrinya and Tigrai-speaking Christians. Negro cultivators live south of the Mareb river. Beja and other nomads wander over the intensely dry hot plains bordering the Red Sea, wearing practically nothing and, as Doresse describes them, always vaguely on the move, pulling a camel behind them. Arabs have long been established in Massawa and Assab. Italian influence persists in Asmara.

With such a variety of tribes, religions, and languages it is not surprising that national feeling scarcely developed at all. Nevertheless, after the war a minority of the population, chiefly Muslims, was opposed to close association with Ethiopia, and the United Nations granted Eritrea a degree of autonomy within the Ethiopian Empire, the local administration retaining powers analogous to those of a state in the U.S.A. These powers are slowly being eroded away. Little investment is taking place in Asmara and attention has mainly been devoted in recent years to Assab, which was reconstructed by Yugoslav engineers from 1958 to 1961 with the intention of making it the main port for Addis Ababa.

Political and economic development

The supreme authority in Ethiopia is the Emperor Haile Selassie, a man of outstanding energy and devotion to the advancement of his country. In the past he has appointed all his subordinates and has taken a personal hand in all policy decisions. The provinces are no longer ruled by semi-autonomous chiefs but by governors, appointed by the Emperor and responsible to him through a minister. In recent years steps have been taken under his guidance towards introducing a constitutional form of government. A Parliament now exists but it is only partly elected and the Emperor can still exercise his veto. Although centralization of authority is helping to bind together a country which because of its diversity might otherwise fall apart, complaints are often made by foreign advisers about lack of co-ordination at high levels in government. Defects of this kind are strongly marked in many African states, but in Ethiopia such problems are particularly severe because a colonial administration did not last long enough for criteria of efficiency to become widely accepted and so tradition and status are even more firmly embedded guides to conduct than elsewhere.

The lack of educated people at all levels magnifies the administrative difficulties. Most of the people are unconcerned about progress and content to live much as their forefathers did; no more than 10 per

Africa House, Addis Ababa. This was built to house pan-African assemblies and it is also used by the United Nations Economic Commission for Africa.

cent. are literate, and the number in secondary schools could be accommodated in a score of large schools in Britain or the United States. In this land of many tongues, much of a student's time is taken up in acquiring a grounding first in his own language, then in Amharic, and finally in English before advanced studies can begin. Few people are properly trained for the top levels of government and much reliance has to be placed on foreign experts who are not always familiar enough with the ways and needs of the country. In these circumstances a great deal depends on the university at Addis Ababa producing an educated class capable of running the country and bridging the gap between ancient traditions and modern needs.

Poor communications have hindered political and economic development in the past. Merchants and travellers still rely on mules, donkeys, and pack-horses which are estimated to do three-quarters of all the carriage of goods in the country. Reed boats still operate on Lake Tana, though metal ones are slowly replacing them. The rivers are useless for navigation with the sole exception of the short stretch of the Baro or Sobat which can be used by steamboats in the wet season for a few tens of miles from the Sudanese frontier up to Gambeila. The only two railways in the country have unusually steep gradients and freight rates are high.

The Italians recognized that development depended mainly on improving communications and partly for this reason, partly to strengthen their hold on the country, spent about £80 million on roads during their short-lived occupation of the country, a sum unprecedented in colonial Africa. About 4,000 miles had been completed by the time the country was liberated by British troops in 1941. Subsequently they fell into disrepair and some of them are still unusable. However, a big programme of road building began in 1950, with aid from the World Bank and the United States, and increasing numbers of buses and heavy lorries are using the main roads radiating from Addis Ababa.

A little cargo is carried by air and Ethiopian Airlines, operated under an agreement with Trans-World Airlines, have done a great deal to reduce the country's isolation.

The railway running inland from Massawa was built in the hope of tapping Sudanese trade, but the construction of the line to Port Sudan put an end to this prospect and in the present state of the Eritrean economy traffic is very limited. With the development of Assab it appeared for a time that the Djibouti line might be uneconomic. However, the Ethiopians have been granted a 50 per cent. interest in the company, which is now called the Franco-Ethiopian Railway, plus certain transit privileges through Afar and Issa Territory (formerly called French Somaliland), and since 1958 it has been showing a profit. Tonnage passing through Djibouti has grown to about 2 million tons annually, and France has made available £4 million for extending the line to the Sidamo grain-growing region close to the Kenya border.

In spite of the improvements in transport, the Ethiopian economy remains self-contained in the sense that most people's wants are supplied by the local countryside and by local craftsmen. Cotton cloth has always been the most important item in imports and the textile industry has expanded in recent years to meet the demand. Plants established by the Italians at Asmara and Diredawa have been enlarged and new factories have been opened at Addis Ababa. Except in the largest towns, there is little opportunity for stimulating demand by advertising, and people remain conservative in their tastes. Retailing is in the hands of Greeks, Armenians, and Arabs; the Amhara disdain trade.

Mining is at present unimportant and imports are paid for by sales abroad of a few agricultural products notably coffee, hides and skins, cereals, pulses, and oil seeds. Coffee is outstandingly important, constituting half the exports by value in the early sixties. Most of the 60,000 tons exported and the 25,000 tons consumed in Ethiopia is *arabica* or *mocha*, grown mainly at high altitudes in the south-western parts of the country, farthest from the coast. The coffee consumed locally is used not only as a beverage but also for eating, being fried in butter. Most of it is shipped to the U.S.A. for blending with beans from other countries. The quality used to be poor, much of it in Jimma being grown wild and dried casually. Yields and quality are improving. There are now many plantations in the Harar highlands and foreign plantations have been started in the Kaffa area.

Large-scale irrigation is mainly confined to the area below the Zula dam east of Asmara, where several square miles are under corn and cotton crops, and the Awash valley in the rift. The latter is likely to be the main scene of development. Two large Dutch-owned sugar plantations downstream of the Koka dam 60 miles from Addis Ababa are supplied by water from the river and in 1962 the mill associated with them produced nearly 60,000 tons of sugar. This is considerably more than current Ethiopian consumption. Cotton is being grown on a large scale, and new schemes are planned to make the country self-sufficient.

Most of the country is free of tsetse-fly and the livestock numbers in Ethiopia are believed to be very large. Quality is poor and animal products, mostly hides and skins, constitute only about 5 per cent. of total exports. The opportunities for developing a meat-export trade to the eastern Mediterranean countries would appear to be considerable if ever the Suez Canal is reopened.

Industrial activity is slight but is gradually increasing. In addition to the textile and sugar plants already mentioned, more than a hundred grain-milling and coffee-cleaning plants are scattered over the interior and a few other factories, mainly operated in Addis Ababa by Greeks and Armenians, and in Asmara by Italians, produce shoes, cigarettes, matches, soap, and beer. The Koka dam with a capacity of 54 MW built by Yugoslavia, with money from Italian reparations, supplies electricity to Addis Ababa 50 miles away, and to Diredawa at four times that distance. The power is used in new plywood and cement factories at Addis Ababa. Other big dams on the Awash river are envisaged which will increase capacity there to 140 MW. It may be some time before additions are required to the 14 MW capacity of the new generating station on the Blue Nile near Lake Tana. The potentialities of the river for power production are immense, but the region is as yet remote and development, as in the case of other parts of Ethiopia, will come slowly. The country's biggest industrial plant for some time to come is likely to be the new Russian oil refinery at Assab.

Ethiopia appears to be a country with great potentialities. It is large, fertile, and well populated. If the energies of its people can be aroused and guided by the progressive elements to make a peaceful transition from the old feudal order, it may emerge as one of the most prosperous as well as being perhaps the most interesting and beautiful country in Africa.

SOMALIA

The Horn of Africa projecting south of Arabia 400 miles into the Indian Ocean is a poor, dry land, comparable both climatically and topographically with south-west Africa. In contrast to the latter it lacks any known mineral wealth. Less than a hundredth of the area is under cultivation, and yields from this small part are uncertain because of locusts and the unreliability of the rainfall.

Aridity is nowhere as extreme as in the Namib desert, but a general shortage of surface water presents difficulties everywhere. As much as 50 inches of rain have been recorded in a year at Daloh, 6,000 feet up in the highlands projecting east from Harar and close to the Gulf of Aden, but this is quite exceptional; even at Daloh the mean annual rainfall is only 25 inches. The plains to the north are much drier and the Guban plain resembles the Eritrean coast in receiving 2 to 10 inches of rain in showers between December and March, probably derived from depressions that have escaped south-east from the Mediterranean. Mean annual temperatures are amongst the highest in the world. In southern Somalia the brief rains come in the summer months.

Of the two million inhabitants, about three-quarters are pastoral nomads or semi-nomads living mainly on milk, blood, and a little corn, speaking the Somali tongue, but often claiming descent from immigrant Arabs. The agriculturalists in the south include the negroid Sab people, the descendants of slaves, despised by the Somali both for their lowly origin and because they are cultivators.

The lands bordering the Gulf of Aden are sparsely settled, and the area under cultivation hardly reaches 50,000 acres in all. The people are nearly all pastoralists spending the cooler months of winter near the coast where the grazing is excellent after rains, and then moving up into the highlands, the men riding on horseback, the women helping to carry the equipment. With their herds of camels and flocks of sheep and goats they move from one grazing ground to another according to the season and to take advantage of the new growth following individual heavy storms. Many are accustomed to spending the early summer rains and some later months on the rolling grass plains of the Haud which stretches for a hundred miles across the frontier with Ethiopia. According to an agreement made between Ethiopia and Britain in 1954, Somali tribes are allowed to cross the border, but the tribesmen are extremely adverse to any interference on the part of Ethiopian officials, especially tax-collectors, and murderous attacks on them are all too common. Further south, Somali pastoralists move from Ogaden into Somalia and back again, across a broad zone where the Ethiopian frontier has never been defined. Although the United Nations has offered its assistance in solving the frontier problem no solution has been found acceptable to both sides.

The mountains of the Midjurtein in the north-east seem to have been a source of migrants to the more humid south for centuries. Somali pushing south from this area drove the Galla south-west and into Ethiopia in the sixteenth century. Mohammed Gran, a deadly enemy against whom the Abyssinians requested help from the Portuguese, was ruler of the Arab-Somali sultanate of Zeila. The Ethiopians are in large part Christian, the Somali Muslims. The two are traditional enemies and no doubt the Haud and Ogaden will be the scenes of shootings and massacres for many more years.

Grazing in the north is steadily deteriorating, a succession of drier years than normal may have been to blame, or the numbers of livestock may be too large. Some of the people get a little cash by collecting and selling the gum frankincense, the sap obtained from *Boswellia* trees that grow in the foothills and for which a market exists in Arabia and Roman Catholic countries. With this they buy corn or cloth. They are primarily dependent on their camels and other beasts and so are always on the look-out for better pastures. One group infringes on the grazing grounds of another and the friction that develops is usually followed by murder and fighting.

In the south the rainfall gradually increases, allowing steppe vegetation to grow on the higher ground and fringing forest along the main water-courses. The two largest rivers, the Shebeli and Juba, both more than a thousand miles long, carry flood water for several weeks but are otherwise dry or reduced to a trickle. Between the two rivers live the Sab tribes, about a quarter of a million people who are primarily pastoralists but have taken up cultivation to a varying degree. They grow rather poor crops of *dura*, the sorghum common to much of northern Africa, plus some maize and beans. In many cases the cultivators are vassals of the pastoralists, but this is not always the case.

The land below the western plateau on the alluvial deposits of the rivers is poorly drained and during the rains of May to August the people are much afflicted with malaria and their cattle by tsetse-fly. Some of the Sab move east at this season to a belt of ancient dunes, lying inland of the barren coastal sandhills, where the ground is well drained and wells can reach sub-surface water. The grazing grounds on the consolidated dunes are also visited by herds owned by the town-dwellers of Mogadishu and Kismayu.

Alongside the main rivers farms are cultivated by Bantu negroes some of whom may be the descendants of pre-Somali communities, and others are the descendants of slaves brought from the south-west and kept by local Arabs and Somali instead of being exported with the majority of their kind to Arabia and elsewhere. Here the village is the social unit rather than the family, and houses are permanent structures with cylindrical mud walls and thatched conical roofs. Some of the cultivators have taken to irrigated cotton which fetched good prices in the 1950's. Corn is planted on land flooded by the rains for harvesting late in the dry season and the crop residues are fed to cattle, much as in the western Sudan.

The total area under irrigation, believed to be less than 50 square miles, has decreased in recent years. Several thousand Italian settlers organized the irrigation of twice this area between the wars, using pumped water and canals, but most of them departed long ago. The Somali were never fond of the arduous and unhealthy life of the cultivator: they thought it demeaning, suitable only for slaves, and preferred to go back to their flocks and herds.

Irrigation farming remains an important feature of the country's economy, plantations on the Juba river, owned and operated by Italians, providing the most important export, bananas. Production and packing is largely in Italian hands and until 1966 the crop obtained preferential treatment on the Italian market; now it may not be easy to dispose of it. The Somalia government is anxious to extend the irrigated area. Sugar-cane and cotton seem to offer the best opportunities for the future and a large scheme has been instituted involving the irrigation of about 30 square miles on the Shebeli river, 100 miles from Mogadishu. It employs about 90 Italians and 4,000 Somali, is operated by an Italian company, and supplies the domestic market with sugar and cotton.

Economic and political development

The main wealth of the country lies in its livestock; 4 million camels, 12 million goats and sheep,

and $1\frac{1}{4}$ million cattle. These provide the milk and blood on which the nomads largely depend for food. Occasionally they sell off or kill an old male animal, and with the cash from the sale of beasts, hides and skins, milk and ghee they are able to purchase corn and beans. Livestock exported to Jeddah and to Aden bring into the country about £3 million annually, and attempts are being made to increase sales to Egypt.

Standards of living are low. The people suffer from tuberculosis, probably the main cause of death, and half of them are infected by yaws, syphilis, malaria, or bilharzia. The huts and tents of the nomads are well suited to their needs, but housing in the towns is poor. Everywhere money is required to improve water supplies. Education has been fostered with some care and in 1958 some 35,000 children were attending school, but the cost has been borne in large part by the British and Italian governments, and may be difficult to meet in the future. As yet the Somali language, in spite of its rich oral folk-literature, is not usually written. Arabic is normally used for government business or, in the north, English, and in the south Italian.

The townspeople, who are mainly Arabs and Indians, have gained some political experience, and in the 1959 municipal elections voting was extended to women, a sign at least to some observers of real progress. In the Provinces and Districts the officers in charge are almost entirely Somalis. The people they administer are mainly very tough nomads. Their loyalty is to the tribe or family, not the state; blood feuds persist interminably, taxation is practically impossible and the control of the administrators is very uncertain. It is not surprising that the government's policy is to settle the nomads and encourage agriculture.

In the international sphere, the idea of a state embracing all Somalis has won strong support amongst the politically minded young people in the towns. This has led to trouble with France, Kenya, and the traditional enemy, Ethiopia. There is no doubt that Somali nationalism plus the movements of pastoralists and their unruly behaviour will continue to provide frontier incidents for many years.

Since independence, Somalia has been fortunate in receiving aid from many countries, notably Italy, Russia, the U.S.A., and China. Egypt has also taken a good deal of interest in the region. But unless oil is discovered in large quantities Somalia will always be a poor country.

11

East Africa

THE countries on the Indian Ocean side of the western rift differ in many respects from those on the Atlantic side. They are for the most part higher and cooler, drier, and far less heavily forested. Only about one-quarter has a chance of obtaining regularly, year by year, more than 30 inches of rain, the minimum amount required by many crops. Long droughts are liable to occur. Those of 1960-1, which caused particularly heavy losses of stock and crops, were followed by torrential rains that did as much damage as the droughts.

The region, though it includes great lake basins, is essentially a source area for rivers; its plateaux and highlands give rise both to the Congo and to the Nile. The watersheds, coast, and lakeshore are generally well watered and well populated; the upland plains are in comparison arid and empty, left for the most part to nomadic pastoralists.

The succession from coast to western rift of plains, plateaux, lake basin, and highlands, imposes a meridional zoning of climate and land use, less clear-cut than the latitudinal banding of west Africa, but providing a basic regional pattern on which national boundaries are superposed.

The east coast and offshore islands are fringed with coral reefs, mangrove swamps border creeks and inlets, and uplifted coral rocks underlie the coastal lowlands. Near Zanzibar and for some distance to the north the rainfall is great enough to support high forest, but most of the heavier woodland has been cleared for agriculture.

Crops grown on the coast, such as cloves, peppers, and coconuts, and the mixed character of the population, remind one of Indonesia as much as Africa. The towns, forming part of the Indian Ocean trading network, gained much from the Arabs, and Swahili, an arabized Bantu language which evolved on the coast, has become a lingua franca for most of east Africa.

Towards the interior the rainfall diminishes very rapidly giving a belt of dry steppe that narrows in the middle, where the Usambara mountains approach the coast, and widens over the low plateaux of south-east Tanzania and northern Kenya. This inhospitable country, infested with tsetse-fly in the south and with fierce nomads in the north, deterred early visitors from penetrating far inland almost as effectively as did the falls of the lower Congo on the west side of the continent. When at length Arab traders began to push inland, they followed routes across the narrowest part of the dry belt, running west from the coast opposite Zanzibar.

Much of the interior plateau in central and southern Tanzania and on the south-east flank of the Kenya highlands receives too little rain for successful arable farming. The most productive lands are in the vicinity of Lake Victoria and on the volcanic highlands bordering the rifts, east and west of the lake plateau.

The peoples of east Africa are very varied, both racially and culturally. In Tanzania, Bantu-speaking peoples are overwhelmingly in the majority, the Masai in the north-east being the main Nilo-Hamitic intruders. Further north, Nilo-Hamitic pastoralists penetrated south between the peoples of the coast and the Kenya highlands splitting the Bantu into different groups. Others entered the eastern rift and west Kenya highlands thereby separating the Kikuyu from the Nilotic Luo and Bantu-speaking Baluheya on the Nyanza plateau. Consequently ethnic as well as physical divisions run mainly north and south.

Until the Arab traders came in search of slaves about 1830, the peoples of the interior seem to have been affected scarcely at all by events on the coast. They had made no contact with either Islam or Christianity and so were in a very different position from the peoples of the Sudan zone and west Africa. It was some decades before the missionaries followed in the footsteps of the slave-traders. Hard on their heels came the soldier-administrators, and soon afterwards the railways began to extend west from Mombasa, Tanga, and Dar-es-Salaam. Most of the economic development and the contact with outside cultures has been confined to the twentieth century.

All the countries in east Africa are rather poor, average incomes per head varying from £35 annually in Kenya to less than £25 in Tanzania. These figures take into account the much higher incomes of the non-African population. Minerals are relatively unimportant products, constituting less than

10 per cent. of total exports; over a half of the total production is in the form of crops and livestock. In some areas commercial agriculture is largely in European hands, in others Africans produce for the market, the balance varies from one territory to another. Although Africans have had greater opportunities than in the Congo to take some initiative and reach the higher positions in government and industry, many activities such as wholesale trading and manufacturing are still owned or controlled mainly by non-Africans, either Indian or European.

Zanzibar, which always seems to receive the impact of outside interference most sharply, has recently been transformed from an Arab sultanate into what appeared at first to be an outpost of eastern-style socialism operated by the African majority. It has since joined up politically with Tanganyika and the two together form the state of Tanzania.

Independent Kenya is now an African state. There are still many white farmers, but one can no longer refer to the 'White Highlands', for African farmers are taking up land in the areas once reserved for Europeans and the political privileges of the white settlers have disappeared. The consequences of European initiative still mould the economy. Nairobi, the capital of Kenya, retains a large European population and is well established as the main industrial and commercial centre for the whole of east Africa.

Physical conditions in Uganda were in many ways ideal for the development of European plantations, but alienation of land was prevented after 1916 by order of the Secretary of State for the Colonies and a settler problem never arose. Plantations established before the First World War were badly hit by the slump of the thirties, many were abandoned, and less than 1 per cent. of the entire country is now owned by Europeans and Indians. Uganda remains essentially a land of peasant cultivators and farmers, resembling in some ways the more progressive and prosperous parts of west Africa, but handicapped by its great distance from the sea and longer sea-routes to Europe and America.

The histories of Tanganyika, Rwanda, and Burundi differ from those of the other countries in that they formed a German colony for many years and were subsequently Trust Territories.

In Tanganyika only a small proportion of the land fell into the hands of European settlers, about 1 per cent. as in Uganda, but as late as 1960 this small area was producing nearly a half of the country's exports. Economic and political develop-ment until the late fifties was no faster than in other parts of east Africa, but Tanganyika became independent earlier, largely because of its status as a Trust Territory and also because inter-tribal dissension was less than in the other countries.

Kenya, Uganda, and Tanganyika were associated under British rule in the East Africa High Commission, under which certain services common to all of them were operated jointly. These included railways, telephones, and research. Together they formed an east African common market, with no customs barriers between them, but with high external tariffs to protect infant manufacturing industries. These developed mainly in Nairobi, especially in the fifties, and Kenya seems to have benefited more from the common market than the other members. Kenyans have taken most of the jobs on the railways, and exports from Kenya to the other two countries have been much greater than her imports from them.

It remains to be seen whether the economic ties between the territories forming the East African Community will strengthen. In 1964 an agreement was signed providing for the continuance of the customs union but setting limits to Kenya's advantageous position as regards secondary industry. Other countries, including Ethiopia, have expressed interest in joining the common market. Although a road north to Ethiopia has been started from Isiola in Kenya, communications between the two countries are still poor and it is unlikely that trade between them will be of any considerable volume for a long time to come. More effective links are likely to be established with Rwanda and Burundi, and above all with Zambia.

The closure of the Suez Canal in June 1967 has harmed the economies of the east African countries by increasing costs of transport to western Europe and affecting the ability of crops like sisal to compete on world markets.

TANZANIA

Zanzibar and Pemba

Zanzibar and Pemba are fragments of uplifted coral reefs lying 30 to 40 miles offshore. Zanzibar island, with an area of 640 square miles, is nearly twice as big as Pemba and has a larger population, 180,000 as compared with 130,000 on Pemba. They are hot, humid islands. The temperature fluctuates between 75° and 85° F. (24° and 29° C.) on the whole, rising a little higher in March before the passage of the Intertropical Convergence and the onset of the rainy season. After the rains, south-westerlies bring cooler, dry weather until November

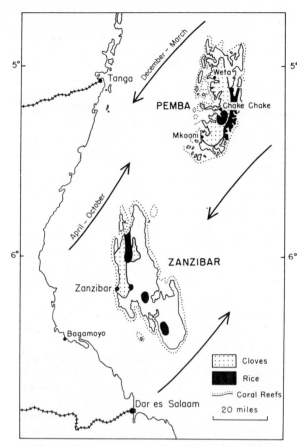

FIG. 47. *Zanzibar and Pemba, lying off the coast of mainland Tanzania.*

and December, when light rains signal the return of the convergence zone to the southern hemisphere and the dominance of the north-easterly monsoon (Fig. 47).

With a climate so different from that of Arabia, it seems a little odd that this should ever have been the most arabized state south of the Sahara. On both islands Arabs have always been a minority. Most of the people have been known as Shirazis, a name that implies consciousness of a Persian element in their origin. They are predominantly Africans none the less, descended from the people who were living on the islands when the Arabs arrived in large numbers a century and a half ago. Since much earlier times they had interbred with Arabs and with other peoples coming from around the shores of the Indian Ocean; today they speak Swahili and are almost without exception Muslims. There are also about 50,000 Africans from the mainland, mainly pagans and Christians who have immigrated from Kenya and Tanganyika in recent decades. In

addition, about 10,000 Indians are living in Zanzibar town, and a few hundred Europeans and Chinese hold technical, commercial, and military posts.

The Sultan of Muscat took up residence at Zanzibar town when he arrived from Oman with a large number of followers in 1837. The site he occupied was a triangular spit almost converted into an island at high tide. It had excellent springs of water for the town-dwellers to use, and ships called in to water on their way up and down the coast and crossing to Oman and India. The harbour was one of the best along the coast, sheltered from the surf and swell of the Indian Ocean and affording safe anchorage no matter which monsoon was blowing.

Behind the town, low ridges were covered in dense forest. Most of the indigenous people, the Shirazi, lived in fishing towns and villages scattered around the coast, or in farming settlements, confined to patches of good soil, on the east side of the island. Most of eastern Zanzibar is coral waste where shifting cultivators have difficulty in raising any crops. Pemba is different; the soils are more fertile, settlement is more evenly distributed, and agriculture was always more productive than on the larger island.

The economy and land use were transformed by cloves. They were introduced from Mauritius in 1818 and cultivation rapidly expanded after the arrival of the Sultan who recognized their potential value and, it is said, ordered Arab landlords to plant three clove trees to every coconut palm. He gave Arabs land in the western forests of Zanzibar and they used slave labour to establish clove plantations. Before long they grew wealthy on the proceeds from the crop and built themselves large houses which are still to be seen in Zanzibar town and the country round about. The slaves settled down on the estates as squatters, growing food crops for themselves and working for the Arabs at the clove harvest.

The Arabs on Pemba, where spare land was more widely distributed in smaller patches, had land cleared and planted by the local Shirazi and rewarded them with a proportion of the land and trees. So Arab and Shirazi plantations were intermingled all over Pemba, whereas on Zanzibar the Shirazis remained subsistence cultivators until the end of the century, by which time the Arabs had already planted up most of the land suitable for cloves.

When a hurricane struck Zanzibar in 1872, it destroyed almost all the clove plantations on that island while Pemba escaped damage. Since then the smaller island's economy has been dominated by clove production much more than that of Zanzibar. Pemba's climate is more favourable, with 77 inches of rain at Wete compared to 62 inches at Zanzibar, it has a greater area of suitable soils, and today has four-fifths of all the clove trees. Ommaney describes them as giving the island 'the aspect of a garden, formal and arranged, almost a graveyard because of its close-growing habit and dark foliage'.

After slavery was abolished in 1897, the Shirazi were much in demand for harvesting the cloves. By this time they were developing their own copra industry and demanded high wages, so mainland Africans were brought over as clove-pickers as well. The Shirazi who had moved from the eastern villages to the plantations in the west settled as squatters either on the plantations themselves or in villages on the eastern fringe of the main clove area and there they have remained.

Land tenure has caused considerable friction on the islands. Problems have arisen because both Muslim law and customary law have been recognized. Elements of the old usufructuary rights survived while land in the plantation areas was bought and sold and the rights of squatters on Arab plantations and of tenants in Shirazi villages were never entirely clear. The new government of Zanzibar, having got rid of the Sultan, has ousted the Arab landlords, nationalized the land and distributed it amongst the peasants. The land problem may yet prove more difficult to handle than the Sultan.

On both islands improved roads and bus services have made it much easier to move about. Distances are not great, and seasonal migration for the clove harvest and to grow rice on the valuable patches of heavy soil has become a part of the way of life. In the east of Zanzibar, where some inland villages have decayed as a result of people moving to the capital, efforts were being made under the British administration to redevelop the area. A cattle ranch was started and attempts were being made to plant up the coral wasteland with casuarina and eucalyptus.

The future of the island depends a good deal on political developments. The economy is not very securely based. Fungus diseases have devastated the clove plantations in recent decades and prices for cloves and coconuts have declined and show few signs of recovering. Half the clove crop is purchased in Indonesia for mixing with tobacco in the manufacture of cigars, and Indonesia is not an entirely reliable market. Limes and cocoa are being grown in an attempt to diversify production but cloves must remain the chief source of income for several years. Eventually, the islands may benefit from their position in relation to the mainland, but at present there is little sign of Zanzibar becoming the Hong Kong of the east Africa coastline, except in a curiously inverted political sense.

Mainland Tanzania

Tanzania's great size is an embarrassment. Much of it is either tsetse-ridden or too dry for cultivation and the population of 12 million is scattered around the periphery of the country in clusters nowhere quite large enough to form a sound basis for large-scale economic development. The railways pass through long stretches of empty country providing no business; they lose money and so there is little economic stimulus to build new lines to open up promising country at present undeveloped commercially. A 1,000-mile rail link from the central line to Zambia, to make the latter country independent of the Rhodesian railways, is being built and an oil pipeline to Ndola in Zambia was completed in 1968.

Dar-es-Salaam

The capital of Tanzania and the starting-point of the railway and main roads to the west, Dar-es-Salaam, is a fast-growing city (Fig. 48). Its population increased from 51,000 in 1948 to 92,000 in 1957 and 190,000 in 1968. The Zaramo, whose tribal area surrounds the city, constitute about one-third of the population, Asians about one-quarter, and migrants have come in from all parts of the country, but especially up the coast from the south. Many of them are finding jobs in industry which now employs about one-third of the working population. The harbour, which is an excellent one, handles a very large part of the country's overseas trade and a newly constructed line links Dar-es-Salaam to the productive country south of Kilimanjaro, so that it is well situated for importing raw materials and distributing manufactured goods throughout the country. A meat-canning factory capable of handling 100,000 cattle annually and an oil refinery are but two of the largest plants established.

Tanga and its hinterland

Tanga's hinterland is more restricted, for the railway only goes as far west as Arusha, and some of the traffic from the productive areas on the slopes of Kilimanjaro and Meru moves east to Mombasa or south to Dar-es-Salaam. It has been suggested that the railway might be extended west of Arusha to the dry country near Lake Manyara to allow a large phosphate deposit at Minjingu hill to be

178

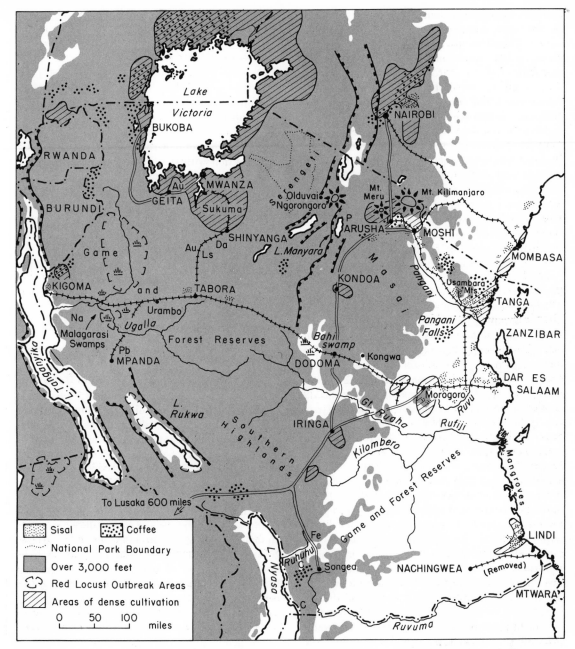

FIG. 48. *Tanzania. The productive areas of Tanzania are distributed round the periphery of the country.
C—coal, Fe—iron, Pb—lead, Au—gold, Da—alluvial diamonds, Ls—limestone, Na—salt, P—phosphate.*

worked. This formed an island when the lake stood at a higher level in the past, and the droppings of birds accumulated to the extent of some millions of tons of guano. If normal freight rates were to be charged the phosphate could hardly compete in world markets, but it could probably be developed for use in east Africa at least, if freight rates were to

be reduced to a minimum to allow large-scale exploitation and the economies this entails.

The main crop produced in Tanga's hinterland is sisal, a native of the dry part of Yucatan which was introduced to east Africa from Florida in 1892. For very many years it was the mainstay of the Tanganyikan economy and production in the

179

1950's increased from about 120,000 tons to nearly 200,000 tons, some 40 per cent. of the world's output. Expensive machinery is needed to process the leaves and a minimum of several thousand acres under the crop is required to make its installation worth while, so most of it has been grown on European estates. The fibre is costly to transport and production is therefore concentrated in a relatively small area near the railways and decortication factories. Two-thirds of Tanzania's production is exported through Tanga. In the past it has been customary to grow sisal continuously on the same land for several years without fertilizers, and to take in new land as yields diminished, but no great areas of suitable land remain, and efforts are being made to intensify production. At present sisal finds employment for about 120,000 people; reduction of costs, very necessary to meet competition from synthetic fibres, may entail reducing the labour force and increased mechanization. In 1967 the Tanzanian government stated that it intended to take a controlling interest in the industry.

About half of Tanzania's coffee is also produced in Tanga's hinterland, mainly by African farmers of the Chagga tribe. They live on the fertile volcanic soils of a dissected platform extending east and south from the slopes of Kilimanjaro. It is thickly populated, mountainous country, where steep narrow paths wind through a cultivated jungle, and clear rivers fall over fern-covered rocks in fine cascades. Thomson, one of the early European explorers in the area, was much struck by its remarkable fertility and described the system of irrigation channels leading water from the high streams over the mountain slopes. At that time the Chagga grew plenty of bananas, as they still do on the lower slopes, but after the last war coffee was planted extensively on the higher slopes and has brought in a great deal of money. All the producers belong to a co-operative which deals with marketing the crop and maintaining quality. Yields could probably be increased considerably by using better strains and by more careful mulching and pruning; this would allow the Chagga to persist in a highly competitive industry.

Forty miles west of Moshi, the centre of this progressive African area, lies Arusha, the main centre for a number of European settlers growing maize, coffee, pyrethrum, and other cash crops. Its chief industry is a very specialized one, tobacco pipes worth £100,000 annually being produced from soft Meerschaum rock mined nearby. The town has many hotels, for it lies on the main north–south road and is an important communications centre. Arusha has been selected as the capital of the East African Community.

Less successful ports and railways

No other coastal towns can compete with Dar-es-Salaam and Tanga. The traffic through Lindi amounts to only about 50,000 tons annually and it will probably be closed as an ocean-going port. Its place has been taken by Mtwara, a few miles down the coast with a better harbour, which was developed in connexion with the Groundnut Scheme as the port for the railway running 154 miles west to Nachingwea. Though it was completed as recently as 1959, the line has been closed down for lack of traffic; the country near the railway is tsetse-ridden and has a rainfall of less than 30 inches, and west of Nachingwea there are very few people. This is not the first line to fail in Tanganyika. A branch line from Manyoni to Kinyangiri opened in 1934 was a failure economically and the track was taken up and used for a new line to serve lead mines being developed at Mpanda. Now the lead has run out and the lines are rusting once more.

Sukumaland

The railway running north from Tabora to Mwanza has benefited from mining. Diamonds were discovered at Mwadui near Shinyanga in the thirties and by 1962 the value of the gems produced exceeded £5 million annually, of which the Tanganyika government received over £½ million in mining royalties. A new gold-mine has been opened in the Lake Region from which exports were valued at £1·2 million in 1962.

Sukumaland lying nearer Lake Victoria is a country of rolling plains and rocky hills with a mean annual rainfall of about 30 inches. Once it was covered with savanna woodland, but its population of a million and a half cultivators and stock-raisers has spread continuously in the last fifty years to occupy nearly 20,000 square miles, reducing it to a cultivation steppe where the only trees surviving are either useless for firewood or bear edible fruits.

The people suffered severely at the end of the last century under the German administration. When they began to spread out from the hills to which they had been confined earlier, they were attacked by sleeping-sickness. Then rinderpest killed off their cattle, famines occurred, and forced labour reduced numbers still further. Sleeping-sickness was eventually brought under control by concentrating settlement into relatively small areas and clearing the woodland round about. For the last few decades the tsetse-fly have been retreating and the numbers of cattle and sheep have increased so rapidly that Sukumaland is now one of the most heavily stocked areas in the whole of the continent. Droughts kill off cattle by the thousand from time to time, but it was realized after the last war that positive measures were required to reduce pressure on the land. After water supplies had been improved and thickets sheltering *Glossina morsitans* had been cleared, tens of thousands of people from the most congested districts were persuaded to move into the Geita area to the north-west, relieving the situation temporarily. The provision of new land, however, did not encourage the Sukuma to intensify their cultivation practices.

The future well-being of the area depends on increasing yields per acre rather than extending the land under cultivation. There is practically no new land left. Planting at the right time, ridging to conserve soil and moisture, the use of manures or artificial fertilizers could double or triple the production of cotton and other crops. Sukumaland is even now the main cotton-producing region of Tanzania and one of the major sources of meat. Cotton, formerly shipped across the lake to Kampala for railing to the coast, is now sold to co-operative unions that own several ginneries and arrange transport to Dar-es-Salaam, and a textile mill has recently been opened at Mwanza. Cattle are sold to the heavily settled districts on the eastern and western lakeshore.

Bukoba

West of Lake Victoria most of the people live within 20 miles of the lakeshore, where the rainfall locally exceeds 70 inches. Long sandstone ridges with intervening clayey valleys run north and south. The ridge crests with sandy soils have been reduced by grazing and burning to exceptionally poor grassland. Settlements have grown up near hollows in the slopes, where deep soils occur, and have been built up by careful husbandry to support banana gardens and Robusta coffee, leaves from the bananas being used to mulch the soils around the coffee bushes. At distances more than 20 miles from the lake, the country is dry, tsetse-ridden, and sparsely settled.

The western and southern highlands

These highlands are potentially productive areas, but at present their remoteness prevents them contributing very much to the economy of the country as a whole. The highlands adjoining Burundi, though far from the coast, are within reach of Bukoba on Lake Victoria and Kigoma on the

railway, but the southern highlands are less fortunate, being 250 miles from the railway and twice as far from the coast by road. Malawi, Zambia, and Rhodesia are more easily reached than the rest of Tanzania and thousands of Nyakyusa go away to find work on the Copperbelt. Now the southern highlands are likely to profit from Zambia's need for an outlet to the sea through Dar-es-Salaam by rail and road. Work began in 1968 on both these projects and by 1971 a 24-foot wide highway should run all the way from Dar-es-Salaam to the copperbelt by way of Iringa.

The most productive and heavily settled country rises from the alluvial plains bordering Lake Nyasa. It resembles Chagga country in some ways. The soils are derived from volcanic rocks and grow a wide variety of crops; rice on the plains, maize, bananas, tea, and coffee at higher levels, wheat, barley, and beans above 6,000 feet. The cost of transport to the coast cuts prices for farmers to a level which gives them little encouragement to increase production. Minerals occur in the same area. Coal in the Ruhuhu valley is not far from abundant iron-ore with a 50 per cent. metal content. However, remoteness is not the only difficulty here, for the iron-ore contains impurities that are difficult to deal with by normal methods, and the coal is not suitable for coking.

One of the more isolated massifs lies east of Lake Nyasa, the Umatongo highlands which are separated from the rest of the highlands by the Ruhuhu trough. They provided a place of refuge for the Matezo people who were suffering at the hands of raiding Ngoni. Living in caves on the steep hillsides, and forced to find a way of cultivating intensively in order to survive, the Matezo worked out a system of pit cultivation that still persists. Holes are dug in the ground, about 3 feet in diameter. Crops are grown on the excavated earth built up into ridges between the holes, and the pits are filled with waste and rubbish to benefit the crops in succeeding years. Hard work and intensive methods have allowed the people to remain self-sufficient in foodstuffs and even to produce coffee for export.

Possibilities for economic development

After the last war it was believed in some quarters that the empty tsetse-ridden country that forms so much of central Tanzania could be made to produce crops profitably if development were to be carried out on a big enough scale. Millions of pounds were spent clearing thousands of acres of savanna woodland in three main areas, near Urambo west of Tabora, Kongwa near the railway line east of Dodoma, and Nachingwea in Southern Region. The scheme failed for a variety of reasons. Experienced personnel and proper equipment were scarce in the early post-war years; rainfall is marginal and unreliable; the soils are difficult to cultivate and set too hard to allow cultivation in the dry season, and the woodland is dense with long tough tree roots making clearance very costly.

There is little to show now for the great expenditure of money and effort. At Nachingwea tenants given 10 to 50 acres of the cleared land have not been able to make a profit great enough to persuade them to stay on. Experiments at Urambo with larger farms employing labour and growing tobacco have been rather more successful. At Kongwa, where 90,000 acres were cleared, the rains are inadequate for arable farming, and ranching seems to offer the best possibilities.

Future development of agriculture in Tanzania is likely to take place in two directions: firstly, in stock-rearing; secondly, in irrigation and flood control.

In the Central Region a large scattered population relies on rearing cattle. Productivity is low, possibly because of the dry conditions and above all because the people are not commercially minded. European ranchers operating in this type of country have shown that improving water supplies, controlling disease, and castrating poor-quality bulls can allow the annual 'take off' for slaughter to be increased by 20 per cent. Greater profits could be obtained without increasing the number of stock, by these means and also by improving transport to market and by providing holding grounds where the cattle could be fattened on oil-seed cake, before slaughter.

Tanzania's rivers are not amongst the largest in Africa, but they can be developed for irrigation. At first sight the Pangani basin would appear to be the best suited for development, for the river is fed by a number of strong springs and never falls very low, and there is an ample supply of labour in the Kilimanjaro–Meru–Usambara area to the north. However, the Pangani's water is rather salty, soils on the valley floor are shallow or impermeable, and in any case the water is needed to generate electricity downstream. Turbines already installed can utilize all the mean low water flow and other generating plants are under construction. The greatest scope seems to be provided by the Rufiji basin which occupies about one-fifth of the entire country. Enough water is available to irrigate 200,000 acres in the Botoro and Pawaga flats and provide employment for people from the overcrowded highlands

nearby. A dam on the lower river, about 100 miles south-west of Dar-es-Salaam in Stiegler's gorge, would not only allow the lower basin to be irrigated but would also prevent flooding which is often dangerous. In the Ruvu basin it has been estimated that storage reservoirs would allow 300,000 acres to be irrigated and at a later stage half a million acres might be developed in the Kilombero valley. The total irrigable area in Tanzania might be put as high as 4 million acres—comparable with that of Egypt.

Other opportunities for development are provided by the fisheries, some of which are already very productive. Lake Kitangiri, for instance, yields about 2,000 tons of fish annually and gives seasonal employment to about 1,500 fishermen. At present the fish bring $\frac{1}{2}d.$ per lb. to the fisherman but cost the consumer 10$d.$ per lb., mainly because of high transport costs.

The country derives one benefit from its underdeveloped state. In the dry, sparsely settled steppe country on either side of the rift valley in the northeast, there is an abundance of game. In its Serengeti National Park, Tanzania claims to have the largest concentration of plains game animals left in the world, and the Ngorongoro crater to the east provides a dramatic setting, perhaps the most spectacular of any reserve in Africa. A journey from Tanga to Lake Victoria calling in at Kilimanjaro, Ngorongoro, Olduvai gorge, and a final camp-site on the Serengeti plains could not fail to provide something of interest for the most hardened tourist.

KENYA

Kenya is a very varied country with striking scenic contrasts within short distances. The cool highlands in the south-west are backed by humid country on the lakeshore and bordered on the north and east by steppe country passing into desert. A cross-section north from Mount Kenya runs from glaciers capping the mountain at 17,000 feet through montane moist forest near Meru at 6,000 feet, to desert conditions in the vicinity of the Ewaso Nyiro river (Fig. 49). The coast is another distinctive region with its own ethnic patterns and economic problems, more akin to Zanzibar than the interior.

The coast

The coastal people are very mixed indeed. By far the majority are black Africans. They number about 300,000 and include migrants from the west and the descendants of various groups of people who have been driven south by invading Galla and

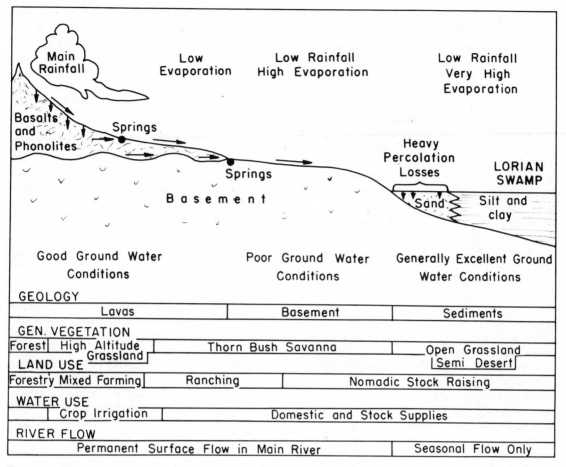

FIG. 49. *A Kenya transect. This runs 200 miles north-east from the Aberdares and Mount Kenya at altitudes of between 7,000 and 10,000 feet, to the Lorian Swamp about 1,000 feet where waters draining from the high areas spread over the flat land and sink into the ground. (Taken from* An Investigation into the water resources of the Ewaso Nyiro basin, Kenya. *Ministry of Works, Nairobi, 1962, p. 4.)*

Somali. There are 40,000 Muslim Arabs and Swahili-speaking peoples of mixed Arab and African ancestry, about 50,000 Indians and 5,000 Europeans, mostly living in the towns. All these have lived side by side without any great friction developing between them.

Except for a forested strip about 10 miles wide along the western boundary of what used to be called the Coast Protectorate and which is still inhabited by elephant and buffalo, most of the land is under cultivation. Coconut, mango, cashew, citrus, and other trees have been planted widely. Many of the landowners are absentees living in Mombasa or Nairobi and their lands are occupied by African squatters who pay a rent or perform some services in return for the right to stay and grow crops. Many of the squatters are Nyika who have been attracted

from the dry hinterland in recent years by the chance to grow cotton and to earn cash as labourers.

Mombasa is by far the most important coastal town, containing about half the coast population. It serves Uganda as well as Kenya and is becoming an important industrial centre. In addition it plays an important part in coastal trading. Dhows still bring Persian rugs and other goods to the old port under Fort Jesus, and the inhabitants of Lamu and the Bajun islands in the north depend on receiving many of their staple requirements by dhow from Mombasa because the roads are closed for three months in the year during the long rains. Dhows carry cement, food, and paraffin oil north and south along the coast from Mombasa and return with firewood, grass mats, and mangrove poles. The smaller ones will probably be used for some time to come

Masai women. They are packing up the family belongings before moving from an overnight camping spot.

but the long-range coastal dhows will soon disappear in face of competition from long-distance lorries. Trade with Muscat has dwindled to very small proportions.

Modern shipping is accommodated in the deepwater harbour of Kilindini on the other side of the island from Fort Jesus. Petroleum has formed a large proportion of the imports for many years and in 1963 a refinery was completed with an annual capacity of 2 million tons which will meet the needs of much of east Africa for some time to come. A cement factory is another important new industry, helping to supply Tanzania's demands as well as those of Kenya. Built on the edge of an old uplifted coral reef it uses local shale and the coral rock as raw material. The railway workshops are old established and have given the local people an opportunity to gain some skill in handling machinery. Various light industries such as aluminium and enamelware are being established on a new industrial estate situated at Changamwe on the mainland, and the Japanese have opened a large rayon

factory. Electricity is provided by thermal power-stations using oil imported from the Middle East. Fresh water is rather short and may limit future development; at present it is brought 150 miles by pipeline from springs at Mzima.

The drylands

The northern and eastern parts of Kenya are only sparsely watered by the summer rains and for the rest of the year are baked red and brown by the hot sun. Only two rivers reach the sea through the year; the Tana and Galana. The dry watercourses show up as white and yellow lines from the air, threading through the tawny plains, with greener patches marking the isolated crystalline and volcanic hills, and the highlands of Marsabit standing out as an unusually large green island.

The dry plains are roamed by nomad pastoralists; Boran, Samburu, and Turkana on the plains stretching away from Lake Rudolf, Somali and Galla immigrants further east. The Somali have been anxious to form some kind of union with Somalia.

It remains to be seen how long a 'Memorandum of Understanding', signed by the two countries in 1967, will be observed.

The Masai used to roam over wider areas until early in this century when, their numbers reduced by famine and disease, they were persuaded by the Kenya government to move away from the high plateaux. Now they are confined to the country stretching south of the railway to the Serengeti plains in Tanzania. Rich in cattle, Masai are poor in material goods and seem to care little for them. Their diet is still largely milk and blood, though maize and millet flour are increasingly important. They stick to their traditional ways, moving from the floor of the rift valley where they spend the rains to the better-watered shoulders of the rift for the dry season. They lost many of their cattle in the drought of 1959-61 and suffered severely in the heavy rains and floods that followed.

In the middle of Masai territory lies Magadi, one of the strangest lakes in the world, a petrified lake, covered to a depth of several feet by a crust of sodium carbonate derived from volcanic springs on the floor of the rift. A large bucket dredge floating on the water chews away at the crust and pumps the slurry to a refinery where it is purified, dried, and bagged for export by way of a specially built railway to the main line and Mombasa. This sodium carbonate is one of the main industrial exports of Kenya, worth about £1 million annually. The market is limited at the present time by Kenya's refusal to trade with South Africa.

According to the International Bank Mission to Kenya there are good prospects for irrigation on the lower Tana. Near Galole some 75,000 acres could be irrigated without storage reservoirs, and if dams were to be constructed the total might be four times as great. In view of the steadily increasing population on the highlands this would seem to offer a valuable outlet for settlement, capable of providing eventually for upward of 75,000 families on the land, plus a large supporting population providing services and engaged in trade and commerce. Preparations for such a scheme involve hydrological studies of the whole Tana catchment and the detailed contour mapping of more than 1 million acres of desert. A tenant farmer scheme has started with families from several different tribes growing cotton on 4-acre holdings and each with an acre for maize and other food crops (Fig. 50).

The highlands

The hills and plateaux rising above the 5,000-foot contour, with their great relief, well-watered

Floating dredger on Lake Magadi. It is scooping up the soda crust which is then ground up and pumped through pipes to a factory at the edge of the lake where it is processed and bagged for carriage by rail to Mombasa.

valleys, deep soils, and richer vegetation form a striking contrast to the monotonous arid plains and plateaux at lower levels. They occupy about 65,000 square miles and support about 3 million people belonging to several different tribes of which the largest is the Kikuyu.

When the British arrived on the highlands and built the railway to Lake Victoria, the Kikuyu were dwelling in wooded country that stretched south from the east side of Mt. Kenya to about the site of Nairobi. Kamba people occupied the drier country at somewhat lower levels to the east as they do today. The open grassy country was the domain of the Masai who were in a feeble state as result of cattle epidemics and smallpox so that the great pasturelands of the highlands appeared almost free of native peoples to the white newcomers.

At the beginning of the century, soon after European settlement began, it became clear that country seemingly unoccupied was not without African claimants. The Kikuyu had been subdued in the nineties by armed patrols and like the Masai had suffered severely from diseases. Now their numbers were increasing again they wished to move out and occupy lands vacated by the Masai, only to find they had been included in European farms. The colonial administration set aside certain areas as native reserves to protect African rights but sporadic boundary alterations removed any sense of security

Market scene in Meru District, Kenya.

these might have inspired. In 1933 the area of native reserves on the highlands was increased to 50,000 square miles, but at the same time, an irregularly shaped block of 12,000 square miles was set aside within which land ownership was reserved for European farmers. This was known as the White Highlands. It included a large part of the best land, the higher well-watered country on either side of the rift, as well as the drier steppe on the floor of the valley in the vicinity of lakes Nakuru and Naivasha. Some of this country, on the Aberdares, Mt. Kenya, and elsewhere was reserved for forests, but much of the rest was amongst the best farmland in the country with good soils and the great advantage of lying within 30 miles of the railways.

In the early decades of the century European farmers learned to cope with the climate and with the many pests to which they were unaccustomed. They trained African staff and gradually extended the area under cultivation. Efforts were made at the same time to improve African agriculture but after

early attempts to encourage cotton-growing in Nyanza Province had proved unsuccessful the Kenya government ceased to regard native farming as likely to provide a basis for the country's money economy. East African tariffs were fixed to help Kenya settlers produce wheat, cheese, milk, and butter. Coffee and sisal were planted on suitable land by farmers with capital; maize by farmers not in this position. The land was improved by degrees, in spite of setbacks in the thirties from the slump and locusts. Some of the land was naturally unsuitable for agriculture and remained unused; some was never fully developed either from lack of capital or lack of effort; but many of the farms were and still are a delight to the eye, with fields of grain, coffee, tea, and pyrethrum, fine herds of cattle grazing amongst scattered trees, and roads leading through the parkland to big rambling farmhouses.

The White Highlands supported many more than the 12,000 Europeans who lived there. Africans who came to live on the farms obtained squatters

Cattle on a European farm in the highlands of Kenya.

rights, being allowed to farm a patch of land for themselves and graze a few cattle, and altogether the Africans on European farms in 1948 numbered about 150,000. Of these about two-thirds were Kikuyu whose own lands were overcrowded and confined between the areas set aside for European occupation.

The situation was greatly modified as a result of the Mau-Mau troubles of 1952–6 when the political leaders of the Kikuyu provoked a rebellion against British rule. Many Europeans and hundreds of non-compliant Kikuyu were murdered before Mau-Mau was broken.

Amongst the most important steps taken by the Kenya government at that time was the decision to force the Kikuyu to move off the white farms and from the scattered homesteads where they normally lived in the reserves and to assemble them in new villages. The aim was to exert effective control and to prevent terrorists intimidating isolated families. In little over a year, nearly one million people were moved into 845 villages, thereby helping to break the power of the terrorists and transforming at least temporarily the settlement pattern on the highlands.

It had long been recognized that Kikuyu land-holding was unsatisfactory economically and the opportunity was taken by the government to re-organize it. A single Kikuyu's holding of, say, 5 or 6 acres had in the past been split into small parts, it might have been seven or eight, and the fragmentation prevented agricultural methods being improved. Furthermore, many of the holders had no real security of tenure. This situation sprang from the traditional rules of inheritance amongst the Kikuyu. For example, a stretch of land (an *mbari*) over which rights had been acquired from another tribe would be divided amongst close relations and also amongst tenants. The latter could be bought out at will. This resulted in hundreds of land cases being brought before the courts at a cost of thousands of pounds in litigation annually.

A new village in Kenya. On a shelf of the eastern scarp of the eastern rift valley, this village was built in the 1900's when Kikuyu were collected into nucleated villages as part of the effort to deal with Mau-Mau.

Attempts started in 1948 to consolidate holdings, but the government knew that any attempt to force the pace would be used by nationalist leaders to foment unrest and opposition. The Mau-Mau 'Emergency' presented the opportunity to carry consolidation into effect. In the villages records of existing rights to land were compiled and each *mbari* was surveyed and then redivided to give each landholder a single block of land equal in area to all the bits he had previously held, plus a plot of building land in one of the new villages. A large part of Kikuyuland was redivided in this way. But systems of inheritance are not easily altered and unless laws against it are enforced subdivision will no doubt recommence.

A few years later the approach of independence brought new problems. The prospect of living under an African government did not appeal to many European settlers and they sold their farms and left the country. Others were anxious to leave but unwilling to sell their farms for a low price. At the same time the land was wanted by Africans, many of whom were landless and unemployed, and had no cash. The problem was solved in part by the British government providing funds worth £19 million for settling 20,000 African families on subdivisions of former European farms, the poorer ones on small holdings, those with some capital, say £500, on larger holdings where they can grow cash crops and employ labour. More than half the African settlers are Kikuyu.

It is by no means certain that resettlement schemes of this kind will relieve the employment and land problems to any great extent. The Europeans with their greater capital resources were able to farm relatively intensively and employ labour on a large scale. If the Africans replacing them were to farm the former White Highlands in the way they farm their reserves the land would support fewer Africans than it did when the Europeans employed them as labourers and there would be no surplus crops for sale overseas. Smallholding schemes of this kind are quite out of line with most current ideas on agricultural development which visualize larger units better able to take full advantage of modern methods of cultivation and marketing. It is hoped that co-operatives will help to overcome the disadvantages of the small unit by procuring equipment, providing marketing facilities, and reducing production costs generally. Some such schemes are operating successfully; several have suffered from inefficient book-keeping and corruption.

A good deal of progress in agriculture has been made outside Kikuyu areas. The Kamba to the east have constructed miles of terraces and numerous dams to conserve soil and water on their dry, eroding tribal lands. Elgeyo farmers on the high country near Eldoret are rearing high-grade cattle and growing pyrethrum for sale to the manufacturers of insect sprays. (The crop grows well on the volcanic plateaux at 6,000 to 8,000 feet, continuing to flower for nine months and giving a prolonged harvest.) North of Eldoret the slopes of the Cherangani hills have been largely fenced in by progressive African stockfarmers. Wherever holdings have been consolidated, land use has improved and production has increased.

At present the economy is very dependent on agricultural exports. Coffee, almost all *arabica*, worth £19 million, was the main source of the country's foreign exchange in 1966. Tea exports, of which a growing proportion is being produced on smallholdings, were worth nearly £9 million. Livestock products £6 million, sisal, pyrethrum, wattle bark, cotton, fruit, and vegetables brought the total up to about £45 million. Of the total, over a half was produced by European and Asian farmers. The share of Africans is slowly rising, but if they were to take over all the farmland the surplus for export would almost certainly drop considerably. It could be argued that this is not a very serious matter because the level of African incomes would still be higher than before. But this is not necessarily so, and what is more important, the ability of the country to invest in capital equipment would be curtailed.

Although agriculture is the basis of the Kenyan

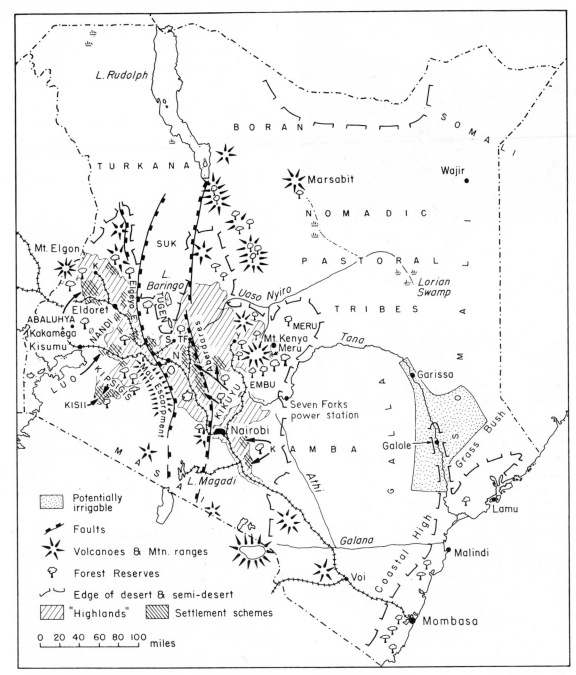

FIG. 50. *Kenya. The south-west is the productive part of Kenya: most of the rest is desert or semi-desert. The potentially irrigable land on the lower Tana covers 3 million acres, from which about 300,000 will probably be selected for development. On the highlands, land formerly farmed by Europeans is being taken over by Africans. People from the many different tribes are being permitted to move into particular areas set aside for them under settlement schemes. The arrows indicate the directions in which different tribes have been able to expand. N—Nakuru, with the lake of that name and Lake Naivasha to the south; K—Kitale, S—Solai, T.F.—Thomson's Falls, Y—Nanyuki. Seven Forks is the site of a new power station on the Tana river with a capacity of 40 MW. The scheme will ultimately provide about 340 MW and supply most of Kenya's needs for electricity for several years to come.*

Nairobi. The central business district of the city.

economy, <u>about one-fifth of the male population over 16 are now engaged in industry and the public</u> services. Most of the men employed in this way live in Nairobi.

Seventy years ago Nairobi was no more than a camp-site on the new railway. Now overseas firms have their head offices in tall blocks lining the wide streets of the city centre. Hundreds of Indian shops lie further out, and beyond lie the European and African residential areas. At the outskirts of the town a number of new factories produce textiles, shoes, and various kinds of household goods to supply the east African market. The new enterprises are protected from overseas competition by tariffs, their profitability depends on the prosperity of east Africa as a whole, and they require continued investment from abroad. The Kenyan government cannot ignore the requirements of these industries, because if they are unable to compete and expand, the number of unemployed in Nairobi will increase and this would endanger any government.

<u>Nairobi is also the centre of tourism,</u> an industry that is already the second biggest money-maker in the country worth over £14 million in 1966. The attractions are provided by Nairobi itself as an English-speaking town with good hotels and shops, the scenery, and above all by the game animals that can be seen in the reserves, one of which is just outside the capital.

West to the lakeshore

West of Nairobi the railway and road to Uganda descend the rift escarpment and swing round the north shore of Lake Nakuru at the foot of the crater of Menengai. Along the rift valley 60 miles to the north, about 2 or 3 square miles of the hot arid country south of Lake Baringo is irrigated from the Perakera river, yielding about 1,000 tons of onions in 1964 and bringing an average net income of £75 to the 334 tenants. Nakuru is an important market and shopping centre for the rift valley area and looks something like a small prairie town in western Canada. Nearby the railway branches, the newer line to Uganda passing through the maize fields and wattle plantations of the European farming area of Uasin Gishu near Eldoret, the older line dropping down to Kisumu at the head of the Kavirondo gulf on Lake Victoria.

Kisumu, which was in Uganda when it became the terminus of the railway, acquired considerable importance as a regional commercial centre, with canoes, dhows, and steamers carrying goods to and from the other lake ports. Since then Kisumu has become part of Kenya and with the construction of the railway to Kampala in the twenties and its more recent extension west, Kisumu's trade has diminished while that of the lake region as a whole has greatly increased. For a time in the thirties the town was enlivened by the discovery of gold at Kakamega, but this soon petered out. Now Kisumu is rather a dull town, still the major lake port with a few small factories processing local-grown rice, maize, and groundnuts and acting as the commercial centre for the populous district nearby, but a place that looks backwards rather than to the future.

The low-lying Nyanza district around the Kavirondo Gulf supports 200 to the square mile, even 1,000 locally in the central areas. The people are mainly Luo, a Nilotic people, second in number to the Kikuyu amongst Kenyan tribes. They were herdsmen who entered the country bordering the lake from the north many decades ago. Towards the end of the last century when they were already settled in Nyanza, vast numbers of their cattle were wiped out by the rinderpest epidemic and other diseases, forcing them to adopt a sedentary way of life, farming and fishing like their Bantu neighbours. They still have many cattle but their herds are small today and their pastures limited in extent because they are hemmed in by strong tribes to the east and by the lake to the west. The lakeshore Luo are fishermen, selling a part of their catch in order to pay taxes and to import grain. Those living away from the lake depend on sorghum for their staple food and grow maize, rice and cotton as cash crops. In the higher wetter areas to the east bananas are an important foodstuff and coffee brings in cash.

The Luo seem to have a reputation amongst Europeans for obstinacy and awkwardness. We find Elspeth Huxley writing that land consolidation began to go forward in Nyanza only because it was stated officially that the people were not yet ready for it. Michael Whissom, too, in his study of social and economic change amongst the Luo, *Change and challenge* (1964), mentions the opposition which most of them feel for all measures proposed and implemented by the administration, with regard to economic development generally and the growing of cash crops, cotton in particular. Usually, as he makes clear, it is found that such attitudes have a rational basis. In the colonial period, one of the most effective ways in which people could demonstrate their dislike for the regime was by ignoring advice and disobeying agricultural regulations. Furthermore, there were often good reasons why the advice proffered should have been rejected.

Pressure on the land in Luo areas is high and food is expensive at certain times of the year, the price of maize and millet commonly doubling in the period between the harvest, in August, and early June which is a hungry period. For a couple of months in the year many people have to depend on cassava. This helps to explain why many of them are not anxious to grow cotton. The soils are suitable, returns are often quite good, but rainfall distribution is uncertain and if their cotton crop fails they may be left destitute.

Subdivision and fragmentation of land is a serious matter, the result of systems of inheritance and the doubling of the population in the last forty years. But consolidation presents many problems. Families short of land have been able to graze their cattle on the stalks on their neighbours' land after the harvest or beg a piece of land to grow crops for a season or two. They are afraid that they would no

longer to be able to do this after rationalization and might be unable to survive as independent farmers. In any case, equitable division of the land is not easy to arrange where soils vary considerably over short distances and difficult problems arise in the Luo country because there has been so much emigration.

Some Luo have moved into the Musoma area of Tanzania but have retained rights to land in Nyanza. Much larger numbers have emigrated to European farms on the highlands. It has been easier for them to earn money in this way than by growing cash crops in their home areas and their families depend on the money sent home by the migrants for buying food, paying taxes, and sending the children to school. Many have settled in Nairobi and Mombasa; several are cabinet ministers and university professors. But the results of emigration on social life in Nyanza have in other ways been far from beneficial; the old order has been disrupted, first by the loss of the herds which once played such an important part in the life of the Luo and then by the departure, at least temporarily, of the most active and energetic members of the tribe. This may help to explain why the people in the home area sometimes give the impression of being conservative and obstinate.

LAKE VICTORIA

Lake Victoria occupies a shallow hollow of the plateau between the two arms of the rift. It is believed to have been formed by uplift of the margins of the western rift ponding back rivers that originally flowed to the site of the rift and may once have drained across it to the Congo. The lake is

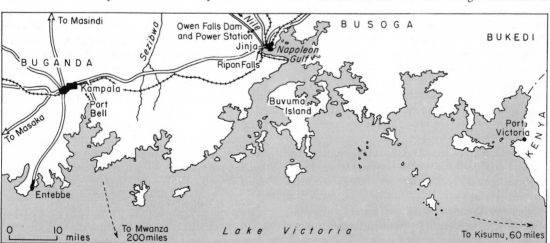

FIG. 51. *Lake Victoria, north shore. The indented shoreline and numerous islands are the outcome of submergence of a dissected land surface in late Pleistocene times. The Owen Falls power station is near the main road and railway from Kampala to Nairobi and the coast.*

Steamer on Lake Victoria. A dhow in the foreground.

scarcely anywhere more than 200 feet deep. Its outline is indented by drowned river valleys, except in the west where barrier beaches have been built up by waves under the influence of south-east winds. Flat-topped islands, the cliffed remains of old mesas and buttes, rise high above the surface.

This inland sea is about the size of Ireland. Its outlet to the north over the Owen falls is now controlled by a dam of which it has been claimed, quite rightly, that nowhere in the world is such an enormous mass of water held up by so little masonry (Fig. 51). As it happens, the supply of water to the lake by rain falling on its surface and rivers flowing into it, is on the whole just in excess of the losses of water by evaporation from the surface. Consequently it is rather sensitive to fluctuations in climate. If the mean annual rainfall were to diminish by a few inches and the mean annual evaporation losses were to increase, there might be very little water to drive the Owen

falls turbines. However, there seems to be no sign at present that the output of electricity will be restricted on this account. On the contrary, in the years after 1961 the lake began to rise and by 1964 had reached the highest levels in this century, possibly the highest level for over 4,000 years. The water in storage in 1965 was greater than the entire discharge of the Nile at Aswan in a normal year so it should be enough to keep the turbines turning for some time to come. In fact the high levels have been creating problems by submerging harbour works and farmland.

The lake divides the peoples living along its shores rather than uniting them, most of the lakeshore dwellers are peasants with a greater liking for their own staple foods than those of other people, and until this century trade around Victoria's shores was on a very small scale. Commerce was first stimulated by Indians and the traffic reached its peak early in the 1920's when the economy of Uganda was booming. It declined when the railways reached Mwanza in 1928 and Kampala in 1931: now most of the crops produced on the lake shores are carried directly to the coast by rail. A new steamer was put into service on the route between the main ports, Jinja, Kisumu, and Mwanza in 1961, capable of carrying 500 passengers and with a refrigerated cargo capacity of 100 tons to carry meat from Tanzania to Uganda. Many of the smaller lake ports closed in 1964 as a result of declining trade and flooded piers.

The lake is important economically as a source of power and as a source of protein. The Owen falls scheme produced 400 million units of electricity in 1961, which at 1d. per unit would be worth £1⅔ million. The Uganda fisheries in the same year produced about £4 million worth of fish.

The Lake Victoria fish differ in some respects from those in the Nile downstream of the Murchison falls. The Nile perch, for example, was not present in the lake until its introduction a few years ago. As a predator it will no doubt feed on the *Tilapia* which constitute a large proportion of the total catch, but as the perch's food is mainly inedible smaller fish and the perch themselves are very good eating, the outcome of the introduction is likely to be beneficial in the long run. Catches of fish in the lake increased at first after the adoption of nylon nets but yields in some of the richer areas have diminished recently, possibly as a result of overfishing. The local elimination of crocodiles has also reduced catches because they used to kill lung fishes that eat the fish sperm on the bottom. The use of outboard motors will allow more of the lake to be fished than was possible in the past, but careful control is evidently necessary if yields are to be maintained at an optimum level.

UGANDA

You often get the impression in Uganda of being in a low-lying country, and yet the altitude is generally between 3,000 and 5,000 feet. The explanation is to be found in the great area in the centre occupied by marshes and lakes and the distant views of high mountains distributed round the rim (Fig. 52A). In the west, the low country bordering Lakes Edward and George to the south and Lake Albert and the Nile to the north, is dominated by the immense bulk of Ruwenzori, a block mountain range, faulted in the west, with its serrated crust usually shrouded in mists and cloud. The Nangeya mountains stand on the frontier with the Sudan Republic in the north, and the frontier with Kenya runs across the massive volcano of Mount Elgon in the east. The depressed centre is largely occupied by a drowned river system forming Lake Kyoga, which provides a passage for the waters flowing out of Lake Victoria on their way by the Murchison falls to Lake Albert. The drainage system has been disrupted by the earth movements that ponded back Lake Victoria, and the western part of the country is traversed by a number of valleys that used to carry water to the west, possibly into the Congo system and which have been interrupted by uplift along an axis parallel to the western arm of the rift system and about 25 miles to the east of the rift scarp.

Climatically the country shows a greater uniformity than Kenya. Only small areas receive less than 20 inches or more than 60 inches of rain annually, but the differences are still important as far as land use is concerned. The most productive and well-populated country, forming a narrow band along the west side of Lake Victoria and a broader one on the north side, receives an annual rainfall of more than 33 inches in nine years out of ten, the rain falling in two distinct seasons (Fig. 52B). This is the heavily settled banana and coffee growing country of Buganda, originally under rain forest and now largely cultivated or under elephant grass. The highlands of western Ankole and Kigezi in the south-west receive a similar rainfall and are also heavily settled, but between them and the lakeshore, the country is drier probably because this western part of Uganda receives its rain mainly from westerly air streams and the dry areas lie in the rain shadow of the highlands bordering the rift. The open rolling country with less than 30 inches of rain in the south-west is roamed by Hima pastoralists, living in scattered kraals and avoiding the areas infested with tsetse-fly. North of Lake Kyoga, in West Nile and Acholi, rainfall peaks draw closer together and seasonal contrasts are stronger than on the northern shore of Victoria. This is millet and cattle country, deteriorating to semi-desert in the extreme north-east, comparable in many respects to the Sudan zone of west Africa.

Communications between north and south are hampered by wide stretches of swamp and lakes. There are differences between the people too, with most of the northerners, including the Acholi and Lango, together numbering well over half a million, belonging to the same linguistic group as the Luo while the Ganda, Nyoro and Nyankole are Bantu. But the main causes of fission in Uganda are less physical and ethnic than historical. Europeans have always been too few to present any

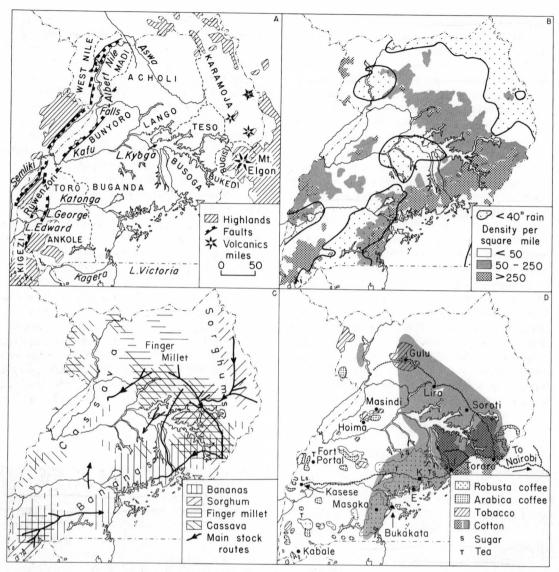

FIG. 52. *Uganda. A. Relief and drainage, B. Climate and population, C. Staple food crops and stock routes, D. Export crops. K—Kampala, E—Entebbe, J—Jinja, Ls—limestone, Cu—copper. (After* Atlas of Uganda.)

serious minority problems. Asians are more numerous; there were about 90,000 of them in 1966. They are prominent in trade, they run cotton gin-neries and factories and have developed sugar and other plantations. Africans who compete with them on a similar level are inclined to resent their pre-sence in the country. However, the main source of friction dates from happenings in the nineteenth century that mainly affected the Africans themselves and the traditional states that together form modern Uganda.

Buganda

The largest and most progressive tribe or nation in Uganda are the Ganda of the fertile banana and coffee belt on the lakeshore and inland. The land-scape is characterized by flat-topped hills with ferricrete cappings forming the remnants of an erosion surface at 4,500 to 4,200 feet; a newer sur-face on which the hills stand declines gently to the lake-shore and forms part of its floor. High forest is confined mainly to a narrow zone near the lake; north of the forest tall grasses predominate, with large trees clustered near compounds and at the base of old termite mounds. Swampy river valleys and hollows are widespread.

The Baganda are mainly engaged in farming, living on farmsteads dispersed along tracks and lanes often long distances from the main roads, scattered over the red soils of the hill flanks and the darker soils down towards the swamps. There are few large towns or even villages, just the beginnings of nucleated settlements around shops originally established by Asians and now usually operated by Africans, typically located at road junctions. Surrounding the compounds are permanent banana gardens—plantains are the staple food—with sweet potatoes, cassava and vegetables near Kampala where such crops find a ready sale. Beyond the gardens are fields of maize, cotton, and coffee, the main cash crops.

In the eighteenth and nineteenth centuries the Baganda formed a powerful military state, tyrannizing neighbouring tribes and enriching themselves with livestock, women, and slaves. The first European explorers found them well clad in bark cloth, living in large houses and making use of good roads. Their supreme ruler was the Kabaka. Beneath him local rulers enjoyed unlimited jurisdiction and unrestricted rights to the services of the people. The chiefs who surrounded the king's court were quite ready to avail themselves of the European innovations, being appreciative it would seem of both firearms and Christianity. It was with these chiefs, grown more mature and powerful, that the British signed the Uganda Agreement of 1900, a treaty which has had long-lasting consequences.

The agreement provided for a good measure of Buganda self-government under the Kabaka and his council of ministers and, when Uganda eventually became independent, the Ganda state retained its identity and the Kabaka became the country's first President. This arrangement was not to last very long, however. In 1966, the Kabaka was ejected by the central government, and the Prime Minister, a northerner, Dr. Obote, assumed the Presidency and ended Buganda's autonomy.

The British occupation did not eliminate tribal friction. In the early days the Buganda system of government was applied by the British administration to neighbouring tribes; Ganda were often used as intermediaries and this did nothing to improve relations. In the case of Bunyoro the situation was aggravated by a territorial dispute that dates from the end of the century when the Ganda helped the British to subdue the Nyoro and were rewarded with a slice of conquered territory. These 'lost

Kiganda market. Mainly plantains for sale in this section of the market.

Sugar cane in Uganda. Production in 1967 was 134,000 tons, well in excess of local consumption, and some difficulty may be experienced in disposing of the surplus now that Kenya and Tanzania are self-sufficient.

counties' have been a source of grievance to the Nyoro ever since and it was with much reluctance that they withdrew their claim in 1962 to four of the counties where Ganda are now in the majority, on condition that the other two counties should be administered by the central government until such time as the inhabitants express their decision whether to remain in Buganda or to return to Bunyoro. Subsequently in 1964, a referendum was held which revealed a desire amongst the local people for return to Bunyoro.

The tenurial system in Buganda by which land is held by individuals and can be bought and sold, also derives from the early years of the Protectorate, to the Uganda Agreement, according to which nearly half the land in Buganda was divided between 4,000 people: the Kabaka, his chiefs, and other notables. Since then, holdings have been subdivided on inheritance and plots have been sold to pay survey fees or buy cars or houses. Now there are reckoned to be some 130,000 landowners in Buganda, some with large holdings, others merely landed peasants. On the larger holdings, tenants have acquired squatters rights that are carefully protected by law and so few of the *mailo* estates, as they are called, especially the large ones, are actually at the disposal of their owners. The rest of the land in Buganda is administered by the Buganda Land Board and is occupied by individuals on lease or licence.

About half the people are not really Baganda. The farmers are usually assisted in their work by paid employees, the majority of whom are immigrants from Ankole and the Western Region of Uganda, and also from Rwanda and Burundi. Some act as herdsmen looking after the cattle belonging to Ganda farmers. Others work on the coffee and cotton farms.

Buganda has always dominated the economy of the country and is likely to continue to do so, partly because of its initial lead and partly because of its greater resources. The expansion of coffee and sugar production in post-war years, possibly helped in the case of the former by the security of tenure offered by the *mailo* system, has taken place mainly in the lakeshore region. The market provided by Kampala has attracted new industries to Buganda, and the construction of the hydroelectric power plant at Jinja has accentuated the concentration of economic activity in the region. Cattle imports to Jinja and Kampala from the north are increasing and dairying is beginning to develop in Buganda. Cotton is one of the few commodities which has declined in importance in the lakeshore region and expanded elsewhere, and in this case an explanation can be found in the fixing of cotton prices by the marketing board, irrespective of the distance the crop has to be moved for ginning and railing to the coast. Coffee prices are fixed in a similar way, but climatic conditions are unsuitable for this crop in the north. In Buganda coffee has replaced cotton as the chief crop.

Kampala, the chief town in Uganda, is built on a number of low hills, one of which was the site of the Kabaka's palace when the British arrived. In recent decades, following the extension of the railway and with growing commerce and prosperity, people have been attracted from all parts of the country by the amenities and the chance for wage labour. The majority are not Baganda. Light industries depending on electricity from the Jinja power-station 50 miles away are springing up at Kampala and at Port Bell on the lakeshore, and a trading estate has been established on the railway linking the two places (Fig. 51).

The earlier seat of colonial government was established at Entebbe on a peninsula of Lake Victoria about 20 miles outside Kampala, for reasons of health and safety. Some departments of government are still there, and the international airport, but Kampala is now the capital. The College of Makerere, part of the University of East Africa, is also in Kampala.

Jinja was visualized by Winston Churchill early in the century as destined to become a very important place in the economy of central Africa. 'In years to come the shores of this splendid bay may be covered with long rows of tropical villas and imposing offices, and the gorge of the Nile crowded with factories and warehouses.' His prophecy is at last being fulfilled. A dam was built across the channel in 1954, flooding the rapids and enabling the falling waters to drive turbines with a capacity of 150 MW. Jinja, with a population of about 50,000 in 1966, now has a textile mill, brewery, a smelter to deal with Kilembe copper, a small steel rolling mill, and plants for processing locally grown groundnuts and other crops. The rate of expansion has been slower than had been hoped. At first cloth produced at Jinja was no cheaper than cloth imported from India, and other manufacturers have had difficulty in competing with imported goods. In 1960 the demand for electricity was still only half the installed capacity in spite of the export of large quantities of energy to Kenya. Since then, sales to Kenya have remained steady, but Uganda's own electricity consumption has steadily increased. The Owen falls now supply nearly all Uganda towns of any size. A vigorous rural electrification policy is being pursued and a new scheme is being prepared for a hydroelectric station at the Murchison falls which would have a capacity of some 600 MW.

Other heavily settled areas

Heavy settlement with more than 250 people to the square mile extends east of the Nile towards Mount Elgon, leaving to the south about a quarter of a million acres of potentially highly productive land in south Busoga sparsely settled. It was depopulated by sleeping-sickness at the end of the nineteenth century and has never been reoccupied. The completion of the railway reducing the track distance from Jinja to the Kenya border should help to reopen the area to settlement, and an International Bank Mission recommended its development as a planned farming area producing such crops as sugar.

Bugisu occupies the slopes of Elgon to the east of Busoga. Long ridges with narrow valleys extend west from the great volcano like the fingers of an outstretched hand and further south lies a jumble of hills, with one main valley and a number of smaller ones leading away from the higher forested slopes to the closely cultivated, short-grass country at lower levels. The plains are well suited to cotton and cattle; coffee, cotton, and a variety of other crops will grow in a middle zone where there are also water meadows excellent for grazing. On the highlands, coffee and potatoes grow side by side, with cattle grazing the uncultivated slopes nearby. Local farmers like to have land in each of these zones and some of the clan lands run from high up on the mountains down to the plains. By borrowing, buying, renting, and exchanging land a man can achieve his ideal and so the prosperous Mugisu is the owner of many strips in various places, and if he is a large cattle-owner, part of his herd will be kept on the plains stretching perhaps outside Bugisu territory.

Kigezi in the extreme south-west of Uganda is another densely settled highland area with 800 people to the square mile in parts of the southern

Kigezi, Uganda. Carefully terraced slopes in one of the most densely settled parts of east Africa.

counties. With only 3 acres for a family, competition for land is very keen and it is no wonder that the Bakiga have the reputation for being amongst Uganda's most competent agriculturalists. The population increased from a quarter of a million in 1931 to 400,000 in 1948, partly as a result of immigration from Ruanda-Urundi. There were signs that fertility was declining and so an area suitable for resettlement was chosen above the Lake Edward escarpment, in northern Kigezi. The settlers inspected the land well beforehand, other careful preparations were made, and some 15,000 people agreed to move to the new area. They have been followed by others. In the home area the intention is to consolidate the old fragmented holdings into larger blocks and contour cultivation is the rule.

In recent years Uganda has permitted refugees from Rwanda and the Sudan to enter the country. Tutsi refugees from Rwanda are being settled in the Oruchinga valley in Ankole District. This is on one of the main routes by which tsetse-fly enter Uganda from Tanzania. It is hoped that the refugees will clear the bush and provide a barrier against the tsetse and so protect the country to the north, which includes a proposed ranching area.

Northern and western Uganda

Economic progress in the north and west has been much slower than in the lakeside districts, and the cash income per head of the people is only a fraction of that in Buganda. McMaster has shown how subsistence cropping has been modified, with banana cultivation expanding westwards, and cassava replacing finger millet in many areas. Cotton is now very widely grown; sugar, tea, and tobacco are important locally (Fig. 52).

Industrial development in the north and west has been very limited. The extension of the railway to Kasese at the foot of the Ruwenzori range in 1956 allowed Kilembe copper to be mined and this now forms about one-tenth of the country's exports by value. But little development has taken place at Kasese itself, or along the line to Kampala. A cement factory built at Tororo in the east in 1952, before the high-grade limestones near Kasese were accessible, supplies all the country's needs, and being

Picking cotton in West Nile, Uganda. Notice that the trees were not completely cleared before the crop was planted.

Ankole cattle on the grass-lands of western Uganda. Livestock contribute some £12 million annually to the country's economy.

Virunga volcanoes. On the shoulders of the western rift the highest of these peaks rises to nearly 15,000 feet.

near the source of power at Jinja and the main markets is better placed than a plant at Kasese would ever have been. The same arguments apply to most other industrial development.

RWANDA AND BURUNDI

Two of the smallest and most densely settled of the African mainland states lie astride the Congo-Nile watershed, a little south of the equator. Until the First World War, when they were occupied by Belgian forces, they formed a remote corner of German East Africa. Between the wars Belgium administered them as the mandated territory of Ruanda–Urundi, and after the Second World War they formed a trust territory until independence came in 1962.

From the thalwegs of Lakes Kivu and Tanganyika and the Ruzizi river, they stretch across the eastern shoulder of the rift valley to the Kagera, the main feeder of Lake Victoria. This river, generally regarded as the ultimate source of the Nile, rises nearly 4° south of the equator in the hills of Burundi. The main watershed with the Congo is formed by a group of mountain masses rising to more than 8,000 feet, well forested, and receiving annually over 50 inches of rain (Fig. 53A). In the north, on the frontier with Uganda and the Congo, are the great active volcanoes known as the Virunga or Mfumbiro mountains, the highest of which, Karasimbi, reaches 14,786 feet. Elephant, gorilla, and chimpanzee live in the bamboo and montane moist forests of the

upper slopes which are included in a national park. Another park of quite a different character has been established in the north-east corner of Rwanda where the human population on the savanna plains is small, because of the low rainfall, and quite a large area is roamed by herds of zebra, roan antelope, impala, and water buck.

The longitudinal arrangement of the relief and rainfall pattern is reflected in the distribution of population (Fig. 53B). While the lowlands in the east and west have less than 100 people to the square mile, plateaux and hills at 5,500 to 6,500 feet just to the east of the main watershed support more than 450 people to the square mile. In this populous belt, cropland and pasture form a complicated mosaic. There are few villages, merely groups of huts situated often on hill-tops, surrounded by banana plantations and patches of coffee, with fields of beans, sweet potatoes, sorghum, and fallow land further afield. The farmers have pressed westwards into the highlands, clearing the upland forests and avoiding the swampy valley floors, which are often underlain by several feet of papyrus peat.

The political frontier between the two states cuts across these longitudinal zones, and yet there is no great ethnic or language difference between Rwanda in the north and Burundi to the south. The two countries are in fact remarkably alike, both having rather curious ethnic and social structures. In both about 85 per cent. of the people are Hutu, similar in appearance to the generality of peasant cultivators in east Africa. Living amongst them, until recently as their superiors, are the Tutsi, one of the tallest human groups in the world; a slender, long-legged people with a mean height of about 5 ft. 9 in., narrow heads, long, narrow noses, and thick lips, a people who have something in common with the Masai and the Fulani. The Twa, in complete contrast to the Tutsi, are a short stocky people, round-headed with short, wide noses and thin lips, morphologically related to the pygmies of the Ituri forest who live not so very far to the north. The Twa were probably the aboriginal inhabitants of the region; now they trap and net animals in the forest, or engage in primitive crafts on the open plains. They form only about 1 per cent. of the total population.

The Tutsi are related to the Hima who make up the ruling caste in all the interlacustrine kingdoms from Bunyoro to Buhaya and are believed to have come from the east as invading pastoralists about the fifteenth century. The Tutsi moved on to the highlands west of Lake Victoria, and after a series of struggles against the Hutu clans and amongst themselves, succeeded in establishing two states, each ruled by a king called a Mwami.

The Tutsi were, and still are, devoted to their cattle and they seem to have inspired a similar devotion amongst the Hutu, who were thereby brought under subjection. Amongst the Tutsi a system of patronage operated by which a man in need of cattle was granted one or more cows by a patron in return for performing certain services over a period of a year or two. He could use the cows as he liked and the calves belonged to him, but he still had to carry out certain duties for his patron such as helping him to cultivate his fields, build his dwelling, and guard his herds. He could not sell his cattle without permission, but if he died without an heir then the cattle returned to the patron. This type of cattle contract was part and parcel of the Tutsi social hierarchy, all cattle patrons being tied to more important patrons up to the highest levels, where they were direct clients of the Mwami.

The Hutu, also being desirous of cattle, were willing to enter into this client relationship with the Tutsi, who alone had the cattle. So in time the Tutsi came to occupy the top of the social and political pyramid in both Rwanda and Burundi, and the Hutu formed the base of it. To all of them cattle were the symbol of power and wealth. In Burundi the dead Mwami was sewed into the skin of a black bull for burial. One person greets another in Rwanda with 'amashyo', may you have herds, to which the reply is 'amashongure', I wish you herds of females. The Tutsi were in turn influenced by contact with the peasant life of the Hutu, becoming sedentary stock-owning cultivators, no longer nomads living on blood and milk.

With the approach of independence in the fifties this caste system began to collapse. Educated Hutu came to form a new *élite* which had little sympathy with the Tutsi establishment. Attempts were made to abolish *ubuhake*, the cattle contract system, clients being given two-thirds of the cattle, which they had formerly held on trust, as their own property. In Rwanda, the Mwami who had always been very autocratic was driven out by the Hutu; about 150,000 Tutsi fled as refugees to Uganda and Burundi and thousands are reported to have been murdered since then. In Burundi the principal leaders of the Hutu were executed at the end of

FIG. 53. *Rwanda and Burundi. A. Relief and rainfall, B. Minerals and population distribution.*

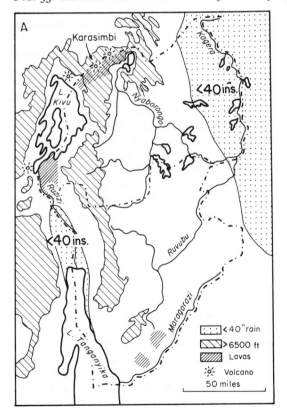

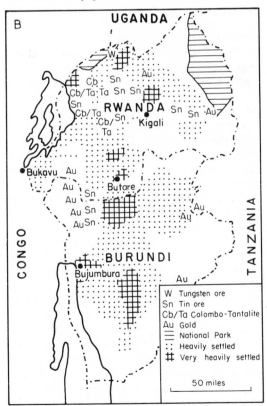

1965 after an unsuccessful rising against the Tutsi king. A few months later he was deposed by his own son who was himself deposed in November 1966.

It had been made clear to United Nations representatives visiting the Trust Territory before independence, that in spite of all the economic advantages of being under one government, the two states had no desire to remain united. The people of the two countries knew little of each other, and apparently what they knew they did not like. So Rwanda became a Hutu republic governed from Kigali, a village that was once the home of the Mwami, while Burundi has become a Tutsi republic, ruled from the old capital at Bujumbura, the only truly urban centre in either territory.

Both countries badly need stable, capable governments to enable them to cope with their social and economic problems. They are still remote. They have no railways and the nearest point on the coast is 750 miles away to the east. Yet their economies must somehow provide for the needs of large and growing populations. In each country about 3 million people are living off 10,000 square miles, a situation in striking contrast to that in neighbouring Congo and Tanzania, where densities are less than one-tenth as great.

Emigration would seem to offer a possible solution to the population problems. People have been moving out for several decades, many going to Uganda even before the Belgian mandate, especially in time of famine and war. The numbers of migrants increased in the twenties of this century, when Uganda's economy was expanding rapidly, and it has been estimated that some 50,000 men annually found seasonal employment, mostly in the coffee and cotton plantations of Buganda. Many of them settled down there and some 300,000 are believed to have emigrated permanently. There are smaller seasonal movements into Tanzania, but the opportunities for finding work are more limited there. A few thousand have left for the Congo each year, to work for two or three years at a time in mines and on plantations. The migrants return with goods and money thereby helping to relieve pressure on the land in the home country. It remains to be seen whether the flow of labour will increase or diminish now that all the countries concerned are independent.

Both Rwanda and Burundi are primarily dependent on their agricultural resources. Most people grow their own food, only a small proportion of the food crops produced coming into the market. For a cash income they rely on coffee. About half a million peasants, each with 50 to 100 trees, were growing about 30,000 tons of coffee annually in the late fifties, thereby obtaining a cash income of £5 to £10 each. Fortunately the climate is suitable for growing high-quality *arabica* which is in demand for blending with Brazilian coffee, so the price may remain attractive. In recent years coffee has made up four-fifths of the total exports by value. Cotton, grown in the drier alluvial areas, is much less important, only about 5,000–7,000 tons being produced annually and the proportionate costs of transport being higher than for coffee. There is some room for expanding production of both these crops by increasing yields and acreage, but demands on the land are already heavy. For each family there are only 5 to 12 acres of cropland and for each cow only 4 acres of grazing land. In response to this situation the concept of individual ownership of land is spreading and this is raising many problems of land tenure which remain to be solved. The Belgians made some attempt to deal with the problems of fragmentation and erosion by redistributing land holdings in selected areas, so that each family should have a section of land at least equal in size to what it had previously, but arranged to allow contour cultivation and with crops planted in strips marked by anti-erosion hedges. In the sparsely settled alluvial lowlands, swamps were drained and agricultural settlements established on thousands of acres. Each farmer has about 10 acres of land, half of it under crops, half fallow, and incomes of the settlers are reckoned to be twice those of most other farmers.

The most difficult problem to solve is overstocking. It has been estimated that the cattle population multiplied about ten times under the Belgian administration, and many areas are now suffering from overgrazing. The cattle have beautiful long horns but their yields of milk are low, the beasts are in poor condition and the industry is not very rewarding economically. Attempts have been made to stimulate meat consumption and possibly as a result of this, numbers of cattle in the two territories together remained at about the million mark during the fifties; sheep, goats, and pigs continued to increase.

Fisheries have developed considerably since the last war. Nylon nets and metal canoes replaced dug-outs, and annual catches by native fishermen increased from about 1 or 2 tons to 3 or 4 tons per head. European commercial firms began to operate on Lake Tanganyika in the fifties and using seine nets were able to take 2 or 3 tons in a night. To protect the local fishermen the numbers of European operators were restricted, and new techniques worked out for the Africans. Two of the new type of metal boats are tied together side by side and the 'catamaran' is towed by night to the middle of the lake, where fish are more plentiful, by a third boat. Fires are lit on the bows according to custom to attract the *ndagara* fish, and a large square net is lowered to a depth of 100 to 300 feet. When this is hauled up, the fish are scooped out with smaller nets and in this way 400 to 600 lb. of fish may be caught in a single night. The fisheries on the other smaller lakes are also being developed, but the nutrient content of the water is not very high, so yields are not very good.

The resources for industrial growth are limited. Alluvial tin-ore is produced at a rate of about 2,000 tons annually and less-important quantities of tungsten, gold, columbite, and tantallite. These together make up about one-fifth of exports by value. The prospects for the discovery of other valuable mineral deposits cannot be considered promising. The only fuel supplies that might be developed are peat and methane gas. Great thicknesses of papyrus peat occur in many of the upland valleys. The methane is in Lake Kivu where the gas is believed to be produced by the decomposition of plankton in the absence of oxygen. A little methane is present in all lakes, but in Kivu the dissolved gas has accumulated over the centuries, presumably because the density stratification of the water is such as to prevent disturbance of the layer of water in which the gas is produced. The heating equivalent of about 50 million tons of coal is believed to be available, dissolved in the lake waters, and attempts are being made to pipe it to the shore for industrial use. More important potentially is hydroelectric power. A large plant has already been constructed on the Ruzizi river and the high relief and rainfall of both countries would allow many small plants to be constructed if finance were available.

Manufacturing is on a limited scale at present. Coffee and cotton are processed for export at a number of points; factories producing foodstuffs, saucepans, and blankets for local use have been erected in Bujumbura. This is the main commercial centre of both countries, having road links with Bukavu in the Congo, and with Kigali, the main town in Rwanda. It is also conveniently near the power station on the Ruzizi river. Its population increased from 10,000 in 1944 to 67,000 in 1966, and if conditions in the Congo do not impede communications with the outside world, it will probably continue to grow. (The rise of Lake Tanganyika caused some flooding of the factory area in 1961–5.) Even this modest urban expansion shows little prospect of attracting local people off the land. Many of the town-dwellers are Congolese or Swahili speakers from the coast and the industries were, at least until independence, almost entirely in the hands of Europeans. If standards of living are to be maintained in these two countries, with populations growing at 3 per cent. annually, development will have to accelerate considerably.

12

South Central Africa

A LARGE part of Africa between 10° and 20° south of the equator is drained by the Zambezi, which rises on the high plateau of eastern Angola and flows across the continent to reach the sea half-way along the coast of Mozambique. The construction of the Kariba dam provided a physical and economic bond between Zambia and Rhodesia, for the two countries, though they have drifted apart politically, remain very reliant on the river as a source of power for their industries and mines. Scarcely used by river craft on account of rapids the Zambezi does little else to link together the countries along its course, in fact it might well have been chosen as the boundary between two of the regional blocks distinguished in this book. Rhodesia could have been attached to South Africa, Angola to the Congo, and the other countries to east Africa. But the countries of south-central Africa have some common features and interdependence resulting from their positions and history, and so they have been grouped together here.

The former British territories depend heavily on the railways reaching the sea through Portuguese territory, the lines to Beira and Lourenço Marques in Mozambique, and to a lesser degree on the Benguela railway to Lobito in Angola. Labour migration to the Copperbelt and Rhodesia is another feature of their interdependence. Finally, the five states can be seen as constituting a zone of political uncertainty and tension between the newly independent equatorial territories and the white-dominated Republic of South Africa.

Since the dissolution of the Central African Federation in 1963, the two northern states, Zambia (formerly Northern Rhodesia) and Malawi (formerly Nyasaland) have become independent states within the Commonwealth. The position of Rhodesia (formerly Southern Rhodesia) is still in the balance. At the time of writing it is in most respects an independent state with its government provided by the European minority. In Angola and Mozambique, which are officially described as provinces of Portugal, African nationalists have created some disturbances, but the Portuguese continue to maintain their hold.

This region of south central Africa is quite well endowed with natural resources both mineral and agricultural, but economic activity is mainly restricted to a few scattered, relatively small and specially favoured areas where Europeans have taken the initiative in developing resources. The African population, almost entirely Bantu, is sparse on the whole, except in southern Malawi, parts of Mozambique, and in the neighbourhood of European mining, industrial, and agricultural enterprises elsewhere, but in all five countries together the Africans outnumber the whites by about forty to one.

ANGOLA

Angola is some fourteen times the size of Portugal and has a somewhat smaller population. Until the twentieth century there were seldom more than a thousand Portuguese living there and the wonder is that they ever managed to persist. After their early successes in the Kingdom of the Congo they found the warm humid climate and the cannibal tribes of the north too unhealthy for comfort and confined their settlements to the coast and particularly to Luanda. For many decades their rule was exercised from Brazil, and in Luanda, the capital, seventeenth-century houses can still be seen that are poor relations of the mansions of Bahia and Rio de Janeiro. Even the local cuisine is Brazilian. For these acquisitions Angola paid dearly. Over a million natives were shipped across the Atlantic to the Brazilian plantations in the seventeenth century and 2 million more before the collapse of the slave trade about 1850.

A narrow plain with a very dry climate stretches all along the coast and is overlooked by a prominent escarpment. The rolling uplands of the interior are underlain by crystalline rocks and further east by sandstones declining gently towards the Kalahari and Congo basins. Most of the country is dry savanna woodland, deteriorating to thorn scrub in the south where the rainfall is less than 20 inches, and with high forest restricted to Cabinda, the small Portuguese enclave north of the Congo mouth, and to the valleys of the Kasai and Kwango tributaries (Fig. 54).

The Benguela railway, which is largely owned by a British company and was constructed in the first three decades of this century to provide access to the copper-mines of Katanga and Northern Rhodesia, provides a representative transect of the country. Lobito, the ocean terminus, is a good example of an African town that has grown up solely because it was chosen to be the port of a railway. A magnificent harbour is provided by a north-pointing sandspit, one of many along the Angolan coast (Fig. 55). Since the Lobito port was formally opened in 1928 the population has grown to 70,000, a number which includes over 10,000 *civilizados*, the term used to cover both Portuguese and non-Europeans who have adopted a European way of life. After the interruption of normal transport services in the Congo, traffic increased because nearly all Katanga's copper was exported through Lobito. In spite of the fact that Lobito is 3,000 miles nearer to Europe than Beira, shipping companies maintained freight rates from Lobito at a higher level than from east coast ports until 1965 when, under pressure from Zambia, they were equalized. This is likely to lead to a big expansion of traffic on the railway and through the port. Restrictions on the movement of Zambian copper through Rhodesia in 1966 and 1967 resulted in much of it being exported by way of the railway to Lobito. Several industries have been established at the port such as the manufacture of cement, extraction of salt from sea-water, and timber mills.

The railway runs south along the coast at first, crossing the Catumbela river which is believed to have carried down the sand building the spit at Lobito. The line passes Benguela, which was the chief port in the days of the slave trade and is now eclipsed by Lobito, and strikes east towards the escarpment. The coastal plains stretching far to the north and south are dry and desolate, unproductive except for irrigated sugar plantations near the larger rivers. Towards the scarp foot the rainfall increases to about 20 inches and thorn scrub with occasional baobabs gives way to thicker woodland. The first step of the scarp is so steep that the original line required a rack and pinion section 5 miles long, and in spite of subsequent improvements to the alignment, steep gradients, notably at Cubal, still limit maximum loads and thereby increase transport costs between coast and hinterland.

East of the scarp crest the railway slowly climbs over the *planalto* for 150 miles, traversing rather empty country that provides little traffic. Quite suddenly it reaches the outskirts of Nova Lisboa,

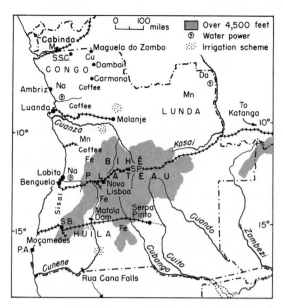

FIG. 54. *Angola. M.—Matadi, S.S.C.—São Salvador do Congo, S.P.—Silva Porto, S.B.—Sá da Bandeira, P.A.—Porto Alexandre, Cu—copper, Na—salt, Da—alluvial diamonds, Mn—manganese, Fe—iron.*

Port of Lobito in Angola. The terminus of the Benguela railway, serving Katanga and the Zambian Copperbelt.

the second largest city in Angola, more than 5,000 feet above sea-level and with a climate not unlike Portugal's. On account of its climate and central position plans were made at one time to make it the capital. They have never materialized, but Nova Lisboa has grown to be a thriving town at the centre of a productive region. A wide variety of crops,

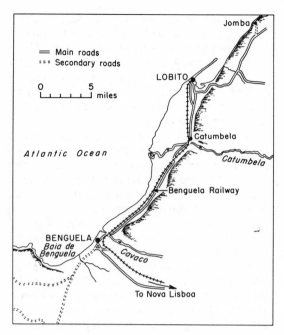

FIG. 55. *The port of Lobito and the Benguela railway.* (*Taken from an article thus entitled by W. A. Hance and I. S. Van Dongen*, Geographical Review, *46, 1956, p. 460.*)

similar to those of the Rhodesian highveld, are grown on African and European farms; factories in the town produce starch, dextrose, and flour from local produce.

Population densities decline from more than fifty to the square mile around Nova Lisboa to sparsely settled areas at a distance where most of the people are shifting cultivators. These people belong to the Ovimbunda who are descended from an immigrant group that arrived from the northeast three centuries ago and now occupy much of the *planalto* and the nearby coastal plains. In consequence this whole area in Angola has a single language with only minor dialectical differences.

From the highlands rising above the *planalto* to heights of over 5,000 feet, streams descend rapidly to the Atlantic and in a more leisurely fashion to the Zambezi and towards the Okavango swamps. The railway follows the watershed running east between the tributaries of the Cuanza and the headwaters of the Cubango, crossing rolling savanna uplands providing grazing for a million and a half cattle, mostly owned by Africans. At Silva Porto a mill grinds locally grown corn but can hardly compete with flour imported from America. East of the Cuanza valley, the land slopes gently down towards the east, with flat-floored valleys on either side

draining to the Congo and Zambezi systems. The line is bordered by eucalyptus, originally planted to provide fuel for the locomotives, and on either side stretch sisal plantations, deliberately established near the railway to keep transport costs low. Further away from the railway the country is practically empty, with small, widely separated settlements and no large markets. The Ganguella people who live here are shifting cultivators, clearing patches of woodland to take a crop of bulrush millet and perhaps another the following year, and then moving on to fresh land.

South of the Benguela railway the rainfall gradually diminishes and south of latitude 14° irrigation is needed for successful cropping. In spite of its aridity, the Portuguese have made greater efforts to develop Huila Province than any other part of the country. Until recently it was difficult to reach from the coast. In fact, the first European settlers were Boer trekkers, about 300 of whom made their way to Angola from Mafeking about 1880. By the time the Portuguese arrived in force the Boers were well established but in the 1920's, by which time the colony had grown to about 1,500, most of them were persuaded by the Union government to move down into South-West Africa where a vigorous policy of white settlement was being pursued.

The Portuguese have made most effort in the headwaters of the Cunene, one of the few perennial rivers in southern Angola. The railway from Moçamedes to São Bandeira is being extended to Serpa Pinto and may eventually be carried through to join the Rhodesian system. The improved access should stimulate agriculture and a colony of 200 families, mainly Portuguese, has been induced to settle in an area prepared for them at Cela. In this scheme, which was intended to be a pattern for the future, the farms are small and the owners provide all the labour themselves, living in the same kind of style as peasants in Madeira or Portugal itself. A large barrage has been built at Matala, where the railway extension crosses the Cunene river in order to generate electricity for Bandeira and its neighbourhood and to store water for irrigating several thousands of acres. The Quitere–Mucopa depression, 20 miles west of the Cunene, is another potential site for irrigation. Some day, the Rua Cana falls, tenth largest in the world will be harnessed for generating electricity.

The coastal lowlands in the south are extremely dry with extensive dunefields between Porto Alexandre and the Cunene river. The Benguela current which causes this aridity, is also the source of wealth in this area for its fisheries are very rich

206

indeed. Boats mainly operated by Portuguese and Madeirans land about 400,000 tons of fish annually. Some is salted or dried and sent to the Copperbelt, but most of it is converted into fish meal for cattle food. The Japanese and other nations are beginning to operate large fishing vessels which are capable of freezing and transporting very large volumes of fish from the Benguela fishing grounds.

Moçamedes, as well as being a fishing port, also benefits from the exploitation of iron-ore in the Cuima and Cassinga areas. Half a million tons were exported in 1961 mostly to Germany, and production was expected to exceed 3 million tons in 1967.

The greatest contribution to the Angolan economy is made by Luanda and the regions lying north of the Benguela railway. The biggest money-maker is coffee which accounts for nearly half the exports. It is grown mainly in the hinterland of Luanda in the Congo Province. The most productive area lies at 3,000 to 4,000 feet between Malanje, at the terminus of the Luanda railway, and Carmona, which is linked by road to Luanda. About three-quarters of the coffee is grown on plantations owned by Europeans, notably the Companhia União Fahil. Native producers, who are said to be less careful and to produce a poorer sample, receive only about half the price paid to the planters. In Congo Province the plantations of coffee and other crops occupy only a tiny proportion of the whole area. Much of it is practically uninhabited, labour is scarce, and methods used for recruiting labour have been harsh.

Although the initiative in commercial agriculture lies entirely with the Portuguese, Africans are not prevented from taking up land and at least in theory anyone, Portuguese or Angolan, with moderate resources can procure a thousand-acre holding. But if a plantation is to pay, heavy expenditure is needed for housing and roads, and only Portuguese companies are capable of raising the necessary capital. The most practical steps taken to improve native farming methods resemble those taken in other colonies. South of Dambai, for example, 7,500 acres of land have been cleared, ploughed, and terraced under European supervision, and African farmers allotted 25 acres each to grow cassava, maize, peanuts, and fruit. At present tsetse prevent cattle being kept, but sheep, goats, pigs, and poultry are reared having sufficient resistance to the disease to survive. Schemes like this are intended to wean the people away from shifting cultivation; so far they have made little impression.

Mineral production is far less valuable than in neighbouring territories and is not increasing markedly. Diamonds won from alluvial formations in the north-east come second in the list of exports and are worth about £13 million per year. About a thousand tons of copper are produced annually from ores mined about 15 miles south of Maquela do Zombo. Oil companies prospecting in the coastal zone have had some success and production exceeded 750,000 tons in 1966.

In the future the economy of Angola must depend mainly on agriculture, and as in so many other African territories the excessive reliance on coffee must be corrected by greater diversification. Cotton, oil-palms, rubber are grown locally but hardly enter into international trade at present.

Over all looms the spectre of rebellion. Opposition to the Portuguese in any organized form seems to have originated mainly outside the country with new African states seeing Angola as another colony ripe for independence, and the Bakongo in the north-east of Angola receiving arms and assistance from their brothers in the Congo. In 1961 several hundreds of Europeans and many thousands of Africans were killed in disturbances that affected mainly the north-east. In addition far larger numbers fled from their homes, some to the Congo, most to the bush. The outlook is indeed gloomy in what might well be a prosperous country, given time and money and goodwill; but all three are scarce in central Africa.

RHODESIA

Towards the end of the last century, Rhodes's Pioneer Column making its way north from the Cape, between the Kalahari on the one side and the Transvaal on the other, found the way to the highveld north of the Limpopo impeded by the Matabele. They were a fighting people, a Zulu horde that had been defeated by the Boers in the Transvaal and had settled across the Limpopo under their chief Lobengula. They lorded it over the neighbouring tribes, sending raiding parties out to the wetter eastern highveld to steal the cattle and women of the Mashona, the tribes amongst whom the white men had come to settle. When in 1893 they also attacked a post of the British South Africa Company, war broke out with the settlers, the Matabele were defeated by British troops and Lobengula was killed. The way lay open for increasing numbers of settlers to make their way north in search of gold and farmland.

The settlers were energetic people and found the highveld between the Limpopo and the Zambezi very attractive country. On the high plains above 4,000 feet, mean annual temperatures are not much

RHODES

Rhodes's statue in Salisbury, capital of Rhodesia. Cecil Rhodes landed in the Cape in 1873 and became one of the main organizers of the South African diamond and gold-mining industries. As the head of the British South Africa Company he was mainly responsible for the construction of the railway to the north through Bechuanaland and for the settlement of Rhodesia. He died in 1902.

above 70° F., comfortable for Europeans and Africans alike. The open woodland is dominated by species of *Brachystegia*, with foliage that changes from red and russet before the rains to green later in the year. The ground, before the grasses grow tall, is covered with flowering plants. It is good country for cattle, and though many of the soils developed from the granites are light and sandy, they are well suited to some crops, particularly tobacco, and the heavier reddish soils give good yields of corn.

The Europeans knew there was gold to be won, for the native people had mined it for hundreds of years, long before the empire of Monomotapa flourished on the eastern highveld, way back in the time when the towns and walls of Zimbabwe were built. Early white travellers had been shown hundreds of pits from which gold had been mined till the workings had got too deep for primitive methods. This might be a new Witwatersrand waiting to be developed, or so it seemed to the settlers, and gold was in fact found widely, but never in such quantities as in the Transvaal.

The gold and other minerals worked in Rhodesia are associated with igneous rocks formed a thousand million years ago when ancient volcanic and sedimentary rocks that had accumulated earlier in the earth's history were invaded by immense volumes of magma that devoured great masses of the sedimentaries and altered others by heat and pressure. The molten rocks cooled down and solidified, and by degrees were eroded away to reveal granite bosses with their metamorphic aureoles. Gold, asbestos, and chrome are found in the altered rocks. The most conspicuous feature on the geological map of the country is the Great Dyke, an elongated mass of basic rocks from 3 to 6 miles wide, and 320 miles long, trending north-east through the centre of the territory (Fig. 56). It seems to consist of four separate igneous complexes, flaring out towards the surface and aligned along a gigantic fault system that may have been a precursor of the rift valley. Seams of chromite and a big deposit of asbestos are associated with this intruded mass.

The oldest fossiliferous rocks in Rhodesia belong to the Karroo formation. Sandstones in the lower division of the Karroo include the coal measures at Wankie, and the upper division lavas displayed in the Victoria falls and the winding gorge downstream. At one time the Karroo formation may have covered the whole country, but following rift faulting in early Mesozoic times, rocks of Karroo age were planed off the plateau area and are mainly preserved in the rifts extending along the Zambezi-Luangwa depression and the lower Zambezi and the Sabi-Limpopo valleys. Uplift of the continental mass allowed rivers to cut wide troughs in the downfaulted Karroo formations. These were filled with Cretaceous sediments and later re-excavated; and their floors now form the lowveld. Towards the end of Mesozoic times continental sediments, the

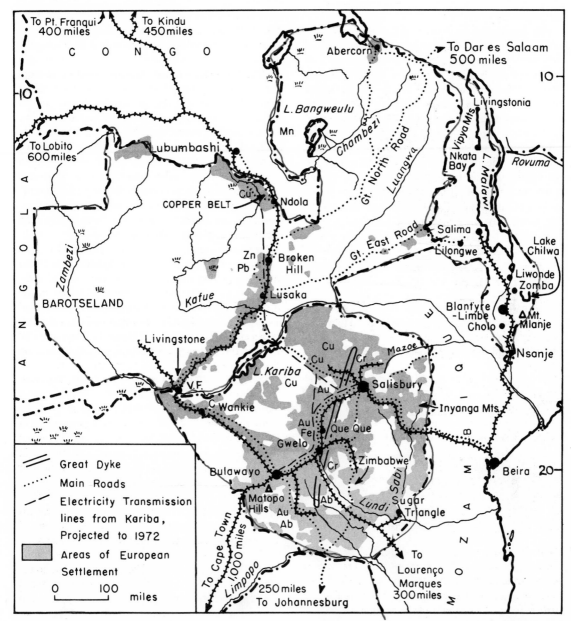

FIG. 56. *Rhodesia, Zambia, and Malawi. Note Zambia's dependence on railways through Rhodesia, Angola, and Mozambique. Hence the desire for a link to the coast via Tanzania, by a line following the Great North Road. V.F.—Victoria Falls, W.N.—West Nicholson, Au—gold, Cr—chromite, Fe—iron, Ab—asbestos, Cu—copper, Pb—lead, Zn—zinc, Mn—manganese, C—coal.*

Kalahari sands, were laid down over a wide area stretching westwards from Rhodesia into Botswana and Angola. It forms sparsely settled country with light sandy soils.

The lowveld country near the Mozambique frontier, where the floors of the Zambezi, Limpopo, and Sabi valleys decline to about a thousand feet is characterized by mopani woodland. The leguminous tree *Colophosphermum mopani* is dominant, and other trees include the baobab, fan-palm, and various species of acacia. It is unhealthy country, malarious, tsetse-ridden, hot and humid in comparison to the highveld and offered few attractions until agricultural developments in the last decade.

European settlement

The healthiest and most productive part of Rhodesia is the highveld, above 4,000 feet. To the early settlers it seemed to offer land in plenty and they obtained from the Company grants of thousands of acres for their farms. The Mashona tribes, whom the Matabele had regarded as subjects and a convenient source of women and cattle, were looked upon by the South Africa Company and the settlers as a source of labour. They had been saved from the depredations of the Matabele, it was argued, and in return they should be willing to pay taxes in support of the new and more benevolent administration. To pay their taxes they could earn money by working for the Europeans. The settlers paid the Mashona ridiculously low wages and allowed them to farm patches of land for themselves, so long as they paid a rent. So at an early stage class distinctions evolved that almost inevitably had a racial or colour bias.

The natives found the taxes and rules of their white masters irksome and were disinclined to work, but they were worn down by natural disasters. 'Droughts and plagues of locusts had come when the Pioneers had entered Mashonaland and never gone', writes Philip Mason in *The birth of a dilemma*, 'next came rinderpest and the cattle died, those the rinderpest didn't kill the Company's veterinary officer shot to prevent its spread.' Both Matabele and Mashona rebelled in 1896-7 and were decisively beaten. So the country settled down.

A railway was built along the watershed, following the natural routeway taken by the Pioneers to Fort Salisbury in Mashonaland. Another line was built to the north, crossing the Zambezi at the easiest and at the same time the most spectacular bridging point possible, the gorge below the Victoria falls, so close to the falls that the spray sprinkles the trains as they cross the bridge. By 1902 Salisbury was linked by rail to Beira as well as the Cape.

European companies and individuals had acquired nearly 22 million acres of land in Southern Rhodesia by 1913, four-fifths of it within 25 miles of the railway. Nearly 25 million acres had been set aside as native reserves, of which less than a third were as favourably placed. This setting aside of land for native reserves was not looked upon at first as

The Victoria Falls. Discovered by David Livingstone in 1855, they are over a mile wide and 300 feet high, and now attract thousands of visitors every year. In April and May, at the end of the rains when the river is at its highest level, clouds of spray often obscure the falling waters. Below the falls the river zigzags 60 miles through basalt lava rock before it widens out again into the wide middle Zambezi valley. From archaeological evidence it seems that the Falls have cut back 5 miles since the beginning of the Upper Pleistocene.

a permanent division of the soil but as a device to shield the African until he should be ready for assimilation. But gradually segregation and discrimination instead of diminishing took on more formal aspects. Natives going to live in the towns were confined to special locations, the sale of liquor was restricted, and there was discrimination in education. Natives had to carry passes, very few had votes, none were members of parliament. By 1923, when certain areas were set aside as European areas, it was widely felt that the place for the natives was the reserves. In that year, Southern Rhodesia became a self-governing colony.

In the early years gold was the most important export, but there were no opportunities for large-scale operations and after the late thirties production ceased to expand. Tobacco, which had been recognized as the most paying crop before the First World War, continued to be the mainstay of the European farmers and after the Second World War, Britain and other Commonwealth countries bought Rhodesian tobacco in order to conserve American dollars, and the crop became Rhodesia's most valuable export worth about £30 million annually by the early sixties. The pace of development as a whole was quickened during the war. Base metals were required for armaments and production greatly increased. Many people from the British Isles were introduced to the country by the air-training schemes and after the war, between 1945 and 1960, the number of whites in Southern Rhodesia increased from about 80,000 to more than 200,000. The newcomers were mainly skilled and energetic young and middle-aged people from the United Kingdom and the Union of South Africa, bringing capital with them and attracting capital from outside, and the economy expanded faster than ever.

The Central African Federation

In 1953 the Federation of the Rhodesias and Nyasaland was formed. Its main purpose was two-fold; firstly, to create a state in which black and white might be partners; secondly, to stimulate economic development by reducing the costs of administration and providing a larger market.

The first of these aims was never achieved. The people of Nyasaland were always opposed to federation in a state which they believed would always be dominated by the white ascendancy in Southern Rhodesia. They resented the social colour-bar, which many of them had experienced as migrants working in that country, and they were anxious to prevent it appearing in their own. They made it

clear that they wished to break away from the Federation and to rely on their own resources.

The economic consequences of Federation appear to have been satisfactory on the whole, and especially for the whites, though it is difficult to assess how fast the economies of the three territories would have grown without it. Nyasaland, which provided a large share of the labour for the mines and the farms of the Rhodesias, received a subsidy in the form of a larger share of the federal revenue than its contribution warranted. The advantages to Northern Rhodesia are more difficult to discern. Its mines contributed one-fifth of the Federation's revenue. Possibly more skilled and experienced people were led to work in the territory. Certainly industrial production increased and its economy became more diversified. Without a doubt, Southern Rhodesia was the main beneficiary; between 1953 and 1960 its economy grew faster than that of any other part of Africa.

Political development could not keep pace with economic progress; racial prejudice and distrust amongst both blacks and whites were too deep-seated. While, in the northern territories, Africans were taking an increasingly important part in the government, restrictions on them in Southern Rhodesia were becoming more rather than less severe. By the end of 1962 it was clear that Federation was doomed and its dissolution came at the end of the following year. About 51 per cent. of the federal debt and corresponding assets were taken over by Rhodesia, 37 per cent. by Zambia and 11 per cent. by Malawi; Rhodesia Railways and Kariba power assets were shared equally by Rhodesia and Zambia. Several thousands of non-Africans left the country.

It is difficult to tell how much was permanently gained from the ten years of Federation. The most tangible outcome of the union was the Kariba dam which would probably not have been built at all if the Rhodesias had remained under separate administrations. Perhaps the Kafue gorge which lies entirely in Zambia would have been chosen instead as the site for a dam. But Kariba was built and now it forms a very important feature of the environment, so big that slight earthquakes have been caused by the loading of the crust with the enormous mass of water impounded. The dam and various installations cost altogether over £100 million, a sum that constitutes a large part of the debt incurred by the Federation in the course of its headlong economic expansion. The electricity is very important to the mines and industries of Zambia and Rhodesia but it is worth noting that the output of the Rhodesian thermal power-stations, burning coal from Wankie, is not much less than half of electricity output from Kariba.

The transport system of Rhodesia has improved in recent years. Over the twenty-year period 1939 to 1958 goods and passenger traffic on the railways increased fourfold; copper and coal making up much of the goods traffic. A new line was completed from Bulawayo to Lourenço Marques, and bituminized roads were built linking Salisbury to Beira and Bulawayo, and Bulawayo to Lusaka and Johannesburg. Nevertheless communications are still inadequate, and it can be argued that the money invested in Kariba would have been employed more effectively in building more roads and railways throughout the Federation.

Agriculture

In Rhodesia, the two nodes of economic activity are Salisbury and Bulawayo. Salisbury the capital is the centre of the main agricultural area of the country where maize and tobacco are the chief crops. For many years tobacco has exceeded the value of mineral exports with production steadily expanding until the imposition of sanctions in 1966. The climate of the highveld and the light sandy soils derived from granite are ideal for growing flue-cured tobacco. Native labour is well suited to the tasks of harvesting the leaves individually as

they ripen and then tying them for curing. After curing, the leaves are railed for auction at Salisbury and shipment from Beira. Turkish tobacco which has similar climatic and soil requirements, but needs less fertilizer and is dried in the sun, has generally been considered better suited for production by African peasant farmers.

Maize produced commercially is another important crop, worth about £10 million annually. Most of it can be absorbed within Rhodesia. Except in unusual years such as 1961, when Rhodesian yields were high while the east African crop was ruined by excessive downpours, the returns to the producer for exported maize are not very attractive and greater emphasis is being placed on growing other crops.

Sugar was imported until the fifties, but by 1963 over 80,000 tons of Rhodesian sugar were being exported annually and it was estimated that by 1972 sugar would be the country's second export with production reaching a million tons annually. The sugar is being grown almost entirely on the despised lowveld, most of it in the Chiredzi-Hippo-Triangle area (Fig. 57). The mean annual rainfall is below 20 inches and irrigation is required. The first attempts to develop the crop were made about 1930 when a weir was built and a canal 8 miles long was dug to lead water on to land near the Mtilikwe river. A Natal group took over the estate in 1954 and other concerns began to develop

Kariba. The dam is shown in 1961 when it was nearing completion and the lake had still to rise to its present level. Some of the electricity generating plant can be seen on the south, the Rhodesian side of the dam wall. Work was interrupted at an earlier stage in construction by unusually high floods. See the high value for the Zambezi's discharge in 1957–8 in Fig. 59.

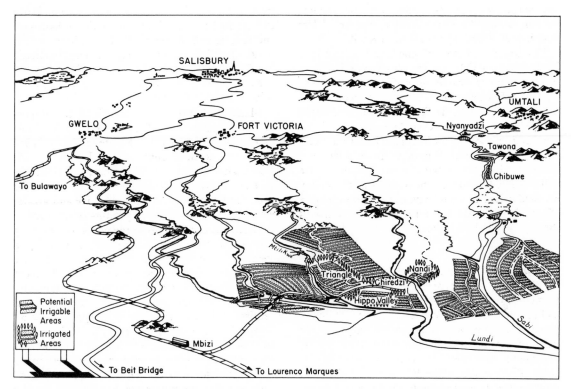

FIG. 57. *Irrigation on the Rhodesian lowveld. The rivers of the Lundi–Sabi system in south-east Rhodesia are being dammed to provide water for growing sugar and other crops in the Triangle, Hippo, Chiredzi area. (From Optima, December 1964.)*

similar schemes. It seemed that by 1967 about £30 million would have been invested in dams, a branch railway line 52 miles long, irrigation systems watering 66,000 acres, and sugar mills, the money being put up by the Rhodesian government and commercial companies. Some difficulties were caused locally by seepage and waterlogging associated with soil conditions, but the main problems were connected with the falling price of sugar on world markets and disposing of crop surpluses in the face of trade sanctions. In 1967 more emphasis was being placed on growing other crops such as maize in these lowveld areas.

Other expanding sectors of the economy include meat and dairy production. Beef cattle are raised mainly in Matabeleland in the drier western parts of the country under ranching conditions. Droughts such as the one of 1965 can inflict severe losses in this region bordering on the Kalahari. Dairying is concentrated near the larger towns, especially Salisbury, and is steadily getting more intensive. Dairy farmers may soon provide a market for cattle feed containing molasses from the sugar refineries of the lowveld. Cotton and citrus from the lowveld,

Rhodesian tobacco field near Umtali, on the lowveld near the Mozambique frontier. Rhodesia's tobacco crop of more than 100,000 tons, worth over £40 million in 1964, normally represents half Africa's production of leaf tobacco.

tea and coffee from the eastern highlands are other crops with bright prospects. The British South Africa Company's Mazoe valley estate north-east of Salisbury is one of the largest single orange groves in the world yielding about 800 tons per year. Wattle, pines, and other plantations have been established on the wet, mist-shrouded eastern slopes of the highlands.

About five-sixths of the national agricultural production comes from European farms. In 1958 there were 6,650 European landholdings with an average size of 4,000 acres of which 140 were arable. African holdings, numbering 312,000, had an average size of about 100 acres of which 9 were cultivated. The Africans are largely concerned with growing food-crops for themselves and their families, but many are growing crops for sale and some are doing well with tobacco and vegetables. The fastest progress is being made on new settlement areas; methods on the reserves are still primitive and progress very slow, and Europeans point to this when called upon to defend their own very large landholdings. If the Africans had the land, they say, they would not use it properly. But it can also be argued that the Europeans are very fortunate in having selected for themselves the best land near the railways. They have been able to borrow money at low rates of interest and they alone have benefited in the past from price control of maize. In the reserves roads are bad, the land is overstocked and over-populated and there is too little capital and knowledge for methods to be improved. It is not surprising that yields of maize in African areas are only two bags per acre and in European areas exceed ten.

Mining

Gold, though it ceased to dominate the mining industry several years ago, is still the most valuable mineral produced, and efforts are being made to increase the size and efficiency of the gold-mining companies. The low world price for gold restricts mining to the highest-grade ores at the present time.

Asbestos has been the main mineral export in some years but in 1963 and 1964 production was worth the same as gold about £6 to £7 million. Rhodesia is one of the world's main producers of asbestos, the raw material is of excellent quality, and there are big reserves near Mashaba and Shabani. Coal is plentiful at Wankie and cheap at pithead, but adequate local markets are lacking. Exports to the Copperbelt slackened when the Kariba dam was completed and diminished still more in the late sixties as Zambia came to rely on its own resources. Chrome has been suffering from Russian competition.

Most of the mining takes place in a belt less than 100 miles wide extending 300 miles from Salisbury to West Nicholson, south-east of Bulawayo. A new development is the construction at Dorowa in the Sabi valley of a new £1 million plant for exploiting rich phosphate deposits which will make the country independent of costly imports from west Africa.

Industry

Industry began much later than in South Africa and only gained momentum in the last war when the Rhodesias were deprived of manufactured goods and local demand was inflated by European servicemen under training.

The Shabani asbestos mine, Rhodesia. Asbestos is quarried from the pit in the foreground; processing plant and waste dumps are in the background. Rhodesia's mineral output was valued at nearly £27 million in 1964.

Aerial view of Salisbury, capital of Rhodesia. Government offices are in foreground, tall office blocks in the background. European residential areas, native locations, and industrial areas lie out on the grassy plains around the central area of the city.

Eighty per cent. of the 100,000 workers employed in industry work in the factories of Bulawayo and Salisbury. Many process locally produced raw materials, such as the meat-canning and flour-milling in Bulawayo. In addition a wide range of consumer goods is being produced under the protection of import duties, the high costs of transport from abroad and trade sanctions. Tyres, textiles, and a host of other industries have sprouted; the clothing industry alone employs 9,000 workers. The two big towns, with a combined population exceeding half a million, contain half the country's European population. Africans in Bulawayo and Salisbury together outnumber Europeans by three to one.

Heavy industry is located in the midlands, about half-way between the two main nodes. The Rhodesian Iron and Steel Company has a large plant at Redcliff near Que Que which was established by the Southern Rhodesian government and taken over in 1957 by a group of British and South African companies. Its three blast furnaces have an output of 900 tons per day, some of which is exported as pig-iron and the rest converted into steel in the same plant. Although large steel sections

Wankie colliery, Rhodesia. Proved coal reserves here are 4,000 million tons. Plant capacity is only 6 million tons a year, and production in the early sixties was only about half this figure on account of the limited home market.

Rhodesian Iron and Steel Company's plant at Redcliff, Que Que. A big expansion programme, involving an investment of about £13 million, was planned to begin in 1965.

cannot be made, a great deal of the structural steel used in the Rhodesias has been made at Que Que and hundreds of tons were used in the Kariba dam. The coking coal has to be brought 300 miles by rail from Wankie but vast reserves of high-grade iron-ore and limestone occur side by side at Redcliff itself. The plant is small compared with those of Europe and North America and at times the product is not much cheaper than imported steel. But in 1964 over a quarter of a million tons of pig iron were exported to Japan, and because of steel shortages in Britain and South Africa, 66,000 tons were exported to those countries. The local market is rather small, absorbing only 60,000 tons of Que Que steel in 1964, but consideration is being given to a scheme that would cost some £14 million and boost production to 1·2 millions tons a year.

One of the most advanced industrial plants in Rhodesia has been erected at Gwelo for treating the chrome ores mined nearby in Selukwe and Kildonan. Although the process is an advanced one, requiring the utmost precision at all stages of operation, it appears to be operating successfully. Electricity is supplied by Kariba, Wankie provides limestone and special high-reactivity coke, and high-quality quartz is mined locally. The product is exported along the direct line to Lourenço Marques.

At Umtali a £10 million oil refinery with a through-put capacity of 20,000 barrels a day was completed in 1964. Its operations have been interrupted by oil supplies being cut off following Rhodesia's Unilateral Declaration of Independence.

In 1964 industrial production was far greater in value than tobacco or mining. Half the exports of manufactured goods went to Zambia, a tenth to Malawi. Possibilities for further rapid growth in the country's economy are very great as far as resources are concerned. The main obstacles are social and political. If Malawi and Zambia raise tariff barriers against Rhodesia's manufactured goods, then the market for them is limited to 4 million, the total population of Rhodesia itself. Of this total, 90 per cent. are Africans. Two-thirds of the adult male Africans are now employed, but their wages are only about £2 per week compared with the Europeans' £20. They have not had the educational opportunities to make full use of their abilities and until recently they have not been organized into trade unions. If economic expansion is to continue, the productivity of the African worker will have to increase in order to provide a market for the goods being produced. It is in the interest of Europeans and the country as a whole that the barriers to the progress of Africans should be broken down. One

216

may hope that it is not too late for this to take place peacefully.

ZAMBIA

On the highveld north of the Zambezi the rainfall is greater than to the south and the woodland is taller with trees a hundred feet high in some places. Much of the country is infested with tsetse-fly, particularly in two broad bands, one following the valley of the Luangwa and the other running parallel and further west. The ground is generally very gently sloping and great areas north-west of an axis running across the plains from the south end of Lake Nyasa to Lake Ngami are covered with swamps. The largest are in the vicinity of Lake Bangweulu, others occupy the flat valley floors of the Kafue river and the upper Zambezi.

The upper Zambezi flows south as if it intended to enter the Makarikari depression or even the Limpopo, as some geologists believe it did at one time. The floodwaters are held up by volcanic rocks outcropping in the Gonya falls, and from January to June great stretches of Barotseland are inundated. The people move away from the riverain flats at this time of year and graze their cattle in the scrub forests at higher levels until the floods recede, leaving pools of water for the cattle to use in the dry season.

After turning to the east at the Katina rapids and forming the northern boundary of the Caprivi strip, the Zambezi plunges over the Victoria falls, the world's largest waterfall, and following a fault-guided valley, broadens out to form the world's largest man-made lake, behind the Kariba dam.

The purpose of the dam and lake is, of course, to even out the seasonal and year-to-year variations in the discharge of the Zambezi and to provide a big head of water for generating electric power. The power-station is situated underground on the Rhodesian side of the river. It attained its installed capacity of 705 MW in 1963 and it was intended that work should commence on the installation of additional turbines on the Zambian bank within a few years. The reservoir is also a useful source of fish and it provides a routeway of some little value. Within two years of the dam's construction weeds called *Salvinia auriculata* and the Nile Cabbage *Pistia stratiatus* spread over one-fifth of the lake's surface. Since then the weed-covered area has been much reduced by wave action and is now mainly confined to sheltered inlets. The dam is one of the main attractions on the tourist circuit, by air, from Salisbury to Kariba, the Victoria falls, and the Chobe and Wankie game reserves.

The Barotse plains of western Zambia. Each year when the plains are covered with the floodwaters of the upper Zambezi the people move to higher ground. This shows the low water home of the ruler, the Litunga, at Lealui.

Mining

With its hot climate, rather infertile soils and tsetse-infested savannas, Zambia is sparsely settled and would be one of the poor countries in tropical Africa, were it not for the minerals in the central zone. The rocks belonging to the Katanga system, which rest on the Basement Complex, have been invaded by granites and highly mineralized. Near Broken Hill they yield lead and zinc, and about 100 to 150 miles further north, copper. In the small area 80 miles long by 20 miles wide between Ndola and Bancroft, declared reserves of 3 to 5 per cent. copper ore exceed 700 million tons. The total value of copper produced in 1965 amounted to £170 million and, as a result, gross production per head of population in Zambia is comparable with that of Rhodesia, making it, by this reckoning, one of the most prosperous countries in Africa.

The copper ore outcrops in six localities arranged along two roughly parallel lines about 80 miles long and 20 miles apart, so that the layout and size of the Copperbelt is not unlike that of the Rand. But there is no dominating city comparable with Johannesburg, nor as yet any large-scale development of manufacturing industries. The seven principle towns, which have a combined population

The Kuomboka; the migration of the people across the flooded Barotse plains.

Roan Antelope copper mine, Luanshya, Zambia. The headworks of the mine can be seen in the distance. In the foreground is the copper smelting and concentrating plant.

of 500,000, remain essentially mining towns, separated one from another by 20 or 30 miles of bush-covered country. Ndola, situated in the east where the railway enters the Copperbelt, is the commercial centre of the region. The Bwana Mkubwa mine at Ndola has closed down, but the main refinery for the Copperbelt is there and about half the other factories in the region. Kitwe, which is in a more central position at the hub of the road network and in the middle of the area where most of the copper will probably be produced in the future, is growing faster than Ndola and is now emerging as the capital of the Copperbelt (Fig. 58).

The mines are owned by two great combines, namely Zambian Anglo American and Roan Selection Trust. In 1966 they employed directly more than 6,000 Europeans and 40,000 Africans, three-quarters of the Africans being Zambian. The average length of service of the latter is five to six years and three-quarters of the workers in the mining towns have their families with them. This contrasts strongly with Rhodesia, where three-quarters of the workers in Salisbury are without their families. Of the £170 million that might be received for the copper in an average year, about one-quarter to one-third is paid out as wages. The European staff receives the lion's share, but it is worth noting that African mineworkers' pay has risen from £160 a year in 1963 to £400 in 1966. Other industrial plants, such as refineries, provide employment for some 20,000 workers, and altogether over 90 per cent. of the people living in the belt are urbanized.

The world price of copper fluctuates violently, reaching £660 in 1966 and being as low as £150 per ton in the fifties. Production is liable to be interrupted from time to time by labour troubles and so the economy of Zambia is not entirely stable. The lead and zinc from Broken Hill and manganese at Fort Rosebery, worth together about £8 million annually, diversify the economy a little, but the importance of copper is overwhelming.

African agriculture

In all about 140,000 Zambians find employment in the mines and in associated tertiary activities and about 60,000 find work in Rhodesia and the Republic of South Africa. Only about half the adult male population is left to work on the land. The women were always accustomed to doing most of the farming, but it was the men who used to carry out the initial clearing before sowing and planting. Now the *citemene* system of shifting cultivation, which may involve clearing 30 to 60 acres for every acre cultivated, is becoming impracticable because of the lack of menfolk, and the old way of life is fading.

Along the Great North Road linking southern and east Africa it has been observed that the Bemba no longer live in small nucleated settlements. They have moved into larger townships along the road and each unit family has its own patches of land mainly distributed along the sides of streams within a few miles of the roads. Millet is no longer the main crop and is grown now mainly for making beer. Crops like maize, cassava, and sweet potatoes requiring less labour are replacing it. Cultivation is more permanent than it was, with crops being planted on mounds of earth incorporating ashes and organic matter. There is more irrigation and produce is no longer merely for subsistence but to make foodstuffs for sale to hungry travellers on the road. Some help is being given to new settlers by government assistance in clearing and stumping. The change-over from shifting cultivation is not the result of over-population and a reduction in the fallow period; it seems to be a response to the shortage of male labour allied with opportunities for production for sale.

Commercial African farming has made a good deal of progress in certain areas in recent years, the performance of the Plateau Tonga being most impressive. Living near the railway, and profiting from the experience of European farmers in the area they have also benefited from the ready market for their produce. There have also been increasing sales of maize, groundnuts, tobacco, and cotton

FIG. 58. *The Zambian Copperbelt. Cu—copper, Co—cobalt, Con—concentrator, Sme—smelter, El—electrolytic refinery. Figures in brackets are the populations of the towns in 1965.*

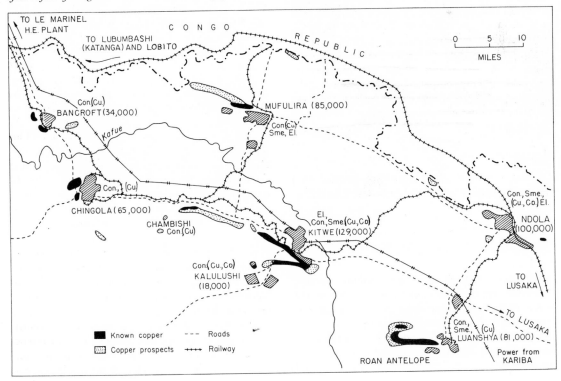

from farmers in the Kafue basin of Southern and Central Provinces and the upper part of the Luangwa basin in Eastern Province, all of which include areas with reasonably good soils. In general, however, returns from small-scale farming have not been great enough to retain the more enterprising men on the land. They have abandoned the rural life and have gone off to the towns.

European farming

Europeans farming in Zambia number less than 1,500 and occupy less than 6 per cent. of the whole country but they probably account for a third of the total agricultural production. The farms are large, about 3,000 acres. They lie near the railway on the watershed where the weathered layer is deep and ground-water can be tapped by boreholes. They include some of the better soils and are not infested with tsetse. The most productive farms are near Lusaka where maize is the principal crop, some tobacco is grown, and cattle are kept to supply the meat and dairy requirements of the capital and the Copperbelt.

The value of commercial agricultural products is only about £5 million annually, far less than in Rhodesia, but the opportunities for development are considerable. Near the eastern margin of the Kafue flats near Mazbuka some 20,000 acres are believed to be suitable for irrigation and pilot projects aimed at controlling the flooding with banks will show the practicability of growing rice in summer and wheat and cattle fodder in winter. Sugar is likely to be one of the first commercial crops. The mining companies are interested in these schemes to produce cheaper food and are also supporting attempts to improve farming methods on the Bemba plateau.

Fishing

About two-thirds of the country is infested with tsetse-fly and cattle number only about 1·25 million, most of them owned by African farmers. State ranches are being developed but at present fish constitutes a large proportion of locally produced protein. Native fisheries on the lakes and rivers of the north already yield about 30,000 tons of fish worth something of the order of £1 million annually. Much of this is smoked for consumption on the Copperbelt. One of the most promising lakes is Tanganyika. Unfortunately a harbour and fishing shed not long built were made useless in the early sixties by the lake rising several feet above its normal level.

Future prospects

The economies of Zambia and Rhodesia are in many respects complementary. The Zambian Copperbelt has depended on the Wankie mines for coal and on the Kariba dam for electricity. Zambia has provided a very important market for Rhodesian industry. However, as soon as it became clear the Federation was about to break up, several new industries were attracted to Zambia, including a shoe factory and Jeep-assembly plant at Lusaka, a Unilever complex at Ndola, and a clothing factory at Kitwe. Later, tariff barriers were erected against Rhodesian manufactures, and between 1964 and 1968 Zambian industrial production more than doubled. Since the Rhodesian Unilateral Declaration of Independence economic co-operation between the two countries has diminished markedly. Movement of coal to Zambia was interrupted from time to time and the Copperbelt is coming to depend on low-grade coal being worked north of the Zambezi at Nkandabwe, about 40 miles north-east of Livingstone. Zambia intends to push ahead with a hydroelectric scheme on the Kafue river and additional generating plant is to be installed on the Zambian side of the Kariba dam. Communications to the east coast are being developed through Tanzania. In August 1968 an oil pipe-line was completed from Dar-es-Salaam to Ndola which makes Zambia entirely independent of supplies through Rhodesia. Roads to the north-east are being improved and preparations are being made for a railway linking Zambia to the Tanzanian central line.

Given a period of peaceful development, Zambia has excellent prospects for economic growth, better than those of almost any other country in tropical Africa. The emphasis must be on providing young Zambians with the education and skills they need to be employable in industry and public services, but it is not unlikely that the emphasis will be placed on the conflict with the white government in Salisbury.

MALAWI

Malawi is a small land-locked country stretching 500 miles along the west side of Lake Malawi and either side of the Shire river almost as far downstream as the Zambezi (Fig. 56). With a land area of 36,000 square miles, it is only about one eighth the size of its three big neighbours. Its population, however, is large in comparison with its size, exceeding 4 million in 1964, giving it an average of more than 100 people to the square mile, a figure more typical of west Africa than of the south-eastern part of the continent.

Occupying the floor and western shoulder of the rift, it is much more varied scenically and climatically than Zambia. Temperatures of 120° F. have been recorded at Nsanje in the lower Shire valley, within sight of the peaks of Mlanje (9,843 feet) which occasionally receive falls of snow. More than 100 inches of rain are recorded on the lakeshore in the extreme north-west, and only a few miles to the south and on the lee side of the Vipya mountains, 40 miles away, mean annual totals are less than 30 inches. Most of the rain comes in months from November to April when winds are north-easterly at the surface but westerly flows converge in troughs at higher levels. The windward slopes of the highlands receive some additional rain from the south-easterly trades bringing moist air from the Mozambique channel in the middle of the year, but this is not much use to crops.

Soil and vegetation vary greatly over short distances; baobab trees and acacias grow on the alluvial and colluvial soils of the dry lowlands while the red, leached soils of the medium level plateaux are largely covered with Brachystegia woodland. Remnants of evergreen forests surviving on the high plateaux are rich in useful timber species, such as the conifer Mlanje cedar, but most of the forest has been cleared and burned, and replaced by mountain grassland. A little over one-third of the country is good arable land and a quarter is quite unfit for cultivation.

The make-up and the distribution of the population is as varied as the physiography. The Nyanja, Chewa, Nsonga, Tonga, and Tumbuka were amongst the most important of several tribes that were already settled in the country by the end of the eighteenth century. They were broken up by two great invasions in the first half of the last century. The Yao moved down the Rovuma valley, killing and burning, and catching slaves for sale to the coastal Arabs, and later on Ngoni groups, that had split off from their own tribes in what is now Swaziland and Zululand, crossed the Zambezi and swept up both sides of the lake, collecting adherents on the way. They eventually settled down to form military kingdoms in several widely scattered areas.

The damage caused by these invasions was still apparent when Livingstone first entered the country and reached the southern end of the lake in 1859. Scottish missionaries who arrived in the country a few years later persuaded merchants to set up stores in an effort to encourage legitimate trade, but it was not until 1890 that Sir Harry Johnston made treaties with the chiefs on the west side of Lake Nyasa as a preliminary to the declaration of the Protectorate. Johnston had financial backing from Rhodes, and in the years that followed a number of European settlers arrived and took up land. They were never so numerous as in the Rhodesias, and their influence in affairs was always less than that of the Colonial Office officials and the missionaries. So there was no racial segregation in Nyasaland, nor was there much economic development.

Malawi lacks rich mineral deposits, and those minerals that are present, notably coal and bauxite, have not been exploited because of the isolation of the country and high transport costs to the coast. It remains predominantly agricultural. Most of the people are still basically subsistence cultivators using hand methods of cultivation and relying on maize, cassava, and other crops that they grow for themselves. Tsetse-fly prevent cattle being kept in many places, especially in the north, though there are some large herds in the Rukuru valley on the north-western plateau and near the lakeshore at the extreme northern end of the lake. Some of the soils are quite productive, but good land is scarce in the heavily settled parts of the country and standards of living are generally low. In 1960 the minimum wage rates were 2s. 6d. per day in Blantyre-Limbe, and only 1s. 5d. in most other areas; enough to buy no more than 12 lb. of maize or 1 lb. of meat. The more energetic and ambitious people are therefore attracted by opportunities for work in the richer countries to the south, where wage rates are much higher than at home.

In the north there is little production for sale or opportunity for employment and most of the migrants are drawn from that part of the country.

Further south the country broadens out and is more accessible by road and rail. Lilongwe, a focal point in the country's road system, has been chosen as the site of the capital to replace Zomba. Around Lilongwe large tracts of good land have been opened up for Africans to grow tobacco which, with tea, is the most valuable export crop. The emphasis is on dark fire-cured tobacco, 80 per cent. of it grown by Africans. In the Central Province, an African tobacco farmer with 5 acres of land might grow a ton of maize, plus a few hundred pounds of tobacco, beans, and groundnuts to get a return of about £50 a year.

Over half the cattle are in the Central Province where they number about 200,000 and have increased 50 per cent. in the fifties. Quite a large number are sold to Africans from the Southern

Plucking tea on one of the estates in the Cholo area of Malawi. Malawi's tea production exceeds ten thousand tons annually and is comparable with that of Kenya and Mozambique. These three account for three-quarters of Africa's production of tea. The crop provides nearly a half of Malawi's export earnings.

Province at the end of the rainy season, to be fattened for four to six months when they are ready for slaughter. Everywhere grazing land is being encroached on by cultivation and cattle are increasingly confined to *dambos*, marshy hollows with heavy soils. In the south, where population densities are highest, cattle are stall-fed with grass and concentrates, and provide valuable manure.

The Southern Province is the most advanced part of Malawi, benefiting from the rail outlet to Beira and the greater extent of cultivable land. Much of the cash cropping is concentrated here, and 80 per cent. of the wage labour. Tea, first grown at the foot of Mlanje mountain before 1900, is still grown mainly on large European estates in this area and near Cholo. Annual production has doubled since the war due mainly to the replacement of older bushes by new high-yielding varieties. The area with suitable soil and climate is limited, the tea estates operate their own factories, and costs

of establishing plantations work out at about £500 per acre, so native tea planting is making slow progress. Virginian tobacco is an important crop on the Shire highlands, and cotton in the lower Shire valley. Bananas and pineapples from the Cholo district are consumed locally or sent to Salisbury. Tung oil is produced on European plantations from the nuts of a tree *Aleurites montana* that thrives at 3,500 to 5,000 feet and needs 40 inches of rain.

The fisheries on Lake Malawi and the upper Shire river yield about 20,000 tons of fish annually, nearly half caught by large non-African commercial firms using motor vessels. Chilwa, quite a small, shallow lake like Lake George in Uganda, is very productive and about 3,500 tons of fish are landed there each year.

The value of Lake Malawi for transport is not very great. A small fleet of steamers, tugs, and barges has been operated by the railways for many years, generally at a loss. Storms on the lake can be dangerous,

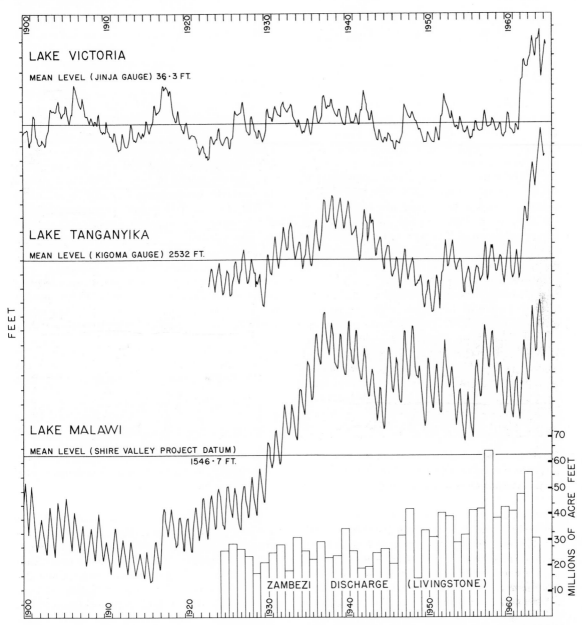

FIG. 59. *The levels of the Great Lakes and the discharge of the Zambezi. The levels of the lakes are controlled firstly by the level of their outfalls, and secondly by the difference between precipitation and evaporation over their catchment areas. Levels normally rise a few feet in the rainy season and fall a similar amount in the following dry season. Unusually heavy and prolonged rains in 1961–2 caused all the lakes to rise and they reached their highest levels of the century in 1964. The level of Lake Victoria has been affected, but probably only slightly by the completion in 1954 of the Owen Falls dam at the outlet. Silting at the Lukuga outlet of Lake Tanganyika may have helped to cause it to rise rapidly in recent years. The Shire outlet to Lake Malawi was blocked by sediment when the lake was very low in 1915 and outflow ceased until 1935. The large fluctuations of Lake Malawi afflict shipping and lakeshore cultivators. Under the Shire Valley Project, it is hoped not only to stabilize the lake level but also to develop power on the middle Shire cataracts and irrigate land alongside the lower river. To carry out all these intentions effectively would involve raising the lake level to 1,568 feet which would flood densely populated areas of the lakeshore. The Zambezi's discharge seems to have been considerably greater in the fifties than in the three preceding decades.*

and an added difficulty is presented by big fluctuations in lake-level which upset harbour facilities (Fig. 59). These fluctuations are probably caused by blocking of the main outlets of the lake into the Shire river, both by sediment brought down by lateral streams and the accumulation of vegetation. The completion of a barrage on the Shire at Liwonde in connexion with the Nkula falls hydroelectric scheme has improved conditions on the lake and opened up other resources. Irrigated sugar, rice, and cotton are being grown on the swampy floor of the Shire valley. The power-station, with a capacity of 24MW, will be a valuable source of energy in a country hitherto dependent on thermal power-stations.

Malawi must make full use of its somewhat meagre resources if it is to survive. In the early sixties its imports cost about £18 million per year, 50 per cent. more than was earned by exports. Some foundation for its economic viability was provided by the Central African Federation in which it was relieved of a part of the costs of administering such services as civil aviation, prisons, health and education, all of which came under the Federal government. But the people disliked the federal idea and persisted in opposing the dominance of the whites in the Federation. When the breakaway came in 1962, about 150,000 Nyasa men were abroad, about three-quarters of them working in Southern Rhodesia, the rest in Northern Rhodesia and the Republic of South Africa. Their remittances totalled some £2 million per year, a contribution to the country's economy which has not diminished in importance since Malawi became independent politically. Estimates in 1968 were of 250,000 to 350,000 Malawians employed in Rhodesia, Zambia, and South Africa.

Apart from a few factories in Blantyre-Limbe, making cloth, cigarettes, cement, and soap, there had been practically no industrial development in Nyasaland. It is not surprising that one of the first acts of the new government was to invite a number of economists to a conference to make suggestions and answer questions on the possibilities for development. The visiting experts were not very encouraging. It is evident that for some time to come Malawi will be very dependent on aid from Britain and other countries. The government, realizing its dependence on Beira for its foreign trade, has pursued a less hostile policy towards Mozambique than some other African countries less exposed to reprisals. It is intended to build a railway linking Malawi to the line through Mozambique reaching the coast at Nacala. Under the leadership of Dr. Banda, the country is beginning to benefit economically from South African investment.

MOZAMBIQUE

Mozambique stretches over 600 miles north-east and south of the lower Zambezi and a similar distance up the river valley from the delta to the head of navigation. It is a country that has only begun to develop since the war and the stage it has reached so far contrasts strongly to that reached by the countries bordering it on the west.

In the seventeenth century, when the Dutch drove the Portuguese from the East Indies, and the Arabs regained many of the east African ports, Portugal was able to hold on to a southern part of the coast, the section generally under the influence of the south-easterly trades. Portuguese settlers were granted large estates to establish plantations and proceeded to rule these *prazeros* carved out of the jungle, in feudal style. Indians came over in considerable numbers. Some were Roman Catholic Goans, trading to the interior, others were Hindus acting as coastal agents for Indo-British trading houses. Many of the *prazeros* came into their hands and it has been asserted that Indians rather than

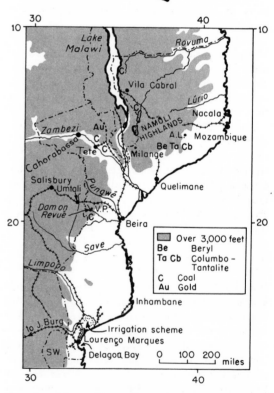

FIG. 60. *Mozambique. Economic activity is concentrated around Lourenço Marques and Beira, and along the railways. V.P.—Vila Pery, A.L.—Alto Ligonha, SW—Swaziland.*

Portuguese were the industrious element in Mozambique society and maintained such links as there were between the coast and the interior.

The high country lies well inland, bordering Rhodesia and the Nyasa rift (Fig. 60). Separated from the coast by wide stretches of nearly empty country, it has attracted little European settlement. The African population is rather sparse in the highlands probably as a result of slave-raiding and intertribal wars, and most of the territory, except for the southern quarter, is infested with tsetse. Over the country as a whole the population density is little over twenty persons to the square mile; about 7 million people over 300,000 square miles. Much heavier concentrations occur in the coastal districts, particularly those facing the south-east, where mean annual rainfall totals exceed 50 inches and the climate is hot and humid throughout the year.

The contrast with the Angolan coast is partly to be explained by the warm Mozambique current, which is about 8° C. (14° F.) warmer than the Benguela current, leading to much greater instability in airmasses moving onshore and heavier precipitation.

The two largest, modern cities, Lourenço Marques and Beira, are both ports which owe a great deal of their importance to the overseas trade of the countries of the interior. Both have populations exceeding 150,000 and white populations of more than 20,000.

Lourenço Marques, the capital, is an unusually attractive city, well planned in the centre, though the development of the outskirts is chaotic. It stands on the shores of Delagoa bay, so named because ships called there on the return journey from Goa. Twelve square miles of sheltered anchorage are connected to the sea by dredged channels, and the quay, which is a mile and a half long, allows twenty-one ships each drawing 30 feet of water to berth at any one time. It is efficiently run and has been well able to cope with the increased traffic resulting from the Limpopo railway, linking it to Bulawayo, and the expansion of the Rhodesian and Swaziland economies. In addition to handling 7 million tons of goods (1965) mainly from the countries inland it produces 40 per cent. of the country's manufactures and also manages to support a thriving tourist industry. Thousands of South Africans are lured by the bright lights and the foreignness of a Portuguese town to spend their holidays at 'L.M.' when the chill winds of July blow across the Rand.

Beira is on the estuary of the Pungwé river. The bar needs constant dredging, the tidal range at maximum springs is 21 feet and the harbour is less well equipped than Lourenço Marques which now takes a much greater proportion of the Rhodesian traffic. Nevertheless Beira was still handling 3·5 million tons of goods in 1965 and as the whole of central Mozambique and Malawi lie within its hinterland as well as Rhodesia, it is unlikely to decline.

Besides these two ports, there is a string of fine deep-water harbours along the coast and development has been concentrated around them, and along railways running inland from them. Communications parallel to the coast are difficult because of the many rivers that have to be crossed. The road system is badly maintained, large tracts in the north have no roads at all, and the total length of tarmac in the whole country runs to only a few hundred miles, so coastal shipping plays a more important part than in many countries. There are plans to link Lourenço Marques and Beira by rail, but this link is unlikely to materialize for many years.

Until recently the Portuguese government has done little directly to develop the country. It was too poor itself, and so concessions were offered to foreign companies as well as Portuguese. The Anglo-Portuguese Mozambique Company had exclusive rights of trade and government north of the Zambezi until 1942 and it in turn granted a British company concessions to build the Beira railway to Southern Rhodesia and to run the railway and the port. Similar concessions were granted by other colonial governments in Africa, but in Mozambique they have persisted longer than elsewhere. In the thirties and during the war the concessionaires were encouraged to press the Africans into growing more cotton and rice to supply the needs of the home country, and production did rise. In Zambesia Province one of the concessionaires has developed tea estates, a cattle ranch, mines, plywood and other factories. But in too many cases the entire profits from concessions have been repatriated and have not been reinvested in Mozambique. Above all, the system lays itself open to abuses of authority over the Africans. In recent years many of the concessions have not shown profits as a result of competition from European planters, and the system is tending to break down from economic as well as political pressure.

A recent application of the concession system has been to game reserves. In post-war years much of the interior was denuded of game by teams of professional hunters shooting the wild animals to sell the meat and hides and tusks. Now the government has set aside reserves, prohibiting hunting in some, leasing others to private companies or individuals as exclusive hunting concessions. In these safari *coutadas* the holders of the concessions are held responsible for controlling the game, running camps, and looking after the comfort of tourists. The application of the system to animals is at least an improvement on the old type of concession.

The most populous and best-developed area in the country lies south of the tropic between Lourenço Marques and Inhambane and includes the lower Limpopo and Incomati valleys. The wide belt of old dune sands along the coast is well suited to cashew and groundnuts which are two of the main exports. The cashew fruit provides a juice which can be distilled giving a very potent drink, stronger than from any other wild fruit; according to C. F. Spence, it makes workers 'almost incapable of working or thinking for days after'. It is the bean, growing outside the fruit, which is of commercial value. Shelling is still commonly done by hand, but mechanized plants for shelling and for extracting the oil have been built. Cashew nuts rank second to cotton as a source of foreign exchange.

The heavier lowland soils are more productive. On the black humus soils of marshy hollows, called *machongas*, lying between the dunes and kept moist by seepage from them, Africans grow rice and other crops. Using cheap ox-ploughs introduced from South Africa they are also growing a good deal of maize on black soils of the valley bottoms too heavy for hoe cultivation. Cotton and sugar, which make up over half Mozambique's exports, are also important. A surprising crop is wheat. Because of the high humidity it is liable to rust, but since flour mills were built at Lourenço Marques, both Africans and Europeans have found it worth growing as a winter crop.

Processing and marketing problems curtail production of several commodities. Bananas, pineapples, and grapefruit grow well, but meet competition from other parts of southern Africa and are at a disadvantage in Commonwealth preference and Common Market countries. Meat is imported into the Republic of South Africa from the Protectorates, not from Mozambique. In time, as Lourenço Marques becomes the natural outlet for beef from Rhodesia and Swaziland, local ranchers may benefit from refrigerated storage that will be needed to store the meat from inland.

The railway from Lourenço Marques to Bannockburn and Bulawayo, crosses the Limpopo about 60 miles above its mouth by a bridge which has been designed to act as a barrage allowing wide plains downstream on the right bank to be irrigated, the floodwaters of the river being stored in a lagoon for use in the dry season. About 74,000 acres are being divided into farms on which Portuguese and Africans are being settled, each settler being granted 10 to 25 acres irrigated, and 64 acres for dry farming. The European settlers are not permitted to employ labour and are supposed to provide an example their African neighbours can follow. The settlers' houses are grouped into small villages to make life more pleasant and also to allow strict control of malaria and bilharzia. Other schemes are afoot to control flooding along the lower Limpopo and Incomati, and to drain the *machongas* in the coastal dune zone.

The Revué and Pungwé valleys behind Beira have also received a good deal of attention. A hydro-electric station on the Revué river, with a capacity of 46 MW, supplies power to textile mills at Vila Pery, 30 miles to the north, and the electricity is also transmitted to Umtali and Beira. The mills operate reasonably successfully but are reported to suffer from a chronic shortage of labour. European planters in the Beira area rely mainly on maize as their main crop and efforts are being made to diversify their production. A sugar-refining and gunny-bag factory have been built at Beira, and it is intended that Portuguese and African settlers in the Pungwé valley shall grow sugar-cane and fibre to supply them.

The Zambezi valley contains greater latent wealth than any other part of the Province. In 1968 it was announced that work was shortly to begin on a dam and hydroelectric project. In the gorge at Cabora Bassa, 86 miles upstream of Tete. The first phase to be completed in 1974 will generate 1,200 MW, and the eventual peak load capacity will exceed 2,000 MW. South Africa is expected to take the bulk of the power generated. Gold and copper are amongst a number of minerals known to occur in the area, but they are scarcely worked at all. Coal is mined near Tete at Moatize, and since the completion of a railway to Mutarara in 1949, production has increased to about a quarter of a million tons. It is good-quality coal, comparable to that from Wankie, and the seams are very thick, but freight rates are high and at Beira coal from Wankie is cheaper than coal from Moatize, so the opportunities for expanding production are limited.

The Zambezi finds its way to the sea through seven different outlets at the margin of a delta covering 2,500 square miles. The people of the delta have cultivated rice for centuries, transplanting seedlings from February until April after which the floodwater of the river combined with spring tides causes the whole delta to be flooded fortnightly for five or six days at a time to a depth of about 6 inches. The people have to live in houses built on stilts, which also accommodate their animals and fowls.

The coastal areas north-east of Quelimane, are well settled. Coconut plantations, mainly belonging to large, internationally capitalized companies, are almost continuous for the 400 miles to Mozambique island; copra, the dried flesh of the coconuts, is one of the country's chief exports. The old settlement of Mozambique from which the country takes its name is an attractive town and it seems likely that the old houses with their tiled courtyards will remain undisturbed, for a place called Nacala some miles to the north is being developed as the main seaport for the northern part of the country. Nacala has a magnificent natural harbour and is linked by rail to Vila Cabral on the Nyasa highlands.

The interior of Mozambique is not very productive. Tea estates have been developed in the Milange area near the Malawi frontier. Asbestos and bauxite are worked on a small scale near the Rhodesian border; beryl and columbo-tantallite in the vicinity of Alto Ligonha, near the Nacala–Vila Cabral railway.

For Africans in the interior life can be hard. The local administration has full power over them and forces them to work on private or public projects unless they can show that they are farming efficiently or are otherwise productively employed. Many of the men are glad to go to work in the Rhodesias and South Africa, and in some villages three out of four adult males are abroad at any one time.

According to a long-standing agreement with the Portuguese government, South Africa is allowed to recruit up to 80,000 Africans annually for work in the Witwatersrand, their contracts lasting a year to eighteen months. The Portuguese benefit from taxes paid by the employers and the migrant labour and from the fact that the deferred pay of the workers, amounting to about £1 million annually, which is paid through the Mozambique authorities,

Chapel and walls of S. Sebastião fortress, Island of Mozambique.

is recoverable in South African bullion. Furthermore, according to the same agreement, Lourenço Marques is guaranteed $47\frac{1}{2}$ per cent. of the transit traffic from the gold-mining region of the Transvaal. In recent years, because of competition from Durban, traffic through Lourenço Marques has failed to reach this level and the South African Government has had to pay compensation. As opportunities for employment increase in Mozambique and mechanization of the mines in South Africa becomes more complete, migration will probably diminish in volume, but at the present time the actual numbers crossing into the Republic exceed the official quota.

It is difficult to estimate the extent to which the people of Mozambique have been influenced by their long contact with the Portuguese. They belong to several different tribes, speaking different languages, and although Swahili is spoken widely in the north and many of the migrants learn English or Afrikaans, Portuguese is the country's main common language. Education has been left mainly in the hands of the Roman Catholic Church. The proportion of children at school is smaller than in most parts of Africa and standards of education are rather low.

13

Indian Ocean Islands

MOST of the smaller islands of the Indian Ocean are merely the coral-encrusted peaks of volcanic heaps rising from oceanic ridges. Some of the volcanoes, on Réunion for instance, are still active. But certain islands in the Seychelles group are granitic and Madagascar, one of the world's largest islands, is evidently continental in character.

The people of the islands are very complex mixtures of physical types. On Madagascar the Negroid element predominates especially in the coastal regions, with Mongoloid elements strongest on the interior plateau and Caucasoids noticeable where Arab or European settlement is known to have taken place. On the smaller islands European languages and peoples are well represented, for until the Suez canal was opened the oceanic islands were stopping places on the sea route to India. Some of the most distinguished immigrants have not come of their own accord. The Seychelles received Archbishop Makarios for a few years, until he became President of Cyprus, and in earlier decades a number of African rulers who made themselves troublesome to British colonial administrations were sent into exile there.

Madagascar is now an independent country, the Malagasy Republic; the other islands are still colonial dependencies, the relics of empires that depended on sailing ships and sugar. Until recently they have been looked upon by the metropolitan powers as problems rather than assets, but with the independence of African mainland territories and increasing pressure from an expansionist China the Indian Ocean has acquired a new strategic significance and the islands a new importance as air and naval bases.

MADAGASCAR

The Mozambique Channel separating Madagascar from the continental mainland is a broad stretch of water ten times the width of the English Channel and the Malagasy do not usually care to be regarded as Africans. It is noteworthy that a political grouping of former French African States was called the O.A.M., Organisation Afrique-Malagasy, underlining the distinctiveness of Madagascar.

The physical separation of Madagascar from the mainland seems to have taken place as long ago as the Mesozoic era and isolated over such a long period of time, the flora and fauna have become somewhat specialized and are less varied than on the continent. Though there are lots of crocodiles in the rivers there are no strictly freshwater fish, few large quadrupeds native to the island, and no poisonous snakes. The local species of lemurs, bats, and spiders are of much interest to biologists.

The origin of the Malagasy people is still uncertain, though many theories have been put forward, postulating, for example, an early Pygmoid occupation. Murdock sees no reason for assuming that the island was other than completely uninhabited when the first Malagasy arrived on its shores and gives reasons for supposing that the first culture was exclusively Indonesian brought by immigrants who arrived by sea, probably from Borneo, via India, south Arabia, and east Africa, before the end of the first millenium A.D. Arabs and other trading peoples who visited the islands from the twelfth century onwards do not seem to have settled in any number or to have had much permanent influence except in the south-east corner, and the main languages are said to have some elements in common with those of Malaysia and south-central Borneo. The crops on the island also resemble those of south-east Asia. Rice is the staple and traditional food, taro and bananas are widely cultivated and Polynesian arrowroot is important on the plains. Bantu and part-Bantu have arrived from time to time, some as slaves others as refugees; their effect on the ethnic composition of the population has been large but their contribution to the total culture relatively small.

The eastern half of the island consists of a plateau of ancient crystalline rocks, that possibly formed a part of the ancient continent of Gondwanaland, covered locally by volcanic rocks. The steeper east side of the plateau is bounded by faults; on the west side, successively younger rocks outcrop, dipping gently towards the Mozambique Channel and forming east-facing scarps (Figs. 62 and 63). In many ways the island is structurally a mirror-image of Mozambique. In spite of the island's great extent, its mineral wealth so far as it is known

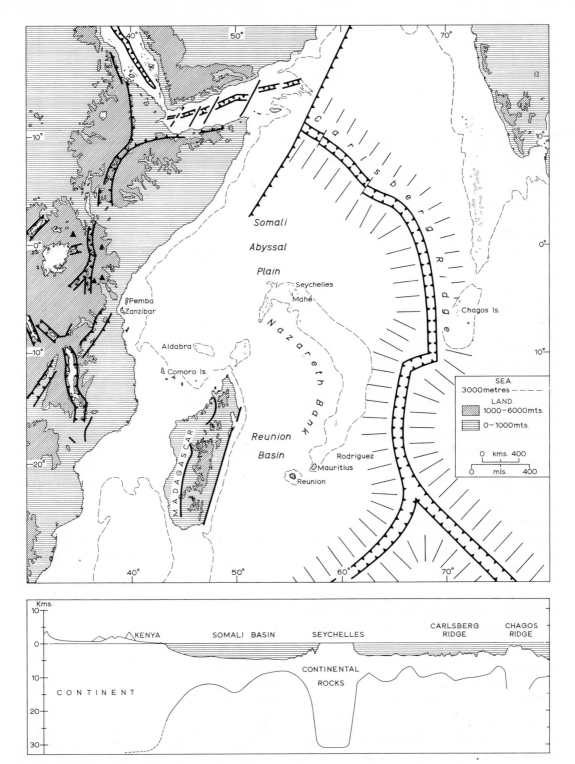

FIG. 61. *The western Indian Ocean. The Carlsberg Ridge, shown diagramatically, is believed to be a zone of rifting in the floor of the Indian Ocean, related to the East African rift system in some way as yet to be determined.*

229

is not very great. Although radioactive minerals discovered in the 1940's seemed to provide a new source of wealth, their importance has turned out to be much less than was originally thought. In the Sahoa basin in the south-west, good seams of coal occur; estimates have been made of 75 million tons within 300 feet of the surface, and ten times that amount within 2,000 feet. To be worth while, extraction would have to be on a scale of at least half a million tons annually but Madagascar is unlikely to be able to absorb this quantity locally, and any exports would have to compete with cheap coal shipped from Durban. Beryl, quartz, and mica are mined on a modest scale, and the island is the world's chief source of graphite. None of these exports is of great value to the country.

The climate varies considerably from one end of the island to the other and allows the production of a wide range of crops. Between November and April an equatorial trough lies over northern Madagascar and periods of deep westerlies cause prolonged rainfall in the northern part of the island. Rain is brought mainly by the north-east monsoon that blows from December to April and the windward corner receives more than 100 inches annually. Drier south-east Trades are dominant for most of the rest of the year, and the south-west corner of the island, which is generally under their influence and lies in the lee of the hills, is semi-desert country, the low rainfall reinforcing the effects of limestone bed-rock.

The east coast is liable to be ravaged by cyclones. Originating to the north-east between early December and March, they approach the island from the east, following curved paths that swing round to the south and south-west and may or may not cross the whole island. They cause damage in belts between 20 and 50 miles wide, with torrential rain, and wind speeds of more than 100 miles per hour. Nine violent cyclones caused severe damage between 1940 and 1960, those of February and March 1959 being particularly destructive; about forty others less severe visited the island in the same period. Half the plantation crops can be destroyed in the path of such storms, ships are sunk and buildings of all kinds damaged. Disasters of this kind seriously discourage investors.

The south-easterly winds blowing over long stretches of the Indian Ocean and driving a heavy surf on to the east coast of the island have built up a series of barrier beaches with lagoons behind, stretching south from Tamatave to Farafangana, a distance of nearly 400 miles. The lagoons are used for coastal traffic but are separated from one

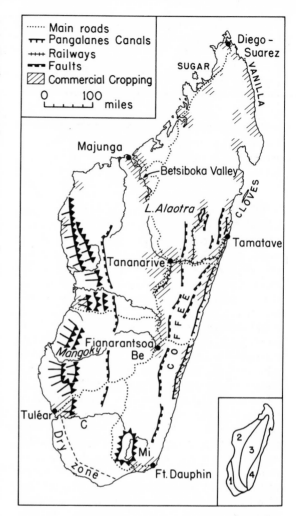

FIG. 62. *Madagascar. Westward dipping sedimentary rocks and east-facing escarpments on the west side of the island are seen in section in Fig. 63. Four main regions are to be distinguished: 1. The semi-arid country in the south-west; 2. The western savanna lands; 3. Grasslands of the central plateaux and highlands; and 4. Humid forest country along the east coast.*

another by low eminences called *pangalanes*, a word which is sometimes used to describe the whole feature. If bigger cuts were to be made through all these obstacles, the lagoon system could be made navigable from one end to the other, and serve a fertile well-populated plain stretching inland for about 25 miles. But it would be an expensive undertaking, there would always be some danger of rivers blocking the route with silt, and boats would have to go very slowly, so a road might be more economical in the end.

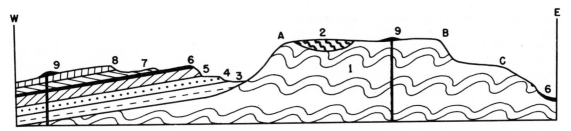

FIG. 63. *A schematic section across Madagascar after H. Besairie, 'La Géologie de Madagascar', Ann. géol. serv. mines, Madagascar, Fasc. No. XII (Paris, 1946), showing granite-gneiss (1), overlain by ancient sediments (2) and rocks of Karroo to Tertiary age (3–8) dipping towards the Mozambique channel. Recent volcanics (9).*

The dominant tribal group in Madagascar are a Mongoloid people, the Hovas (or Merinas), who were originally confined to a small section of the east coast. In the nineteenth century they gradually extended their influence inland, conquering the many independent kingdoms that had existed until that time. By 1820, when the French began to take an active interest in the island, the Hovas were well established in the centre of the island at Tananarive, and their sovereigns were recognized as rulers of the country. The French took over the administration in 1896. By this time, English Protestant missionaries had converted the Hovas to Christianity, and today the Hovas, over 1·6 million strong, hold most of the administrative posts. The coastal peoples, many of whom are Catholic, have made slower progress. Religious differences allied to tribal ones may give rise to political unrest in the future, but on the whole it seems that the people of Madagascar have a greater sense of unity and identity than those of most other large African countries.

Asiatics and Europeans form a small but important part of the population. Chinese are shopkeepers on the east coast, Indians on the west. Europeans, almost entirely French, are involved in commerce and continue to exert considerable influence in affairs. Though Madagascar obtained its independence in 1960, it remains within the French community and depends heavily on an annual subsidy from France. Two-thirds of its trade is with the former colonial power, and is to a large extent in the hands of a few French trading and shipping companies whose finances are controlled by a comparatively small group of people sitting on interlocking company boards in Paris. As a result the country has not benefited greatly from the profits derived from commerce.

The economy of the island is almost entirely based on agriculture; two-thirds of the cultivated land is under food crops, of which by far the most important is rice. More than seventy varieties are recognized, with differing properties and suited to different soils. Some is grown on hill slopes after the bush has been cleared by burning; the best yields are obtained on the alluvial soils of the valley floors, where careful systems of cultivation have developed. Seed-beds in some areas are made on the hill-sides, each bed surrounded by a little wall of earth to keep in the water and to serve as a footpath when the fields are flooded. The men control the watering, and when the rice is ready, women uproot the plants and bundle them up for transplanting in the main paddy fields. There they must be kept free from weeds. In spite of the care taken, yields are low on the whole, only about 1,000 lb. per acre, and it is believed that improved varieties and fertilizers could double or treble them. The central parts of the island manage to produce a surplus over and above the large volumes absorbed by the capital Tananarive; some of it is traded to the north-east and southern extremities of the island where there is a rice deficit and a variable amount, about 30,000 tons annually, is exported.

The most valuable export of Madagascar, as of so many African territories, is coffee. About half of it is grown by native cultivators and the rest on European or Indian plantations. In 1966, coffee represented about 35 per cent. by value of the total exports, most of it being absorbed by the French market. In view of world over-production, the economy of the island cannot be safely based on further extension of this crop. Vanilla and cloves, two other major crops, mainly grown in the humid north-east are no more promising. Madagascar already produces two-thirds of the world's vanilla, and now synthetic substitutes are being put on the market. The price of cloves is low and unlikely to rise very much.

There may be a better future in cotton-growing. In the delta of the Mangoky about 100,000 acres might be irrigated to give high yields, and a similar acreage might be grown relying on the rains. In the

Betsiboka valley in the north-west it has been estimated that cotton could be grown on 50,000 acres of alluvium in the period of the year after the retreat of the annual flood waters. France is poorly supplied with cotton from its associated territories at present, and the crop should find a market there and, at a later stage, in local textile industries.

Pastoralism offers considerable opportunities. The total number of cattle on the island is put at about 6 million. During the last war meat and meat products were exported, but since then both the number of cattle and meat production have declined. The reason sometimes given is the extension of the area under rice, particularly into the dry-season pastures of the valley floors. In the south and south-west of the country, cattle stealing is so much an accepted part of the lives of the people that it is said to constitute a sport. However this may be, it is certainly the custom to herd the cattle together near the settlements every night, with the result that grazing is not used to the best advantage. Development of the livestock industry should reduce the dependence on imported animal products, which are valued at over £1 million annually.

Rice cultivation could probably be expanded and be made more efficient. Most of the crop is produced on holdings of only 2 to 5 acres and is more expensive on the urban markets than rice imported from south-east Asia. European farmers are using mechanical equipment near Lake Alaotra and Malagasy farmers are beginning to use ploughs. If these methods reduce costs of production it should be easier to dispose of a surplus than would be the case under present conditions. Yields of cassava could also be boosted from the present 4 tons per acre obtained on native plots to nearer the 40 tons obtained on European plantations. But the market for tapioca, semolina, and other derivatives is limited.

In recent years the Malagasy have seen the terms of trade turn steadily against them, and it is difficult for them to see in which direction they should turn to increase their incomes. The country is hampered by its remoteness from European and American markets and the high costs of transport this involves. Furthermore, production is scattered widely over the country, so that the existing roads and ports are costly to maintain in relation to their traffic; so freight rates are high. The situation is changing slowly. People are moving towards the north from the drier, less-productive parts of the island. Tananarive (or Antananarivo), the capital, is growing rapidly. Its port, Tamatave, which already handles 40 per cent. of the foreign trade by volume

is now the only modern harbour in the country and is increasing its dominance. This process may lead to greater efficiency for it can be argued that the country as a whole is underpopulated and should benefit from this kind of concentration of activity in the most favoured areas.

The population of Madagascar increased from about 4 million to about 7 million during the 20 years after 1947 and it is likely to continue to rise rapidly. Immigration from the heavily settled Comoro Islands and Réunion has contributed something to the greater numbers but, as in other African countries, the increase results mainly from the use of DDT and the lower death-rate from malaria.

MAURITIUS

This lovely green island, the size of an average English county, lies 500 miles east of Madagascar. Precipitous rocky peaks rising to more than 2,000 feet in the ranges behind Port Louis, the capital, and in the south-west corner of the island are so steep and devoid of soil that no form of agriculture

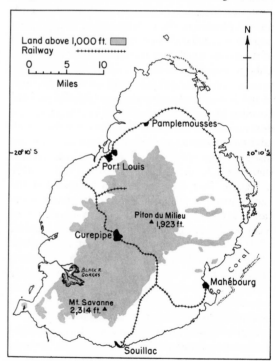

FIG. 64. *Mauritius. The island is built of volcanic rocks extruded and ejected since mid-Tertiary times. The latest craters form the main watershed running from north-east to south-west. A land-use map on a scale of 1 : 300,000 has been produced by the Directorate of Overseas Surveys, Tolworth, Surrey.*

or even forestry is possible (Fig. 64). The lower slopes of the mountains are occupied by forests and grasslands. On the coast, a ring of protective trees is preserved in a strip about 100 yards wide around the whole island. Known as the Pas Géometriques, it was land reserved by the French for military purposes. Nearly all the rest of the country, about 46 per cent. of the whole, consists of sugar-cane fields, separated from each other by windrows of great basaltic boulders and stones, collected from the fields over several decades at the cost of much labour. On the produce of these fields, covering 215,000 acres, depends the livelihood of 750,000 people (1965).

The Dutch, the first European settlers, cleared the ebony forests in the seventeenth century and exterminated the dodo. They left in 1710, and the French arrived five years later. The descendants of the French settlers who arrived in the eighteenth century remain the core of the European population, and in spite of the fact that the island has been a British possession since 1814, all educated Mauritians speak French as well as English. The descendants of African slaves who were brought in to work on the plantations form a second element in the population, called Creoles and speaking a language of their own which is derived mainly from French. Labour was imported from India after the suppression of the slave trade, and largely as a result of the Indian immigration, the population trebled between 1833 and 1861 to reach 300,000. Over the next eighty years numbers increased intermittently, falling occasionally as a result of malaria and other diseases then rising again. The area under cultivation was extended and sugar production steadily increased. Improved stock was developed, fertilizers came into general use, and the milling of the cane was concentrated in a small number of efficient factories. The sugar was sold on the world market, while the Mauritians came to depend to a large degree on imported food. Standards of living, though not very high, were much in advance of those in any other part of tropical Africa.

Society had by this time acquired the stratification on a racial basis that still persists. English people held until recently most of the top positions in the administration; the French own and manage the sugar estates; Creoles of African or mixed African and European descent have most of the white-collar jobs in government and on the estates. The retail trade is largely in the hands of Indian Muslims and Chinese, the vast majority of the small planters are Hindus, and Indians provide most of the labour for the canefields. All the languages spoken by these peoples are used in the schools, and learning them, even imperfectly, takes up an inordinate amount of time. In 1965 preparations were made for Mauritius to become an independent state within the Commonwealth. Friction between the Indians on the one hand and the other races on the other was considerable, and numerous safeguards for the minority peoples have been written into the draft constitution. Mauritius became independent in March 1968, with rather gloomy forebodings.

Far and away the most important problem of the island is the rate of increase of numbers in recent years. Until the last war the birth-rate had been about 4 per cent. of the total population annually, and the death-rate about 3 per cent., so that the population was increasing quite slowly. After the war the birth-rate increased slightly for a few years as it did in many countries, because people had delayed getting married on account of wartime conditions. Much more important in Mauritius was the fall in the death-rate about that time. As a result of a campaign to wipe out malaria it fell from 3 per cent. to a little over 1 per cent., and the population shot up from 500,000 in 1952 to 750,000 in 1965. This was alarming, and it implied that the population would reach a million by 1972 and 3 million by the end of the century if this rate of increase were maintained. Yet practically everything, food, clothing, fertilizers, building materials, and so on, depends on the sale of sugar. Sugar constitutes 97 per cent. of the exports and production of sugar is increasing, but it cannot increase as fast as the population, and even if it could, the markets for it are by no means assured. Furthermore, the demand for labour in the canefields has been diminishing with the introduction of chemical weed killers, so there is a risk of steadily increasing unemployment.

There appears to be no quick solution to this problem. The rate of increase of the population might be checked by emigration, and approaches have been made to various countries including British Guiana, Honduras, Brazil, and Tanganyika, but to no avail. Madagascar would seem to be the obvious potential recipient, but as in other countries its government is primarily interested in the well-being of its own people and is by no means convinced that an influx of Indo-Mauritians would be to its own long-term benefit. Emigrants would have to be specially trained to gain their living in an under-developed country, and the cost of establishing them in their new homes would be very high. This cost could hardly be met by Mauritius. Nor would the island people be happy to lose the best-trained and most energetic sector of the population. In fact, the easiest and cheapest outlet for Mauritian emigrants appears to be the United Kingdom, where they would have to face the same difficulties as the West Indians and compete with them for the least attractive jobs in the country. So it is generally agreed that emigration offers no solution.

Family limitation is another possible palliative, but it is difficult to persuade unsophisticated people to adopt methods of birth control, especially when the majority are Roman Catholics opposed at least until recently to the adoption of some of the methods commonly employed. Nevertheless, attempts are being made. Centres have been set up to propagate information about family limitation, and in time they are likely to have some effect. But unless there is some revolutionary change in the situation, the population seems bound to rise steeply for the next twenty or thirty years.

The economy was already showing signs of stress in 1958. At £81 per head, income was still higher than in most parts of Africa and south-east Asia, but the real value of income had fallen slightly in the six preceding years. The sugar estates complained of a shortage of labour and yet 15 per cent. of the population were reckoned to be unemployed. Many people had inadequate diets. Surplus sugar was beginning to be held over to the following year because the island's quota was already filled. Then in January and February 1960 came the two most destructive cyclones of this century, killing forty-two people and destroying 70,000 homes. For its recovery the island had to rely heavily on grants from the British government. But at least the stocks of excess sugar could be marketed, to supplement the reduced yields resulting from the cyclone damage.

For the future, ways have to be found of increasing production if present standards are to be maintained. The popularity of sugar as a crop, which is somewhat embarrassing, is believed to be due in part to the fixed prices paid by the marketing syndicate, and so it has been suggested that diversification might be encouraged by paying fixed prices for other crops. Tea, for example, is well suited to the island and might be grown more widely.

The main assets of the island are the fertile soils, good resources of water, and abundant fairly low-cost labour. The use of overhead irrigation might allow two crops to be raised from the same plot of land each year; in the 1960's the area irrigated increased by about 13,000 acres, all by overhead irrigation. Thousands of acres of private land are still contributing little or nothing to the island's economy, and labour intensive agricultural developments are feasible. However, wage rates in Mauritius are higher than in competing countries such as Ceylon, so costs in agriculture will have to be kept to a minimum. One way of doing this would be through small family holdings organized into co-operatives.

Deep-sea fishing on the banks of the ridge extending north to the Seychelles might add to the much needed supplies of protein, but additional refrigeration plants would be needed.

Industrial opportunities are less promising. Hong Kong and Puerto Rico have shown what can be done by populous islands lacking raw materials, but they have special advantages of position and markets which Mauritius does not possess. However, much might be done if capital were forthcoming and if the islanders were to show some drive and initiative.

In Mauritius, many of the problems of Africa and Asia are exhibited in an accentuated form. Its relative nearness to Madagascar, and the contrasting conditions in the two countries would suggest that some solution to the problems of both countries might come as the result of closer economic and political association. But racial and national prejudices are likely to be too strong.

RÉUNION

Réunion, the sister island of Mauritius, rises from the ocean about 150 miles to the south-west, at the southern end of the Seychelles ocean ridge. It is smaller than Mauritius and much more mountainous. The volcanic peaks in the north rise sharply to more than 10,000 feet above the sea. In the south-east a volcano more than 8,000 feet high is still active, and lava escapes into the sea from time to time, with very spectacular results. Most of the population, which numbers about a quarter of a million, is distributed in small towns around the coast, the south-east corner of the island being avoided.

Because of the high relief, rainfall totals are much higher than on Mauritius, exceeding 150 inches on the east coast, and more than 250 inches annually at the higher altitudes. The west, lying in a rain shadow, is very much drier with only about 20 inches of rain falling annually, and the cactus and aloes there provide a striking contrast with the remnants of evergreen forest on the east coast 20 or 30 miles away. Several species of plants are peculiar to the island and appear to be adapted to some degree to life on a windy volcanic island.

When the French first arrived in the middle of the seventeenth century, the country was uninhabited.

There were great turtles on the beaches, and big heavy birds unable to fly, relatives of the dodo of Mauritius and the long extinct aepyornis of Madagascar. The early French settlers grew various crops, of which coffee was the most important until the nineteenth century. Then sugar-cane was introduced, requiring the use of slave labour, and by the time slavery was abolished in 1848 (the year when the name of the island was finally changed from Bourbon to Réunion) African slaves numbered about 60,000 out of a total population of 100,000. Muslim Indians, Tamils, and Chinese were brought over producing a very mixed population that was given some cohesion only by its use of the French language, or rather a 'creole patois' derived from it.

The economy of the island is now more or less firmly based on sugar. Production has risen to more than 150,000 tons annually but there is little room for further expansion. As in Mauritius the cane-fields are mainly in the hands of locally owned companies that also operate the factories, and planters who sell their crops to the factories. Some people have moved up into the higher country between the two mountains, where the climate is too cold and wet for sugar, and cultivate plants used for making perfumes.

The island has a great deal of charm. St. Denis the capital is a well-planned French colonial town of the eighteenth century with white-painted wooden houses and elegant modern ones. But most of the people, including many of the whites, are very poor and if the population continues to increase at the current rate of 3·7 per cent. annually they are likely to get poorer. Emigration to Madagascar has been considered as a solution, and some resettlement has been attempted with French financial assistance. But the numbers involved have been too small so far to have had much effect on a situation that closely parallels the one in Mauritius.

THE COMORO ISLANDS

Grand Comore is the largest of a group of small volcanic islands between Madagascar and the African mainland. In area and rock structure they compare with Fernando Po and the other islands south-west of Cameroon mountain, but they lie 11° to 13° south of the equator and experience a marked dry season with south-easterly winds that have lost much of their moisture on Madagascar. The Comoro Islands have been much more affected by Arab influence than their big neighbour to the east, and the population, which numbered a quarter of a million in 1968, though very mixed, is mainly

Islamic and Swahili-speaking. The islands are mainly dependent on sugar-cane, and also produce sisal, copra, and vanilla for export, and extracts of plants such as lemon grass, citronelle, and patchouli, used in making perfume.

Large plantations occupy about one-third of the total land area and the pressure on farming land is very heavy indeed. About 25,000 people from the islands are known to have settled on the west coast of Madagascar in recent years and more are likely to follow.

THE SEYCHELLES

Several groups of islands are strewn across the Indian Ocean over a distance of about 750 miles north-east of the Comoro islands. Most of them in the south-west are coral, rising only a little above sea-level, and with no permanent inhabitants. The

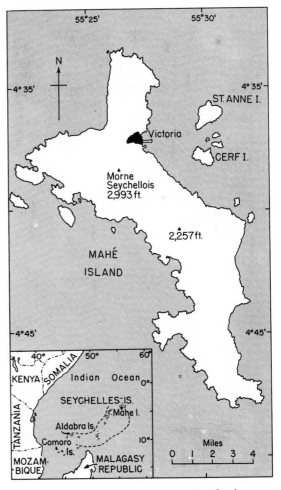

FIG. 65. *Seychelles. Mahé, the granite island.*

235

largest is Aldabra, a very large atoll, the last refuge of giant tortoises that have been wiped out on the other islands.

The group of islands lying furthest north-east, the Seychelles Archipelago, is quite different. The islands are built of granite, which is unexpected in oceanic islands, and have hills and mountains rising to nearly 3,000 feet. The rainfall is 90 inches a year at sea-level, and much more on the high peaks, as compared with 20 inches on Aldabra. The largest individual island, Mahé, is almost 17 miles long and 3 miles wide (Fig. 65). About 40,000 people live on Mahé, about three-quarters of the population of all the islands, and Victoria the chief town is headquarters of the British colonial administration for the whole of the Seychelles Archipelago.

The Seychelles were uninhabited until the French established a settlement on Mahé in 1777. Within little more than a decade the islands' magnificent forests had been destroyed and thousands of giant tortoises had been shipped from Mahé or slaughtered for home consumption. The French settlers, coming from Mauritius, brought with them large numbers of slaves and by the time the islands were formally ceded to Britain, in 1814, French language and customs were well established. A creole language is now spoken as mother-tongue by 94 per cent. of the people.

In many respects the Seychelles are well favoured.

They lie outside the cyclone belt, and diseases such as malaria and yellow fever are unknown. There has been a good deal of miscegenation but society, as in Mauritius, is well stratified, with white landowners at the apex of a social pyramid of which the base is provided by landless labourers descended from slaves.

The main crops grown on the plantations are coconuts, cinnamon, and vanilla. These go to pay for imported foodstuffs, above all rice, flour, and sugar, on which the islanders depend, plus cotton piece goods. The increase in the size of the population is creating problems of unemployment and efforts are being made to attract tourists to the islands. At present there is no airport and boats call too infrequently to offer great prospects for the future in this direction. The present dependence on imported foodstuffs could no doubt be reduced by producing milk, meat, and other items locally. At present the authorities are mainly concerned about melittoma, a disease attacking the coconut palms and greatly reducing yields of the Seychelles' chief crop.

A recent development which made a great impact on the islands' economy was the construction of a United States Air Force tracking station for satellites. Spending on Mahé by the staff attached to the station has created trade and employment in the vicinity.

14

South Africa

AFRICA south of Capricorn is dominated by the Republic of South Africa, easily the richest and most powerful state in the continent. Its population, 19 million in 1968, is only 6 per cent. of the total population of Africa, but its power stations generate over half the continent's electric power and over a third of the continent's motor vehicles run on South African roads.

As the Union, South Africa was a member of the Commonwealth. Then, in 1961, when it decided to adopt a Republican form of government, the hostility of other African and Asian members to its racial policies was so great that South Africa refrained from seeking readmission.

South-West Africa, which is still regarded by the United Nations as a Trust Territory, was administered more or less as a part of the Union for several decades and has now in effect been incorporated in the Republic. Bechuanaland, Basutoland, and Swaziland, lying alongside or within Republican territory, were British Protectorates until they attained self-government in the 1960's. Economically they are very dependent on their powerful neighbour.

The physical environment

Nearly all the region lies outside the tropics and most of it consists of plateaux rising above 3,000 feet so the climate is cooler than elsewhere in Africa. On the plateaux the air is dry, sunshine is abundant, and the daily range of temperature is considerable, with night temperatures in winter commonly falling below freezing. This is particularly true of the Kalahari where the author had it firmly impressed on his mind when sleeping out in the open in July. At midday shade temperatures rose into the eighties, but at sunrise on more than one occasion buckets of water were frozen and the thermometer indicated -6° C. The coastlands are more cloudy and humid, and have a smaller daily and monthly range of temperature.

Lying between latitudes 17° and 35° S. the region is under the influence of dry descending air for much of the year, and lack of rain limits the agricultural potential of extensive areas. On the east side of the region, humid air masses from the Indian Ocean move inland in summer, swinging anti-clockwise round a weak cell of high pressure centred south of the Limpopo. Frontal lifting and convection combine to give showers which are heaviest along the coast and on the rugged escarpments of the Great Escarpment in Lesotho and the eastern Transvaal. All the eastern half of the Republic receives on average over 20 inches of rain annually, but the westerly half of the region, where northerly and north-easterly airstreams predominate, is arid or semi-arid country as Map 4 demonstrates. In this dry country extensive pastoralism is the rule. Only the south-western corner benefits from rain brought by eastward moving depressions. Within

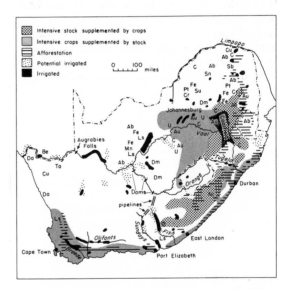

FIG. 66. *Land use and minerals in South Africa. The pipelines from the Orange river to the Great Fish and Sundays rivers are under construction (1965). Ab—asbestos, Au—gold, Be—beryllium, C—coal, Cr—chrome, Cu—copper, Da—alluvial diamonds, Dm—diamonds in kimberlite rock, Fe—iron, Ls—limestone, Mn—manganese, Ni—nickel, Pt—platinum, Sb—antimony, Sn—tin, Ta—tantalum, U—uranium. Notice that most of the agricultural and mineral resources are on the east side of the country and in the south-west Cape.*

about 100 miles of Cape Town mean annual totals exceed 20 inches, but the relief is high, with mountainous ridges of sandstone rising up to 6,000 feet separating shaly basins, and so the rainfall is very unevenly distributed with the highest totals in areas too rugged for cultivation. From the Cape eastwards, towards Port Elizabeth, the proportion of rain carried in by warm northerly airstreams increases and that derived from depressions diminishes. At East London most of the rain falls in the summer months.

Except in the southern Cape, rainfall is unreliable and long periods of drought are normally to be expected each year. Evaporation rates are high, particularly in the summer months when most of the region receives most of its rain. Consequently few of the rivers are perennial and much reliance has to be placed on underground supplies of water. Fortunately, extensive areas are underlain by water-bearing rock strata. Half the farms in the Republic depend on borehole water for domestic use and watering stock and the sites of many towns were chosen originally because strong springs were near at hand. Bloemfontein, capital of the Orange Free State, was founded, as its name suggests, near a perennial spring. Pretoria, capital of the Transvaal and administrative centre of the Republic, for long depended on strong springs issuing from dolomite rocks. Other settlements have been less fortunate. Johannesburg stands on a watershed. The main ports, growing up at the few places along the coast where there were good harbours, depend on supplies carried long distances by pipeline. Many of the mining towns are supplied in the same way and the water pumped from the deep gold-mines can sometimes be worth far more than the cost of pumping.

In most parts of South Africa crops benefit from irrigation. The main irrigated farms lie in the upper valleys of the Limpopo in the Transvaal and near the Olifants and Breede river in the Cape (Fig. 66). Most of the more easily dammed sites are now being utilized. The rivers carry heavy loads of sediment and many reservoirs have lost their original capacity as a result of silting. Further expansion of irrigation involves large-scale diversion of rivers.

The Orange river scheme

The main water-control project involves the Orange river which rises a little to the west of the Drakensberg in Lesotho and discharges 9 million acre-feet (11 milliards) annually into the Atlantic at Alexander Bay. Its main tributary, the Vaal, flows through the industrial complex of the southern Transvaal about 40 miles south of Johannesburg and is already carefully controlled, both for irrigation and to supply the industries of the Rand and Vereeniging. The Orange river itself is more deeply entrenched and offers few opportunities for irrigation. The new project, which will be carried out over the next twenty-five years at a cost of over £200 million, involves diverting a large part of the discharge of the Orange river through a tunnel $51\frac{1}{2}$ miles long and $17\frac{1}{2}$ feet in diameter into the upper reaches of the Great Fish river. From the Great Fish, water will be led by another tunnel into the valley of the Sundays river (Fig. 66). These tunnels plus various dams and pipelines will allow about three-quarters of a million acres of the south-east Cape to be brought under cultivation. A network of twenty hydroelectric stations, with a total potential of 177 MW, is to be constructed as part of the project to provide power for industry and to pump water from the new dams to cities in need of additional supplies. The scheme is expected to make an important contribution to the nation's economy, making land available for at least 9,000 new farms and increasing the annual production of fruit, cotton, wheat, livestock, and other agricultural products by some £60 million.

The pattern of economic activity

The greatest concentration of population and industry in southern Africa lies on the interior plateau, far from the coast or any navigable river. Within 50 miles of Johannesburg, on the watershed between the Limpopo and the Vaal, lies the only industrial complex in Africa comparable with the conurbations of Europe and North America. Its location and development were determined primarily by the existence of the Witwatersrand goldfield, secondly by the proximity of raw materials, and thirdly by the availability of good supplies of labour and capital and a large market created by the gold-mining industry.

The two chief ports, Cape Town and Durban, are foci of other populous regions producing agricultural and industrial goods on a large scale. Of lesser importance are the ports of the south-east Cape, namely East London and Port Elizabeth, and the diamond mining town of Kimberley (Figs. 67 and 68).

The southern Transvaal industrial complex, with a population of 3 million, is greater than all the other centres of industry put together. It contributes about a half the Republic's industrial output and provides a livelihood not only for the people dwelling on the Rand and in its vicinity but also for the families of workers whose permanent homes are hundreds of miles from the mines and factories, in Mozambique, Malawi, Botswana, and Ovamboland.

The concentration of industry in South Africa in a few large urban centres is to be ascribed mainly to the need for industries to be near their chief markets. The freight and traffic-sharing policies of the railways, which were and are state-owned, have had considerable influence. Agreements were made at the beginning of the century to spread traffic with the interior over the several rail routes to the coast in order to make full use of the rail tracks already in existence and the facilities at the different ports. This allowed all the main ports in the Union, and Lourenço Marques as well, to function economically and all of them continued to expand, though at different rates. The freight rates were designed to promote agricultural and industrial development in the interior by charging low tariffs for the carriage of raw materials, and high ones for mining equipment and other finished products. As a result, industries established near their markets were at a great advantage because of the low costs of distributing finished goods and so industrial development was confined mainly to the original urban centres, namely the coastal ports plus Johannesburg and Kimberley.

The railways remain the chief means of freight transport because of the big distances between the big population clusters. The most valuable commodities like gold and diamonds go by air, being flown from the big mining centres to Europe and North America, but most of the freight is iron-ore, coal, and other bulky goods. Passenger traffic is also maintained at a high level on the railways, on both long-distance and local services, because the railways also run the bus services and ensure that the two do not compete directly. While the non-white population is dependent to a large extent on public transport, the number of cars per head of the white population is one of the highest in the world; one car per 3·3 persons in 1963. Most of the non-whites live in locations situated long distances from the town centres and have to travel to work daily by overcrowded trains and buses.

The most productive agricultural districts in southern Africa are situated in the vicinity of the main industrial centres. Here the land is farmed by whites, mainly Afrikaners, growing crops and raising stock for sale. The less productive agricultural areas include the dry lands of the west and the native reserves, where commercial farming is the exception and subsistence farming, little different from that in tropical Africa, is the rule.

Racial patterns and problems

Society and economy in South Africa are more clearly stratified than in most other parts of the world, because class differences there correspond so closely with colour differences. The policy of apartheid, or separate development as it is now known, involves an attempt to convert the horizontal stratification that now exists into a regional distribution, by demarcating European and Bantu areas. The policy appears to have the support of the majority of both the Afrikaans and English-speaking whites. It is claimed that it will prevent exploitation of the economically weak Africans by those who have greater skill and resources, and will thereby lessen the danger of interracial friction. All the various population groups will be given the opportunity to evolve as independent nations while retaining their own cultures and identities. It is difficult to accept that such a division of the country can be effective for the interdependence of the different races is increasing not diminishing, and the measures taken in pursuit of the policy cause friction that many fear could lead to an explosion.

Since 1948 laws have been passed against marriages between people of different races. Everyone must carry an identity card indicating his race. Certain jobs are set aside for particular population groups, and Bantu cannot form trade unions or go on strike. The coloured people of the Cape have been put on a separate roll of voters. The universities are no longer open to all races but each race has its own. Comparable infringements of the rights and freedom of the individual are not unknown elsewhere, but in most other countries racial discrimination is being gradually eroded away; in South Africa it is gradually being reinforced.

Of the total population of the Republic, 19 million in 1968, nearly a fifth were European, 60 per cent. speaking Afrikaans and the rest English. In the sixties the Europeans were increasing in number by 1·7 per cent. annually; the Bantu, forming two-thirds of the population, were increasing by 2·65 per cent., the Coloureds by 3·4 per cent., and the Asians by 2·9 per cent. Thus the whites are being increasingly outnumbered by the other peoples, and this may help to explain the separate homelands policy.

The distribution of the white population corresponds very closely with the pattern of economic activity. They are concentrated in the cities

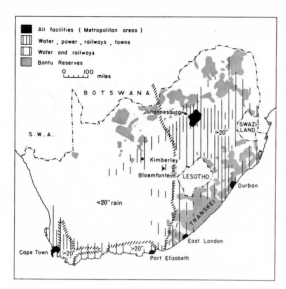

Legend on map:
■ All facilities (Metropolitan areas)
▦ Water , power , railways , towns
▯ Water and railways
▧ Bantu Reserves

0   100 miles

BOTSWANA

Johannesburg

SWAZILAND

S.W.A.

Kimberley

Bloemfontein LESOTHO

Durban

<20" rain

TRANSKEI

Cape Town   >20"   >20"

East London

Port Elizabeth

Fig. 67. *Facilities for development and native reserves in South Africa.*

(84 per cent. were town-dwellers in 1960) and in the most productive agricultural areas. The distribution of the non-whites on the other hand is discordant with the economic pattern. Over three-quarters of a million work permanently on European farms, a similar number are casually or seasonally employed on farms, and over 5 million are urbanized. But about 40 per cent. of the Bantu live in reserves, mainly in the south-east Cape, Natal, and northern Transvaal. Occupying about 13 per cent. of the total area of the Republic, the reserves are mainly in the well-watered part of the country, some of them are in easy reach of the coast and railways, but they all lack industries and other opportunities of employment; they have few large towns, modest mineral resources, and little manufacturing on any considerable scale (Fig. 67).

The Bantu in the reserves are unable to make more than a bare living from the land for their territory is overstocked and eroded, holdings are small, methods obsolete and yields low. The people have responded by leaving to work in the mines and industries and on the farms of the European areas. Average earnings of African employees in 1961 were about £185 per year in manufacturing and construction as compared with about £34 in agriculture. Not surprisingly Africans prefer to find work in factories and workshops, but the government uses the pass system to guide labour from the reserves and from outside the country into the mines and on to the farms. It is considered that the gold-mining industry cannot be allowed to decline rapidly because it is too important to the economy of the country as a source of foreign exchange and revenue, and since the price of gold has not risen as fast as that of other commodities the industry must be supplied with cheap labour if the mines are to be run profitably.

Immigration to the towns, it has been argued, would get quite out of hand as it has in many under-developed countries, if there were no restrictions on labour movement, and the whole policy of separate development would be undermined. In Pretoria the number of Bantu increased by 80,000, that is by 65 per cent. between 1951 and 1961, but in Johannesburg the increase of 157,000 was only 34 per cent. and in other cities the percentage increase was a little less. Thus the rate of expansion of the urban Bantu population over the ten-year period, neglecting city boundary changes, would not appear to have been much greater than the national increase in Bantu numbers. The situation contrasts strongly with that of the newly independent African countries where the rate of increase of the urban population has been more than twice that in South Africa.

In spite of the control on the movement of Bantu into the cities housing the newcomers has presented many difficulties. Appalling slums developed with dangers to health and of political unrest. Huge programmes of native housing have been undertaken to deal with the situation, with recreation centres, school buildings, and other accessories.

In every large town in South Africa the population is composed of Europeans and a larger, growing proportion of Bantu, plus Coloureds in the Cape and, except in the Orange Free State, Asians (Indians). Each racial group is confined by law to its own location or group area. Outside the reserves and the former Protectorates, the best land belongs to Europeans and the Africans provide the labour on the farms. The mines, owned by companies financed from Britain, North America, and now dominantly local sources, are staffed by Europeans at the higher levels, the labourers are Africans. Trying to separate the elements of such a plural society would seem to be attempting the impossible.

SOUTHERN TRANSVAAL AND NORTHERN
ORANGE FREE STATE

The industrial complex of the southern Transvaal is composed of the Rand which stretches 30 miles east and west of Johannesburg, the Witbank coalfield to the east, Vereeniging on the Vaal river to the south, and Pretoria near the margin of the

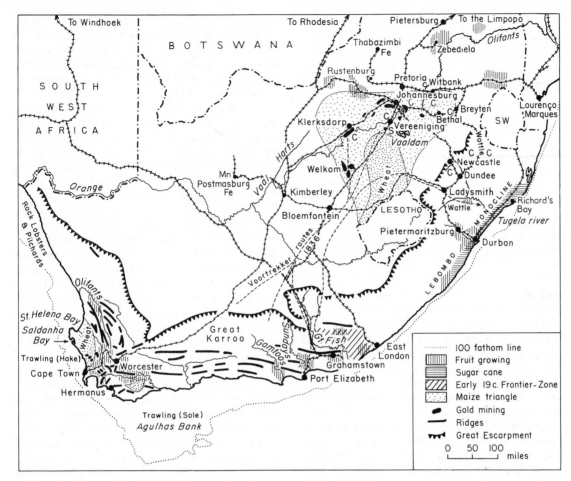

FIG. 68. *Location map of South Africa. Fe—iron-ore, C—coal-mining.*

Map legend (Fig. 68):
.... 100 fathom line
Fruit growing
Sugar cane
Early 19c. Frontier-Zone
Maize triangle
Gold mining
Ridges
Great Escarpment
0   50   100   miles

FIG. 69, right. *Bushveld basin, Bankenveld (or Bankeveld), and Vaal river. The Karroo beds in the south-east, which include coal measures, overlie dolomites and igneous rocks of the Bushveld complex. In the north, where the Karroo sediments have been stripped off the older rocks, the drainage has been superimposed and rivers breach the quartzite ridges as at Pretoria (P) and Thabazimbi (T), thereby providing routeways and damsites. The gold-bearing rocks of the Rand and Klerksdorp goldfields belong to the Witwatersrand system, hard and varied sediments, older than the dolomites and the Bushveld complex, folded into a large syncline of which the northern limb forms the ridges of the Rand running east-west through Johannesburg (J). South of Johannesburg the Witwatersrand beds are overlain by andesitic lavas and are too deep for mining. PB—Pietersburg, LM—Lourenço Marques, W—Witbank, V—Vereeniging, Ba—Balfour, Br—Breyton, M—Mafeking, Z—Zebediela, Sr—Strydpoort Range.*

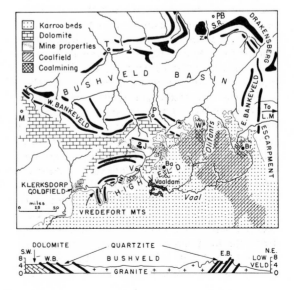

Map legend (Fig. 69):
Karroo beds
Dolomite
Mine properties
Coalfield
Coalmining

Bankenveld and Bushveld basin in the north (Fig. 69).

On the highveld south of the Bushveld basin the altitude exceeds 4,000 feet and the climate is fresh and invigorating with cloudless winter skies and strong daily and seasonal temperature contrasts. The rainfall, coming mainly as thunderstorms in the summer, varies between 20 and 40 inches, enough for maize and pasture grasses. Agriculturally as well as industrially this region is the most important in the Republic.

The greater part of the highveld is monotonously level, being underlain by horizontally disposed beds of sandstone and shale interleaved with sheets of dolerite all belonging to the Karroo system. These old rocks were planed down in Mesozoic times and then uplifted by Tertiary earth movements along an axis from Griqualand to the Transvaal. Rivers cutting down through the Karroo beds were superimposed on the underlying rocks and as the Karroo sedimentaries were stripped away extensively, former land surfaces were revealed that had developed on the ancient rocks before the Karroo sediments accumulated. These exhumed landscapes, developed on the dolomites and other rocks of the Transvaal system, appear north and west of Johannesburg. In the Bankenveld they retain a high relief with great quartzite ridges running east and west for mile after mile. The northward flowing tributaries of the Limpopo cut across them and dams for storing irrigation water have been built in many of the gaps. Pretoria commands a pair of gaps in these ridges, gaps used by the railway line running north from Johannesburg; other lines converging on the town, from Lourenço Marques and the iron-ore mines of Thabazimbi, follow strike depressions between the ridges.

North of the Bankenveld a remarkably level plain coincides with the surface of a mass of igneous rocks, mainly granites and norites, which seem to have been injected into the Transvaal system in such a way that the older beds of the system form the floor of the igneous complex and curve up at the margins to form a high rim, outcropping on the east side in the Drakensberg Escarpment. Around the rim of the basin are a number of strongly mineralized zones of which the most important economically are the iron-ore of Thabazimbi. In addition copper, antimony, platinum, asbestos, tin, and chrome ores are being worked. About 150 miles east of Pietersburg, not far from the Kruger National Park, half a million tons of phosphate concentrate is produced annually. Diamond mining is important near Pretoria; the largest diamond in the world, the Cullinan diamond weighing nearly $1\frac{1}{2}$lb., was found in the Premier mine there.

Still greater mineral wealth lies south of the Bankenveld in the pre-Cambrian conglomerates and quartzites of the Witwatersrand, containing the world's most important gold-bearing reefs. East and west of Johannesburg these old metamorphosed sediments, dipping south from a granite mass north of the city, outcrop to form long parallel ridges rising 500 to 1,000 feet above the general level of the highveld plateau. They are obscured to the east by Karroo beds, stretching south-west across the Vaal river, that include the southern hemisphere's greatest coalfield. Its thick seams of coal are extensively worked near Witbank, Balfour, and Vereeniging. The gold-bearing conglomerates and quartzites extend south into the Orange Free State where they lie concealed beneath several thousands of feet of Karroo beds and other sedimentary rocks.

Some of the most valuable water-bearing rocks in southern Africa, Ventersdorp lavas and massive dolomites of the Transvaal system, immediately overlie the Witwatersrand system and outcrop widely near the Rand and further west. Boreholes sunk into them give very high yields, holes less than 100 feet deep commonly giving more than 100,000 gallons per day. The dolomite areas are important economically for another reason in that diamond-bearing gravels occur locally.

This assemblage of valuable minerals, precious metals and stones, base metals, coal, and underground water, all within an area of a few thousands of square miles is scarcely to be rivalled anywhere else in the world, and it goes far towards explaining why South Africa is such a prosperous country in comparison with other Afro-Asian states.

The gold, which is of primary importance, occurs in a very finely divided state, as a powder in bands of quartz-pebble conglomerates, called bankets, which are believed to have accumulated as shoreline pebble deposits. In the central districts of the Rand near Johannesburg the reefs lie quite close to the surface, but at most places they are at great depths and some mine shafts go vertically down for 2 miles, where temperatures exceed 43° C. and rock bursts are liable to occur. The workings at the eastern and western extremities of the Rand are endangered by flooding from the large volumes of waters in the dolomites overlying the Witwatersrand system; pumping is essential, shafts passing through the water-bearing beds have to be lined with concrete, and subsidence is liable to occur as a result of collapse into caves at depth.

The difficulties involved in extracting a great

volume of rock from a considerable depth under such conditions calls for exploitation by large concerns. Expensive equipment and large skilled staffs are needed to prospect for new reefs, to sink shafts over 25 feet in diameter, pump out water at rates of tens of millions of gallons per day, ventilate deep workings, and extract the gold from the tough ore-bearing rocks. To deal with such problems large companies evolved on the Rand, organized at first by the Kimberley diamond-mining magnates, and financed by them and by thousands of private investors in South Africa, Britain, and North America.

Gold production was first centred at Johannesburg and shifted later to the east end of the Rand. In recent years the most productive mines have been about 40 miles west of Johannesburg. There are still great reserves of gold on the Witwatersrand but much of it is too deep for profitable working, at least with present techniques and prices and it is estimated that by 1980 only about eight mines are likely to remain open in this part of the Republic's goldfields.

The increase in the value of gold in relation to the world's currencies in the 1930's initiated a comprehensive series of geological surveys which revealed new goldfields south of the Witwatersrand and since 1950 a number of new mines have been brought into operation in this southern area. The most important are at Klerksdorp, 100 miles southwest of Johannesburg, and near Odendaalsrus and Welkom, 70 miles south of Klerksdorp (Fig. 68). The ores are remarkably high yielding and as a result of the opening of these new mines and others on the eastern Transvaal highveld, and the introduction of more efficient methods, production of gold in South Africa increased from £200 million in 1959 to £390 million in 1965. The fields already being worked ensure that gold-mining will continue well after the end of the twentieth century, if by that time it is still necessary to use a material won with such great expenditure of effort to lubricate world trade.

Some £200 million has been spent in the last two decades on developing the Orange Free State goldfields. Sleepy corn and cattle country has been turned into a bustling industrial belt; new towns have sprung up with populations numbered in tens of thousands where ten years before there were merely hamlets. Welkom, which has arisen since 1950 on the flat, windy maizelands and by 1962 was serving six mines, is a good example of a new-style mining town, with a four-lane road sweeping round a central park, residential suburbs radiating from the town centre and green wedges of open space between them. On the east side of the town, a trading estate of 500 acres has attracted over a hundred assorted industrial plants.

Johannesburg. A view over the city showing the mining dumps. Johannesburg lies at the centre of the Witwatersrand metropolitan region which extends nearly 50 miles from Randfontein in the west to Springs in the east, and has a population of about three million. This is the largest and wealthiest industrial and commercial concentration on the continent.

A factory at Germiston on the eastern Rand. The wheel, a giant sheave used in mining equipment, is being prepared for delivery. Metal engineering trades were stimulated by the demands of the mines and the distance to overseas sources of supply. Now Johannesburg supplies Rhodesia and Zambia with mining gear. Other industries have grown up in the inner metropolitan zone and already by 1951 secondary industry was providing employment for greater numbers than gold-mining.

While the Witwatersrand mines continue to depend on migrant native labour mainly from beyond South Africa's own frontiers, a start has been made on the Free State mines to house the native worker with his wife and family. Only a small proportion of the labour force benefits at present, partly because of government restrictions, but the practice is likely to become more common, for labour is getting scarcer and must be attracted to the mines by amenities of this kind.

For each ounce of gold, about 3 or 4 tons of rock have to be dug out, hauled to the surface, crushed, and sorted. Under these conditions, it is worth while extracting other economic minerals from the ore, even if they only occur in small quantities, because the extra cost is relatively small. Uranium is one of the most important of these other minerals in the ore, and for some years after 1952 uranium to the value of £50 million annually was extracted, prolonging the economic life of some mines and increasing the profitability of others. However, European and American purchasers had over-estimated their requirements, prices fell and by 1962 only one mining company was still producing uranium. With the expansion of the atomic energy industry demand has revived and production is increasing.

While the centre of the gold-mining industry has moved south, Johannesburg has continued to grow with the momentum it acquired in earlier years. It is now the commercial and industrial metropolis of southern Africa, at the centre of the transport web of the sub-continent with thriving industries all around. The first factories were built on confined sites between the ridges and mine dumps in and around the city as subsidiaries of the mines. Now the central parts of Johannesburg are crowded with skyscrapers and the new industrial areas lie out on the Rand to the east where there is more room and industrial estates allow orderly development. James Morris in *Cities* has contrasted the white housing with the black townships around the city's peri-meter. 'There are perhaps no suburbs more brazenly luxurious than the white highlands on the northern edge of the city', he wrote, but many whites live extremely modestly. And the hideously

Natives ploughing on the contour.

jumbled slums which he deplored have now been swept away, replaced by the modern planned locations, more orderly and sanitary but, as he described them, 'with a terrible impersonality'.

In the latter part of the nineteenth century mining developments absorbed all the available capital and until the 1930's industries were mainly serving the mines and there was little general manufacturing. Expansion began with the establishment of Iscor, the South African Iron and Steel Corporation with government backing, at Pretoria in 1928. Production began in 1934 and expanded during the Second World War. Afterwards a second fully integrated plant was built at Vanderbijlpark, near Vereeniging, 75 miles south of Pretoria. Production is now about 4·5 million tons annually and is competitive in cost and quality with that of the major steel-producing countries.

With locally produced iron and steel available, metal-working and engineering industries were established on the Rand and developed very rapidly under wartime conditions. By 1951 secondary industry there was a bigger employer than gold-mining. Heavy engineering has concentrated around Vereeniging, with the steel works at hand, plus water from the Vaal river, electric generating stations and coal and coke readily available. In 1955 the world's largest oil-from-coal plant was com-

pleted on a coalfield just south of the Vaal at Sasolburg and this now supplies about a tenth of South Africa's oil requirements. A big oil refinery is due to come into operation at Sasolburg in 1970. All this industrial expansion has easily absorbed the labour freed by the reduced needs of the Witwatersrand goldfields.

The great numbers of people attracted to the mines and factories of the southern Transvaal and northern Free State provide a big market for agricultural produce from the surrounding country. Until 1890 the highveld had been essentially a land of large stock-farmers; wool was the Union's chief export. Then the farmers began to grow maize, or mealies as it is called, the staple food of the African mine-worker. Natural conditions for the crop are not ideal. Black clayey soils in the Bethal area, derived from dolerites, have an unusually high plant nutrient content and yields of 1,000 lb. to the acre are normally obtained. But on the prairie soils of the maize-growing triangle pointing south from the Witwatersrand, the yield is 500 or 600 lb. to the acre or even less in drought years. Such yields are no better than those 'normally obtained by African subsistence cultivators. They could be increased considerably and they are rising as more fertilizers are used and newly developed varieties are introduced to suit local conditions, but this maize triangle is not to be compared in productivity with the maize belt of the U.S.A.

Towards the east, in the neighbourhood of the Escarpment, many farms remain under grass. Pastures are suitable for dairying, and farms situated close to the railways radiating out from the Witwatersrand to Breyton, Durban, Bloemfontein, and Ladysmith specialize in milk production.

Labour on the farms is traditionally provided by native squatters occupying labourers' houses who are paid in cash and also have the use of some land and grazing. Farming is constantly becoming more mechanized and intensive. Tractors have almost entirely replaced oxen and on the small farms near Johannesburg cattle are now fed mainly on lucerne, hay, and oil-cake concentrates. Workers on the farms are more skilled and have to be paid more, but fewer are required than formerly.

Irrigation in the southern Transvaal is most important to the north of the highveld proper, at the margins of the Bushveld basin where *poorts* through the quartzite ridges provide excellent dam sites and alluvial soils on the valley floors are suitable for citrus, tobacco, winter wheat, and vegetables. The most extensive groves of citrus in the

country lie south of the Strydpoort range on the Zebediela estates where half a million trees have been planted (Fig. 69). At the other end of the scale are small irrigated plots of vegetables to be found round nearly every town. A large irrigation scheme in the Harts valley, a tributary of the Vaal, depends on water stored far to the east behind the Vaalbank dam, but the Vaal's water is much more valuable to industry than to agriculture and the scheme is unlikely to expand any further.

SOUTH-WEST CAPE

The Karroo (or Karoo) in the interior of Cape Province is arid with a low and uncertain rainfall. It is overgrazed, eroded country where bush has encroached on grassland and little of the climax vegetation survives. Much of it is used for sheep farming, helping to make South Africa second only to Australia as a supplier of Merino wool.

Cape Town and the country nearby is very different from the interior. Scenically and culturally it is closer to Europe than any other part of Africa. Its climate can be compared to that of Portugal; its steep ridges and valleys remind one of Provence; its shoreline is varied with bays and headlands and long white beaches.

The sandstones building the mountain ranges running parallel to the coast and the shales flooring the valleys belong to the early Palaeozoic Cape System of rocks that were pressed east and north and folded against the old continental block in Karroo times. The two systems of folds meet in an area of complex relief between Ceres and Elgin. The rivers were superimposed on the folded rocks from a Mesozoic cover and now Table Mountain Sandstones in the cores of the upfolds are exposed as spectacular ridges and Bokkeveld Shales are preserved in the intervening basins. Archaean rocks that formed the floor on which the Cape System was laid down have been exposed by erosion locally or are covered by Cretaceous sediments. They generally give flat or gently undulating country but in the western lowlands intruded granites form great isolated mountains, and huge relict masses of Palaeozoic rocks rise sharply from the plains. These receive more rain than the surrounding dry lands and are bordered by highly productive farmland.

Cape Town is set against the magnificent backdrop of Table Mountain, perhaps the most spectacular of all the residual hill masses just mentioned. The original settlement site, as in so many cities, is now the commercial centre. Railway yards and offices occupy land reclaimed from Table Bay in the course of dock construction. The suburbs of

Citrus farms in the Rustenburg area, Transvaal. A farmer's house in the foreground, with established groves on the left and newly planted trees on the right. Rustenburg lies west of Pretoria in an area very rich in iron-ore and with the largest platinum-producing mine in the world.

A The Devils Hill
B The Table Hill
C The Lyons Hill
D The Lyons Fort
E The Dutch Fort
F The Companies Garden
G The Hottentot Hutts

H House of ye Dutch
I The Church
K The Hospital
L a Landing place
50 Paces long

Cape Town in the early eighteenth century. From P. Kolben, The Present State of the Cape of Good Hope, *London, 1731.*

Cape Town from the air. Table Mountain occupies the centre of the photograph and the Cape of Good Hope appears in the top left-hand corner.

the city cluster on the northern slopes of the mountain foot and stretch several miles south, with Table Mountain on one side and the sandy Cape Flats on the other. Fashionable resorts are dotted along the west side of the peninsula but this is not the best side to go bathing, the sea is too cold, for the Benguela current sweeps along the west coast and sea temperatures rarely rise above $14°$C. Much more attractive from this point of view is the more crowded and less-fashionable beach at Muizenberg on False Bay, where warm waves roll in from the Indian Ocean and you can surf bathe in comfort at $20°$C. Few places in the world can offer hot and cold on this scale.

The city of Cape Town is steadily becoming less European. In the first sixty years of this century, while its population trebled, the proportion of whites declined from 60 per cent. to 40 per cent. As Europeans have moved out of the older residential areas, factories have been built and coloured folk, who form the majority of the city's non-white population, have moved in. More and more Bantu, attracted by the opportunities for getting jobs in the port and factories, have settled in and around Cape Town. According to the law they should stay in Langa and other African townships, but building in the locations has not kept pace with immigration and so they too have crowded into the central

districts turning them into slums sadly at variance with the natural beauty of the bay.

The port is second in the Republic to Durban, handling some 3 million tons annually. Cape Town's share of the country's trade might well have been smaller, for it is much further than Durban from Johannesburg, but it was protected by the agreement sharing the rail traffic that has already been mentioned. Much of its export trade consists of fruit from its immediate hinterland, whereas Durban and Lourenço Marques handle much greater quantities of minerals from the distant interior. Following the closure of the Suez Canal in June 1967, the tonnage of ships using Cape Town harbour more than doubled.

The agricultural economy of the lowlands stretching east and north from the Cape is based on wheat and wool. On the big farms of the dry Sandveld near the west coast, two-thirds of the land is used for grazing (Fig. 70). As the rainfall increases towards the fold mountains, the proportion of wheat increases. Vineyards climb the lower slopes of the granite Paardeberg and Kasteelberg near Malmesbury and fringe the sandstone Piketberg north of the Great Berg river and the Constantia mountains south of Cape Town. The moderate summer temperatures and light-textured soils in this part of the Cape produce grapes suitable for making light wines.

Municipal flats in the Malay quarter of Cape Town, on the slopes of Signal Hill, looking across to Table Mountain.

At the foot of the fold mountains near Stellenbosch the area under intensive cultivation is greater still and the valley slopes are covered with vineyards and orchards, tobacco grows on the lighter soils derived from granite, and grain on the heavier soils developed over the Malmesbury slates. Stellenbosch itself is the second oldest town in South Africa, a mellow university town with oak trees lining the streets, and gabled houses in the Dutch colonial style.

Elgin, 20 miles to the south and to the eastward of False Bay, lies in a secluded valley well supplied with water from the surrounding ranges. Its low winter temperatures and cool summers are ideal for apples, and about half those grown in the Republic come from the Elgin area. The apple orchards are deliberately sited on the heavier soils of the valley floor where cold air collects on clear winter nights. Peach trees are grown on the more stony soils of the hill slopes, vegetables and irrigated pasture occupy the wetter *vlei* lands.

The main railway line to Kimberley and Johannesburg bypasses Stellenbosch and makes its way across the Drakenstein range to the rapidly growing town of Worcester near the Breede river. The power-station constructed nearby on the Hex river to provide power for the electrified section of the railway between Cape Town and Beaufort West also supplies power for pumping irrigation water to the fruit-growing areas nearby. Great quantities of fruit are also produced in the Ceres basin, much of it being canned or dried for export. The Hex river valley a few miles to the south-east has better rail services and so its fruit is sent fresh to Worcester and Cape Town. Further down the Breede valley the rainfall diminishes to about 10 inches. Short streams entering the river on the north side are used to water vineyards and orchards, but the low-lying land is left uncultivated because the main stream is braided and liable to flood. The grapes are for the most part used to make wines which are generally heavy and sweet because of the high sugar content of the fruit which results from the high summer temperatures. The Great Berg river is rather like the Breede; the Tulbagh basin in the headwaters of the Berg produces a range of crops like Ceres; further downstream cultivation avoids the bottomland and fruit, wheat, and tobacco are grown on the lower hill slopes. As the old farmhouses denote, this was the scene of early Dutch settlement.

Agricultural produce forms the basis for local industrial plants, brandy and cigarettes being made at Paarl, woollen cloth and preserves at Worcester.

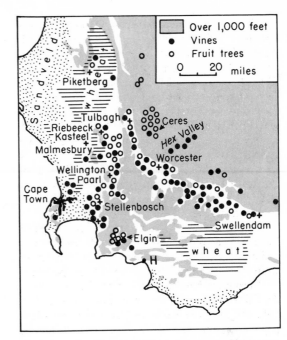

FIG. 70. *The south-west Cape. H—Hermanus.*

In Cape Town the range of industries is naturally much wider; some, like textiles and clothing, cater for the national market but the majority supply the needs of the south-west Cape. The market offered by the city's hinterland is limited, costs of power and distribution are rather high, and the growth rate of industry is consequently more restricted than in some other centres. Nevertheless, the value of industrial production in this region already exceeds that of agriculture by two or three times.

One of the fastest-growing economic activities in the Cape has been the fishing industry. Fish are caught by line fishermen off the entire south African coast, but the main catch is made by trawlers on the Agulhas Bank and above all in the waters off the west coast (Fig. 68). An area of 750 square miles within a few miles of the shore, either side of the frontier with South-West Africa, yields half a million tons of fish annually, the maximum permitted by existing conservation restrictions. The majority are pilchards and anchovy, great shoals of which feed on the phytoplankton utilizing mineral salts brought to the surface by the upwelling Antarctic water on coming into contact at the southernmost tip of the continent with the Agulhas current. Since the war, a fleet of 800 fishing vessels has been built up to supply nineteen canneries. Fish meal and oil are also produced, but of recent years they have suffered from competition from Peru where similar physical conditions have allowed an even more rapid increase in production. A very remunerative export in recent years has been rock-lobsters, frozen for sale in America and flown live to France.

DURBAN AND THE EASTERN PLATEAU SLOPES

Physiographically this region is dominated by the Great Escarpment which is formed in this section by the upper beds of the Karroo system, notably the Stormberg lavas building the Basuto highlands. The lower Karroo beds form great irregular platforms, sloping down towards the Indian Ocean from a level of about 5,000 feet at the foot of the Escarpment. They consist of sandstones bent down to the east along an axis forming the Lebombo monocline. Erosion along this axis has revealed still older beds beneath. Rivers rise on the Escarpment and cut across the sandstone steps, with reaches alternately gentle and entrenched. Their middle courses, superimposed on the old rocks revealed in the Lebombo monocline, are flanked by towering mesas of Table Mountain Sandstone and gentler hills of older granite. The coastline, characterized by dunes and sandspits, is scarcely broken by inlets of any size.

Durban, standing at the edge of a lagoon affording one of the few sites suitable as a harbour along the Natal coast, has required port improvements costing millions of pounds. The mouth, formerly only a few feet deep, has been dredged to take vessels drawing 42 feet, and breakwaters have been required to divert silt-laden currents. The harbour is now the best equipped in the country and handles more traffic than any other in Africa, about $14\frac{1}{2}$ million tons in 1965. An oil pipeline to Johannesburg was completed in 1965.

A city with a population now in excess of half a million, Durban owes its importance to its harbour and above all to its position in relation to the Rand, the rail haul being shorter than to any other port except Lourenço Marques. Its hinterland is more extensive than Cape Town's, and also more varied, with productive farming areas stretching far along the coast to north and south and also bordering the railway nearly all the distance to Johannesburg (Fig. 68). The Klip River coalfield is less than 150 miles away. The big native population of the reserves in Natal and the neighbouring parts of the south-east Cape provide a large market for cheap manufactured goods and a pool of migrant labour. Numbers in the city are growing rapidly, partly on account of African immigration, partly because of the large Indian population numbering about 200,000.

Durban's site presents even greater obstacles to expansion than that of Cape Town. Visitors from congested Johannesburg are envious of the wide main streets, but level land for industrial expansion remains scarce, in spite of reclamation works near the harbour. Most of the European houses are built on the higher ground; Indians have been attracted by the possibilities for growing fruit and vegetables at the lower levels. The Africans are the late arrivals on the scene and the majority have to live a few miles behind the coast. The separation has not prevented friction between Africans and Indians and from time to time it leads to serious bloodshed.

The road running along the coast through the rolling country north and south of Durban passes through mile after mile of sugar-cane. It was first cultivated in Natal in the middle of the last century and production grew intermittently, being stimulated by Indian labourers arriving in the 1860's, by the extension of the railways a few years later, and then by duties imposed on imported sugar. About 85 per cent. of the annual output, which amounted in 1965 to 1·34 million tons, comes from a few large estates owned by Europeans. Extraction of the sugar is concentrated in seventeen large factories, the largest of which are in Durban. The area suitable for the crop is limited. It becomes too dry to the north of the present cane-growing area and too cool to the south. Conditions are marginal in the main producing area, the crop taking about two years to mature, considerably longer than in competing countries nearer the equator. Furthermore, labour is short. The Indians have found more profitable occupations long ago and the Africans, who have never been keen to work in the canefields, would much rather get jobs in industry. Mechanical equipment is being introduced but is difficult to operate in the hilly country, so the costs of sugar production are relatively high and at times difficulty has been experienced in disposing of the surplus on a world market generally amply supplied from other countries with more suitable climates.

Local supplies of sugar have formed a basis for fruit processing and confectionery industries in Durban. In addition, textile, soap, rubber, fertilizer, oil refineries, and other factories have been established and the value of Durban's industrial output is now at least equal to that of Cape Town. These developments are based on the use of electric power generated from Newcastle coal and plentiful supplies of water from the Umlaas and Umgeni rivers.

The city remains a very attractive place and tourism is one of its main sources of income. The beaches near the city, up and down the coast, attract thousands of visitors every year, especially in the winter when the plateau can be cold and windy, and the Europeans of the Witwatersrand are glad to escape to the warm sunshine of Durban.

The road and railway running inland from Durban pass through a countryside of rolling granite hills, streams, and waterfalls. In the river valleys small intensively cultivated Indian farms produce fruit and vegetables for sale. Fifty miles from the coast stands Pietermaritzburg, the capital of Natal, a much smaller town than Durban, but with growing industries amongst which is a big aluminium plant. A number of industries are based on the wattle-tree which has been planted widely on the misty valleys to north and south, notably in the Umkomaas valley about 40 miles away from Pietermaritzburg. The trees thrive at an altitude of about 2,000 to 4,000 feet. When they reach an age of about 10 years the bark is stripped off and sent to factories for the tannin to be extracted, the timber is sold to mines for pit-props. To reduce transport costs most of the plantations are sited near railways. At Pietermaritzburg a large plant extracts tannin. Stock-rearing is important in the area and so a tannery has been established capable of treating 150,000 hides and 120,000 skins annually. With so much tanned leather available other manufactures have developed, notably the largest shoe factory in the Republic.

Three-quarters of the manufacturing in Natal is concentrated in the Durban area, and Pietermaritzburg accounts for much of the rest. Yet there are other areas which would appear to be well provided with raw materials, labour, and transport facilities where industrial development until now has been very limited. Amongst them, the Tugela basin has attracted a good deal of attention from planners in recent years (Fig. 68). It has good supplies of water which are not required for irrigation because there is little suitable flat land in the basin. Steam and coking coal are available from mines between Ladysmith and Newcastle that already provide about half Natal's annual production of 6 million tons of coal. Fairly heavily populated native reserves in the upper and lower basin would provide ample unskilled labour, and the main railway line from the Rand to Durban runs across the broadest part.

The Tugela basin might thus provide an alternative location for industries which cannot be established in the southern Transvaal on account of limited water supplies. The three biggest markets in the Republic, on the Rand, in the northern Free State, and at Durban, lie equidistant from it. Iron is already produced at Newcastle and larger quantities could readily be produced at low cost. This would seem to be the ideal place for a new industrial centre to relieve the pressure on the existing ones.

Much of the basin is evidently unsuitable for industry. The western fringes, wet and cold and poorly served by roads and railways, are suitable for dairy farming and growing conifers but for little else. The lower river valley, hot and dry and deeply dissected, offers few resources that are worth exploiting. Industrial development, if it is possible at all, would appear to have the best prospects in the zone of tall grassveld and sandy sourveld at 3,000 to 4,000 feet, crossed by the railway from Durban to Johannesburg. There the towns of Newcastle, Dundee, and Ladysmith are the most important of several settlements standing where the eastward-flowing tributaries of the Tugela cross this route. The largest of them, Ladysmith, has a total population of less than 25,000, and the total population engaged in manufacturing industries is only about 6,000. Newcastle's iron industry has received a boost from the demands of the Japanese steel industry, and production is rising. But most of the factories in the area are engaged in processing local raw materials, and few ancillary industries have been attracted.

So we have here an area which is under-developed, appears to have considerable natural and installed advantages, and yet where industrial growth is slow. The question arises as to whether growth should be artificially stimulated by government intervention. It is a question that arises in most countries these days, and it is not at all easy to answer. The advantages of the area that have already been mentioned would seem to present a good case in favour of industrial expansion in the Tugela basin. But industrialists wishing to expand their production by setting up new plants are inclined to prefer the big established industrial centre with its great advantages of having highly integrated assemblage of specialized producers, with familiar marketing and financing facilities. A move to a new area introduces new and unfamiliar risks and inconveniences. Furthermore, artificial stimulation of development may well prove inefficient and in the end might undermine the country's economy, for the concentration of industrial activity into a few very large centres appears to be the norm of economic growth at the present stage of technical and communications development. So the Tugela basin may remain an under-developed area for a long time; this conclusion may lead one to ponder on the uncertain future of many other promising areas on which great hopes of industrialization rests—the cost of countering industrial inertia is great, in what circumstances is it worth while?

Industrial growth has mainly concentrated in the country's principle urban areas. Apart from those already mentioned, the only places where manufacturing is of any importance are Port Elizabeth, East London, Kimberley, and Bloemfontein, and the value of production in all four towns put together is much less than a third that of the southern Transvaal. The concentration of activity has created problems of housing, water shortages, and, it has been claimed, higher costs and reduced efficiency. The government is therefore trying to decentralize industry, attracting development to new areas, where climatic conditions, the availability of water, power, raw materials, and transport facilities are favourable. It was announced in 1967 that £300 million is to be invested in northern Natal, mainly in the area around Richard's Bay where a harbour, oil refinery and aluminium smelter are to be constructed.

THE BANTU HOMELANDS

In 1954 a Commission which had been appointed to inquire into the rehabilitation of the native areas in South Africa presented its report. Usually known by the name of its chairman as the Tomlinson Report, it has had a great influence on the policy adopted by the Nationalist government, though it has not been adopted as a whole. Its proposal to bring together some of the reserves, which in all number 254, into a smaller number of larger units has been rejected. Nevertheless, one of its most important recommendations, advocating separate territories for the Bantu, was accepted in principle and is being put into effect.

Of the 13 million Africans in the Republic, belonging to many different tribes, nearly a half live in reserves. The Tomlinson Report allotted them 65,000 square miles of land, of which over a half is too dry for crop production without supplementary irrigation and much of the rest is impoverished and eroded. At present its carrying capacity is probably no more than 3 million people.

The largest and most populous of the reserves was the Transkei, a land of 16,330 square miles in the south-east corner of Cape Province (Fig. 67). This is the homeland of the Xhosa, a people numbering about 3½ million, who have been in contact with Europeans for a longer period than any other Bantu in South Africa. This is to become the first 'Black Nation' of a new South African Common-

wealth. It has its own wholly Black Parliament and Cabinet and the University College for Africans established in 1916 at Fort Hare, near Alice in the Cape Province, has become the university of the Xhosa people. At present about a million Transkeians have to live outside the territory, finding work in the mines and on white farms for lack of employment opportunity at home.

The Transkei has a rainfall of 30 to 45 inches and is ideally suited to pastoral farming. Maize, sugarcane, Kaffir corn, and pineapples grow well; there are good deposits of copper, nickel, coal, and marble; road and rail communications are moderately good and so the Transkei's prospects would seem to be better than those of most independent African territories, despite its small size. A development programme is in hand involving the spending of about £10 million on housing, irrigation, water supplies, fencing, and planting fast-growing exotic trees.

At present the main requirements for such schemes, apart from the co-operation of the Africans themselves, which cannot necessarily be relied on, is an adequate supply of capital. The Tomlinson Commission, which looked forward to increasing the carrying capacity of the reserves from the present 3 million to 9 million over a period of 25 to 30 years, advocated an expenditure in the first 10 years of over £100 million. Between 1962 and 1967 the government invested £57 million in an attempt to diversify the economy of the reserves. In the light of Swaziland's economic development in recent years, this sum would seem to be inadequate. Shortage of technicians is an even more serious problem and for a long time many if not most Africans will have to rely on cash earned in the European areas.

The government envisages the development of industries owned by Europeans at the periphery of the homelands allowing Africans to commute to work daily. It has made tax concessions and established industrial townships to attract industrialists to these border areas. Commercial, technical, and professional services associated with them are owned by Bantu. It was estimated that 126,000 Bantu were employed in the border industrial undertakings in 1968 and that another 600,000 were directly supported by them, mainly in the vicinity of Durban, Pretoria, and East London. More recently attention has been turned to regions well removed from the large urban markets, places like Pietersburg. It will be interesting to follow the fortunes of the decentralization programme. The reserves are distributed in a horseshoe around the

Orange Free State and southern Transvaal, many of them long distances from ports and markets, and it would seem that a good deal of state direction of industry will be needed to carry out the programme effectively.

The South African economy has been expanding rapidly in the sixties. Some of the old sources of wealth have dried up but others continue to contribute to the country's prosperity and new sources of wealth are constantly being tapped. It is difficult to believe that ostrich feathers will ever again bring in £3 million a year, but dress fashions are exceptionally unpredictable. Diamonds, of course, are always fashionable and continue to earn over £15 million annually. Stones from mines in the Kimberlite pipes account for 80 per cent. of the output in carats but the superior alluvial gemstones, from the western Transvaal and Atlantic coast, realize the highest prices.

European farm production has expanded nearly everywhere, partly by cultivating more land but chiefly as a result of improving farming methods and higher yields. In the score of years before 1958 the total area planted by European farmers increased by one-third; the volume of crops produced nearly doubled. In much the same way, cattle and sheep numbers remained more or less stationary while livestock products increased in volume by two-thirds. Wool, meat, and maize constitute half the gross value of farm production and will probably continue to do so. In 1968, wool, fruit, maize, hides, and skins together constituted about one-third of exports, excluding gold.

Manufacturing is developing rapidly and between 1963 and 1967 the physical volume of industrial production rose by nearly 40 per cent. Growth was especially marked in the industries manufacturing transport equipment, textiles, paper, chemicals, metal products, and machinery. The future of the gold mining industry is undertain, with prices for gold remaining low on the open market.

In the political field the policy of separate development is being applied in a deliberate fashion. The Ciskei and Tswanaland are to follow the Transkei and become self-governing, and it is intended that other territories should evolve as semi-independent homelands; notably the Sotho, the Shangaan people, the Venda, and Swazi. No matter how critical or doubtful one may be of the policy of separate development one may at least hope that these territories will make peaceful progress.

Though isolated politically from much of the

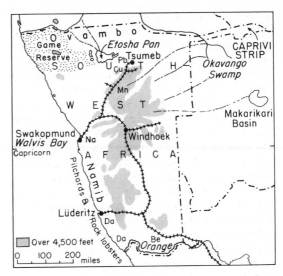

FIG. 71. *South-West Africa.*

world, South Africa continues to play a full part in world trade, with Britain still its main trading partner. In Africa its position seems to be stronger than ever. The International Court's refusal to decide against the Republic's position in South-West Africa has confirmed its hold on that country. The governments of the former Protectorates are on the whole co-operative. The Rhodesian situation is not developing unfavourably. In Malawi the South Africans are providing financial assistance for the building of the new capital at Lilongwe. The part being played by South Africa in the construction of the giant dam at Cabora Bassa on the Zambezi in Mozambique, and its intention to take most of the power generated, represents an important extension of economic and political influence in that direction. South Africa's dominance in Africa south of Capricorn is by degrees becoming more apparent.

SOUTH-WEST AFRICA

South-West Africa is a sparsely settled country, with 600,000 people unevenly distributed over 300,000 square miles. About 75,000 are whites of whom the majority speak Afrikaans or German.

Windhoek, the capital of the territory, standing on the highveld at an altitude of over 6,000 feet, has a higher proportion of Europeans than almost any other town in Africa. About a quarter of all the whites in the country live there with a roughly equal number of non-whites. Besides being an administrative centre, it is the market for the surrounding pastoral region where cattle and sheep are raised on big ranches.

The railway from Cape Province runs north through Windhoek to the copper- and lead-mining area at Tsumeb in the far north. The rest of the north lacks transport facilities and is scarcely touched by European influence. In the extreme north, the Ovambo people, numbering more than 270,000 and constituting some 45 per cent. of the total population, are to become self-governing like the Transkei. It is planned to develop the Cunene river for hydroelectric power and use some of the electricity to pump water to the interior of Ovamboland where there are no perennial streams. In the region of the Etosha Pan, a great tract set aside for wildlife is said to be the largest game reserve in the world.

Only the north-east corner has a rainfall of more than 20 inches. Kalahari Sands occupying the area declining to the Okavango basin absorb nearly all the rain falling on them and give rise to very few perennial streams. Towards the south-west, mopani woodland and tall grasses merge into thornveld and on the plateau into grassy steppe. Pastoral farming is dominant. As the rainfall diminishes towards the south-west, so does the variability of the rainfall increase. The coastal strip, beneath the Escarpment, receives very little rain at all, being occupied almost permanently by extremely stable air. Occasionally stratus cloud at about 5,000 feet produces a light drizzle, but this is almost immediately evaporated.

In spite of its aridity the coastal strip contributes about half of the territory's exports by value. The raised beaches of gravelly material, brought down by the Orange river thousands of years ago from some source as yet undiscovered, and carried north along the coast towards Walvis Bay, contain diamonds. This coastal zone is fenced off with barbed wire and carefully guarded for it yields about £35 million worth of diamonds annually, chiefly gem stones. Diamonds are also being recovered from sea-bed deposits offshore.

Huge numbers of pilchards thrive in the cold waters of the Benguela current and these, together with rock lobsters, caught in quantity south of Walvis Bay, provided another £25 million in 1966.

An unusual product is the curly black fleece of the Karakul sheep. This has to be taken from lambs killed and skinned within 36 hours of birth. The industry is peculiarly well suited to an arid area where the pasturage and browse is very sparse indeed, because the lambs do not have to be fattened for market, nor do the ewes have to provide for more than a small proportion of their young. Typical Karakul farms range from 20,000 to 60,000 acres

in extent, with the largest tending to occur in the driest districts in the extreme south and along the Namib border at the foot of the western Escarpment. Carrying capacities range from 15 to 20 acres per animal.

All these products provided in 1965 an average of £180 per head for all races living south of the Ovambo reserve. The chief beneficiaries are the Europeans, but standards amongst the Africans are higher than they are in other parts of the continent with a comparable climate and population density.

SWAZILAND

Swaziland is a small but varied country occupying the Escarpment and eastern plateau slopes. Several rivers rising in the mountainous west flow down to the lowveld and cut across the Lebombo

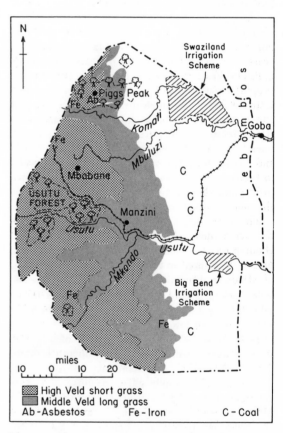

FIG. 72. *Swaziland. The new railway links Mbabane, the capital in the hills, and Manzini to Lourenço Marques. These two towns, the most important in the country, have combined populations of only about 10,000, of whom a quarter are white.*

hills into Mozambique. Though the smallest of the former Protectorates, and only half the size of the Transkei, Swaziland is easily the most advanced economically. Its development which has mainly been since the war is the result of experienced people studying the country, seeing the possibilities of its considerable natural resources and investing in them.

It was recognized that conditions on the western mountains, which receive up to 80 inches of rain annually were comparable to those in the Transvaal nearby where it had been found that softwoods could be grown commercially. Difficulties arose in acquiring land for planting in Swaziland because some of it belonged to sheep farmers from the eastern Transvaal who bring their flocks in for winter grazing. But most of the land in the west is unfit for grazing; better land was bought from European farmers for the few Swazi who were settled there, and within about twelve years some 200,000 acres were planted with conifers. The plantations can be worked on a fifteen-year rotation which is very short compared with the forty years of Scandinavia and the British Isles. Sawmills and box factories have been built and a large proportion of the wood from plantations in the Usutu valley is absorbed by a pulpmill with an annual capacity of 100,000 tons. Until the early sixties there was no railway in the territory, the lines from Johannesburg to the coast passing north and south, and the Usutu pulp was taken by lorry to Goba, the railhead in Mozambique. The other main plantation is in the vicinity of Piggs Peak in the more isolated north of the territory.

The territory is rich in minerals. Asbestos from the neighbourhood of Piggs Peak accounted for about a quarter of the 1965 exports. Large-scale mining of haematite ores at Ngwenya, north-west of Mbabane, began in 1964 and reached 2 million tons in 1967. To export the ore it has been necessary to build a railway, 150 miles long, west from Goba and entirely traversing the country. This is of great benefit to Swaziland, for it links the most promising part of the country to the coast and allows big coal deposits to be exploited.

The main agricultural areas are the middle and lowveld. The narrow north-south zones of the middleveld and the Lebombos are suitable for cattle-breeding, citrus plantations, rice, and vegetables, and the broader stretch of lowveld, though mainly too dry for anything but grazing land, presents some good opportunities for irrigation on a large scale. The Colonial Development Corporation, which was in large part responsible for the

successful afforestation and has invested over £21 million in development projects in Swaziland since 1948, purchased more than 100,000 acres of land from a European company in 1950 for irrigation from the Komati river. A canal was constructed and now various European and Swazi companies produce about 45,000 tons of sugar annually. Another scheme on the Usutu river near Big Bend also produces about 40,000 tons of sugar annually plus a variety of fruit and vegetables.

Economically, what had been a backward and neglected territory, is now expanding and flourishing. The Swazi themselves are involved in the changes, but it is significant that the developments have taken place almost entirely on land owned by whites and that during the fifteen-year period of expansion after the war the European population of Swaziland increased from about 3,000 to nearly 10,000. About 15,000 jobs were provided for Africans over the same period, thereby reducing the need to emigrate to find work in the Republic. Half the Swazi people remain subsistence cultivators and have still to be integrated in the new economy of the country.

LESOTHO

Lesotho is a mountainous country of 12,000 square miles, entirely surrounded by the Republic, with few resources and poor communications. Much of the cool, high country to the east is used for grazing and crops are grown on any considerable scale only in the low country of the west. To supplement locally grown foodstuffs, corn has to be imported from the Republic.

The economy is not soundly based. Out of a total population of a million, about 100,000 are temporarily absent at any one time, mainly working in the mines of the Transvaal and Orange Free State. This brings a good deal of money into Lesotho and another important source of revenue is the share of the South African government's customs duties received by the Lesotho government. Nevertheless an annual grant of some £2 million is required from Britain to balance the budget. In the future South Africa may be prepared to pay for water and water power needed for the industrial areas of the Orange Free State.

From the South African point of view, Lesotho is very much like a large native reserve. A politically independent Lesotho presents dangers as a refuge for political agitators and a base for African subversion in the heart of the continent. For its survival it depends to some degree on British protection but its

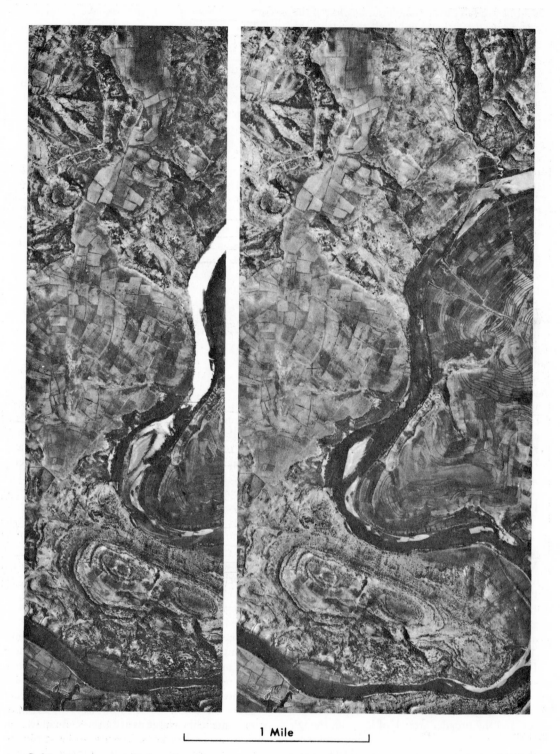

1 Mile

Cultivation patterns in Lesotho. The river winds through dissected lavas; traditional square fields on the left of the picture and contour strips on the right.

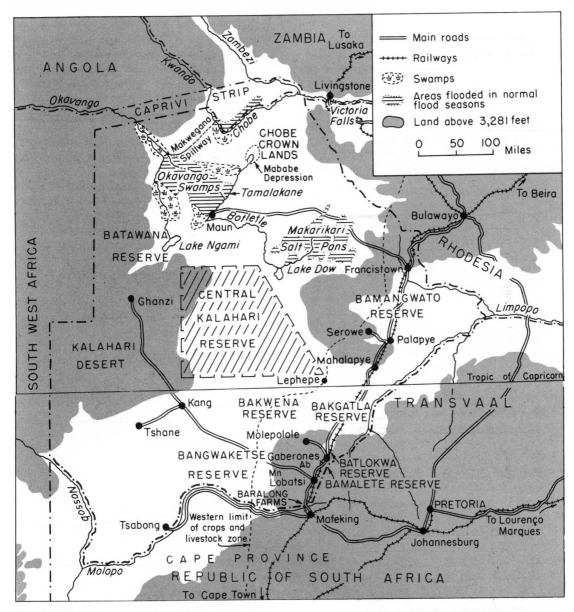

FIG. 73. *Botswana*.

economic dependence on the Republic necessitates co-operation with the government of that country.

A high proportion of the children attend school, about 95 per cent. of the total. At Roma, a University has been established which caters for all three of the former Protectorates.

BOTSWANA

With an area of about a quarter of a million square miles and a population of some 600,000, Botswana (Bechuanaland until October 1966) is the largest and the most sparsely settled of the three former Protectorates. The greater part of the country is made up of the Kalahari thirstland and much of the north is swamp. The majority of the people live a short distance from the south-eastern border where the railway from Cape Town to Bulawayo runs close to the western rim of the Limpopo basin.

The aridity of the Kalahari is to be attributed as much to the sandy character of the surface as to the low rainfall. Typical desert is confined to the extreme south-west where there is little vegetation of any kind and the mean annual rainfall is less than 10 inches. Most of the so-called desert has a mean annual rainfall of 10 to 20 inches, and consists of undulating sands covered with acacia and thorn scrub, or with much taller trees where underground water lies close to the surface. Because of the lack of surface water, and the long dry season, most of the region is unsuitable for livestock rearing. There are about 160 European farms in the Ghanzi area, but the Kalahari is first and foremost the habitat of the Bushmen; the little yellow men who live on wild roots and fruits and hunt the game with bows and arrows. For water they depend at least in part on sip-wells, sucking water out of the sand, as Debenham has described them in *Kalahari Sands*, and storing it in empty ostrich egg-shells. An area of 20,000 square miles in the centre of the country has been declared a game reserve, not for safari hunters, but to preserve the natural food and habitat of the Bushmen.

In the north-west, the Okavango river enters the country from Angola, across the Caprivi strip, and subdivides into many distributaries forming a great inland delta that ends suddenly at a low rise, possibly formed by a fault dislocation, running north-east to south-west through Maun. Instead of the complete absence of surface water of the Kalahari, this area has an embarrassing superfluity. The floods that reach their peak several weeks later than the peak of the rains produce thousands of square miles of grass, but it cannot be used for profit to man because tsetse-fly infest the whole of the central swamp area of Ngamiland and the Chobe. The fly have been advancing, spreading south and west in recent years, and efforts are being made to halt the encroachment by clearing bush and spraying with residual insecticides.

The people of eastern Botswana are compounded of a succession of invading groups who entered the area from the east and drove their predecessors west into the thirstland and swamps or kept them as serfs. The Batawana of the Okavango swamps are an offshoot from the Bamangwato of the eastern Kalahari who again are an offshoot of the Sotho tribes on the other side of the present Transvaal. They form a ruling class far less numerous than their serfs, the Makoba, the typical fisher-people of the swamps.

The Bamangwato, Bakwena, Bangwaketse, and other peoples living in the south-east are primarily pastoralists. A feature of their way of life is the large size of the villages, with the cultivated lands 10 or 20 miles away from the villages and the rainy season grazing lands five times as distant. The main settlements are fully occupied in the winter months only, and with the commencement of the cultivating season the people scatter to their fields, only the schoolchildren and some of the older people staying behind. The lads of the family and hired hands look after the livestock kept out at the cattle-posts through the year.

In the highest, most fertile parts of the country along the eastern border, about 4,000 square miles of land in four blocks granted in perpetuity to the British South Africa and Tati Companies have been divided into farms and sold to Europeans. They grow maize and breed cattle.

The mineral resources of the territory are not well known or developed. Old mineral-bearing rocks are exposed in the east of the country, where asbestos, valued at about £300,000 annually, is mined at Kanye and manganese worth rather less is produced in the same area. Near Mahalapye, two thick seams of coal may be worked in the future to feed a thermal power station. Power will be needed for working copper, nickel, and diamonds recently discovered in the Francistown area and elsewhere. By 1972 Botswana should have a substantial mining industry.

The economic future of the country will continue to depend heavily on the livestock industry, the products of which constitute about 80 or 90 per cent. of current exports. New bore-holes and wells allow stock to be kept ever more widely, but the most important development has been the building of an abattoir at Lobatsi in 1954 by the Colonial Development Corporation. Stockowners market stock direct to the abattoir and in 1962 over 93,000 cattle were slaughtered there. The carcasses, hides, and various by-products, almost all sold to the Republic of South Africa, bring in about £3 million annually.

The opportunities for wage employment in Botswana are scanty and ever since the opening of the Kimberley diamond-mines the men have been accustomed to seek work outside the country, mainly in the South African gold-mines. They spend most of their income where they are employed but between £¼ million and £½ million are brought back to the territory annually by migrants.

Economically, Botswana is evidently very much at the mercy of the South African government. The administration has only recently moved from Mafeking in Cape Province to Gaberones, and to the South Africans Botswana appears to differ very little from one of the Republic's reserves or Bantustans.

15

A Summing Up

FEW generalizations can be made about Africa; the regional differences are too great. Indeed this book is mainly concerned with demonstrating the diversity of the continent and attempting to explain the variations from place to place in historical and environmental terms.

The initial division into High and Low Africa appears to be associated with certain broad physical and economic differences. The high plateaux of the east and south, relatively cool and healthy, never seem to have been used very intensively by the Bantu and Hamitic peoples. They were interested in pastoralism as much as agriculture and seemed to have lacked suitable crops and implements to support a dense population. To Europeans on the other hand, the highlands were the most attractive part of the continent and white immigrants settled mainly in the south, and east while the hotter, malarious lands of Low Africa knew only traders, missionaries, and government employees, most of whom regarded Europe as home.

The greater abundance of economic minerals in the ancient rocks of High Africa accentuated the contrast between the two parts of the continent south of the Sahara. Gold, diamonds, copper, and other minerals attracted European capital as well as settlers, above all to South Africa and the lands extending north into Katanga. Up to 1936, two-thirds of the capital invested in Africa found its way to the Union, South-West Africa, the Rhodesias, and the Belgian Congo and at present 90 per cent. of the white population is in those countries.

Industry in the mining areas of the south gained a great impetus from the urban markets with their wage-earning populations, well-developed communications and the presence of Europeans anxious to create profitable enterprises. Whereas tropical Africa as a whole remains poor and undeveloped, with the majority of the people primarily subsistence cultivators, in the lands south of the Zambezi a high proportion of the total labour force, some 10 per cent., is employed in industry. The Republic of South Africa gives employment to almost as many wage- and salary-earners in non-agricultural occupations as all the rest of the continent south of the Sahara put together. Average incomes amongst the native population are higher than in the tropical territories, and those of the Europeans are amongst the highest in the world.

In Africa as a whole, economic development is going ahead as rapidly as in the rest of the world, but the level of activity, at present, especially in tropical Africa is very low with *per capita* incomes of between £10 and £60, compared with £500 in the United Kingdom and £1,000 in the U.S.A. At present rates of growth it will be 50 to 100 years before the mass of the people attain current European standards, and it is impossible to predict whether present rates will be maintained or exceeded in the future. Environmental factors are important, the lack of coal for example. Vast areas are still inaccessible, some 80 per cent. of the people are illiterate, and much depends on how quickly such situations can be corrected. Perhaps most important is the need for a long period of political stability to allow personal and economic links to become established within and between individual countries, and to create an atmosphere favourable to investment and long-term planning.

A century ago, most of the people lived in small, self-contained communities with wants and activities adapted to each other, the people in equilibrium with the environment and knowing little of the outside world. Some tribal groups had been incorporated in large ephemeral states such as those that developed in the Sudan zone and had acquired long-distance commercial and cultural ties. The spread of Islam from the north, which accelerated under colonial rule, helped to break down tribal barriers and widen horizons. The spread of Christianity inland from the coast has also undermined the traditional societies and brought people more closely into touch with the rest of the world. The use of money, the development of markets, and improvement of communications have all operated to bring local economies together and link them to the world economy. The languages of the imperial rulers are displacing many of the indigenous languages. Schools, newspapers, and the radio employ the more important African languages, but many of those less widely spoken are dying out. English, French, and Portuguese are the imported common languages; Afrikaans and Swahili local hybrids. These and a few other languages like Arabic, Amharic, and Hausa are becoming dominant not only for official purposes but also in commerce and everyday life. The fine texture of the old ethnic diversity is still there but it is rapidly becoming more difficult to detect beneath the new bolder patterns imprinted on the continent.

As European values are ever more widely and thoroughly absorbed and transmuted, African intellectuals have become more aware of their distinctiveness and speak of their negritude and of the 'African personality'. In what this consists it is not for me to say. It seems to me to be something rather vague at present, synthetic rather than traditional, but none the less of potential importance.

In politics, Pan-Africanism is more than an empty slogan. The Organization of African Unity established a permanent secretariat in 1963. Such sense of common purpose as exists, however, is directed mainly against the white-dominated states of southern Africa, and though the organization does something to unite the states north and south of the Sahara, it has deepened the political rift between South Africa and the rest of the continent.

Regional groupings of states for political and economic purposes are quite numerous; some are derived from the colonial era, for example the customs union in East Africa; others have risen in recent years. In each state a large part of total production, an average of about 30 per cent., is for export and in each state the bulk of trade is with the U.S.A. and a few European countries, notably the former metropolitan countries. By far the greatest trade between African states involves Rhodesia, Zambia, and the Republic of South Africa. The Commonwealth countries have certain preferential trade arrangements amongst themselves and share in joint technical educational and financial arrangements; all are in the sterling area. The former French territories have a special relation with France within the European Economic Community (Common Market) and have received substantial economic aid from France and other member countries. The economies of Angola, Mozambique, and Portuguese Guinea are closely tied to Portugal. The Sudan has bilateral trading agreements with the Soviet bloc. Ethiopia, Liberia, and other states are increasingly dependent on American aid. Communist China is actively engaged in the politics and economies of various states. All these outside linkages promote centrifugal tendencies and are stronger in many cases than regional groupings formed since

independence, such as the short-lived Guinea–Ghana–Mali Union and the so-called Monrovia and Casablanca groupings. Partly in consequence of the colonial period and the monetary, transport, and commercial systems established in the first half of the century, partly on account of the competitive natures of the economies of the African states and the complementary nature of the industrial and primary producers, international links do not hold the continent together but tend to separate the national units.

Political fragmentation in Africa has increased as a result of independence. While some of the smallest states such as Zanzibar are being absorbed into their neighbours, many countries which formerly belonged to federations, shared currency boards, legal systems, and defence arrangements have established their own special institutions since independence. They are consequently burdened with greater administrative expenses than formerly, for supporting representative assemblies, diplomatic missions abroad, armed forces, and so on. Some former federal capitals are now too big for the unitary states in which they are situated and the states themselves are too small to provide the market required to support new industries. In some cases countries in the interior are cut off from the sea and have special transport and customs difficulties. In general economic efficiency has been sacrificed to political expediency.

Within each country regional differences are marked and seem to grow stronger with the growing contrast between urban and rural areas. Although populations are increasing at rates of 2 and 3 per cent. annually and are likely to grow faster as mortality rates are reduced, there do not seem to be many signs of the empty areas filling up. In some places, the Middle Belt of Nigeria for instance, agricultural settlement is expanding into areas still unoccupied, but in general migration to the towns is accentuating contrasts in population density. Improvements in communications may help to even out settlement. More railways have been built in Africa since the war than in most parts of the world and the standards of the roads are rapidly improving. Nevertheless, transport costs in Africa are likely to remain high because of the long overland distances, the high cost of keeping up roads, and the steep gradients in the coastal escarpments and rift zones. Furthermore, the initial advantages of the areas of early economic development at the ports and transport nodes disappear very slowly, if at all.

As people congregate in the towns the contrast between urban and rural areas increases and land use everywhere becomes more strongly differentiated. Instead of the same piece of land being used for crops one year, grazing another, and sylvan produce a decade later, it is reserved for a special purpose and so the pattern of land is becoming fixed and permanent. As more and more land is built up, or improved by irrigation and the planting of perennial crops, land is acquiring a cash value and freehold tenure is being slowly accepted more widely in rural as well as urban areas.

The populous, productive areas in Africa are relatively small islands of economic activity based, it may be, on a particular crop, irrigation scheme, minesfield, port, administrative centre, or source of power. In a few places several of these coincide. Some countries have only one such node, usually the capital, others have several. The question arises as to whether these nodes or islands of activity are likely to remain economic enclaves, expanding, but leaving the rest of the country little disturbed, or whether their influence will permeate the whole. At present, the rate of economic and social change in rural areas is slow. Agriculture is still in many areas a way of life rather than an economic activity, yields per head and per acre are low and the influence of the economic islands does not reach beyond a certain radius, leaving the traditional economies of the interior little altered.

The monetary economies of the tropical African countries depend on a limited number of exports, largely made up of five agricultural crops; coffee, cocoa and cotton, palm products and peanuts, with three minerals—copper, iron-ore and petroleum. At the time of writing most of the crops are in surplus world supply, and prices are low compared with the early fifties when demand was stimulated by the Korean crisis. Since then, the terms of trade have turned against African countries, the prices for manufactured goods having increased while those of farming products have fallen. Future demand is difficult to forecast, because it depends a good deal on international relations; the high prices for sugar in the early sixties because of the Cuban situation is an illustration of this. The continued growth of world population would seem to offer possibilities for the future, and markets in the U.S.S.R. and China are as yet scarcely tapped. But the need for African produce is greatest in underdeveloped countries, such as India, which are too poor to afford to pay for them.

In most African countries the possibilities for economic development in the future are believed, in those countries, to lie mainly in industrial growth. To this, there are all manner of obstacles in the form of lack of managerial and technical skills, entrepreneurial ability, capital, transport, and markets. The greatest opportunities would appear to lie in the mineralized zone of southern Africa, the densely settled Guinea coastlands, and the populous region around Lake Victoria.

Much would seem to depend on regional groupings to enlarge potential markets and allow rational use of resources, but at present there are few signs of these evolving. Labour still moves fairly freely backwards and forwards annually from rural areas where people are under-employed in agriculture to the developing areas mentioned above. In South Africa labour movements of this kind have been going on for almost a century and they are unlikely to cease here or elsewhere for some time to come, in spite of the policy of apartheid in the Republic and the increasing definiteness of national boundaries. Trade in foodstuffs, above all cattle, between the savanna and the forest lands is also active and crosses state boundaries. Overseas trade between the coastal ports and the interior necessarily crosses frontiers too. In most respects, however, countries in Africa are less interdependent than countries in Europe and political developments are causing frontiers to become more, not less, divisive.

Guide to Further Reading

THE number of societies and journals devoted to African studies has increased enormously in recent years and it is very difficult to keep track of all the books and articles relating even to quite restricted topics or regions. In this guide attention is directed mainly towards recent books and only a few articles are mentioned.

Articles on African Geography

These appear from time to time in a vast number of journals. The main ones in Britain are the *Geographical Journal*, *Geography*, the *Transactions of the Institute of British Geographers*, and the *Scottish Geographical Magazine*. Popular articles with many illustrations appear in the monthly *Geographical Magazine*. In America mention may be made of *Economic Geography* and the *Geographical Review*. The issues of *Focus*, each devoted to a single country or region and published by the American Geographical Society, monthly, are handy sources of up-to-date information. The *Journal of Tropical Geography* (Singapore), the *Tijdschrift voor economische en sociale geographie* (published in the Netherlands but with many of its articles in English), *Europe-France Outre-Mer* (Paris), *Cahiers d'études africaines* (Paris), and *Cahiers d'outre-mer* (Bordeaux) are all important sources. Other non-geographical British quarterlies which commonly have articles of interest to geographers are *Africa*, which is the journal of the International African Institute, and the *Journal of Modern African Studies*. The Royal African Institute publishes a quarterly, *African Affairs*, which often includes papers read at conferences of the African Studies Association of the United Kingdom. The Association, an object of which is to co-ordinate activities by and between persons and institutions concerned with the study of Africa, produces a cyclostyled news bulletin twice a year. A number of banks issue handbooks from time to time on individual territories.

In *Geographers and the Tropics*, edited by R. W. Steel and R. M. Prothero (London, 1964), Steel gives a useful list of recent papers on Africa by British geographers. A bibliography of modern works is also given by E. S. Munger in a review article entitled some African Geographies, *Annals of the Association of American Geographers*, 53, 1963, pp. 235-47.

African Studies Centres

These have been established at a number of universities in the United Kingdom:

School of Oriental and African Studies, University of London—publishes *Bulletin of the School of Oriental and African Studies*.

Institute of Commonwealth Studies, University of London.

Institute of Commonwealth Studies, University of Oxford.

Centre of African Studies, University of Edinburgh.

African Studies Unit, University of Leeds—publishes *Leeds African Studies Bulletin* (mimeo).

Centre of West African Studies, University of Birmingham.

African Studies Centre, University of Cambridge.

School of African and Asian Studies, University of Sussex.

Of centres in America the following are amongst the most important:

Africa Collection, Hoover Institution, Stanford University—publishes various series on Africa, including a Bibliographical Series. Number XXIX of this Series, 1967, by Peter Duignan, is a *Handbook of American Resources for African Studies*, published 1967.

African Department, Northwestern University, publishes joint acquisitions list of Africana of nineteen libraries in Evanston, Illinois, U.S.A., Canada, and U.K.

African Collection, Yale University.

African Studies Centre, Boston University.

Committee for the Comparative Study of New Nations, University of Chicago.

Committee on African Studies, University of Chicago.

African Studies Centre, University of California, Los Angeles.

Programme of East African Studies, Syracuse University—publishes bibliographies.

Centres in other countries include the following:

Committee on African Studies in Canada, University of Alberta.

Scandinavian Institute of African Studies, University of Uppsala—publishes miscellaneous items.

Geneva - Africa Institute — publishes *Génève-Afrique*.

Afrika-Studiecentrum, Leyden, Holland—publishes quarterly *Kroniek van Afrika*.

Afrika-Studien, IFO Institute for Economic Research, Munich—publishes monographs in English and German.

Centre of African Studies, Universytet Warszawski —publishes *Africana Bulletin*.

These institutes and others throughout the world are listed in the SCOLMA (Standing Conference on Library Materials in Africa) *Directory of libraries and special collections on Africa*.

Bibliographies

Several bibliographies of Africa have been produced amongst which are the following:

African affairs for the general reader: a selected and introductory bibliographical guide 1960-1967. Council of the African-American Institute, New York, and African Bibliographic Center, Washington, 1967.

GLAZIER, K. M. *Africa south of the Sahara, a select and annotated bibliography, 1958-63*. Hoover Institution Bibliographical Series, 16. Stanford, 1964.

JONES, R. *International African Institute. African Bibliography Series: North-East Africa, 1959; East Africa, 1960; South-East Central Africa and Madagascar, 1961*.

Agricultural development schemes in sub-Saharan Africa: a bibliography. Pp. 189. Library of Congress, Washington, 1963.

UNITED NATIONS ECONOMIC COMMISSION FOR AFRICA, *Bibliography of economic and social development plans of African countries*. Pp. 40, mimeo. Addis Ababa, 1968.

UNITED NATIONS ECONOMIC COMMISSION FOR AFRICA, *Bibliography of African statistical publications*. Pp. 206, mimeo. Addis Ababa, 1962.

A bibliography of African bibliographies, covering territories south of the Sahara, has been prepared in mimeograph form as *Grey Bibliography No. 7* by the South African Public Library, Cape Town, 1963. Another bibliography of bibliographies, covering the whole of Africa, has been prepared in limited numbers, mimeographed, by the African Studies Centre in Cambridge.

Le Centre d'Analyse et de Recherche documentaires pour l'Afrique Noire (CARDAN) issues bibliographical publications. Since 1965 CARDAN has been publishing cards with abstracts of periodical articles and other works on Africa covering about 800 periodicals, as well as books, theses, government documents, conference proceedings and cyclostyled material, in English and all European languages. The African Studies Centre, Cambridge, maintains a comprehensive bibliography in card form, classified according to author, subject and region.

General

LORD HAILEY, *African Survey, revised 1956*. London, 1957.

WORTHINGTON, E. B. *Science in the development of Africa*. London, 1956.

KIMBLE, G. H. T. *Tropical Africa*, 2 vols. New York, 1962.

WOLSTENHOLME, G., and O'CONNOR, M. (eds.). *Man and Africa*. London, 1965.

THOMAS, M. F., and WHITTINGTON, G. W. (eds.). *Environment and land use in Africa*. Pp. 554. London, 1969.

HODDER, B. W., and HARRIS, D. R. (eds.). *Africa in transition*. Pp. 364. London, 1967.

PROTHERO, R. M. (ed.). *A geography of Africa*. Pp. 480. London, 1969.

HUNTER, G. *The new societies of tropical Africa*. London, 1962.

ROBINSON, E. A. G. (ed.). *Economic development of Africa south of the Sahara*. London, 1964.

1. *The Physical Environment*

HAUGHTON, S. M. *The stratigraphic history of Africa south of the Sahara*. Edinburgh, 1963.

DE KUN, N. A. *The mineral resources of Africa*. Amsterdam, 1965.

KING, L. C. *South African Scenery*, 3rd ed. revised. Pp. 308. New York, 1963.

FLINT, R. F. 'On the basis of Pleistocene correlation in East Africa', *Geol. Mag.* 96, 1959, pp. 265-84.

BARGMAN, D. J. (ed.). *Tropical meteorology in Africa*. Pp. 446. Switzerland, 1965.

THOMPSON, B. W. *The climate of Africa*. O.U.P., Nairobi, 1965. 132 pages of maps and 22 pages of text.

RODIER, J. *Bibliography of African hydrology*. Pp. 166. UNESCO, Paris, 1963.

PEREIRA, H. C., *et al.* 'Special issue on land-use hydrology experiments', *E. Afri. agric. for. J.*, 27, 1962, pp. 1-131.

HURST, H. E. *The Nile*. London, 1952.

NEDECO, *River studies and recommendations on improvements of Niger and Benue*. Amsterdam, 1959.

WARREN, W., and RUBIN, N. (eds.). *Dams in Africa*. London, 1968.

2. *Vegetation, Soils, Fauna, Pests, and Diseases*

KEAY, R. W. J. *Vegetation map of Africa south of the Sahara*. 1959.

RATTRAY, J. M. *The grass cover of Africa*. F.A.O. Agricultural Studies No. 49. Rome, 1960.

RICHARDS, P. W. *The tropical rain forest, an ecological study*. Pp. 450. Cambridge, 1952.

UNESCO. 'Humid tropics research', *Tropical soils and vegetation*. Proceedings of the Abidjan Symposium of 1959. Paris, 1961.

MAIGNIEN, R. *Review of research on laterites*. UNESCO, 1966.

MOSS, R. (ed.). *The soil resources of tropical Africa*. London, 1968.

LINNEAN SOCIETY. 'A discussion on the distribution of plants and animals in Africa', *Proc. Linn. Soc. London*, 165, 1954, 25-75.

WORTHINGTON, E. B. *The wild resources of east and central Africa*. Colonial No. 352. Pp. 26. H.M.S.O., 1961.

SKAIFE, S. H. *African insect life*. Pp. 387. Cape Town, 1953.

MOREAU, R. E. *The bird faunas of Africa and its islands*. London, 1966.

BUXTON, P. A. *The natural history of tsetse flies: an account of the biology of the genus Glossina (Diptera)*. Pp. 816. London, 1955.

PROTHERO, R. M. *Migrants and malaria*. Pp. 142. London, 1965.

DAVIS, D. H. S. (ed.). *Ecological Studies in southern Africa*. Pp. 415. The Hague, 1964.

3. *The People*

MURDOCK, G. P. *Africa: its people and their culture history*. New York, 1959.

OTTENBURGH, S. and P. (eds.). *Cultures and societies of Africa*. New York, 1960.

GREENBERG, J. H. *The languages of Africa*. Bloomington, Indiana, Research Centre in Anthropology, Folklore and Linguistics, 1963.

SPENCER, J. (ed.). *Language in Africa*: papers of the Leverhulme Conference on Universities and the language problems of tropical Africa, held at the University College, Ibadan. Pp. 167. London, 1963.

LORIMER, F. *Demographic information on tropical Africa*. Pp. 207. Boston, 1961.

BARBOUR, K. M., and PROTHERO, R. M. (eds.). *Essays on African Population*. Pp. 336. London, 1961.

BRASS, W. *et al*. *The demography of tropical Africa*. Pp. 540. Princeton, 1968.

CALDWELL, J., and OKONJO, C. (eds.). *The population of tropical Africa*. Pp. 457. London, 1968.

BASCOM, W. R., and HERSKOVITS (eds.). *Continuity and change in African cultures*. Pp. 308. Chicago, 1959.

SOUTHALL, A. *Social change in modern Africa*: studies presented at the first International African Seminar, Makerere College, Kampala, 1959. Publ. for International African Institute. London, 1961.

GROVES, C. P. *The planting of Christianity in Africa*, 4 vols. London, 1948–58.

BAËTA, C. G. *Christianity in tropical Africa*. Pp. 449. London, 1968.

LEWIS, I. (ed.). *Islam in tropical Africa*. London, 1966.

MINER, H. *The city in modern Africa*. Pp. 364. London, 1967.

4. *Traditional Herding, Farming, and Fishing*

ALLAN, W. *The African husbandman*. Pp. 505. Edinburgh, 1965.

BIEBUYCK, D. (ed.). *African Agrarian systems*: studies presented and discussed at the Second International African Seminar. Lovanium University, Léopoldville, January 1960. Pp. 407. London, 1963.

BOHANNAN, P., and DALTON, G. (eds.). *Markets in Africa*. Pp. 762. Evanston, Illinois, 1962.

CHURCH, B. M. 'Some methods for livestock survey work in Africa', *Agricultural Economics Bulletin for Africa*, No. 2, 1963, pp. 27–44.

DESHLER, W. 'Cattle in Africa: distribution, types and problems', *Geographical Review*, 53, 1963, pp. 52–58.

JOHNSTONE, B. F. *The staple food economies of western tropical Africa*. Pp. 305. Stanford, 1958.

JONES, W. O. 'The food and agricultural economies of tropical Africa: a summary view', *Food Research Institute Studies*, vol. 2, no. 1, 1961. Pp. 20.

GULLIVER, P. H. *The family herds*. London, 1955. This is concerned with the Jie and Turkana in Kenya and Uganda.

HARRISON, A. C. *Fresh-water fish and fishing in Africa*. Johannesburg, 1963.

HICKLING, C. F. *Tropical inland fisheries*. London, 1961.

MORGAN, R. *World sea fisheries*. London, 1956.

MURDOCK, G. P. 'Staple subsistence crops of Africa', *Geographical Review*, 50, 1960, pp. 523–40.

PHILLIPS, J. *The development of agriculture and forestry in the tropics: patterns, problems and promise*. London, 1961.

SCHLIPPE, P. DE. *Shifting agriculture in Africa: the Zande system of agriculture*. Pp. 336. London, 1956. South-west Sudan Republic.

STENNING, D. J. *Savannah nomads*. London, 1959. This is an anthropologist's study of Fulani pastoralists in Northern Nigeria.

TRAPNELL, C. G., and CLOTHIER, J. N. *The soils, vegetation, and agricultural systems of north-western Rhodesia: report of the Ecological Survey*. Lusaka, 1937. Reprinted 1959.

—— *The soils, vegetation and agriculture of north-eastern Rhodesia: report of the Ecological Survey*. Lusaka, 1943. Reprinted 1959.

UNFAO. *The possibilities of African rural development in relation to economic and social growth*. Pp. 235. Rome, 1962.

UNFAO. *African agricultural development. Reflections on the major lines of advance and the barriers to progress*. Pp. 243. New York, 1966.

DE WILDE, J. C. *et al*. *Experiences with agricultural development in tropical Africa*, Vol. I, *Synthesis*; Vol. II, *Case studies*. International Bank for Reconstruction and Development, Baltimore, 1967.

5. *African Prehistory and History*

HOWELL, C., and BOURLIÈRE (eds.). *African ecology and human evolution*. Pp. 400. London, 1964.

BISHOP, W. W., and CLARK, J. D. (eds.). *Background to evolution in Africa*. Pp. 935. Chicago, 1967.

DAVIDSON, B. *Old Africa rediscovered*. Pp. 287. London, 1959.

—— *The African past: Chronicles from antiquity to modern times*. London, 1965.

OLIVER, R. A., and FAGE, J. D. *A short history of Africa*, 2 vols. London, 1962.

WIEDNER, D. L. *A history of Africa south of the Sahara*. Pp. 578. New York, 1964.

BOVILL, E. W. *The golden trade of the Moors*. Pp. 281. London, 1958.

ROBINSON, R., GALLAGHER, J., and DENNY, A. *Africa and the Victorians; the official mind of Imperialism*. Pp. 491. London, 1961.

COHEN, SIR ANDREW. *British colonial policy in changing Africa*. Pp. 118. London, 1959.

FAGE, J. D. *An atlas of African history*. London, 1963. Pp. 64.

HAZELWOOD, A. *African integration and disintegration: case studies in economic and political union*. Pp. 414. London, 1967.

HATCH, J. *A history of postwar Africa*. Pp. 432. London, 1967. See the *Journal of African History*, London, published quarterly.

6. *The Sudan Republic*

HILL, R. L. *Bibliography of the Anglo-Egyptian Sudan*. 1939.

NASRI, ABDUL RAHMAN EL. *A bibliography of the Sudan 1938–1959*. Pp. 171. London, 1963.

BARBOUR, K. M. *The Republic of the Sudan: a regional geography*. Pp. 292. London, 1961.

HOLT, P. M. *A modern history of the Sudan from the Funj Sultanate to the present day.* Pp. 242. London, 1961.

TOTHILL, J. D. (ed.). *Agriculture in the Sudan.* Pp. 974. London, 1948.

—— 'Population growth and manpower in the Sudan. A joint study by the United Nations and the government of the Sudan', *Population studies No. 37.* United Nations. New York, 1964.

TRIMINGHAM, J. S. *Islam in the Sudan.* London, 1949.

GAITSKELL, A. *Gezira: a story of development in the Sudan.* London, 1959.

LEBON, J. H. G. *Land use in Sudan, World Land Use Survey, Regional Monograph*, No. 4. Bude, 1965.

—— and ROBERTSON, V. C. 'The Jebel Marra, Darfur and its region'. *Geogr. Jour.* 1961, pp. 30–49.

HAMDAN, G. 'The growth and functional structure of Khartoum'. *Geogr. Review*, 1960, pp. 21–40.

Sudan Notes and Records, Khartoum, a periodical, is a very valuable source of information.

7. The Southern Sahara and its Borderlands

BLAUDIN DE THÉ, B. M. S. *Essais de bibliographie du Sahara français et des régions avoisinantes.* Paris, 1960.

CAPOT-REY, R. *Le Sahara français.* Pp. 564. Paris, 1953. A very comprehensive volume with an excellent bibliography.

BRIGGS, L. C. *Tribes of the Sahara.* Pp. 295. Princeton, 1960.

WILLARD, J. *The Great Sahara.* London, 1964.

HESSELTINE, N. *From Libyan sands to Chad.* Pp. 208. London, 1960.

LE ROUVREUR, A. *Sahariens et Sahéliens du Tchad.* Pp. 468. Paris, 1962.

BONARELI, P. *La République du Niger, naissance d'un État.* Paris, 1960.

BRASSEUR, P. *Bibliographie générale du Mali.* IFAN, Dakar, 1964.

PORGES, L. *Éléments de bibliographie sénégalaise, 1959–63.* Pp. 141. Dakar: Archives Nationales — Centre de documentation.

DESCHAMPS, H. *Le Sénégal et la Gambie.* Pp. 125. Paris, 1964.

BOUTILLIER, J. L., and others. *La Moyenne Vallée du Sénégal* (étude socio-économique). Pp. 368. Paris, 1962.

GAMBLE, D. P. *Bibliography of the Gambia.* London, 1958.

WOOLF, B. S. (Lady Southorn). *The Gambia.* London, 1952.

HASWELL, M. R. *The changing pattern of economic activity in a Gambian village.* H.M.S.O., 1963.

8. West Africa

RYDINGS, H. A. *The bibliographies of west Africa.* Pp. 36. Ibadan, 1961.

JOUCLA, E. A. *Une Bibliographie de l'Afrique-Occidentale française.* Paris, 1937.

HARRISON CHURCH, R. J. *West Africa: a study of the environment and man's use of it.* 5th edition. London, 1967.

MORGAN, W., and PUGH, J. *West Africa.* Pp. 687. London, 1969.

RICHARD-MOLARD, J. *Afrique-Occidentale française.* Paris, 1956.

THOMPSON, V., and ADLOFF, R. *French West Africa.* Pp. 626. London, 1956.

JOHNSTON, B. F. *The staple food economies of western tropical Africa.* Stanford, 1958.

KUPER, H. (ed.). *Urbanization and migration in West Africa.* Pp. 227. London, 1967.

Les Guides Bleus, Afrique de l'Ouest; les republiques d'expression française. Pp. 542. Paris, 1958.

The weekly journal *West Africa* presents a news digest and a variety of biographical, economic, and other articles mainly on English-speaking west Africa.

JARRETT, H. R. *A geography of Sierra Leone and Gambia.* London, 1961.

PORTER, A. T. *Creoldom: a study of the development of Freetown society.* Pp. 151. London, 1963.

Atlas of Sierra Leone. Freetown, 1953.

Articles in *Sierra Leone Studies*; Bulletin of the Sierra Leone Geographical Society.

MARINELLI, L. A. *The New Liberia; a historical and political survey.* London, 1965.

CLOWER, R. W., et al. *Growth without development: an economic survey of Liberia.* Evanston, Illinois, 1966.

FRAENKEL, M. *Tribe and class in Monrovia.* Pp. 256. London, 1964.

TEIXEIRA DA MOTA, A. *Guiné Portuguesa*, 2 vols. Lisbon, 1954.

Essai d'une bibliographie sur la Côte-d'Ivoire. Pp. 122. Organisation de Co-opération et de Développement, Paris, 1964.

JOHNSON, A. F. *A bibliography of Ghana 1930–1961.* Pp. 210. London, 1964.

DICKSON, K. *A historical geography of Ghana.* London, 1969.

BOATENG, E. A. *A geography of Ghana.* Pp. 205. London, 1959.

HILTON, T. E. *Ghana population Atlas: the distribution of population in the Gold Coast and Togoland under United Kingdom Trusteeship.* London, 1960.

HILL, P. *Migrant cocoa farmers of southern Ghana.* Pp. 320. London, 1963.

WILLS, J. B. (ed.). *Agriculture and land use in Ghana.* Pp. 503. London, 1962.

LA ANYARE, *Ghana agriculture. Its economic development from early times to the middle of the twentieth century.* London, 1963.

MANSHARD, W. *Die geographischen Grundlagen der Wirtschaft Ghanas.* Wiesbaden, 1961.

GÉRARDIN, B. 'Le développement de la Haute-Volta', *Cahiers de l'Institut de science économique appliquée.* Supplement No. 142. Pp. 207. 1963.

HARRIS, J. *Books about Nigeria: a select reading list*, 3rd edition. Ibadan, 1962.

BUCHANAN, K. M., and PUGH, J. C. *Land and People in Nigeria.* Pp. 242. London, 1961.

FORDE, D., and SCOTT, R. *The native economies of Nigeria.* London, 1946.

HODGKIN, T. *Nigerian perspectives.* Pp. 362. London, 1960.

KIRK-GREENE, A. H. M. *Barth's travels in Nigeria.* Pp. 300. London, 1962. Edited selections from Heinrich Barth's account of his travels in the western Sudan in the mid-nineteenth century.

BAUER, P. T. *West African trade.* Cambridge, 1954.

MABOGUNJE, A. *Urbanization in Nigeria.* London, 1968.

MARRIS, P. *Family and social change in an African city.* Pp. 180. London, 1961. Lagos and its slum-clearance programme.

FLOYD, B. *Eastern Nigeria: a geographical review.* London, 1969.

STAPLETON, G. B. *The wealth of Nigeria.* Pp. 264. London, 1967.

The following journals are mainly devoted to Nigeria:
Farm and Forest, The Nigerian Field, The Nigerian Geographical Journal.

9. The Congo Basin and Cameroon

HEYSE, T. *Documentation générale sur le Congo et le Ruanda-Urundi* (1955–8), *Bibliographia Belgica*, 39. Brussels, 1958.

ACADÉMIE ROYALE DES SCIENCES D'OUTRE-MER. *Livre blanc*, 3 vols. Brussels, 1963.

BELGIAN CONGO AND RUANDA-URUNDI INFORMATION AND PUB-
LIC RELATIONS OFFICE. *Belgian Congo*, 2 vols. Brussels,
Inforcongo, 1960.
ROBERT, M. *Le Congo physique*, 3rd edition revised. Liège, 1946.
BÉZY, F. *Problèmes structurels et l'économie congolaise.* Louvain,
1957.
MIRACLE, M. *Agriculture in the Congo basin: tradition and change
in African rural economies.* Madison, Wisconsin, 1967.
ENCYCLOPÉDIE ET L'UNION FRANÇAISE, *L'Encyclopédie coloniale
et maritime: Afrique française.* Paris, 1950.
DELAVIGNETTE. *French Equatorial Africa.* Pp. 126. Paris, 1957.
Afrique centrale, les republiques d'expression française. *Les Guides
Bleus.* Pp. 533. Paris, 1962.
THOMPSON, V., and ADLOFF, R. *The emerging states of French
Equatorial Africa.* Stanford, 1960.
VENNETIER, P. 'La population et l'économie du Congo', *Cahiers
d'outre-mer*, 15, 60, 1962, pp. 360-80.
KALEK, P. *Réalités oubanguiennes.* Paris, 1959.
WEINSTEIN, B. 'Gabon, a bibliographic essay', *Africa Newsletter*,
vol. 1, no. 4, 1963, pp. 4-9.
HILLING, D. 'The changing economy of Gabon: developments
in a new African republic', *Geography*, 48, 219, 1963, pp.
155-65.
COUSINS, N. *Doctor Schweitzer of Lamberéné.* Pp. 168. London,
1961.
MVIENA, P., and CRIAUD, J. *Géographie du Cameroun.*
Spain in equatorial Africa. Spanish Information Service. Pp. 91.
Madrid, 1964.

10. *Ethiopia and Somalia*

ABUL-HAGGAG, Y. *Physiographical aspects of northern Ethiopia.*
1960.
MOHR, P. *Geology of Ethiopia.* Mimeo. Addis Ababa, 1964.
DELANEY, A. *Ethiopia survey: a selected bibliography.* African
Bibliographic Center, Washington, 1964.
ULLENDORFF, E. *The Ethiopians: an introduction to country and
people.* London, 1965.
DORESSE, J. *Ethiopia.* (Translated from the French by E. Coult.)
London, 1959.
PANKHURST, S. *Ethiopia: a cultural history.* Pp. 747. London,
1959.
LIPSKY, G. A. *Ethiopia: its people, its society, its culture.* Pp. 376.
New Haven, 1962.
HUFFNAGEL, H. P. *Agriculture in Ethiopia.* F.A.O. Pp. 484.
Rome, 1961.
SIMOONS, F. J. *North-west Ethiopia: peoples and economy.*
Madison, 1960.
CHEESMAN, R. E. *Lake Tana and the Blue Nile.* Pp. 400. London,
1936.
Articles in the *Ethiopian Observer* and the *Ethiopian Geographical
Journal.*
INTERNATIONAL BANK. *The economy of the Trust Territory of
Somaliland.* Washington, 1957.
LEWIS, I. M. *Peoples of the Horn of Africa: Somali, Afar and
Saho.* London, 1955.
——*A pastoral democracy.* London, 1961.

11. *East Africa*

MOLNOS, M. *Sources for the study of East African cultures and
development.* East African Research Information Centre,
Circular No. 1, Nairobi, 1969.

For special aspects of the region and maps of the geology, etc., see

RUSSELL, E. W. (ed.). *The natural resources of East Africa.*
Pp. 144. Nairobi, 1962.
East Africa Royal Commission 1953-55 Report, Cmd. 9745,
H.M.S.O., London, 1955.
MARSH, Z. A., and KINGSNORTH, G. *A history of East Africa.*
Pp. 263. London, 1961.
MATHEW, A. G., and OLIVER, R. (eds.). *History of East Africa*,
vol. 1. London, 1962.
HARLOW, V., and CHILVER, E. M. (eds.). *History of East Africa*,
vol. 2. London, 1965.
HOYLE, B. S. *The seaports of East Africa.* Pp. 137. Nairobi,
1967.
O'CONNOR, A. M. *Economic geography of East Africa.* Pp. 310.
London, 1966.
TRIMINGHAM, J. S. *Islam in East Africa.* Pp. 198. Oxford, 1964.
HOLLINGSWORTH, L. W. *Asians of East Africa.* London, 1960.
Yearbook and Guide to East Africa is published annually in
London. Publication of an *East African Geographical Journal*
commenced in 1963 (Makerere).
INGRAMS, W. H. *Zanzibar, its history and its people.* London,
1931.
OMMANEY, F. D. *Isle of Cloves.* London, 1955.
MIDDLETON, J. *Land tenure in Zanzibar.* Colonial Office Research
Studies No. 33. H.M.S.O., 1961.
INTERNATIONAL BANK. *The economic development of Tanganyika.*
Pp. 548. Baltimore, 1961.
MOFFETT, J. P. (ed.). *Handbook of Tanganyika.* Dar-es-Salaam,
1958.
LESLIE, J. A. K. *A survey of Dar-es-Salaam.* Pp. 305. London,
1963.
Kilimanjaro. A collection of papers on the mountain. *Tan-
ganyika Notes and Records*, No. 64, March 1965.
Atlas of Tanganyika, Survey of Tanganyika, 1956.
A Bibliography on Kenya, East African Studies Program, Syra-
cuse University. New York, 1967.
International Bank. *The economic development of Kenya.* Balti-
more, 1963.
HUXLEY, ELSPETH. *A new earth.* New York, 1960. A number of
other books by Elspeth Huxley, some of them at least in part
autobiographical, make very good reading.
COLE, S. M. *An outline of the geology of Kenya*, London,
1950.
SOJA, E. *The geography of modernization in Kenya, a spatial
analysis of social, economic and political change.* Syracuse, 1968.
African land development in Kenya. Ministry of Agriculture.
Nairobi, 1962.
MORGAN, W. T. W. (ed.). *Nairobi: city and region.* Nairobi,
1967.
——and SHAFFER, N. M. *Population of Kenya, density and dis-
tribution*, Nairobi, 1966.
Atlas of Kenya. Survey of Kenya, 1959.
FORDE, V. C. R. *The trade of Lake Victoria.* East African Studies
No. 3. Kampala, 1955.
INTERNATIONAL BANK. *The economic development of Uganda.*
Baltimore, 1962.
TOTHILL, J. D. (ed.). *Agriculture in Uganda.* London, 1940.
RICHARDS, A. I. (ed.). *Economic development and tribal change.*
Cambridge, 1954.
WRIGLEY, C. C. *Crops and wealth in Uganda; a short agrarian
history.* East African Studies No. 12. Kampala, 1959.
MCMASTER, D. N. *A subsistence crop geography of Uganda.*
Geographical Publications Ltd., Bude, 1962.
Atlas of Uganda. Survey of Uganda, 1962.

Ruanda-Urundi. Geography, Economy I and II, and Social achievements. Four pamphlets translated from the French. Inforcongo, Brussels, 1960.

UNITED NATIONS. *The population of Ruanda-Urundi.* Population Studies No. 15. New York, 1953.

MAQUET, J. J. *The premise of inequality in Ruanda: a study of political relations in a central African Kingdom.* London, 1961.

LEURGUIN, P. *Le niveau de vie des populations rurales de Ruanda-Urundi.* Publications de l'Université Lovanium de Léopoldville, 1960.

HEIMO, M. C. 'Réflexions sur les conditions et les perspectives du développement économique au Rwanda', *Genève-Afrique*, 7, 1968, pp. 7-29.

12. *South Central Africa*

Bibliography of general works on Portuguese Africa published since 1945. *Africana Newsletter*, vol. 1, No. 3, 1963, pp. 24-28.

DUFFY, J. V. *The Portuguese in Africa.* (Penguin.) Harmondsworth, 1962. Duffy is far less favourably impressed by the Portuguese activity than F. C. C. Egerton.

EGERTON, F. C. C. *Angola in perspective.* London, 1957.

HOUK, R. J. 'Recent developments in the Portuguese Congo', *Geogr. Review*, 1958, pp. 201-21.

VAN DONGEN, I. S. 'Coffee trade, coffee regions and coffee ports in Angola', *Economic Geography*, 37, 1961, pp. 320-46.

TEIXEIRA PINTO, L. M., and MARTINS DOS SANTOS, R. 'Problems of economic development of Angola: poles and prospects', in *Economic development for Africa south of the Sahara* (E. A. G. Robinson, ed.—listed under general books).

URQUHART, A. W. *Patterns of settlement and subsistence in southwestern Angola.* National Academy of Sciences—National Research Council Publication 1096, 1963, Washington.

SPENCE, C. F. *Mozambique, East African Province of Portugal.* Pp. 147. London, 1963.

HANCE, W. A., and VAN DONGEN, I. S. 'Beira: Mozambique gateway to central Africa', *Annals of the Association of American Geographers*, 1957, pp. 307-35.

—— 'Lourenço Marques in Delagoa Bay', *Economic Geography*, 1957, pp. 237-56.

Atlas of Mozambique. Lourenço Marques, 1962.

NG'OMBE, R. M. S. *A selected bibliography of Rhodesia and Nyasaland.* Rhodes-Livingstone Institute, Lusaka, 1957.

Rhodes-Livingstone Journal: Human problems in British Central Africa and the papers and communications of the Institute contain numerous valuable articles.

BRELSFORD, W. V. (ed.). *Handbook to the Federation of Rhodesia and Nyasaland.* Pp. 803. London, 1960.

Atlas of the Federation of Rhodesia and Nyasaland. Survey Department, Salisbury.

MASON, P. *The birth of a dilemma, the conquest and settlement of Rhodesia.* London, 1959.

FLOYD, B. N. 'Changing patterns of African land use in Southern Rhodesia', *Rhodes-Livingstone Journal*, 25, pp. 20-39.

An agricultural survey of Southern Rhodesia, 2 vols. Government Printer, Salisbury, 1962.

YUDELMAN, M. *Africans on the land. Economic problems of African agricultural development in southern, central and east Africa, with special reference to Southern Rhodesia.* Pp. 352. Harvard University Press, 1964.

COLLINS, M. *Rhodesia, its natural resources and economic development.* Salisbury, 1965.

RICHARDS, A. I. *Land labour and diet in northern Rhodesia. An economic study of the Bemba tribe.* Pp. 425. Reprinted London, 1961.

KAY, G. *A social geography of Zambia.* Pp. 160. London, 1967.

DUFF, C. E. *Regional survey of the Copperbelt.* Government Printer, Lusaka, 1959.

WILLIAMS, S. *The distribution of the African population of Northern Rhodesia.* Rhodes-Livingstone Communication Paper No. 24. Lusaka, 1962.

PIKE, J. G., and RIMMINGTON, G. T. *Malawi: a geographical study.* Pp. 229. London, 1965.

Two of the contributions to Barbour and Prothero's *Essays on African population* (listed under further reading for Chapter 3) deal with this part of the continent, namely, 'Demographic features of central Africa' by J. R. H. Shaul, and 'Wage labour and African population movements in central Africa' by J. C. Mitchell.

13. *Indian Ocean Islands*

CHEVALIER, L. *Madagascar, population et ressources.* Paris, 1952.

ROBEQUAIN, C. *Madagascar et les bases dispersées de l'Union française.* Paris, 1958.

THOMPSON, V., and ADLOFF, R. *The Malagasy Republic, Madagascar today.* Pp. 504. Stanford, 1965.

STRATTON, A. *The Great Red Island: a biography of Madagascar.* London, 1965.

The physical geography of Madagascar and especially its physical relationships with southern Africa are outlined in *Southern Africa* by J. H. Wellington. (See reading for next chapter.)

Report on Mauritius, 1960. Pp. 167. H.M.S.O., 1961.

MEADE, J. E. *The economic and social structure of Mauritius.* Pp. 246. London, 1961.

TITMUSS, R., and ABEL-SMITH, B. *Social policies and population growth in Mauritius.* London, 1960.

OMMANNEY, F. D. *Shoals of Capricorn.* London, 1959. Popular book on Mauritius and the Seychelles.

BROOKFIELD, H. C. 'Problems of monoculture and diversification in a Sugar Island: Mauritius', *Economic Geography*, 1959, pp. 25-40.

—— 'Population distribution in Mauritius', *The Journal of Tropical Geography*, 1959, pp. 1-22.

BENEDICT, B. *People of the Seychelles.* Overseas Research Publication No. 14. H.M.S.O., London, 1966.

14. *South Africa*

WELLINGTON, J. H. *Southern Africa, a geographical study,* 2 vols. Pp. 528 and 283. London, 1955.

COLE, M. M. *South Africa.* London, 1961.

DE BLIJ, H. J. *Africa south.* Pp. 399. Evanston, Illinois, 1962.

ANDREWS, H. T., *et al. South Africa in the sixties.* Johannesburg, 1962.

GREEN, L. P., and FAIR, T. J. D. *Development in Africa: a study in regional analysis with special reference to southern Africa.* Pp. 203. Johannesburg, 1962.

HOUGHTON, D. H. *The South African economy.* Pp. 272. London, 1964.

—— *The Tomlinson Report. A summary of the findings and recommendations in the Tomlinson Commission report.* South African Institute of Race Relations. Pp. 76. Johannesburg, 1958.

FAIR, T. J. D., and SHAFFER, N. M. 'Population patterns and policies in South Africa, 1951-1960', *Economic Geography*, 40, 1964, pp. 261-74.

MacMillan, W. M. *Bantu, Boer and Britain: the making of the South African native problem.* Oxford, 1963.

The Transkei and the case for separate development. Pp. 31. London, 1963.

Hill, C. *Bantustans.* London, 1965.

Board, C., *et al. The Border Region, Natural Environment and Land Use in the Eastern Cape.* Pp. 238. Cape Town, 1962.

Horwitz, R. *The political economy of South Africa.* London, 1967.

Atlas of the Union of South Africa, by A. M. Talbot and W. J. Talbot.

See articles in the quarterly review, *Optima, South African Geographical Journal,* and in the *Journal for Geography.*

South West African Survey, 1967. Government Printer, Pretoria.

Wellington, J. *South West Africa and its human issues.* Oxford, 1967.

Basutoland, Bechuanaland and Swaziland. Economic Survey Mission Report, H.M.S.O., 1960.

Barker, D. *Swaziland.* H.M.S.O., London, 1965.

Holleman, J. F. (ed.). *Experiment in Swaziland.* London, 1964.

Sillery, A. *The Bechuanaland Protectorate.* London, 1952.

Schapera, I. *Native land tenure in the Bechuanaland Protectorate.* Loveday Press, 1952.

Debenham, F. *Kalahari Sands.* London, 1953.

Bechuanaland Protectorate 1961 and 1962. London, H.M.S.O., 1964.

Index

Aba, 138-9.
Abadan, 146.
Abakaliki, 136.
Abako, 151.
Abbai river (Blue Nile), 168.
Abeché, 51, 96.
Abeokuta, 132-4.
Aberdare highlands, 183, 186.
Abidjan, 76, 99, 114, 120, 122, 123, 124.
Abuna, 166.
Abyssinia, *see* Ethiopia.
Acacia albida, 88, 147.
Accra, 15, 48, 76, 113-21.
Achimota, 116.
Acholi, 193.
Acioa barteri, 59.
Adamawa, 145, 147, 161, 162, 163.
Adangbe people, 116.
Addis Ababa, 47, 166-72.
Adowa (Aduwa), 72, 78.
Afar, 166, 170, 172.
Afrikaans people and language, 43, 70, 236, 237, 251, 258.
Agadès, 98.
Agaw people, 167.
Agriculture, 16, 26, 27, 46, 52, **57-62**, 152, 153, 158, 160, 169,
    186-8, 198, 212-14, 219, 220, 231, 248, 253, 261.
Agulhas bank, 249.
Ahaggar (Hoggar), 1, 2, 93, 94.
Aïr, 2, 67, 93, 98.
Akan people, 122.
Akim Abuakwa, 115.
Akjoujt, 102.
Akosombo, 119.
Akoumapé, 126.
Aksum, *see* Axum.
Akwapim hills, 115, 116, 119.
Aldabra island, 236.
Alexander Bay, 238.
Alice, 252.
Alto Ligonha, 224, 227.
Aluminium, 111, 119, 163, 184, 251, 252.
Ambas, 168.
Amhara people and Amharic, 43, 166, 167, 168, 171, 260.
Anambra river, 139.
Anecho, 125.
Angola, 1, 5, 6, 17, 20, 39, 41, 42, 43, 46, 62, 69, 81, 149, 151,
    154, 157, 165, **204-7**, 209, 260.
Ankober, 170.
Ankobra river, 115.
Ankole, 38, 193, 196, 198.
Annobon, 165.
Ansongo, 97, 98.
Antimony, 237, 242.
Apapa, 125, 134, 135.
Apartheid, 239, 261.
Apples, 249.
Arabic, 41, 43, 64, 91, 92, 174, 260.
Arabs, 41, 62, 66, 69, 72, 73, 83, 87, 88, 90, 92, 95, 96, 145, 149,
    171-8, 183, 224, 228, 235.
Armenoid, *see* Caucasoid.
Artesian water, 7, 98, 145, 146.
Arusha, 178-80.

Asbestos, 208, 209, 214, 227, 237, 242, 254, 255, 258.
Asesewa, 121.
Ashanti, 69, 74, 75, 79, 116, 117, 121, 144.
Asians, **41**, **42**, 72, 79, 174, 176, 177, 178, 183, 188, 192, 194,
    195, 224, 228, 231, 233, 235, 239, 240, 250.
Asmara, 170-2.
Assab, 170-2.
Aswan, High Dam, 20, 21, 86, 90, 192.
Atbara river, 20, 84, 86, 90.
Awash river, 166, 172.
Awaso, 118.
Awdaw river, 59.
Awka, 22, 59, 128, 138.
Axim, 115, 120.
Axum, 72, 166, 168.

Babanusa, 90.
Bacita, 147.
Baganda (Ganda people), **193-7**.
Baggara people, **55**, 87.
Bahar Dar, 170.
Bahima (Hima people), 193, 200.
Bahr-el-Ghazal, 20, 87.
Baikie, W. B., 75.
Bajun islands, 183.
Bakiga people, 198.
Bakongo people, 149, 150, 151, 155, 160, 207.
Bakwanga, 154.
Balante people, 111.
Balfour, 241, 242.
Baluba people, 149, 155.
Baluhya people, 175.
Balunda people, 149, 155.
Bama, 132, 146.
Bamako, 65, 98, 99, 102.
Bamangwato people, 258.
Bamba, 94.
Bamenda, 55, 161, 164.
Bamiléké, 162, 164, 165.
Bamoun, 164.
Bananas, 57, 58, 60, 69, 114, 123, 160, 163, 164, 174, 180, 181,
    190, 193, 194, 195, 198, 200, 222, 228.
Bancroft, 217.
Bandama river, 122.
Bandiagara, 100.
Bangala people, 151.
Bangui, 96, 158, 159, 164.
Bankets, 242.
Bankenveld, 241-2.
Bannockburn, 226.
Bantu, 40, 41, 43, 69, 70, 71, 72, 80, 149, 174, 175, 190, 193, 204,
    228, 239, 240, 248, 252, 259.
Bantustan and Bantu Homelands, **252-3**.
Baraka wadi (Barca), 90.
Barley, 169, 181.
Baro, 79, 124.
Baro river, 171.
Barotseland, 36, 217, 218.
Basutoland (*see* Lesotho), 235, 250.
Bata, 165.
Batawana people, 258.
Batéké plateau, 160.

Bathurst, 76, 105.
Batutsi (Tutsi people), 198, 200, 201, 202.
Batwa (Twa people), 200.
Bauchi, 145, 147, 148.
Bauxite, 2, 100, 107, 110, 111, 114, 115, 118, 119, 161, 163-5, 221, 227.
Bawku, 122.
Bechuanaland (*see* Botswana), 77, 78, 208, 237.
Beira, 5, 13, 151, 154, 210, 212, 222, 224, **225**, 226.
Beja people, 90, 171.
Belgian Congo, 43, 82, 149, 155, 259.
Belgians, 41, 63, 75, 77, 80-82, 149-51, 155, 156, 160, 200, 202.
Bemba people, 219, 220.
Benguela current, 13, 62, 206, 225, 248, 254.
Benguela railway, 204, 205, 206, 207.
Benin, 68, 125, 134, 135, 136.
Benin sands, 125.
Benito river, 165.
Benniseed, 128.
Benue river, 4, 7, 11, 19, 20, 25, 37, 55, 75, 76, 79, 96, 128, 129, 130, 132, 144, 147, 148, 161.
Benue-Plateau, 148.
Berlin Conference, 76, 77.
Beryl, 224, 227, 230, 237.
Bethal, 255.
Betsiboka river, 232.
Bia river, 123.
Biafra, 82, 127, 140, 147.
Bida, 144.
Bilharzia, 38-39, 174, 226.
Bini people, *see* Edo.
Birim, 118.
Black Pod disease, 116, 134.
Blantyre-Limbe, 221, 224.
Bloemfontein, 238, 246, 252.
Blue Nile, 17, 20, **21**, 72, 83-87, 168, 170, 172.
Bo, 108.
Bobo-Dioulasso, 124.
Bodélé depression, 20, 95.
Boers, 70-72, 77, 206, 207.
Boké, 111.
Bolgatanga, 122.
Boma, 150, 152, 153.
Bomi hills, 112.
Bondoukou, 124.
Bong hills, 112.
Bongor, 96, 132.
Bonny, 136, 137.
Bonsa, 118.
Bonthé, 107, 108.
Boran people, 184.
Borku, 53, 94.
Bornu, 7, 73, 74, 96, **145-7**, 161.
Botletle river, 20.
Botswana, *see also* Bechuanaland, 11, 20, 209, **257-8**.
Bouaké, 123.
Bouali falls, 159.
Bourem, 20, 100.
Brachystegia woodland, 25, 208, 221.
Brazil, 69, 125, 135, 204.
Brazzaville, 77, 95, 96, 149, 158, 159, **160**, 161, 162, 164.
Breede river, 238, 249.
Breyton, 241, 246.
British, 41, 70, 71, 75-82, 113, 127, 150, 161, 172, 174, 176, 178, 185, 187, 188, 195, 204, 205, 207, 211, 233, 240, 255.
British South Africa Company, 207, 208, 210, 214, 258.

Broken Hill, 78, 217, 219.
Brong-Ahafo, 117, 121.
Bruce, James, 72.
Buchanan, 110, 111.
Buduma people, 96.
Buganda, 47, 73, 193, **194-8**, 202.
Bugisu, 197.
Buhaya, 200.
Bujumbura, 202, 203.
Bukavu, 203.
Bukoba, 181.
Bukuru, 130, 146, 148.
Bulawayo, 78, 212, 214, 215, 225, 226.
Bunyoro, 193, 195, 198, 200.
Burundi, 46, 80, 176, 181, 196, **200-3**.
Burutu, 96, 136.
Bushmen, **40-42**, 46, 70, 258.
Bushveld basin, 241, 242, 246.
Busoga, 197.
Bussa, 20, 73.

Cabinda, 157, 203.
Cabora Bassa, 226, 253.
Cacheu river, 111.
Cadmium, 154.
Caillié, R., 67, 100.
Calabar, 126, 136.
Calcrete, 10, 11, 27.
Camels, 54, 55, 94, 98, 100, 173, 174.
Cameroon highlands, 2, 6, 18, 23, 55, 128, 149, 163.
Cameroon, Mount, 6, 23, 161, 162.
Cameroon Republic, 14, 39, 43, 55, 65, 77, 79, 95, 96, 106, 111, **146-8**, 158.
Canaries current, 13, 62, 103.
Cape Coloured people, 40, 42, 239, 240.
Cape of Good Hope, 68, 247.
Cape Province, South Africa, 11, 23, 26, 39, 40, 63, 71, **237-40**, **246-50**, 252, 254, 258.
Cape Three Points, 113, 114.
Cape Town, 3, 42, 70, 77, 78, 237, 238, **246-50**, 257.
Cape Verde, 103, 104, 105.
Caprivi strip, 217, 253, 258.
Capsid disease, 116, 134.
Carmona, 207.
Casamance, 102.
Cashew, 183, 226.
Cassava, 57, 58, 59, 60, 69, 120, 123, 152, 160, 163, 191, 194, 195, 198, 207, 219, 221, 232.
Cattle, 38, 39, **52-56**, 60, 96, 108, 110, 111, 120, 122, 124, 130, 141, 145-7, 153, 160, 164, 165, 169, 172, 174, 178, 181, 182, 185, 186-8, 190, 191, 193, 196, 197, 198, 199, 201, 202, 206, 208, 213, 217, 220, 221-3, 232, 246, 251, 253, 255, 258.
Cattle trade, 97, 100, 106, 120-2, 124, 125, 139, 162, 194, 261.
Catumbela river, 205.
Caucasoid, 40, 41, 43, 228.
Cela, 206.
Central African Federation, *see* Federation of the Rhodesias and Nyasaland.
Central African Republic (formerly Ubangi-Shari), 60, 95, 96, 149, **158**, **159**, 161, 162.
Ceres, 246, 249.
Chad basin, 2, 4-7, 20, 26, 29, 53, 83, 144, 149.
Chad Republic, 39, 41, 53, 88, **95-96**, 106, 158, 161.
Chagga people, 180, 181.
Chaillu mountains, 157.
Chalawa river, 132.

Chamba people, 164.
Chambezi river, 20.
Changamwe, 184.
Cheesman, R. E., 166.
Cherangani hills, 188.
Chewa people, 221.
Chinese, 65, 177, 231, 235, 260.
Chipya woodland, 25.
Chiredzi, 212, 213.
Chobe river, 217, 258.
Cholo, 221, 223.
Christianity, 43-45, 64, 69-73, 83, 91, 124, 135, 138, 148, 151, 166-8, 171, 173, 175, 195, 231, 259.
Chromite, 107, 110, 208, 209, 214, 216, 237, 242.
Cinnamon, 236.
Ciskei, 253.
Citemene, 60, 219.
Cities and towns, 16, **47-49**, 132-4, 239, 240.
Citrus, 110, 183, 213, 246, 255.
Civilizados, 205.
Clay plains, 26, 29, 30, 88, 119, 130, 132, 146.
Climate, **12-16**, 167, 230, 237-8.
Climatic change, **7-10**, 13, 18, 26, 30, 104, 130, 132.
Cloves, 73, 175, **177-9**, 231.
Coal, 4, 78, 128, 138, 139, 140, 181, 208, 209, 212, 214, 215, 220, 221, 224, 226, 230, 239, 241, 245, 250, 251, 252, 255, 258, 259.
Coasts, 6, 13, 15, 106, 107, 113, 120, 175, 251.
Cobalt, 154, 219.
Cocoa, 27, 29, 46, 49, 78, 79, 106, 108, 114-19, 121, 123-7, 132, 134, 136, 137, 142, 150, 153, 158, 160, 163-5, 178, 261.
Coconuts, 175, 178, 183, 227, 235, 236.
Coffee, 24, 46, 106, 108, 110, 114, 123, 126, 150, 159, 163, 164, 165, 170, 172, 180, 181, 186, 188, 190, 193, 194, 195, 196, 197, 200, 202, 203, 207, 214, 231, 235, 261.
Columbite, 114, 128, 130, 144, 201, 203, 224, 227.
Common Market, 123, 226, 260.
Comoro Islands (Comores), 232, 235.
Conakry, 76, 99, 111.
Concessions, 225, 226.
Congo basin, 1, 2, 5, 13, 15, 23, 25, 29, 40, 41, 47, **149-61**, 204.
Congo Brazzaville, 149, 156, 157, **159-61**.
Congo Kinshasa, 41, **149-56**, 157, 160.
Congo Free State, 75-78.
Congo river, 13, **17-18**, 20, 75, 76, 95, 149, 151, 159, 175, 199.
Congo, Republic of the (*see* Congo Brazzaville), 77.
Congo Republic (*see* Congo Kinshasa, formerly Belgian Congo), 42, 46, 49, 63.
Conifers, 255.
Constantia, 248.
Copper, 78, 81, 102, 154, 155, 194, 197, 205, 207, 209, 212, 217-19, 226, 237, 242, 252, 254, 258, 259, 261.
Copperbelt (Zambia), 37, 41, 46, 48, 63, 81, 181, 204, 205, 207, 214, **217-20**.
Coptic Church, 166, 168.
Coral, 6, 175-8, 184, 228, 235.
Cotonou, 97, 113, 114, 125.
Cotton, 25, 34, 46, 51, 84-91, 96, 99, 104, 124, 128, 142, 143, 145, 147, 150, 151, 159, 161, 170, 172, 174, 181, 183, 186, 188, 190, 194-9, 213, 219, 222, 224, 225, 226, 231, 232, 261.
Creoles, 108, 191, 233, 235.
Cross river, 128, 136, 137.
Crystal mountains, 2, 156.
Cuando river, 20.
Cuanza river, 206.
Cubal, 205.
Cubango river, 20, 206.

Cunene river, 40, 206, 254.
Cyclones, *see* hurricanes.

Dagomba people, 76, 122.
Dahomey, 46, 69, 97, 119, 124, **125-6**, 156.
Dairying, 186, 213, 246, 251.
Dakar, 46, 79, 98, 99, **102-5**, 106.
Dallol, 20.
Daloh, 173.
Dambai, 207.
Danakil, 166, 170.
Danes, 113.
Dankali, *see* Danakil.
Dar-es-Salaam, 79, 175, 177, **178**, 180-2, 220.
Darfur, 53, 55, 83, 88, 95.
Date-palm, 25, 57, 61, 62, **94**.
Debenham, F., 258.
Debra-Behran, 170.
Dega, 168, 169.
Delagoa Bay, 225.
Densu river, 115, 116, 121.
Desiccation, 26, 132.
Dessye, 170.
Dhows, 183, 184, 190, 192.
Diamonds, 77, 81, 107, 109, 110, 114, 115, 118, 123, 154, 157, 159, 179, 180, 205, 207, 237, 238, 239, 242, 253, 254, 258, 259.
Dinka people, 36, 90.
Diredawa, 172.
Dixey, F., 5.
Djibouti, 77, 166, 172.
Dodoma, 182.
Dorowa, 214.
Dosso, 97.
Douala, 96, 111, 158, 159, 161-5.
Drakensberg, 5, 40, 71, 238, 242.
Dschang, 164.
Dundee, 251.
Dunes, 7, 19, 87, 94, 95, 99, 104, 131, 132, 144, 146, 174, 226.
Dunkwa, 118.
Durban, 13, 46, 71, 78, 227, 230, 238, 246, **250-2**.
Duricrusts, **10**, **11**, 29.
Dutch, 41, 69, 70, 113, 172, 224, 232, 249.

Earthquakes, 6, 113.
East Africa Community, 180.
East Africa High Commission, 176.
East London, 46, 70, 237, 238, 252.
Edea, 162, 163.
Edo people (Bini), 127, 135.
Egba people, 133.
Egypt (U.A.R.), 20, 42, 61, 64, 72, 73, 75, 77, 83, 84, 85, 86, 87, 90, 166, 174.
Eichornia crassipes, 18.
Eldoret, 188, 190.
Elephants, 9, 31, 32, 94, 111, 183, 200.
Elgeyo people, 188.
Elgin, 246, 249.
Elgon, Mount, 193, 197.
Elmina, 68, 120, 121.
El Obeid, 51, 87.
English, 43, 106, 171, 174, 190, 233, 239, 259.
Enjera, 169.
En Nahud, 87.
Ennedi, 95.
Enneri Bardagué, 95.

Ensete edule, 170.
Entebbe, 197.
Enugu, 48, 128, 138, 139, 140, 148.
Equatorial Guinea, 165.
Eritrea, 12, 78, 166, 168, 170, 171, 172.
Erosion surfaces, 5, 10, 25, 138, 194.
Eseka, 164.
Ethiopia (Abyssinia), 1, 5, 12, 34, 39, 40, 43, 45, 46, 65, 68, 69, 72, 78. 81, 82, **166-73**, 174, 176, 260.
Etosha Pan, 254.
Eucalyptus, 168, 169, 178, 206.
Evaporation, 14–16, 19, 61, 238.
Ewaso Nyiro river, 182, 183.
Ewe people, 62, 76, 120, 122, 125.

Falasha people, 162.
Fang people, 158, 165.
Farafangana, 230.
Faro river, 161.
Fashoda, 75.
Faya, 95.
Federation of the Rhodesias and Nyasaland, 82, 204, **211-12**, 224.
Fernando Po, 6, 78, 149, 165, 235.
Ferricrete, **10**, 11, 29, 36, 194.
Fezzan, 53, 95.
Fires, 25, 113.
Firestone Rubber Company, 27, 81, 107, 112.
Firki, 132, 146.
Fish and fishing, 6, 52, **62-63**, 96, 102, 103, 108, 120, 121, 123, 125, 139, 145, 146, 153, 158, 160, 182, 190, 193, 202, 203, 206, 207, 220, 222, 234, 239, 249, 254.
Food and Agricultural Organization (F.A.O.), 169.
Forest, 23–24, 57.
Fort Archambault, 96, 161.
Fort Gouroud, 101.
Fort Hare, 252.
Fort Jesus, 68, 183, 184.
Fort Lamy, 51, 95, 96, 146, 159, 161.
Fort Rosebery, 219.
Foumban, 161.
Fourah Bay College, 108, 110.
Fouta Djallon, 55, 75, 107, 110.
Frafra, 122.
Francistown, 258.
Frankincense, 173.
Freetown, 46, 70, 75, 106, **108**, 109, 110, 111, 135.
French, 43, 70, 75–81, 82, 92, 93, 95, 96, 99, **101-3**, 123, 124, 125, 144, 149, 156, 159, 160, 161, 231, 233, 234, 235, 236, 259, 260.
French Equatorial Africa, 93, 95, 149, 156, 158, 159.
French Somaliland, 166, 170, 172.
French Sudan (*see* Mali).
French West Africa, 102, 105.
Fresco, 113.
Fulani people, 51, **55-56**, 61, 74, 75, 95, 97, 100, 104, 107, 110, 111, 119, 124, 126, 127, 130, 133, 141, 142, 144, 145, 147, 158, 162, 164, 200.
Fung, 83, 90.
Funtua, 130, 142.

Ga people, 116, 122.
Gaberones, 258.
Gabon, 14, 149, **156-8**, 160, 162, 165.
Galana river, 184.
Galla people, 43, 72, 166, 170, 173, 182, 184.

Galole, 185.
Gambeila, 171.
Gambia, 75, 76, 102, 103, 104, 105.
Gambia river, 25, **105**.
Game cropping, 32, 33.
Game reserves, *see* National Parks.
Ganda people, *see* Baganda.
Ganguella people, 206.
Ganoa, 52.
Gao, 14, 20, 67, 100.
Gari, 139.
Garoua, 96, 161.
Gash delta, 90.
Gaya, 97.
Géba river, 111.
Gedaref, 89.
Geidam, 98.
Geita, 181.
Germanium, 154.
Germans, 70, 76, 77, 78, 79, 81, 125, 126, 161, 163, 176, 180, 207, 253.
Gez, 166.
Gezira, 21, 51, 83, 84–86, 99.
Ghana, *see also* Gold Coast, 3, 6, 13, 15, 18, 27, 30, 36, 43, 46, 48, 49, 65, 67, 79, 100, 106, 113, **114-22**, 123, 124, 125, 126, 134, 260.
Ghana (ancient state), 65, 66, 67, 98.
Ghanzi, 258.
Glaciation and glaciers, 3, 4, 5, 8, 9, 10.
Glossina, *see* trypanosomiasis.
Goats and sheep, 53, 60, 94, 108, 120, 124, 141, 146, 153, 173, 174, 202, 207.
Goba, 255.
Gobir, 142.
Gojjam, 167, 168.
Gold, 2, 77, 78, 79, 81, 98, 100, 107, 110, 114, 115, 118, 123, 154, 157, 179, 190, 201, 203, 207, 208, 209, 211, 214, 224, 226, 227, 237, 238, 239, 240, **241-4**, 253, 258, 259.
Gold Coast, *see also* Ghana, 65, 69, 75–80, 82, 113, 116, 122.
Gombe, 147, 148.
Gondar, 170.
Gondwanaland, 4, 5, 6, 228.
Gongola river, 129, 130, 147.
Gonya falls, 217.
Gowon, 127.
Grand Bassam, 123.
Grand-Lahou, 123.
Grand Popo, 125.
Graphite, 230.
Grasslands, 25, 26, 94, 128, 164, 173, 185, 194, 199, 230.
Great Berg river, 248, 249.
Great Dyke, 208.
Great Fish river, 70, 237, 238.
Groundnut Scheme, 180.
Groundnuts (peanuts), 25, 29, 46, 60, 69, 78, 79, 87, 91, 95, 97, 102–5, 111, 122, 124, 128, 130, 141, 145, 146, 160, 161, 190, 197, 219, 221, 226, 261.
Ground-water, *see also* Artesian water, 15, 16, 61, 220, 238, 242.
Guban plain, 173.
Guinea, Republic of, 76, 82, 98, 99, 100, 101, 106, 107, **110-11**, 123, 260.
Guinea-worm, 38.
Gulara River reserve, 32.
Gulf of Aden, 5, 166, 173.
Gulf of Guinea, 2, 6, 15, 17, 46, 62, 76, 78, 106, 113–41, 261.
Gum arabic, 25, 84, 87, 91, 98, 102.

Guraje people, 170.
Gurma, 126.
Gusau, 143, 145.
Gwari people, 143.
Gwelo, 216.

Haartz river, 246.
Hadj Omar, 75, 76.
Hamitic, 40, 41, 43, 166, 167, 175, 259.
Harar, 170, 172, 173.
Harbel, 112.
Harbours and ports, 6, 78, 79, 113, 120, 125, 134, 180, 250.
Haud, 173.
Hausa people, 40, 43, 51, 53, 56, 60, 74, 97, 126, 127, 141, 142, 144, 147, 260.
Hausaland, 46, 67, 75, 87, 95, 144.
Hermanus, 249.
Hex river, 249.
Hides and skins, 46, 102, 161, 172, 174, 251, 253, 258.
Highveld, 207-10, 212, 217, 241, 242, 245, 246.
Hill, P., 115.
Hima people, *see* Bahima.
Hippo, 212, 213.
Hookworm, 38.
Hopetown, 77.
Horn of Africa, 13, 34, 37, 166, 173, 174.
Hottentots, 31, 40, 41, 42, 53, 70.
Hova people (Merinas), 231.
Huila province, 206.
Humidity, 14, 15.
Hunter, J. M., 116.
Hurricanes, 14, 177, 230.
Hutu people, 200, 201, 202.
Huxley, Elspeth, 190.
Huza settlements, 116, 121.
Hydro-electricity, 17, 111, 123, 130, 145, 148, 150, 154, 160, 163, 170, 182, 189, 192, 193, 197, 203, 206, 211, 212, 217, 219, 220, 224, 226, 237, 238, 254.

Ibadan, 47, 132, 133, 134, 145, 148.
Ibibio people, 126.
Ibo people, 57, 59, 126, 127, 135, **136-40**, 148.
Iboland, 127, 136, 140.
Idah, 140.
Idoma, 126, 148.
Iforas, 100.
Igbo, 69.
Ijaw, 126, 127.
Ikom, 136.
Ikot-Ekpene, 126, 136.
Ile-Ife, 134.
Ilorin, 126, 132, 134, 148.
Imperial British East Africa Company, 77.
Incomati river, 226.
Independence, political, 80, 81, 82, 155, 188, 201, 207, 260.
Indian Ocean, 14, 40, 65, 68, 175, 177, 228-36, 248, 250.
Indians, *see* Asians.
Indonesia, 40, 41, 42, 175, 178.
Industry, 51, 91, 118, 123, 134, 135, 136, 138, 142, 143, 148, 163, 172, 178, 180, 184, 190, 197, 198, 203, 211, 214-16, 220, 234, 238, 239, 243, 244, 249, 250, 251, 252, 253, 259, 260.
Inhambane, 226.
Inselbergs, 2, 10, 11, 29, 109, 119, 127.
Inter-tropical convergence, discontinuity, or front, 12, 13, 14, 34, 113.

Iringa, 181.
Iron and steel industry, 112, 119, 140, 148, 197, 215, 216, 245, 251.
Iron ore, 2, 10, 11, 93, 101, 102, 107, 109, 110-14, 128, 140, 157, 164, 179, 181, 205, 207, 209, 215, 239, 241, 242, 245, 251, 254, 255, 261.
Ironsi, 127.
Irrigation, 16, 20, 21, 61, 84-91, 99, 104, 120-2, 143, 145-8, 172, 174, 182, 185, 189, 190, 205, 206, 212, 213, 219, 220, 226, 234, 237, 238, 242, 246, 249, 252, 255, 261.
Isioli, 176.
Islam (Muslims), 43, 44, 45, 50, 51, 64, 66, 68, 72, 73, 74, 83, 84, 91, 92, 110, 124, 126, 141, 144, 147, 161, 166, 171, 173, 175, 177, 178, 235, 259.
Issa, 166, 172.
Italians, 72, 78, 81, 82, 84, 171, 172, 174.
Itsekiri people, 127.
Ituri, 153, 200.
Ivory Coast, 27, 75, 100, 106, 113, 114, 122-4, 125, 128.
Iwo, 134.

Jadotville, 154.
Japanese, 207, 216, 251.
Jebba, 20, 79, 130, 145, 147.
Jebel Aulia dam, 20, 87.
Jebel Marra, 1, 18, 65, 83, 87, 88, 89.
Jie people, 54, 55.
Jimma, 170, 172.
Jinja, 193, 197, 200.
Johannesburg, 46, 48, 212, 238, 239, 240, 241, **242**, 248, 249, 250, 255.
Johnston, Sir Harry, 221.
Jonglei, 21, 90.
Jos, 130, 146, 148.
Jos plateau, 25, 49, 55, 79, 127, 129, 130, 147, 148.
Juba, 84, 90.
Juba river, 173, 174.
Jukun people, 130, 148.

Kabaka, 195, 196.
Kabré people, 126.
Kade, 116.
Kaduna, 143, 144, 145, 148.
Kaduna river, 130, 144.
Kafanchan, 148.
Kaffa, 172.
Kafue river, 22, 211, 217, 220.
Kagera river, 200.
Kainji, 97, 130, 144, 145, 148.
Kakamega, 190.
Kalahari, 2, 5, 7, 11, 20, 21, 40, 46, 60, 204, 237, **257-8**.
Kalahari Sands, 209, 254.
Kamba people, 185, 188.
Kampala, 47, 48, 176, 181, 190, 191, 193, 195, **197**, 198.
Kanem, 95, 96, 161.
Kankan, 99.
Kano, 37, 51, 61, 74, 79, 97, 98, 130, 132, 141-8.
Kanuri people, 51, 96, 126, 145.
Kanye, 258.
Kaolack, 104, 105.
Karakul sheep, 254.
Karasimbi mountain, 200.
Kariba dam, 18, 20, 204, 208, **211**, **212**, 214, 216, 217, 220.
Karroo, 26, 246.
Karroo system of rocks, 4, 5, 149, 208, 241-3, 250.
Kasai, 149, 153, 154, 155, 205.

Kasese, 198, 200.

Kassala, 51, 90.

Kasteelberg, 248.

Katanga, 46, 50, 77, 78, 79, 81, 102, 149-55, 205, 217, 259.

Katiola, 123.

Katsina, 53, 142, 143.

Kavirondo Gulf, 190.

Kayes, 94, 98.

Kayes-Jacob, 161.

Kedia d'Idjil, 101.

Kenya, 5, 13, 32, 34, 35, 41, 42, 49, 54, 65, 79, 81, 82, 174, 175-6, **182-90**, 197.

Kenya highlands, 175, 176, 182, 183, **185-90**.

Keta, 120, 125.

Khartoum, 20, 51, 64, **83-87**, 90, 91.

Khashm el Girba, 20, 86, 90.

Khoisan, 40.

Khor Abu Habl, 87, 88.

Kigali, 202, 203.

Kigezi, 65, 193, **197, 198**.

Kigoma, 79, 181.

Kikuyu people, 175, 185-90.

Kildonan, 216.

Kilembe, 197, 198.

Kilimanjaro, Mount, 9, 26, 73, 79, 178, 180, 182.

Kilindini, 184.

Kilombero river, 182.

Kilo-Moto, 154.

Kimberley, 77, 78, 238, 239, 243, 249, 252, 258.

King, L. C., 5.

Kinshasa (*see also* Léopoldville), **149-53**, 154, 160.

Kinship, 43, 44.

Kipushi, 154.

Kisangani, 151, 153.

Kismayu, 174.

Kisumu, 79, 190, 193.

Kitale, 46, 189.

Kitwe, 218, 220.

Kivu, 153, 154.

Klerksdorp, 241, 243.

Koforidua, 116, 121.

Koka dam, 172.

Kola, 24, 46, 123, 127, 132, 134.

Kolwezi, 154.

Komati river, 255.

Kongwa, 181, 182.

Konkouré, 111.

Kordofan, 55, 83, 87.

Kosti, 55, 84, 87.

Koudougou, 124.

Kouilou dam, 157, 160.

Koulikoro, 98.

Kouroussa, 98.

Kribi, 164.

Krobo people, 115, 119, 121.

Kruger National Park, 242.

Kufra, 53.

Kumasi, 47, 79, 115, 116, 118, 120-2, 124, 125.

Kumba, 163.

Kumbi Saleh, 65, 67.

Kuntaur, 105.

Kwahu plateau, 121.

Kwango, 205.

Kwara, 147-8.

Kwolla, 168.

Labour migration, *see* migrant labour.

Ladysmith, 246, 251.

Lagoons, 6, 113, 120, 121, 122, 123, 125, 127, 230.

Lagos, 6, 23, 25, 75, 79, 125, 126, 127, **132-6**, 138, 141, 143, 145, 148.

Lake Alaotra, 232.

   Albert, 18, 72, 193.

   Bangweulu, 20, 63, 217.

   Baringo, 190.

   Bosumtwi, 113.

   Chad, 1, 7, 19, 20, 55, 63, 73, 75, 76, 77, 89, **94-98**, 119, 130, 132, 144, 145, 146, 147, 161, 162.

   Chilwa, 222.

   Edward, 5, 198.

   Faguibune, 100.

   George, 62, 193, 222.

   Iyiocha, 59.

   Kitangiri, 182.

   Kivu, 62, 63, 153, 200, 203.

   Kyoga, 192-4.

   Leopold II, 149.

   Magadi, 185.

   Malawi (Nyasa), 5, 39, 77, 181, 217, 220-4.

   Manyara, 178.

   Mweru, 18, 33, 62.

   Naivasha, 62, 186, 189.

   Nakuru, 186, 189, 190.

   Ngami, 20, 217.

   Rudolf, 5, 54, 166, 184.

   Rukwa, 33, 63.

   Tana, 69, 84, 167, 168, 170-2.

   Tanganyika, 5, 33, 63, 73, 79, 200, 202, 203, 220, 223.

   Tumba, 149.

   Victoria, 2, 18, 36, 41, 46, 48, 64, 75, 77, 79, 175, 180, 181, 182, **190-3**, 197, 200, 223, 261.

Lakes, 7, 9, 14, 15, **16-22**, 99, 191, 192, 221.

Lama-Kara, 126.

Lamu, 183.

Land tenure, 178, 187, 188, 191, 196, 202.

Langa, 248.

Language, **43**, 44, 171, 259.

Lasta, 167.

Laterite and lateritic soils, 11, 29, 111, 132, 140, 142.

Lawra, 122.

Lead, 78, 128, 179, 209, 217, 219, 254.

Leakey, L. S. B., 64.

Lealui, 217.

Lebombo hills and monocline, 250, 254, 255.

Legon (University of Ghana), 116, 118.

Lengo, 38.

Leo Africanus, 100.

Leopold II, 75, 76, 78, 149.

Léopoldville (*also see* Kinshasa), 78, 79, 155, 159, 160.

Lesotho (Basutoland), 4, 16, 237, 238, **255-7**, 260.

Liberia, 27, 70, 81, 106, 107, 110, **112-13**, 123, 150.

Libreville, **156-8**.

Lilongwe, 221, 253.

Limba timber, 160.

Limpopo river, 2, 71, 77, 207, 208, 209, 217, 225, 226, 237, 238, 242, 257.

Lindi, 180.

Linyanti channel, 20.

Litunga, 217.

Livingstone, David, 73, 75, 77, 210, 221.

Livingstone (Zambia), 220.

Liwonde, 224.

Lobatsi, 258.
Lobé river, 164.
Lobengula, 207.
Lobito, 151, 154, 155, 204-6.
Locusts, **33-34**, 173, 179, 210.
Logoné river, 18, 96, 132, 161.
Lokoja, 75, 140, 148.
Loma mountains, 107.
Lomé, 76, 114, 125.
Lorian swamp, 183.
Los islands, 111.
Loudima, 157.
Lourenço Marques, 78, 204, 212, 216, 224, **225**, 226, 227, 239, 241, 242, 248, 250, 254.
Lower-Buchanan, 112.
Lowveld, 208, 209, 212, 213, 241, 255.
Lualaba river, 20, 75, 155.
Luanda, 204, 207.
Luangwa river, 5, 208, 217, 220.
Luanshya, 218.
Luapula river, 20.
Lubilash river, 154.
Lubumbashi, 154.
Lufira river, 154.
Lukuga river, 223.
Luo people, 175, 190, 191.
Lusaka, 212, 220.
Luvera river, 20.

Macina, 34, 99.
Madagascar, 6, 14, 23, 40, 77, 158, **228-32**, 233, 235.
Mafeking, 241, 258.
Mahalapye, 258.
Mahdists, 73, 77, 83, 84, 170.
Mahé, 235, 236.
Maiduguri, 96, 132, 145, 146, 148, 161.
Mailo estates, 196.
Maize, 55, 57, 58, 60, 69, 87, 106, 122, 123, 169, 173, 180, 181, 186, 190, 191, 195, 207, 212, 213, 214, 219, 220, 221, 226, 241, 242, 245, 252, 253, 258.
Majabat al-Koubra, 100.
Makarikari depression, 20, 217.
Makerere University College, 197.
Makoba people, 258.
Malagarasi swamps, 63.
Malagasy Republic, *see* Madagascar.
Malakal, 21, 90, 91.
Malanje, 207.
Malaria, **36**, 37, 75, 174, 209, 226, 232, 233, 259.
Malawi (formerly Nyasaland), **46**, 50, 181, 204, 209, 211, 216, **220-4**, 253.
Mali (ancient state), 66, 67, 68, 98.
Mali Republic (formerly French Sudan), 67, 76, 97, **98-101**, 105, 106, 120-4, 260.
Malinké people, 110, 111, 124.
Malmesbury, 248.
Mamfe, 163.
Mamu river, 59.
Managil, 85.
Mandara mountains, 147, 161.
Mandates, 79.
Mandingo people, 67, 76, 100, 111, 124.
Manganese, 2, 114, 118, 123, 154, 157, 160, 205, 209, 219, 237, 258.
Mangoky river, 231.
Mangroves, 23, 105, 109, 111, 127, 175.

Mano river, 171.
Mantap, 161.
Manzini, 254.
Maquela do Zombo, 207.
Maradi, 97, 149.
Marampa, 109.
Marble, 252.
Mareb river, 171.
Markets, 79, 169, 186, 195.
Maroua, 161, 162.
Marquesia woodland, 25.
Marsabit, 184.
Masai people, 49, 175, 184, 185, 200.
Masakwa, 146.
Mashaba, 214.
Mashona people, 207, 210.
Mason, Philip, 210.
Massawa, 169, 170, 171, 172.
Massina, 75.
Matabele people, 77, 207, 210.
Matadi, 17, 78, 149, 152, 205.
Matala, 206.
Matezo people, 181.
Mau-Mau, 82, 187, 188.
Maun, 258.
Mauretania, 100, **101**, **102**, 106.
Mauritius, 6, 14, 37, **232-4**, 235.
Mayumbe, 57, 159.
Mazbuka, 220.
Mbabane, 254, 255.
Mbandaka, 151, 153.
Mboshi people, 159.
Meerschaum, 180.
Mekambo, 157, 158.
Mende people, 57, 108.
Menelik, 166, 170.
Menengai, 190.
Merina people, *see* Hovas.
Meru, 79.
Meru, Mount, 178, 182, 186.
Meröe, 64.
Methane, 203.
Mfumbiro mountains, *see* Virunga.
Midjurtein, 173.
Migrant labour, **49-51**, 95-96, 99, 100, 111, 125, 138, 144, 148, 151, 155, 163, 173, 178, 191, 196, 202, 221, 224, 227, 240, 244, 250, 255, 258.
Milanje, 227.
Milingué, 157.
Milk, 141, 145, 174, 185, 186, 202, 246.
Millet, 46, 55, 56, 58, 60, 61, 69, 98, 104, 105, 108, 111, 122, 130, 141, 145, 146, 193, 194, 198, 206, 219.
Minjingu hill, 178.
Minna, 79, 141.
Missionaries, 73, 80, 121, 175.
Mlanje mountain, 221, 222.
Moanda, 157, 160.
Moatize, 226.
Moba, 126.
Moçamedes, 206, 207.
Mogadishu, 174.
Mokanji hills, 110.
Mokwa, 130.
Mombasa, 48, 68, 73, 79, 175, 178, **183**, 185, 191.
Mongalla, 21.
Monod, Th., 100.

Monomotapa, 68, 208.
Monrovia, 70, 106, 110, 112, 113, 260.
Montane vegetation, 23, 26, 200, 221.
Moors (from Morocco), 68, 101.
Mopani woodland, 209, 254.
Morel, E. D., 149.
Moroto river, 38.
Morris, James, 244-5.
Moshi, 180.
Mossi people, 49, 124.
Mounana, 157.
Mount Kenya, 5, 8, 73, 182, 183, 185, 186.
Mozambique, 6, 14, 41, 42, 43, 45, 65, 81, 165, 204, 209, **224-7**, 228, 253, 255, 260.
Mozambique Channel, 2, 65, 221, 225, 228.
Mozambique current, 225.
Mozambique island and town, 227.
Mpanda, 180.
Mtilikwe river, 212.
Mtwara, 180.
Muizenberg, 248.
Mumuye people, 129, 130.
Mungo, 162.
Muni river, 165.
Murchison falls, 18, 32, 193, 197.
Musa, 67.
Muslims, *see* Islam.
Mutarara, 226.
Mwadui, 180.
Mwanza, 180, 181, 193.
Mzima, 184.

Nacala, 224, 227.
Nachingwea, 180, 182.
Nairobi, 41, 46, 48, 176, 183, 185, **189-91**.
Nakuru, 189, 190.
Namib desert, 13, 173, 254.
Nandi, 65.
Nangeya mountains, 193.
Natal, 42, 71, 72, 240, **250-2**.
National Parks, 31, 32, 179, 182, 190, 200, 201, 217, 225, 226, 242, 254.
Native Reserves, 185, 211, 214, 240, 250, 252-3.
Natural gas, 2, 93, 127, 136, 140, 145, 148.
Navigation, *see* river transport.
Navrongo, 15, 122.
Ndama cattle, 108, 110, 124, 160.
Ndola, 178, 217-20.
Negroes, 40, **41**, 42, 170.
Newcastle, 250, 251.
Ngamiland, 258.
N'Gaoundéré, 159, 161, 162.
Ngoni people, 181, 221.
Ngorongoro crater, 64, 182.
N'Guigmi, 97.
Nguru, 98, 143, 146.
Ngwenya, 255.
Niamey, 20, 97, 98, 100, 145.
Niari valley, 157, 160, 161.
Nickel, 237, 252, 258.
Nieuwveld range, 70.
Niger basin, 1, 2, 5, 26, 55.
Niger dams project, 130, 145, 147.
Niger delta, coastal, 23, 69, 126, 136, 140, 147.
Niger delta, inland, 19, 22, 97, **99-100**.
Niger Republic, 39, **97-98**, 100, 106, 124, 125, 142, 145, 146.

Niger river, 2, 6, 16, 17, 19, 20, 22, 23, 59, 73, 75, 76, 79, 94, 97, 98, 100, 107, 124, 127, 129, 130, 145, 147, 148.
Nigeria, 2, 9, 27, 38, 39, 42-45, 46, 47, 49, 55, 56, 64, 69, 79, 82, 96, 97, 106, 125, **126-48**.
Eastern Nigeria, 22, 48, 161.
Middle Belt, 25, 37, 45, 129, 130, 142, 145, 147, 260.
Northern Nigeria, 2, 4, 15, 28, 31, 46, 51, 53, 56, 74, 98, 161.
Twelve States, **132-48**.
Benue-Plateau, 148.
East-Central State, 136-41.
Kano, 141-2.
Kwara, 147-8.
Lagos, 134-5.
North-Central State, 142-4.
North-Eastern State, 131, 145-7.
North-Western State, 50, 144-5.
Midwestern State, 135-6.
Rivers State, 127, 136.
South-Eastern State, 136, 162.
Western State, 132-4.
Nile, 1, 2, 5, 6, 17, 18, 20, 21, 26, 49, 55, 61, 63, 64, 72, 73, 75, 83-91, 175, 192, 193, 196, 199.
Nilotic people, 40, 41, 63, 90-91, 170, 175, 190.
Nimba mountains, 107, 111-13.
Nitti island, 110.
Nkalagu, 139.
Nkandabwe, 220.
N'Kongsamba, 162.
Nkula falls, 224.
Northern Rhodesia (*see also* Zambia), 78, 82, 205, 211.
Nouadhibou, 101, 102, 103, 158.
Nouakchott, 101, 102.
Nova Lisboa, 205, 206.
Nsanje, 221.
Nuba mountains, 83, 87, 88.
Nubians, 64, 83, 86, 87, 90.
Nuer people, 55, 63, 90.
Nupe people, 130.
Nyakyusa people, 181.
Nyala, 87, 88, 90.
Nyanja people, 221.
Nyanza, 46, 175, 186, 190, 191.
Nyasaland, *see also* Malawi, 51, 82, 211, 221.
Nyoro, *see* Bunyoro.
N'Zérékoré, 110.

Oats, 169.
Oba people, 133, 134.
Obuasi, 115.
Obudu, 128.
Ocean currents, *see also* Canaries, Benguela, and Mozambique currents, 13, 62, 113, 225.
Ocean Railway, 157, 159, 160, 161.
Odendaalsrus, 243.
Ogaden, 170, 173.
Ogbomosho, 134.
Ogoja, 137, 138, 139.
Ogowé river, 156-8.
Oil, mineral, 2, 62, 93, 95, 127, 136, 148, 156, 160, 207.
Oil-palm, *see* palm oil.
Oil refinery, 104, 119, 136, 156, 172, 178, 183, 216, 250, 252.
Oil Rivers, 73, 75, 136.
Ojukwu, 127.
Okavango basin, 20, 21, 206, 254, 258.
Oko, 59.
Okoume timber, 156, 165.

Olduvai Gorge, 64, 182.
Olifants river, 238.
Omdurman, 73, 83, 84.
Onitsha, 138, 139, 140, 142.
Orange Free State, 39, 71, 238, **240-6**, 253, 255.
Orange river, 2, 71, 237, 238, 254.
Orange River Scheme, 238.
Organization of African Unity (O.A.U.), 39, 82, 106, 260.
Orlu, 127, 128, 138.
Oruchinga, 198.
Oshogbo, 134.
Ouagadougou, 124, 125.
Oubangui river, 158, 162.
Ouesso, 160.
Ovambo people, 239, 254.
Ovimbunda people, 206.
Owen Falls dam, 191, 192, 193, 197.
Owendo, 156.
Owu, 133.
Oyo, 47.

Paardeberg, 248.
Paarl, 249.
Palm kernels, 128, 134, 139, 153.
Palm oil, 24, 46, 57, 58, 60, 69, 75, 78, 90, 108, 110, 121, 123, 126, 127, 128, 136-40, 150, 151, 153, 159, 160, 163-5, 261.
Pangalanes canals, 230.
Pangani river, 182.
Park, Mungo, 73.
Pas Géometriques, 233.
Pastoralists, 16, 23, 38, 39, 50, **52-56**, 60, 90, 92, 94, 98, 100, 167, 170, 173, 174, 184, 190, 193, 232, 237, 252, 258.
Peaches, 249.
Peasant farming schemes, 152, 153, 188, 206, 207.
Pemba, 176-8.
Pepel, 109.
Perkerra river, 190.
Petroleum, 100, 102, 136, 161, 184, 261.
Peuls, *see also* Fulani, 110.
Phosphates, 104, 114, 126, 178, 179, 214, 242.
Pietermaritzburg, 251.
Pietersburg, 241, 242, 252.
Piggs Peak, 255.
Pigs, 108, 141.
Piketberg, 248.
Plantations, 42, 112, 123, 126, 135, 140, 150, 153, 155, **163-4**, 177, 178, 194, 207, 214, 224, 231, 251, 255.
Plateau Tonga, 219.
Platinum, 237, 242, 246.
Pobé, 125.
Pointe Noire, 96, 157, 159, **160**, 161.
Polygamy, 44.
Population distribution, **45-51**, 126, 137-8, 159.
Ports, *see* harbours.
Portuguese, 41-43, 57, 64, 65, **68, 69**, 72, 73, 76, 81, 82, 108, 113, 125, 135, 149, 157, 165, 169, 173, 204-7, 224-7, 259, 260.
Portuguese Guinea, 106, 107, **111**, 112, 260.
Port Bell, 197.
Port Bouet, 122, 123.
Port Elizabeth, 70, 78, 238, 252.
Port Étienne (*see* Nouadhibou).
Port Francqui, 154.
Port Gentil, 156-8.
Port Harcourt, 48, 96, 127, 136, 140, 141, 143, 162.
Port-Kakandé, 111.
Port Louis, 232.

Port Sudan, 84, 85, 90, 91, 172.
Porto Alexandre, 205, 206.
Porto Novo, 76, 125, 126.
Potash, 157, 160.
Potiskum, 56.
Poto-Poto, Brazzaville, 159.
Prazeros, 224.
Precipitation, *see* rainfall.
Prester John, 68.
Pretoria, 238, **240-2**, 252.
Principe, 165.
Pungwé river, 225, 226.
Pygmies, 40-42, 46, 200, 228.
Pyrethrum, 153, 180, 186, 188.

Qoz, 55, 87-89.
Quartz, 21, 130, 230.
Quelea birds, 33, 146.
Quelimane, 227.
Que Que, 215-16.
Quitere-Mucopa, 206.

Race, **40-42**, 48, 80, 209, 210, 227, 231-4, 237.
Radium, 154.
Railways, 42, 48, **78, 79**, 80, 84, 106, 115, 117, 125, 138, 143, 146, 148, 149, 151, 154, 157, 159-62, 172, 178, 180, 204, 205, 206, 208, 210, 211, 212, 224, 239, 242, 249, 255, 257, 260.
Rain and rainfall, **12-16**, 20, 53, 113, 173, 175, 178, 193, 221, 230, 242, 254.
Rain forest, **23-25**, 57-60, 114, 117, 126, 156.
Rand (Witwatersrand), 2, 48, 51, 77, 78, 227, 238, 239, **240-6**, 250.
Redcliff, 215, 216.
Religion, *see also* Christianity and Islam, 44-45.
Réunion, 6, 14, 228, 232, **234-5**.
Revué river, 226.
Rhodes, Cecil, 77, 207, 208, 221.
Rhodesia, formerly Southern Rhodesia, 5, 22, 38, 39, 41, 49-51, 65, 78, 181, 204, **207-17**, 219, 220, 226, 244, 259, 260.
Rice, 57, 69, 90, 96, 99, 104, 105, 107-11, 121-4, 130, 136, 137, 139, 146, 148, 158, 160, 161, 177, 178, 181, 190, 220, 224, 226, 227, 228, 231, 232, 236, 255.
Richard Toll irrigation scheme, 104.
Richard's Bay, 252.
Rift valley, East African, 5, 6, 23, 166, 182, 185, 186, 188, 193, 194.
Rima river, 97, 144, 145.
Rinderpest, **39**, 78, 108, 164, 180, 190, 210.
Rio Muni, 149, 165.
River blindness (*Onchocersiasis*), 38, 121.
River transport, 16, 18, 73-79, 84, 136, 145, 147-50, 151, 158, 161, 171.
Rivers, **16-22**, 72, 113, 145, 148, 171, 238.
Rivers State (*see* Nigeria).
Roads, 79, 80, 100, 106, 112, 116, 143, 146, 148, 171.
Rock engravings and paintings, 9, 30, 40, 52, 53, 64.
Roma, 257.
Roseires dam, 20, 85, 87.
Rovuma river, 221.
Royal Niger Company, 76.
Rua Cana falls, 206.
Ruanda-Urundi, *see also* Rwanda and Burundi, 79, 198, 200.
Rubber, 27, 108, 110, 112, 113, 127, 128, 135, 136, 150, 153, 158, 159, 163, 207.
Rufiji river, 22, 182.
Ruhuhu river, 181.

Rustenburg, 246.
Rutile, 110.
Ruvu river, 182.
Ruwenzori, 4, 9, 27, 193, 198.
Ruzizi river, 200, 203.
Rwanda, 46, 80, 176, 196, **200-3**.

Sab people, 173, 174.
Sabaloka gorge, 86.
Sabi (Save) river, 22, 208, 209, 213, 214.
Sahara, 1, 2, 4, 7, 9, 11, 13-15, 20, 21, 23, 27, 33, 34, 40, 46, 51, 53, 61, 64, 65, 67, **92-95**, 130, 132.
Sahel, 94, 95, 99, 119, 161.
St. Denis, 233.
St. Isabel, 165.
St. Louis, 79, 102-4.
Salisbury, 208, 210, 212, 213, **214, 215**, 217, 218, 220.
Saloum river, 104.
Salt, 65, 66, 67, 94, 100, 103, 104, 115, 120, 121, 158, 179, 205.
Salvinia auriculata, 18, 217.
Samburu people, 184.
Samveboi, 118.
San Pedro, 124.
Sanaga river, 161, 162.
Sandveld, 248.
Sangha river, 160.
Sansanding, 99.
São Bandeira, 205, 206.
São Salvador do Congo, 205.
São Tomé, 165.
Sapele, 135, 136.
Sasolburg, 245.
Savanna, 9, 11, 24, 25, 28, 37, 38, 60, 128, 130, 182, 230.
Scarcies river, 109.
Scramble for Africa, 75-78.
Ségou, 99.
Séguéla, 123.
Sekondi, 115, 116, 121.
Selukwe, 216.
Semien mountains, 168.
Senegal Republic, 6, 12, 62, 67, 69, 76, 78, 79, 95, 98, 99, 100, **102-5**, 106, 111, 123.
Senegal river, 1, 65, 75, 94, 98, 101-5, 106.
Sennar, 20, 21, 74, 83-85, 87.
Serengeti, 182, 184.
Serpa Pinto, 206.
Seychelles, 228, 234, **235-6**.
Shabani, 214.
Shai people, 115, 116, 119, 121.
Shari river, 18, 96.
Shea-butter, 25, 124.
Shebeli river, 173, 174.
Shehu dan Fodio, 144.
Shendam, 25, 148.
Sherbro island, 106-8.
Shifting cultivation, 29, 57, 60, 145, 152, 159, 206, 207, 219.
Shilluk people, 90.
Shinyanga, 180.
Shirazi people, 177, 178.
Shire river, 220, 221, 222, 223, 224.
Shiroro gorge, 130, 144, 145.
Shoa, 167, 170.
Sidamo, 172.
Sierra Leone, 57, 70, 76, 105, 106, 107, **108-10**, 111, 123, 165.
Siguiri, 98.
Silcrete, 10, 11, 27.

Silva Porto, 205, 206.
Silver, 154.
Simandou mountains, 111.
Simbili, 109.
Sisal, 123, 151, 159, 176, **179, 180**, 186, 188, 206, 235.
Slavery and slaves, **69, 70**, 73-75, 78, 126, 135, 144, 149, 165, 174, 175, 178, 195, 205, 225, 228, 233, 235.
Sleeping sickness, *see* Trypanosomiasis.
Sobat river, 20, 171.
Sodium carbonate, 96, 185.
Sofala, 65.
Soil catenas, 29, 30.
Soil erosion, 10, 22, 24, 26, 28, 29, 56, 58, 95, 99, 132, 138, 144, 202.
Soils, 16, 23, 25, **26-30**, 104, 115, 117, 121, 127, 132, 134, 137, 144, 146, 159, 164, 191.
Sokoto, 14, 50, 73, 74, 76, 142, 144, 145.
Sokoto river, 130, 132, 144, 145.
Somali people, 72, 170, **173, 174**, 183, 184.
Somalia, Somali Republic and Somaliland, 2, 13, 14, 26, 33, 34, 39, 77, 78, 166, 167, **173, 174**, 184.
Songhai, 66, 67, 68, 100, 124.
Sorghum (Guinea-corn), 58, 60, 69, 88, 89, 105, 141, 145, 146, 173, 190, 194, 200.
Sotho people, 253, 258.
Souanké, 160.
Sourveld, 251.
South Africa, Republic of (formerly Union of), 20, 39, 41, 42, 45, 49, 50, 70, 77, 80-82, 204, 211, 219, 224, 227, **237-53**, 259-61.
Southern Rhodesia (now Rhodesia), 78, 80, 81, 210, 211, 224.
South-West Africa, 34, 62, 63, 77, 79, 206, 237, 253, 254, 259.
Spaniards, 149, 165.
Spanish Guinea (Spanish Equatorial Africa), 149, 158, **165**.
Stanley, H. M., 75, 76.
Stanley Pool, 17, 20, 75, 149, 157.
Steel, *see* iron and steel.
Stellenbosch, 249.
Stenning, J. D., 56.
Stone line (in soils), 36.
Strydpoort Range, 241, 246.
Suakin, 51, 84.
Sudan Republic, 1, 18, 26, 29, 34, 36, 41, 42, 43, 51, 55, 60, 63, 64, 67, 72, 73, 77, 78, 82, **83-91**, 198, 260.
Sudan zone, 7, 13, 15, 23, 29, 40, 44, 51, 53, 60, 65, 68, 73, 74, **92-105**, 124, 132, 259.
Sudd, 18, 21, 64, 84.
Sugar and sugar-cane, 72, 143, 147, 148, 153, 161, 165, 172, 174, 194-7, 198, 205, 212, 213, 220, 224, 226, 228, 233, 234, 235, 241, 250, 252, 255, 261.
Sukumaland, 46, 180-1.
Sulphuric acid, 154.
Sundays river, 237, 238.
Suni, 87, 88.
Swahili, 43, 149, 175, 177, 183, 203, 227, 235, 260.
Swaziland, 221, 224, 225, 226, 237, 252, **254-5**.
Swollen shoot disease, 116, 117, 134.

Table Mountain, 3, 246, 247, 248.
Tabora, 73, 79, 180, 181.
Tafo, 117.
Taiba, 104.
Takoradi, 113, 114, 116, 117, 118, 120.
Tamale, 121.
Tamatave, 230, 232.
Tana river, 184, 185, 189.

Tananarive, 231, 232.
Tanga, 79, 175, **178-80**.
Tanganyika (*see also* Tanzania), 14, 34, 73, 82, 176-82.
Tanzania (*see also* Tanganyika and Zanzibar), 22, 26, 33, 42, 45, 63, 64, 65, 79, 175, 176, **176-82**, 184, 191, 193, 198, 202, 209, 220.
Tarkwa, 79, 115, 118.
Tassili des Ajjers, 3.
Tati Company, 258.
Tayiba, 84.
Tchibanga, 158.
Tea, 164, 181, 186, 188, 194, 198, 214, 221, 222, 225, 227, 234.
Teff, 169.
Tema, 48, 114, 119, 120, 121.
Temne people, 108.
Temperature, 14, 28, 170, 207-8.
Termites, 29, 35, 36, 94, 195.
Terre de Barre, 125, 126.
Tesissat falls, 170.
Tété, 226.
Thabazimbi, 241-2.
Thiès, 104.
Tibesti, 1, 3, 6, 9, 53, 93-96.
Tibu people, 53, 54, 62, 95.
Tigrai people, 166, 167, 170, 171.
Tigrinya people, 167, 171.
Tikar people, 164.
Tiko, 163.
Tilapia, 63, 153, 193.
Tilemsi Wadi, 20, 100.
Timber, 115, 118, 121, 123, 135, 136, 150, 156, 158, 160, 163, 164, 165, 170, 205, 221.
Tin, 79, 81, 98, 128, 130, 148, 154, 201, 203, 237, 242.
Titanium, 114.
Tiv people, 126, 129, 130, 132.
Tobacco, 46, 55, 60, 61, 90, 123, 148, 160, 180, 194, 198, 208, 211, 212, 213, 214, 219, 220, 221, 222, 246, 249.
Togoland and Republic of Togo, 46, 76, 79, 106, 113, 119, 120, 125, 126, 156.
Tokar delta, 90.
Tombouctou (Timbuktu), 20, 34, 67, 68, 73, 100.
Tonga people, 221.
Tororo, 198.
Touareg people, 62, 68, 98, 100.
Tourism, 110, 182, 190, 217, 225, 226, 236, 250.
Towns, *see* cities.
Transkei, 252, 253, 254, 255.
Transvaal, 39, 71, 77, 78, 80, 207, 208, 227, 237, 238, **240-6**, 252, 253, 255, 258.
Trekkers, 71, 72.
Triangle, 212, 213.
Tribes and tribalism, 44, 49, 57, 79, 160, 195.
Trypanosomiasis (Sleeping sickness), 25, 32, 37, 38, 39, 46, 53, 60, 108, 110, 130, 180, 181, 197.
Trust Territories, 79, 161, 176, 198, 200, 237.
Tsetse fly, 32, 37, 38, 39, 46, 60, 121, 162, 172, 174, 175, 180, 193, 198, 209, 217, 220, 225.
Tshikapa, 154.
Tsumeb, 2, 254.
Tswanaland, 253.
Tugela basin, 251.
Tulbagh basin, 249.
Tumbuka people, 221.
Tung oil, 222.
Tungsten ore, 201, 203.
Turkana people, 54, 55, 184.

Tutsi, *see* Batutsi.
Twa, *see* Batwa.

Uasin Gishu plateau, 190.
Uaso Nyiro river (*see* Ewaso Nyiro river).
Ubangi river, *see* Oubangui.
Ubangi-Shari (now Central African Republic), 158-9.
Udi plateau, 128, 138-40.
Uganda, 18, 32, 36, 38, 39, 42, 46, 47, 49, 54, 65, 79, 82, 91, 176, 183, 190, **193-200**, 202.
Uganda Agreement, 195, 196.
Ujiji, 73.
Umatongo highlands, 181.
Umgeni river, 250.
Umlaas river, 250.
Umtali, 212, 216, 226.
Umuahia, 138, 139.
United Africa Company, 136.
United Nations, 82, 124, 155, 171, 173, 202, 237.
Universities, 80, 171, 197, 239, 252, 257.
Upper Volta, 49, 100, 106, 113, 114, 120, 122, 123, **124, 125**.
Urambo, 181, 182.
Uranium, 98, 157, 237, 244.
Urhobo people, 127.
Usambara mountains, 175, 182.
Usuto river, 255.
Uyo, 136.

Vaal river, 20, 30, 238, 240-2, 245, 246.
Vanderbijlpark, 245.
Vanilla, 231, 235, 236.
Vegetation arcs and similar patterns, 26, 89, 94, 113.
Vereeniging, 238, 240-2, 245.
Victoria, 236.
Victoria-Bota, 103.
Victoria Falls, 208, 209, 210, 217.
Vila Cabral, 227.
Vila Pery, 224, 226.
Vili tribe, 159.
Vines, 248, 249.
Vipya mountains, 221.
Virunga mountains, 200.
Volcanoes, 6, 23, 129, 164, 165, 168, 181, 189, 201, 227, 228, 232, 234.
Volta basin, 115, 121, 122.
Volta dam, 48, 49, 115, 116, **119**.
Volta delta, 113, 119-21.
Volta river, 18, 114, 124.
Vridi canal, 122, 123.

Wad Medani, 84, 85, 90, 91.
Wadai, 95.
Wadi Halfa, 84, 86.
Walvis Bay, 63, 254.
Wankie, 78, 208, 212, 214, 215, 216, 217, 220, 226.
Wattle, 26, 188, 190, 214, 251.
Wau, 90.
Welkom, 243.
Wenchi, 121, 122.
West Nicholson, 209, 214.
Wete, 178.
Wheat, 96, 169, 181, 186, 220, 226, 238, 246, 248, 249.
White Highlands, *see also* Kenya highlands, 176, 185, 186, 188.
White Nile, 5, 18, 20, 21, 29, 75, 83-91.
White settlers, 80, 81, 185-8, 207, 208, 210-11, 220, 259.

Windhoek, 253, 254.
Winds, 12, 95, 113.
Witbank, 240-2.
Witwatersrand, *see* Rand.
Wolof people, 104.
Wool, 246, 248, 253.
Worcester, 249.
World Bank, 172, 185, 197.
Worthington, E. B., 32.
Wot, 169.
Woyna dega, 168.
Wuri river, 162.

Xhosa people, 250.

Yabassi, 162.
Yams, 57, 58, 59, 69, 118, 120, 121, 122, 123, 137, 139.
Yangambi, 153.
Yao people, 221.
Yaoundé, 158, 161, 162, 164.
Yellow fever, 36, 37.
Yelwa, 145.
Yemen, 166.
Yengema, 109.
Yobe river, 145, 146.

Yoruba people, 125, 126, 127, 130, **132-4**.
Yorubaland, 47, 75, **132-5**.

Zambezi river, 2, 5, 18, 20, 39, 49, 68, 75, 204, 206, 207, 208, 209, 210, 212, 217, 220, 221, 223, 224, 225, 226-7, 253.
Zambia, formerly Northern Rhodesia, 20, 22, 25, 26, 36, 37, 41, 46, 48-50, 60, 176, 178, 181, 204, 205, 209, 211, 214, 216, **217-20**, 224, 244, 260.
Zamfara, 145.
Zande people, 60, 90, 159.
Zanzibar (now part of Tanzania), 14, 73, 77, 78, 175, **176-8**, 182, 260.
Zaria, 10, 61, 130, 132, 142, 143, 144.
Zaroma people, 178.
Zebediela, 241, 246.
Zebu, 52, 53.
Zeila, 173.
Ziguinchor, 105.
Zimbabwe, 65, 208.
Zinc, 78, 127, 154, 209, 217, 219.
Zinder, 97, 98.
Zomba, 221.
Zouar, 95.
Zulu, 71, 207, 221.
Zulu dam, 172.
Zungeru, 143.

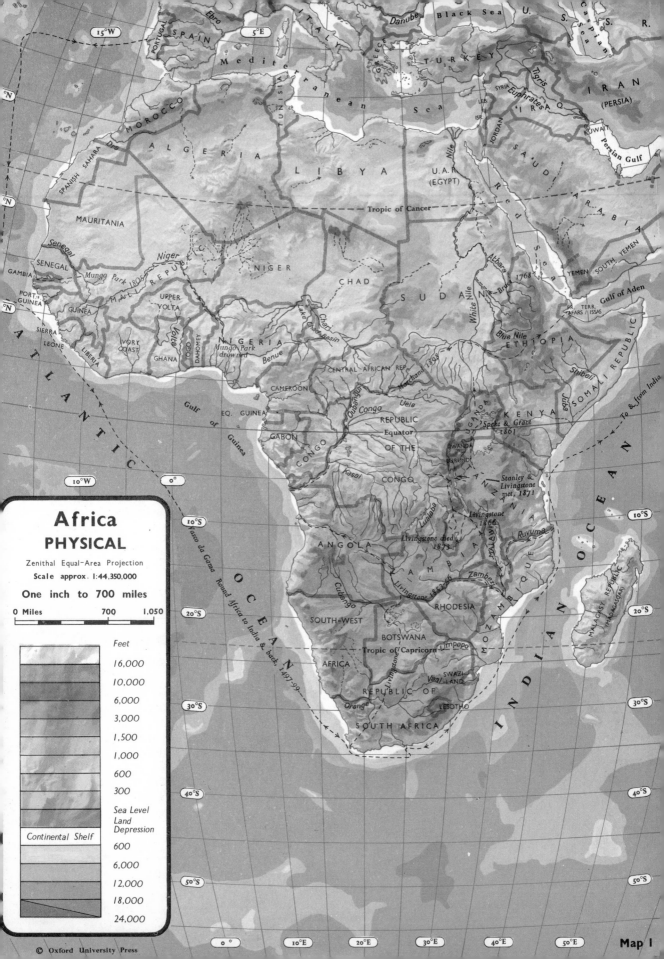

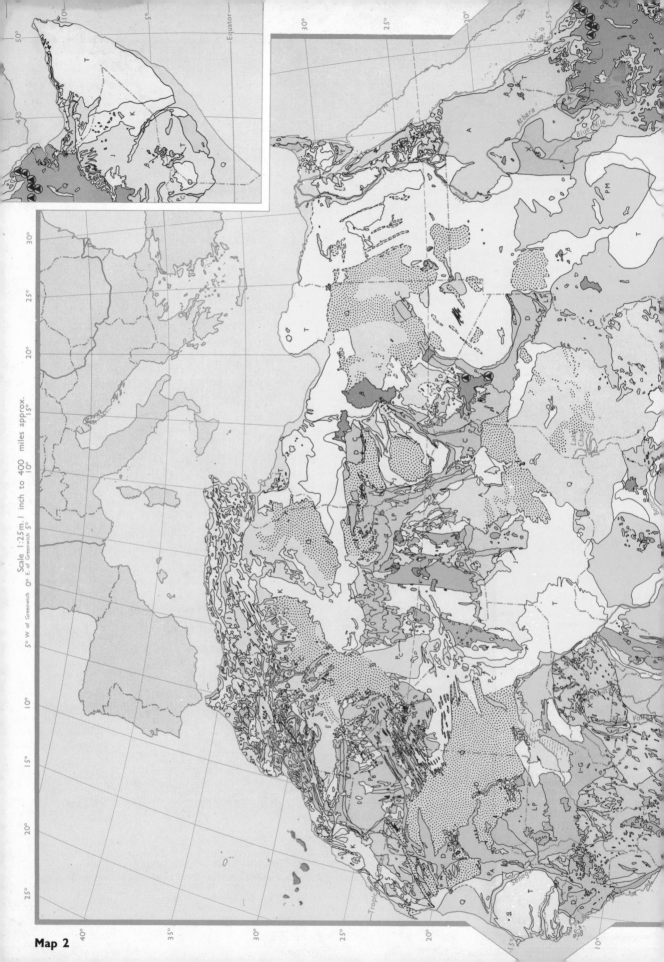

Scale 1:25 m. I inch to 400 miles approx.

5° W of Greenwich   0° E of Greenwich 5°

Map 2

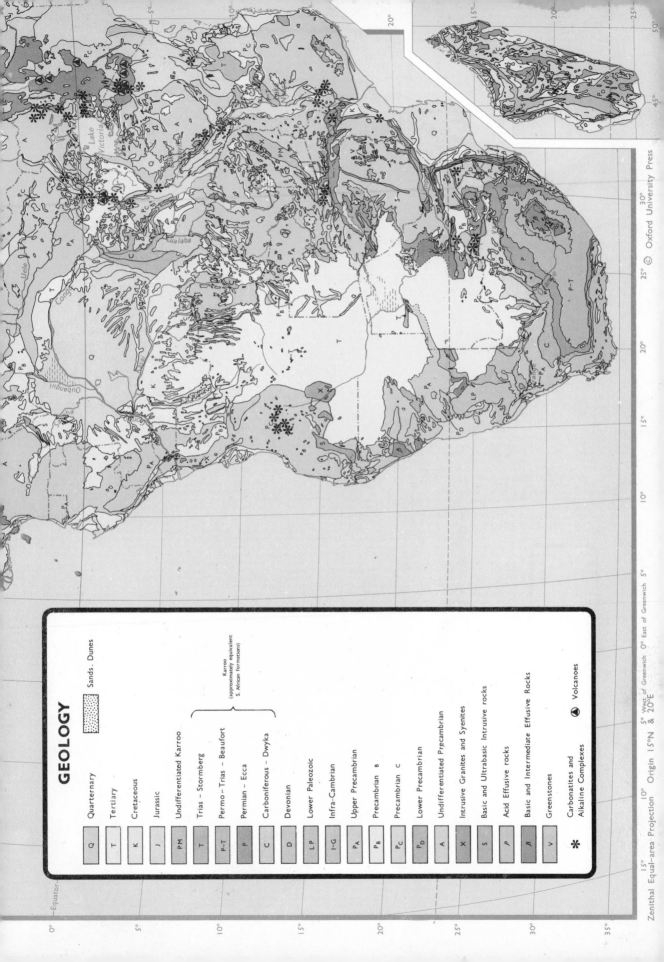

GEOLOGY

Sands. Dunes

Q	Quarternary
T	Tertiary
K	Cretaceous
J	Jurassic
PM	Undifferentiated Karroo
T	Trias – Stormberg
P-T	Permo – Trias – Beaufort
P	Permian – Ecca
C	Carboniferous – Dwyka
D	Devonian
LP	Lower Paleozoic
I-G	Infra-Cambrian
PA	Upper Precambrian
PB	Precambrian B
PC	Precambrian C
PD	Lower Precambrian
A	Undifferentiated Precambrian
X	Intrusive Granites and Syenites
S	Basic and Ultrabasic Intrusive rocks
P	Acid Effusive rocks
ß	Basic and Intermediate Effusive Rocks
V	Greenstones
*	Carbonatites and Alkaline Complexes
◭	Volcanoes

Karroo (approximately equivalent S. African formations)

Zenithal Equal-area Projection   Origin 15°N & 20°E

5° West of Greenwich 0° East of Greenwich 5°

© Oxford University Press

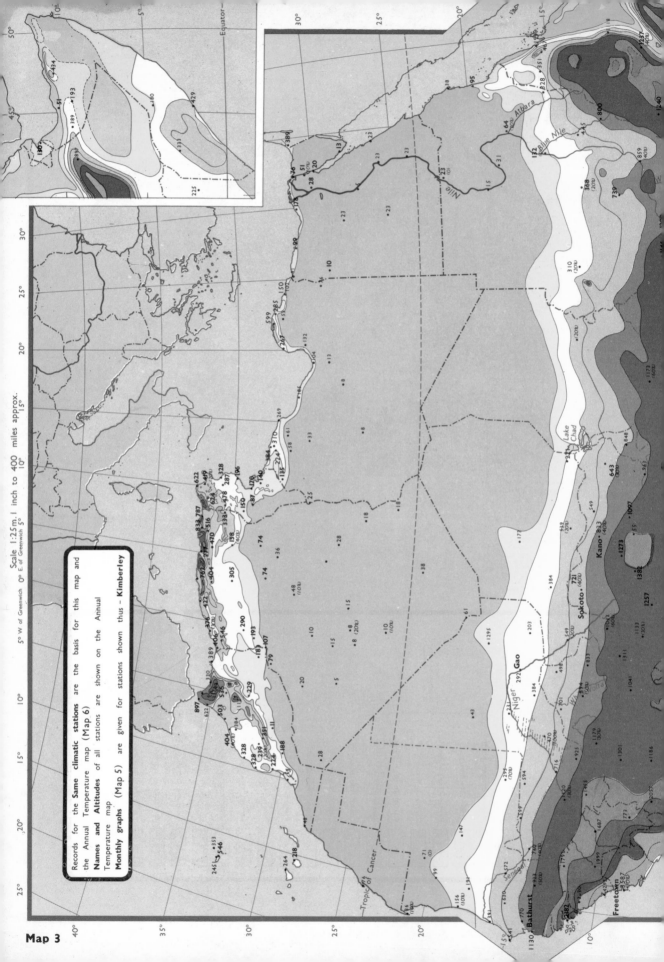

Map 3

Scale 1:25 m. 1 inch to 400 miles approx.

Records for the **Same climatic stations** are the basis for this map and the Annual Temperature map (Map 6)

Names and Altitudes of all stations are shown on the Annual Temperature map

Monthly graphs (Map 5) are given for stations shown thus – **Kimberley**

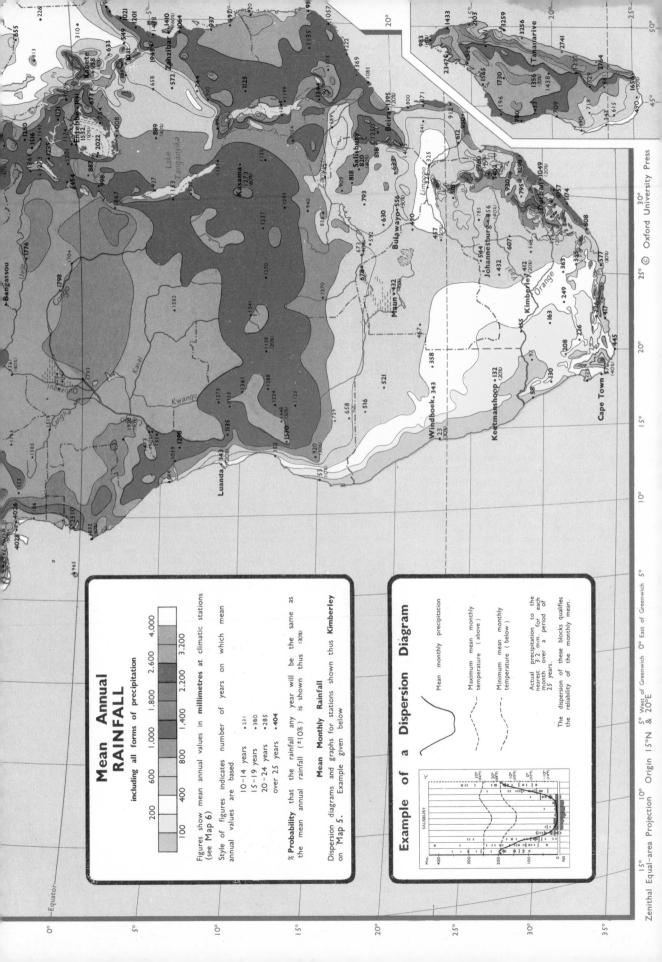

Mean Annual RAINFALL

including all forms of precipitation

	100	200	400	600	800	1,000	1,400	1,800	2,200	2,600	3,200	4,000

Figures show mean annual values in **millimetres** at climatic stations (see Map 6)

Style of figures indicates number of years on which mean annual values are based

10–14 years   •231
15–19 years   •380
20–24 years   •285
over 25 years   •404

% **Probability** that the rainfall any year will be the same as the mean annual rainfall (±10%) is shown thus **Kimberley** (90%)

Mean Monthly Rainfall

Dispersion diagrams and graphs for stations shown thus **Kimberley** on Map 5. Example given below

Example of a Dispersion Diagram

—— Mean monthly precipitation

– – Maximum mean monthly temperature (above)

– – Minimum mean monthly temperature (below)

Actual precipitation to the nearest 3.2 mm. for each month over a period of 25 years.

The dispersion of these blocks qualifies the reliability of the monthly mean.

SALISBURY

Zenithal Equal-area Projection   Origin 15°N & 20°E

5° West of Greenwich 0° East of Greenwich 5°

Map 4

Scale 1:25 m. 1 inch to 400 miles approx.

Over 100mm. each month from Apr. to Aug.
Over 100mm. each month from October and November
Over 100mm. each month in April

Over 100mm. for each of the following months NOV. TO DEC.
DEC. TO MAR.
OCT. TO DEC.
NOV. TO FEB.
OVER 100mm. IN DEC
OVER 100mm.
NOV. TO MARCH
IN DECEMBER
Over 100mm.
OCT. TO MARCH
Over 100mm. for each of the following months

Equator

Nile
Atbara
Blue Nile
White Nile

JULY TO SEPTEMBER
OVER 100mm. IN AUGUST
OVER 100mm. EACH MONTH FROM JULY TO SEPTEMBER
OVER 100mm. EACH MONTH FROM JUNE TO SEPTEMBER
OVER 100mm. EACH MONTH FROM

Lake Chad

Benue

OVER 100mm. IN AUGUST
OVER 100mm. EACH MONTH FROM JULY TO SEPTEMBER
OVER 100mm. EACH MONTH FROM JUNE TO SEPTEMBER

Sokoto
Kano.
OVER 100mm. EACH MONTH IN OCTOBER

Gao
Niger

White Volta
Black Volta

OVER 100mm. IN AUGUST
OVER 100mm. EACH MONTH FROM JUNE TO SEPTEMBER
OVER 100mm. EACH MONTH FROM MAY TO OCTOBER
OVER 100mm. EACH MONTH FROM APRIL

Tropic of Cancer

Senegal

Bathurst

NOVEMBER

Freetown

5° W of Greenwich   0° E. of Greenwich 5°

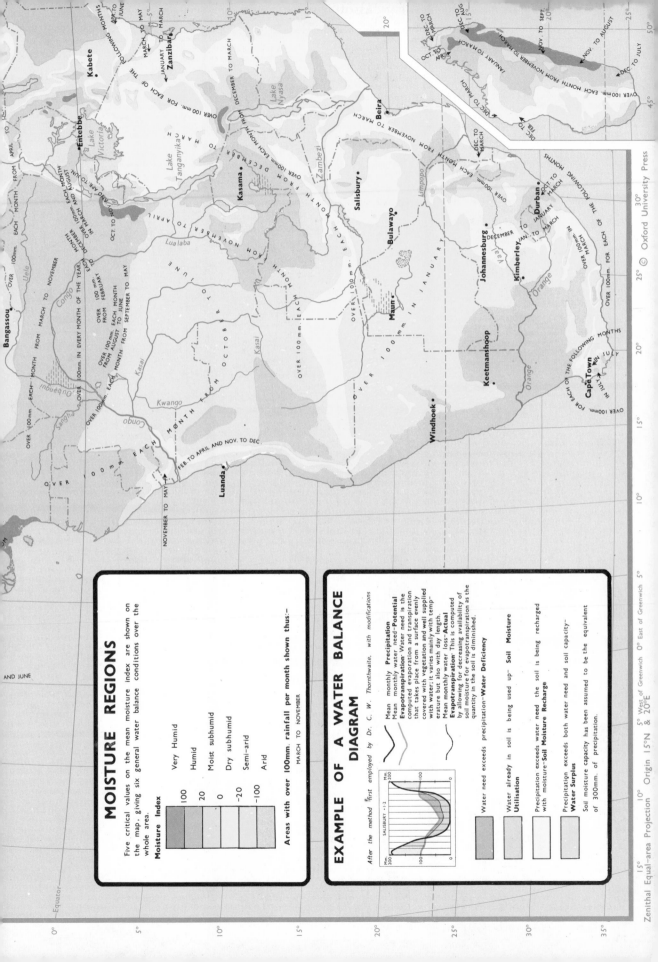

MOISTURE REGIONS

Five critical values on the mean moisture index are shown on the map, giving six general water balance conditions over the whole area.

Moisture Index

100	Very Humid
20	Humid
0	Moist subhumid
-20	Dry subhumid
-100	Semi-arid
	Arid

Areas with over 100mm. rainfall per month shown thus:—

MARCH TO NOVEMBER

EXAMPLE OF A WATER BALANCE DIAGRAM

After the method first employed by Dr. C. W. Thornthwaite, with modifications.

Mean monthly **Precipitation**

Mean monthly water need—**Potential Evapotranspiration**· Water need is the computed evaporation and transpiration that takes place from a surface evenly covered with vegetation and well supplied with water; it varies mainly with temperature but also with day length.

Mean monthly water loss—**Actual Evapotranspiration**· This is computed by allowing for decreasing availability of soil moisture for evapotranspiration as the quantity in the soil is diminished.

Water need exceeds precipitation—**Water Deficiency**

Water already in soil is being used up—**Soil Moisture Utilisation**

Precipitation exceeds water need· the soil is being recharged with moisture—**Soil Moisture Recharge**

Precipitation exceeds both water need and soil capacity—**Water Surplus**

Soil moisture capacity has been assumed to be the equivalent of 300mm. of precipitation.

SALISBURY ÷12

Zenithal Equal-area Projection   Origin 15°S   Origin 15°N & 20°E

© Oxford University Press

ACCRA Alt.88′

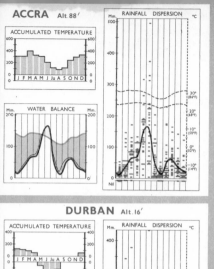

BANGASSOU Alt.1,640′

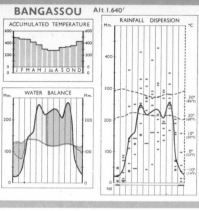

BATHURST Alt.90′

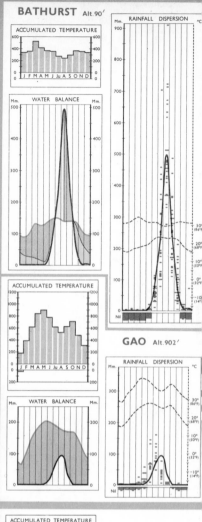

DURBAN Alt.16′

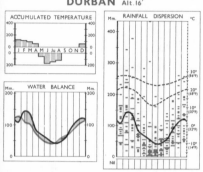

ENTEBBE Alt.3,878′

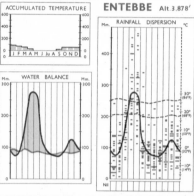

GAO Alt.902′

KANO Alt.1,533′

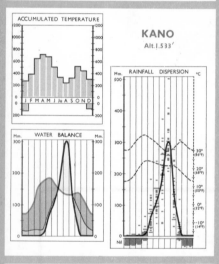

KASAMA Alt.4,544′

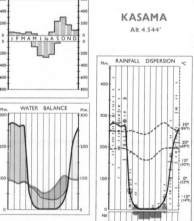

MAUN Alt.3,091′

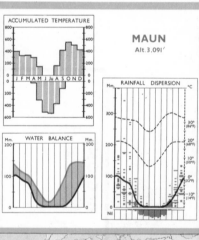

ZANZIBAR Alt.61′

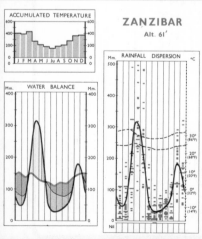

LAGOS Alt.10′

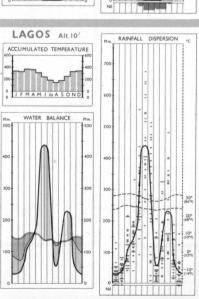

CLIMATIC DIAGRAMS

Explanations: Temperature Map 6
Rainfall Map 3   Water Balance Map 4

Map 5

© Oxford University Press

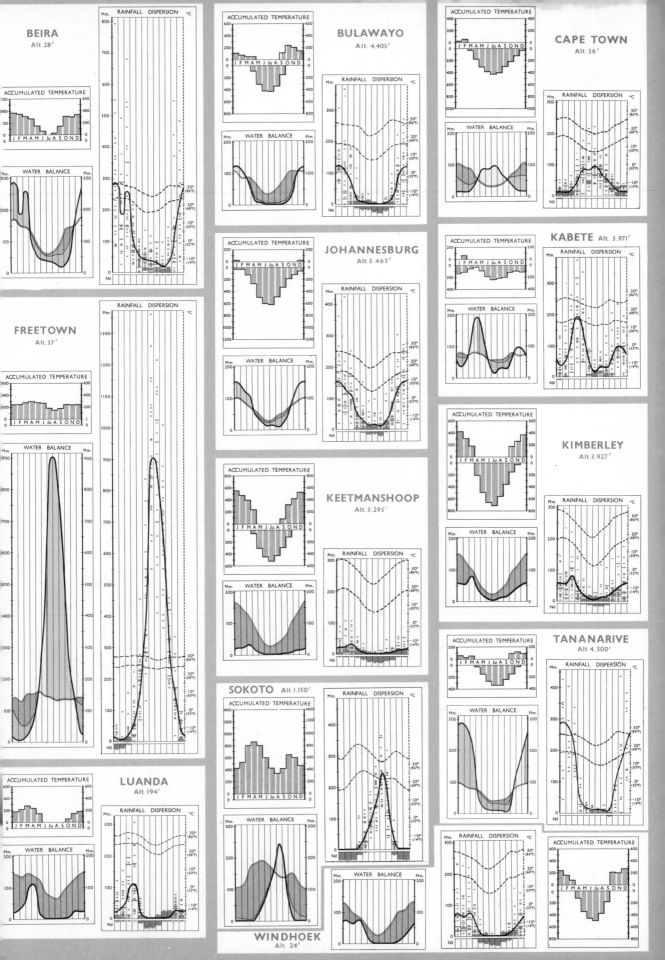

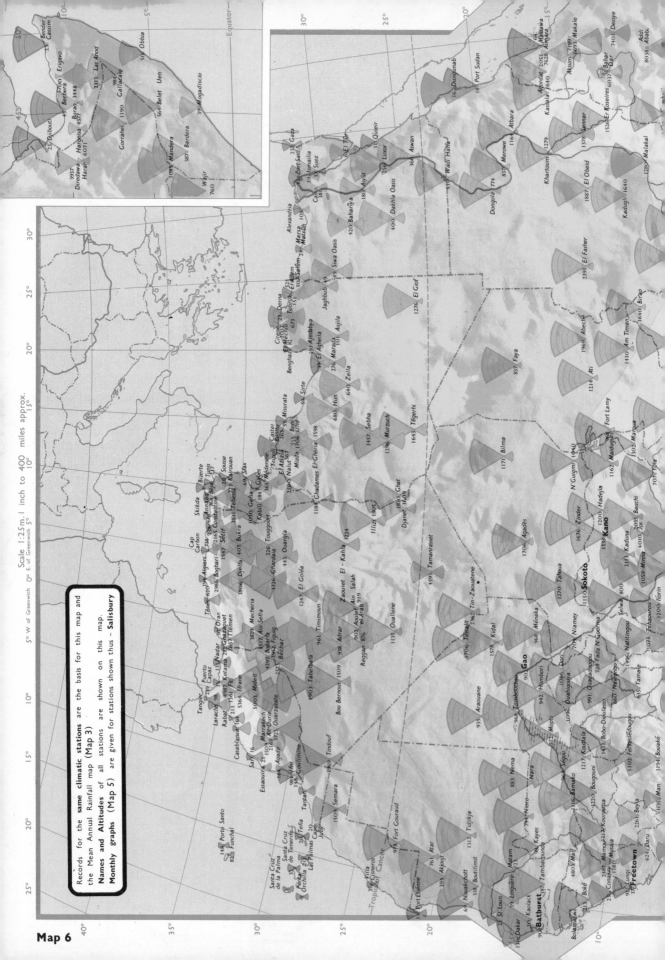

Map 6

Scale 1:25 m. 1 inch to 400 miles approx.

Records for the same climatic stations are the basis for this map and the Mean Annual Rainfall map (Map 3). Names and Altitudes of all stations are shown on this map. Monthly graphs (Map 5) are given for stations shown thus – Salisbury

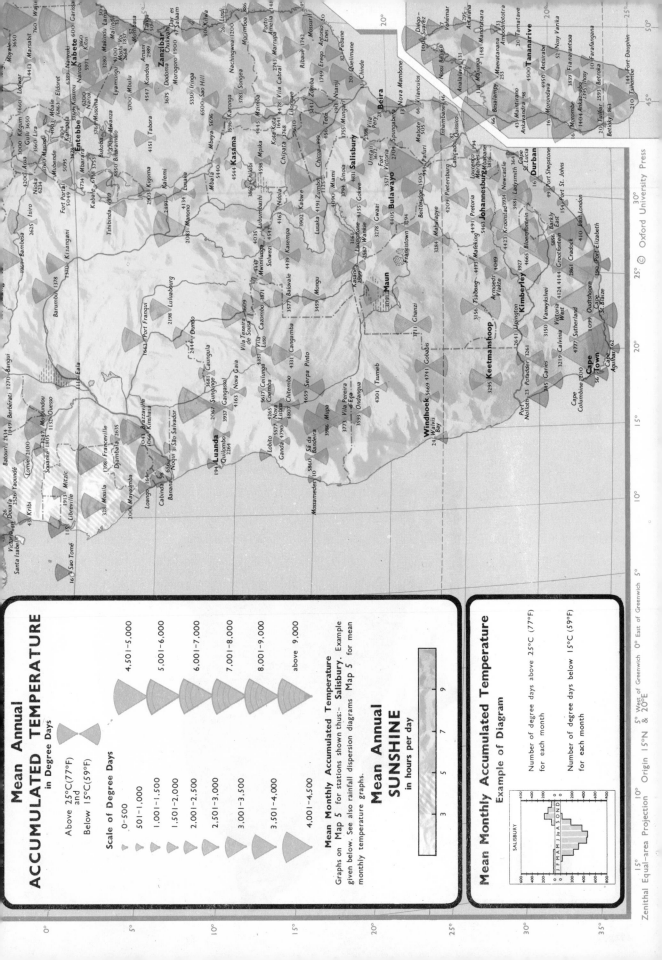

Mean Annual ACCUMULATED TEMPERATURE
in Degree Days

Above 25°C(77°F) and
Below 15°C(59°F)

Scale of Degree Days

0–500
501–1,000
1,001–1,500
1,501–2,000
2,001–2,500
2,501–3,000
3,001–3,500
3,501–4,000
4,001–4,500
4,501–5,000
5,001–6,000
6,001–7,000
7,001–8,000
8,001–9,000
above 9,000

Mean Monthly Accumulated Temperature

Graphs on Map 5 for stations shown thus:– Salisbury. Example given below. See also rainfall dispersion diagrams Map 5 for mean monthly temperature graphs.

Mean Annual SUNSHINE
in hours per day

3   5   7   9

Mean Monthly Accumulated Temperature
Example of Diagram

Number of degree days above 25°C (77°F) for each month

Number of degree days below 15°C (59°F) for each month

SALISBURY

Zenithal Equal-area Projection   Origin 15°N & 20°E

15°   10°   5° West of Greenwich   0° East of Greenwich   5°   10°   15°   20°   25°   30°

© Oxford University Press

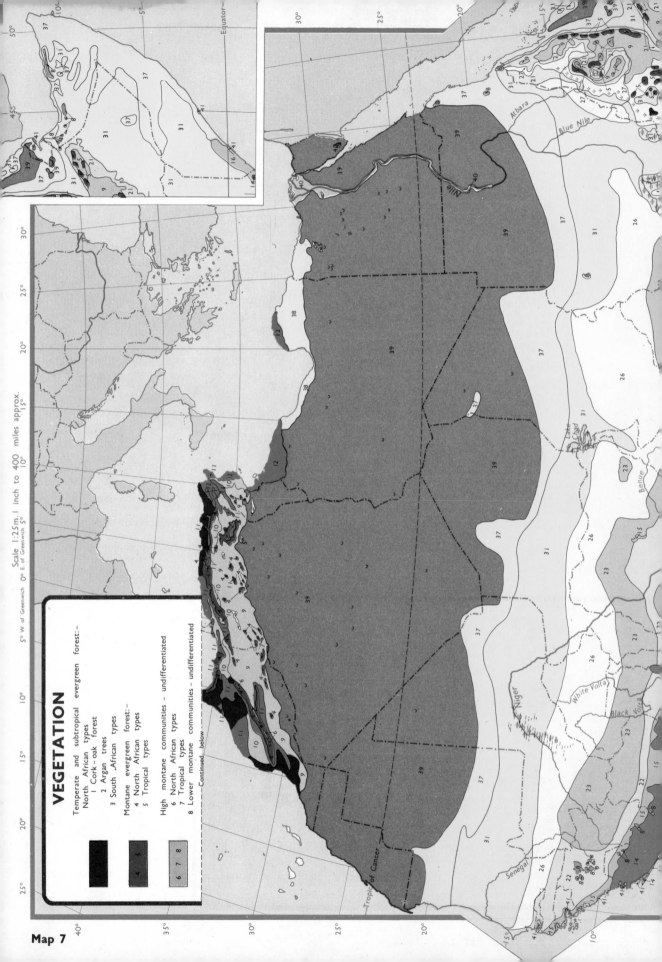

VEGETATION

Temperate and subtropical evergreen forest:—
North African types
1 Cork-oak forest
2 Argan trees
3 South African types

Montane evergreen forest:—
4 North African types
5 Tropical types

High montane communities – undifferentiated
6 North African types
7 Tropical types
8 Lower montane communities – undifferentiated
—— Continued below ——

Scale 1:25m. 1 inch to 400 miles approx.

5° W of Greenwich 0° E. of Greenwich 5°

Map 7

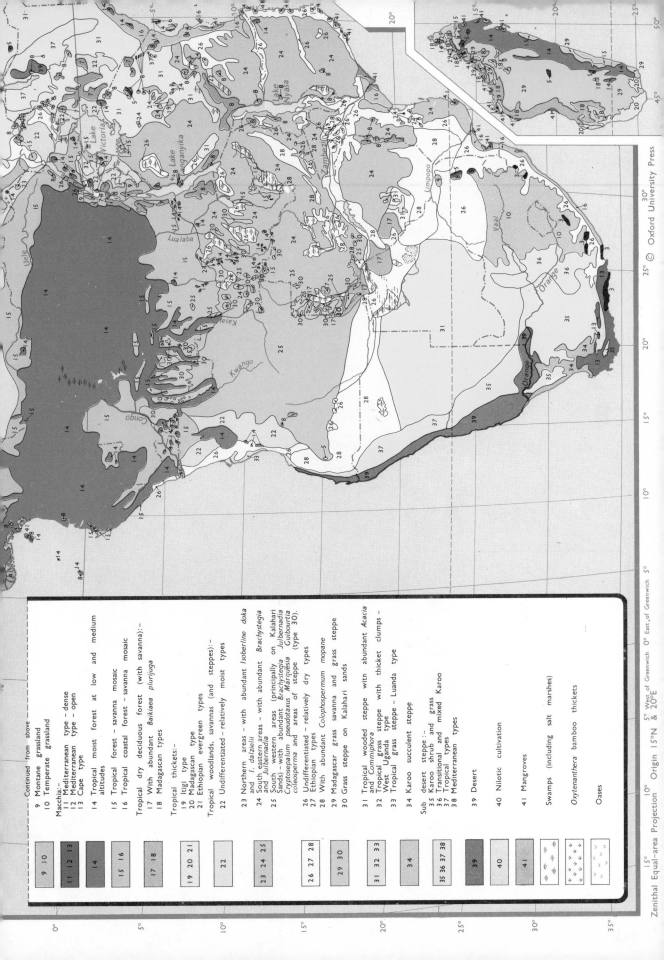

© Oxford University Press

Zenithal Equal-area Projection   Origin 15°N & 20°E

Legend:

- - - Continued from above
9 Montane grassland
10 Temperate grassland

Macchia:-
11 Mediterranean type – dense
12 Mediterranean type – open
13 Cape type

14 Tropical moist forest at low and medium altitudes
15 Tropical forest – savanna mosaic
16 Tropical coastal forest – savanna mosaic

Tropical dry deciduous forest (with savanna):-
17 With abundant Baikiaea plurijuga
18 Madagascan types

Tropical thickets:-
19 Itigi type
20 Madagascan type
21 Ethiopian evergreen types

22 Undifferentiated – relatively moist types

Tropical woodlands, savannas (and steppes):-
23 Northern areas – with abundant Isoberlinia doka and I. dalzielii
24 South eastern areas – with abundant Brachystegia and Julbernadia
25 South western areas (principally on Kalahari Sands) – with abundant Brachystegia Julbernadia Guibourtia Cryptosepalum pseudotaxus Marquèsia coleosperma and areas of steppe (type 30).

26 Undifferentiated – relatively dry types
27 Ethiopian types
28 With abundant Colophospermum mopane

29 Madagascar grass savanna and grass steppe
30 Grass steppe on Kalahari sands

31 Tropical wooded steppe with abundant Acacia and Comminphora
32 Tropical grass steppe with thicket clumps – West Uganda type
33 Tropical grass steppe – Luanda type

34 Karoo succulent steppe

Sub desert steppe:-
35 Karoo shrub and grass
36 Transitional and mixed Karoo
37 Tropical types
38 Mediterranean types

39 Desert

40 Nilotic cultivation

41 Mangroves

Swamps (including salt marshes)

Oxytenanthera bamboo thickets

Oases

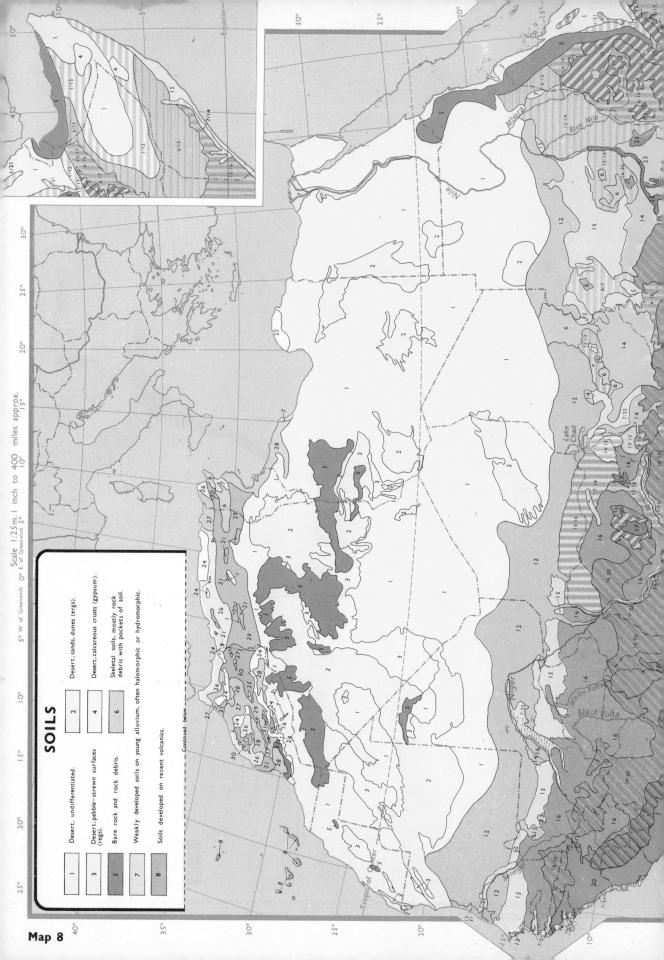

SOILS

1	Desert, undifferentiated.
2	Desert, sands, dunes (erg).
3	Desert, pebble-strewn surfaces (regs).
4	Desert, calcareous crusts (gypsum).
5	Bare rock and rock debris.
6	Skeletal soils, mostly rock debris with pockets of soil.
7	Weakly developed soils on young alluvium, often halomorphic or hydromorphic.
8	Soils developed on recent volcanics.

Continued below

Scale 1:25 m. 1 inch to 400 miles approx.

Map 8

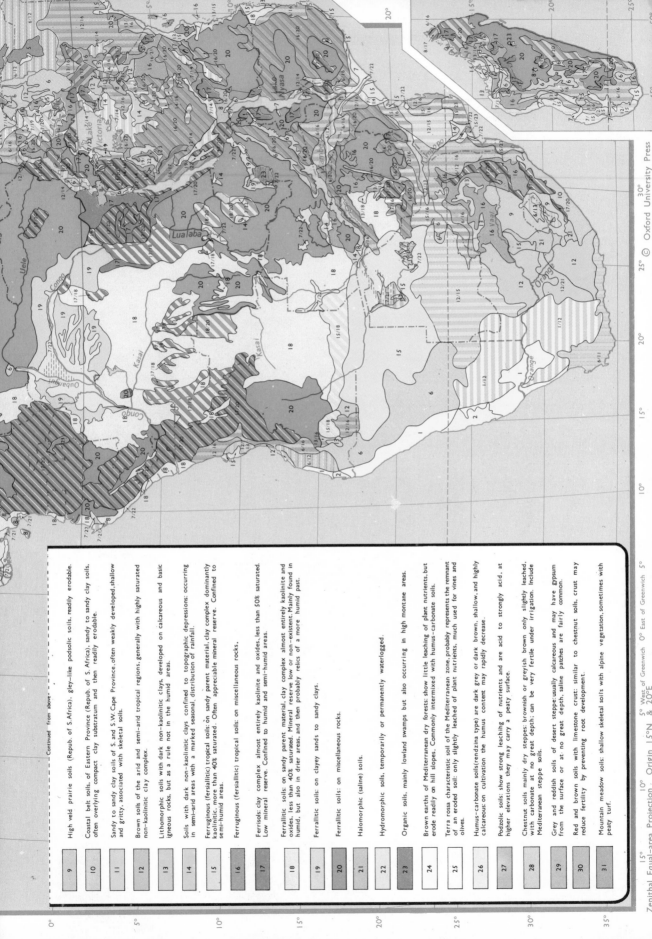

© Oxford University Press

- - - Continued from above - - -

9   High veld prairie soils (Repub. of S.Africa). gley-like podsolic soils, readily erodable.

10   Coastal belt soils, of Eastern Province (Repub. of S. Africa), sandy to sandy clay soils, often overlying compact clay substratum and then readily erodable.

11   Sandy to sandy clay soils of S. and S.W. Cape Province, often weakly developed, shallow and gritty, associated with skeletal soils.

12   Brown soils of the arid and semi-arid tropical regions, generally with highly saturated non-kaolinitic clay complex.

13   Lithomorphic soils with dark non-kaolinitic clays, developed on calcareous and basic igneous rocks, but as a rule not in the humid areas.

14   Soils with dark non-kaolinitic clays confined to topographic depressions: occurring in semi-arid areas with a marked seasonal, distribution of rainfall.

15   Ferruginous (fersiallitic) tropical soils: on sandy parent material, clay complex dominantly kaolinitic, more than 40% saturated. Often appreciable mineral reserve. Confined to semi-humid areas.

16   Ferruginous (fersiallitic) tropical soils: on miscellaneous rocks.

17   Ferrisols: clay complex almost entirely kaolinite and oxides, less than 50% saturated. Low mineral reserve. Confined to humid and semi-humid areas.

18   Ferrallitic soils: on sandy parent material, clay complex almost entirely kaolinite and oxides, less than 40% saturated. Mineral reserve low or non-existent. Mainly found in humid, but also in drier area, and then probably relics of a more humid past.

19   Ferrallitic soils: on clayey sands to sandy clays.

20   Ferrallitic soils: on miscellaneous rocks.

21   Halomorphic (saline) soils.

22   Hydromorphic soils, temporarily or permanently waterlogged.

23   Organic soils, mainly lowland swamps but also occurring in high montane areas.

24   Brown earths of Mediterranean dry forests: show little leaching of plant nutrients, but erode readily on hill slopes. Commonly intermixed with humus-carbonate soils.

25   Terra rossa characteristic soil of the Mediterranean zone, probably represents the remnant of an eroded soil: only slightly leached of plant nutrients, much used for vines and olives.

26   Humus-carbonate soils (rendzina type) are dark grey or dark brown, shallow, and highly calcareous: on cultivation the humus content may rapidly decrease.

27   Podzolic soils: show strong leaching of nutrients and are acid to strongly acid, at higher elevations they may carry a peaty surface.

28   Chestnut soils mainly dry steppes: brownish or greyish brown only slightly leached, with carbonate at no great depth: can be very fertile under irrigation. Include Mediterranean steppe soils.

29   Grey and reddish soils of desert steppe: usually calcareous and may have gypsum from the surface or at no great depth, saline patches are fairly common.

30   Red and brown soils with limestone crust; similar to chestnut soils, crust may reduce fertility by preventing root development.

31   Mountain meadow soils: shallow skeletal soils with alpine vegetation, sometimes with peaty turf.

15° West of Greenwich   0° East of Greenwich

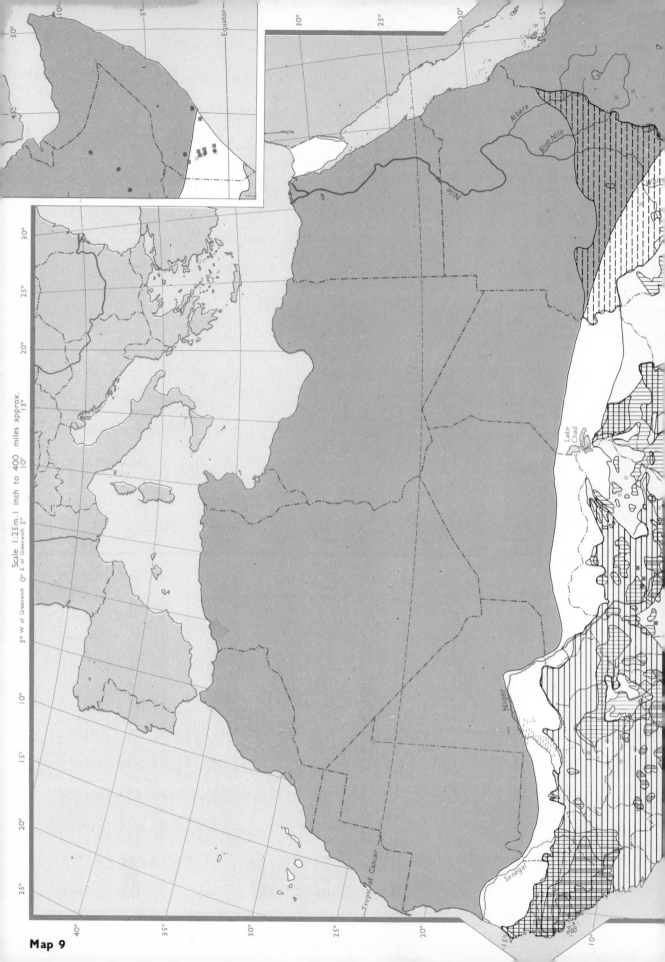

Scale 1:25 m.1 inch to 400 miles approx.

Map 9

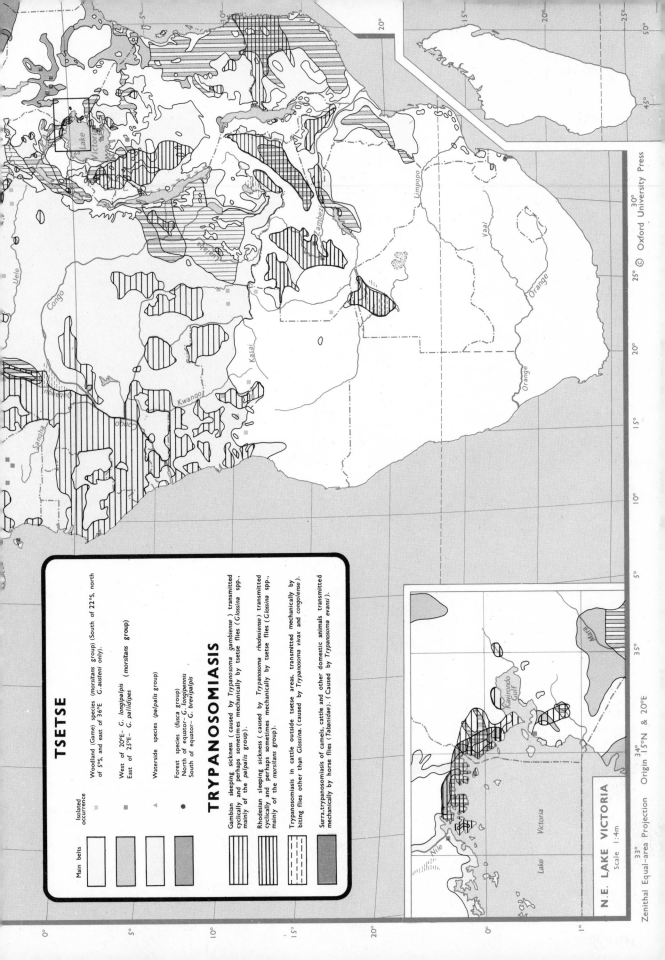

TSETSE

Main belts

Woodland (Game) species (*morsitans* group) (South of 22°S, north of 5°S, and east of 36°E   *G. austeni* only).

West of 20°E– *G. longipalpis*   (*morsitans* group)
East of 15°E– *G. pallidipes*

Waterside species (*palpalis* group)

Forest species (*fusca* group)
North of equator– *G. longipennis*
South of equator– *G. brevipalpis*

Isolated occurrence

TRYPANOSOMIASIS

Gambian sleeping sickness (caused by *Trypanosoma gambiense*) transmitted cyclically and perhaps sometimes mechanically by tsetse flies (*Glossina* spp.), mainly of the *palpalis* group).

Rhodesian sleeping sickness (caused by *Trypanosoma rhodesiense*) transmitted cyclically and perhaps sometimes mechanically by tsetse flies (*Glossina* spp.), mainly of the *morsitans* group).

Trypanosomiasis in cattle outside tsetse areas, transmitted mechanically by biting flies other than *Glossina*. (caused by *Trypanosoma vivax* and *congolense*.)

Surra.trypanosomiasis of camels, cattle and other domestic animals transmitted mechanically by horse flies (*Tabanidae*). (Caused by *Trypanosoma evansi*).

N.E. LAKE VICTORIA
Scale 1:4m

Zenithal Equal-area Projection   Origin 15°N & 20°E

© Oxford University Press

Map 10

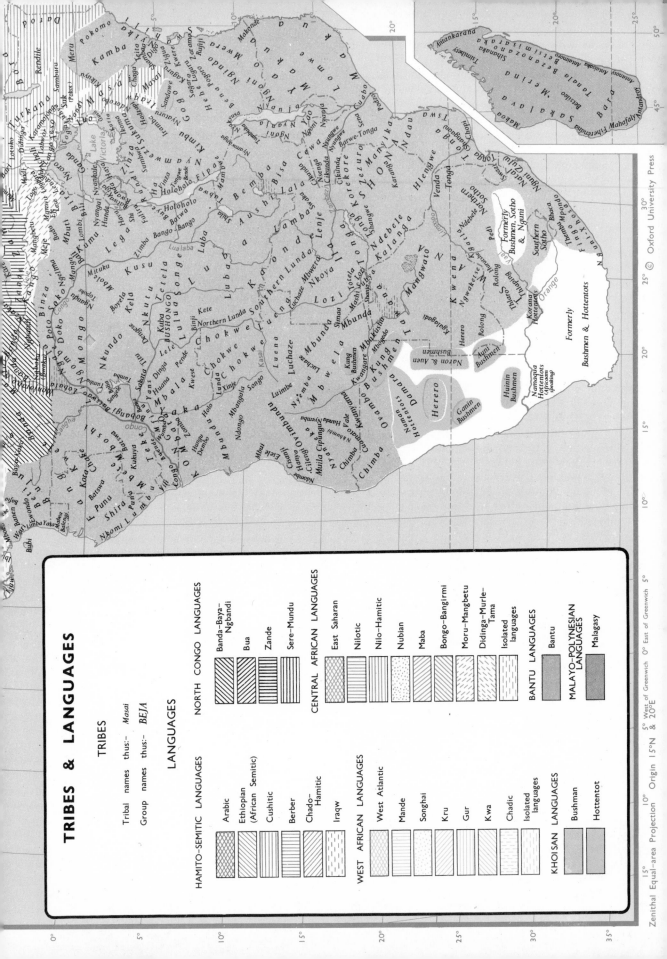

TRIBES & LANGUAGES

TRIBES

Tribal names thus:- *Masai*

Group names thus:- BEJA

LANGUAGES

HAMITO-SEMITIC LANGUAGES

- Arabic
- Ethiopian (African Semitic)
- Cushitic
- Berber
- Chado-Hamitic
- Iraqw

WEST AFRICAN LANGUAGES

- West Atlantic
- Mande
- Songhai
- Kru
- Gur
- Kwa
- Chadic
- Isolated languages

KHOISAN LANGUAGES

- Bushman
- Hottentot

NORTH CONGO LANGUAGES

- Banda–Baya–Ngbandi
- Bua
- Zande
- Sere–Mundu

CENTRAL AFRICAN LANGUAGES

- East Saharan
- Nilotic
- Nilo–Hamitic
- Nubian
- Maba
- Bongo–Bangirmi
- Moru–Mangbetu
- Didinga–Murle–Tama
- Isolated languages

BANTU LANGUAGES

- Bantu

MALAYO–POLYNESIAN LANGUAGES

- Malagasy

Zenithal Equal-area Projection   Origin 15°N & 20°E   © Oxford University Press

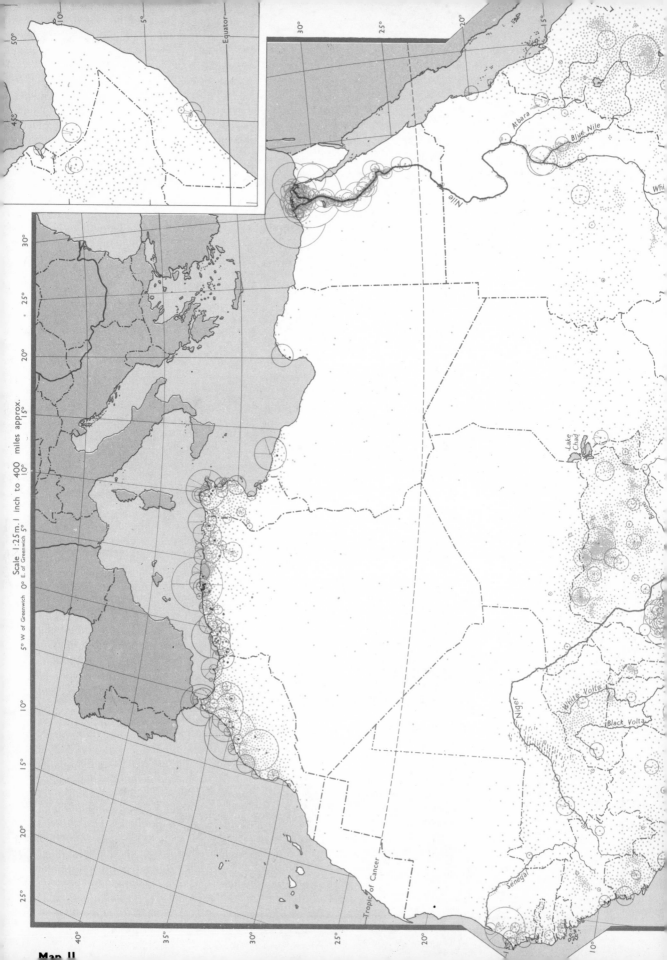

Map II

Scale 1:25 m. 1 inch to 400 miles approx.

5° W of Greenwich   0° E. of Greenwich 5°

Equator

30°

25°

20°

Tropic of Cancer

Nile

Atbara

Blue Nile

Whi

Lake Chad

Benu

Niger

Senegal

White Volta

Black Volta

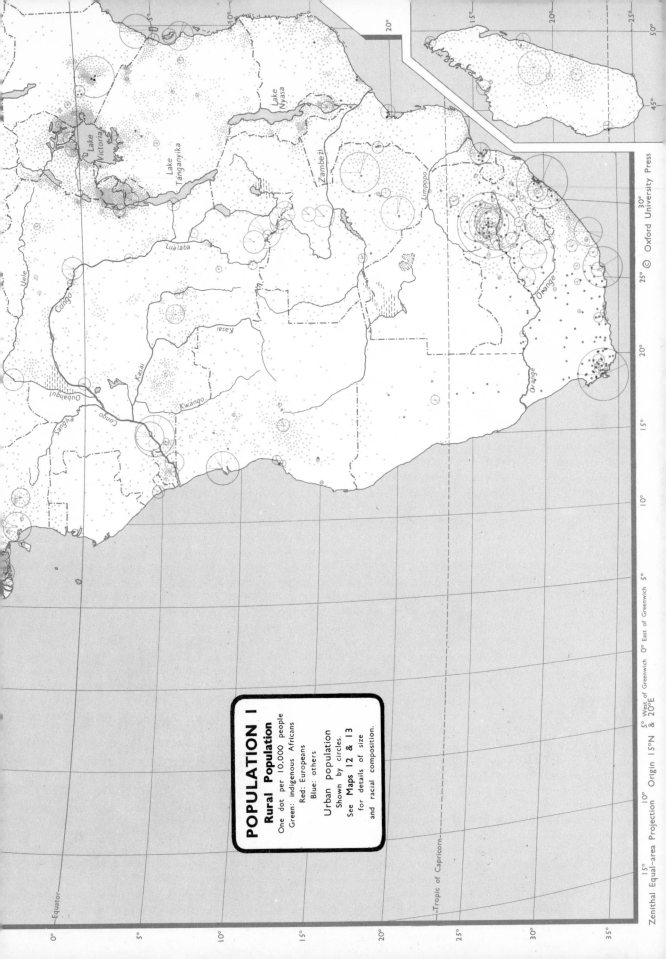

POPULATION I
Rural Population

One dot per 10,000 people
Green: indigenous Africans
Red: Europeans
Blue: others

Urban population
Shown by circles.
See Maps 12 & 13
for details of size
and racial composition.

Equator

Lake Victoria
Lake Tanganyika
Lake Nyasa

Uele
Congo
Lualaba
Kasai
Kasai
Ubangui
Congo
Sangha
Kwango
Zambezi
Limpopo
Orange
Orange

Tropic of Capricorn

5° West of Greenwich   0° East of Greenwich   5°
Zenithal Equal-area Projection Origin 15°N & 20°E

© Oxford University Press

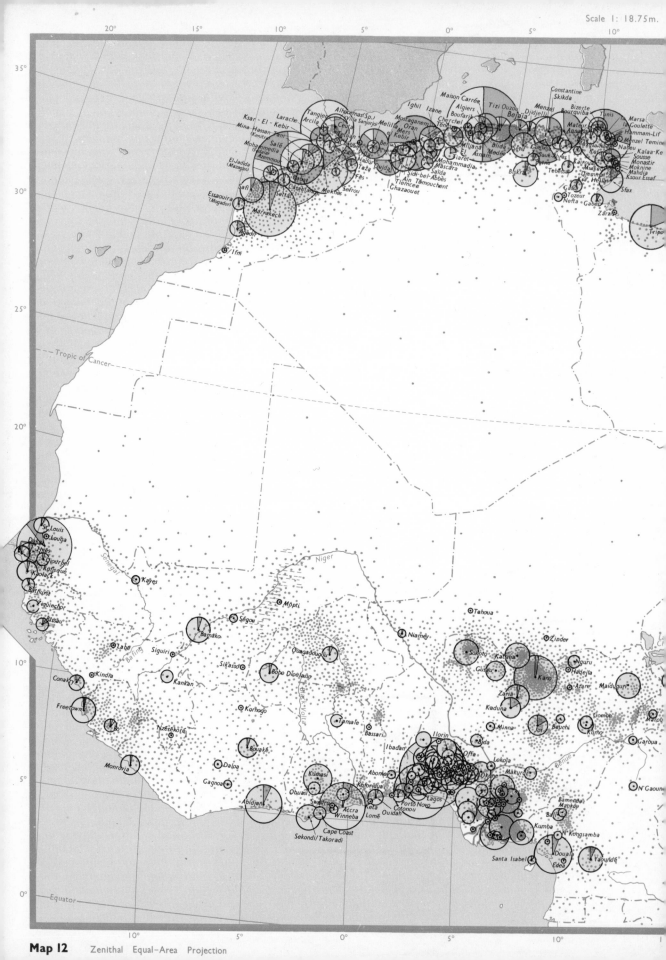

Scale 1: 18.75m.

Map 12 Zenithal Equal-Area Projection

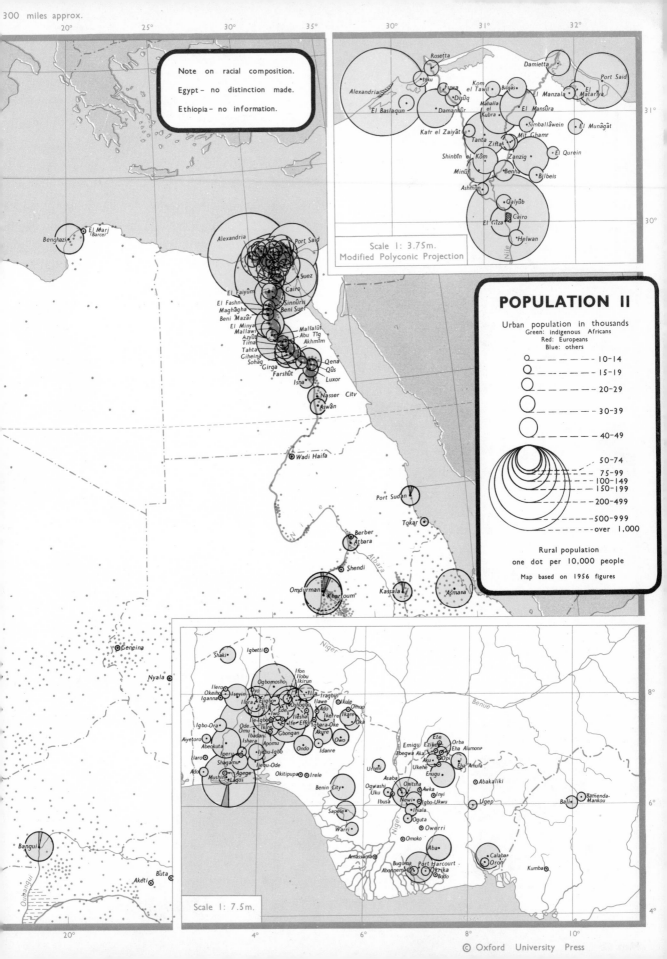

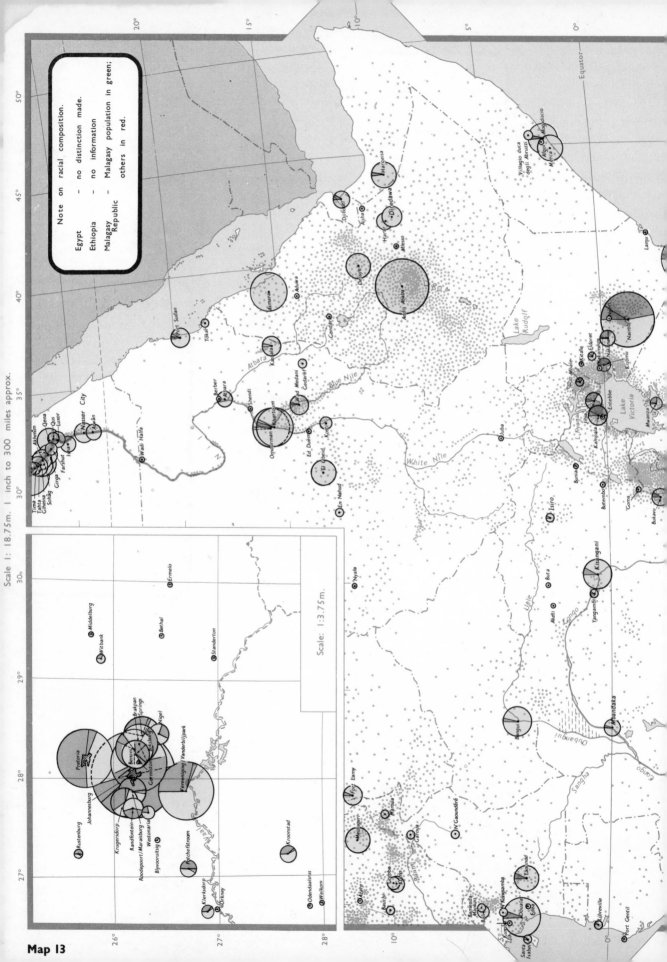

Map 13

Scale 1: 18.75m. 1 inch to 300 miles approx.

Scale: 1:3.75m.

Note on racial composition.

Egypt   – no distinction made.
Ethiopia   – no information
Malagasy   – Malagasy population in green;
Republic   others in red.

POPULATION III

Urban population in thousands

Green: indigenous Africans
Red: Europeans
Blue: others

50–74	
75–99	
100–149	
150–199	
200–499	
500–999	
over 1,000	

10–14		
15–19		
20–29		
30–39		
40–49		

Rural Population one dot per 10,000 people

Map based on 1956 figures

© Oxford University Press

Zenithal Equal-Area Projection. Origin 15°N & 20°E.

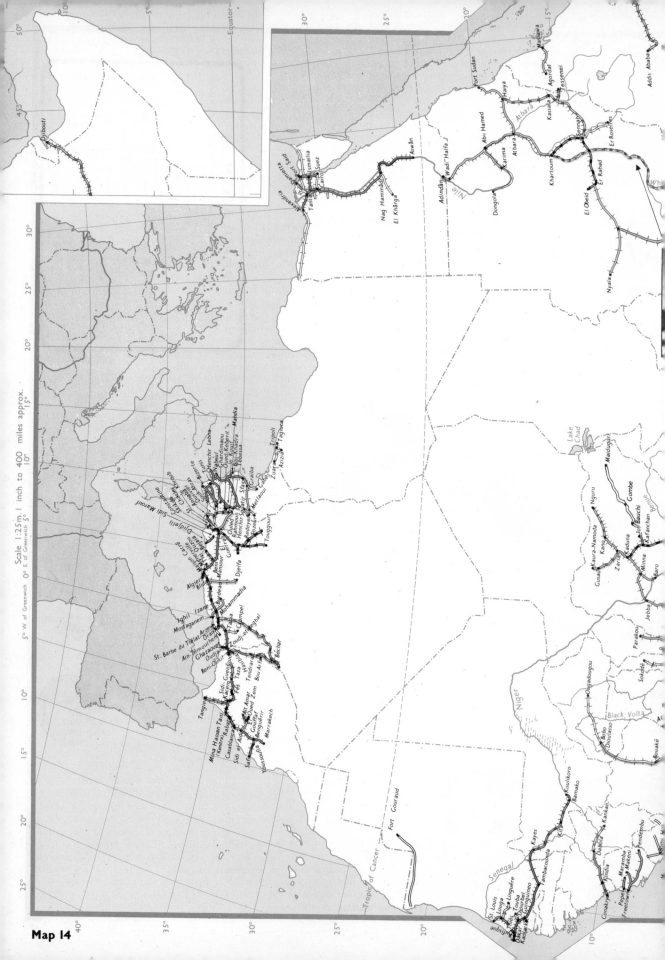

Map 14

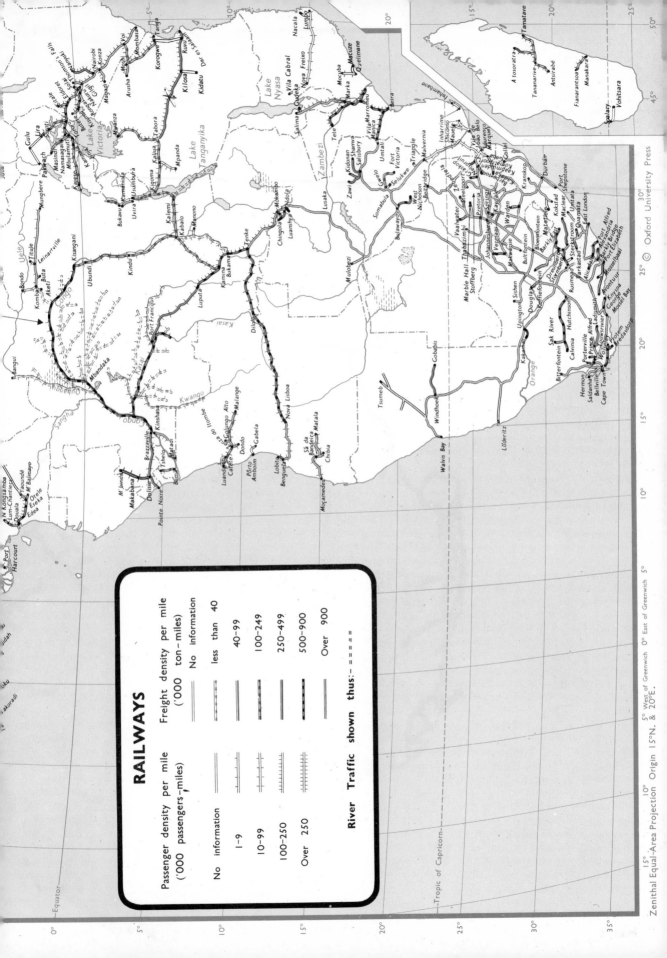

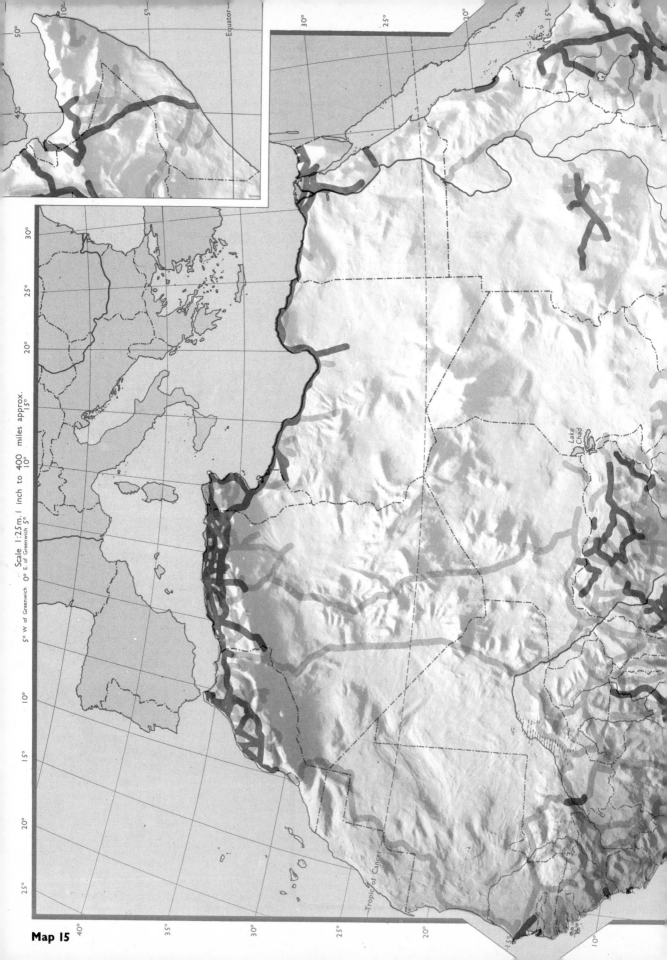

Map 15

Scale 1:25m. 1 inch to 400 miles approx.

5° W of Greenwich   0° E. of Greenwich   5° E. of Greenwich

Tropic of Cancer

Lake Chad

Equator

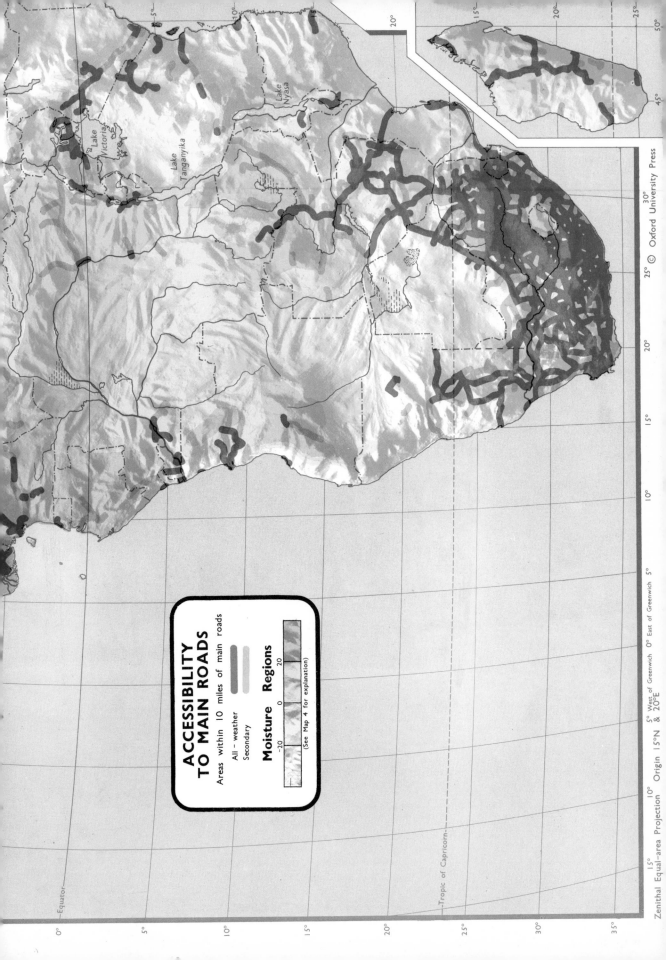

ACCESSIBILITY TO MAIN ROADS

Areas within 10 miles of main roads

All – weather

Secondary

Moisture Regions

-20   0   20

(See Map 4 for explanation)

Lake Victoria

Lake Tanganyika

Lake Nyasa

Equator

Tropic of Capricorn

Zenithal Equal-area Projection Origin 15°N & 20°E

5° West of Greenwich 0° East of Greenwich 5°

© Oxford University Press

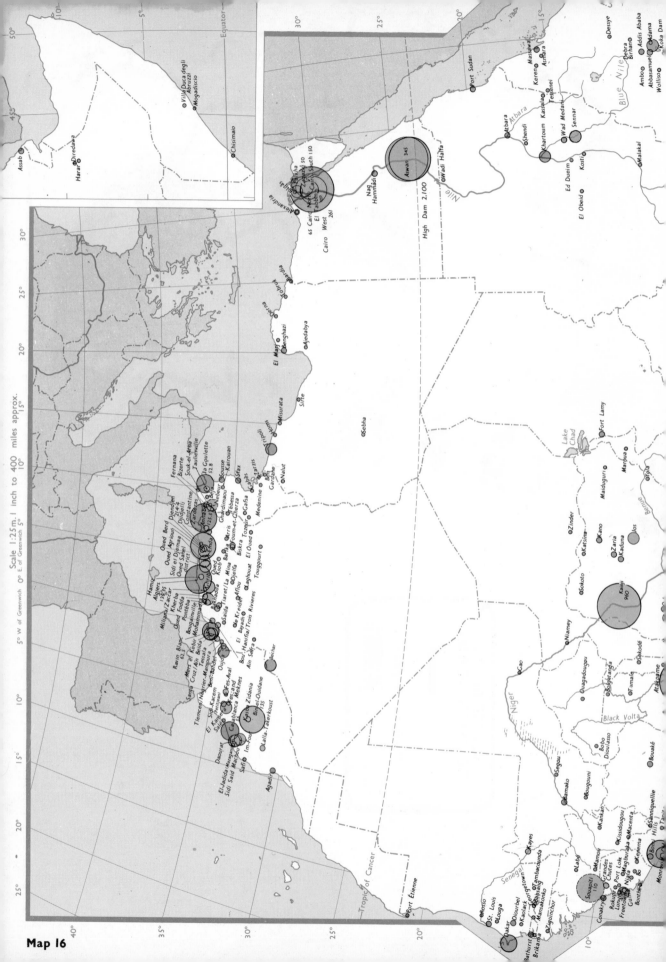

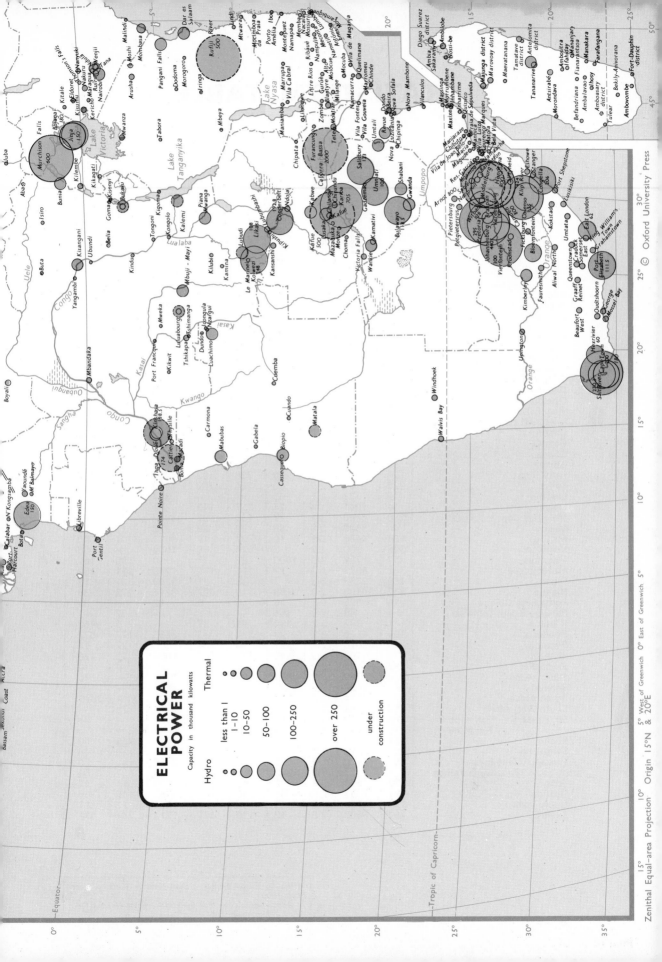

ELECTRICAL POWER

Capacity in thousand kilowatts

Hydro   less than 1
         1-10
         10-50
         50-100
         100-250
         over 250

Thermal

under construction

Zenithal Equal-area Projection   Origin 15°N & 20°E
© Oxford University Press

STATISTICAL TABLE

	1 Area in thousands of square miles.	2 Population in thousands, 1964	3 Percentage Annual Increase in Population, 1958–1964	4 Number of People per square mile, 1964	5 Imports 1964. Millions of U.S. $	6 Exports 1964. Millions of U.S. $	7 Number of Cattle in thousands, 1962	8 Installed Electricity capacity in Mw., 1963 or 1964.	9 Energy consumed. expressed as coal equivalent in Kg per head.
Angola	481	5084	1·4	11	164	204	1220	334	98
Botswana	220	543	3·1	2	—	—	1319	—	—
Burundi	11	2800	—	255	—	—	500	—	14
Cameroon	184	5103	2·1	28	116	122	1750	152	71
Central Afr. Rep.	241	1320	2·2	5	30	29	500	8	29
Chad	496	3300	1·5	7	34	27	4000	10	15
Comoro Islands	0·8	212	2·5	252					
Congo (Brazzaville)	132	826	1·6	6	65	47	20	—	157
Congo (Kinshasa)	906	15300	2·1	17	285	337	1035	—	79
Dahomey	43	2300	2·9	53	31	13	300	8	30
Ethiopia	472	22200	1·8	47	124	106	22450	111	10
French Territory of Afars & Issas	10	81	—	8	—	—	12	6	383
Gabon	103	459	1·6	4	56	90	—	13	196
Gambia	4	324	2·4	81	12	9	143	5	31
Ghana	92	7537	2·7	82	340	292	500	143	120
Guinea	95	3420	2·8	36	49	43	1505	—	101
Ivory Coast	124	3750	3·3	30	238	302	289	—	107
Kenya	225	9104	2·9	40	214	150	7460	101	129
Lesotho	12	733	1·7	63	—	—	377	—	—
Liberia	44	1041	1·4	24	117	143	11	118	231
Malagasy Rep.	230	6180	3·1	27	136	92	6387	73	37
Malawi	46	3900	2·8	85	20	28	372	13	36
Mali	464	4485	2·3	10	37	17	3513	—	20
Mauritania	398	900	2·2	2	16	46	1000	—	56
Mauritius	0·7	722	2·9	1000	82	77	40	96	151
Mozambique	302	6872	1·3	23	156	106	746	211	132
Niger	489	3237	3·3	7	33	21	3500	—	13
Nigeria	357	56400	2·0	158	710	602	3212	272	38
Portuguese Guinea	14	525	0·2	38	15	5	12	—	63
Principe & São Tomé	0·4	58	2·0	156	—	—	—	2	—
Réunion	1	382	3·2	394	91	37	—	9	162
Rhodesia	150	4140	3·3	28	238	233	3563	1177	577
Rwanda	10	3018	3·1	297	—	—	500	22	14
Senegal	76	3400	2·3	45	172	123	1500	70	136
Seychelles	0·2	46	2·9	295	—	—	—	—	70
Sierra Leone	28	2240	2·1	81	100	95	180	—	70
Somalia	246	2420	3·5	10	—	—	842	—	25
South Africa	473	17474	2·4	37	2150	1456	12327	—	2576
South West Africa	318	564	2·0	2	—	—	2117	79	—
Sp. Equat. Gu. : Fernando Po	0·8	70	3·3	89	—	—	—	—	—
Rio Muni	10	193	1·5	19	—	—	—	—	—
Sudan	967	13180	2·8	14	274	198	7000	59	60
Swaziland	7	288	2·5	43	—	—	535	—	—
Tanzania : Tanganyika	362	9990	1·9	28	123	197	8016	}70	50
Zanzibar & Pemba	1	335	1·9	328	11	11	48		54
Togo	22	1603	2·8	73	42	30	139	11	41
Uganda	91	7367	2·5	81	92	186	3383	148	36
Upper Volta	106	4750	2·5	45	—	—	1800	11	11
Zambia	291	3600	2·9	12	120	441	1219	261	431

SOURCES 1,2,3,4,5,6,8,9: United Nations *Statistical Yearbook, 1965*
7: *Agricultural Economics Bulletin for Africa-No, 6* E.C.A./F.A.O. Addis Ababa 1964.